GENDER AND JUDGING

Does gender make a difference to the way the judiciary works and should work? Or is gender-blindness a built-in prerequisite of judicial objectivity? If gender does make a difference, how might this be defined? These are the key questions posed in this collection of essays, by some 30 authors, from 15 countries representing all five continents, whose answers draw on various theoretical approaches, including gender, feminist, and sociological theories.

The book's pressing topicality is underlined by the fact that well into the modern era male opposition to women's admission to, and progress within, the judicial profession has been largely based on the argument that their very gender programmes women to show empathy, partiality and gendered prejudice—in short essential qualities running directly counter to the need for judicial objectivity. It took until the last century for women to begin to break down such seemingly insurmountable barriers. And even then, there are a number of countries where even this first step is still waiting to happen. In all of them, there remains a more or less pronounced glass ceiling to women's judicial careers.

Oñati International Series in Law and Society

A SERIES PUBLISHED FOR THE OÑATI INSTITUTE
FOR THE SOCIOLOGY OF LAW

Recent titles in this series

Feminist Perspectives on Contemporary International Law:
Between Resistance and Compliance?
edited by Sari Kouvo and Zoe Pearson

Challenging Gender Inequality in Tax Policy Making:
Comparative Perspectives
edited by Kim Brooks, Åsa Gunnarson, Lisa Philipps and Maria Wersig

Emotions, Crime and Justice
edited by Susanne Karstedt, Ian Loader and Heather Strang

Mediation in Political Conflicts
Soft Power or Counter Culture?
edited by Jacques Faget

Criminological and Legal Consequences of Climate Change
edited by Stephen Farrall, Tawhida Ahmed and Duncan French

Managing Family Justice in Diverse Societies
edited by Mavis Maclean and John Eekelaar

Making Human Rights Intelligible: Towards a Sociology of Human Rights
edited by Mikael Risk Madsen and Gert Verschraegen

For the complete list of titles in this series, see
'Oñati International Series in Law and Society' link at
www.hartpub.co.uk/books/series.asp

Gender and Judging

Edited by

Ulrike Schultz
and
Gisela Shaw

Oñati International Series in Law and Society

A SERIES PUBLISHED FOR THE OÑATI INSTITUTE FOR THE SOCIOLOGY OF LAW

·HART·
PUBLISHING
OXFORD AND PORTLAND OREGON
2013

Published in the United Kingdom by Hart Publishing Ltd
16C Worcester Place, Oxford, OX1 2JW
Telephone: +44 (0)1865 517530
Fax: +44 (0)1865 510710
E-mail: mail@hartpub.co.uk
Website: http://www.hartpub.co.uk

Published in North America (US and Canada) by
Hart Publishing
c/o International Specialized Book Services
920 NE 58th Avenue, Suite 300
Portland, OR 97213-3786
USA
Tel: +1 503 287 3093 or toll-free: (1) 800 944 6190
Fax: +1 503 280 8832
E-mail: orders@isbs.com
Website: http://www.isbs.com

British Library Cataloguing in Publication Data
Data Available

ISBN: 978-1-84113-640-0

Typeset by Compuscript Ltd, Shannon
Printed and bound in Great Britain by
TJ International Ltd, Padstow

MIX
Paper from
responsible sources
FSC® C013056
FSC
www.fsc.org

Preface

Compiling a comprehensive international collection of contributions such as this one on the topic of 'Gender and Judging' represents a demanding task. The idea to set up a specific research group on the subject was born early in the new millennium. It was sparked off by the realisation of a striking difference between common law and civil law countries regarding not only women's entry to and career progression within the judiciary, but particularly remarkable, the respective reception of this process. In common law countries (mainly the United States, the United Kingdom, Canada, Australia and New Zealand) the gradual increase in the number of women who made it to judicial office including the higher echelons has been accompanied by considerable media and political attention. By contrast, civil law countries that had actually seen a much earlier and more rapid access of women to such offices and where in countries such as France, Italy and the Netherlands, the share of women by now even exceeds that of men, there has been a marked absence of any real public interest in these developments.

This opens up a fascinating field of study for legal sociology around questions such as: what exactly are the processes that have taken place in the two judicial systems? What are their causes and effects? And what, more generally, can we learn from a comparative study of developments in common and civil law countries? This volume attempts to respond to this challenge.

Our work began with a first special session on 'Gender and Judging' at the 2006 Law and Society Association (LSA) meeting in Baltimore. This has been followed by a number of subsequent events: a conference for women lawyers in April 2007 organised by Beatriz Kohen in Buenos Aires; the large international socio-legal conference in 2007 in Berlin jointly organised by the LSA, the Research Committee on Sociology of Law (RCSL) and various national socio-legal organisations, where our five panels presented a total of 18 papers; the LSA conferences in Montreal (2008), Denver (2009), Chicago (2010) and San Francisco (2011); the RCSL conferences in Milan (2008) and Oñati (2009); the meeting of the RCSL Working Group for the Comparative Study of Legal Professions in Berder, France (2008) and in Paris (2010). All in all, this has added up to some one hundred papers on the subject of 'Gender and Judging', not including those presented at numerous national socio-legal conferences—overwhelming evidence of the topic's profound and lasting interest to socio-legal scholars. In acknowledgment of this, the status of a Collaborative Research Network (CRN) of the LSA was conferred on our research group in 2008.

An international venture of this kind involving contributors from around the world requires a wealth of contacts and is the result of intensive networking. The 'Gender and Judging' project builds on the work of the Women and Gender in the Legal Profession Group. Established in 1994, this group can by now point to a range of publications, most prominently the collection *Women in the World's Legal Professions*.[1] It is a sub-group of the RCSL Working Group on Legal Professions, which, for its part, can look back at a 30-year tradition of collaboration.

Having concluded this comprehensive and complex volume, both editors of *Women in the World's Legal Professions* felt at the time that tackling another one of its kind would be inconceivable. And yet, driven by sheer fascination with the topic and having put together an editorially less demanding (much shorter) study on 'Gender and Judging' in the form of a special issue of the *International Journal of the Legal Profession* (2008),[2] we decided to bite the bullet and proposed to the increasing number of scholars working in this area the production of a large-scale collection of contributions on the subject.

Work on this volume was finally brought together at a special workshop on 'Gender and Judging' at the International Institute for the Sociology of Law in Oñati, Spain, in June 2009, jointly organised by Ulrike Schultz, Sally Kenney[3] and Gisela Shaw. The bulk of the contributions included here originated as papers presented at this meeting.

In all, the book comprises 30 contributions by 32 scholars, of these 28 female and four male. Nineteen countries from the world's five continents, as well as from its two major legal systems—common law and civil law—are represented here. Common law countries included are Australia, Canada, India, Israel, Kenya, South Africa, the United Kingdom and the United States. Respective civil law countries are Argentina, France, Germany, Italy, Japan, the Netherlands, Syria and Switzerland. Additionally, there are contributions on the Philippines and Cambodia. The collection is truly interdisciplinary, its authors including lawyers, sociologists, political scientists, historians, psychologists and philosophers, among them specialists in feminist subjects and researchers with a keen interest in feminist and/or gender studies.

[1] U Schultz and G Shaw (eds) (Oxford, HartPublishing, 2003). Also a special issue of the *International Journal of the Legal Profession* has been edited: *Women in the Legal Profession* (2003) 10(2) *IJLP* and many articles in books and journals have been inspired by the work of the group.

[2] In 2012, this issue was reproduced by Routledge under the title *Women in the Judiciary*. Five papers on 'Gender and Judging' were compiled and edited by Dermot Feenan in a special issue of *Feminist Legal Studies* (1/XVII, April 2009). Further articles have since been written and will eventually appear in published form.

[3] Sally Kenney runs a blog on 'Gender and Judging' which gives details on 120 colleagues who have subscribed to it and where a lively exchange of ideas and information is taking place: genderandjudging.com.

All academic ranks and age groups are represented. There is evidence of some considerable continuity of work given that seven of the authors were also contributors to the volume on *Women in the World's Legal Professions*.

Producing an international collection, especially when, as is the case here, fewer than half of the authors are not native English speakers, requires some hard work on all sides regarding language. In this context it is worth mentioning that occasional idiosyncratic phrasing may actually help to emphasise differences in national writing and citing cultures.

We—editors and authors—would like to acknowledge invaluable help received from various sources: the ILSL offered (for the second time) a venue and structural framework for our crucial final meeting; Malen Gordoa Mendizabal provided generous structural assistance and endless patience, managing to retain her equanimity even at the fifth change in our programme; the IISL and the LSA both lent support to this project; Gunther Gerl helped with expert editorial work. We are grateful to the Center on Women and Public Policy, Hubert H Humphrey Institute of Public Affairs, University of Minnesota, and to the Society of Friends at Fern Universität in Hagen, Germany, for their generous sponsorship of breakfasts and evening meals in Oñati—a not to be underestimated ingredient ensuring fruitful collaboration and communication among the project team. Finally, our thanks go to Richard Hart for accepting this volume for publication in the Oñati series.

Summary of Contents

PART 5: QUOTAS AND DIVERSITY

PART 6: GENDER AND JUDICIAL EDUCATION

Contents

PART 1: PIONEERS AND EMINENT WOMEN JUDGES

PART 7: GENDER AND JUDICIAL EDUCATION

List of Contributors

M Angela Amante is a lawyer, attorney at law (UBA, Argentina) and UBA assistant professor focusing on law research methodology.
aamante@cvi.com.ar

Beverley Baines is a Professor in the Faculty of Law and cross-appointed to the School of Policy Studies and the Department of Gender Studies in the Faculty of Arts & Science, Queen's University, Canada: law.queensu.ca/facultyAndStaff/facultyDirectory/baines.html
bainesb@queensu.ca

Maria Rita Bartolomei is a lawyer and a legal mediator with a PhD in Sociology of Legal and Political Institutions, working as adjunct professor of Cultural Anthropology (University of Macerata) and Sociology of Law (University of Messina), Italy. She has conducted many anthropological fieldworks in Italy as well as in India (Kerala) and Africa (Ivory Coast, Tanzania and Zambia). Her fields of interest are: the survival of traditional institutions in black Africa; migration processes and legal adaptation; and, especially, the role of women jurists in changing legal cultures and empowering women's and children's (human) rights.
m.bartolomei@unimc.it

Anne Boigeol is a French sociologist, senior researcher at the Centre national de la recherche scientifique (Institut des sciences sociales du politique, Ecole normale supérieure de Cachan) working on questions of gender in the legal professions and the judiciary and, more recently, on women at the Bar. She was President of the RCSL from 2006 to 2010 and a member of the Oñati International Institute for the Sociology of Law governing board from 2001 to 2010.
aboigeol@gmail.com

Monique C Cardinal is an Associate Professor of Islamic Studies at the Faculté de théologie et de sciences religieuses of the Université Laval in Quebec, Canada. Her main areas of interest are the history of Islamic law, its teaching and institutions. She has done extensive fieldwork in the Arab world, particularly in Syria since 1992. Her present research focuses on the history of the judicial system in modern Syria.
monique.cardinal@ftsr.ulaval.ca

Ruth B Cowan is Senior Research Fellow (The Ralphe Bunche Institute for International Studies, City University of New York) concentrating on South Africa's transformation to democracy with focus on gender equality. She

created *Courting Justice*, a documentary featuring South African women judges; and is the Founding President and board of directors' member of Pro Mujer—a women's empowerment organisation serving poor women in Latin America. She has extensive economic and social development experience in Latin America and Afghanistan. Her current project focuses on two Native American women tribal court judges in California.
ruthcowan@aol.com

Bregje Dijksterhuis is a Research Fellow in the School of Social Work and Law, University of Applied Sciences in Amsterdam, the Netherlands. Her PhD thesis in Law (Leiden University) dealt with national judicial cooperation in the field of alimony law (Leiden University Press 2008). She researches and teaches family law and sociology of law. She has a particular interest in women judges and in questions of gender and divorce law.
bregjedijksterhuis@planet.nl

Andrea L Gastron holds a postdoctoral degree in gender studies (UCES, Argentina), a PhD in sociology (UBA, Argentina) and a degree in law (UBA). She is a Professor and Researcher at UBA/UCES focusing on law research methodology and gender studies.
andreagastron@hotmail.com

Reg Graycar is a barrister practising in NSW, and is Emeritus Professor of Law at the University of Sydney, Australia. She was Professor of Law at the University of Sydney from 1997 to 2012, prior to which she was Professor of Law at UNSW. She is a former full-time commissioner of the NSW Law Reform Commission, a former part-time commissioner of the Australian Law Reform Commission and was also a part-time hearing commissioner with the national Human Rights and Equal Opportunity Commission. She has published extensively on a range of legal issues including, with Jenny Morgan, *The Hidden Gender of Law*, Federation Press, 1990; 2nd edn, 2002. Since 1986, her work has been supported by a number of grants from the Australian Research Council for research on, among other things, the gendered nature of personal injury damages assessment, law reform in changing societies and the subject of this article, legal responses to systemic and historical injuries.
rgraycar@stjames.net.au

Ruth Herz is a former judge at the local court of Cologne, Germany. From 2007 to 2010 she was an associate researcher at the Centre of Criminology, University of Oxford, and is now a visiting professor at Birkbeck College, University of London. She is a member and co-founder of the international interdisciplinary network 'Images of Justice'. Her latest book *The Art of Justice* was published by Hart Publishing, Oxford, 2012.
rherz@gmx.net

Rosemary Hunter is Professor of Law at the University of Kent, UK. She was one of the organisers of the UK Feminist Judgments Project, and is currently chair of the UK Socio-Legal Studies Association, a founding editor of the online journal feminists@law and a member of the executive committee of the Equal Justices Initiative, a lobby group whose aim is to promote the equal participation of women and men in the judiciary in England and Wales.
r.c.hunter@kent.ac.uk

Winifred Kamau (LLB, LLM, PhD) is a Senior Lecturer at the School of Law, University of Nairobi, Kenya. Her research interests are in gender, law and dispute resolution with a focus on how the interaction between formal and informal dispute resolution structures impacts on women.
winkamau@hotmail.com

Eyal Katvan holds PhDs in law and in history of medicine. He is a lecturer at the Academic Center of Law and Business in Israel. His major interests are bioethics, law and medicine (gender perspectives); the legal and medical professions; legal history and the history of medicine. He specialises in medical, physical and mental examinations, women's legal history and the history of law and medicine.
katvan@biu.013.net.il

Sally J Kenney is the executive director of the Newcomb College Institute of Tulane University where she holds the Newcomb College Endowed Chair and is a Professor of Political Science. Her first book, *For Whose Protection? Reproductive Hazards and Exclusionary Policies in the United States and Britain*, examined how courts and judges construct rather than discover gender differences through law by examining cases on women's exclusion from hazardous work. Her latest is *Gender and Justice: Why Women in the Judiciary Really Matter* (New York, Routledge Press, 2013). She co-chairs the Collaborative Research Network on Gender and Judging for the Law and Society Association (genderandjudging.com/), co-founded the Infinity Project whose mission is to increase the gender diversity of the federal bench to ensure the quality of justice in the Eighth Circuit (www.theinfinityproject.org), and works closely with the academic network of the National Association of Women Judges.
skenney@tulane.edu

Beatriz Kohen is a sociologist and a researcher on gender and judging with a PhD from the University of Durham on gender differences in the family law courts of the city of Buenos Aires. She teaches at postgraduate level at the University of Palermo Law School where she is in charge of the Law and Gender Program. She coordinates a programme on human trafficking of the Argentine Association Judges in association with the International

Association of Women Judges and collaborates with the recently created Gender Observatory of the Judicial Council of the city of Buenos Aires.
bkohen@fibertel.com.ar

Juan LaLlave is a clinical psychologist practising analytical psychotherapy and Jungian analysis with an added focus on forensic and political psychology as well as criminology. His research interests include competence versus bias in moral, legal, ethical judgments, moral dilemma, and boundaries in the work of expert witnesses. He is a research member affiliated with the programme in Psychiatry and the Law at Harvard Medical School and works with the Competence Center for Forensic Psychology at the IRP, University of St Gallen in Switzerland.
lallave.hms@gmail.com

Revital Ludewig is a psychologist and therapist. She teaches legal psychology at the University of St Gallen, Switzerland. Her current research includes a project on 'Difficulties, moral dilemmas and coping strategies in the work of judges and lawyers'. She also teaches continuing education for judges and lawyers in Switzerland and Germany with the German Academy for Judges, Institute University Kurt Bösch and others. She serves as forensic consultant, evaluator and supervisor for various courts and is founder of the Competence Center for Forensic Psychology at the IRP, University St Gallen. Among other subjects, her publications look into victim psychology, knowledge base in psychology, moral dilemmas and decision-making.
revital.ludewig@unisg.ch

Kathy Mack, BA Rice, JD Stanford, LLM Adel is Professor of Law, Flinders Law School. She is the author of a monograph, book chapters and articles on Alternative Dispute Resolution and articles on legal education and evidence. With Sharyn Roach Anleu she has conducted empirical research involving plea negotiations. Since 2000,they have been engaged in a major socio-legal study of the Australian judiciary.
www.flinders.edu.au/law/judicialresearch
judicial.research@flinders.edu.au

Kate Malleson is Professor of Law at Queen Mary, University of London. Her main research interests are the judiciary, the constitution and the legal system. She has a particular interest in judicial selection processes and the challenge of increasing diversity in the composition of the judiciary. She has recently completed a three-year Research Council funded project on the selection processes of the international judiciary and is currently working on a project on the politics of judicial independence.
k.malleson@qmul.ac.uk

Elaine Martin is Professor of Political Science at Eastern Michigan University. Her teaching interests comprise women and politics, gender and the judiciary, politics in fiction and film, sex and justice, global issues, state and local politics and local government management.
elainemartin@yahoo.com

Kayo Minamino is Professor of Law at Kyoto Women's University Faculty of Law in Kyoto, Japan. Her major research interests are gender and law and judicial education on gender issues.
minamino@kyoto-wu.ac.jp

Atsuko Miwa is currently a researcher at the Kyoto Human Rights Research Institute, Kyoto, Japan. She was formerly Programme Officer at the United Nations Development Fund for Women (UNIFEM) Bangkok Office and has been researching and writing in the field of gender, development and human rights.
kokusai@kyoto.email.ne.jp

Leslie J Moran is Professor in the Law School, Birkbeck College, University of London. His research on the judiciary has two main strands: first, the politics and practice of judicial (especially sexual) diversity; secondly, judicial image making and image management.
l.moran@bbk.ac.uk

Mary Jane Mossman is Professor of Law at Osgoode Hall Law School of York University in Toronto, Canada, and was Director of the Institute for Feminist Legal Studies at Osgoode from 2002 to 2010. Her current research focuses on the history of women lawyers in Ontario from the 1890s to the 1970s.
mjmossman@osgoode.yorku.ca

Erika Rackley is a Professor in the Law School at Durham University, UK. She has written widely in the area of judicial diversity and is author of *Women, Judging and the Judiciary: From Difference to Diversity* (Routledge, 2013). She is co-organiser (with Rosemary Hunter and Clare McGlynn) of the Feminist Judgments Project in England and Wales and co-editor of *Feminist Judgments: From Theory to Practice* (Hart, 2010). She is also on the executive committee of the Equal Justices Initiative (www.law.qmul.ac.uk/eji/index.html), a group which works to promote the equal participation of women and men in the judiciary in England and Wales.
erika.rackley@durham.ac.uk

Sharyn L Roach Anleu, MA Tas, LLB Adel, Ph D Conn is Matthew Flinders Distinguished Professor of Sociology at Flinders University, Adelaide and a Fellow of the Australian Academy of the Social Sciences in Australia. With Kathy Mack, she is currently engaged in socio-legal research in the

Australian Judiciary and their courts. She has contributed to the Masters programme at the International Institute for the Sociology of Law, Oñati, Spain.
www.flinders.edu.au/law/judicialresearch
judicial.research@flinders.edu.au

Rubén Rodríguez is a psychologist (UBA, Argentina) and specialist in quali-quantitative market, opinion and publicity research. He is currently Professor and Researcher at UCES/UBA/CAECE University.
rodriguez.rubenjose@gmail.com

Marion Röwekamp is a historian/lawyer at the Freie Universität in Berlin. After various stays in the US (Columbia University/Mount Holyoke College/Harvard University), she is now working at CIESAS, the Colegio de México as well as at the Instituto de Investigaciones Históricas of the UNAM in Mexico City. Her main interest is in gender and law in a historical perspective.
roewekamp@zedat.fu-berlin.de

Keiko Sawa is Associate Professor of Sociology of Law in the Faculty of Contemporary Society, Kyoto Women'sUniversity, Japan. She specialises in gender and minorities issues.
sawa@kyoto-wu.ac.jp

Ulrike Schultz is a lawyer and Senior Academic at the FernUniversität in Hagen, Germany. She specialises in questions of gender and law, the sociology of the legal profession, and didactics and professional communication. She has taken part in many international socio-legal projects, and conducted big empirical studies on, for example, women's careers in the judiciary and women in the legal academy. She heads the International Working Group on the Comparative Study of Legal Professions and has been a member of the Oñati International Institute for the Sociology of Law governing board since 2006. She co-chairs the Collaborative Research Network on Gender and Judging for the Law and Society Association.
www.ulrikeschultz.de
ulrike.schultz@fernuni-hagen.de

Gisela Shaw is Emeritus Professor in German Studies at the University of the West of England, Bristol (UK), where she held the post of Director of Research for Modern Languages and European Studies (1996–2002). She chaired the British Women in German Studies Association (1995–2001) and has worked in philosophy, literature and legal sociology (with a special interest in women jurists).
gisela@giselashaw.com

Hilary Sommerlad is Professor of Law, Centre for Professional Legal Education and Research (CEPLER), University of Birmingham. Her extensive work on

woman lawyers includes a study (with colleagues) of diversity in the legal profession undertaken for the Legal Services Board: www.legalservicesboard.org.uk/what_we_do/Research/Publications/pdf/lsb_diversity_in_the_legal_profession_final_rev.pdf.
h.a.k.sommerlad@bham.ac.uk

Ann Stewart is Reader in Law and Associate Professor at the School of Law, University of Warwick, UK. She is director of the International Development and Human Rights programme and specialises in gender, law and development issues. She has researched and been involved with judicial training in India on gender issues since 1996.
ann.stewart@warwick.ac.uk

John Grisham *A Time to Kill* (London, 1989; Arrow edition 1992)

In the novel, an African American father shoots two white men who have raped and seriously injured his little daughter on the stairs of the county court house, expecting that they will be acquitted. The question is how his case will be dealt with in court.

p 116

'Can Carl Lee Hailey receive a fair trial in Ford County?'
'Why couldn't he?' Jake asked.
'Well he's black. He killed two white men, and he will be tried by a white jury.'
'You mean he will be tried by a bunch of white racists.'
'No, that's not what I said, nor what I implied. Why do you automatically assume I think you are all a bunch of racists?'
'Because you do. We're stereotyped, and you know it.'

p 329

'Women', said Lucien. 'Always pick women for criminal trials. They have bigger hearts, bleedings hearts, and they're much more sympathetic. Always go for women.'
'Naw', said Harry Rex. 'Not in this case. Women don't understand things like taking a gun and blowing people away. You need fathers, young fathers who would want to do the same thing Hailey did. Daddies with little girls.'

p 384

'White females, white females', Harry Rex said. 'The worst possible jurors in the world. White females.'
Ellen stared at him. 'I think fat white men are the worst jurors.'
'Don't get me wrong, Row Ark, I love white females, I've married four of them. I just hate white female jurors.'
Ellen … 'Women, as a general rule, will have more sympathy. We're the only ones who get raped, remember?'

p 117

'The system reflects society. It's not always fair … It's as fair as biased, emotional humans can make it.'

Introduction: Gender and Judging: Overview and Synthesis[1]

ULRIKE SCHULTZ AND GISELA SHAW

> Whichever way you put it, the message is clear: the incorporation of difference on the bench subtly changes and, ultimately, improves the judicial product (Brenda Hale, the first female Law Lord in the UK).[2]

1. WHAT THE BOOK IS ABOUT

1.1. General Overview

This volume deals with most aspects of gender and judging relevant to discussions on the subject around the world. It tells the story of women in the judiciary in 19 countries of the five continents of the world—representative of their history and national and global developments. Half of the countries concerned are common law countries, the other half civil—law countries, countries with mixed jurisdiction, or countries (like many in Asia) that have received and transformed elements of both major legal systems. Contributions include those from both developed and so-called underdeveloped countries.

Just to list them—for Europe: Germany, Switzerland, The Netherlands, France and Italy; for North America: the USA and Canada; for South America: Argentina; for East Asia: India, Japan, the Philippines and Cambodia; for the Middle East: Syria. Finally, and perhaps most remarkably, for Africa: Ivory Coast, Kenya and South Africa. We are particularly delighted to have attracted contributions from countries in Asia and Africa, given that, with the exception of Japan, the sociology of law remains for them a burgeoning subject as yet little explored.

[1] In references to contributions in this volume the author's name is given in brackets (as there are two articles by Ulrike Schultz they are numbered 1 and 2). References to the entries in the bibliography take the form of the author's name plus year of publication, again in brackets.

[2] Quoted in Rackley 2008, 49.

The book is structured by subjects currently dominating academic debates.

Pioneers and Eminent Women Judges; the history of women in the judiciary: Why were women kept away from judicial office? How did they finally manage to break into the judicial ivory tower? What were their early contributions to the dispensation of justice?

Women Judges' Work and Careers: How does the judicial selection process work? What are the career paths and career options? What are women judges' experiences, their attitudes towards judging and their psychological experiences in their daily work?

Gender Perspectives in Judging: To what extent does gender matter in judging? Do women judge differently from men? Do they contribute to a more gender equal society? Are they inclined to specialise in particular areas of law?

Gendered Construction of the Judiciary: How does the judiciary view itself? How do women fit into this picture which, after all, has traditionally been determined by men?

Feminist Judges and Feminist Adjudication: What makes a female judge a feminist judge? What are the expectations (s)he is confronted with? Is there such a thing as a feminist adjudication process? How do we explain the reluctance on the part of many female judges to identify themselves as feminists?

Quotas and Diversity: How can the share of women in the judiciary be increased? Why does it matter? Do we need quotas? What is the significance of diversity within the judiciary?

Gender Training for the Judiciary: Ought legal training to include gender training? If so, what form should it take? What are the issues arising?

Contributions to this volume have been classified under subheadings according to their main focus. This goes particularly for chapters in sections 2, 3 and 4, as they could have been included under various subheadings. The common denominator of all contributions is their preoccupation with the issue of the gendered image of the judiciary, and that of the particular contribution made by women.

Three areas are obviously of greater significance for common law than for civil law countries. These are: quotas and diversity, the gendered construction of the role and personality of a judge, and feminist judges and adjudication.

1.2. Approaches to the Subject

Approaches and styles vary depending on the authors' personalities as well as on their professional backgrounds. A historian handles her subject differently from a psychologist. A sociologist tends to go for a more theoretical approach than a jurist. The various national cultures also play their part. Some contributions are rather more narrative and descriptive, others more argumentative, and yet others designed to provide specific views on certain issues, such as, for instance, a treatise on diversity. Ruth Herz, who for decades worked as a judge, chooses the form of an autobiographical piece reflecting on her own personal gendered experiences during her judicial career.

Some contributions incline more towards the sociology of organisations, others towards that of the professions. Authors differ in their handling of feminist and also of queer theory, which impacts particularly on their discussion of the changes brought about by the feminisation of the judiciary.

A number of articles are based on authors' empirical quantitative and qualitative research, their arguments frequently supported and illustrated by quotations from interviews with judges and prosecutors of both sexes. Andrea Gastron uses linguistic analyses to extract gender arguments from judicial sentences. Similarly, Ruth Cowan, Les Moran and others make use of textual and image analysis.

The majority of contributions approach the object of their investigation in a critical mode; be this the judiciary as an institution that has, historically, tended to disregard or even reject women as a resource and that even today regards them with some suspicion, denying women complete equality of opportunities; be it the practice of adjudication that fails to do justice to women and lacks the necessary gender sensitivity. Some contributions, such as the one about Gender Education in Japan, also pursue a political aim (ie towards gender justice), and do not shy away from openly criticising their judicial system.

1.3. Differences between Civil and Common Law Judiciaries

In comparing developments regarding women judges in different countries it is important to keep in mind a number of relevant fundamental differences between civil law and common law systems. (Schultz/Shaw 2012, 2) In civil law countries a judicial career is one of a number of separate career paths open to law graduates, which means that judges start their careers at the age of between 25 and 35. As they are public servants, entry later in life is, as a rule, not possible, and formal qualifications are crucial to access to the judiciary. By contrast, in common law countries, judges are chosen from among experienced legal practitioners. These tend to be appointed in middle age (40–50 years), the key criterion being professional achievement, or, as in many states in the United States, they are elected.

Another key difference between the two judicial systems is that of the number of judges, with civil law countries having much higher numbers, a situation reinforced by the distinction in common law countries between recorder, magistrate and judge. The need for higher numbers of judges in civil law countries is also partly due to the fact that their judges produce extensive and detailed written reasonings for their decisions. A civil law judge's position in the legal field is high but not to be compared to that of a common law judge who commands a higher social status as well as a higher income in a more exclusive judicial system than his or her civil law counterpart. Both factors may work as hidden mechanisms to keep women out or hinder them from getting in. In civil law countries it is easier for women to enter the judiciary, as here key access criteria for judicial office, such as formal qualification and examination results, are more rational and transparent and therefore more easily met by women than those in the common law world, where professional visibility, favourable evaluations of professional achievement, and access to—traditionally male—networks are of crucial weight. The increase in the number of women in the judiciary therefore happened about two decades earlier in civil law countries than in common law countries, and more of them have by now reached career positions.

In the two big legal systems of the world, the very process of judicial decision-making is governed by contrasting ideologies. In common law countries a judge, according to convention, is a passive arbiter, an umpire (Mack/Roach Anleu). In civil law countries, judges have a more active role, they direct the proceedings. They act as anonymous interpreters of the law according to specified interpretation rules (Boigeol, Schultz 2) and pass judgments in the name of the state or the people.

Judges in common law countries have greater discretion in reaching their decision by 'distinguishing' the case in hand from precedents. They 'make the law' (Rackley). The judgment is therefore more closely connected to their personality, and the reasoning in the decision will be more often scrutinised and criticised with a view to their personal character and background, ie financial status, political affiliation, life experience as a man or woman, religious belief, sexual orientation, ethnicity and personal qualities. In both systems the final judgment is the product of a process of communication, hence the importance of a gendered view of this process.

All of these differences explain why problems of women's access to judicial careers have been more frequently analysed and discussed in the common law than in the civil law world. One further important reason is that the civil law ideology of the impersonal neutral judge applying the law in strict compliance with formalised rules, makes it almost a taboo to discuss influences of gender on judging in civil law countries. In countries like France the question of gender and judging is all the more unpopular, given the seemingly unstoppable feminisation of the judiciary (Boigeol, Le Feuvre/Lapeyere 2005).

1.4. Judges and Prosecutors

The judiciary in civil law countries comprises judges as well as prosecutors, although the focus in the book is mainly on judges and judging. In many countries the practical training for the two positions differs. In others, such as some German states, Syria and Pakistan, members of these professions may or even have to switch from one to the other. Where judges and prosecutors are elected, as is the case in many states of the USA, women and men may hold judicial office at one time and become prosecutors later or vice versa. Their respective role, however, differs fundamentally. In common law, ie adversarial, systems, prosecutors act as equal opponents to defending counsel. In civil law, ie inquisitorial, systems, such as Germany, the ideology requires that prosecutors, judges and counsel should jointly work to achieve, or at least aim to achieve, justice. Yet another role of prosecutors is that practised in countries in Latin America where the prosecution is a political institution. Overall the number of prosecutors is small compared to that of judges.

2. THE ADVANCEMENT OF WOMEN IN THE JUDICIARY

2.1. Access and Early Development

There are two main reasons for the long delay in modern times to allow women access to legal professions. One was the increasing emphasis on academic qualifications that in many countries remained closed to women until the early twentieth century. The other is the fact that the constitutions of nineteenth-century nation states reserved the right to equality for only one sex, ie men.

It was only late in the nineteenth century that the struggle of the first women's movement for the right of entry to higher education as well as for civil rights for women paved the way for the first women to become lawyers. Access to the judiciary proved to be even harder to achieve. In all countries heated debates took place as to whether women could act as judges. It was frequently argued that women would not be able to judge objectively due to their emotionality and their biologically-based mood swings. Therefore it would be unthinkable to let them pronounce judgment in court. Another argument repeatedly put forward was that women would be too precious for the tough legal world and that they would need to be protected from it (Schultz 2004, 117).

The judiciary was a men's club (in East Asia it was sometimes referred to as 'the Sacred Family' (Kim 2012)), based on idea(l)s of masculinity that had developed over centuries, if not millennia. The first female judges were, at best, stared at with amazement, but also openly attacked. They were helped by the fact that they exercised an authority derived directly from the state, made visible by their robes that helped to blur the difference between them and their male colleagues (Röwekamp).

To help women gain a foothold in the judiciary required not only action on the part of women's groups and political parties but also the relentless struggle of a number of individual women for equal rights and economic independence, a struggle that in some states dragged on for decades. Eyal Katvan, in his contribution, refers to this as the two 'parallel ladders'. In some countries (a number of states in the USA, from 1869, as well as Israel) one helpful device was the professional involvement of women without academic qualifications in the capacity of Justices of the Peace in lower courts, thereby demonstrating their ability to reach objective judgments. Political regimes also played a role, ie left-wing socialist governments were more inclined than conservative governments to consider the possibility of gender equality. Finally, political upheavals in the wake of the two World Wars favoured the cause of women (Burrage 2006).

While in a number of countries women were permitted to become lawyers at the end of the nineteenth century, in many cases admission to the judiciary occurred a good deal later (Menkel-Meadow 1989, Schultz 2003a, xxxiii). Taking on public office as a judge presupposed the right to vote in political elections. Even in states such as Italy and France this was granted to women only following constitutional reform after World War II. The first female judge was appointed in France in 1946, in Italy in 1963 and in Portugal only in 1974. In some countries legislative action was needed to legalise the appointment of women to public office, eg in Germany in 1922.

Almost a century separates the admission of the first women to the judiciary in the USA and in Cambodia and the Philippines. By way of comparison: Russia 1917; Germany 1922 (by 1933 only 26 in post and over 100 in training); USA 1920s (9 judges in 1931); Czechoslovakia 1930; Denmark 1933; Turkey 9 judges in 1932; Poland 11 prior to 1939.

In many central and southern African countries, judges of both sexes met with particularly serious obstacles, given that during the colonial period judicial matters were in the hands of the whites trained in their respective homelands, while natives were only allowed to deal with informal matters in tribal courts. Some 50 years ago, the first law faculties were set up in these regions, which laid the foundation for institutionalised academic legal training. However, only the modern constitutions of recent decades have guaranteed legal equality for women and therefore the right of women to be admitted to the judiciary. In South Africa, it took until the regime change at the end of apartheid, before the first female black women could gain admission as judges.

In Muslim countries, too, women had to wait a very long time for this to happen. However, even in countries under strict Islamic rule, such as Kuwait and the United Arab Emirates, there are now female judges (in the UAE since 2008). Ever since the First International Conference on Women's Rights in Mexico in 1975, NGOs working for equality of rights for women had vociferously demanded the admission of female judges, thereby building up political pressure. This was reinforced by donor countries making development aid dependent on legal equality for women being put into practice. As of 2012, in Egypt, 42 of 12,000 judges are women (Lindbekk 2012). Since the European Union stopped its funding in 2007, no further female judges have been appointed. Development politics was also of significance in East Asian states such as the Philippines (Miwa) and Cambodia (Sawa).

Yet, there are still countries without any female judges. In Saudi Arabia, Sharia law bans women from participation in public life, including any legal profession. The same applies to Iran.

Table: Women in the Judiciary[3]

Nation	Legal system/ Legal Culture	Geographical Location	1st Female Judge	Share of Women in %
Germany 2011	Civil law/ Germanic	Europe	1927 (Dr Maria Hagemeyer)	Judges: 38% Prosecutors: 41% Judges on probation: 57% Prosecutors on probation: 53%

(Continued)

[3] The data in this table (the best available, but obviously incomplete) stem from the contributions to this volume, the cited literature, an internet research of December 2012, the 'European Commission for the Efficiency of Justice Report 2012' for the Council of Europe, 276–87, a global circular mail to ministries of justice, and information provided at a workshop on Women Judges in the Muslim World in Oslo in December 2012. The latter will be documented in a collection of articles being prepared by Monika Lindbekk, University of Oslo, Norway, and Nadia Sonneveld, Leiden University, the Netherlands. In Council of Europe states as a whole the judiciaries enjoy gender equality, with an average of 52% men and 48% women. In four former communist states women make up more than 70% of the judiciary, while in six other states, amongst them the UK and Ireland, men still represent a majority of over 70%. With the exception of some Supreme Courts, the proportion of female judges in higher courts tends to decrease the higher the level in the hierarchy. Significantly fewer women than men are court presidents. The prosecution service overall is less feminised than the courts, while it shares the feature of an inverse proportion of women to rising hierarchical status. Striking differences between data for judges and those for prosecutors may have to be interpreted in the light of these professions' varying political importance, social ranking and prestige.

Table: *(Continued)*

Nation	Legal system/ Legal Culture	Geographical Location	1st Female Judge	Share of Women in %
Austria 2011	Civil law/ Germanic	Europe		Judges: 51% Judges on probation: >60% Court presidents: 29% (2010) Prosecutors: 47% (2010) Heads of prosecution service: 27% (2010)
Netherlands 2010	Civil law	Europe	1947	Judges aged 60–70: 30% aged 50–60: 45% aged: 40–50: 60% aged >40: 76% Court presidents: 11% Prosecutors: 53% Heads of prosecution service: 16%
Belgium 2012	Civil law	Europe		Judges: 47% Court presidents: 23% Prosecutors: 47% Heads of prosecution service: 27%
France 2010	Civil law/ Romance	Europe	1946	Judges: 64% Court presidents: 28% Prosecutors: 47% Heads of prosecution service: 19%
Italy 2010	Civil law/ Romance	Europe	1963	Judges: 48% Court presidents: 13% Prosecutors: 38% Heads of prosecution service: 9%

(Continued)

Nation	Legal system/ Legal Culture	Geographical Location	1st Female Judge	Share of Women in %
Portugal 2010	Civil law/ Romance	Europe	1974 (also 1st female public prosecutor)	Judges: 55% Lower Courts: 63.5% (2011) Superior Courts: 32% (2011) Prosecutors: 59%
Denmark 2010	Civil law Scandinavian-German	Europe	1933	Court presidents: 28% Prosecutors: 64% Heads of prosecution service: 45%
Norway 2010	Civil law Scandinavian-German	Europe	Supreme Court: 1968	Judges: 36% Court presidents: 27% Prosecutors: 47% Heads of prosecution service: 8%
Sweden 2010	Civil law Scandinavian-German	Europe		Judges: 44% Court presidents: 25%
Poland 2010	Civil law Formerly communist	Europe	<1939	Judges: 63% Court presidents: 44% Prosecutors: 53% Heads of prosecution offices: 40%
Czech Republic 2010	Civil law Formerly communist	Europe	1930	Judges: 61% Court presidents: 37% Prosecution: 52% Heads of prosecution offices: 48%
Slovenia 2010	Civil law Formerly communist	Europe		Judges: 78% Highest ratio of female judges in Europe Court presidents: 65% Prosecution: 67% Heads of prosecution offices: 57%

(Continued)

Table: *(Continued)*

Nation	Legal system/ Legal Culture	Geographical Location	1st Female Judge	Share of Women in %
Russian Federation 2010	Civil law Former communist	Europe/ Asia	1917	Court presidents: 37% Prosecutors: 45% Heads of prosecution offices: 6%
Turkey 2012	Civil law	Asia Minor		Judges: 32% Court presidents: 6% Prosecutors: 7% Heads of prosecution offices: –
Syria 2007	Civil law/ Islamic	Near East	1975	Judges: 12%
Egypt	Islamic (fiqh)/ Civil law	Near East	2003 (Tahany El-Gebaly)	Judges: 0.34%
United Arab Emirates	Civil law/ Islamic	Near East	2008	
China 2009	Civil law/ Romance-Germanic, Soviet law, USA, Banking law	East Asia	>1926 (Yuxiu Zheng)	Judges: 24.8% Public prosecutors: 24.6%
Japan 2007	Civil law/ Romance Germanic	East Asia		Judges: 15% Assistant judges: 21.5%
Philippines 2005	Civil law/ Common law (US)	South East Asia	Cecila Munoz Palma (1952)	Judges: 27.8%
Great Britain 2010	Common law	Europe	1945 (Sybil Campbell) or 1956 (Rose Heilbron)	Judges: UK England and Wales: 23% Scotland: 21%

(Continued)

Nation	Legal system/ Legal Culture	Geographical Location	1st Female Judge	Share of Women in %
Ireland 2010	Common law	Europe		Supreme Court: 25% High Court: 16% Circuit Court: 29% District Court: 25% Court presidents: 25% Prosecutors: 60%
USA 2010	Common law	North America	1870 (Esther Morris)	Federal district (or trial) court judges: approx 30%
Canada 2012	Common law (mixed)	North America	1943 County Court: Helen Kinnear 1971 Supreme Court of Ontario: Mabel Van Camp	Judges: 33%
Australia 2011	Common law	Oceania	1965 (Roma Mitchell)	Judges: 28.9%
New Zealand 2009	Common law	Oceania	1975 (Augusta Wallace)	Judges: 26%
Israel 2010	Common law (mixed)	Near East	1948	Judges: 52.4%
South Africa 2008	Common law (mixed)	Africa		Judges: <18%
Kenya 2006	Common law	Africa	<1974 (Effie Owuor)	Chief magistrates: 40% High Court: 20%
India 2010	Common law	South Asia		Magistrates: 26% Superior Court: 7%
Pakistan 2012	Common law	Southern Asia	1974	Judges >1/3

2.2. The Situation Today

In many countries the number of women judges, once they had been admitted in principle, grew very slowly. In Continental Europe it was only in the late 1970s that significant increases were recorded, as growing economic prosperity and women's increasing share in education and training led to equivalent developments in the number of female law students. A veritable explosion of numbers has been happening since the 1990s. In many countries women now represent more than half of all students in legal education. Even in countries such as South Korea and China the 50 per cent mark is now being reached, although generally speaking, women's share in academic studies has remained less vibrant than elsewhere.

The number of female judges has risen in tandem with these developments. In many countries women judges now represent at least one third of the total. This is true even of a Muslim state such as Pakistan, the first to call itself an Islamic Republic, where the first appointment of a female judge took place in 1974. Similar developments have occurred in many states of South and East Asia, such as India (Stewart) and the Philippines (Miwa), where women's access to judicial office was delayed for a long time.

In a steadily increasing number of European states the share of women in judicial posts by far exceeds that of men. Intriguingly, this is precisely the case in countries such as France and Portugal where the first women judges were admitted as late as after World War II. The proportion of women among young judges can reach 75 per cent (as it does in the Netherlands), which suggests a further feminisation of the judiciary, at least partly due to the fact that in civil law countries success in being appointed depends on performance in academic examinations and in assessment centres, where women do just as well as men. Not surprisingly, calls can be heard in a number of countries for preferential treatment for men in appointment processes in order to safeguard gender equality (Boigeol for France, Dijksterhuis for the Netherlands), although the decrease in the number of male appointees is actually due, not to discrimination, but to a lack of interest on the part of men. Men with top examination results tend to prefer positions in large international law firms where salaries are significantly higher than in the judiciary.

In the Anglo-American world the picture is less favourable for women, due to the fact that judges are selected from experienced lawyers either by way of elections or through judicial appointment committees. It remains unclear why and in which states the share of women judges develops faster or more slowly. In the USA there exists a substantial body of research into questions of female representation on the bench which, however, has, so far, not produced generally-agreed results (Kenney).

In Arab countries with a pro-Western orientation, such as Syria, women have also gained their share in the judiciary (Cardinal). Yet, this has to be seen in the light of the move towards traditional values and the reinforcement of Sharia, the religious laws of Islam, and the coming to power of Muslim brotherhoods. Islamist governments generally resist the acceptance of constitutionally-grounded equality rights of women, fighting the modernisation of family law in the direction of equal rights and duties of both sexes in marriage and family. This raises the question whether the progress made in women's participation in education and work will at some point be reversed.

An interesting development has occurred in the context of European and international courts. By now the International Criminal Court in the Hague has more female than male judges,[4] while the European Court of Human Rights has around one third female members.[5] However, the courts of the European Union lag well behind. At the European Court of Justice only 6 out of the 36 judges are women; at the General Court (Court of First Instance) it is 6 out of 27; at the Civil Service Tribunal 3 out of 8. This demonstrates that, leaving aside the differing appointments processes, the share of women decreases with a court's growing importance and prestige.

2.3. Gender Factors in Recruitment and Entry to the Profession

In civil law countries entry to the judiciary immediately follows the completion of legal education and training. The following are some prototypes: In Germany, having completed their academic studies, candidates undergo two years of practical training in the various fields of legal work, and then sit a state examination under the aegis of the respective state ministry of justice that awards the qualification for judicial office (also needed by lawyers), followed by three years of practice 'on probation'. In France, access is gained by passing the entry examination of the judicial college. In East Asia where traditionally the civil law model has been adopted and the selection of jurists was extremely strict (Kim 2003), a new training system for judges, prosecutors and lawyers was recently introduced that is broadly based on the American graduate law school system (Korea in 2009, Japan a few years earlier).

As a rule, in civil law countries success in examinations determines access to the profession. This is a rational criterion that can be expected not to discriminate against women. In Continental Europe, this has indeed resulted

[4] At the ICC the 2012 annual *Gender Report Card* examined the Court's internal policies, recruitment and personnel statistics, as well as its institutional development.

[5] In total, 164 judges from 47 states have so far sat at the ECtHR, of whom 31 have been women.

in the currently high and growing number of women in judicial posts. However, examination and later assessment results are also affected by gendered factors. In France, at the judicial college men achieve better results than women. Where written examination papers are anonymised, gender factors cannot be at play. However, regarding oral examinations the question arises whether the (mostly largely still male) examiners grant women a bonus (on the simple principle that men like women), or whether they are inclined to give preference to men. Regarding the French judicial examination Anne Boigeol states: 'There is no doubt that in the light of the diminishing number of male applicants, juries in the oral entrance examination pay particular attention to their performance, particularly in the context of discussions on "general culture"'. There might be even greater feminisation if male and female candidates received exactly the same treatment. A similar phenomenon has been observed in Germany where women's success rate in the second state examination equals that of men, but at their first assessments during their probationary period in the judiciary after 6, 16 and 36 months, their grades suddenly drop.

In China job adverts and appointments reveal traditional patterns of gender discrimination, when male applicants are preferred because the jobs involve 'working in harsh conditions, travel and on-site investigation'. In European Union Member States such practices are banned through anti-discrimination regulations. Job advertisements have to be formulated in a gender neutral way, and open as well as hidden discrimination are unlawful and entitle those affected to compensation. However, this does not mean that gender-based considerations do not occur backstage.

In Muslim countries the opportunity for women to get into higher political and also judicial positions is linked to their offering an alternative to their male colleagues. In many African and Asian countries the participation of women has helped to restore public trust in the judiciary (Kamau for Kenya, Owor 2013 for Uganda). Women are less prone to bribery which raises the question whether they are more virtuous than men. In any case it is easier for them than for men to resist corruption as they do not need to earn the money for the family: they are not the breadwinners (Cardinal)[6]. In Arab states (such as Syria and Egypt, but also in Pakistan) it is customary (most likely as an anti-corruption measure) for judges' period of office at one and the same court to be limited to a number of years. They are regularly moved to other courts and cities, which for women in particular,

[6] Cf also Holden, Livia and Holden, Marius (2012) *Lady Judges of Pakistan*, Insights Productions, documentary-film. www.insightsproduction.net. In these countries, donor-country pressure results in female judges not necessarily being selected from a pool of judges according to their performance but appointed by high ranking officials, which again opens up the possibility of nepotism.

owing to the traditional family structures in these countries, represents a considerable hardship as it frequently involves separation from families and complications in providing for them.

In Commonwealth countries where judges are mostly appointed by Judicial Appointment Commissions the last two decades have seen growing attempts at procedural reform in order to counteract the low participation rate of women (consistently well below international averages). Efforts have been made to rationalise appointment criteria to reduce the influence of classical gatekeepers, such as old boys' networks and clubs. In the United Kingdom the vetting of judges used to be carried out by the Judicial Appointment Boards for Scotland and England and Wales by informally canvassing senior lawyers, occasionally referred to as a process of 'secret soundings' (Malleson). While this system did ensure a homogeneity amongst judges as they were chosen from a narrow range of educational backgrounds often with family connections to the legal profession (Blackwell 2012) and along with it stability through self-replication, it excluded women and potentially talented applicants who were not sufficiently well-known to the judiciary and the bar. Now selection by a 'tap on the shoulder' guided by candidates' social characteristics and background is to be replaced by selection by merit.

The problem lies in translating the concept of merit into practice. What constitutes merit and potential? (Thornton 2007) What criteria are to be applied in the absence of any positive description of the realities of work? (Genn 2009) Or in other words: what are the key qualities required for a good judge? Do women have these to the same extent as men? (Mack/Roach Anleu) In Canada, judicial selection reform efforts only showed success for women when the definition of merit was rethought. However, if superficially neutral looking criteria are defined, it often results in men being better able to meet them than women. That applies especially to elite credentials. In this case the result runs counter to the original intention. In the UK the proportion of women in post has remained static or has even decreased (Malleson).

In so far as judicial elections take place, as is the norm in many states in the US, the recruitment process is even harder to influence. Electors are not likely to appoint women unless social movements and interest groups mobilise and articulate appointing women as a demand (Kenney). And women themselves have to push and demand to be appointed. Here the issue is still partly to break the mould. In the US, for instance, there are still courts without any female or black female judges.[7] And if finally a first woman were appointed, this does not mean that she will be followed by a second such appointment (Kenney).

[7] *Cf* Information in the Gender and Judging Blog http://genderandjudging.tulane.edu/.

The question is whether the selection process in common law states needs a wholly new approach, as has happened for instance in Kenya where, since the new constitution of 2010, the selection of judges has been transformed into a public, competitive and transparent process (Kamau).

The judiciary is an employer particularly favoured by women. In the course of a recent study of careers in the legal academy in Germany[8] many interviewees voiced the opinion that it is difficult to retain women in academic legal positions given the highly attractive alternative of the judiciary, a position offering prestige, respect, good gender-neutral pay, secure employment, a regular work schedule with a manageable workload, all of which helps to achieve a good work-life balance (different for Argentina, Junqueira 2003 and for Brazil, Bonelli 2012). In addition the judiciary offers maternity and parental leave, and very flexible part-time working patterns (Bartolomei), operating as 'pull' factors as well as 'push' factors given that these conditions are rarely available for lawyers (Sommerlad). This runs through the volume's contributions like a red thread. For moral reasons women also prefer the role of decision-maker to that of partial counsel.

2.4. Careers in the Judiciary—Chances and Impediments

Women in the judiciary share with women generally the difficulties in reaching higher or leadership positions. In recent years, the topic has been the subject of numerous research projects. Yet, nation-specific insights and results regarding specific problems in the judiciary remain limited.

In civil law countries the bulk of women is gathered in courts of first instance, in common law countries the larger part hold positions as magistrates or recorders, ie lower judicial functions. In civil law countries a career in the judiciary runs from courts of first instance via appellate courts to supreme courts and to positions of court president and vice-president, the latter two groups being also or even largely charged with administrative functions. Frequently, judges in supreme courts are being elected. The various contributions in this volume outline the respective procedures in the countries concerned. Even the higher and highest courts do by now comprise an increasing number of female judges and also court presidents,[9] while in common law countries their number remains extremely modest (Kenney). Brenda Hale, who was appointed as the first female law lord to the House of Lords in England and Wales in 2003 (now the Supreme Court of the United Kingdom) is still the only female member out of 11 judges. In Germany, with the setting up of the Federal Constitutional Court in 1951,

[8] *Cf* www. fernuni-hagen.de/jurpro.

[9] *Cf* details in the blog on Gender and Judging, http://genderandjudging.tulane.edu/?page_id=23.

one woman was nominated, and there remained just one for decades until 1987. Currently, there are 5 out of 16 judges who are women, almost a third. At the level of courts of first instance and the appeal courts the percentage of presidents stands much lower (Boigeol, Schultz 1).

All in all, higher courts are far from achieving equality of numbers and a fully gender-integrated bench. Feminisation is happening, but in all countries the principle still applies that the higher the position, the smaller the share of women, even in states where women currently represent over 60 per cent of all judges. This cannot be explained away by the so-called trickle-up effect (Schultz 1, Malleson 2003), ie the theory that it is only a question of time until women take on the higher positions. Some common law countries have even recorded a backlash (UK, Australia, Canada).

Which factors play a part in these developments? The main and official argument used to explain the scarcity of women in higher and top positions is that women do not apply, that it is a choice voluntarily entered into. This is a way of attributing responsibility for women's exclusion to women themselves. In Germany as well as in France and the USA women have demonstrated an equal desire for promotion as men (Boigeol, Kenney, Schultz 1), albeit fewer apply. How is this to be explained? One explanation offered is that men are more strongly career orientated, that women avoid early career decisions, that for women bringing up children takes precedence over careers (Boigeol) that women have competing life targets. Another explanation is that women anticipate failure to be appointed and therefore decide not to apply. Some people claim that women lack the necessary qualities and commitment. It is therefore not surprising that women have lower perceived efficacy—ie they are as motivated as men to make a career but have more doubts as to their ability to do so. Also, their perception of self-efficacy—their trust in their own abilities—falls short of those of men. This is a feature shared by female judges and prosecutors with other women in higher-ranking professions. And they often lack support from their partners who need them at home for their own support—a classical male career criterion.

But even if women do apply for senior posts they encounter difficulties in being selected. The glass ceiling continues to exist. Why should that be so? Many states have produced catalogues of competencies, qualities and abilities (Schultz 1, Malleson, Sommerlad) by which applicants are to be measured. The real problem is the actual ranking, as naturally subjective assessments come into play, as well as the tendency towards system self-replication, which results in men being preferred for exposed and visible positions. In addition, there tends to be a lack of transparency in the process, so that in case of doubt, ultimately the (often male) candidate, the 'one' preferred in the first place, is selected.

Appointment and selection committees, which in many countries hold a key role in the selection process, remain in male hands. Many reports state that the promotion criterion is for the candidate 'to be visible and then to be asked to apply' by court presidents or the selection committees or whoever is in charge of promotion—in the UK and Commonwealth countries captured in the famous phrase of 'tap on the shoulder'. Various networks of power and influence (from which women are often excluded) provide information about colleagues and their abilities, thus allowing the construction of a picture of the persons most suited to the post and, of course, ensuring the system's homogeneity and stability. Whatever procedure is applied, there is one feature which remains in place, ie that men control access and resources, and stereotypical perceptions of masculinity and femininity play an import part (Boigeol, Dijksterhuis, Schultz 1, Bonelli 2012).

The high quality of an applicant's work is a sine qua non. Beyond that what matters are commitment above the call of duty, and (depending on the respective judicial system) mobility within the judicial district, as the number of higher courts is limited and these courts lie in cities far apart. Both requirements are particularly harsh on women with children not only in those societies where men traditionally continue to feel socially less responsible for children and family jobs (eg Arab states like Egypt and Syria, but also Pakistan and Brazil etc). Women who become pregnant are assumed to be on the 'Mommy track' and to have given up any professional ambitions; part-time work is seen as an indication of reduced commitment.

In civil law countries, where career paths are strictly prescribed, slightly older women find it almost impossible to catch up on any career ladder. Years 'lost' due to family duties are difficult to make up. It is not surprising that significantly more women than men believe that their private lives are obstacles to achieving their professional goals. Over half of women, but only five per cent of men think that women experience greater professional disadvantages due to gender discrimination (Ludewig/LaLlave). Yet it is precisely in civil law countries that we find narratives negating the persistence of gender differences in the careers of women in leading positions. Also those who do gain access to positions of power and thereby raise the social status of women frequently deny gender-based disadvantages. In common law countries women are much more aware of them.

What is not wholly clear is whether alongside vertical stratification there exists also a horizontal stratification, with female enclaves within the judiciary that work as a career impediment. It seems that only in a few countries are there clearly marked tendencies to shunt women into special jurisdictional courts (mainly family or juvenile law, or rural courts that hear small claims) (eg Bartolomei for Italy). This represents a difference vis-à-vis law firms that produce a gendered stratification and segmentation accompanied by heightened gender identity. There are therefore more discourses about differences amongst lawyers than amongst judges (Bonelli 2012, Bolton and Muzio 2007).

In spite of any shortcomings of the judiciary regarding the treatment of women, women (like men) enjoy a high degree of professional satisfaction. Indeed, women's satisfaction, considering their standard of living, exceeds that of men (Ludewig/LaLlave). As in other instances, this may partly be explained by the fact that, as a rule, they are not the main breadwinners in their family.

2.5. Biographical Factors: Age, Origin, Sexual Orientation

As women judges began to be appointed later than men, and only recently in larger numbers, their average age is significantly below that of men.

There are few differentiated studies on the social origins of male judges, and very few data on those of women. We know that in the 1970s in Germany, female law students came from higher social strata than their fellow male students (Schultz 2003 b). In England, senior judges as a body are characterised by an establishment background, often with family connections with the legal establishment, and it seems that this applies even more strongly to the small number of women amongst them (Blackwell 2012, 426). It can be assumed that in countries where the history of women judges is still a very short one, especially countries with a culture dominated by the upper classes, such as Arab and Central Asian states, larger numbers of women than men judges and public prosecutors are from higher social strata. In Pakistan, for instance, female judges tend to be the wives and daughters of the liberal elite upper class.

Little is known of the sexual orientation of male or female judges and public prosecutors. In some countries, especially in the Near, Central and Far East, this has remained a taboo topic. In parts of Europe, North America and Latin America there are legal institutions for same-sex cohabitation thus indicating that sexual orientation other than heterosexual is accepted to a degree. But whether members of the judiciary of same-sex orientation are open about their sexual orientation is a different question.

In the UK, discussions about diversity in the judiciary have led to data being collected regarding the sex, ethnicity, disabilities and professional background (solicitor or barrister) of judges. Issues of sexual orientation were disregarded as irrelevant to the conduct of professional roles (Moran 2013). However, there is an InterLaw Diversity Forum for Lesbian, Gay, Bisexual and Transgender (LGBT) in the judiciary, and meanwhile data have also been collected about sexual diversity. Being female and being disabled are identified by those of same-sex orientation and by heterosexuals alike as key factors in discrimination, with membership of a network of people of same-sex orientation having an aggravating effect. 'Gender and ethnicity in combination with sexual orientation may have an amplifying effect, making elite positions seem more entrenched and the barriers to change even higher' (Moran 2013).

2.6. Promoting Women in the Judiciary: Quotas and Demands for Diversity

How can we achieve gender justice? Due to antidiscrimination guidelines and the European Court of Justice's adjudication, both positive action and quotas are legal in countries within the European Union. In England and Wales as well as France, quotas are restricted to political elections and are not applicable to professional elections, recruitment and career advancement (Boigeol, Malleson, Rackley). In Germany target quotas are laid down by law. To achieve gender parity women have to be given preference in appointments and promotions in case of equal qualifications and where there are no specific distinguishing factors on the part of the competing candidate. However, in practice, in the judiciary these quotas hardly ever have any bearing on actual appointment decisions (Schultz 1). On the other hand, Kenya for instance operates a one third gender requirement for public offices. What might be more effective than quotas would be to make gender balance an implicit goal and a benchmark by which commissioners and personnel heads are assessed.

The argument put forward by lawyer organisations, that gender parity pays in economic terms, the so-called 'business-case for equality', is of no relevance to the judiciary. Here a more appropriate question would be that of quality, ie, to once again quote Brenda Hale, whether an increase in the share of women, 'the incorporation of difference on the bench', would change or even improve the 'judicial product'.[10]

Which other policies might enhance women's careers? First of all, the recruitment pool should be expanded through a culture of encouragement and targeted approaches to suitable female candidates, or at least by the identification and removal of discouragement strategies. Precise job descriptions are of the essence.[11] Defining the job profile, advertising judicial posts, setting up interviews to ensure transparency of the process; ensuring gender parity among commission members, training decision-makers in gender-neutral personnel assessments, inspiring gender sensitivity, and alerting them to implicit bias, especially in the context of assessment and evaluation would improve the likelihood of women applying for and gaining senior posts. On the other hand it is important to reduce the pressure of work eg by means of mentors during the introductory phase, providing collegial advice and supervision, help with stress management, reinforcement

[10] *Cf* n 1.
[11] These exist in Germany, however, intriguingly, not for top positions.

of self-perception (Schultz 2012). In the case of elections of judges and prosecutors, there is also a need to raise self-awareness within the committees and, ultimately, within the public at large.

In Germany, presumably as in a number of other countries, the judicial system as a whole as well as the entire public service, provide for equal opportunities officers in all courts and prosecution organisations. Women judges and prosecutors are appointed to look after their female colleagues' interests. As a rule they tend to operate with some caution due to pressures within the judiciary to conform, and for fear of spoiling their own career chances. So far it is only amongst lawyers in Canada that there are gender-bias task forces charged with documenting discrimination and gender bias.

For any such measures to be successful it is important that the promotion of women goes beyond mere lip service and becomes an aim supported by society as a whole. Yet we observe worldwide that this is very rarely the case, irrespective of on-going efforts to create gender equality. In particular in Anglo-American countries, the aim of gender equality has been integrated into the diversity discourse, with the risk that the aim of gender justice gets buried under efforts to stop discrimination of other kinds.

Why does gender diversity matter over and beyond the aim of gender justice that follows from basic rights and the principle of equal rights? A number of rationales for diversity have been developed: 'These include the need for equal participation, namely that equal participation of men and women in the justice system is an inherent and essential feature of a democracy without which the judiciary cannot enjoy public confidence and legitimacy' (Kamau). Similar to equal participation is the concept of inclusive diversity which describes the idea of the equal representation of judges with diverse background on the bench, with the judiciary as the third power better reflecting society and representing litigants irrespective of their sex, sexual orientation and ethnicity. Other arguments used are that women bring to the judiciary different perspectives based on their different life experiences, different attitudes and values, which add richness and texture to the judicial system. Diversity has also been advocated in order to counterbalance the traditional perception of judging as a 'masculine' enterprise (Rackley,[12] Malleson 2003, Feenan 2009, Kenney 2013).

Countries with an intense colonial past, multi-cultural societies and migration had their diversity discussions earlier as well as experiencing diversity on the bench at an earlier point. Due to its apartheid history, South Africa has made the latter a clear priority (Cowan). Judges in these countries may also have experienced discrimination more intensely, particularly

[12] Erika Rackley distinguishes between facial diversity which is about appearance, hardship diversity which is about life experience deviating from the group norm, transformative diversity which means that all the differences are brought into the judges' substantive work including their judgments, and inclusive diversity.

if there is an intersection with other features prone to creating discrimination (religion, sexual orientation, age, ethnicity)—so-called intersectional discrimination.

Important advocates for the advancement of women in the judiciary are women judges associations (eg Kamau for Kenya). These are most frequent in common law countries. In civil law countries, women have opted to join forces in women lawyers' associations some of which can look back at a long tradition. The German Women Jurists' Association was founded in 1914. It runs, for example, an initiative to increase women's participation in the federal courts under the heading 'Women into the red robes!'[13]

3. THE JUDICIARY: STILL A GENDERED ORGANISATION?

> *But as one of the most powerful mechanisms for reinscribing the conventional social script, the law is also pivotal to both the construction of women as irrational, disorderly and hence inherently unsuited for judicial office and the naturalisation of masculinised legal authority. As a result the judiciary is symbolic of hegemonic masculinity (Sommerlad).*

Resistance against women in the judiciary is the product of its purely masculine image and impact that has lasted until very recent times. 'The exercise of authority whether in the family or in society was a masculine prerogative, linked to such features as physical strength, a louder voice, the habit to give orders and take decisions' (Boigeol). Male gender was part of the judicial model, deeply inscribed in the judicial script. Female judges in interviews conducted by Hilary Sommerlad, refer to meetings which are 'still predominantly male-dominated by public school/Eton type blokes', wearing 'unimaginative clothes', men who 'all seemed big and imposing', 'drank like fish', a 'sea of grey men—pompous, with loud voices'. Hence her conclusion that 'the judiciary is symbolic of hegemonic masculinity.'[14]

The traditional prototype of a judge was an outstanding white male bourgeois personality of high morality, humanistic, mild, the loving father of a happy family. This adds 'heterosexuality as a silent norm inherent to the system' (Moran).

(Male) judges were (and are) representatives and servants of the state, exerting authority, incorporating the ideal of objectivity covering their individuality with a black robe. In a 1956 portrait of one of the first judges at

[13] http://www.djb.de/Themen/RoteRoben/.

[14] It is worth pointing out that this summary, in its radicality, no longer applies to (for instance) Germany, where class-related questions such as 'What club do you belong to?' or 'Do you go yachting?' are hardly conceivable any more.

the German Federal Constitutional Court, Karl Heck, we find an idealised description of a judge in Germany:

> A cross between a monk and an officer, characterized by selfless dedication but little creativity ... severe, precise, earnest and more or less identical looking beings wholly devoted to their duties; advancing in strictly trained parade step—you almost see before your eyes the 'Old Fritz' of Prussia with his crooked stick ensuring that the judge who dares oppose the Imperial Court's decisions or even, absolutely unforgivably, overlooks a higher court's precedent, remains in rank and file order and regains his good sense (Hänlein 1996).[15]

How were women to fit into this picture, women about whom a female appeal court president in Germany recently said, 'They have made justice livelier and more colourful.'? Admittedly, the robe that attracts respect from the outside world helps women to adapt to the ruling image thereby turning themselves into 'asexual beings' (Junqueira 2003). Yet, women remain the 'other' who cannot be entrusted with certain activities and functions and who must be feared as undermining the familiar judicial image,[16] given that from time immemorial women as a group have been suspected on the basis of their emotionality of being incapable of objectivity. Les Moran observes that concerns about judicial subjectivity are only raised if the judge or judicial nominee is a woman or somehow other.

In the eyes of their superiors and colleagues, motherhood in particular imparts women with classical female qualities such as empathy, mercifulness, indulgence and tolerance, qualities that run directly counter to the image outlined above. In other words, femininity threatens the familiar and established image of the judiciary.

This, in turn, leads to a tendency towards self-replication by means of conscious or unconscious defence mechanisms and strategies to maintain at least the outer appearance of masculinity. Hence the attempts to fill mostly with men leadership positions that are crucial to determine the judicial public image.[17] Thus men's domination is protected (Syria, France, Germany) and the institution as the traditional male (France) and public elite institution maintained (Bonelli 2012 for Brazil). Somewhere in the background there is also the secret fear that feminisation of the judiciary might bring about the devaluation of the institution.

Masculinity was and continues to be displayed and reinforced by means of symbolic actions and ceremonies. Les Moran has analysed the wording of public oaths in the Supreme Court of New South Wales, Australia. He

[15] This conjures up the mediaeval principle of *Fiat justitia pereat mundi.*

[16] Feminisation of the judiciary as one of the usurpationary projects of women (Witz, 1992).

[17] In France, the option of lateral access to the judiciary has opened up opportunities for the recruitment of more men.

concludes that they serve 'the purpose of identifying and mapping the personal and professional qualities of the subject onto the newly made judicial subject. They formulate and fashion the subject as the embodiment of judicial virtues', which creates hagiographic images of the judge. As Maria da Gloria Bonelli puts it, the judge is transformed into a public existence (Bonelli 2012). This process is reinforced by judges' traditional theatrical attributes such as the cap and gown or, in common law countries, the wig, as well as by the awe-inspiring architecture and decor adorning classical law court buildings (Herz, Resnik 2011). In this way the perception of judges' personalities is reduced to a small number of striking symbols. Photos and images of the judiciary are amazingly monotonous, hardly variable and static.[18]

The public therefore perceives the judiciary as an organisation that is characterised by masculinity and would be in danger of losing legitimacy if feminisation went too far. Bregje Dijksterhuis describes media discussions about the feminisation of the judiciary in the Netherlands, which resulted in the demand for preferential male appointments under the label of the need for diversity. In this context, female judges received dubious praise: 'When a female judge is judging, you are sure to be home early, because the potatoes are waiting.'

The question is whether the entry of large numbers of women together with the diversity discourse are capable of producing new judicial subjectivities (Sommerlad). Intriguingly, we can observe a cultural shift in civil law states, albeit not in proportion to feminisation. Nor is it clear where this shift will lead. Sommerlad comments, in the face of the durability and deep embeddedness of gender in socio-structural arrangements and cultural practice,

> The relative autonomy of masculine domination despite historical transformations in patriarchy also shows us that new social forms do not supplant their predecessors; rather, different temporalities are co-enacted in social practice.

4. DO WOMEN IN THE JUDICIARY MAKE A DIFFERENCE?

These conceptions of masculinity demonstrate that rather than asking, 'Do we just count heads?', ie treating the increase in the number of women in the judiciary as a mere formality, we should ask, 'Is substantial change happening?'

[18] Gender aspects of judicial iconography were the focus of discussions at a panel on 'Gender, Judging and Popular Culture' at the Law and Society Association meeting in Chicago in May 2010. Key contributions were from L Moran on 'Masculinity, TV and the visual delights of judicial authority: Reflections on Judge John Deed', and N Marder on 'Judging Judge Judy and Other Television Judges'. A further paper by J Resnik addressed the issue of 'Representing Justice: Gender, Race and the Iconography of Courts'.

4.1. Views of Pioneering and Eminent Female Judges

The first female judges in the Weimar Republic of Germany, appointed in the 1920s, were convinced that their entry into the profession would have a marked influence on jurisprudence. They thought they would not 'switch off their emotional considerations as completely as the majority of male judges' and would 'comprehend the case more intuitively.' They also 'saw their best chances to unfold their special "feminine and motherly character" in those legal fields that were thought to be suitable for women.' At the same time they never doubted that their legal education ensured that their feelings were governed and controlled by exact, objective, logical juridical thinking (Röwekamp).

The first female judges at the Federal Court of Justice after World War II described this in terms of women wanting to make greater use of the option to develop the law, while men were more inclined to adhere to its exact wording. Or, as Marion Röwekamp puts it:

> While strictly adhering to the norms, standards and traditions of their profession and wanting to assimilate to the profession, they [the female judges] also wanted to reveal the 'human' side of the law and thus stressed the essentialist views propagated by the bourgeois women's movement that women should work in the spirit of a caring or welfare morale. Indeed, these female judges felt hurt if, as professional women, they were regarded as lacking in feminity.

Elaine Martin reaches similar conclusions in her biographical study of three American female judges, called to office in the 1980s, when women judges were no longer a rarity in the United States. These three women (who on appointment were quite a bit older than their colleagues in Germany who were career judges) equally stress the unique perspective women bring to the bench. Thus Judge Nelson is said to talk of 'the qualities of mental alertness, intuition, and the spiritual qualities of love and service in which women are strong and how they can positively influence the adversary system'. Throughout her career as academic and judge, Nelson promoted the idea of Alternative Dispute Resolution (ADR), as a legal approach that fits neatly with the notion of women as contextual thinkers. Another female judge, Judge Barkett, even goes further. Her profile illustrates the contention that women judges may be more likely to practise feminist jurisprudence and ask 'the woman question'—that is, to ask 'how a particular rule or outcome may have different consequences for men and women.'

In our time, too, women judges have argued along similar lines. The first British Law Lord, Brenda Hale, thought that, 'the incorporation of difference on the bench subtly changes and, ultimately, improves the judicial product'.[19] Judge Sonia Sotomayor (the first Latina Supreme Court Judge

[19] Note 2 above.

in the USA) remarked in her now notorious Berkeley speech of 2001, 'I would hope that a wise Latina woman with the richness of her experiences would more often than not reach a better conclusion than a white male who hasn't lived that life.', a remark that, as the press had it, 'launched a thousand tantrums' during her nomination to the Supreme Court in 2009. Ruth Bader Ginsburg, the second female Supreme Court Judge in the USA, expressed her view of the matter as follows, 'There are perceptions that we have because we are women. It's a subtle influence. We can be sensitive to things that are said in draft opinions that (male justices) are not aware can be offensive.'[20]

As reported by Mary Jane Mossman, two of the first female judges in Canada did not focus on gender. Helen Kinnear was the first woman in the British Empire appointed to a County Court in 1943, and Mabel Van Camp was the first appointed to the Supreme Court of Ontario in 1971. Reflecting on the gendered context for women in law, Mossman comments:

> Even though their successes may have resulted from pressure on the gatekeepers on the part of the women's movement, these successful women lawyers [firmly distanced themselves from the women's movement and] continued to deny that gender had any significance in the practice of law … [They] were always required to work within the traditions of the 'gentleman's profession' of law, and to accept gender neutrality as fundamental to the ideals of modern legal professionalism.

These Canadian women illustrate a stance frequently seen in relation to women in leadership positions, that is, they take care to adapt as closely as possible to male standards, thus providing a masculinised performance in the attempt to avoid any criticism linked to their femininity.

Ruth Herz, the first Jewish female judge in Germany after World War II and one of the few female judges generally in the 1970s, writes in her autobiographical report in this volume about her adoption of a self-critical approach as well as her reflections regarding her own social role and alternative strategies for action as a judge. This may be typical of a woman reflecting on her position in the context of a dual minority position. However, her legal sociological approach is also typical of women jurists in Germany who went to university at the time.

In sum, there is a whole variety of possible starting-points for a discussion about whether there is an essential difference between women and men judges and their respective work.

[20] Lithwick, Dahlia (2009) White Men Can't Judge? Why Sonia Sotomayor might really believe that Latina women make better judges, http://www.slate.com/articles/double_x/xxfactor_xxtra/2009/06/white_men_cant_judge.html.

4.2. The Issue of Gendered Judging

This question is as controversial as that whether intelligence is innate or a product of education and training, that is the environment.[21] Are women's characters gendered by nature? Do they have generally shared qualities that are typically female (empathy, mercifulness, lenience, tolerance, gentleness)? Or are they and their attitudes and judgements formed by cultural environments and typical of women and their life experiences? Or, again, are any differences merely the product of individuals' characters, education, life circumstances, financial situation, family status, political views etc?

When, in the late 1980s we were planning the comparative project 'Women in the World's Legal Professions', we began by asking: Do women change the legal profession? Does the legal profession change women? These questions followed in the wake of the feminism of difference current in the 1980s. Then, in the 1990s, feminism committed itself to structuralism and deconstruction of gender. Its aim was to overcome social gender with traditional gender roles and character constructed by patriarchy, although paradoxically enough many feminists cherished a 'we, the women' rhetoric which in itself presupposes difference. The vast majority of the authors in that volume[22] discuss—most of them critically—the thesis advanced by Carol Gilligan, the pioneer of difference feminism of those years, i e that women's voice differs from that of men and their ethic is one of care as opposed to a male ethic of justice. In this volume, too, most of the authors refer to, discuss and illustrate this thesis.

The problem is and remains that if the emphasis is on differences between men and women, then one inevitably drifts towards the 'patriarchal dilemma', providing ammunition for those men who 'have always known that women are different', ie weaker, and thereby weakening the position of feminists attempting to define and describe such differences. Yet, the question remains central to any study of women's path towards access to the professions, denied to them on the basis of their being different.

After the turn of the millennium, the predominance of diversity discourses has given preference to approaches emphasising individualisation and subjectivisation. This facilitates discussions about gender differences while also depriving them of some of their previous weightiness.

Tracking down and providing evidence for effects of difference due to the gender of the judge is always made harder by the fact that male and female gender intersects with other aspects of difference as described in section 2.5

[21] This was the subject of an embittered debate in Western Europe in the 1970s, between the psychologist van Eysenck and those stressing the prime significance of the social environment.

[22] Note 9 above.

on diversity, such as age, race/ethnicity, family background, class/social stratum, sexual orientation, religion. Besides, personality traits such as looks, manners and behaviour, which determine human interaction have an influence on personal value systems and take concrete form in individuals' life experience. Thus it is conceivable that the early generations of female judges and public prosecutors may, due to obstacles in the way of advancement, have adopted attitudes different (possibly more rigorous) to those of later generations (Schultz 1990).

Where, then, can we find starting-points for discussions of potential gendered difference?

4.3. Difference in Habitus and Social and Legal Qualities

Regarding male and female judges, do we find differences in their 'habitus', their physical being, their presentation, visible life-style, language (body language included), clothes and taste?[23] Do we detect differences in their social habitus, their attitudes or are female and male judges a homogeneous group with identical or comparable forms of thinking, feeling and acting?

Regarding self-presentation, there can be no disagreement. Female corporeality differs from that of males. In our reports, we read about female judges pondering how to dress, whether to dress in a way that signals femininity or to veil it. Ruth Herz describes her struggle with a robe which was too big for her, and being told that she would certainly have to grow into it, the robe, of course, covering up the wearer's individuality and sex and outwardly signalling uniform dignity of office.

Regarding male judges' body language, one of Hilary Sommerlad's female interview partners commented that 'the men convey that sense of self-importance in their body language, there's no sense of awkwardness or embarrassment—they look you straight in the eye and demand attention.' On the other hand Maria Rita Bartolomei observed women judges using their sex appeal and feminine charm to capture male attention.

Observations of (male) judges in leadership positions have given the impression that leadership goes with a specific sense of self and habitus (Schultz/Peppmeier/Rudek, 2011), while this was less clearly visible in the case of female court presidents. However, performance of professional roles generally tends to blur such differences; individuals adapt to and imitate existing patterns as well as responding to organisational normative requirements. Several of our female contributors note that women judges may even go for greater harshness and give a masculinised performance in order to counteract gendered expectations.

[23] What Bourdieu also calls 'hexis'.

Issues of individual responses to professional practice are dealt with by Revital Ludewig/Juan Llave who investigate men's and women's ways of handling professional stress caused by such factors as time pressure, problems with colleagues and the pressure to reach decisions, the latter an in-built feature of judicial work. They conclude that both sexes report similar experiences and that there are no differences in the impact of professional stress on their private lives. Also both develop coping strategies such as distraction or suppression and objective distancing. However, female judges referred more frequently than their male colleagues to the use of social support (discussion of cases and conversations with family and friends) as a coping strategy as well as being more likely to consider mediation as a suitable means of solving a case.

Anne Boigeol quotes a former (female) general prosecutor at the Cour des Comptes:

> Neither men nor women hold a monopoly on a particular behaviour, but a quality encountered perhaps more frequently with women than men is a capacity to listen. They are happy to consult with others, discuss issues with their team, and make sure that questions have been fully explored, without this impeding their ability to take a decision.

The comprehensive socio-legal study of the entire Australian judiciary by Kathy Mack/Sharyn Roach Anleu provides insights into what male and female judges consider to be important for their work. Kathy Mack/Sharyn Roach Anleu asked magistrates and judges, both male and female, about their assessment of the importance of qualities and skills needed for their everyday work, such as legal knowledge, problem-solving skills, fact-finding skills, empathy, communication, and being a good listener. Their study showed that women magistrates, that is, women in judicial functions in lower courts, differed in some ways in their views from their male colleagues and from female and male judges. Of the four cohorts women magistrates attached the highest importance to interactive qualities and legal skills. Of the other cohorts, male magistrates attached the lowest importance to legal skills while male judges gave the least emphasis to interactive qualities. The views of female judges generally ranked between the views of female magistrates on the one hand and male magistrates and judges on the other. The evaluation of this pattern is difficult. Do women magistrates attach more importance overall to their work? Or are women magistrates and judges more enthusiastic about their work (or, merely, more conscientious about answering survey questions)?

Mack/Roach Anleu conclude that the results at least show that women in lower courts constitute a stronger gendered presence than female judges:

> While the dominant story is one of shared or similar attitudes across all four cohorts on many dimensions, the differences, where they exist, form varied

> patterns. These findings sometimes challenge and sometimes reinforce the binary construction of male/female judicial differences and the importance of court hierarchy in understanding judging.

Research in Germany from the late 1980s and the 1990s about women's perception of gender differences in their professional work produced somewhat different results. Female judges and prosecutors claimed that their style of working was different to that of their male colleagues. The women specified certain feminine elements that in their view should be incorporated into the administration of justice in general: improving the emotional climate, strengthening communication and cooperation between the parties involved in the trial, reducing both the hierarchical distance from the parties and competitiveness among colleagues (Schultz 2003c). Surprisingly congruent were statements from male judges and prosecutors in Germany who in the 1990s attended further judicial training courses. Characteristics they considered specifically feminine were: emotionality, a high level of sensitivity, empathy, preparedness to solve problems on an emotional level, a lower risk of restricting oneself to juristic dogma.[24]

In the past 10 years the notion in seminars and gender training in the Academies for the Judiciary has been that such perceptions may have become less marked amongst course participants, but they still exist. In any case, talking about them has become more difficult, as any mention of gender meets with hostility on the part of numerous members, although most women have signalled their perception of the existence of gendered differences in style and behaviour (Schultz 2003c).

These subjective perceptions are being supported by socio-linguistic analyses of communication in court hearings in Israel. Female attorneys were more likely to deal with the emotional needs of their clients during the court proceedings than their male counterparts (Bogoch 2003, Bogoch et al 2007). The question is whether female judges and prosecutors, too, have a more agreeable style of dealing with people in court. Could it be that the parties in the proceedings feel better if they are conducted by women? Or is it rather that female judges and prosecutors have greater problems in properly enacting power in the courtroom?

'Differences with male colleagues are to be found more in the process rather than the outcome of the judgment', Maria Rita Bartolomei writes citing a judge of appeal in the context of her fieldwork in Italy. Referring to Hanne Petersen's theory of 'home-knitted law', she discusses 'how with female judges we can easily find intuitive-unofficial legal practices, where values like bargaining, sympathy, sharing and solidarity are widespread'. She bases her study on results of participant observation at law courts in the Marche region of Italy, coupled with research into the survival of traditional

[24] Comparable results can be seen in Bartolomei's interviews in Italy.

procedures for conflict resolution in Ivory Coast, where women judges can be found to have their own courts of justice. Here indeed the home-made law phenomenon can be qualified. 'To manage the needs of social change in everyday life Abron women creatively re-interpret and adapt traditional wise practices' and apply the mentioned key values. She concludes that in both societies women occupy their role as judge in a constructive way to imagine and build a more complete vision of the law and its impact on people's everyday lives, developing strategies for articulating an alternative vision of the real, thereby re-drawing the boundary between the legal and the social.

Maria Rita Bartolomei also finds in women judges a greater sensitivity to, and advocacy of, human rights and minority groups' claims and needs. Can we, then, conclude that rather than merely introducing different working styles and behaviours, women in the judiciary do indeed make a specific contribution to the forensic world? Is the assumption justified that women judges promote substantive justice? That they take a more interdisciplinary approach, avoiding the rigid application of universal rules and narrow doctrinal issues? And that they therefore might reach more balanced decisions, avoid contentious solutions, search for win/win solutions, pass more lenient sentences and try alternative sanctions? In other words, do women judge better?

These are key issues discussed in this volume from varying perspectives and with varying results.

4.4. Gender and the Quality of Judgments

Judgments are hard to evaluate, and judicial quality hard to measure. In their analysis of the nature of judgments, Choi, Gulati, Holman and Posner (2011) dealt with elements of 'production, influence and independence' and tried to identify gender effects. Production was determined by the number of opinions and pages published per judge and per year, while influence was defined by citation counts and the number of citations of state High Court decisions by out of state courts. Neither criterion produced specific gender differences, except that in family law courts women were quoted more frequently than men, which gives greater influence to their opinions in this area. Choi *et al* concluded: 'Here we find indications that female judges not only wrote in a pro-women fashion but expand more effort than men do in shaping the law in areas of greater interest to women.'

These findings are underlined by those of a study on 'The Publication of Judicial Decisions in Family Law in Israel' by Bogoch, Halperin-Kaddari, Katvan, which states that female judges wrote longer and more detailed judgments (Bogoch, Halperin-Kaddari, Katvan).[25]

[25] Similarly, Eliane Junqueira (2003) discovered that female judges in Brazil provide more thoroughly elaborated reasonings than men.

Choi *et al* did find differences regarding independence from or resistance to partisan pressure. Republican men judges emerged as least independent. Republican women and Democratic men judges were more likely to agree with judges of their own political party. And Democratic women proved the most independent group. The authors consider this as solid evidence that gender differences may affect the outcome of a case, accepting that an interpretation requires taking into account a number of other factors (*cf* above list of possible causes of difference).

It is important to point out that it is difficult to relate these results to civil law systems, as in most civil law countries the deciding judge remains anonymous in published judgments. Added to this, publication practices in common law and civil law systems do not allow comparison, and in most civil law countries allegiance to political parties plays a part only in the case of leadership positions.

4.5. Impact of Gender in Gender-coded Cases

As Rhode states in the context of the discussion about the nomination of Judge Sotomayor to the Supreme Court of the USA in 2009, in the USA a 'cottage industry of empirical work has tried to disentangle the influence of gender on judging'.[26] However, findings tend to be sparse and widely dispersed. Also they tend to derive from research on common law rather than civil law countries, as explained by the differing scope given to judicial decision-makers in the two systems. Here we shall summarise the main findings.

Workplace Sexual Harassment

Rhode discusses primarily US studies of panel effects and the impact of the gendered composition of panels on judgments in sexual harrassment cases. Peresie (2005) has shown that in cases of workplace sexual harassment, male judges were more likely to find for plaintiffs when at least one female judge was on the panel, and that both liberal and conservative female judges were more likely than their male counterparts to support plaintiffs. Boyd, Epstein, and Martin (2010) also identified these panel effects in sexual harrassment cases. Panel effects were also reported to Bartolomei in court observations in Italy, but interviewees qualified this observation by adding that the influence of women's view on men's was unpredictable.

[26] Rhode, Deborah, 'In a "Different" Voice: What Does the Research About How Gender Influences Judging Actually Say?' Slate.com, June 10, 2009, http://www.slate.com/articles/news_and_politics/jurisprudence/2009/06/in_a_different_voice.html.

Similar results as those by Peresie and Boyd *et al* have been reported for racial harassment cases. Chew and Kelly (2009) found that judges' race significantly affects outcome in workplace sexual harassment cases, that African American judges as a group and white judges as a group perceive racial harassment differently: Race affects judges' ability to appreciate a plaintiff's perspective and African American judges are more sensitive to a plaintiff's needs of whatever race (s)he is (1161).

The explanations Peresie offers for panel effects are: deliberation on the one hand, deference—that male judges see female colleagues in gender-coded cases as more credible and persuasive—logrolling (trading of decisions in the hope that female judges will follow their decisions in other cases), and finally moderation, that the presence of a female judge moderates male judges' opinions.

Immigration Law

Menkel-Meadow has found a gender gap in asylum judging. Women immigration judges were 44 per cent more likely to grant asylum than their male colleagues. But she sees the danger that such findings might be used to proclaim women judges too 'soft' or 'lenient' in an era of hardened immigration policies. The results might even influence immigration judges to overcompensate by increasing denial rates to prove their even-headedness and neutrality (Menkel-Meadow 2010).

In an asylum case in the UK, the so-called *Fornah* Case, the first female Law Lord Brenda Hale, pushed her colleagues towards extending the concept of asylum, originally intended to help the politically persecuted, to include those threatened by female genital mutilation (Rackley 2008).

Family Law

In family courts there is evidence that female judges tend to be less generous than their male colleagues with respect to women asking for alimony (Fuszara 2003, Junqueira 2003, Schultz 2003 a, 2004).The obvious explanation is that female judges as professional and financially independent women feel less sympathetic towards women who rely financially on their husbands.

At least the fear that women prefer women does not seem to be justified. Bregje Dijksterhuis, who attended the meetings of the Dutch Judicial Alimony Commission,was astonished to find that, as far as she could see, female judges did not argue in favour of their sisters. She concluded that although the quantitative feminisation of the Dutch judiciary has been looked at with fear by the media, this trend has not led to qualitative feminisation. Until now not even in the 'gendered' family law has a unique female tone been found in the Dutch judiciary.

Social Law

In social courts in Germany, women's votes differed from those of their male colleagues in the decision relating to whether Viagra should be paid for by health insurers (Schultz 2).

Another indicator for a female voice in social law could be that the German judge and General Attorney at the European Court of Justice, Juliane Kokott, has proactively promulgated the introduction of uniform insurance tariffs for men and women.

Criminal Law

In criminal law the question was and is: Do women pass more lenient sentences? A positive answer would fit in with the gender stereotype hypothesis of women's greater emotionality, compassion and sensitivity to offenders' specific situations.

A German study of 1993 concluded that women showed no more openness or willingness to take into account individual circumstances in apportioning sentences than did their male colleagues (Schultz 2003 c, 314f). On the contrary, several other countries have reported (as mostly expected) that female judges tend to support more stringent penalties than their male colleagues in cases of violence and sexual violence, a fact explained by reference to a stronger identification, or even solidarisiation, with victims (Bartolomei). An Israeli study reached the opposite conclusion, ie that female judges passed more lenient sentences for men's sexual offences, but explained this not by women's natural leniency but by their desire to avoid signalling any special sympathy for the victims (Schultz 2003 a, lv).

A further German study of 1995 concluded that the participation of a female judge basically made no difference in the expected results, but that the participation of a female prosecutor tended to lead to more lenient sentences and the participation of a female defence lawyer to stricter ones. Here the explanation could be that both had problems in achieving their professional aim (harsh sentence for the prosecutor, lenient sentence for the defence lawyer), which means that their professionality was undermined (Schultz 2003c, 315).

A third German study of attitudes and everyday theories of male judges vis-à-vis female offenders found indications that in criminal proceedings women were more leniently sentenced when they showed a behaviour conforming to stereotypical gender roles, while role breakers ("tough women") ran the risk of less sympathetic treatment and stiffer sentences. This means that cross-gender preferences work and they could work both ways from men to women and women to men (Schultz 2003c, 315).

Supreme Court Judgments

Cowan's contribution discusses the difference women have made as judges of the Supreme Court in South Africa by means of an analysis of Constitutional Court cases from 1994–2009 in which women's sentences differed from those of men's.[27] One of these cases involved the interpretation of rules of criminal law relating to sexual violence, extending the crime of rape to non-consensual anal penetration. In another, the women judges held that prostitution should not only incriminate prostitutes but also their customers. In a case of pension law, women argued that widows' benefit rules should also apply to non-married partners. Women also made a difference in cases not relating to women's issues, but in these cases they did not speak in unison. For Ruth Cowen, these are cases where women's voices can be heard. They have provided perspectives previously absent, thereby confirming the general expectation that with the end of apartheid in 1994, African, Coloured, Asian and women judges 'would add value to and advance the Constitution's promises'.[28]

Claire Belleau and Rebecca Johnson have, over the years, kept careful track of female dissenters in the Supreme Court of Canada, concluding that dissenting and concurring votes (ie dissenting reasoning but consent in the result) were much more frequent amongst women than men. As in recent years the number of such votes has declined, the question is whether this is a consequence of key issues in the context of women's rights having been settled (Belleau, Johnson 2008).

An analysis of judgments of the Federal Constitutional Court in Germany from the 1950s to the 1990s has not lead to tangible results, perhaps with the slight exception of the two judgments on abortion, although even here no clear women's voice can be identified.[29]

All cases mentioned are just examples of decisions reported in the literature on gender and judging. At first glance, gender issues are expected to occur in criminal and family law, most particularly in the context of rape, sexual harassment, domestic violence and child abuse. However, the listing shows that, in fact, gender issues go well beyond these confined areas. They can be found hidden in all areas of law, from tax law, to property law, law of succession, administrative law, social and labour law (Schultz 2).

[27] Ruth Cowan has documented the development in the South African Supreme Court in her documentary 'Courting Justice'. http://www.courtingjustice.com/.

[28] The cases outlined by Ruth Cowan provide yet another illustration of the considerably greater discretion afforded to common law as opposed to civil law judges, the latter being authorised only to declare a ruling as unconstitutional and in breach of fundamental rights, but not to replace this by a different ruling.

[29] In Germany dissenting and concurring opinions were only introduced in 1970 and only for the Federal Constitutional Court. Their use has remained the exception (1% of cases).

In summarising our findings relating to gender-coded cases, it becomes clear that even they fail to produce an unambiguous answer to the question whether women judge differently from men. Although, for instance, participants in mediation courses in Germany tend to be mainly women, in their judicial practice women judges have not been found to behave in a more conciliatory fashion than men. Nor can it be said that judges' gender allows any prediction as to how they will judge in particular cases (Bartolomei). Rather, we have to accept that individual female judges' decisions reflect both their particular mix of individual characteristics and life experience on one side, as well as their shared features based on their professional education, training and experience (*formation professionelle*) on the other side.

5. FEMINIST JUDGES AND JUDGING

In the light of these diverging results, Rosemary Hunter suggests that speculation as to the contribution women judges might make to the judiciary should cease, and rather the impact of the presence of feminist judges should be examined. Is there a deliberate impact or should there be one?

The first question to ask is: Who is a feminist judge? Not necessarily only women but also men may be included. It depends on a 'chosen' difference in attitude and mind related to a political opinion and even message, which implies that the women's question has always to be kept in mind and asked (Hunter 2012).

In Sommerlad's interviews in England neither feminism nor social justice were cited as motivations for becoming judges. Kohen found judges in Argentina reluctant to identify themselves as feminist, as this could be misunderstood as revealing a tendency to bias, a fear that is particularly true of civil law countries.

Yet the demand that judges should self-identify as feminists is put forward by feminist scholars. Bev Baines deals with the limits of self-identification as well as with the limits of feminist adjudication. Feminist adjudication can be qualified as a 'particularity model' of judging. It involves feminist practical reasoning with contextualisation (Hunter, Baines): The focus is placed on the person before the court, while drawing on a wider base of legal and social knowledge as well as emotional insight, and putting a greater emphasis on legal values such as a sense of fairness and protecting legal rights.[30] In a case study dealing with the jurisprudence of Justice Marcia Neave from the Court of Appeal in Victoria, Australia, Rosemary Hunter asks in what ways her judgments may differ from those of other judges of the court who

[30] This echoes Hanne Petersen's notion of home-knitted law and Bartolomei's findings in her field work.

do not identify as feminists, and analyses the contributions Neave has made to the jurisprudence of her court.

And yet, can women expect feminist judges to defend women's causes and to act according to a pro-care agenda? Where women are denied civic rights and treated as inferior to fathers, husbands, sons and other men, this could be a necessity. As documentaries such as 'Lady Judges of Pakistan', 'Sisters in Law' about Cameroon as well as 'Courting Justice' about South Africa[31] demonstrate most impressively, in these instances female judges, public prosecutors and lawyers attempt to help their sisters proactively. Obviously, such strategies become dubious if the law of the land opposes them, an issue addressed by Beatriz Kohen in her analysis of the *Tejerina* case.

Reg Graycar asks whether the decision-making process could be deconstructed to develop a space for introducing feminist insights into decision-making processes before they get to an adjudicative forum, and whether a feminist approach can help to articulate harm in a more effective way. She deals with the Canadian redress package designed in the Grandview adjudication process, which was to respond to the harms perpetrated on the women and girls who had been held in the Grandview Training School for Girls in the middle of the twentieth century.

Women's initiatives for gender justice exist in a number of countries with restitution commissions and people's tribunals, where a public space is created for justice outside the national court system. One example is the Women's International War Crime Tribunal in Tokyo of 2000 for victims of Imperial Japan's sexual slavery system (concerning so-called 'comfort women') during World War II, set up as a critical alternative to the current system of Japanese courts.

There are also a number of academic projects that not only criticise but also rewrite judgments incorporating feminist perspectives. To mention two of these, there is firstly a feminist judgments project in which a group of feminist socio-legal scholars led by Rosemary Hunter, Erika Rackley and Clare McGlynn have written alternative feminist judgments in a series of significant cases in English law[32] (Hunter, McGlynn, Rackley 2010). Secondly, in 2004 the Women's Court of Canada/Le Tribunal des Femmes du Canada started the work of rewriting the Canadian Charter of Rights and Freedoms equality jurisprudence.[33]

[31] http://www.insightsproduction.net/ljp.html; http://www.ventura-film.de/page/filmeneu/vorberei/sistersinlaw.htm; http://www.courtingjustice.com/.

[32] http://www.kent.ac.uk/law/fjp/. Similarly, in the Irish Feminist Judgments Project set up by Mairead Enright and Aoife O'Donoghue, a group of academics and practitioners write 'the missing feminist judgments' in a series of important Irish and Northern Irish cases, http://www.kent.ac.uk/law/research/projects/projects.html.

[33] http://womenscourt.ca/home/.

An organisationally anchored form of routine gender review of key judicial decisions is practised at the International Criminal Court (ICC) as part of the Gender Report Card issued annually by the Women's Initiatives for Gender Justice—an initiative that deserves to be drawn to the attention of and recommended to other courts and court systems.[34,35]

6. GENDER TRAINING FOR THE JUDICIARY

Gender awareness in the judiciary is still low. In relation to Argentina, Andrea Gastron, Angela Amante, and Ruben Rodriguez analysed 105 decided cases in fields of law where gender issues necessarily arise.[36] They assessed these cases in order to determine whether gender aspects were in fact taken into consideration. They found that the presence of gender arguments, as well as of a gender perspective, is still rare in Argentine judgments, and that as a general rule women judges handle them no differently from men. 'Whenever it arises, it merely reflects the opinion of individual members.'

What else can be done to enhance the quality of judgments in cases where gender questions are implicit, beyond the described feminist critique?

Is diversity by itself the solution? It can be expected that the greater the number of judges with different backgrounds and experiences, the greater the range of ideas and information that will be contributed to the procedure. But the question is how diversity on the bench may colour a specific judgment. Reg Graycar, drawing on her experience as a barrister, warns that we need to pay careful attention to what judges know about the world and how the things they know translate into activities as a judge (Graycar 2008). In other words, otherness does not guarantee that other perspectives and standpoints are included in a judgment. Nor can the individual position and opinion of a judge ever be predicted and taken for granted.[37] However, gender consciousness should not be treated as a private matter but as a prerequisite for judicial office.

How can gender sensitivity be achieved in the judicial process? The easiest, most effective and least contested way would be to include it in the

[34] http://www.iccwomen.org/.

[35] In civil law countries, the more common approach is via critical comments on judgments in journals. In Germany this happens, for instance, in the feminist legal journal STREIT (meaning 'argument', 'quarrel').

[36] Such as abortion, adoption, child support, concubinage, marriage conventions, alimony obligations, crimes against marital status, crimes against honour, crimes against honesty, crimes against sexual integrity, crimes against freedom, the right to privacy, the right to health and personal integrity, the right to life, the right to visits, labour law, discrimination, divorce, filiation, paternity challenge, marriage, parental rights and legal separation.

[37] The appointment of judges, such as, eg, the black judge Clarence Thomas to the US American Supreme Court, has shown that they do not necessarily live up to the expectation attached to their ethnicity, sex or political standpoint.

law school curriculum. Unfortunately, this requirement for mainstreaming gender aspects has hardly been put into practice, although in Europe it ought to be taken into consideration as it is a requirement for all course accreditation. This also goes for the systematic inclusion of gender training in continuing legal education. Specific gender training is opposed by judges especially in well-developed legal systems as a possible attempt to introduce ideological re-education (Schultz 2). Such training, if it exists at all, takes a minimalist form. In Japan, judges attend a one-hour lecture on women's rights—a kind of fig leaf, as Kayo Minamino, initiator of an international comparative project on gender training for the judiciary argues, although it is of central importance: 'While Japanese courts are generally believed to enjoy a considerable degree of credibility, they remain unable to render appropriate judicial judgments in newly emerging legal issues associated with gender.' (Sewa).

Countries have to submit, in their regular reports to the UN for CEDAW (UN Convention on the Elimination of all Forms of Discrimination against Women), answers regarding 'the implementation of education for judges especially focusing on indirect discrimination' (Minamino for Japan). In developing countries donors include gender training in projects on judicial development as one criterion for the allocation of financial support, as gender justice is not only considered as an integral part of the realisation of human rights, it also promotes countries' economic success. Programmes aim to ensure proper representation of women in the judiciary, making the judiciary more gender-sensitive and gender-responsive, analysing any differential treatment of men and women, promoting the use of gender-fair language in court, and facilitating a change of attitudes and behaviours in the handling of cases. For this a gender-responsive database on the judicial system in each country would be highly desirable.

India (Stewart), the Philippines (Miwa) and Cambodia (Sawa) as well as numerous other developing countries have implemented programmes for the development of gender responsiveness in the judiciary. Contributions to this volume present the respective programmes. In 2002, the Philippine Judicial Academy introduced an Action Programme for Judicial Reform entitled 'Gender Sensitivity in the Court System', accompanied by a Committee on Gender Responsiveness in the Judiciary, as well as a Gender Justice Award for judges who wrote gender-responsive decisions.

In Cambodia, gender training is of particular importance following the era of Pol Pot and the Khmer Rouge, requiring the setting up from scratch of a new legal and judicial system—a tall order given the poor quality of and often hardly existing judicial personnel in an environment traditionally dominated by an ideology of women's subordinate status. Similar requirements will emerge in other countries currently embroiled in and devastated by warfare.

In this context, it is important to stress the significance of judges' economic independence in terms of adequate remuneration, job security and independence from instructions from above, these not being a matter of course in countries with authoritarian governmental and administrative structures.

How effective will gender training be given the many practical and psychological problems obstructing it? And how long-lasting the stereotypes in the face of their deep-rootedness in societies and individuals alike? Encouragingly, Ann Stewart's assessment of the programme in India as to its long-term effect on individual participants concludes that efforts made have been well worthwhile, attitudes have been changed, and behavioural change has been encouraged.

7. CONCLUSION

In most of the Western industrialised world women have found their place in the judiciary, the civil law world leading the way ahead of the common law world. Women's presence has become a matter of course, their competence is being recognised, albeit questioned more frequently than that of their male colleagues. Gender stereotypes remain deeply engraved in social collective memory. Women have tended to remain the 'other'. Hence the suspicions regarding a further feminisation of the judiciary. The path into higher positions remains stony.

In developing countries, too, female judges are respected due to the status and dignity provided by their office, even if their professional opportunities remain more limited.

Fifteeen years ago Bryna Bogoch analysed communication processes in lawsuits and discovered that male statements towards female parties to the proceedings were geared towards establishing male power and hierarchical status. Also women's statements (be they of witnesses or female judges) towards other women (prosecutors or lawyers) were less respectful than those towards men, and the statements made by women met with less consideration (Bogoch 2003, Schultz 2003a). This kind of disparagement of women has not disappeared, but it has become more subtle. It still reflects, depending on the country and its cultural tradition, the continuing ambivalent situation of women in society where different views of gender roles prevail.

Legal systems and the practice of law continue to display deficits regarding the principle of gender equality and the observance of civil and women's rights. Judges' gender awareness remains fairly weak. Traditional thinking and argumentation ignorant of gender as an issue tends to prevail, women featuring as late-comers having to adapt. If gender bias in judiciaries is to be avoided they must be sensitised to gender issues.

Contributions to this volume taken as a whole neither confirm nor refute Gilligan's thesis of women's other voice. And yet we know that women in the judiciary make a difference, however difficult to measure. They have changed the style operating in the judiciary, obviously supported by other aspects of social modernisation, such as de-formalisation, a generally stronger service orientation, and the gradual waning of the concept of the male breadwinner. Women have made an impact on the organisation as well as on the outcome of cases as they bring along different biographical patterns and life experiences. But of course gender is not the only factor shaping the interpretation and application of rules. Other factors such as race, origin, religion and political persuasion matter as well.

Overall, we have to agree with Mack's and Roach Anleu's argument that

> the findings challenge the monolithic image of the generic disembodied judge as well as the binary construction of male/female differences within the judiciary ... Women judges ... may experience several possible gendered and judicial identities: Assimilation to masculine judicial norms, the ideal of the disembodied neutral judicial officer who is neither male nor female, a gender aware female judge, or a feminist judge.

Women are no longer seen as 'deviant', as dangerous outsiders as there is no longer a uniform image for them to fall outside of and to threaten. But they are still regarded as the 'others'.

Diversity has entered the judiciary—to a degree. But there is some way to go for gender equality in terms of professional opportunities and career diversity to become a political goal, and gender training is needed.

In our synthesis in *Women in the World's Legal Professions* we argued that there is no such thing as a feminist professional project. However, there remains the challenge to create the ideal of a judge, a judge who is not only professionally qualified but also empathetic, a judge keen to introduce feminist insights into judicial decision-making processes and embodying the qualities which, according to many contributions should characterise the decision maker: common sense, compassion, patience, being a good listener, courtesy, a pleasant manner in court and broad life experience.

Change is also required regarding legal procedures. In her article on asylum in another voice Menkel-Meadow proclaims that the procedure should be changed away from binary 'yes' or 'no' decisions to

> more inclusive, less formal hearings, consideration of family connections and emotions, and a generous benefit of the doubt in credibility determinations rather than overly harsh cross-examinations—for those who have usually undergone enormous hardship (Menkel-Meadow, 2010, 219).

This harks back to the conception of women's other voice, as first formulated by Carol Gilligan, a voice that follows a logic of care and turns against blind justice drawing on abstract universal principles.

Change can happen in small steps. Winifred Kamau provides a delightful example of the ethic of care at the High Court in Nairobi, Kenya: 'On Friday no criminal cases are held at the High Court. It is the day for adoption matters, creating a family friendly environment in the court.'

What remains is the age-old question whether the presence of women in the judiciary affects the profession's status and social prestige. Over the last decades society has changed at breathtaking speed. Yet, change in gender relations has lagged behind. Female judges like all women have to continue in their efforts to break down gender stereotypes. Sometimes they may ask themselves whether the world has really moved on, as demonstrated by two German documents, dating from 1923 and 1912 respectively. A mentoring judge of the first female legal trainee in Germany attested in a reference of 27 January 1923:

> She (Miss ...) has fulfilled in the most pleasing and delightful manner all expectations directed at her in her role as the first female law trainee, through her modest and truly feminine demeanour in personal relations as well as through objectivity and clarity in official contexts. Her powers of comprehension and attention even to detail, as for instance in taking down court minutes, put her well ahead of most of her male predecessors; added to this she has a sound knowledge and an obvious desire to expand this as well as her life experience whenever possible. For this reason, her period at the criminal court X has also been truly stimulating for me, her mentoring judge.[38]

Almost a century later, Ulrike Schultz was asked to write an editorial for the journal for judges and prosecutors in Northrhine-Westfalia, based on her research on women in judicial leadership positions. The (male) judge in charge of editing the piece commented in an email to a female colleague, 'Herewith suggestions for the editorial the style of which strikes me as masculine and harsh rather than feminine and gentle. Never mind.'

8. REFERENCES

Belleau, M-C and Johnson, R (2008) 'Judging gender: difference and dissent at the Supreme Court of Canada' 15 (1–2) *International Journal of the Legal Profession* 57.

Blackwell, MC (2012) 'Old Boys' Networks, Family Connections and the English Legal Profession' *Public Law* 426.

Bogoch, B (2003) 'Lawyers in the Courtroom: Gender, Trials and Professional Performance in Israel' in Schultz, Ulrike and Shaw, Gisela (eds), *Women in the World's Legal Professions* (Oxford, Hart Publishing) 247.

[38] http://www.personalbeurteilung.de/soziale_erwnschtheit.html.

Bogoch, B and Halperin-Kaddari, R (2007) 'The Voice is the Voice of Mediation, but the Hands are the Hands of the Law: Mediation and Divorce in Israel' 49 *Hapraklit* 293 (Hebrew).

Bogoch, B, Halperin-Kaddari, R, Katvan, E (2009) *Exposing Family Secrets: Judicial Decision Making and the Publication of Family Court Decisions in the Age of Computerized Databases,* Final Report submitted to the Israel Science Foundation (Jerusalem, Israel).

Bolton, SC and Muzio, D (2007) 'Can't live with 'em; Can't live without 'em: Gendered segmentation in the Legal Profession' 41 (1) *Sociology* 47.

Bonelli, MG (2012) 'Gender and Difference among Brasilian Lawyers and Judges: Public and Private Practice in the Global Periphery' *Conference paper, International Socio-Legal Meeting Honolulu.*

Boyd, CL, Epstein, L, Martin, A (2010) 'Untangling Causal Effects of Sex on Judging' 54 (No 2 April) *American Journal of Political Science* 389.

Burrage, M (2006) *Revolution and the Making of the Contemporary Legal Profession: England, France, and the United States* (Oxford, Oxford University Press).

Chew, P, and Kelley, R (2009) 'Myth of the Color-Blind Judge: An Empirical Analysis of Racial Harassment Cases' 86 *Washington University Law Review* 1117–166, http://lawreview.wustl.edu/inprint/86/5/kelley.pdf.

Choi, SJ, Gulati, M, Holman, M, Posner, E, (2011) 'Judging Women' 8 (3) *Journal of Empirical Legal Studies* 504.

Darbyshire, P (2011) *Sitting in Judgment: The Working Lives of Judges* (Oxford, Hart Publishing).

European Commission for the Efficiency of Justice cepej (2012) *European judicial systems. Efficiency and quality of justice (2012 data)* (Strasbourg, Council of Europe Publishing) http://www.coe.int/t/dghl/cooperation/cepej/evaluation/2012/Rapport_en.pdf.

Feenan, D (2009) 'Editorial Introduction: Women and Judging' 17 *Feminist Legal Studies* 1.

Feuvre, N & Lapeyere, N (2005) 'Les 'sexués' de carrière dans les professions juridiques en France'. in Giannini, Mirella (ed) *The Feminization of the Professions, Thematic Issue. Knowledge, Work & Society*, Vol 1, No 3, 101.

Fuszara, M 'Women Lawyers in Poland under the Impact of Post-1989 Transformation' in Schultz, Ulrike and Shaw, Gisela (eds), (2003) *Women in the World's Legal Professions* (Oxford, Hart Publishing) 371.

Genn, H (2009) *Judging Civil Justice, The Hamlyn Lectures 2008* (Cambridge, Cambridge University Press).

Gilligan, C (1982) *In a Different Voice: Psychological Theory and Women's Development* (Cambridge, MA, Harvard University Press).

Graycar, R (2008) 'Gender, Race, Bias and Perspective: OR, how otherness colours your judgment' 15 (1–2) *International Journal of the Legal Profession* 73.

Hänlein, A (1996) 'Richter des BVerfG a.D. Dr. Karl Heck' *Neue Juristische Wochenschrift* 3131.

Hecht Schafran, L (2005) 'Not from Central Casting: The Amazing Rise of Women in the Judiciary' *36 University of Toledo Law Rev*iew 953.

Hunter, R (2008) 'Can Feminist Judges Make a Difference' 15 (1–2) *International Journal of the Legal Profession* 7.

Hunter, R, McGlynn, C, Rackley, E (2010) *Feminist Judgments. From Theory to Practice* (Oxford, Hart Publishing).
Junqueira, EB 'Women in the Judiciary: a Perspective from Brazil in Schultz, Ulrike and Shaw, Gisela (eds), (2003) *Women in the World's Legal Professions* (Oxford, Hart Publishing) 437–50.
Kenney, S (2013) *Gender and Justice. Why Women in the Judiciary Really Matter* (New York, Routledge).
Kim, H (2003) 'Lee Tai-Young (1914–1998): The Pioneer Woman Lawyer of South Korea' in Schultz, Ulrike and Shaw, Gisela (eds), (2003) *Women in the World's Legal Professions* (Oxford, Hart Publishing) 451.
—— (2012) 'Winds of Change: A New Reality for Women Jurists in Korea', *Conference paper, Internatinal Socio-Legal Meeting, Honolulu,* Hawaii (USA).
Lindbekk, M (2012) 'Women Judges in Egypt: Discourse and Practice', Conference Paper, *Workshop, Women Judges in the Muslim World,* Oslo (Norway).
Liu, X (2012) 'Chinese Women in Legal Education and in the Legal Profession' *Conference paper, International Socio-Legal Meeting, Honolulu*, Hawaii (USA).
Malleson, K (2003) 'Prospects for Parity: The Position of Women in the Judiciary in England and Wales' in Schultz, Ulrike and Shaw, Gisela (eds), (2003) *Women in the World's Legal Professions* (Oxford, Hart Publishing) 175–89.
Marder, N (2009) 'Judging Judge Judy' in Asimow Michael (ed), *Lawyers in Your Living Room! Law on Television* (Chicago, American Bar Foundation).
Menkel-Meadow, C (1989) 'Feminization of the Legal Profession: the Comparative Sociology of Women Lawyers' in Abel, Richard L and Lewis, Philip SC (eds), *Lawyers in Society: Comparative Perspectives* Volume 3, (Berkeley, University of California Press) 196.
—— (2010) 'Asylum in a Different Voice: Judging Immigration Claims and Gender' in *Refugee Roulette. Disparities in Asylum Adjudication and Proposals for Reform,* Georgetown University Law Center, Public Law & Legal Theory Research Paper No 10–24 and University of California, Irvine School of Law, Legal Studies Research Paper No 2010–14, http://papers.ssrn.com/sol3/papers.cfm?abstract_id=1586402.
Moran, L (2013) 'Sexual Diversity in the Judiciary: Research on Barriers to Judicial Careers' *International Journal of the Legal Profession* (forthcoming).
Owor, M, Musoke, HD (2013) 'Neglect of Gender Questions in the Vocational Stage of Judicial Education in Uganda' *International Journal of the Legal Profession* (forthcoming).
Peresie, JL (2005) 'Female Judges Matter: Gender and Collegial Decisionmaking in the Federal Appellate Courts' 114 *Yale Law Journal* 1759–790.
Petersen, H (1996) *Home Knitted Law. Norms and Values in Gendered Rule-Making* (Aldershot, Dartmouth).
Rackley, E (2008) 'What a Difference Difference Makes: Gendered Harms and Judicial Diversity' 15 (1–2) *International Journal of the Legal Profession* 37–56.
—— (2012) *Women, Judges and the Judiciary. From Difference to Diversity* (New York, Routledge).
Resnik, J, Curtis, D (2011) *Representing Justice: Invention, Controversy, and Rights in City-States and Democratic Courtrooms* (Newhaven, CA, Yale University Press).

Schultz, U (1990) 'Wie männlich ist die Juristenschaft?' in Battis, Ulrich and Schultz, Ulrike (eds), *Frauen im Recht* (Heidelberg, CF Müller) 319–59.

—— (2003a) 'Women in the World's Legal Professions. Overview and Synthesis' in Schultz, Ulrike and Shaw, Gisela (eds), *Women in the World's Legal Professions* (Oxford, Hart Publishing) xxv–lxii.

—— (2003b) 'The Status of Women Lawyers in Germany' in Schultz, Ulrike and Shaw, Gisela (eds), *Women in the World's Legal Professions* (Oxford, Hart Publishing) 271–91.

—— (2003c) 'Women Lawyers in Germany: Perception and Construction of Femininity' in Schultz, Ulrike and Shaw, Gisela (eds), *Women in the World's Legal Professions* (Oxford, Hart Publishing) 295–321.

—— 2004 'Richten Richterinnen richtiger?' in *Frauenbilder. Handbuch für die Aktionswochen der kommunalen Gleichstellungsbeauftragten 2005* (Ministerium für Gesundheit, Soziales, Frauen und Familie NRW. Düsseldorf) 117–26.

—— 2012 'Frauen in Führungspositionen der Justiz' *Mitteilungsblatt des Schleswig-Holsteinischen Richterverbandes* 4–22.

Schultz, U, Peppmeier, I, Rudek, A (2011) 'Frauen in Führungspositionen der Justiz. Eine Untersuchung der Bedingungen von Frauenkarrieren in den Justizbehörden in Nordrhein-Westfalen', Abschlussbericht (Hagen, IGG, Institut für Geschlechterforschung und Gleichstellungsrecht und -politik).

Schultz, U and Shaw, G (eds), (2012) *Women in the Judiciary* (Abingdon, Routledge) reprint of the special issue 15 (1–2) *International Journal of the Legal Profession on Gender and Judging.*

Thornton, M (2007) '"Otherness" on the Bench: How Merit is Gendered' 29 (3) *Sydney Law Review* 391–413.

Witz, A (1992) *Professions and Patriarchy* (London, Routledge).

Part 1

Pioneers and Eminent Women Judges

1.1

Becoming the First Women Judges in Ontario: Women Lawyers, Gender and the Politics of Judicial Appointment

MARY JANE MOSSMAN

Abstract

This chapter explores issues about gender and feminism in relation to the appointment of two of the first women judges in Canada, along with the failure to appoint a third, arguably equally outstanding, woman lawyer to the bench. In doing so, the chapter examines the stories of the professional lives of these three women, and their accomplishments in the context of societal factors that may have influenced decisions about judicial appointments. Moreover, while gender was a barrier to judicial appointment for much of the twentieth century, the chapter considers how the feminist movement eventually resulted in making (female) gender a 'bonus' by the 1970s. In this context, the chapter explores how women who wished to achieve judicial appointment often downplayed their connections to the women's equality movement, suggesting that their strategies reveal the cultural strength of ideas about 'professionalism' in law. In reflecting on gender and professionalism in the context of judicial appointments for women, the chapter explores the myriad and nuanced ways in which individual women negotiated their professional aspirations as lawyers and as women.

1. INTRODUCTION

Take a young man and a young woman of equal intelligence. Give them the same social background and opportunity. Put them into the same business. And there will be little to choose between them ... Only the fact that I am a lawyer matters. That I am a woman is of no consequence. I make a point of not knowing how many women lawyers there are in Canada.[1]

[1] 'The Legal Lady' Maclean's Magazine (1949) 15, 23.

Asked if she is disappointed not to be a Supreme Court judge, she replied: 'I have been at peace over unfulfilled ambitions for 20 years. Not appointing a woman judge has been discrimination. It was broken with the appointment of Mabel Van Camp. Again, as in most top jobs, a woman has to be much better than a man. This applies to women judges'.[2]

BOTH THESE COMMENTS to the press were made by Margaret Hyndman, a prominent woman lawyer who was called to the Bar in Ontario in 1926. Significantly, her circumspect comments in the first excerpt about being a *lawyer*, not a *woman lawyer*, were made in a magazine article about her excellent accomplishments in 1949, about 25 years after her call to the Bar. By contrast, the second excerpt reflects her views in an interview published in a newspaper in 1973, nearly 50 years after her call to the Bar and almost 25 years after her earlier comments.

The juxtaposition of these quite different comments—both public statements by a prominent woman lawyer but at two different points in time—necessitates some explanation. One possibility, of course, is that Hyndman's views had simply changed over time—although any such explanation requires some additional information to understand why and how this change in her perception occurred. More significantly, I want to suggest that it is also possible that these differing comments reflect changes in *what it was possible to say in public* about the experiences of women who gained admission to the legal profession. In this way, I argue that it is changes in the relationship between gender and ideas about professionalism that account for Hyndman's very different public comments 25 years apart.

In reflecting on ideas about the relationship between gender and professionalism, this chapter explores some aspects of the lives of three women lawyers, two of whom succeeded in being 'the first' to be appointed judges. Their experiences suggest that Hyndman was correct when she used the word 'discrimination' in 1973 to explain why women had not become judges before the appointment of Mabel Van Camp to the Superior Court of Ontario in 1971, just two years prior to Hyndman's public accusation. Yet, almost 30 years before Van Camp's appointment, another woman lawyer, Helen Kinnear, had succeeded in becoming the first woman in the British Empire to be appointed to a county court in 1943. In this context, this chapter examines the experiences of these three women, Helen Kinnear, Margaret Hyndman and Mabel Van Camp, all of whom became outstanding members of the 'gentleman's profession' of law. What factors contributed to judicial appointments for Kinnear and Van Camp? How do we explain the '30-year gap' between these two appointments? And what factors resulted in earlier patterns of discrimination being 'broken' with the appointment

2 'Margaret Hyndman Still Fights for Equal Rights' Ottawa Journal (16 March 1973).

of Van Camp? This chapter first focuses on the experiences of these three women in law, and then reflects on these intriguing questions.

2. STORIES OF THREE WOMEN IN LAW: HELEN KINNEAR, MARGARET HYNDMAN AND MABEL VAN CAMP

Helen Kinnear was the daughter of a lawyer who practised in Port Colborne, about an hour south of Toronto in the Niagara Peninsula. She first graduated from the University of Toronto and then completed the law course at Osgoode Hall; she was called to the Bar of Ontario in 1920 at the age of 26. Kinnear returned to Port Colborne, practising with her father as 'Kinnear and Kinnear'; she was probably the first woman to practise law in the Niagara Peninsula. When her father died suddenly just a few years later in 1924, Kinnear continued the general law practice in Port Colborne on her own (Corbett and Corbett, 1996: 129–30; Mather, 1993).[3] Kinnear's practice was generally successful, and she became the first woman to appear as counsel in the Supreme Court of Canada; in addition, in 1934, she became the first woman in the British Empire to be appointed King's Counsel[4] (Corbett and Corbett, 1996: 131).

In addition to following her father into the legal profession, Kinnear also followed in his footsteps with a passion for politics. Like earlier generations of the Kinnear family, she became active in the Liberal Party, travelling around the Niagara Peninsula 'organizing campaigns, chairing committees, and holding offices in local and regional branches of the Liberal Party' (Corbett and Corbett 1996: 130). Kinnear was tireless in her efforts to overcome women's inequality in Canadian society as well as in the Liberal Party, serving on the executive of the Ontario Women's Liberal Association in the 1920s, and as President of the Hamilton District Women's Liberal Association from 1925 to 1935. In addition, she made repeated efforts in these years to obtain the Liberal nomination to the House of Commons[5] (Corbett and Corbett 1996: 129–31).[6]

Finally, in 1941, Kinnear succeeded in gaining the Liberal nomination for Welland riding.[7] It was a three-way race in which Kinnear was the

[3] *Canada Post* issued a commemorative stamp in 1993 in honour of the 50th anniversary of Kinnear's appointment.

[4] 'First Woman KC is Congratulated' The Globe (22 December 1934).

[5] 'Liberal Women Name Officers' The Globe (25 July 1935); 'Out-of-Town Delegates Lining up for Convention' The Globe (1 May 1937); 'Tolerance Urged on Liberal Women' The Globe (7 April 1937).

[6] Corbett and Corbett (1996) noted, at 129, that Kinnear would respond to anyone who asked her political affiliation: 'Liberal by birth and Liberal by conviction'.

[7] Welland riding was situated in the Niagara Peninsula, about one hour from Toronto.

only woman candidate. As *The Globe* reported somewhat ambiguously: 'Before voting took place, Miss Kinnear pleaded with the delegates not to allow the fact that she was a woman to influence the vote'.[8] After two ballots, Kinnear succeeded in gaining the nomination, and seemed poised to win election to the House of Commons in the upcoming by-election.[9] To everyone's surprise, however, just a few months later, Kinnear withdrew as the Liberal candidate in the by-election in favour of the newly-appointed Minister of Labour, Humphrey Mitchell, who did not yet have a seat in the House of Commons; according to press reports, Kinnear's decision was prompted by the national situation in relation to Canada's war effort.[10] Then, as early as April 1942, a rumour began to circulate about Kinnear's appointment to the bench;[11] and in June 1943, she was sworn in as county court judge for Haldimand County in Cayuga. For Kinnear, this appointment was 'more than a personal achievement'; she regarded it as a 'victory' for women, and an acknowledgment that women had a 'definite place' in Canadian legal administration (Corbett and Corbett, 1996: 132).

Kinnear served as a judge for almost two decades, retiring in 1962. Her prominence as a woman in public life in Canada was demonstrated frequently, and her activities and public lectures were widely reported. Indeed, when she attended the eight-day Commonwealth and Empire Law conference in London in 1955, along with 500 Canadian lawyers, magistrates and judges, the press reported that there were 22 judges at the conference, singling out the chief justices of Quebec, Ontario and Alberta—'and Helen A Kinnear of Cayuga, Ont, the only woman in the Commonwealth to have been made a county court judge'.[12]

Kinnear was one of 63 county court judges in Ontario, with jurisdiction to hear criminal cases of all kinds, as well as summary trials involving landlord and tenant matters and other issues pursuant to a variety of provincial statutes. As a county court judge, she was also a judge of the Surrogate Court, with jurisdiction over estates and in relation to guardianship and custody of children. She was also a Juvenile Court judge, and her interest in juvenile justice resulted in her becoming founding president of the Juvenile and Family Court Judges' Association in the early 1950s (Corbett and Corbett, 1996: 133). Overall, as Kinnear herself explained, the scope of a county court judge's jurisdiction was 'the Jack of all trades in the administration of

[8] 'Woman KC Nominated as Liberal Candidate' The Globe (27 October 1941a) 13.

[9] Agnes MacPhail was the first woman elected to the House of Commons in 1921: see Wyatt (2000); and Sharpe and McMahon (2007).

[10] 'Refused Permission to Resign Candidacy' The Globe (24 December 1941b).

[11] 'Report Woman Slated for Bench' The Globe (23 April 1942).

[12] 'Lawyers Study Fusion of Two Professions' The Globe (27 July 1955).

justice in Ontario' (Kinnear, 1954).[13] In addition to her judicial functions, Kinnear was appointed, along with Chief Justice McRuer in Ontario and Dr Desrochers of Quebec City, to two related Royal Commissions in 1954; these Commissions concerning insanity as a defence in criminal cases and the criminal law relating to sexual psychopaths resulted in final reports in 1958 that pioneered arguments for the segregation and treatment of sexual offenders (Corbett and Corbett, 1996: 133–34).

Like many women lawyers called to the Bar just after the First World War, Kinnear never married. For most of her life, she shared a home with her sister, Jennie, with whom she travelled as well. She was active in a wide variety of organisations, including organisations of women lawyers in Canada and the United States, and she was frequently involved in public lectures and community activities. For example, when the Local Council of Women in Toronto organised a series of presentations about law in 1945, Kinnear was the first speaker in the series; her presentation on 'The Machinery of Law' drew 500 women to hear about the administration of civil and criminal law.[14] In addition, however, Kinnear exuded a 'straightforward and fair approach,' suggesting in a press interview that the 'judicial costume' needed renovation to replace the 'antedeluvian attire we wear at the moment'; noting how 'it wears the fingernails to the bone to struggle daily with a judicial collar-button', she argued that women should get together and 'work out some kind of feminine attire that would be dignified but easier to wear'.[15] Kinnear died in 1970 at the age of 76; by that time, although a few other women had been appointed to the county court, it was not until the following year that Mabel Van Camp was appointed to the Supreme Court of Ontario. Before turning to Van Camp, however, it is necessary to examine the experiences of Margaret Hyndman, called to the Bar in Ontario just six years after Kinnear in 1926 (LSUC records).

Margaret Hyndman's father was a town clerk in Palmerston, Ontario. When she moved to Toronto to attend Osgoode Hall, Hyndman supported herself with secretarial work and tutoring. In addition, she experienced a rather eclectic succession of articling positions before her call to the Bar. She completed the final stage of her articles with FW Wegenast KC, with whom she continued to practise in partnership for several years; significantly, she assisted Wegenast in writing an influential book on company law, initially published in 1931 (Hyndman transcript: 25–29).[16] Although

[13] According to Corbett and Corbett (1996) 133, 'county courts in Canada tried four times as many criminal cases as the Supreme Court'. The county courts were merged with the Supreme Court of Ontario in 1990.

[14] 'Machinery of the Law Theme to Judge Kinnear' The Globe (4 October 1945).

[15] 'Uncomfortable Clothing Annoys Judge Helen Kinnear' The Globe (19 April 1948).

[16] The treatise is FW Wegenast, The Law of Canadian Companies (Toronto, Burroughs, 1931).

she was engaged in a general law practice, Hyndman's work focused particularly on company law and insurance; as she explained in a later interview:

> Mine has never been a ... promoters' business. I have never acted for promoters. I have acted for solid business people who are out to manufacture something and sell it to the public, or to gather capital and discover something. But not to play high-jinks. And I have had a great many private companies, although I have been associated with public companies [too] (Hyndman transcript: 58).

Over several decades, Hyndman established a flourishing career as a company lawyer, becoming the first Canadian woman appointed to the board of a trust company, the London and Western Trust Company Ltd, in 1945 (Hyndman transcript: 108).

Yet, Hyndman was never just a company lawyer, and some of her work actively promoted the interests of Canadian women. For example, she assisted Wegenast in the 1930s in his defence of Dorothea Palmer, after Palmer was charged with the Criminal Code offence of providing information about birth control.[17] Hyndman also represented the Consumers' Association of Canada in its case challenging the ban on the sale of margarine; in the latter case, Hyndman appeared in the Supreme Court of Canada and then became the first Canadian woman lawyer to appear before the Privy Council in the successful appeal in the late 1940s.[18] In addition, as President of the Business and Professional Women's Association, Hyndman provided important leadership in the struggle to gain Ontario's first equal pay legislation in 1951 (Tillotson, 1991: 545–49),[19] and she also provided representation to some aboriginal women in their constitutional challenges in the 1970s.[20] More generally, Hyndman initiated a programme during the Second World War, by which the Canadian Bar Association provided free legal services to military personnel and their spouses, the beginning of legal aid services in Canada; and she received the City of Paris Medal for helping to publicise in Canada the cause of the Free French movement during the Second World War (Hyndman transcript: 102–05 and 161–64). After Helen Kinnear

[17] *R v Palmer* [1937] 2 DLR 609 (Ont Mag Ct); [1937] 3 DLR 493 (Ont CA); and Hyndman transcript, 74–78.

[18] Reference as to the Validity of s 5(a) of Dairy Industry Act, RSC 1927, chapter 45 (Margarine Case) [1949] SCR 1; Canadian Federation of Agriculture v AG Québec [1951] AC 179 (PC). Hyndman appeared in the Supreme Court of Canada as counsel to the Canadian Association of Consumers; although the record of the case indicates that no Canadian counsel participated in the Privy Council, Hyndman reported that she appeared: Hyndman transcript, 92–102.

[19] Hyndman was later involved in the 1967 *Bell Canada* equal pay case: see Kates (1990–91).

[20] *Canada (AG) v Lavell; Isaac v Bédard* [1974] SCR 1349. Hyndman and Frances Smookler appeared as counsel for Rose Wilhelm, Alberta Committee on Indian Rights for Indian Women Inc; see also Hyndman transcript, 149–53.

became the first woman in the British Empire to be named King's Counsel in 1934, Hyndman became the second in 1938.[21]

Partly as a result of Hyndman's involvement with international business and professional women's clubs, she also acquired many women friends and legal colleagues outside Canada. One was Helena Normanton, who became the first woman admitted to the Middle Temple in London in 1922).[22] When Normanton decided to retire in 1947, plans were made to hold a party in her honour with the Lord Chief Justice and other dignitaries from the Inns of Court in attendance. Hyndman's recollections of her unique contribution to this celebration in postwar London clearly reveal her national and international legal prominence at that time, as well as her well-known social acumen and generosity:

> [I]t was going to be a great big splash. But I knew that one thing that they wouldn't have much of would be cake, and I have a recipe for a wonderful light fruit cake ... and I sent it over to a firm of confectioners in London ... famous for [their] icings on cakes ... So I wrote to them about it and they said, ... they couldn't possibly do their best, they needed so many pounds of icing sugar ... and so many pounds of butter, and they couldn't possibly get that, and so many eggs to make the icing. So I sent them all over by airmail, and ... they decorated them. And the Lord Chief Justice was asked to cut the cake, with the Sword of Justice, and they found it didn't have any edge to it, it couldn't cut. And they had to bring the chef in from the kitchen with his big knife to cut the cake. And that just brought down the house (Hyndman transcript: 128).

Although Hyndman never married, this account of her ability to create a special occasion for a colleague reveals that her social life was extraordinarily active, not only in relation to her professional work, but because of her extensive volunteer activities, both in Canada and beyond.[23]

Much later, Hyndman was present when a group of prominent women met at the University Women's Club in 1966 to formulate plans to request the Canadian Prime Minister to establish a Royal Commission on the Status of Women; and when its report was released in 1970, Hyndman was prominent among the women who lobbied continuously for the implementation

[21] M Strauss, '61 Years of Practicing Law' Globe and Mail (14 February 1987) B1.

[22] 'Helena Normanton' The Times (16 October 1957). Like other aspiring women lawyers in Britain, Normanton had completed her law studies some years before women were permitted to become barristers and solicitors after the First World War; she was the first woman to be briefed at both the High Court of Justice and the Central Criminal Court.

[23] A Barnes, 'Lawyer Margaret Hyndman was a Women's Rights Pioneer' Toronto Star (21 January 1991) A11. Hyndman's social activities, and parties for large numbers of guests at her home, were well known, as was her humourous quip that she regretted not having married—every time she had to queue up in the liquor store—as she did not have a husband to do this job for her.

of its recommendations (Macpherson, 1994: 150–52).[24] Indeed, it was during one of her visits to Ottawa to speak about the need for women to continue to press the government to implement the recommendations of the report that she was interviewed by the Ottawa newspaper in 1973. Moreover, her published comment in that report—which suggested that discrimination in the legal profession had been broken with the appointment of Mabel Van Camp to the Supreme Court of Ontario two years earlier—is noteworthy because it clearly identified her own 'unfulfilled ambitions' 20 years earlier. By 1973, Hyndman was already in her early seventies, and too old for consideration in relation to an appointment to the bench. Yet, in the context of her many accomplishments, both within and outside the legal profession, there is a need to reflect on her lack of a judicial appointment; in fact, Hyndman went on practising law, in spite of increasing blindness in old age, until her death at the age of 89 in 1991.[25]

Like both Kinnear and Hyndman, Mabel Van Camp also grew up outside Toronto in a small community, where her father ran a local business as a garage mechanic. After finishing high school and then waiting a year until she was 17, Van Camp attended the University of Toronto, living with the Sedgwick family (a prominent lawyer's family) and providing some babysitting for them. She graduated in 1941 and then began to study education so that she could earn the funds necessary to attend Osgoode Hall; however, just six weeks into her education programme, she was asked to replace a teacher in a small community outside Ottawa because the teacher had fallen ill, and she taught Latin and home economics there for a year and a half. After another year of teaching in the town of Norwood, Van Camp entered Osgoode Hall in the fall of 1944, one of five women in a small class just before the end of the the Second World War (Van Camp transcript: 2–47).

Interestingly, Van Camp had met Dean Falconbridge a year earlier to seek his advice about studying law at Osgoode Hall; as Van Camp recalled:

> I went to see Dean Falconbridge ... and he persuaded me in the gentlest of terms that law was no profession for a lady, and I would be much happier if I did not take it. So I went away at that time. And over the year decided that I would try it. That was the only comment at any time all the way through law school about whether you should be in law or not (Van Camp transcript: 48–49).

Van Camp articled with Macdonald and Macintosh, doing research, and filing and serving papers; she recalled being the first student at the firm

[24] Macpherson identified Margaret Hyndman as one of a small group of women who met at the University Women's Club, and then contacted government leaders to arrange for the group's request for a Royal Commission to be presented to the Prime Minister.

[25] Just prior to her death, Hyndman became the first woman to receive the newly-established Law Society Medal, the highest honour of the Law Society of Upper Canada.

who did not pay for the privilege of being a student (Van Camp transcript: 62–70). Eventually, she was called to the Bar in September 1947. However, following her admission, Van Camp experienced great difficulty in finding a job—although she obtained interviews, she could not find employment because she was a woman. Some months later, with Sedgwick's help, she joined the firm of Gerard (Gerry) Beaudoin, a lawyer from Penetang, a small community north of Toronto. Beaudoin was active in providing legal services to the French Canadian community in Toronto, and Van Camp was useful to Beaudoin because, as a practising Catholic, he was not permitted to do divorces for Catholic clients. As Van Camp explained, 'it was handy when I came in, because I now could act for Roman Catholics who wanted a divorce' (Van Camp transcript: 86–93).

Van Camp worked in Beaudoin's firm, undertaking primarily family law and particularly counsel work in family law appeals, until 1962, when Beaudoin became ill; eventually, she and another lawyer took over Beaudoin's practice together and Van Camp continued her family law work, including advocacy in the courts (Van Camp transcript: 95). Years later, she vividly recalled the problems of inadequate robing rooms for women barristers: it was not just that the space was about 'twice the size of a clothes closet', but also that male lawyers often discussed their cases and negotiated settlements in their own robing rooms. Indeed, as Van Camp recalled, one woman lawyer had tried to overcome this problem when she was appearing in cases in Toronto by '[robing] in the men's robing room and that caused great furor' (Van Camp transcript: 174). Although Van Camp was involved in general practice, including some criminal law and negligence work, the Beaudoin firm became particularly well known for its family law activity, and the firm prepared a lot of separation agreements for spouses who did not wish to divorce, as well as divorce litigation (Van Camp transcript: 108–11 and 134–37). In addition, Van Camp was, for decades, active in the Women's Law Association of Ontario (Van Camp transcript: 77–78 and 152–60) and also in a variety of social service organisations, including the YWCA. According to Van Camp, it was the 'Y' which submitted her name for judicial appointment, even though she claimed to have no expectation of appointment because of her lack of political involvement (Van Camp transcript: 240–42).

Nonetheless, in spite of her lack of political connections, Van Camp was appointed to the Supreme Court of Ontario in November 1971. Years later, Van Camp recalled her first meeting with Chief Justice Gale, and their telephone consultation with judges in England and Australia about what to call her; eventually, they rejected 'Miss Justice Van Camp' and several other possibilities, and decided on 'Madam Justice'—without an 'e'. Van Camp's appointment also raised practical issues about washroom facilities for women judges and she later laughed about the challenges for Harcourts when she needed to be measured for judicial robes: 'they had never measured a woman for a gown' (Van Camp transcript: 246–50).

Van Camp retired in 1995 at the age of 75; like Kinnear and Hyndman, she never married and like them, she had been actively involved in numerous legal and other organisations.[26] All these women also seem to have been highly competent practitioners. In this context, it is puzzling that both Kinnear and Van Camp were appointed to the bench, while Hyndman was not. It is also puzzling that Kinnear was appointed a judge so many years before Van Camp. That is, in a context in which Kinnear had clearly demonstrated women's competence as judges, why was it almost 30 years before Van Camp was appointed to the Supreme Court in 1971? How can we explain the relationship between gender and ideas about professionalism in this context?

3. THE PUZZLE OF JUDICIAL APPOINTMENT: GENDER, FEMINISM AND THE LEGAL PROFESSION

In reflecting on these questions, research about women's appointment to the judiciary in the United States sheds some light on the appointment of Van Camp to the Ontario Supreme Court in 1971. According to Beverly Cook, the appointment of women judges is connected to a number of related but independent factors. In the first place, she identified the need for a pool of eligible women and an increase in the number of positions. Secondly, Cook suggested a need for 'gatekeepers' to recognise the presence of eligible women and the legitimacy of their claims for appointment to the bench. In addition, however, Cook argued that a third factor was essential: '*Without a woman's movement and specialized organisations of women lawyers and judges*, the pool of women eligible for law jobs would not increase and the gatekeepers would not be reminded of their claims' (Cook, 1984: 575, emphasis added; Cook, 1981).

Although Cook's analysis did not focus on the Canadian context, there are obvious similarities in the intersection of these three variables in Ontario in the early 1970s when Van Camp was appointed. First, the pool of women lawyers began to increase significantly in the late 1960s and early 1970s. According to Law Society records, only a few women were being admitted to the Ontario Bar in the early decades; indeed, even in the period from 1960 to 1968, fewer than a dozen women gained admission in each of these years (LSUC records). Then, quite rapidly, these numbers began to change: 32 women were admitted to the Bar in 1969; 19 in 1970; 33 in 1971; and 20 in 1972. In 1973, however, the numbers began to increase even more substantially: 51 women were admitted to the Bar in 1973; 50 more

[26] T Claridge, 'Retiring Ontario Judge, 75, Ready for the Next Course' Globe and Mail (13 May 1995) A5.

gained admission in 1974; and then 85 women were called to the Bar in 1975 (LSUC records). Indeed, overall, it is significant that slightly more women were admitted to the Ontario Bar between 1969 and 1975 than had been admitted to same Bar between 1897 and 1968.[27] To some extent, these increasing numbers reflected the expansion of university law schools in the 1960s and 1970s. Yet, as Richard Abel noted, the rate of expansion for women law students across Canada greatly exceeded that of males in these years: while the number of male law students doubled nationally between 1962–63 and 1980–81, the number of female law students increased twenty-four times in the same period (Abel, 1985: 23). As Abel concluded, the highly accelerated rate of women's entry to the legal profession was 'nothing short of revolutionary' (Abel, 1988: 202).

Secondly, there is evidence that most law graduates in this period had little difficulty obtaining employment in the profession, as law jobs increased in number and variety, particularly as the economy prospered, the rate of legislative activity increased, new roles for governmental intervention resulted in the creation of an array of agencies and tribunals and programmes for legal aid and assistance for the poor and disadvantaged were established (Arthurs, Weisman and Zemans, 1988: 123; Stager with Arthurs, 1990; White, 1987). In this context, the number of judicial appointments also seems to have started to increase (Stager with Arthurs 1990: 299). Thirdly, and perhaps most significantly, it appears that some of the traditional gatekeepers must have changed their attitudes (at least in public) about women on the bench.

As Cook argued, however, the critical factor was *the presence of a women's movement that exerted pressure on the gatekeepers*. In this context, Mabel Van Camp's later recollections of her appointment to the bench in 1971 identified the feminist movement as a significant factor in creating pressure for the appointment of a woman to the Supreme Court of Ontario; as she reflected:

> There was pressure. There had been pressure, I think, of about maybe two years. I have forgotten what [exactly] was happening in the feminist movement at that time. But many [feminist] groups were not so much [determined] to have a woman on the Court, as to have women in public life in some way or other. And Trudeau was very receptive to it. Chief Justice Gale would have liked it to commence somewhere else ... And in some other court. But they were going to add five [judges] and it was difficult to add five and not have one of them a woman at that time ... And I sat down and tried to think what I wanted to do about it, but ... what influenced me was that ... all through my life I had sort of gone where things led ... I was terrified at how I would ever prepare myself for the job ... But

[27] According to the Law Society records, there were 273 women lawyers admitted to the Ontario Bar up to the end of 1968; between 1969 and 1975, a total of 279 women lawyers were called to the Ontario Bar.

> I thought well, I have done everything else and I have been scared [of] doing it, so I will try this one too (Van Camp transcript: 243–45).

Van Camp's acknowledgment of the pressure to appoint women to public life and her sense of personal responsibility to respond positively in this context appear to be important factors to explain why women began to be appointed as judges in higher courts in Canada in the 1970s.

Moreover, her reflections are consistent with the Report of the Royal Commission on the Status of Women in 1970, which had noted that there were 889 judges and magistrates in Canada, of whom only 14 were women; moreover, only one, Réjane L-Colas of Quebec, was then a member of a superior court (Royal Commission Report 1970: 342). The Commission strongly recommended that both federal and provincial governments should appoint more women judges, citing the comments of Chief Justice McRuer a few years earlier. Significantly, Chief Justice McRuer had commented that women should not be appointed *only* because they were women, but he had also pointedly suggested that 'many women who are practising at the Bar of Canada ... would make better judges than some of the men that have been appointed' (McRuer, 1968). McRuer's public comments are especially important in identifying the attitudes of (some) gatekeepers in the early 1970s, although there were undoubtedly different views among some of his male contemporaries. Yet, as Van Camp's reflections reveal, there was also political support in Ottawa for her appointment, spurred on to some extent at least by the demands of the women's movement and the recommendations of the Royal Commission (Van Camp transcript: 240).[28]

In this context, it is arguable that timing explains why Van Camp was appointed to the judiciary, when Hyndman was not. Although both women had demonstrated their qualities as legal practitioners, and both had been involved in public and community activities, Hyndman was older than Van Camp and already in her seventies by the time that all the factors identified by Cook were finally in place. Yet, although these arguments usefully explain the context for Van Camp's judicial appointment (and Hyndman's lack of appointment), how is it possible to explain Kinnear's appointment 30 years earlier in the 1940s?

Clearly, none of the factors identified by Cook were in place in 1943, when Kinnear was appointed as a county court judge. Indeed, very few women were then becoming lawyers, and there was not a strong feminist

[28] Van Camp's appointment was probably influenced by a number of factors: she was an active and well-respected advocate in the courts; her expertise in family law was a particular asset in the context of the enactment of federal divorce legislation three years earlier in 1968; and her lack of personal political connection may have been helpful. Like most women lawyers of her generation, moreover, she practised law alongside men, some of whom may have been willing to support her appointment because of her competence and her legal and community service activities.

movement in place—so there was little pressure on gatekeepers to appoint women. At the same time, it seems likely that Kinnear's willingness to relinquish the Liberal nomination in the by-election in 1941 was highly significant. It was early in the Second World War and there was a pressing need for the Minister of Labour to be in the House of Commons and at the Cabinet table. In this context, it seems likely that Kinnear's decision to stand aside to allow the minister to run in the by-election resulted in her appointment to the bench two years later in 1943. Yet, since neither Kinnear nor the Canadian government ever acknowledged a connection between Kinnear's decision to stand aside and then her subsequent appointment to the bench, how should we understand this aspect of her professional life?

In trying to respond to this question, it is useful to take account of Jill Ker Conway's analysis of 'silences' in the lives of early professional women. Conway argued that

> Pioneer women professionals were silent about their ambitions and recounted their lives as though their successes just happened to them, rather like the soprano's chance meeting with the tenor in the first act of an opera ... [In telling her story,] the woman professional ... seems to have chanced upon the causes which elicit a lifetime commitment from her. She never acknowledges strategizing about how to advance the cause, she is as surprised as anyone else when success is at hand ... What are we to make of such silences? (Ker Conway, 1999: 15–16).

As Ker Conway argued, such women may engage in 'censorship for public self-presentation', a perspective that may be useful in understanding Kinnear's judicial appointment. Thus, recognising that Kinnear had been active in Liberal politics for at least 15 years by 1941, and that she had been seeking the Liberal nomination in the Niagara region for some years, it seems reasonable that she acceded to the request to stand aside to enable the Minister of Labour to obtain a parliamentary seat only after negotiating for some recognition of her agreement to do so. Clearly, the exigencies of the Second World War may also have encouraged the appointment of a woman judge in the context in which many women were already engaged in non-traditional work; and the relative absence of qualified male lawyers for the judiciary during the War years may also have been a factor in Kinnear's appointment. Yet, as Ker Conway's comment suggests, Kinnear's appointment downplayed overt ambition or strategising: judicial appointment 'just happened' to her in 1943. While much of this assessment is speculative, of course, it suggests that Kinnear's timing was propitious along with her abilities as a lawyer, and that she was ready to respond to such an opportunity.

By contrast, Hyndman's outstanding accomplishments were only beginning to be revealed during the Second World War, and the relative decline of the feminist movement, in the context of ideas about women's 'proper roles' after the Second World War, ensured that no similar opportunities were ever presented to her. And then, when the feminist movement revived and the pool of women lawyers increased, creating pressure on the gatekeepers, it was Van Camp whose timing was right. Poignantly, Hyndman's comment that she had been 'at peace over unfulfilled ambitions for 20 years' suggests that she was finally prepared to break her 'silence', both about her own ambition for a judicial appointment and also with respect to discrimination in the legal profession.

Yet, two aspects of Hyndman's comment about discrimination in the legal profession are worthy of note. One is that her 1973 comment is almost unique, at least for its time. Indeed, it is striking how often women who were successful in gaining appointments to the bench and to positions of public office in the 1970s and 1980s continued to deny the relevance of gender to the practice of law. Particularly in a context in which the strength of the women's movement and its pressure on gatekeepers created opportunities for women to achieve new levels of success in the legal profession, it is curious that many women in law so firmly distanced themselves from the women's movement. For example, Laura Legge, the first woman to be elected a Law Society Bencher in 1975 and then its Treasurer in 1983, always avoided being identified as a 'woman lawyer', declaring 'I don't know what a feminist is ... Women have had equality for all my life. It's a question of them getting on with the job. I think the fact that I'm now treasurer proves it' (*Toronto Star*, 1983). Similarly, as her biographer reported, Bertha Wilson was always firmly and 'avowedly not a feminist' (Anderson, 2001: 135), even though she became the first woman appointed to an appellate court in 1975 and to the Supreme Court of Canada in 1982. Thus, even in the context of successes never achieved by earlier cohorts of women lawyers, and even though their successes may have resulted from pressure on the gatekeepers on the part of the women's movement, these successful women lawyers continued to deny that gender had any significance in the practice of law. Indeed, as Hyndman's earlier comment in 1949 reveals, she too firmly declared the irrelevance of gender to the practice of law at that time.

In addition, however, Ker Conway's perceptions about 'silences' in women's lives, particularly with respect to public self-presentation, is crucial in understanding the denial of the relevance of gender and feminism for women lawyers; and it also helps to explain the significance of Hyndman's differing views in 1949 and 1973. For all these successful women in law, such comments are not at all curious in *the context of ideas about legal professionalism*. Indeed, they confirm how women lawyers were always required to work within the traditions of the 'gentleman's profession' of law (Gidney and Millar, 1994: 239),[29] and to accept gender neutrality as

[29] As the authors stated succinctly, an occupation could not be called a profession 'if it was filled with women'.

fundamental to the ideals of modern legal professionalism (Cott, 1987: 233–34).[30] Put more bluntly, for a woman like Hyndman to succeed in the legal profession in mid-twentieth century Canada, it was fundamentally necessary to be a 'lawyer,' not a 'woman lawyer'. Or, as Legge explained when she was first elected a Bencher, it was important for a woman to demonstrate that she was not a 'monster' and that she was not going to 'make a lot of waves' (Legge transcript).

Thus, as Glazer and Slater explained in relation to women who entered the professions in the late nineteenth and early twentieth century:

> In trying to sort out the reasons for professional women's successes or failures, it is far too facile to say that there were prejudices against women that they had to overcome. The ways in which prejudice manifested itself were extremely complex and insidious ... As determined, aspiring professionals, women were not easily deterred. They found a variety of ways to respond to the discrimination they faced (Glazer and Slater, 1987: 12–14).

As these American researchers concluded in relation to the prejudice experienced by earlier generations of women in the professions, women lawyers who were 'determined, aspiring professionals', were not 'easily deterred' and they utilised a number of strategies to pursue their aspirations as members of the legal profession in the period of transition in the 1970s and 1980s (Glazer and Slater, 1987). For many of these women in law, changes in the status of women created by the women's movement opened up new professional opportunities, but the cultural traditions of the 'gentleman's profession' continued to define them as 'lawyers' (ungendered).

At the same time, it is clear that we need to be as attentive to the 'silences' in their lives as well as their public self-presentation. On this basis, it is possible that Kinnear's appointment reflects both propitious timing, but also astute negotiation on her part. In contrast, for Hyndman, gender was always a barrier to judicial appointment, in spite of her exceptional accomplishments. And significantly, Van Camp's appointment is arguably the first in which gender is no longer a barrier; indeed, it may have become a 'bonus': that is, Van Camp was appointed because she was a woman, in a context in which a strong feminist movement was creating increasing pressure on gatekeepers to appoint women to the judiciary, a pressure that could no longer be ignored. As a result, in examining the experiences of women lawyers, and particularly those who were the 'first' to be appointed to the bench, we need to attend carefully to the circumstances of their appointments, not

[30] As Cott concluded, 'the professional ethos, with its own promise of freedom from sex-defined constraints, was released to flourish in aspiring women's minds.' Although Cott's assessment was particularly directed to the 1920s and 1930s after women's suffrage was achieved, it seems that these ideas continued to flourish into the 1970s and after.

only to understand how they accomplished their successes, but because their 'silences' in relation to their 'public self-presentation' provide important evidence about invisible, but nonetheless powerful, ideas about the relationships between gender and the 'gentleman's profession' of law.

4. REFERENCES

Abel, R (1985) 'Comparative Sociology of Legal Professions: An Exploratory Essay' 1 *American Bar Foundation Research Journal* 5.

—— (1988) 'United States: The Contradictions of Professionalism' in R Abel and P Lewis (eds), *Lawyers in Society: The Common Law World*, vol 1 (Berkeley, University of California Press).

Anderson, E (2001) *Judging Bertha Wilson: Law as Large as Life* (Toronto, University of Toronto Press).

Arthurs, HW, Weisman, R and Zemans, FH (1988) 'Canadian Lawyers: A Peculiar Professionalism' in R Abel and P Lewis (eds), *Lawyers in Society: The Common Law World*, vol 1 (Berkeley, University of California Press).

Cook, BB (1981) 'Will Women Judges make a Difference in Women's Legal Rights? A Prediction from Attitudes and Simulated Behaviour' in M Rendel (ed), *Women, Power and Political Systems* (London, Croom Helm).

—— (1984) 'Women Judges: A Preface to their History' 14 *Golden Gate University Law Review* 573.

Corbett, M and Corbett, D (1996) 'Helen Kinnear (1894–1970)' in RM Salokar and ML Volcansek (eds), *Women in Law: A Bio-Bibliographical Sourcebook* (Westport Conn, Greenwood Press).

Cott, N (1987) *The Grounding of Modern Feminism* (New Haven, Yale University Press).

Gidney, RD and Millar, WPJ (1994) *Professional Gentlemen: The Professions in Nineteenth-Century Ontario* (Toronto, University of Toronto Press).

Glazer, PM and Slater, M (1987) *Unequal Colleagues: The Entrance of Women into Professions, 1890–1940* (New Brunswick, Rutgers University Press).

Kates, C (1990–91) '"Identical or Substantially Identical": Bell Canada and the Struggle for Equal Pay 1967–1976' 4 *Canadian Journal of Women and the Law* 133.

Ker Conway, J (1999) *When Memory Speaks: Exploring the Art of Autobiography* (New York, Vantage Books).

Kinnear, H (1954) 'The County Court Judge in Ontario' 32 *Canadian Bar Review* 21 (Part I).

—— (1954) 'The County Court Judge in Ontario' 32 *Canadian Bar Review* 128 (Part II).

Macpherson, K (1994) *When in Doubt, Do Both: The Times of My Life* (Toronto, University of Toronto Press).

Mather, M (June/July 1993) 'Judge Helen Kinnear: A Woman of Many Firsts' *Canadian Lawyer* 14–18.

McRuer, JC (1968) 'The Task Ahead', National Conference on Human Rights, Ottawa.

Royal Commission on the Status of Women (1970) *Report of the Royal Commission on the Status of Women* (Ottawa, Information Canada).
Sharpe, R and McMahon, P (2007) *The Persons Case: The Origins and Legacy of the Fight for Legal Personhood* (Toronto, University of Toronto Press).
Stager, D with Arthurs, HW (1990) *Lawyers in Canada* (Toronto, University of Toronto Press).
Tillotson, S (1991) 'Human Rights Law as Prism: Women's Organizations, Unions, and Ontario's Female Employees Fair Remuneration Act, 1951' 72 *Canadian Historical Review* 352.
Wegenast, FW (1931) *The Law of Canadian Companies* (Toronto, Burroughs).
White, G (1987) 'Lawyers in Government: A Preliminary Study' in RJ Matas and DJ McCawley (eds), *Legal Education in Canada* (Montréal, Federation of Law Societies of Canada).
Wyatt, R (2000) *Agnes MacPhail: Champion of the Underdog* (Lantzville BC, XYZ Publishing).

Archival Sources

'Laura Legge' in Archives of the Law Society of Upper Canada (Legge transcript).
'List of Women Barristers and Solicitors in Ontario' in Archives of the Law Society of Upper Canada (LSUC records).
'Mabel Van Camp' transcript of oral history, Osgoode Society for Canadian Legal History, Archives of Ontario (Van Camp transcript).
'Margaret Paton Hyndman' transcript of oral history, Osgoode Society for Canadian Legal History, Archives of Ontario (Hyndman transcript).

1.2

Profiles in Leadership: Eminent Women Judges in the United States

ELAINE MARTIN

Abstract

There are two major ways in which women judges in the United States have had a significant, measurable and gendered impact on the course of justice. The first has been well-documented and focuses on the cumulative impact on law, especially family law, made through case decisions by an increasing number of women judges. A second line of research, focusing on individual women's judicial behaviour both on and off the bench, is the one chosen here. Three women are selected from the first generation of women federal judges to illustrate three different theories drawn from the gender and judging literature.

1. INTRODUCTION

A NEW ERA in the study of women judges in the United States was ushered in by virtue of President Carter's unprecedented appointment of 40 women to the federal courts, during his only term in office from 1976 to 1980. In the old pre-Carter days, nearly three decades ago, there had been so few women judges that they were studied mostly from a biographical perspective, as opposed to a more statistical and theoretical methodology. Thanks to Carter's signal determination to appoint women to the federal bench, and the subsequent following of his lead by all succeeding presidents, the number of women federal court judges has increased substantially. When Carter took office, only four women were active sitting judges, by September 2009 there were 247 women out of 1286 active and senior status sitting judges, or 19.2 per cent. Following Carter, scholars no longer had to discuss small numbers of individual women judges and their uniqueness, but instead were able to compare women and men judges in aggregate to examine their possible differences in voting behaviour. Despite some very suggestive findings over the years indicating that there are differences between men and women judges in certain types of cases, it is not clear why such differences may occur, although there are a number of competing theories. It is the premise of this chapter that a return to qualitative research may shed some light on the competing theories of gender differences in judging.

Selecting the women judges to be included in this study was not an easy task. Many women judges have been honoured by legal associations, most particularly the National Association of Women Judges that gives an annual award to an outstanding woman judge. Many are well-known legal scholars, leaders in the National Association of Women Judges and other legal associations, as well as influential in establishing gender bias task forces in their jurisdictions. Many have been viewed as mentors or role models by up-and-coming women lawyers and judges, and have broken new ground in deciding cases that impact women's lives. However, relatively few have written about their gendered life experiences and perspectives on the bench. The judges selected for discussion here are among those few.

All three of the women selected were appointed to the United States Appeals Courts by Democratic presidents.[1] Two were appointed by President Carter: Judge Patricia M Wald (DC Circuit) and Judge Dorothy W Nelson (Ninth Circuit). Judge Rosemary Barkett (Eleventh Circuit), after serving many years on the Florida State Supreme Court as an Associate Justice and four years as Chief, was appointed by President Clinton. As individuals they are very different from one another, but all have spoken and written about gender issues and have been acclaimed as role models and mentors for other women lawyers, and all are at the end of their long and full careers.

No claim is made that they are representative of other women judges. However, each woman's profile is illustrative of various research conclusions that have been offered to explain judicial gender differences: (1) Judge Wald's profile demonstrates the ways women's paths to the bench differ from those of men and how that might impact their behaviour (Martin, 1982; Martin, 2004; Martin and Pyle, 2002); (2) Judge Nelson's profile demonstrates that women, as women, may bring a unique perspective to the bench (see generally Goldstein, 1992); and (3) Judge Barkett's profile illustrates the contention that women judges may be more likely to practise feminist jurisprudence and ask 'the woman question'—that is, to ask how a particular rule or outcome may have different consequences for men and women (Martin and Pyle, 2005).

Despite what some have called mixed results, the clear message of quantitative research to date is that gender does have an impact on case decisions by judges (Boyd, Epstein and Martin, 2010). That impact, however, is

[1] The 94 US judicial districts are organised into 12 regional circuits, each of which has a United States court of appeals. A court of appeals hears appeals from the district courts located within its circuit.

probably limited to those cases in which gendered experience is relevant to understanding and interpreting the facts and law at hand, and in which the use of judicial discretion is appropriate. It can be seen in differences between men and women judges in deciding cases, but it can also be seen in appellate courts with mixed gender panels.

Qualitative research upholds these empirical findings and adds a richer human dimension by focusing more narrowly on individual judges or groups of judges, and by telling more about the context in which gender experiences might be germane (for example, Martin, 2009). In this chapter each of the women selected will be examined in light of the three theories described above.

2. PATRICIA M WALD: HER GENDERED PATH TO THE BENCH

Patricia M Wald's history presents an interesting illustration of the way in which gendered experiences may be filtered through an individual's own personality and self concept. She is intellectually aware of certain drawbacks she experienced due to her gender, but equally aware of her personal ability to interact with possible mentors and develop support networks to overcome these drawbacks. She refers to herself as 'adventurous'[2] and that appellation certainly seems accurate. It also re-enforces literature which has concluded that women judges tend to be risk-taking extroverts, and those traits have aided them in their efforts to be accepted in a male-dominated profession (Kennedy, 2005). Wald explicitly credits her gendered life experiences for making her the kind of judge she became (Wald, 2005).

Wald's history is a story of contrasts. Born in 1928, she was an only child raised by a single mother, but also part of a large Irish Catholic extended family of blue-collar workers. She joined her family members in the factory at the age of 16, but took college-track classes in high school at her mother's insistence. There was no money for college expenses, but with the aid of merit scholarships, Wald became the first in her family to go to college. She had never seen a woman lawyer, but determined to pursue a career in law after observing factory labour union efforts.[3]

Her first problem, after graduating from college (Connecticut College for Women) in 1948 was to find a law school that would admit women. Ultimately, she graduated from Yale with the help of a Pepsi-Cola scholarship and part-time work, one of 11 women out of 200 students. At Yale, as she did throughout her life, she networked and made long-lasting friends and mentors, who were to serve her well in her career. Unlike Supreme

[2] L Greenhouse, 'Public Lives; War Crimes Tribunal Appeals to Unconventional Judge' *New York Times* (12 July 1999) A8.

[3] Ibid.

Court Justice Ruth Bader Ginsberg, who has spoken of the 'chilly climate' for women in law school in the 1960s, Judge Wald says she experienced no derogatory putdowns in class by virtue of her gender and was chosen as a student editor of the *Yale Law Journal*, one of the two women in her class to do so (Wald, 2005).

The 'chills' began, however, when she attempted to find work in private sector law. She was told such things as, sorry we've already hired 'our woman' and when she did get an offer it was at 20 per cent less pay than her male counterparts. She wisely decided to try other avenues. There were no women professors at Yale during her time there, but two of her male professors enabled her to get a very prestigious clerkship with Second Circuit Appeals Judge Jerome Frank. She learned much from Frank, and formed an enduring friendship with him. When her clerkship ended, Frank was instrumental in getting her a job with the law firm of Arnold, Fortas and Porter. Wald again felt no discrimination on the job, but adds that she chose not to join the local Bar association as it was sex-segregated.

Shortly thereafter, she married a former Yale Law classmate and became pregnant. She decided to leave the law and would not return for 10 years. This decision was fuelled by the birth of five children in seven years, one of whom suffered a serious illness for nearly a year. She acknowledges that her choice may also have been affected by the fact that there was no such thing as maternity leave at the time, and societal standards definitely emphasised the importance of full-time motherhood.

When her youngest child began kindergarten, she eased her way back into law by joining friends in research activities, soon writing her own manuscript for the Office of Economic Opportunity Conference on Law and Poverty. She continued writing policy papers until she landed a presidential appointment to the DC Crime Commission.

Her experience there strengthened her determination to go into legal service law where she served for a number of years. She notes that she won the first case in Washington DC granting divorces for indigent women (the US Supreme Court followed suit many years later). After publishing a book on drug abuse, she was appointed to the Ford Foundation Board where she continued lobbying for money for public interest law and organisations litigating for women's and children's rights.

Partly as a consequence of contacts made during that time, she was offered a position as Assistant Attorney General for the Office of Legislative Affairs in the Department of Justice in the Carter administration. A big part of her job was to lobby for legislation wanted by the Department of Justice and the President. As it happened, her boss was Attorney General Griffin Bell who played a major role in helping President Carter meet his goal of appointing women and minorities to the federal bench. Bell and back door lobbying by women's groups helped her get the nomination she coveted to the DC Circuit Court of Appeals.

She felt the 'chills' again during the Senate confirmation process, when she was targeted by right-wing opposition, and Senator Humphrey (Rhode Island) led the charge claiming she was a 'wild and wooly woman' and anti-family (Wald, 2005). Once again, friends and colleagues she had cultivated in her past came to her support, including such Republicans as Barry Goldwater and she was affirmed easily.

Once on the Court, she plunged enthusiastically into her caseload, and felt welcomed by her all-male colleagues. While there, she accumulated multiple honours and continued a record of scholarship, quite extraordinary for a sitting judge. There is no requirement of scholarship for judges, and many do not publish at all. Of the 106 legal publications authored by Judge Wald to be found through a search on *Google Scholar*, six deal explicitly with her experiences as a woman judge. She wrote 820 published opinions. A *Westlaw* search demonstrates that her writings have been cited 1486 times in law reviews and journals, an indication of her widespread influence on legal scholarship. She also wrote several great dissents that were ultimately held correct by the US Supreme Court. Wald was frequently mentioned as a possible candidate for a US Supreme Court appointment. In her decisions, and perhaps especially in her dissents, she revealed herself as an advocate for civil rights and the interests of members of minority groups (Beiner, 2005).

In 1998, at the age of 70, when many judges take senior status, she was offered an appointment to serve on the International Criminal Tribunal for the Former Yugoslavia for two years. As she states: 'my adventurous instincts took over' and off she went to The Hague (Greenhouse, 1999). While there, in addition to her other assignments, like helping build legal systems for strife-torn countries like Rwanda, Cambodia and Yugoslavia, she also attempted to make women and children more visible as victims of war crimes, and to make rape a war crime. At the end of her two years, she continued to be active, filling her days with writing, teaching, arbitration, working with NGOs on international justice and human rights issues and serving on presidential commissions.

3. DOROTHY M NELSON: HER UNIQUE PERSPECTIVE AS A WOMAN LEADER

Judge Dorothy M Nelson seems not to have had, or at least not spoken of, the kind of specifically gendered experiences that Judge Wald had. However, in many respects she personifies the leadership style and manner that has been assumed to be, in many quarters, the expected hallmark of women's rise to power (Sherry, 1986; Resnik, 1988; Peresie, 2005). She is said to have 'emphasized collaboration and teamwork, forging alliances between people with common interests' (Kay, 2002). She was reputedly extremely friendly, approachable, kind and solicitous of others' opinions. She was inclined to 'serve and honour others, rather than be served or honoured' (Kloppenberg, 2001: 100). Throughout her career in academe and on the bench she promoted the concept of Alternative Dispute Resolution (ADR), claiming the limitations of the adversarial system.[4] She also promoted the notion of family-friendly practices in the workplace, especially law firms. She has contended that women have special characteristics that amount to an ethics of care.

Judge Nelson was born in 1928 to a middle-class family in Southern California. Her mother was a classroom teacher in an era of stay-at-home mums. She had two experiences while in high school that were to have an impact on her later life. She decided to become a lawyer and she met the man she would later marry. During an annual 'Law Day' in her senior year in high school, she sat on the bench alongside a juvenile court judge, and afterwards she determined to pursue a career in law. She met James Nelson when the two were working as camp counsellors; they went on to become friends, took the Law School Admission Test together, became a rare two-attorney family in the 1950s, and then an even rarer two-judge family. She credits her husband as instrumental in her ability to balance both a career and family (Chuang, 1999).

Nelson came to the US Ninth Circuit Court of Appeals from academia. She received a Master of Law from the University of Southern California Law School in 1956, and shortly afterwards, became a member of the faculty. She moved quickly up the ranks until 1969 when she became Dean of the Law School, at that time the only woman Dean of an ABA (American Bar Association) accredited law school.

She tells the following story of how she got into teaching law:

> When I was getting my master's at USC (University of Southern California) I was in a seminar called Judicial Administration. The Professor of that seminar was called away to Europe ... I was asked to teach the last nine weeks of the course. The course had not been very interesting, to put it mildly, and I said, 'We're going to leave the Law School and we're going to go downtown and start at the drunk tank, and we're going to move through the criminal justice system. One day a week is going to be a field trip. Everyone is going to do a paper (every week) on how to improve the system, either in the juvenile courts, the traffic courts, the probate courts, whatever they are, and then we are going to do the same with the civil justice system' (Nelson, 1989: 108)

[4] Alternative Dispute Resolution (ADR) refers to processes such as: negotiation; early neutral evaluation, where a neutral third person evaluates a case's worth before trial; mediation, where a neutral third person helps the parties to arrive at a mutually agreeable solution; and arbitration, where a neutral third person is selected to resolve a dispute.

At the course's end, the students marched into the Dean's office and demanded that she be hired, and thus, she became the first woman faculty member at USC. That experience was not dissimilar to the manner in which she was appointed Dean. After two years of effort at finding a male Dean, the law faculty informed the President that they wanted Nelson. She describes her first meeting with the faculty as Dean:

> When I became the first woman Dean, one of the senior faculty members called me into his office and advised me to arrive at the next faculty meeting 15 minutes late to show the faculty who was boss. Instead, I rushed home and baked 5 dozen chocolate cookies and arrived 15 minutes early to greet everyone. I also announced that we would have food at all faculty meetings henceforth.[5]

She continues: 'I have always found that in meetings and in crisis situations, food brings people closer together and improves communication immeasurably'.[6]

She has certainly followed her instincts with regard to the importance of food. For example, during the student sit-ins of the 1960s she ordered the school cafeteria to send over sodas and snacks. As a new appellate court judge, she hosted dinner parties at her home for the other judges when the court sat in San Francisco (Martin, 2009). She also held a monthly luncheon in her chambers when court was in session for all the judges and their staffs (Schroeder, 2002).

A former student, and a law school Dean, says of Nelson (Kloppenberg, 2001: 100): 'She listened carefully and brought other people along on her initiatives, forming coalitions among diverse groups. People soon saw that she was tough in a less authoritarian way—she was ambitious, purposeful, persistent, optimistic and full of energy'.

Nelson did not just 'talk the talk' but 'walked the walk'. For example, during her US Senate confirmation hearings after being nominated to the federal bench, she was praised for her efforts as USC Dean to improve the academic climate for minorities. She took the initiative for expanding affirmative action programmes, for establishing a Western Centre on Law and Poverty, a National Senior Citizens Law Centre, a Chicano Law Centre and a Black Students' Law Association (Nelson, 2007: 113). Nelson took student concerns on campus very seriously, engaging in frequent dialogue with students, and hiring a new Dean of Student Affairs (Kloppenberg, 2001).

Her promotion of the idea of Alternative Dispute Resolution (ADR) is a legal approach that fits neatly with the notion of women as uniquely contextual thinkers, and was viewed by her male colleagues as a 'woman's thing'. Her view was that justice would be better served by the implementation

[5] 'First Women: Dorothy W Nelson' *Ms JD* at: ms-jd.org/first-women-dorothy-w-nelson/.
[6] Ibid.

and expansion of systems of ADR. She claims, 'The adversarial system is too costly and too inefficient for many types of disputes' (Nelson, 2004: 168).

In the 1950s, as a new law school faculty member and the first woman, she determined to insert ADR materials into the curriculum. Her faculty friends advised her not to rock the boat. As a member of the Bahá'í Faith, she believed in the process of consultation to resolve conflicts peacefully, and was not convinced of the efficacy of the adversary system. She inserted materials on mediation, the closest thing to consultation, in her seminar on the administration of justice. One day at a faculty meeting, she overheard a faculty member say to another: just what is this thing called mediation that Dorothy is teaching in her seminar? The response was: 'Oh, it's a woman's thing. She is trying to get everyone to love each other' (Nelson, 1980: 13).

Nelson laughed and carried on with her plans, but she does believe that women have unique perspectives and great opportunities to advance the legal field. She talks of the qualities of mental alertness, intuition and the spiritual qualities of love and service, in which women are strong and how they can positively influence the adversary system. She asserts that

> While men and women must achieve full equality with respect to education, employment, salaries, and advancement opportunities, men and women have some distinct attributes, which must be present if we are to have a just and peaceful society.[7]

Nelson has observed that many women opt out of the legal profession because they feel that it is necessary to conform to a male model which values long hours and neglect of family in pursuit of material wealth. She suggests that female attorneys who also want families should not back down from their perspectives and values as women, but instead work to alter workplace values. She describes her own efforts in that regard in successfully advising a former law clerk, torn between her new-born child and her legal career. She told the young woman lawyer to ask if she could return to work part-time and not to worry about not making partner as soon as her male peers. The firm agreed, and shortly thereafter, three young male associates asked to be allowed to cut their hours to spend more time with their families. In some agitation, the senior partner of the law firm called Nelson and said: 'Judge, what are you doing to my law firm?'[8] She persuaded him that this development was a good thing, and pointed out that the local Bar association was spending $200,000 a year to provide drug and marital counselling to young associates who might be okay if they didn't work so

[7] Ibid.
[8] Ibid.

many hours. The senior partner agreed and the environment of the entire law firm was changed.[9]

She points to this as an example of how women lawyers have much to offer in improving the workplace. She urges that laws and practices need to be radically different in all areas, allowing such things as parental leave times, flexibility in schedules, interrupting careers for raising children, perhaps employment type benefits for parents who are engaged full-time in raising children, such as social security, health insurance and disability coverage.[10]

As a judge, Nelson states that she is not an 'originalist'—a judge who determines how a case should go by looking to the intent of the original writers of the Constitution. She points out that 'those forty-four men' wrote what was originally a four-page document that left out the rights of women and minorities, and did not even contain the Bill of Rights until four years later (Nelson, 1989: 112).

4. ROSEMARY BARKETT: HER FEMINIST JURISPRUDENCE

Judge Rosemary Barkett is presented here as an example of a woman judge who practises what has been called feminist jurisprudence (Holbrook, 1992). Judge Barkett never married, so has not experienced the kind of competing demands of family and career that Wald and Nelson faced. She also has not written as extensively about her gendered experiences. However, her appellate opinions provide a rich source for identifying her feminist jurisprudence, and will be the primary source for her profile.

Her narrative is compelling. She was born in Mexico, in 1939, of Syrian parents, one of 16 children, only seven of whom survived to adulthood. She immigrated to the United States at the age of five. At the age of 17, she became both a citizen and a Roman Catholic nun. As a nun she obtained an undergraduate degree and taught in elementary and middle schools. She left her order after 11 years to go to law school. After graduating from the University of Florida Law School, she went into private practice for eight years, and then started up the judicial ladder. She began as a Florida circuit court judge, then a judge on the Florida Court of Appeals, moving on to the state Supreme Court, and serving two years as Chief Justice (the first woman) before being appointed to the US Court of Appeals for the Eleventh Circuit, where she still sits. Barkett is extraordinarily active on and off the bench. She has served on numerous commissions and associations, addressing child welfare matters, court management, criminal justice, family law, legal education and the role of women in the law.

[9] Ibid.
[10] Ibid.

A universal definition of feminism is hard to find, and no contention is made here that Judge Barkett is a feminist, but instead that she is a judge who practises feminist jurisprudence. That, too, is hard to define, but would seem to be primarily a *reasoning* process that emphasises understanding of experiences, relationships and the relative power of individuals in reaching legal decisions (Holbrook, 1992). In addition, feminist jurisprudence should seek to expose how the substance of law may silently, and without justification, submerge the perspectives of women and other excluded groups (Bartlett, 1990). These features, in turn, would seem to include certain judicial temperament attributes: a willingness to take controversial stands, exercise judicial discretion, examine judicial questions in situational context and write opinions exposing the lack of neutrality in law.

Barkett is by all accounts a strong-minded jurist devoted to both a sense of justice and the necessity of careful legal reasoning. She stands foursquare for the position that judges should and do exercise their discretion in deciding cases: 'The exercise of discretion is a constant and recurring feature of the work that judges do' (Barkett, 2005: 2). She is also a strong believer in carefully examining judicial neutrality: 'the questions we ask are almost never entirely disconnected from the context in which we ask them' (2005: 2). As a curb to the arbitrary use of judicial discretion, she urges that 'judges give reasons for all their decisions, including their discretionary calls, in order to better maintain confidence in our judiciary' (2007:2). She practises what she preaches, writing extensive opinions. Judicial scholars recently rated her 'number one' among federal appellate court judges for her independence, that is, the number of dissenting and concurring opinions she writes (Choi and Gulati, 2004: 47). Her opinions also have a feel for the human aspects and evolutionary nature of the law.[11]

In these opinions, often dissents, she has spoken openly of the reasoning process and values she holds dear. The cornerstone of any practice of feminist jurisprudence is the necessity of asking the woman question (Martin and Pyle, 2004). That is, going beyond the surface of the law or facts to ask if women (or other minorities) are disadvantaged as a consequence of the application of the law or standard. It is in this respect that Judge Barkett excels. For example, she testified before the Florida Gender Bias Task Force (1988) that the Florida no-fault divorce law, permitting an allegation of adultery to be used to reduce or preclude an alimony award, is not as gender neutral as it appears. She stated:

> 95 or 99 percent of (alimony) receiving spouses are women, and therefore the language in this statute in this day and age, I believe, effectively says that you can punish a wife for adultery by giving her less than she needs, but you cannot correspondingly punish an adulterer husband (Tannen, 1990: 177).

[11] A Quindlen, 'Justice for Justice Barkett' *New York Times* (16 Feburary1994) A18.

Selections from Barkett's opinions (mostly dissents) in five cases are offered below as examples of her feminist jurisprudence. The first three cases are from the US Court of Appeals, Eleventh Circuit, and the last two from Barkett's tenure on the Florida Supreme Court.

Florida state law forbade gay and lesbian couples to adopt children (although they were permitted to act as foster parents). The court majority upheld the law, finding that since most adopted children are heterosexual, heterosexual parents were better able to provide education and guidance to their children during their sexual development. Barkett, in her dissent, ridiculed the majority's opinion:

> There is certainly no evidence that the ability to share one's adolescent dating experiences (or lack thereof) is an important, much less essential, facet of parenting. The difficult transition to adulthood is a common human experience, not an experience unique to human beings of a particular race, gender, or sexual orientation. It is downright silly to argue that parents must have experienced everything that a child will experience in order to guide them.[12]

The constitutionality of an Alabama statute prohibiting commercial distribution of any device primarily used for stimulation of human genitals (apparently believing they were only used by lesbians) was challenged. The District Court granted plaintiffs' motion for permanent injunctive relief, and the state appealed. The Court of Appeals held that there is no fundamental due process right of consenting adults to engage in private sexual conduct. Judge Barkett in her dissent emphatically claimed:

> This case is not, as the majority's demeaning and dismissive analysis suggests, about sex or about sexual devices. It is about the tradition of American citizens from the inception of our democracy to value the constitutionally protected right to be left alone in the privacy of their bedrooms and personal relationships.[13]

Former city lifeguards (female) sued the city and their supervisors (male) for sexual harassment, battery, and negligent retention and supervision. The Federal trial court found hostile environment sexual harassment to have occurred and permitted the victims' claim against the city for compensation. The Appeals Court majority held that the city was not liable for the harassment, which was undisputed. Barkett's dissent pointed out that the city could not isolate itself from liability by placing its lifeguards in a remote location to be supervised by someone who made their work life miserable and had unchecked supervisory authority with no contact with higher city officials, and then claim immunity because it didn't know

[12] *Lofton v Sec'y of the Dept of Children & Family Servs*, 358 F.3d 804 (11th Cir. 2004) 804.
[13] *Williams v Attorney General of Alabama*, 378 F.3d 1232 (11th Cir. 2004) 1232.

what was going on. She argued that under those circumstances, and without dissemination of a sexual harassment policy, the supervisors should be considered to be acting within their scope of employment, making the city liable. In her words:

> [I]t is clear that the City had divested itself of all responsibility for the social climate of the lifeguards' work environment, that (the supervisors) essentially were given unfettered responsibility for and control over that environment, and that the lifeguards had no effective avenue of redress with the City.[14]

The facts in *Wright* were compelling. The father had vanished to Idaho, abandoning the mother pregnant in Florida. The mother and child had neither power nor resources. The mother sued for child support. The father denied paternity. The majority concluded that Florida had no jurisdiction over the father and therefore could not compel payment. Kogan and Barkett dissenting argued:

> The majority's adherence to outdated and limited concepts ignores the general, overriding policy of insuring that support is provided to children. Under modern thought, it is no longer the child that is 'illegitimate', but rather the father who has acted illegitimately. The majority opinion discards this updated and more reasonable line of thought by forcing the child to chase the father to Idaho to litigate paternity. It is far more fair and within reason to allow Florida courts to do so.[15]

In the *Mize* case, a divorced mother, who had primary custody of her daughter, petitioned the court for permission to relocate with her child to California. The trial court found that the mother had well-intentioned reasons for moving and had no vindictive desire to interfere with the father's visitation rights, and therefore could make the move. The decision was reversed on appeal and the mother's subsequent appeal went to the Florida Supreme Court. The Supreme Court overruled the appellate court's decision. Barkett in her concurring opinion enthusiastically endorsed the majority opinion's specific acknowledgement that the best interests of children are served by frequent and continuing contact with both parents. However, echoing Judge Dorothy Nelson, she goes further than the majority, to urge that such issues should be settled through mediation. She comments:

> Sadly, the adversarial system, which too often fosters hostility and bitterness, frequently prevents parents from engaging in the types of discussions that are necessary to reach a mutually acceptable arrangement.[16]

[14] *Faragher v City of Boca Raton*, 111 F.3d 1530 (11th Cir. 1997) 1530.
[15] *Department of Health v Wright* 522 So.2d 838 (Fla. 1988) 838.
[16] *Mize v Mize*, 621 So. 2d 417 (Fla. 1993) 420.

5. CONCLUSION

This discussion of Judges Wald, Nelson and Barkett contributes to existing research on gender and judging by giving an up-close and personal glimpse of why women judges may behave differently from men judges. In no case is it contended that the judges profiled are representative of anyone other than themselves; however, each was selected to illustrate one of three leading explanatory theories of why gender influences judging: gendered life experiences, women's unique perspective and feminist jurisprudence. Judge Wald, most obviously because of her 10 years' sabbatical from her legal career to bear and raise children, has clearly lived through many of the gendered experiences common to women of her generation. Yet, she has overcome these obstacles with a pioneering spirit and an enviable ability to form strong supportive attachments. Judge Nelson has had greater ease in combining family and career than many women, due in part to a supportive husband. However, she illustrates the contention that women have an ethics of care, most clearly with her support of Alternative Dispute Resolution, but also with her approach to leadership and to modifying the workplace to be more family-friendly. Judge Barkett has lived a non-traditional life, migrating to the US at an early age as a non-English speaker. She has a clear and no-nonsense vision of what it means to be powerless, and to have one's state in life overlooked by the law, laying a foundation for her feminist jurisprudence.

6. REFERENCES

Barkett, R (2005) 'The Tyranny of Labels' 38 *Suffolk University Law Review* 749.

—— (2007) 'Judicial Discretion and Judicious Deliberation' 59 *Florida Law Review* 905.

Bartlett, KT (1990) 'Feminist Legal Methods' 103 *Harvard Law Review* 829.

Beiner, TM (2005) 'Female Judging' 36(4) *The University of Toledo Law Review* 821.

Boyd, CL, Epstein, L and Martin, A (2010) 'Untangling the Causal Effects of Sex on Judging' 54 *American Political Science Review* 389.

Chuang, TD (1999) 'Judge Profile: the Honorable Dorothy Nelson' 46 *The Federal Lawyer* 14.

Choi, SJ and Gulati, M (2004) 'Choosing the Next Supreme Court Justice: An Empirical Ranking of Judge Performance' 78 *Southern California Law Review* 23.

Goldstein, L (ed) (1992) *Feminist Jurisprudence: The Difference Debate* (Rowman and Littlefield).

Holbrook, L (1992) 'Justice Barkett's Feminist Jurisprudence' 46 *University of Miami Law Review* 1161.

Kay, HH (2002) 'Women Law School Deans: A Different Breed, or Just One of the Boys?' 14 *Yale Journal of Law and Feminism* 219.

Kennedy, J (2005) 'Judging, Personality and Gender: Not Just a Woman's Issue' 36 *The University of Toledo Law Review* 905.

Kloppenberg, L (2001) 'A Mentor of Her Own' 33 *The University of Toledo Law Review* 99.
Martin, E (1982) 'Women on the Federal Bench: A Comparative Profile' 65 *Judicature* 306.
—— (2002) 'Feminist Judges: Challenging the Status Quo' in S Carroll (ed), *The Impact of Women in Public Policy* (Indiana State University Press).
—— (2004) 'Gender and Presidential Judicial Selection' 26 *Women and Politics* 109.
—— (2009) 'US Women Federal Court Judges Appointed by President Carter: Ongoing Relevance' 17 *Feminist Legal Studies* 43.
Martin, E and Pyle, B (2002) 'Gender and Racial Diversification of State Supreme Courts' 24 Women *and Politics* 35.
—— (2005) 'State High Courts and Divorce: The Impact of Judicial Gender' 36(4) *The University of Toledo Law Review* 923.
Nelson, DW (1980) 'Why Are Things Being Done This Way' 19 *Judges' Journal* 13.
—— (1989) 'Reflections on Becoming a Judge' 2 *Western Legal History* 107.
—— (2004) 'Which Way to True Justice? Appropriate Dispute Resolution (ADR) and Adversarial Legalism' 83 *Nebraska Law Review* 167.
Peresie, JL (2005) 'Female judges matter: Gender and collegial decision-making in the federal appellate courts' 114 *Yale Law Journal* 1759.
Pudlow, J (2000) 'Women in the Florida Bar' 74 *Florida Bar Journal* 56.
Resnik, J (1988) 'On the bias: Feminist reconsiderations of the aspirations for our judges' 61 *Southern California Law Review* 1877.
Schroeder, MM (2002) 'Judging With a Difference' 14 *Yale Journal of Law and Feminism* 255.
Sherry, S (1986) 'Civic Virtue and the Feminine Voice in Constitutional Adjudication' 72 *Virginia Law Review* 543.
Tannen, R (1990) '1990 Symposium: Women and the Law, Goals for the 1990s' 41 *Florida Law Review* 163.
Wald, P (2005) 'Six Not-So-Easy Pieces: One Woman Judge's Journey to the Bench and Beyond' 36 *The University of Toledo Law Review* 979.

1.3

The Entry and Integration of Women into Judicial Positions in Israel

EYAL KATVAN*

Abstract

From a numerical point of view, women are today a majority in the judiciary in Israel. The beginning of the change and feminisation of the legal profession in Israel is usually dated as the 1970s. The question is when did women's entry into these positions begin, what enabled it and what prevented or halted their integration? I wish to show that the seeds for this success story were not sown in the 1970s, but in the time of the British mandate of Palestine, at the end of the First World War. Although at that time women's integration into the formal legal state systems was not possible, women did serve as judges in informal, non-state courts. I propose that this served as the foundation and training for their subsequent own, or their successors', legal activities after the foundation of the State. The process of integration was largely enabled by and due to: (1) the involvement of women's organisations, which recognised the potential of integrating women within legal frameworks—both during the Mandate and shortly after the foundation of the State; and (2) the private action and independent initiative of the first women lawyers, called to the Bar during the Mandate years. I demonstrate the existence of two ladders—private and collective—which women climbed in order to reach the top of the legal pyramid.

* The author wishes to express thanks for the generous access provided to him by the Central Zionist Archives (CZA), Israel State Archives (ISA), Tel Aviv Municipality Archives (TAMA), Haifa Municipality Archives (HMA), and Yad Tabenkin Archives (YTA). All archival material cited herein is originally in Hebrew and has been translated by the author. The author also wish to thank the Hadassah-Brandeis Institute, Brandeis University for supporting this research, and to Bryna Bogoch, Silvia Fogel-Bijawi, Ilan Fuchs, Ruth Halperin-Kaddari, Assaf likhovski, Amichai Radziner, Gisela Shaw, Margalit Shilo, Ulrike Schultz, for their very important remarks.

1. INTRODUCTION

IN THE PAST hundred years, Israel has undergone two periods of governmental transition: the first, on the termination of Ottoman rule and the start of the British Mandate over Palestine in 1917; and the second, on the conclusion of British rule and the establishment of the State of Israel in 1948. Some Israeli historiographers, including legal historians, view this periodisation as obvious; others argue that this dichotomy is not clear, and that the Israeli legal system should be viewed instead as a result of continuous processes that began during the pre-State period.[1] It is my contention that the latter approach is also applicable to the entry and integration of women into judicial positions, and that earlier processes had a direct influence on developments following statehood, leading to the current reality in which women constitute a majority of the Israeli judiciary.[2] In other words, the high percentage of women judges in Israel today is mostly attributable to the fact that women were already appointed to judicial roles prior to the establishment of the State and immediately thereafter. This reality, as I will demonstrate, is the fruit of two separate initiatives: an individual or private initiative and a collective initiative (primarily, that of the Union of Hebrew Women for Equal Rights). As I will show, these initiatives were sometimes combined.

2. FRAMEWORK AND SOURCES

The unique nature of the process whereby women have been admitted and become integrated into judicial positions in Israel, both prior to and

[1] Likhovski, A (1998) 'Between "Mandate" and "State": Re-thinking the Periodization of Israeli Legal History' 19 Journal of Israeli History 39, 44, at: www.tau.ac.il/law/likhovski/the%20journal%20of%20israeli%20history.pdf.

[2] Based on the judges list (Israeli Judiciary website), as for February 2010, there were 668 judges in Israel's general court system: 318 men, 350 women judges (52.4%), for a general population of 7,500,000 people: www.court.gov.il/heb/home.htm [Hebrew].

	Men judges	Women judges
Supreme Court	10	5
District Court	81	59
Magistrates' Court (including Registrars and Traffic Court judges)	181	204
Regional Labour Courts	18	43
National Labour Court	4	3
Juvenile Court	4	9
Family Court	20	27

following the establishment of the State, is illustrated by several interrelated facts:

1. In Ottoman and Mandatory Palestine, women were appointed to positions on informal or quasi-judicial panels even before they were allowed to practise law.[3]
2. Following the establishment of the State of Israel, women were immediately appointed to official judicial positions. Moreover, their admission to the judiciary occurred within only 18 years after they had first been allowed to practise law (while having been denied appointment to official courts during the British Mandate). This sharply contrasts with the situation in other countries, where there was a significant delay between the admission of women to the practice of law and their entry into the judiciary.[4]
3. The current percentage of women in the Israeli judiciary (50.8 per cent as of 2008) is among the highest in the world compared to the generally low percentages in other countries.[5]

Given the singularity of the Israeli case it is hard to draw comparisons with other countries. Even if we limit ourselves to the judiciaries of common law countries such comparisons are problematic, since the percentage of women judges in these nations is still low compared with their number in some civil law countries (Schultz, 2003: xlvi–xlvii). Furthermore, the explanations given for the differences between common law and civil law countries are not relevant to the dynamic of the process that took place in Israel.[6] However, it is my hope that these very differences will provide general insights regarding the methods, patterns and dynamics related to the integration of women into public positions in the legal field. Of course, there are also similarities between the Israeli case

[3] Nevertheless, it should be noted that women serving as lay magistrates were also a familiar phenomenon in England (Public Record Office, London, LCO2/350, Justices of the Peace (Qualification of Women) Bill (1919)) following a similar, largely successful, struggle primarily conducted by women's organisations (Logan, 2007). However, this accomplishment in England was apparently not translated into a successful integration of women into 'real' judicial positions, which was only accomplished after many years of struggle.

[4] The delay, in several European countries, was as follows: the Netherlands—44 years; France—46 years; Italy—44 years (Schultz, 2003: xxxiv).

[5] Comparative figures in the synthesis to this book.

[6] The Israeli Judiciary today is composed hierarchically of three court instances: the Supreme Court, the District Courts and Magistrates' Courts (which includes at this level, also the Family Court, the Juvenile Court and the Traffic Court). There are also special tribunals, such as the Regional Labour Courts and the National Labour Court. There is also the Religious Court system (including, for example, the Rabbinical Courts and the Sharia (Moslem) Courts). This structure stems from the Ottoman period with some changes and adaptations during the British Mandate period and after the foundation of the State of Israel. That is part of the reason why Israel considers itself having a mixed legal system: common and civil law.

and the nomination of women judges around the world as this chapter will show.

Research in Israel has barely addressed the questions raised in this chapter. Bogoch (2003: 250) notes that:

> The history of women in the legal profession in Israel has yet to be charted. In fact, to date there has been no survey of the legal profession, and very little demographic data are available in the official sources.

In recent years, several studies have been devoted to the state of women in the Israeli legal profession, mostly dealing with the current situation of women lawyers and the feminisation of the legal profession, dating this process to the 1970s (Bechar, 1999). As Cook observed:

> The notion that women will fill the legal positions, from the entry level to the most prestigious judgeship, in proportion to their presence in law school and the bar takes account of the eligibility factor only and does not fit the historical experience of women (1984: 574).

In this chapter, I will examine both the historical process and the 'numbers'—until the 1970s within the framework of the Israeli court system.

Other studies relevant to this investigation focus on some of the specific issues that women in the Israeli legal professions face, such as: the 'work–family challenge' (Elias and Shitrai, 1998); wage discrimination (Rachman-Moore, Almor and Kogman, 2006); and discrimination within the framework of the legal process itself, as well as the other, or different, voice that women lawyers bring to the legal system (Bogoch and Don-Yechiya, 1999).[7] Comparative research, dealing with the integration of women into other professions—like specialised medicine—also provides explanations for a rise in the number of women lawyers since the 1970s (Holtzman and Izraeli, 2000). The insights emerging from these studies reveal the importance of the presence of women in a particular profession as a basis for their further admission (Izraeli, 1999: 206) and the significance of activity by women's organisations or feminist movements for the integration of women into the professions (Izraeli, 1999: 214). Another central argument for the gradual acceptance of women in the field of law is that both organised and unorganised activities by women have led to a process of desensitisation to their presence in previously barred professional positions, not dissimilar to the gradual process leading to the acceptance of breastfeeding in public.[8]

The present chapter is based primarily on archival material found in Israel and abroad, various statistical data and interviews of the first

[7] The present chapter does not deal with the issue of a possibly different/other voice of women.

[8] S Colb, 'Public Breastfeeding: When Legal Protection Isn't Enough' at: writ.news.findlaw.com/colb/20040714.html.

42 women lawyers (or their relatives) admitted to practice from 1930[9] up until just before the establishment of the State in 1948 (Katvan, Halperin-Kaddari and Trau-Zitnitski, 2009).[10] These combined sources offer detailed profiles of the first women lawyers, including the first women judges.

3. WOMEN JUDGES PRIOR TO THE ESTABLISHMENT OF THE STATE

During the Ottoman and Mandatory periods, official judicial positions were reserved for men alone. However, during this pre-State period, informal or quasi-judicial institutions existed in which women did participate. This informal arena facilitated interesting and important developments. There were three such judicial frameworks: the Hebrew Courts of Peace, the 'comrades' tribunals of the General Federation of Hebrew Workers in Eretz Israel (Histadrut)[11] and the municipal courts. In what follows, I shall address the struggle of women to be appointed as judges within these three frameworks—primarily the Hebrew Courts of Peace—and also focus on the related struggles over their right to vote and be elected to Yishuv[12] institutions and their right to practise law.

3.1. Hebrew Courts of Peace

The Hebrew Law of Peace was applied by an elaborate system of community justice tribunals scattered throughout the cities and villages of the Yishuv—known as Hebrew Courts of Peace (HCP)—which were designed to provide Jews with the means for resolving disputes without the interference of the colonial power (Shamir, 2000). This alternative, informal judicial system was comprised of public representatives who were not necessarily jurists. It already operated under Ottoman rule and, as far as we know—at least in the Rishon LeZion colony—one woman, Nehamah Pukhachewsky, served as an HCP judge during this period (Berlovitz, 2011). This system

[9] This year marked the admission to the Bar of two women in Mandatory Palestine. The first was Freda Slutzkin. The second was Rosa Ginzberg, who led the struggle over the right of women to practise law (Katvan and Halperin-Kaddari and Trau-Zitnitski, 2009).

[10] For similar methodological studies, see: Soh (1993); Ietswaart (2003: 353).

[11] When the pre-State period is discussed in Hebrew writing—and sometimes in English writing as well—the geographic area then known as Palestine is generally referred to as *Eretz Israel* (literally, the 'Land of Israel'), a term adopted by the Zionist movement. The *Histadrut* was established as a 'trade union' of the Jewish workers.

[12] The Jewish community in Palestine (approximately 84,000 Jews in 1922; 175,000 Jews in 1931) prior to the establishment of the State of Israel, is commonly referred to by the Hebrew term *Yishuv* (literally, 'settlement'). A distinction is generally made between the Old *Yishuv*, referring to the community of mostly religious Jews already living in the Holy Land prior to 1882, and the New *Yishuv*, referring to Jewish immigrants arriving from 1882 onwards. Population in Israel: May 1948—a total of 800,000 people; 1949, a total of 1,174,000.

was revived following the First World War, accompanied by a struggle on the part of women seeking to be appointed as judges on these tribunals. In January 1919, Attorney Daniel Auster, secretary of the legal department of the Delegate Committee (the representative body of the World Zionist Organisation in Mandatory Palestine), who had visited the various regions in order to reorganise the HCP, wrote to Ya'akov Thon, one of the Yishuv leaders, as follows:

> The women's problem was raised and I don't know how to respond. General elections are needed for judges, and the women, of course, demand both the right [to vote and be elected]. I understand that, in principle, we cannot object, but I cannot imagine 'women judges' in reality. I do not understand why something that does not even exist in America and England is appropriate here in Eretz Israel. Indeed, I tried not to raise the question in the cities ... however, in the rural settlements ... I was forced to transfer the appointment of judges to a general assembly. And this was really very difficult for me. The women demanded both a right [to vote and be elected]. I wanted to object but saw that this would not look proper, I had to arrange it in this way, because I gave them all of the rights and tried to ensure that women would not be elected, and that is how it actually turned out. However, this question must be resolved in principle and it is to this that I request an answer, for in a short while the same question will arise in the villages of the Lower Galilee, and women there can be elected. I do not view this as a tragedy, but in my opinion, it is still too early.[13]

This quote presents an interesting picture. On the one hand, Auster understands that, in outward appearance, he cannot present the New Yishuv—with its Zionist principles extolling equality—as being opposed to the right of women to vote for and be elected as judges. On the other hand, he accepts that he is expected to prevent such a development, as evidenced by his apologetic tone. Auster succeeded in temporarily resolving the 'problem' since, in fact, women were not elected. His argument that it was 'still too early' to give women the right to be elected as judges is interesting, and Auster treats this as equivalent to a right to serve on an official judiciary at a time when, as he mistakenly believed,[14] this was still not possible in other Western nations. The response by Thon was brief: 'This problem (the question of "women judges") should not be resolved as long as it has not been resolved in the Supreme HCP in Jaffa' (ie, the highest instance of the HCP).[15] Thus, Auster was given authorisation to continue acting as he had

[13] CZA, L2/193, Auster to Thon, 31 January 1919. [in Hebrew]

[14] Regarding a case in the United States, where a petition by women to be allowed to practise law was dismissed based on the *belief* that they were not permitted to do so in England, without the submission of any evidence on this matter, see Drachman (1998: 20). Incidentally, Auster argued that in the United States there were still no women judges, whereas, in fact, a female judge had already served there in 1870: for further detail, see *Corcos (1998)*.

[15] CZA, L2/193, letter to Auster (apparently, from Dr Thon) 14 February 1919.

been expected to do up to that point.[16] Nevertheless, several days later, Thon reconsidered his position and wrote that 'regarding the question of women, it is our opinion that this question must be left open to be decided in each locality'.[17] And, in fact, that same year women were already elected as judges on the HCP in the villages of the Upper Galilee.[18]

The situation in the cities was different. The Union of Hebrew Women for Equal Rights (UHWER), founded in 1918 in order to achieve equality for women, including the right to vote, led by Rosa Welt-Strauss, protested against women not having been invited to participate in the reorganisation of the Jerusalem HCP.[19] Yitzhak Nofech (the father of one of the first women lawyers) who was in charge of the Jerusalem HCP, explained that his hands were tied in this matter, by force of a decision by the Supreme HCP at the time the branches had been established in the cities.[20] However, the situation was somewhat different in the city of Haifa. The municipal elections committee published a list of candidates for the HCP, but it did not include women, so members of UHWER sent a letter to the elections committee requesting that several women be added to the list.

This time, Auster tried to avoid embarrassment. He acknowledged the right of women to vote for and be elected as judges, while also recognising that, due to possible opposition from the Old Yishuv, granting this right might lead to the collapse of the HCP. Such opposition was reflected in the general struggle over the right of women to vote for and be elected to Yishuv institutions. A compromise was reached that initially appeared acceptable to UHWER, that is, to wait until the general elections.[21] However, several days later, the UHWER committee met to discuss this question, and 'unanimously decided not to concede our just right and demand'.[22]

It is unclear how this particular issue was resolved, but, for our purposes, it is important to understand the relationship between the struggle over the appointment of women to the HCP and the wider battle over their general right to vote for and seek office to Yishuv institutions (Shilo, 2005). These struggles had a similar dynamic and, in both cases, nation-building interests were perceived as outweighing women's rights (Izraeli, 1979: 2). Both concerned political equality—ie, representation and equal citizenship (see also Logan, 2007)—and not professional equality. After all, appointment to the

[16] CZA, L2/193, Auster to Thon, 21 February 1919.
[17] CZA, J1/52, Thon to Auster, 26 February 1919.
[18] CZA, J1/42, list of judges on the HCP at the end of 1919.
[19] CZA, J1/52, Welt-Strauss to the 'Organising Committee for the Jerusalem HCP,' 7 December 1919.
[20] YTA, Division 15 (Sarah Azaryahu), Container 1, File 1, Nofech to UHWER, November 1920. This was probably Thon's decision.
[21] CZA, J1/45, Auster to the Haifa elections committee, 26 February 1920.
[22] HMA, Division 8, Community Committee, UHWER to the Haifa elections committee, 29 February 1920.

HCP did not require any legal training, but involved a political role including participation in the public life of the Yishuv and the 'education' of the community regarding the existence of this alternative dispute resolution system.

It should be noted that the fight by women to practise law in Mandatory Palestine was a public–political struggle, unlike that of women in some other countries, where it assumed the form of a private–economic struggle (Corcos, 1996: 443). This struggle continued up until 1930, when the High Court of Justice ruled that women could practise law. It was led by Rosa Ginzberg and actively supported by UHWER. It was fought against the British and, for this very reason, was considered a national, public and political struggle of the entire Yishuv—including its male members, who based their support on arguments opposite to those that they had used to delay the appointment of women to the HCP. Essentially, all these struggles were conducted concurrently and were perceived as public rather than private struggles. Thus, from the viewpoint of women lawyers, there was an advantage to British opposition. The fact that women were admitted to the profession already during the British Mandate, as part of the revolt against the British, created a good basis for the ostensible equality achieved later on, establishing their status and facilitating their integration into the profession. By contrast, the opposition of male attorneys in other countries was more pronounced and, thus, served as an inhibiting factor. That is to say, notwithstanding the disadvantages of British rule—which prevented women from being appointed to official judicial positions—the political situation in Mandatory Palestine facilitated their admittance to the practice of law. For this very reason, women were considered the equal of men in the legal profession, which subsequently laid the foundations for their appointment to the bench on the establishment of the State.

3.2. Women on the HCP—Formal Recognition

In 1927, the question of women judges on the HCP arose once again. The decision to appoint women was reached by the HCP administrative body, under the orchestration of Mordechai Ben-Hillel Hacohen, Rosa Ginzberg's father.[23] In 1929, 'following considerable efforts (by UHWER), the Tel Aviv HCP invited three women to serve as judges'. Given the election of women judges in the villages of the Galilee in 1919–20, ostensibly, there was nothing new in this. However, based on the precedent set in the Galilee, this was the first time that women judges were also formally appointed in the cities:

> In the debates, the question of the right of women to serve as judges was raised; although this right basically existed beforehand and, in several places, there

[23] 'Hebrew Court of Peace Conference (Report)' (1927) 1 *Ha'Mishpat* 97, 98. [in Hebrew]

> were already women judges, the overwhelming majority of conference members expressed the opinion that the regulations should be interpreted in a manner leaving no doubt that men and women had the same right.[24]

Aware of the significance of this formal recognition, UHWER requested that a declaration be issued concerning the right of women to serve on the HCP and that practical steps be taken to appoint more women judges. This raising of public awareness regarding female representation in Yishuv institutions is one of UHWER's most important contributions, and also characterised its later efforts on behalf of women when there was not just a precedent for appointing women judges to the HCP, but the public was already accustomed to their presence on these tribunals.

The overall number of women judges on the HCP was still relatively limited, and UHWER members were heavily represented. Thus, perhaps for the first (and not the last) time, UHWER members had succeeded in situating themselves in key legal positions. One of these women was Miriam Shtrakman-Varlinski, then a lawyer and, in time, the second woman judge in the State of Israel. Marginal as HCP as a judicial instance is sometimes perceived to have been, and notwithstanding the apparently small part played by women in its activity, their participation eventually carried significance, contributing to the future appointment of women to judicial and quasi-judicial positions following the establishment of the State. In all of the aforesaid struggles, UHWER stood guard over the rights of Yishuv women, thus establishing an important infrastructure for the future, if only by bringing the subject to public awareness and by placing women, even non-jurists, in judicial positions. The importance of this process of desensitisation—accustoming the public to the fact that women 'had arrived and were here to stay'—cannot be understated.

3.3. The Participation of Women on other Quasi-judicial Bodies

Desensitisation was also accomplished thanks to the presence of women 'judges' in two other, alternative, judicial instances. One of these, established in 1923 by the Histadrut (General Federation of Hebrew Workers in Eretz Israel) was the so-called 'comrades law' system, designed to resolve conflicts and disputes among Histadrut members themselves and between members and Histadrut institutions. Many women, primarily workers, served as judges on these Histadrut tribunals, among them women who would eventually become leaders of the Yishuv and the State of Israel.

[24] Ibid.

A second such alternative institution was the municipal courts. Section 2 of the Mandatory Municipal Courts Ordinance authorised the High Commissioner to 'appoint fit persons of education and standing to be magistrates of a town'. This provision was not designed to fill permanent judicial positions, but rather to allow for the appointment of 'public representatives' or 'honorary judges'. As far as we know, women were not appointed as 'town magistrates' in mixed cities (with both Jewish and Arab populations), where the British denied women the right to vote in municipal elections, while in Tel Aviv, which was not a mixed city and where women did have voting rights, this judicial instance became a sort of community tribunal. Given the numerous requests by organisations and individuals for participation in the Tel Aviv Municipal Court, the absence of such requests by women's organisations is puzzling[25] and resulted in a significant delay in the appointment of a woman to this body. In other words, UHWER's failure in this instance illustrates the importance of its activity in achieving the appointment of women to judicial positions in the other instances mentioned. It was only in 1944 that Attorney Rivka Danon was appointed as a town magistrate on the Tel Aviv Municipal Court.[26] Apparently, this was not a political appointment and did not arouse any interest or problem. Rivka Danon was appointed regardless of her gender, simply because she was a lawyer. The struggle over the right of women to practise law had borne fruit.

In conclusion, the participation of women on these unofficial or quasi-judicial bodies helped to establish a cadre of women involved, in one way or another, in the field of law. At the very least, their appointment contributed to the process of desensitisation. Some of these women continued their involvement following the establishment of the State, in formal or informal judicial positions, or in legislative functions (as legal advisors or as Parliament (Knesset) members themselves) (Yishai, 1997: 42). The appointment of women judges was facilitated by their public activity or the fact that, following a public struggle, they had been allowed to practise law. Perhaps it was also due to the shortage of town magistrates and the need for persons (including women) proficient in the law or with practical legal experience. One way or another, it entailed involvement in the public life of the Yishuv and laid the foundations for the process of the desensitisation of the populace to the presence of women in the developing legal life of the state about to be established.

[25] See 'Questions of the Hour' *Davar Hapoelet* (23 January 1936) 210: 'After 50 years of the existence of the New *Yishuv* ... and an investment of the considerable powers of the woman in its establishment—there is not one woman representative among the 15 members of the Tel Aviv Municipality'.

[26] TMA, M 1173, File 2801, Mayor to the Regional Officer, 17 May 1944.

4. WOMEN JUDGES IMMEDIATELY FOLLOWING THE ESTABLISHMENT OF THE STATE

During the Mandatory period, not a single woman served on an official judicial body. On the establishment of the State of Israel in May 1948, UHWER sent a letter to the Minister of Justice requesting to 'meet on urgent matters' signed, among others, by Attorney Shtrakman-Varilinski.[27] This was followed immediately by a second letter stating: 'We know that new judges are about to be appointed in most parts of the country. We demand that several women be appointed as judges'.[28]

The first appointment of a woman to a quasi-judicial position was made shortly thereafter, in July 1948, when Attorney Rivka Danon became a magistrate on the Tel Aviv Municipal Court.[29] However, this was not a professional appointment, but rather a continuation of Danon's activity on this court during the Mandatory period. UHWER once again petitioned the Minister of Justice to appoint a woman to the district court for the specific purpose of adjudicating women's issues—particularly, family matters—which, in UHWER's opinion, required 'considerable expertise, dedication, and special understanding of a woman's heart'.[30] UHWER's executive committee submitted the name of Attorney Hemda Nofech-Moses, 'who, for 12 years now, has acquired considerable experience regarding these issues'. Her name was also included on a list of female candidates for positions on the Tribunal for the Prevention of Profiteering and Speculation, along with that of Tehila Matmon and Hemda Giladi. Regarding the latter, it was noted that she had 25 years of judicial experience on the HCP.[31] That is to say, experience in the practice of law or on judicial bodies during the Mandatory period was cited as a basis for the candidature of women to judicial posts following statehood. Thus, the achievements attained in the struggles conducted by Rosa Ginzberg and UHWER had created a pool of potential candidates in the years to follow.

[27] ISA, Division 74, File 32 (C-5672/4), UHWER to the Minister of Justice, 17 June 1948.

[28] ISA, Division 74, File 32 (C-5672/4), UHWER to the Minister of Justice, 25 June 1948. During the Mandate period, the High Commissioner appointed the judges, after consulting with judges and lawyers. Most of the judges held legal qualifications (Rubinstein, 1980: 24). After the foundation of the State of Israel, most of the Jewish judges continued in their positions or were promoted to higher courts. New judges were appointed by the Minister of Justice, as non-political nominations (ibid: 56). Following this, the Judicial Selection Committee was established, composed of nine members (the President of the Supreme Court, two Justices, the Minister of Justice, an additional Minister, two Members of Parliament, and two representatives of the Israeli Bar). This committee appoints judges in Israel nowadays. The nomination process for the religious courts, such as the Rabbinical Court, is different. There are no women serving as judges (*Dayanim*) in the Rabbinical Courts, although women's organisations argued for that right during the Mandate period and after the establishment of the State of Israel.

[29] *Official Gazette* (28 July 1948).

[30] CZA, J75/38, UHWER Executive Committee to the Minister of Justice, 1 August 1948.

[31] CZA, J75/35, UHWER to Pearlson, 23 August 1948.

One month later, Nofech-Moses was appointed as a member of the Tribunal for the Prevention of Profiteering and Speculation.[32] Up to this point, women were only granted 'innocuous' peripheral appointments, but this provided a basis for continued activity and ultimately led to the appointment of additional women judges.[33]

In 1948, Eugenia Winogradow was appointed to the Haifa Magistrates' Court, becoming the first woman judge in the State of Israel,[34] shortly to be joined by Miriam Shtrakman-Varilinski. The submission of Nofech-Moses's name and Shtrakman-Varilinski's appointment is unsurprising. Both were veteran members of UHWER and had thus situated themselves at the forefront of the public stage. As an organised body, UHWER was able to submit 'recommendations.' However, questions remain. Why were women only appointed to the magistrates' courts? Why only in Haifa? Why didn't they handle matters of personal status (such as alimony)? And why only two such appointments?

4.1. Climbing up from the Bottom of the Ladder: The Magistrates' Court

One possible answer to the question of why women were appointed to the magistrates' courts and not the district courts is related to the limited number of available positions in the district courts. Rubinstein (1980: 56–57) points out that, following the establishment of the State, male judges who had served during the Mandatory period were generally promoted to the district courts and the Supreme Court. This fact may explain, even if only partially, the absence of women in these judicial instances. The first two appointments of women judges, and several subsequent appointments, were solely to the magistrates' courts. In this way, the gap created during the Mandatory period was perpetuated.

4.2. Why only in Haifa?

Lahav (1999: 119) explains that '[t]he departure of Arab and British judges emptied the Haifa court of most of its staff', creating open judicial positions—but this still does not explain why appointments were not made in other places.[35] Perhaps it is because Haifa, more than other cities,

[32] *Official Gazette* (8 September 1948).

[33] ISA, Division 74, File 32 (C-5672/4), UHWER Legal Department to the Minister of Justice, 29 July 1950.

[34] *Official Gazette* (31 December 1948).

[35] See, eg, ISA, C-275/35, correspondences from 1948 regarding the shortage of judges in Jerusalem.

had already become accustomed to the presence of women judges within the framework of its HCP. It is also possible that Eugenia Winogradow's appointment had removed inhibitions and enabled the entry of additional women judges. In other cities, such as Jerusalem, women were first appointed to the magistrates' court in 1975—only then did the floodgates open for the admission of additional women judges.

4.3. Why didn't Women Handle Matters of Personal Status?

The answer to this question is related to the fact that UHWER had requested that Nofech-Moses be appointed to hear personal status cases (in the district court), a request viewed as fundamentally flawed because, although women could offer a unique perspective in such cases, this was no longer a gender-neutral consideration. There was a clash between UHWER's organised activity and the individual efforts of some of the first women lawyers. Whereas UHWER sought to involve women in fields related to the special condition of women, particularly regarding personal status issues, this led to an antagonistic reaction on the part of women themselves. Raday (1996: 533) notes that many women members of the legal profession were vehemently opposed to any form of affirmative action for women. Some of the first women lawyers tried to distance themselves from a 'feminine' label. For example, several days after being appointed as a district court judge, the president of the court suggested that Hana Evenor should deal with family matters, perhaps because male judges had expressed a lack of interest in such cases. Like them, she too refused:

> I was very angry with the proposal and said: 'You think that as a woman I am fit only to be a judge for family matters. You are mistaken. I am ready to hear all kinds of cases, except family disputes'. I won that time and persuaded my colleagues that a woman can be as good a judge as a man.
>
> When I met women colleagues from other countries, I was astonished to learn that most of them were judges in juvenile courts or family courts. We overcame this obstacle in our courts (Evenor, 1998: 94–95).

4.4. Why Only Two Women Judges?

Regarding the limited number of women judges appointed, we should examine the 'supply and demand' for judicial positions during this period. One important statistic indicates that from among the 33 Jewish judges who had served in the judicial system during the British Mandate, 21 continued on the bench following the establishment of the State. In 1950, among the 53 judges serving in the Israeli courts, there was only one woman (1.9 per cent), and in 1951, out of 65 judges no more than three were women

(4.6 per cent)—two in Haifa and one in Tel Aviv. The percentage of women judges was consistent with that of women lawyers (3.6 per cent in 1948 and about six per cent at the beginning of the 1950s). That is to say, statistically, this was ostensibly 'just'. An examination of the numbers for the years immediately following statehood (1948–50) reveals that not all the first women lawyers were active in the profession, and some of them were considered too young for judicial positions. Among those not engaged in legal work, some returned to the profession on the establishment of the State. Approximately 20 women lawyers entered the public sector primarily in legal positions, as prosecutors, or legal advisors in government offices (or public bodies), and some even took on judicial roles within the framework of military service. The remainder practised law in the private sector, and some even refused judicial appointments. This indicates that there were very few women who could have been appointed as additional judges.

5. DEVELOPMENTS SINCE THE ESTABLISHMENT OF THE STATE

Parallel to its vigorous efforts for the appointment of women judges, UHWER was also seeking to achieve the integration of women into various legal and public occupations, primarily related to women's issues. UHWER relied on the considerable experience acquired by its members in the years preceding the establishment of the State. The pressure exerted by UHWER led to various appointments, and even those who were not appointed as judges immediately following statehood found places as district and state attorneys, as well as positions in the Ministry of Justice, making a later transition to the judiciary much easier. In this sense, UHWER activity once again laid a foundation for the continuing professional development of these women. However, this was also characterised by a high degree of personal initiative taken by women lawyers, given the fact that there was a shortage of personnel for these positions.

Within several years of statehood, the situation had stabilised. From among the first women lawyers, 18 (53 per cent) had found places in public practice (including judicial positions), four (12 per cent) had found non-legal positions (including several very senior public positions) and 12 (35 per cent) were in private practice. The occupations of five of the first women lawyers are unknown. Out of the 42 first women lawyers, nine became judges. For most of them, it was a solution for the 'work-family challenge': All but one was married, but none of them to a male lawyer. This sets them apart from the majority of the first women lawyers, who had a high divorce rate and were mostly married to other lawyers. Also, eight out of the nine women judges were not born in Eretz-Israel, but in Russia, Lithuania, Germany and Poland. However, most of them studied law in Eretz-Israel.

The establishment of the State and the need to staff its public institutions facilitated this transition. However, at the same time that this had a 'liberating' effect, it was also, in a sense, restrictive. Although the number of women admitted to the Bar increased, their numbers changed very slowly in the district and state attorneys' offices, the Ministry of Justice and the judiciary. Once quotas had been filled in these institutions, the doors were shut and only those women who had been allowed through were able to climb up the ladder from within. Women lawyers who had found positions as district and state attorneys or in the Ministry of Justice gradually began to advance and sometimes moved on to the judiciary. However, these judicial positions, which have a relatively late 'date of expiration' (the mandatory age of retirement for judges was 70) were then held on to for decades.

Developments were slow, and only in the 1970s was there a significant rise in the number of women holding positions as (senior) district or state attorneys and judges. This may be attributed to the departure of the 'desert generation' from the system, the need for more judges and a rise in the number of women admitted to the Bar. Over the years, the number of women judges has almost doubled each decade.[36] The glass ceiling for women, at least with regard to the judiciary, was not suddenly broken in the 1970s, as is commonly believed. Instead, it has been part of an ongoing process dating from the first days of the British Mandate and gathering steam from the end of the 1950s. It is this gradual process that has facilitated and led to female hegemony in the district and state attorneys' offices, the Ministry of Justice and the courts.

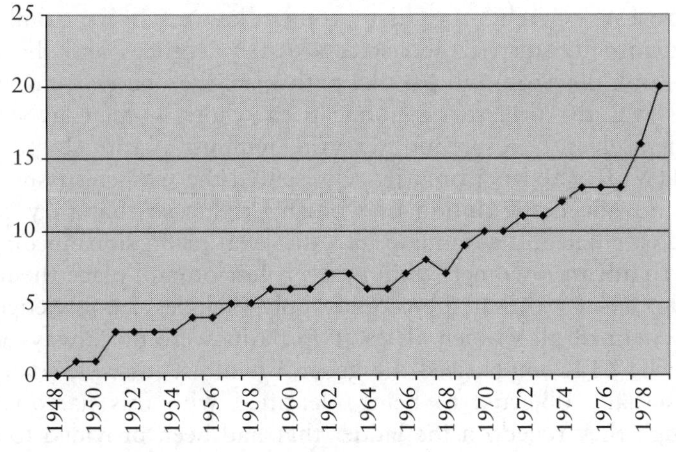

Figure 1: Number of women judges (1948–79)

[36] This 'decade multiple' began to find tangible expression only at the end of the 1970s. Prior to this, although the number of women judges had doubled, their relative proportion compared with male judges was still low. From that point on, the trend continued until numerical equality was achieved between male and female judges.

6. PRIVATE AND COLLECTIVE INITIATIVES

As we have seen, during the Mandatory period, three groups worked for the advancement of women, sometimes in coordination, with identical interests, and sometimes separately, with diverging interests: women who were not jurists, women jurists (lawyers) and UHWER. It is also quite possible that the very existence of a foreign ruler (the British) furthered the process by leading to the support of the rest of the Yishuv in their struggle over the right to practise law.

What then were the operational dynamics and synchronisation among these groups, which eventually facilitated the integration of women, not just in the legal profession, but in the judiciary? It should be remembered that, following the establishment of the State, only lawyers could be appointed to official judicial positions. Therefore, initially, these appointments were made from among the first women lawyers (some were members of the UHWER) who had been excluded from such positions up until then. There is a correlation between active participation in UHWER and appointment to various positions. That is not to say that UHWER operated for the personal advancement of individual members, but the fact that these women were at the forefront of the public struggle for women's rights and equal citizenship did provide them with special opportunities. The feminist issue has provided the groundwork for personal advancement. Apparently, the first women lawyers made use of their legal expertise in this activity, while their own personal benefit dovetailed with the public benefit obtained by the community at large and women in particular.

The process whereby the first women lawyers were admitted and integrated into the district and state attorneys' offices and the judiciary therefore took place on two parallel paths. On the one way, an individual path: this was the private, economic path where women lawyers represented themselves. The second was the feminist, national, public path where UHWER activists primarily represented the women's issue. At first, UHWER advanced the notion of women's rights so that they would be permitted to enter and assimilate into the legal profession. In due course, it sought to advance women within the profession and place them in positions of influence, so that they could apply their legal knowledge for the general benefit of all women. These two paths were not always identical. Whereas UHWER emphasised the general feminist interest, some women lawyers actually objected to being identified with this narrow interest, even though they relied on the ladder that had been provided to them by UHWER. Indeed, sometimes collective and individual struggles coincided when women lawyers were also UHWER activists (very similar to the situation in England, Logan, 2006: 834).

The activity of UHWER was characterised by both an identification of gender issues and the attempt to initiate steps for their resolution (Azaryahu,

1977: 45).[37] UHWER activity was especially significant in the process of desensitisation that helped the community become accustomed to the presence of women in public roles in general and judicial roles in particular. The seeds planted by UHWER during the Mandatory period bore fruit in the first years of the State. It may be assumed that, without this activity, there would have been no basis for the advances achieved later. UHWER did not usually operate with the goal of achieving immediate results, but rather with the intention of patiently initiating a process and waiting for it to bear fruit, even if such fruit would only be enjoyed by the next generation of women, in general, and women lawyers in particular.

The timing of UHWER activity (and that of individual women) was also significant. Both the struggle over suffrage and over the appointment of women judges (1919) represented an attempt by women to 'seize the moment' by taking advantage of the window of opportunity that had opened up following the end of the First World War, allowing them to demand rights based on their partnership during the War.[38] This energetic activity to integrate women in all areas of legal and public activity had far-reaching effects. It continued on the establishment of the State, when women demonstrated that they represented a valuable resource in the nation-building process in general, and in the field of law in particular.

7. CONCLUSIONS

Historical reasons are not the only explanation for the (numerical) equality, or even supremacy, of women in public/legal roles in Israel, but they do illustrate that this is the outcome of a process that began way before the 1970s and 1980s. The appointment of women to the Supreme Court—the highest point of the legal pyramid—is the final stage in this process. The first female Supreme Court justice, Miriam Ben-Porat was appointed in 1976 and Dorit Beinish became president of the Court in 2006. The path was long and full of obstacles, and its outcome was far from obvious (Beinish, 1998). As Fania Oz-Salzberger notes, the very fact that today it is conceivable for women to head all three branches of Israeli democracy—as Speaker of the Knesset, President of the Supreme Court and Prime Minister—'is a tremendous achievement of political correctness in the true and profound meaning of the term' and the outcome of a process that began 'one hundred and twenty years ago'.[39]

[37] See YTA, Division 15, Container 2, File 3, B Mills to UHWER, 28 August 1931.

[38] This was the case all over the world (Schultz, 2003: xxxii).

[39] F Oz-Salzberger, 'The Judge, the Legislator, and the Executive', *Haaretz* (20 September 2008) at: www.haaretz.com/print-edition/opinion/the-judge-the-legislator-and-the-executive-1.254243.

8. REFERENCES

Azaryahu, S (1977) *The Union of Hebrew Women for Equal Rights in Eretz-Israel* (Haifa, Women's Aid Fund) [Hebrew].

Bechar, S (1999) *The Practice of Law in Israel: Feminisation of a Profession* (Discussion Paper No 101, Golda Meir Institute for Social and Labour Research, Tel Aviv University) [Hebrew].

Beinish, D (1998) 'Are Women More Successful in the Public Service than in Private Practice?' in S Shetreet (ed), *Women in Law* (Kluwer Law International).

Berlovitz, Y (2011) 'A Court of One Woman: The Story of Nehamah Pukhachewsky as a Local History of Women (Rishon LeZion, 1893–1933)' in E Katvan, M Shilo and R Halperin-Kaddari (eds), *One Constitution and One Law for Men and Women: Women, Rights and the Law during the Mandate Period* (Bar-Ilan Press) [Hebrew].

Bogoch, B (2003) 'Lawyers in the Courtroom: Gender, Trials and Professional Performance in Israel' in U Schultz and G Shaw (eds), *Women in the World's Legal Professions* (Oxford, Hart Publishing).

Bogoch, B and Don-Yechiya, R (1999) *The Gender of Justice: Bias Against Women in Israeli Courts* (Jerusalem, Jerusalem Institute for Israel Studies) [Hebrew].

Cook, BB (1984) 'Women Judges: A Preface to their History' 14 *Golden Gate University Law Review* 573.

Corcos, C (1996) *'Lawyers for Marianne: An Essay on the Nature of Discourse on the Entry of French Women into the Legal Profession*, 1894–1926' 12 *Georgia State University Law Review* 435.

—— (1998) *'Portia Goes to Parliament: Women and their Admission to the English Legal Profession'* 75 *Denver University Law Review* 307.

Drachman V, (1998) *Sisters in Law: Women Lawyers in Modern American History* (Cambridge, MA, Harvard University Press).

Elias, N, and Shitrai, M (1998) *Women Lawyers are Worth Less: Patterns of Segregation and Inequality in the Legal Profession in Israel* (Discussion Paper No 95, Golda Meir Institute for Social and Labour Research, Tel Aviv University) [Hebrew].

Evenor, H, (1998) 'Women on the Bench' in S Shetreet (ed), *Women in Law* (Kluwer Law International).

Holtzman, O and Izraeli, D (2000) 'The Differential Entry of Women into Specialised Medicine in Israel' 34 *Bikoret U'Parshanut (Criticism and Interpretation)* 65 [Hebrew].

Ietswaart, H (2003) 'Choices in Context: Life Histories of Women Lawyers in the Netherlands,' in U Schultz and G Shaw (eds), *Women in the World's Legal Professions* (Oxford, Hart Publishing).

Izraeli, D (1979) 'The Zionist Women's Movement in Palestine, 1911–1927' (Tel Aviv University, Faculty of Social Sciences, Department of Labor Studies).

—— (1999) 'Gender in the Workplace' in D Izraeli et al (eds), *Sex, Gender and Politics* 167 (Tel Aviv, Hakibbutz Hameuchad Publishing House) [Hebrew].

Katvan, E and Halperin-Kaddari, R (2011) 'When the Woman Becomes a Lawyer': Rosa Ginzberg-Ginossar and the Battle Over Women's Right to Practice Law During the British Mandate in Palestine' in E Katvan, M Shilo and R Halperin-Kaddari (eds),

One Constitution and One Law for Men and Women: Women, Rights and the Law during the Mandate Period (Bar-Ilan Press) [Hebrew].

Katvan, E, Halperin-Kaddari, R and Trau-Zitnitski, T (2009) *The First Women Lawyers in Mandatory Palestine, 1930–1948* (Tel Aviv) [Hebrew].

Lahav, P (1999) *Israel in Law* (Tel Aviv, Am Oved) [Hebrew].

Logan, A (2006) 'Professionalism and the Impact of England's First Women Justices, 1920–1950' 49 *The Historical Journal* 833.

—— (2007) 'In Search of Equal Citizenship: The Campaign for Women Magistrates in England and Wales, 1910–1939' 16 *Women's History Review* 501.

Rachman-Moore D, Almor, T and Kogman, M (2006) 'Equal Investments, Different Rewards: Gender Inequalities Among Israeli Lawyers' 13 *International Journal of the Legal Profession* 189.

Raday, F (1996) 'Women in Law in Israel: A Study of the Relationship between Professional Integration and Feminism' 12 *Georgia State University Law Review* 525.

Rubinstein, E (1980) *Judges of the Land: On the Beginnings and Characteristics of the Supreme Court of Israel* (Jerusalem, Schocken) [Hebrew].

Schultz, U (2003) 'Introduction: Women in the World's Legal Professions: Overview and Synthesis' in U Schultz and G Shaw (eds), *Women in the World's Legal Professions* (Oxford, Hart Publishing).

Shamir, R (2000) *The Colonies of Law: Colonialism, Zionism, and Law in Early Mandate Palestine* (Cambridge, Cambridge University Press).

Shilo, M (2005) 'The Struggle over the Right to be Elected as a Reflection of the View of Women in the *Yishuv* (1918–1926)' 4 *Masechet* 49 [Hebrew].

Soh, CS (1993) 'Fathers and Daughters: Paternal Influence among Korean Women in Politics' 21 *Ethos* 53.

Yishai, Y (1997) *Between the Flag and the Banner: Women in Israeli Politics* (New York, State University of New York Press).

1.4

First Female Judges in the Weimar Republic in Germany: Reflections on Difference

MARION RÖWEKAMP

Abstract

While most of the historical research on women in the legal professions in Germany focuses on their struggle to gain access to the professions, the actual working situation of female jurists after their successful entry has seldom been a topic of research. Nor has much scholarly attention been paid to the differences in gaining access among the various legal professions. Indeed, without mentioning or realising it all studies so far have been based on the history of female attorneys. This chapter is the first to focus on the history of female judges in Germany until 1933. It will explore who were the 'first', which working conditions they found when entering the judiciary and which experiences and impressions they gained. Finally, it will examine whether the first female judges brought about a change in the judicature.

1. INTRODUCTION

COMPARED EVEN WITH medicine or other male-dominated professions, the law was a notoriously difficult field for women to break into in Germany, more so than in most other countries (see generally, Albisetti, 2000: 825, 857; Schultz and Shaw, 2003). It was not only that women were only admitted to practise law in 1922—on average 25 years later than in many other countries; they also had very limited opportunities to establish themselves in legal careers before the Nazi era when they were excluded in principle from exercising their professions. Recent research has dealt with the struggles of European or Anglo-American women to gain access to the legal professions. Most articles or books present the arguments that female jurists in Germany used to overcome the obstacles and the resistance that they encountered from defenders of the status quo. But none of the research has ever distinguished between the different

German legal professions. Although some articles about the history of German female jurists expressly focused on the history of the struggles of female attorneys, for example, Eggert (1998: 133, 157) and Dölemeyer (2003: 151, 164) none so far has to my knowledge concentrated on female judges, at least not on the pioneers. The failure to consider the differences between the various legal professions has led to a misinterpretation in explaining the delay that occurred. This chapter is a first attempt to focus specifically on the first female judges in Germany. Obviously, female attorneys and judges shared common ground and a common struggle, but compared with attorneys, judges-to-be met much stronger resistance. This is due to the fact that in Germany attorneys, although part of the judicature, do not wield the same power as judges who, by definition, pass sentences within a hierarchical order in the power structure of the state. This, in the eyes of many, was not a function that could be performed by women. Thus, in most states women were first admitted to the Bar while the struggle for admission to judicial office continued.

Unlike in the United States in the nineteenth or early twentieth centuries, where aspiring jurists could do a clerkship in a law office or attend night law school and then pass a Bar examination, in Germany all jurists had to be university graduates, and then pass two separate state examinations. Only full-time matriculated students, after completing the required coursework, could sit the first state examination that qualified them for the second examination. The latter, which qualified jurists for admission to the judiciary, normally took place after three years of legal training in a law office, a courtroom or public administration as *Referendare* (law clerks). After passing the second state examination, aspiring jurists were appointed as *Assessoren* (unpaid probationary jurists) and could choose to become attorneys in private practice, apply for a permanent judicial appointment or join the civil service. Since all jurists had to go through exactly the same training, the system featured the so-called *Einheitsjurist*, a jurist who could work, at least theoretically, in any of the legal professions. Thus, access of women to the legal professions proved more challenging in Germany than in other countries where the training for attorneys and judges differed and women primarily applied for the Bar. To prevent women in Germany from taking part in the examinations that would lead to all the executive and legal power positions in the administration and the judicature, the individual state ministries of justice simply excluded women from legal examinations leaving only the option of the doctor in law. As a result, it took another 20 years from the first admission of women to both legal state examinations in the state of Baden in 1900[1] until, in 1922 a national law

[1] In other German states it still took several years longer.

was passed admitting women to all legal careers.[2] The turbulent process preceding this step having been studied by various scholars (for example, Böhm, 1986: 374; Cordes, 2006: 279, 301; Deutscher Juristinnenbund, 2003; Flügge, 1984: 153; Häntzschel, 1997: 194, 213; Röwekamp, 2011),[3] this chapter focuses on the subsequent period.

German women's late access to the legal professions, however, brought about an amazing result: by the late 1920s Germany had become one of the very few countries in the world where women were working as judges. Apart from Germany which had 26 women judges in 1933 and over 100 in training, for example, only the following countries had had women judges: Russia since 1917 (Russia: Anonymous, 1917: 154); the United States had women judges of the peace since 1869 and professionally educated judges since the 1920s (nine judges in 1931: United States: Anonymous, 1921: 27; 1925: 114; Oregon: Anonymous, 1926: 178; New York: Anonymous, 1931: 208; California: Anonymous, 1931: 224; Massachusetts: Anonymous, 1931: 5–6); Canada since 1923 (Canada: Anonymous, 1923: 170); Czechoslovakia since 1930 (Czechoslovakia: Anonymous, 1930: 104); Turkey had nine women judges in 1932 (Turkey: Anonymous, 1932: 39); Denmark since 1933 (just one in 1933, Denmark: Anonymous, 1933: 262–63); and Poland had 11 before 1939 (Poland: Anonymous, 1947: 85).

2. BIOGRAPHICAL DATA ON THE FIRST GERMAN FEMALE JUDGES

As the first female judges are still little known, this chapter provides brief career sketches of the first 10 of them (in chronological order of award of a lifetime judicial position).

Maria Hagemeyer passed her second state examination in October 1924 in Prussia and was appointed an Assessor the same month. First she was employed by the Prussian Ministry of Justice where she worked in the field of criminal law. In May 1927, Hagemeyer was appointed *Amts- und Landrichterin* judge (local and regional judge) in Bonn. In June 1928, she was promoted to a lifetime position and received the first established post as a female judge in Bonn (Röwekamp, 2005: 123).

Dr Gertrud Cichorius was placed in a full post in January 1929, first at the regional court of Chemnitz, and from 1934 at the *Landgericht* (district court) in Dresden. Cichorius was born in September 1897 in Kratzen, the daughter of an owner of a spinning company. Before that, she had passed her second state examination in law in December 1924 in Dresden and

[2] Gesetz über die Zulassung von Frauen zu den Ämtern und Berufen der Rechtspflege von 1922, RGBl. 1922, part 1 No 51, 573f.

[3] Cp for a short summary of the history of women lawyers in Germany, Schultz (1990).

in 1925 worked as a lecturer at the school of social work for women in Dresden and as deputy for an attorney.[4]

Dr Gertrud May in Leipzig passed her second state examination in 1924 in Dresden and then worked for a number of attorneys in Berlin. In January 1925, she was nominated a *Hilfsrichterin* (judge signed up for a fixed period of time) in Wurzen/Saale, later at the regional court in Leipzig. In September 1929, May was appointed a judge for life.[5]

Elisabeth Krumme, who after the Second World War was appointed as one of the first female judges at the Federal Court of Justice, had passed her first state examination in Cologne in June 1924 and the second in Berlin in 1926. After working for the Prussian Ministry of Justice for some months, she was awarded a lifetime position as a judge in Essen in October 1929 (Röwekamp, 2005: 214).

Marie Hurtzig was appointed in April 1930 to the district court in Chemnitz. Born in March 1896 in Stockum close to Bochum as the daughter of a general manager, she passed her two legal examinations in June 1921 in Leipzig and in 1926 in Dresden.[6]

Dr Marie Munk is often wrongly cited as the first female judge, occasionally even as having started work as a judge as early as 1924. In fact, Munk passed her second state examination in January 1924 and was then employed by the Reich Ministry of Justice. When, in consequence of the World Economic Crisis in the wake of inflation and the depreciation of the German mark, her position was abolished after a few months, she was admitted to the Bar as the first female attorney in Berlin. Only in 1929 did she apply for her actual 'dream' position as a judge and was appointed to a lifetime position in August 1930 (Röwekamp, 2005: 275). In 1933, she was dismissed because she was Jewish according to the new national socialist laws.

Dr Hedwig Brann-Frank passed her second state examination in 1926 and was assigned a commission, meaning a temporary position as a judge. Shortly after, she was already working in a presiding function for civil matters at a local court in Frankfurt/Main. In February 1930, she was appointed *Hilfsrichterin* (judge in a fixed term position) and in October 1930 was awarded a lifetime position as a judge (Röwekamp, 2005: 57).

Dr Maria Friedmann was appointed a lifetime judge in December 1931 at the local court of Mannheim in the state of Baden and thus became the eighth female judge in the German Reich. In 1934, Friedmann was promoted to judge at the regional court (Scherner, 1997: 300).

[4] 'Gertrud Cichorius', Bundesarchiv Berlin R 3001 053503.
[5] 'Gertrud May', Staatsarchiv Leipzig, LG 8008.
[6] 'Marie Hurtzig', Bundesarchiv Berlin R 3001 061499.

In 1932 Dr Erna Scheffler (née Friedenthal) received her lifetime judicial post at the local court of Berlin-Mitte. She had passed her exams in 1921 and 1925. She was married and had a child. She was first admitted to the Bar in Berlin. Three years later she was taken on as a regular judge in a fixed-term position and in 1932 was appointed a lifetime judge. After the Second World War she became the first female judge at the Federal Constitutional Court, the highest judicial position in the Federal Republic of Germany (Langer, 2003: 521).

The state of Saxony in 1932 appointed Marianne Krauspe as a lifetime judge in Dresden. She had passed her exams in 1925 and 1929 and was held in such high esteem by the Bar of Dresden that she was the only female judge in Germany who remained in her former position in the 'Third Reich' while all others were moved to less high-profile positions on the orders of Adolf Hitler himself.[7]

Besides these first 10 female judges, Prussia and Saxony appointed one other lifetime judge each. Thus, by 1932 a total of six women in Prussia and five in the progressive state of Saxony held this position. Otherwise Baden and Württemberg had one lifetime female judge, while many other states such as, Thuringia and Hamburg had not yet made any such appointments, and others, such as Bavaria and Oldenburg, refused to appoint female judges altogether. In 1933, Germany had an estimated 13 lifetime judges, 13 assigned fixed-term positions and over 100 in judicial training (Röwekamp, 2011: 451f.). The difference between judges appointed for life and those assigned to fixed-term positions became all too apparent for non-Jewish female judges in 1934. Despite continued prejudices against female jurists and Hitler's antipathy towards female jurists in general, the few with a lifetime position were not fired from their positions but shifted into less publicly visible positions. By contrast to female civil servants in the administration some of whom were forced into early retirement on the basis of a law 'on the restoration of a professional civil service' (*Gesetz zur Wiederherstellung des Berufsbeamtentums*) of April 1933, which could also be directed against women, the legal status of female lifetime judges was respected. It is unclear why this was the case. This was obviously not true of female judges of Jewish descent. Article 136 of the Weimar Constitution had advocated an equal personnel policy in the administration of justice, and a number of members of the judiciary, both lifetime and not yet lifetime appointments, were from this group (contrary to a claim by Freidenreich, 2002: 81). This changed with the *Gesetz zur Wiederherstellung des deutschen Berufsbeamtentums* (Act on the Restoration of the German Career Civil Service) when female jurists of Jewish descent lost their positions. The majority of them left their country and of those who did not, most lost their lives.

[7] 'Marianne Krauspe', Bundesarchiv Berlin R 3001 064600.

3. FIRST IMPRESSIONS AND EXPERIENCES OF FEMALE JUDGES

The opposition towards women in the legal professions, especially towards women in the judiciary, carried on after 1922. The same concerns and arguments that first were used to prevent women from entering the legal profession now served to steer them into certain areas of the law for which, allegedly, they were better suited. Divorce, guardianship, juvenile law as well as the non-contentious jurisdiction were considered to be preferable to criminal and other areas of civil law as well as public and administrative law, all of which were considered male territory (Böge, 1992; 1995: 139; Costas, 1995: 121; Wetterer, 1995: 11). But although this conception existed and had been widely debated, in practice most female judges were assigned posts in any of the legal fields in accordance with the German Judicature Act.

The newly hard-won judicial positions were not easy to fill. Female judges started their careers as judges with more self-doubt as to their abilities than their male colleagues. Elisabeth Schwarzhaupt, one of the *Hilfsrichterinnen* and after the Second World War, the first female minister in Germany, reported:[8]

> But after the second state examination I was suddenly shaken by uncertainty regarding the practical duties and responsibilities of a judge. I may say that I was right in feeling that I lacked the ability to deal with the life and people of social classes different from the one I grew up in (Deutscher Bundestag 1983: 244).

Viktoria Eschke, another *Hilfsrichterin* assigned to the *Kammergericht*, the Prussian appellate court located in Berlin, said in a newspaper interview:

> I concede: I was not only proud but also a bit afraid when I was assigned to the Kammergericht after only eight months working in a civil court. But I was encouraged by the fact that already six female colleagues were working in Berlin (Sims, 1929).

However, it was the competence and ability of female judges that slowly dissolved the suspicion and opposition of male judges towards them. One female judge wrote:

> [E]xperience has proved that a woman who is skilled in logical thinking by university and legal clerkship, never fails to apply the required objectivity, and that impartiality and the elimination of all unobjective moments is as much a matter of course to her as it is to her male colleagues (Koll, 1928: 100).

There is evidence to suggest that female judges worked harder than their male colleagues in order to prove their qualification for their new positions

[8] Originals of the citations are in German and translated by the author.

(Fabricius-Brand, Berghahn and Sudhöffer, 1982: 135). Elisabeth Krumme, for example, reported that she was first assigned a position in cadastral law because nobody was confident that she as a woman would be able to tackle another field of law. Afterwards she was placed into a department dealing with the law of guardianship where 400 files of her predecessor were already collecting dust. Only after she had worked through these files in the shortest time possible was she taken seriously (Kümmel, 1984: 357).

Marie Munk was famous for having heard over 2000 divorce cases between 1929 and 1933 (Mecklenburg, 1996: 297). She reported that she had long and exhausting working days that tended to result in overload.[9] Hedwig Brann-Frank, who from her early days as a *Referendarin* proved herself to be a specialist in legal questions well beyond the average, broke the resistance of her male colleagues with her legal competence. Many of them soon requested her as assessor to their benches for difficult and complicated cases. Earlier in her career than was normal, she was asked to teach younger colleagues and *Referendare*, or to give lectures to legal organisations.[10] One of the very few female *Referendarinnen* to be already tutored by a female judge assessed her tutor Marie Klahr years later:

> I would like to say that Ms Klahr was a very capable judge. Friendly, courteous, and clear in expression, thinking logically, firmly presiding in court, and combining sound knowledge of the law with human empathy. Only very few of her sentences ever went into appeal (Ameln, 1985: 60).

Most female judges described their relationship with male colleagues as good. Viktoria Eschke said, 'Just splendid! There is really no prejudice anymore, the greatest comradeship is to be found in a "mixed" court' (Sims, 1929). Maria Hagemeyer, who mostly dealt with divorce cases, felt that the teamwork between male and female judges worked especially well in this legal field, 'because here first and foremost the ability to understand psychological actions was asked for' (Hagemeyer, 1932: 53). By contrast, Marie Munk described poor teamwork with her male colleagues, which she traced back to political rather than gender differences.[11] Many of the early female judges felt patronised by their colleagues, and anecdotal evidence frequently suggests a different treatment of male and female colleagues. The *Gerichtsassessorin* Koplowitz therefore demanded at the annual conference of Prussian judges in Stettin in 1928 that men should finally stop treating their female colleagues differently and making them feel the exception, as this in particular had a negative impact on their objectiveness (Anonymous, 1928).

[9] 'Marie Munk, Pioneer Women Judge', Sophia Smith Collection, Northampton, MMP, Box 10, V, 6.

[10] Bundesarchiv Berlin R 3001 052554.

[11] Above (n 9) Box 10, V, 7.

The fear expressed before 1922 that female judges would not be able to maintain authority proved to be unfounded. Although the gender of the judge was noticed and comical situations occurred, female judges seem to have managed well (Sims 1929). One *Referendarin* recounted that she and her female tutor were two women behind the Bar, both of them very aware that they had to meet criticism and stares not only by their male colleagues but also the justice-seeking public (Ameln, 1985: 60). Female judges were helped by the fact that those coming to seek a legal solution in court found themselves facing—though 'merely' a woman—an authority derived directly from the state (Koll, 1928: 101; Mahn, 1932: 326). The robe German judges had to wear in court proved to be of help in gaining respect. Summer dresses seemed unseemly, reported one *Assessorin*, and with the robe she did not run the danger of being taken as a mere stenographer or a witness.[12] Another female judge noted that the 'intellectual training in penetrating the legal case and its important moments automatically gave the female judge the necessary security to perform well in hearing her cases and asserting the required intellectual superiority' (Koll, 1928: 102). One assistant judge described the need to impose her authority when hearing a complicated case. Once she managed so well that a witness who had been sanctioned by her called out, 'But we are not at the Prussian military here!' (Proskauer, 1989: 37). Another assistant judge recounted a case when a defendant rebelled against a female judge because he did not want to be sentenced by a woman. She also remembered that an attorney refused to plead his case because he felt it below his dignity to plead in front of a woman (Koll, 1928: 102). An attorney confided in a *Referendarin* that he 'felt an unpleasant chill in his spine when he was put under oath by a woman' (Ameln, 1985: 60).

As the women's movement and female jurists had from the beginning argued in their efforts to gain access to the legal professions, women in particular who were seeking justice seemed glad to be heard by a female judge instead of a male one. Marie Munk said that in many cases when she was an assessor in divorce cases, women were relieved to be able to express themselves freely in front of a woman and to be judged by one. In Germany, divorce cases were heard by a chamber of three judges. In most cases Munk was the reporting judge, meaning the judge who would suggest the solution and hear the witnesses ahead of the two other judges. If two of the three judges agreed on the suggested sentence, it was passed. According to Munk, she often differed in her legal opinion from the other two judges (Munk, 1938: 43).[13] The same was reported by Hildegard Koll who was assigned a position in the field of guardianship and juvenile law. She often was told by social workers and the public that it was considerably easier to

[12] 'Munk', Autobiography, Landesarchiv Berlin, Rep 235-12 (NMM) Fiche 3508, X, 3; Koll 1928, 102.

[13] For the same question in Canada today see M-C Bellau and R Johnson (2008: 57–71).

deal with a female than with a male judge (Koll, 1928: 103). Media reports about the first appearance of female judges at court also give an idea of how important it was to justice-seeking persons that female judges seemed more approachable. Often the media expressed that the hearing of cases by male judges in comparison was thought to be insufficient (see, for example, Hachenburg, 1928: 227). This was true especially for cases in divorce and child law. These reports provide an outsider view of the impact of a female judge, whether they reported in favour of the female judge or not, and can paint another picture of the kind of impression female judges might have made on the public. The following is one example:

> A mother having been divorced and pronounced partially guilty lost custody of her two sons who according to the effective *Reich* laws go with the father, while she keeps custody of the daughter. For many months she goes without news about whether her sons, who are always abroad, might be seriously sick [...] She frequently approaches the guardianship court and pleads for news about the well-being of her children, as well as for alimony for her daughter. Regarding the former, her questions meet with no response at all, and the latter issue is brushed off. The guardianship judge asks the woman in a conversation why she has 'left' her husband, since he had gained a 'very nice impression' of him. It appears to me that this last case, which is only one out of hundreds of similar cases, speaks volumes. The judge gained 'a very nice impression' of the divorced man. That is to him the crucial factor. The feelings and composure of the woman he doesn't understand, which is the reason why he lacks any drive to do something better for her. 'We need more female jurists!' (Harten-Hoencke, 1931: wp).[14]

Another newspaper tells the story of the labour judge Dr Edith Klausner (Röwekamp, 2005: 413):

> 'Madam', 'Madam Councillor', 'Madam Doctor', 'Madam Chairwoman', 'Your Honour'. These or similar phrases are those used by parties or witnesses referring to the first female judge for labour law at the labour court in Berlin, Gerichtsassessor Dr Edith Klausner. She listens with a fine smile but with little attention to the amazed faces of women or the sceptical ones of men. Objectively, calmly and fully in control she hears her case in the way her male colleagues do (Kaja, 1929: 1)

The article goes on to compare judge Klausner to the women that accompanied Goethe, who emphasised their seriousness by austerely combed back hair and kindly looks accompanied by tightly closed lips:

> Undeniably, she exudes the charm of a woman as, her eyes gleaming intelligently, she bends down from the bench and says to an especially adamant employer's

[14] Legal background for this case is that women who were held to be guilty or partly guilty of the marriage breakdown were not entitled to alimony and lost usually the child custody for boys while the had problems getting them for the girls.

> representative, 'How would it be, if you were extending your boss's suggestion of an agreement by adding a 0 to the 50 marks he is willing to pay, making it 500?' Everybody laughs and the employer's representative just doesn't manage to say 'no', after all the case is about a settlement for a worker with 28 years of service in the employer's company. Immediately, contact and trust between the female judge and the audience are established (Kaja, 1929: 1).

In a later hearing the same day several workers from a leather factory were fighting for holiday entitlement. The article reports:

> The factory owner is represented by a shrewd and legally experienced employee. It is interesting to observe how this gentleman is attempting to mislead the woman whom he is only reluctantly acknowledging as the chairwoman with the superior dignity of his virility. 'It seems that you are unaware of current wage agreements and circumstances in the sector', he says tauntingly at one point. The judge pointedly ignores this ill-mannered remark and proves in her short and objective resume that she knows her business very well and is well informed. The sentence she finds after brief consultation is: the holiday entitlements of the workers are legitimate. It is a fair sentence, resulting not only from know-how but also from a strongly pronounced, healthy and natural sense of justice. You cannot praise Madam Gerichtsassessor Klausner more highly for her way of hearing her cases than by repeating the words of a worker's wife who accompanied her husband to court, 'Madam Chairwoman is wonderful!' (Kaja, 1929: 1).

A less positive approach to the female judge is found in a third contemporary newspaper article:

> The attorney who, on behalf of his client, is concerned [...] regarding the female judge's mode of judging sees the woman in the robe of a judge naturally with his own eyes. This one—he must have been especially unlucky—is finding 'too little objectivity' but 'lots of heart' in the judging woman. Another thinks that a woman in the seat of a judge remains first and foremost a female: 'Think about this scenario: petition for alimony. On the bench a female judge, in front of her a girl, a typical brat from Berlin as a young mother, and an apparently affluent, serious businessman who is supposed to have fathered the child. The girl who would never refer to a male judge differently than Mr Judge' or 'Mr Chairman', addresses the female judge off-handedly as 'Miss' or 'Ain't that true, Miss?' In the austere official building the woman sees first the female, feels close to her. 'Ain't that true, Miss?' And the addressee, although aware of wearing her robe of office, still feels the woman in herself. Feels it—and blushes ... The debate becomes very lively. The girl absolutely insists, but the man denies, equally determined. He never has been in a closer relationship with the girl. But she starts to blow the whistle on him and recounts specific details. He still denies flatly and she gets angry, 'What's he saying? No closer relationship? Well, that's something that you after all would feel, ain't that true, Miss?' The woman calls on the judging woman as a witness for genuine feminine feeling, and once again her awareness of being a judge and her judicial augustness are receding within the female judge

in favour of empathy with the woman in front of her. The female judge becomes embarrassed, blushes fiercely and closes the hearing (Anonymous, 1932).

It seems like all statements by men addressed to female participants were directed towards establishing male power and hierarchical status, and statements by women addressed to other women were less respectful than those addressed to men.

4. HAVE FEMALE JUDGES CHANGED JURISPRUDENCE?

Under the chairwomanship of Jutta Limbach, first female President of Germany's Federal Constitutional Court, and following an opening lecture by Renate Jaeger, a judge at the same court, the annual congress of the German Judges' Association in 1995 debated the question 'Do women change jurisprudence?' Has a feminine element of empathy and indulgence entered jurisprudence with the admission of women to judicial office after the Second World War? Renate Jaeger strongly criticised the phrasing of the question fearing that behind this approach there might lurk the same expectation that had obstructed the access of women to the legal professions at the beginning of the century. She was afraid that 'the old gender role models might enjoy a merry resurrection'. Jaeger also emphasised the professional equality of female and male jurists (Schultz, 2004: 119).

By contrast, contemporaries at the turn of century regarded it as a fact that female judges would bring something new to the judicature. When debating whether women would be allowed to participate in state examinations, the President of the Berlin *Kammergericht*, the highest court of Berlin, reported in an internal record to the Prussian Ministry of Justice on other countries' experiences with women in the legal professions. While having a lot to report relating to female attorneys, he could only refer to one report, ie, that by Judge Klingmann from Wyoming, regarding experiences with female judges. In Wyoming, Klingmann concluded, women had proved to be more alert to procedures and more accurate in their search for the right sentence. They also tended to verify evidence better and were less likely to be open to external influence, while men were always influenced by their business connections. Furthermore, women showed greater conscientiousness than men in the fulfilment of their professional duties.[15]

Female judges themselves assumed that their entry into the profession would influence jurisprudence: 'I make a point of not disregarding the

[15] Geheimes Staatsarchiv, I. HA Rep 84 a Nr. 581, Fiche 12990, 12.

human side of the trial alongside the legal assessment, and I try to avoid at any cost the arrogant tone common to officials' said Judge Viktoria Eschke. 'Maybe some things have changed in this regard, especially because "we girls" have entered the judiciary' (Sims, 1929). While her first remark related to the actual sentencing, the latter is more directed at improving the emotional climate in the courtroom, strengthening communication and cooperation with the other participants in the proceedings. Eschke assumed that all female judges, with their understanding of the concept of the 'organised motherhood' created by the bourgeois women's movement,[16] would agree with the last remark about the positive influence of women on the working climate in the judiciary. After all, female jurists had also been demanding access to the legal professions with the argument that justice had proved to be inhumane and their participation could bring about an improvement.

Let us follow up Eschke's first argument regarding the impact of women on sentencing. She was not the only one who expressed the assumption that the participation of women in this process would bring about change. When describing their way of sentencing, female judges usually argued that first and foremost they used a juridical, objective and logical approach, but they also applied a stronger sense of intuition. One female judge noted:

> If she [the female judge] does perhaps not switch off her emotional considerations as completely as the majority of male judges do and occasionally also comprehends the case more intuitively, her feelings and intuition are nevertheless governed and controlled by exact thinking, and both factors are a precious help in the search for a just and equitable decision (Koll, 1928: 100).

Another *Assessorin* thought that the female influence would find its clearest expression where built-in judicial discretion offered an opportunity for another interpretation of the law. While by German law every case had to be interpreted within very strict rules, the judge had discretion in the context of general rules, for example, § 242 (the general rule of bona fide), § 1568 (hardship clause in divorce proceedings) or § 138 (against public policy) of the German Civil Code. The Criminal Code, too, with its broad

[16] The term 'organised motherhood' or 'extended motherhood' was coined in 1870 by Henriette Schrader-Breymann and expressed the view that motherhood in no way presupposed physical maternity. The umbrella organisation of bourgeois women's organisations, the 'Federation of German Women's Associations' (BDF) took it up later and made it refer to demands for employment and participation by childless women, arguing that ('spiritual') maternity was in principle a quality of all women, and expressed not only having a family. For some of the leading feminists spiritual motherhood in fact counted more than physical motherhood (Stoehr, 1983: 221–249).

range of punishment, would give the judge no more than a first indication for determining the penalty:

> What the judge deems to be 'equitable', 'appropriate', 'reasonable', 'public policy' or whatever these abstract expressions might be, will mostly depend on his personal world view, his Weltanschauung, his character, in short his purely human mental attitude to the matter. Up to the present, all decisions of this kind have been influenced by the male nature. Nobody ever doubted that a sentence flowing from this nature was an objective one. If now—through the admission of women to the legal professions—new views can enter legal decision-making and cases may be judged and decided from angles different than hitherto, then this, according to the previous criteria, is equally legal. The special character of a woman is not altering the law as such, it is merely having a possible impact within the range of the legally granted freedom of discretion, in the same way as differences among individual male judges' characters may result in different judgments about the same case (Koll, 1928: 100).

Female judges saw their best chances to unfold their special 'feminine and motherly character' in those legal fields that were thought to be suitable for women:

> 'Furthermore practice had shown', wrote Marie Hagemeyer, 'that women are especially successful in the fields that require a pedagogical impact, such as guardianship and juvenile law, while the office of a criminal judge for adults or of a prosecutor is less likely to be attractive for women' (Hagemeyer, 1932: 53).

Hagemeyer confirmed that areas which male prejudices tended to assign to female judges were also fields they naturally gravitated towards. They thought that it was precisely in these areas that their work as judges could add a human element to jurisprudence, which in turn could result in raising the low prestige German law courts enjoyed in the Weimar years (Koll, 1928: 103). As for the other 'drier' areas of the law, such as land survey, registry, sales by court order, bankruptcy and estate law, female judges knew that they were as able as their male colleagues to handle the cases, but they could not find the same satisfaction in exercising them (Koll, 1928: 104). Marie Munk mentioned another aspect in which she thought she differed from her male colleagues in her judicial work. She liked to mediate her cases because she often found it difficult to decide which party should prevail, even if she took her time to think through the case.[17] Thus, she was

[17] 'Munk', Autobiography, Landesarchiv Berlin, Rep 235-12 (NMM) Fiche 3508, XII, 11.

happy to work in the civil law department in order to avoid inner conflicts. She recounted:

> After passing judgment in these cases [criminal law or juvenile law] I would have been worried and haunted by the question: Was the defendant really guilty? Even if he was, was my sentence perhaps too severe? Should I have allowed probation? What would happen to the defendant and his family while he served his sentence and how would he get on afterwards? The responsibility of being a judge did not weigh as heavily on me in the civil court.[18]

After the Second World War, Gerda Krüger-Nieland and Erika Scheffen, both among the first female judges at the Federal Court of Justice, also described their judicial activity as differing from that of men in as far as they made greater use of the option of developing the law while men were inclined to abide by its exact wording.[19]

Although it seems that the male jurists, the Ministries of Justice as well as female judges had particular views about which legal fields might best be assigned to women, women, in conformity with the provisions of the German Judicature Act, were in fact placed in almost all legal areas. But when Hildegard Kuess, a judge in the criminal division of the court in Berlin-Moabit, held a first hearing in 1928, the media had a field day, with at least nine newspapers publishing a report.[20] Overall, it does look as if despite their pioneering role in the German judiciary, female judges worked in more legal fields in the Weimar Republic than in the first two decades after the Second World War, when they were restricted mainly to certain areas, such as restitution and tenancy law.

5. CONCLUSION

Female judges in Germany appear to have made an impact, albeit an impact that is not really measurable. They understood their work to be more comprehensive in approach than that of most of their male colleagues. While strictly adhering to the norms, standards and traditions of their profession and wanting to assimilate to the profession, they also wanted to reveal the 'human' side of the law and thus stressed the view propagated by the bourgeois women's movement that women should work in the spirit of a caring or welfare morale. Carol Gilligan years later called that approach 'logic of care' (Gilligan, 1984). In medicine, this approach would have been called 'holistic', located somewhere between that of a 'vocation' and

[18] Ibid, XII, 5a.
[19] Erika Scheffen, Oral History Interview, 2001–02.
[20] Bundesarchiv Berlin R 3001 065108.

a 'profession'. Female judges believed that their femininity would improve the workings of the law, they saw it as complementary, as an 'alternative' to the male way of understanding their profession. The law was the tool to guarantee justice and that is how they interpreted it; but they considered that the way the law was applied was too cold, with the feminine element missing. Legal fields like welfare, juvenile or family law shared one thing: they represented the legal expression of the 'supportiveness' of women. Thus, women judges saw themselves predestined to work especially in these fields, which coincided with the view held by male jurists and officials at ministries of justice. Ironically, they indirectly and unwittingly supported the resistance to female judges working in legal areas that men considered to be more important and influential.

Positions in these fields, as well as those in higher ranks, continued to be assigned exclusively to men, with female judges remaining on the sidelines. Had they had more years to further their cause, women might have overcome this problem. The division of work along gender lines logically followed from traditional gender roles and served to exclude women not only from social functions generally speaking, but specifically from positions in the judiciary. However, women judges did not feel marginalised. They saw their judicial role in guardianship, divorce or juvenile law as ideally suited to their talents to serve society. They also realised that they were helping to restructure gender differences in society at large and in the legal professions specifically. Of course they were fully aware that gender differences had been used, and were still being used, to legitimise their exclusion. But they did not mind. Rather, they demanded emancipation based on acceptance of the equality of a female working ethos and style in the continuance of the traditional gender role. They saw the danger in their argumentation that the definition of some legal fields as more feminine than others would lead into a professional blind alley and that overstepping these boundaries would require legitimisation. But the inter-gender frontiers were already moving, and they trusted that their performance would open up all the other fields as their desire to work in them increased. And, intriguingly, although everybody agreed on a gender-based work division, female judges were in fact (in compliance with the Judicature Act) assigned to all legal fields and proved themselves successful in all of them. So in the end practice had overtaken the ideal, which didn't change anything in the theoretical constructs of the 'natural talents' of women for certain legal fields which survived in the heads of female judges, men and society alike and served as arguments to exclude female judges again in national socialism (Schultz, 1990: 325).

It needs to be stressed that female jurists in general had gained access to the legal professions also due to these 'generalising prejudices' by arguing that women would help to improve jurisdiction and society, that they were necessary as a social counterbalance to centuries of male domination of the legal system. More importantly, these prejudices helped individual women to overcome stereotyped gender roles. It is easy to forget today that the decision to study at university already distanced a girl from her background and the traditional understanding of what a woman should be. But the decision to become a lawyer or even a judge represented such a big step that these women needed to be reassured that they remained women and contributed something specifically feminine to masculine professions. This was particularly important to those women (the majority) who chose to remain single and saw their profession as an alternative to having a family—also a concept they had taken over from the bourgeois women's movement. The public perception that female judges had abrogated their femininity, as it was often expressed in the media, hit them right in their hearts and made them feel extremely vulnerable. They felt compelled to point out the 'motherly and caring' aspects of their profession in order to fend off any attack on their femininity. Characteristically, Margarethe von Erffa, in an early article on the French female attorneys, described them as shrewd, serious and clever, but also 'women in the best sense of the word' (Erffa and Richarz-Simons, 1929: 479). Today's criticisms that early female jurists and the women's movement alike were only tentatively able to let go of the arguments used by male society, goes a bit astray in the face of this background. Anyone studying the situation of women pioneers would do well to remember an appeal by Emma Oekinghaus in 1925:

> If today we are trying to present fairly the social and legal situation of women, we can only succeed if we manage to avoid preconceived notions. This is not easy to achieve for men or women, because we are not only interpreting a given situation, but also presenting something we personally either enjoy or suffer. But not being aware of this easily clouds our view (1925: III).

6. REFERENCES

Anonymous (1917) (*Russia)* 'Women Judges' 11 *International Women's News* 154.
—— (1921) (United States) 'A Woman Judge' 32 *The Young Woman's Journal* 27.
—— (1923) (Canada) 'Notes of the Week: Canada Appoints Three Women Judges' 1 *Equal Rights* 170.
—— (1925) (United States) 'Feminist Notes: Her Honor the Judge' 12 *Equal Rights* 114.
—— (1926) (United States) 'Oregon's First Woman Judge' 13 *Equal Rights* 178.
—— (1928) 'Neue Sachlichkeit' 484 *Deutsche Tageszeitung* wp.
—— (1930) (Czechoslovakia) 'Feminist Notes: Training Women to be Judges' 16 *Equal Rights* 104.
—— (1931) (California) 'Feminist Notes: California Judges' 17 *Equal Rights* 224.

—— (1931) (Massachusetts) 'Two "First" Judges' 16 *Woman's Journal* 5.
—— (1931) (New York) 'Feminist Notes: Twenty Candidates for Judges' 17 *Equal Rights* 208.
—— (1932) 'Die Frau als Richter, Schöffe und Anwalt. Zehn Jahre im Dienst der Justitia' *Deutsche Zeitung* wp.
—— (1932) (Turkey) 'Feminist Notes: Women Judges in Turkey' 18 *Equal Rights* 39.
—— (Denmark) 'Denmark appoints Woman Judge' *19 Equal Rights* 262.
—— (1947) (Poland) 'Poland' 41 *International Women's News* 85.
Albisetti, J (2000) 'Portia ante Portas. Women and the Legal Profession in Europe, ca 1870–1925' 22 *Journal of Social History* 825, 857.
Ameln, E (1985) *Köln-Appellhofplatz. Rückblick auf ein bewegtes Leben* (Cologne, Wienand Verlag).
Belleau, M-C and Johnson, R (2008) 'Judging Gender: Difference and Dissent at the Supreme Court of Canada' 15(1–2) *International Journal of the Legal Profession* 57.
Böge, S (1992) 'Weibliche Juristen? Eine historisch-soziologische Analyse des Zugangs von Frauen zu juristischen Professionen' (Master's thesis, Kassel).
—— (1995) 'Geschlecht und "Horizontale" Segmentierungen in der juristischen Profession' in A Wetterer (ed), *Die soziale Konstruktion von Geschlecht in Professionalisierungsprozessen* (Frankfurt/Main, Campus) 139.
Bogoch, B (2003) 'Lawyers in the Courtroom: Gender, Trials and Professional Performance in Israel' in U Schultz and G Shaw (eds), *Women in the World's Legal Professions* (Oxford, Hart Publishing) 147.
Böhm, R (1986) 'Der Kampf um die Zulassung der Frauen als Rechtsanwältinnen und zum Richteramt' 10 *Deutsche Richter Zeitung* 365.
Cordes, O (2006) 'Die Frau als Organ der Rechtspflege? Über die historisch wichtigsten Stationen der Zulassung von Frauen in der deutschen Rechtspflege' in S Meder (ed), *Frauenrecht und Rechtsgeschichte. Die Rechtskämpfe der deutschen Frauenbewegung* (Köln et al, Böhlau) 179.
Costas, I (1995) 'Gesellschaftliche Umbrüche und das Verhältnis von Profession und Geschlecht. Die juristische Profession im Deutsch-französischem Vergleich' in A Wetterer (ed), *Die Soziale Konstruktion von Geschlecht in Professionalisierungsprozessen* (Frankfurt/Main, Campus).
Deutscher Juristinnenbund (2003) (ed), *Juristinnen in Deutschland. Die Zeit von 1900–1998* (Baden-Baden, Nomos).
Dölemeyer, B (2003) 'Die Zulassung von Frauen zur Rechtsanwaltschaft und ihr Ausschluß in der NS- Zeit' in M Ascheri and F Ebel et al (eds), *'Ins Wasser geworfen und Ozeane durchquert'. Festschrift für Knut Wolfgang Nörr* (Cologne, Böhlau) 151.
Eggert, R (1998) 'Rechtsanwältinnen im Bezirk der Rechtsanwaltskammer Frankfurt am Main' in Rechtsanwaltskammer Frankfurt am Main (ed), *Rechtsanwälte und ihre Selbstverwaltung 1878 bis 1998* (Frankfurt/Main, Deutscher Fachverlag) 133.
Erffa, M and Richarz-Simons, I, 'Der weibliche Rechtsanwalt' in J Magnus (ed), *Die Rechtsanwaltschaft* (Leipzig, W Moeser) 471.
Fabricius-Brand, M, Berghahn, S and Sudhöffer, K (1982) *Juristinnen. Berichte, Fakten, Interviews* (Berlin, Elefanten-Pressverlag).
Flügge, S (1984) 'Der lange Weg in die Gerichte. Von der Männlichkeit des Staates und vom Ende holder Weiblichkeit' 4 *Streit* 149, 153.

Freidenreich, H (2002) *Female, Jewish, and Educated. The Lives of Central European University Women* (Bloomington, Indiana University Press).

Gilligan, C (1984) *Die andere Stimme. Lebenskonflikte und Moral der Frau* (München, Piper).

Hachenburg, M (1928) 'Kindmordfall' 33 *DJZ* 227.

Hagemeyer, M (1932) 'Die Juristin' in I Neundörfer (ed), *Frauengedanken zum Beruf* (Münster, Regensberg) 48.

Häntzschel, H (1997) 'Justitia—eine Frau? Bayerische Positionen einer Geschlechterdebatte' in H Häntzschel and H Bußmann (eds), *Bedrohlich gescheit. Ein Jahrhundert Frauen in der Wissenschaft in Bayern* (München, Beck Verlag) 194.

Harten-Hoencke, T (1931) 'Richterinnen und weiblicher Rechtsbeistand' 449 *Kölnische Zeitung* wp.

Kaja, 'Weiblicher Arbeitsrichter' *Berliner Allgemeine Zeitung* (25 June 1929) 1 of the insert.

Koll, H (1928) 'Die Frau im Richterberuf' in *Städtisches Gymnasium und Realgymnasium in der Kreuzgasse zu Köln, 1828–1928: Festschrift zur Jahrhundertfeier* (Cologne, Du-Mont-Schauberg) 99.

Kümmel, H (1984) 'Die Pionierfrauen der Justiz' 62 *Deutsche Richterzeitung* 357.

Langer, E (2003) 'Dr Erna Scheffler, geb Friedenthal (1893–1983)' in J Mezel (ed), *Jahrbuch der Schlesischen Friedrich-Wilhelms-Universität Breslau, Bd XL (2001–2003)* (Berlin, Duncker & Humblot).

Mahn, I (1932) 'Zum Thema: Die Frau als Richter' 24 *Deutsche Richter Zeitung* 326.

Mecklenburg, F (1996), 'The Occupation of Women Emigrees. Women Lawyers in the United States' in S Quack (ed), *Between Sorrow and Strength. Women Refugees of the Nazi Period* (Cambridge University Press) 289.

Munk, M (1938) 'Legal Training in Germany' in *The Double Tau, National League Sorority, July 1938, Vol IX, No 1* 30, 43.

Oekinghaus, E (1925) *Die gesellschaftliche und rechtliche Stellung der deutschen Frau* (Jena, Fischer).

Proskauer, E (1989) *Wege und Umwege—Erinnerungen einer Rechtsanwältin* (Berlin, Verlag Dirk Nishen).

Röwekamp, M (2005) *Juristinnen. Lexikon zu Leben und Werk* (Baden-Baden, Nomos).

—— (2011) *Die ersten deutschen Juristinnen: Eine Geschichte ihrer Professionalisierung und Emanzipation 1900–1945* (Cologne et al, Böhlau).

Scherner, KO (1997) *Advokaten, Revolutionäre, Anwälte. Die Geschichte der Mannheimer Anwaltschaft* (Sigmaringen, Jan Thorbecke Verlag).

Schultz, U (1990), 'Wie männlich ist die Juristenschaft?' in U Battis and U Schultz (eds) *Frauen im Recht* (Heidelberg, CF Müller) 319.

—— (2003) 'The Status of Women Lawyers in Germany' in U Schultz and G Shaw (eds), *Women in the World's Legal Professions* (Oxford, Hart Publishing) 271.

—— (2004) 'Richten Richterinnen richtiger?' *Reader Frauenbilder* (Düsseldorf) 117.

Schultz, U and Shaw, G (eds) (2003) *Women in the World's Legal Professions* (Oxford, Hart Publishing).

Sims (1929) 'Erste Kammergerichts-Richterin' in *Der Montag (Lokal-Anzeiger)* wp.

Stoehr, I (1983) 'Organisierte Mütterlichkeit': Zur Politik der deutschen Frauenbewegung um 1900 in K Hausen (ed), *Frauen suchen ihre Geschichte: Historische Studien zum 19. und 20. Jahrhundert* (München, CH Beck) 221.

Wetterer, A (1995) 'Die soziale Konstruktion von Geschlecht in Professionalisierungsprozessen' in A Wetterer (ed), *Die soziale Konstruktion von Geschlecht in Professionalisierungsprozessen* (Frankfurt/Main, Campus) 11.

Part 2

Women Judges' Work and Careers

2.1

Feminisation of the French 'Magistrature':[1] *Gender and Judging in a Feminised Context*

ANNE BOIGEOL

Abstract

In France the gender imbalance in the magistrature (judges and prosecutors) is not in favour of men, as it is in many common law countries. The question is not the small number of women in the judiciary, but rather the decreasing number of men. The French magistrature is one of the most feminised in Europe. If the presence of women in the magistrature is a commonplace, this does not mean that women's position and practice are exactly the same as those of men. The chapter explores some of the main issues associated with this feminisation, proposing explanations of the process, analysing how this feminisation affects the hierarchical structure of the magistrature and encounters a persistent glass ceiling. It also considers some of the effects of feminisation on gender consciousness and explores the relation between gender and the manner of judging in the specifically French context.

1. INTRODUCTION

A KEY CLAIM of the French cultural code (Lamont and Thévenot, 2000), ie, the republican universalism dogma, with its emphasis on equality and the disembodied nature of the judiciary symbolised by judges' black robes (Garapon, 1997) has long stood in the way of gendered approaches to the judiciary in France. Challenging such a dogma is anything but easy. The question of gender and judging is all the more unpopular as the unstoppable feminisation of the *magistrature* has

[1] *Magistrature* includes magistrates from both the bench and from the public prosecution service.

become a genuine issue for the judicial establishment (Boigeol, 1996). It is for this reason that the concern often voiced in common law countries regarding the absence of women from the bench (Malleson, 2003, 2006) has failed to find an echo in France. Indeed, if there is a concern about uneven gender distribution in the judiciary, it relates to the diminishing number of male judges. Studies on the integration or otherwise of women into the judiciary have remained the exception (Boigeol, 1993, 1996, 2004) and a coherent approach to the issue of gender and judging is as yet missing.

This chapter presents some aspects of the feminisation of the judiciary in France that can be of interest in a comparative perspective. The first part will deal with the process of feminisation. Then follows a discussion of the question why gender consciousness in the judiciary, which seems so important in the common law world, does not appear to be a problem in France. Finally, aspects of gendering the judging will be presented.

2. FEMINISATION OF THE *MAGISTRATURE*

The French judiciary is one of the most feminised in civil law countries, as illustrated in this volume. Women have been allowed to become magistrates—judges and prosecutors—ever since 1946, but it is mainly since the 1970s that their numbers have strongly increased. Between 1969 and 2009, the number of women magistrates has multiplied by 13.7 per cent (from 350 to 4810) while during the same period the number of men has stayed at the same level and has even decreased a little (from around 4000 in 1969 to 3938 in 2009). In 2009, 61 per cent of all judges were women and in the early stages of judicial careers, this percentage rises to 74 per cent. The corresponding figures for the public prosecution service are 47 per cent and 64 per cent respectively.[2]

The feminisation of the *magistrature* is logical if we consider that more than 60 per cent of French law graduates are female. And, more significantly, the number of male applicants for a judicial post among male law graduates is extremely low, reflecting the fact that overall a judicial career is not an attractive proposition for them given the position of the *magistrature* within the legal field (see below) (Bodiguel, 1991). Thus, in 2009, men made up no more than 15.4 per cent of candidates for the *Ecole nationale de la magistrature*. Consequently, the *magistrature* is more feminised than the

[2] Statistics produced by Directorate for Judicial Services in the Ministry of Justice.

Bar (50 per cent) not to mention the *notariat* (26 per cent)[3] and academia (20 per cent of women professors).[4]

The structure of the legal field (Bourdieu, 1986; Dezalay, 1992) can be interpreted in gendered terms. Feminisation is everywhere, but the higher it is, the lower its ranking in the overall field. The position of the French judicial judge in the legal field is high, but not to be compared with that of the common law judge. Bureaucracy and the limited power to interpret the law—even if European community law has widened the scope somewhat—have left the French judge with a relatively restricted position (Garapon and Papadopoulos, 2003).[5] By contrast, law professors have powers to make and impose legal doctrine, although 'there are signs that it [their power] is fraying' (Garcia-Villegas, 2006: 359) and the Bar, with the strong development of the corporate Bar and its international law firms, also occupies an increasingly dominant position in the field (Sandefur, 2001).

Differences in the rate of feminisation between judges and prosecutors are interesting. In previous studies I have tried to explain this by reference to a number of factors: the general perception of prosecution as a male position, availability for work required, relations with the political sphere and with civic police authorities (Boigeol, 1993). It is also true that in France, between the end of the Second World War and the beginning of the Fifth Republic in 1958, an early career as a prosecutor could speed up a later, successful career as a judge (Bancaud, 2002). This is less true today. But there is an interesting difference within the civil law world itself. On the one hand, there are countries where—as in Germany, Spain or Portugal—women may even outnumber men in the prosecution service, and prosecutors are civil servants enjoying in general a lower social status than judges; and on the other, there are countries such as Italy and France, where judges and prosecutors belong to the same group (*magistrature* in France and *magistratura* in Italy) and can move from the judiciary to the prosecution service and vice versa, and where prosecution seems to be the more attractive career for men (Consiglio superior de la magistratura, 2004). However, the degree of feminisation in the judiciary also depends on the way judges (and prosecutors) are selected in civil law (as opposed to common law) countries.

[3] Figures provided by the National Chamber of Notaries (Conseil supérieur du notariat).
[4] INSEE.
[5] The exceptions are judges on the prestigious highest administrative court, the Conseil d'Etat advising the government, and members of the Cour des comptes, the equivalent of the US Government Accountability Office.

2.1. The Selection Process: A Chance for Women

Judges and prosecutors in France are normally appointed through an open door process,[6] their numbers being determined by the Ministry of Justice. The appointment is preceded by 31 months at the Ecole nationale de la magistrature, a college for judges and prosecutors. In theory, personality plays no part in the selection process for the training. This certainly applies to the first part, the anonymous written examination testing knowledge of the law. But this is debatable regarding the second (oral) part, by its very nature not anonymous, involving not only a legal test but a discussion on a topic of 'general culture' to assess a candidate's personality. Also, given that law graduates tend to come from the more privileged professional and upper middle classes, there is a built-in social bias in the judicial selection process.

Over the years, experience has shown that male candidates have consistently, and with very few exceptions, scored better than women in the oral examination. Are men's oral skills really superior to those of women, or is there a slight degree of discrimination in their favour at work? Most female judges and prosecutors subscribe to the latter view, attributing it to a political desire to rectify the judicial feminisation process. Others argue that socialisation in families (Baudelot and Establet, 1992) and schools prepare boys better for competitive situations (Boigeol, 1993). Whatever the reasons, there is no doubt that in light of the diminishing numbers of male applicants, juries in the oral entrance examination pay particular attention to their performance, particularly in the context of discussions on 'general culture'. In other words, feminisation might be even greater if male and female candidates received exactly the same treatment.[7]

There is another path into the *magistrature*, which is by means of a sideways move from a different profession. Since the creation of the Ecole nationale de la magistrature in 1958, this has been the exception, but there is a political will to give it greater emphasis, and lawyers have frequently advocated this form of recruitment (Soulez Larivière, 1987). Over the last five years, the proportion of future judges or prosecutors entering the school of *magistrature* not through the competitive examination but on the basis of professional experience has increased (10 per cent in 2004 to 24 per cent in 2009). They are selected by a special committee composed of judges and prosecutors, 'only' 59 per cent of whom are women (Ecole nationale de la magistrature (ENM) Profil de la promotion, 2009).

[6] A competition which is open to anyone having the required diplomas and credentials.

[7] Since 2009, the selection process has been slightly modified to accommodate an assessment not only of the knowledge of the candidates, but of their judicial competences.

Candidates selected have varied professional experience, but half of them come from the different legal professions.

Overall, however, by comparison with common law countries (Malleson, 2006; Malleson and Russell, 2006) the French system (like most other civil law countries) compares well in terms of fairness to women.

2.2. Feminisation—A Phenomenon at all Levels of the Judicial Hierarchy, but ...

Strong feminisation is common to all categories at almost all levels of the French judicial hierarchy. This includes specialised judges, most particularly judges at juvenile courts, where 76 per cent are women (table 1 below). Only the prosecution service has over 50 per cent of men, but this is likely to change soon as, with the growing numbers of women in the profession, more and more of them are having to embark on a career in the prosecution service, with the result that 64 per cent of young prosecutors at the start of their careers are now women. Old-fashioned arguments trying to demonstrate women's unsuitability for these posts are no longer in circulation.

There are always some differences reflecting both preferences and constraints (mainly family constraints) on the part of women. Some positions of *juge unique* (at tribunaux d'instance dealing with minor civil cases) are more popular with women who find the work more interesting and who appreciate the fact that they retain some control over their working hours.

Even at the Cour de cassation, the French equivalent of the US Supreme Court (though with not exactly the same powers) 34 per cent of judges are women; this is not parity, but it is a move in the right direction.

2.3. The Persistence of a Glass Ceiling

The only positions that still remain strongly in male hands are those of heads of court. Here change is very slow, although recently there has been some improvement (table 2 below). The pool of candidates is feminised, but few women penetrate (what appears to be) the glass ceiling.

Table 1: Feminisation of the different categories of judges and prosecutors (%)

Year	Judge TGI*	Judge TI**	Juvenile judge	Investigating judge	Prosecutor
1999	52.4	63.4	67.0	47.3	35.0
2009	56.9	72.8	76.7	55.2	47.0

* Tribunal de Grande Instance (first instance court)
** Tribunal d'instance (court dealing with small civil cases)

Table 2: Number of women heads of court/heads of prosecution services

Year	Head of court		Head of prosecution service	
	Court of appeal	Courts (total)	Court of appeal	Courts (total)
1999	2	26	1	21
2000	2	29	3	19
2001	2	23	3	19
2002	3	27	3	19
2003	4	32	3	23
2004	4	36	3	17
2005	4	40	2	16
2006	3	46	2	21
2007	5	48	3	24
2008	4	47	7	22
2009	4	47	7	31
Number of courts	35	170+	35	170+

The main and official argument used to explain the scarcity of women at the top is that women do not apply. It is also a way of attributing the responsibility for women's exclusion to women themselves. Looking at this more closely, it is true that only a small number of women (compared with one third of men) apply for such positions. For men this is part of their *habitus*, from the beginning of their careers. As shown by a survey carried out in the Ecole nationale de la magistrature in the late 1980s (Boigeol, 1991) the majority of men have a clear idea of their professional career and are aiming to get to the top, as president of a court of appeal, or as general prosecutor. By contrast, young women are more disposed to keep their careers open and do not want to anticipate, from the very beginning, how they will end their professional lives. Having and bringing up children may take precedence over their careers:

> Life means you have to have a job, and myself and my women friends we consider it very important, but our job is not the only thing in life, really not. This is a very feminine attitude. Men think only of their job. There are other things in life than the last precedent ... At least for our generation (female prosecutor).[8]

[8] Interview quoted in Boigeol (1993: 517).

However, this does not mean that women would not like to head a court or a public prosecution service. In a survey of 2004,[9] a large majority of women (77 per cent) and men (87 per cent) declared they were interested in such a position. But if a majority of men (61 per cent) applied for such a position, only 22 per cent of women did. Family tasks limited their professional activity and their ambitions, while having little effect on men. In relation to women respondents, 68 per cent said that family tasks had no negative impact on the professional lives of their husbands.

Women, so it seems, have less choice than men in their careers. As a result many of them are excluded from leading positions, which often require considerable availability as well as geographical mobility. But the survey also clearly shows that in the case of some women there is a genuine lack of interest in reaching a top position; they prefer to remain as a judge in a court of appeal rather than being president of a court.

But that is not the only reason to explain why so few women apply for top positions; another explanation is that they anticipate failure to be appointed.

The appointment of presidents of courts is controlled, and even initiated, by the Conseil superieur de la magistrature (CSM) which is rather a corporatist institution with a majority of magistrates.[10] The CSM also controls all appointments to the bench, recalling the role of judicial selection committees in common law systems. As for appointments to the prosecution service, the CSM merely offers an opinion, while the final decision rests with the government.

Positions are awarded according to formal criteria (seniority) but also merit and personal preferences on the part of judges or prosecutors involved in the selection process. The CSM is a very masculine institution. Since 1994, it has been composed of 12 magistrates (six from the bench and six public prosecutors) elected by their peers, as well as four members representing (high) civil society (appointed by chairs of the two parliamentary chambers, the State Council and the President of the Republic).[11] These high civil society personalities have always been men, thereby conveying the very strange message that only men represent civil society.

[9] Survey financed by the European Commission in four countries (Italy, France, Spain, Romania) on the equilibrated participation of men and women to posts of responsibility in the *magistrature*. It was carried out for a seminar organised by the Italian Consiglio superior della magistratura in Rome in 2004.

[10] Conseil supérieur de la magistrature-CSM (2004, 2005) Rapports annuels d'activité. www.conseil-superieur-magistrature.fr/node/47.

[11] Until 1993, members of CSM were appointed by the President of the Republic, either directly or on the basis of proposals submitted by the Cour de cassation and the State Council. The first woman was appointed by President Giscard d'Estaing in 1975, who also appointed a second one in 1979. President Mitterand appointed five women, three (exceptionally) in 1983, another in 1987 and the last one in 1991.

The complex election procedure has not favoured women judges or prosecutors either. Presidents of the lower courts—mainly male—elect two members, as do both the presidents of courts of appeal and of the Cour de cassation (all very male dominated). The remaining six are elected by ordinary judges and prosecutors. In 1994, one out of the 16 members was a woman; in 1998 there were two; and from 2002, there were three women. In the current CSM, there are only two women who were elected by the lower electoral body, while the elected representatives of presidents of courts include not a single one. In other words, the CSM is far from being perfectly gender neutral in its assessment of candidates.

Male members of the CSM not only have the majority, but they occupy a dominant position. Beyond the formal equality of the members there is an informal hierarchy, which reproduces the hierarchy of the *magistrature*: being elected by the upper electoral constituency may give the candidate a stronger position than being elected by ordinary judges or prosecutors. The gender composition of the CSM could have been improved a few years ago, when, in 2001, the modalities of election of the CSM members were changed, with the introduction of a list system of election, the list representing the unions and associations of judges and prosecutors. In the wake of the parity law for political elections (2000) the new law introduced parity in the lists of judges and prosecutors. This disposition was accepted by both houses of Parliament, but it was rejected by the Constitutional Court, which argued that the parity law of 2000 concerns only political elections and not professional ones (Giraudou, 2006; Calvès, 2004). The Constitutional Court also maintained that a distinction between women and men is contrary to article 6 of the Declaration of Human and Citizen Rights of 1789, still in force, which stipulates that 'all citizens are eligible to occupy "positions of dignity" (*dignités*) and public functions purely on the basis of their ability and without any distinction other than their virtue and their talent'.[12]

The idea that women could manage courts as well as men is an unfamiliar one to most of the members of the CSM who rather opt for a continuation of the status quo and the preservation of the maleness of these positions. They choose people like themselves and their predecessors, people they consider to be more suitable for the job and more available. That does not mean that they cannot appoint women, nor are they hostile to the idea, but appointments of women remain the exception. And the fact that few women apply confirms for them that they have made the right choice. Indeed, this may be the last male bastion in a feminised profession.

12 See: www.legifrance.gouv.fr/html/constitution/constitution.htm.

2.4. Is Affirmative Action Required to Change the Gender Profile of Presidents of Courts?

To change a reproductive system is not easy. So the question arises: is affirmative action the only way out? There are two interesting precedents, one for the bench and one for the public prosecution service.

The question of parity on the CSM was raised in the commission itself in 2002 by a newly-elected woman. She was *Premier avocat général* (prosecutor) at the Cour de cassation (the first woman ever to be appointed to this position) which allowed her to raise this delicate subject. Having initiated a discussion by the CSM, she met with some resistance, as recorded in a note for a women's association of high civil servants where she mentioned the strong reservations held by male members of the CSM.[13] In the annual report of the CSM, she published a brief account on parity in the *magistrature*, underlining the scarcity of women appointments for presidential posts. At her instigation more precise statistics appeared in the annual report of the CSM providing a measure of the rate of success of men's and women's applications for the position of court presidents. They showed that in 2002–03 men scored 50 per cent higher than women (table 3 below).[14] One year later, the rate of success for women was higher, even higher than men's. There was a progression in the number of women appointed.[15] In the following year, there was a further (slight) increase, but then the publication of detailed statistics was stopped.[16]

The second example deals with the appointment of prosecutors. Prosecutors are political appointments, including the head of public prosecution. Women are not favoured, as they have traditionally been regarded

Table 3: Gender profile of appointments of presidents of courts

Court presidents	Male candidates	Appointed	Male %	Female candidates	Appointed	Female %
2002–03	716	47	6.6	227	10	4.4
2003–04	761	38	5	257	14	5.4

Source: Rapport d'activité CSM, 2002–03; 2003–04

[13] C Petit, Avocat général à la cour de cassation, *Etat des lieux de la situation des femmes dans la magistrature*. Compiled for *Administration Moderne* (women's association of high-ranking civil servants) at: www.administrationmoderne.com/pdf/.../cr_fmagistrature.pdf.

[14] For women, 4.4%; 6.6% for men, of applications to chairs of courts (without court of appeal).

[15] Since 2005 gender-specific information about the number of applications for heads of courts is no longer published.

[16] CSM *Rapport d'activité* (2005).

as less well suited than men, who are more available, have links with political powers and represent (state and other) authority. This goes particularly for the head of the prosecution service of the court of appeal. In 2007, the incoming French President, Nicolas Sarkozy, appointed a woman with a diverse background as Minister of Justice, a genuine newcomer to the world of politics.[17] As soon as she was appointed, she was not only very active, but authoritarian and tough, in putting into practice the reforms wanted by Sarkozy. Her popularity suffered badly among the whole legal community from the political Right to the Left. But she also took the initiative to promote affirmative action in favour of diversity and of women. She organised special training sessions (*classes préparatoires*) in order to help young law graduates from underprivileged classes to prepare for the competitive examination for the school of *magistrature*. She also wanted to appoint more women as heads of prosecution services of courts of appeal, deciding that, among the new appointments, 50 per cent should be women. And she did just that. In 2007, five women and five men were appointed as *Procureus Généraux*. So today, seven *Procureus Généraux* out of 36 are women! But the question of gender and judging is not only a question of the number of heads of court or of judges; it also concerns gender consciousness.

3. GENDER CONSCIOUSNESS—A'PRIVATE' ISSUE

In many common law countries as well as in some civil law countries—mainly in Latin America—gender consciousness is a public affair. By contrast, in France, gender awareness has remained strictly private, lacking any public manifestation. This is compounded by the fact that in France the judiciary's strong feminisation makes many judges and prosecutors feel uneasy when it comes to the gender question.

3.1. No Women Judges' Voices of Support

For a French judge it is surprising to hear judges such as Bertha Wilson (Wilson, 1990) and Claire L'Heureux-Dubé in Canada, and Brenda Hale in England, evoking the 'women's voice' that introduces the different experience of women's and ethnic minorities' lives and increases the impartiality of the court. Admittedly, not all female judges shared this view,[18] and feminist

[17] She was the first political figure appointed to a very important position in the French Government and whose parents are immigrants coming from the Maghreb. In June 2009, Rachida Dati was replaced by another woman, Michelle Alliot-Marie, who has a more classical profile.

[18] Sandra O'Connor, the first woman appointed to the Supreme Court of the United States, did not claim a woman's voice.

positions did provoke strong reactions in the media, which accused them of partiality and even immorality (Rackley, 2007; Hunter, 2008).[19]

In France there is no real 'women's voice' among the highest judges in the Cour de cassation. The first woman to be appointed as its president—and the only one until now—was anything but a feminist. In an interview in a national newspaper she said that

> there is a question which I am sometimes asked and which irritates me considerably, ie, whether being a woman I apply the law differently from men. There is confusion between the law and the judge. I have never done anything in my professional life that has been guided by my being a woman.[20]

3.2. No Women Judges' Associations, but …

In many common law countries gender consciousness is present through the activities of associations of women judges. Women judges are organised as a collective actor to mobilise support for women's and minorities' rights, promote equal access to the judiciary, denounce gender bias and propose solutions to gender inequality. The most important one in the United States is the National Association of Women Judges (NAWJ) created in 1979. Its ambitions are impressive:

> It is the nation's leading voice for women jurists dedicated to preserving judicial independence, ensuring equal justice and access at the courts for women, minorities and other historically disfavoured groups, providing judicial education on cutting-edge issues, and increasing the numbers and advancement of women judges at all levels to more accurately reflect their full participation in a democratic society.[21]

There are associations in Canada, the United Kingdom, Australia, New Zealand and many developing countries where women's rights and gender equality are promoted. There is also the International Association of Women Judges founded in 1991 (IAWJ) aiming to unite women judges from diverse legal/judicial systems who share a commitment to equal justice and the rule of law. This association claims that women judges 'can be catalysts for social transformation'.[22] Its members come mainly from common law countries,

[19] 'The new—and youngest—law lord is a self-confessed feminist, a breaker of tradition by taking an unusual route to the top and a totemic hate figure for the *Daily Mail*, which accuses her of subverting family values' (*The Guardian*, 9 January 2004).

[20] *Libération* (10 April 2007).

[21] See: www.nawj.org/.

[22] The IAWJ believes that women judges are in a unique position to promote the rights of women through the judicial system, and to protect and empower women throughout the world. These judges operate on the premise that through the exercise of informed and united leadership women judges can be the catalysts for social transformation.

with some notable exceptions, such as Argentina and Brazil. In France there are only two judges who are members of IAWJ. In Argentina or Brazil there are associations of women judges, apparently active. Interest in women in the judiciary is also promoted through the organisation by judges and scholars of international seminars on women in the judiciary, as in 1997 in Rio de Janeiro[23] and 2007 in Buenos Aires.[24] An international seminar was organised in 2004 in Rome by a group of women of the Consiglio superior della magistratura about the question of the equilibrated participation of women and men in the allocation of leading positions in courts, with the support of the European Community. The issue of women in the judiciary has become, for the moment, a public matter, a topic attracting more general interest.

In France there are no associations of women judges, although there are associations of women lawyers.[25] Gender is not a category to mobilise judges and prosecutors. There are some important associations of magistrates, two of them having the form of a trade union. These trade unions include many women; especially the more politically Left ones. Women often head the *Syndicat de la magistrature* and are quite numerous on its board. They are also present in the other organisation but seldom as president. Female representation in key positions is given greater emphasis by trade unions of the political Left than those of the Right. They occasionally discuss women's issues in society at large or in courts, but there are no dedicated women sections.

The role of the State in the promotion of gender equality has been brought to the fore by EU legislation. It was in the wake of a European resolution on balanced participation of women and men in the decision-making process[26] that an *Observatoire des carrières de la justice* was set up in France with the aim of analysing the careers of women and men, including their access to leading positions. However gender mainstreaming has been disappointing and is now rejected by many feminists (Jacquot, 2009).

The non-existence of women judges' associations does not mean that there is no gender consciousness. Rather it is treated as a private, individual matter and rarely manifested in public. Women judges experience their gender in their daily lives, in their careers etc. They are familiar with problems of women in society; they are active in trade unions and associations

[23] Organised by Eliane Junqueira and the Association of Magistrates.

[24] Organised by Beatriz Kohen and ELA (Equipo Latinoamericano de Justicia y Género).

[25] There is also an association of women with legal careers, composed mainly of attorneys and including a small number of judges, but it is not very active.

[26] European Parliament resolution on the Commission report on the implementation of Council Recommendation 96/694 of 2 December 1996 on the balanced participation of women and men in the decision-making process (COM(2000) 120—C5-0210/2000—2000/2117(COS)) (18 January 2001).

but not as a professional collective; they are equally aware of the problems in the judiciary. Many of them consider that men are favoured at the oral entrance examination, as they consistently succeed better than women. They also consider that women are facing a glass ceiling for the positions of presidents of courts and that their careers are often affected by discrimination. Republican universalism, an integral part of the judicial ethos, does not allow them to use their gender as a motive for political mobilisation, although feminisation is considered a problem by many judges, male and female. So we are looking at a kind of 'negative gender consciousness'.

3.3. Negative Gender Consciousness?

The feminisation of the *magistrature* is regarded as a problem by many judges and prosecutors, as it is associated with, indeed regarded as the cause of, a certain devaluation of the institution of the judiciary. The question of the devaluation of justice has been around for a long time and first appeared well before women's entry into the profession. One female court president judge recalls:

> Men themselves have contributed to the devaluation of justice by being too accommodating to the political power, for instance during the Second World War. It was men who prostrated themselves before Pétain. I do not think that feminisation has contributed to the devaluation of justice, but rather other problems such as the role of justice in France and the way we French consider the judicial institution.

The valuation of justice and the judiciary has to be understood in relation to other professions in the legal field. More generally, the *fonction publique*, even elite colleges such as the Ecole nationale d'administration, have lost some of their attraction for young ambitious law graduates (mainly men) by comparison with other professions.

But the real problem is not the feminisation but the de-masculinisation of the judiciary. In other words, women should not, once again, be made accountable for the alleged devaluation of the *magistrature*. It is also interesting to note that many legal historians consider that judges today are much more independent from the political power now than they were under the third or fourth Republic (Bancaud, 2002).

Strong feminisation poses the question of the image of the judiciary and of the administration of justice. Does the gender of judges matter to people who are seeking justice? Some judges think so:

> It would be wrong to say that it does not raise a problem. When there were only men in the *magistrature* this was in step with the society of that time. When society began to change, women began to become judges or prosecutors. And today we have the reverse situation [in the judiciary] but without this being in phase

> with society. There are some cases, where too many women do pose a problem, in divorce cases for instance, where men are not comfortable with a decision taken exclusively by women judges. An ethnic and gender mix is fundamental. The same goes for criminal matters (female president of a court).

One female juvenile judge experienced the impact of her gender with the father of a young offender who, coming from the Maghreb, had some difficulty in accepting a woman as the judge. Her reaction illustrates the fact that the person has to withdraw behind the professional: 'The more he treated me as a woman, the more I reacted as a professional'(quoted by Boigeol, 1993). But there is no general survey that would allow a systematic analysis of whether and how gender of judicial personnel affects those going to court.

4. GENDERING JUDGING

The last point to deal with is the question of the impact of feminisation on the way judging is done. Is there such as thing as a gendered approach to judging?

4.1. Gendering the Judges

The relation between gender and judging can be seen through history with the assignment to women of certain categories of magistrate for which they were said to be best fitted. The indirect outcome of, or possibly reason for, this division of labour was also to preserve the masculine nature of certain other professional categories. Until 1946, when women obtained the right to become judge or prosecutor, the male gender was a part of the judicial model. The exercise of authority, whether in the family or in society, was a masculine prerogative, linked with features such as physical strength, a louder voice, the habit to give orders and to take decisions. Magistrates being exclusively male make it highly likely that their gender had some influence on the way they were judging or prosecuting. On the other hand, the stereotype of women was that they needed protection in order to preserve their role within the family as well as protecting men's jurisdiction within and outside the family.

After the Second World War, equality between men and women made important progress. However, gender stereotypes have anything but died out in society at large as well as among judges and prosecutors. The idea that women being different from men made them less well capable of dealing with certain positions in the *magistrature* was still quite popular among some members of the judiciary when the law was discussed and even afterwards when it was voted in.

As it was impossible to prevent women from entering the judiciary, attempts were made to promote gender differentiation within the judiciary (Boigeol, 1996), the principle being that women were best suited to be juvenile or civil judges, that is, for educational rather than repressive roles. The first attempt to put this into practice was made in 1945 when the law was discussed and women were said to have much better qualities for certain cases than men. 'In questions relating to juvenile delinquency and in all the questions relating to the protection of the family, the woman is more competent to find the solutions which justice requires' (quoted by Boigeol, 1996: 115). The second occurred in 1946 when the law came into force. Judges and prosecutors gathered in an exceptional meeting demanding once again the restriction of women's judicial activity to juvenile and civil cases.

From the beginning, there was an assumption that women could work in a specific way, that they had special qualities, which could be put to good use in the judicial system. For instance, in juvenile cases women's competence within the family could be helpful in a professional context. This view has survived into our time. Women increasingly choose to work in juvenile and civil departments, avoiding more repressive positions such as that of investigating judge or member of the prosecution service. Women who choose such roles are expected to perform like men. A high-ranking female judge, who in the 1970s worked as an investigating judge, remembered that she was supposed 'to work like a man and not like a woman investigating judge. The view of authority was absolutely restrictive, authority was linked to force, to the physical presence, to the loudness of the voice. But authority can be something else'. What she herself thought crucial was to be rigorous and professional (Boigeol, 1993: 515).

Beyond the question of the specificity of women and of horizontal differentiation are attempts to limit women's access to certain positions and protect men's domination. This applied, and still applies, to repressive judicial roles, including that of prosecutor, and to higher-ranking positions. The following anecdote is a good illustration.

In 1946, soon after the law was voted in, the Minister of Justice, Henri Teitgen, wanted to send the strong message that, as far as he was concerned, women judges should not be limited to the position of juvenile judge. He therefore appointed at the Cour de cassation the first woman professor of law who fulfilled all the legal requirements. In his own words:

> As soon as Ms Lagarde's nomination had been published, the President and the General Prosecutor of the *Cour de cassation* asked me for an audience. They arrived, all dressed in black and in gloves, insisted on remaining standing [...] The President told me that the judges of the *Cour de cassation*, gathered in a general assembly, requested me respectfully to give up the nomination of Ms Lagarde, adding that in the case of a refusal, he himself and the General Prosecutor would present their resignation. After a moment of silence I asked them if they had

> anything else to add. Then I replied in a very natural tone that, of course, there was no possibility for me to concede to their request. So would they please go to my secretary's office and write their letters of resignation, which they could consider as accepted. They promptly left the Ministry, and I never heard any more of their protest (Teitgen, 1988).

4.2. Gender and Judging

In common law countries, the usual way of thinking about the issue of gender and judging is to look at the relationship between the gender of judges and their sentences (Gruhl, Spohn and Welch, 1981). In civil law countries very little research has been done on the subject. Nor is it a topic easy to approach as the first reaction of judges is always to reject the assumption that there might be any correlation between gender and judging—a reaction not specific to France. 'I challenge you to find any difference between a decision taken by a male judge and a decision taken by a female judge' said a female president of a court in an interview.

A few years ago Robert Badinter, a famous lawyer and former Minister of Justice and chair of the Constitutional Court, excluded all relations between gender and judging, saying 'In judicial matters, this is not conceivable. There is no more a male or a female way of judging or prosecuting than there is a male or a female way of teaching, pleading or governing'.[27] We know that, as all pioneers, the first women judges did their best not to be different from men, sometimes to be like a man. They experienced a lot of pressure, as many male judges were waiting to see them stumble. These pioneers had to demonstrate that they had 'the qualities of authority, legal reasoning, presence of mind and self-control which seem indispensible in the exercise of judicial functions'.[28] Some of their male colleagues were suspicious of their ability to be repressive. But it seems that women were not especially soft in their judging. On the contrary, a former high judge says that in the early 1960s many young female judges were surprised by the benevolence of their male colleagues in the punishment of crimes and offences (Aydalot, 1976) On the other hand, as has been observed in Brazil, women are possibly less paternalistic towards women who are asking for a divorce (Junqueira, 2003).

Another factor has, in France, contributed to homogenising the process of judging or prosecuting irrespective of the gender or other particularities of judges. This is the creation of a college—Ecole nationale de la magistrature (ENM)—where all judges and prosecutors receive their training. Criticism

[27] Quoted by Giraudou (2006: 179).
[28] *Rapport du président du jury de l'examen d'entrée dans la magistrature 1956.*

has been voiced that in this way all judges and prosecutors are shaped in the same mould. After all, those entering ENM, that is mainly graduate students with no professional or life experience, are malleable and easily acquire similar reflexes and ways of thinking (Soulez Larivière, 1987). But they also acquire an 'esprit de corps', the feeling to have a collective identity that political power and the Bar did not appreciate much.[29]

5. CONCLUSIONS

Women are flocking to the *magistrature* thanks to the competitive examination, which guarantees the equality principle, one of the important values of universalism. By their number they have gained quite a strong position in the judiciary. However, this does not mean that all difficulties and discrimination have disappeared: there is still a glass ceiling.

The impact of feminisation in the judiciary and in the courts has still to be analysed. Even if the ideology of the disembodiment of judges in the service of impartiality is very strong, even if judges are all trained in the same way, even if courts' work is more and more standardised, that does not mean that judges are 'social eunuchs' (Griffith, 1977: 193) as illustrated by history. We know that it is mainly in the way of judging that the role of personality, including gender, has been observed in civil law countries. In Argentina, a study of family judges found differences between the work of men and women judges in divorce cases, as women used more interdisciplinary knowledge and generally developed and favoured different personal qualities (Kohen, 2008).

In France, the idea that women do not operate in exactly the same way as men appears from time to time in the media, mostly with reference to successful women, even in the courts. A former General Prosecutor at the Cour des comptes phrased this very cautiously when she said:

> Neither men nor women hold a monopoly on a particular behaviour, but a quality encountered perhaps more frequently with women than men is a capacity to listen. They are happy to consult with others, discuss issues with their team, and make sure that questions have been fully explored, without this impeding their ability to take a decision.[30]

Gender and judging would be a well worthwhile subject for research in the French context. Very recently, there is new interest in the question

[29] Today the new idea proposed to the government is to train all jurists in the same way in some Ecoles des professions du droit, reducing ENM role to the organisation of training in courts (Rapport Darrois, 2009).

[30] Interview with Hélène Gisserot, *Procureur Général honoraire près la Cour des comptes* at: www.femmesaaeena.com/interviews.html.

among PhD students and young researchers, some of them exploring the question of the relevance of gender to analyse the way of judging, mainly in penal justice and in family courts.[31] Another interesting angle for future researches would be to investigate how those seeking justice in civil and criminal courts experience the gender of judges. Does the judge's gender matter to them?

6. REFERENCES

Aydalot, M (1976) *Magistrat* (Paris, Robert Laffont).

Bancaud, A (2002) *Une exception ordinaire. La magistrature en France* 1930–1950 (Paris, Gallimard).

Baudelot, C and Establet, R (1992) *Allez les filles* (Paris, Seuil).

Bodiguel, JL (1991) *Les magistrats, un corps sans âme* (Paris, Presse Universitaires de France).

Boigeol, A (1991) *Comment devient-on magistrat. Enquête auprès de 3 promotions d'auditeurs* (Vaucresson, CRIV, rapport de recherche).

—— (1993) 'La magistrature française au féminin: entre spécificité et banalisation' 25 *Droit et Société* 489.

—— (1996) 'Les femmes et les cours. La difficile mise en oeuvre de l'égalité des sexes dans l'accès à la magistrature' 22 *Genèses* 107.

—— (2004) 'La contribution des magistrates au débat sur la justice' in N Racine and M Trebitsch, *Intellectuelles. Du genre en histoire des intellectuels* (Bruxelles, Editions Complexe).

Bourdieu, P (1986) 'La force du droit. Pour une sociologie du champ juridique' 64 *Actes de la recherche en sciences sociales* 3.

Botelho Junqueira, E (2003) 'Women in the Judiciary: A Perspective from Brazil' in U Schultz and G Shaw (eds), *Women in the World's Legal Professions* (Oxford, Hart Publishing).

Calvès, G (2004) *La discrimination positive* (PUF, Que sais-Je?).

Consiglio Superiore della Magistratura. Commissione per le Pari Opportunità (30 marzo 2004) *Rilevazioni statistiche*.

Dezalay, Y (1992) *Marchands de droit. La restructuration de l'ordre juridique international par les multinationales du droit* (Paris, Fayard).

Faugeron, C and Rivero, N (1982) *Femmes libérées sous conditions: étude des dossiers des condamnées à des peines supérieures à trois ans libérées entre 1973 et 1979* (Paris, SEPC, collection Déviance et contrôle social) 34.

Garapon, A (1997) *Bien juger. Essai sur le rituel judiciaire* (Paris, Odile Jacob).

Garapon, A and Papadopoulos, I (2003) *Juger en Amérique et en France* (Paris, Odile Jacob).

[31] As it can be seen with the organisation of two sessions on 'Justice through the Lens of Gender' at the annual meeting of the French Association of Political Science, at Strasbourg (31 August–2 September 2011).

Garcia-Villegas, M (2006) 'Comparative Sociology of Law: Legal Fields, Legal Scholarships, and Social Sciences in Europe and the United States' 31 *Law and Social Inquiry* 343, 382.

Giraudou, I (2006) 'La magistrature française au miroir de sa féminisation: le trompe-l'œil d'une parité spontanée' in M Tsujimura and D Lochak (eds), *Egalité des sexes: la discrimination positive en question. Une analyse comparative. France, Japon, Union européenne et Etats-Unis* (Paris, Société de législation comparée).

Griffith, JAG (1977) *The Politics of the Judiciary* (Manchester, Manchester University Press).

Gruhl, J, Spohn, C and Welch, S (1981) 'Women as Policymakers: The Case of Trial Judges' 25 *American Journal of Political Science* 308.

Hunter, R (2008) 'Can Feminist Judges Make a Difference?' 15(1–2) *International Journal of the Legal Profession* 7.

Jacquot, S (2009) 'La fin d'un politique d'exception. L'émergence du gender mainstreaming et la normalisation de la politique communautaire d'égalité entre les femmes et les hommes' 59 *Revue française de science politique* 247.

Kohen, B (2008) 'Gender Differences in the Family Law Courts: A View from Within' 13 *International Journal for the Legal Profession* 111.

—— (2009) 'What's in a Label? Argentine Judges' Reluctance to call themselves Feminists' (Onati, Workshop Gender and Judging).

Lamont, M and Thévenot, L (eds) (2000) *Rethinking Comparative Cultural Sociology: Repertoires of Evaluation in France and the United States (*Cambridge, Cambridge University Press).

Malleson, K (2003) 'Prospects for Parity: The Position of Women in the Judiciary in England and Wales' in U Schultz and G Shaw (eds), *Women in the World's Legal Professions* (Hart Publishing, Oxford).

—— (2006) 'Rethinking the Merit Principle in Judicial Selection' 33(1) *Journal of Law and Society* 126.

Malleson, K and Russell, PH (eds) (2006) *Appointing Judges in an Age of Judicial Power: Critical Perspectives from around the World* (Toronto, University of Toronto Press).

Rackley, E (2007) 'Judicial Diversity, the Woman Judge and Fairy Tale Endings' 27 *Legal Studies* 74.

Sandefur, R (2001) 'Work and Honor in the Law: Prestige and the Division of Lawyers' Labor' 66 *American Sociological Review* 382.

Soulez Larivière, D (1987) *Les juges dans la balance* (Paris, Ramsay).

Teitgen, PH (1988) *Faites entrer le témoin suivant: 1940–1958. De la Résistance à la République* (Rennes, Editions Ouest France).

Wilson, B (1990) 'Will Women Judges Really Make a Difference?' 28 *Osgoode Hall Law Journal* 507.

2.2

'I was noticed and I was asked ...' Women's Careers in the Judiciary. Results of an empirical study for the Ministry of Justice in Northrhine-Westfalia, Germany

ULRIKE SCHULTZ

Abstract

'Women in Leadership Positions in the Judiciary' was a research project commissioned by the Ministry of Justice of Northrhine-Westfalia, the largest of Germany's federal states. The aim was to identify factors preventing women judges and prosecutors from having successful careers, and to decide on measures to eliminate such factors as well as to promote women's professional progress. Admittedly, the proportion of women in the profession has reached 40 per cent and is still rising, but they continue to be under-represented in leadership positions. The careers system is now largely regulated by law, and evaluations and personnel decisions can be challenged in court. Yet, important career decisions are taken by court presidents after 'a tap on the shoulder'. Women with children are still assumed to be treating their careers as a matter of secondary importance, or to lack professional ambition. Part-time work is interpreted as part-time commitment. There is no open discrimination, but as shall be shown gender still works under the surface.

1. THE PROJECT

FOR A NUMBER of years 'women in leadership positions' has been the hot topic in women's policy, both at national and at European level. Even in German public service, where regulations for gender equality as well as quota regulations are in place, women continue to lack adequate representation at top levels. That is why, in November 2008, the Ministry of Justice of Northrhine-Westfalia took early steps to commission an investigation into the causes of the under-representation of women in leadership positions in this state's judicial organisations, among judges and in the public prosecution service.

Intriguingly, the uneven distribution of women and men in top positions and an insufficient female potential in leadership positions at the next level down were defined as an issue of personnel management. The project documentation inviting submissions stated:

> Demographic change suggests a medium-term lack of a highly qualified workforce, which will lead to a highly competitive labour market (poaching). The Northrhine Westfalian judiciary will have to take early measures to remain attractive for promising 'high potentials' in their own ranks in order to secure future availability of appropriate candidates for top positions.

The aim of the study was to identify positive and negative factors influencing the progression of women to top positions in Northrhine-Westfalia's judiciary, and to propose measures to promote women's careers. There was an obvious additional motivation (not without historical precedent), ie, to encourage women's presence in the judicial labour market as a kind of reserve army. The project was taken on by a team combining legal, sociological, psychological and economic/human resources expertise.[1]

In 2009, a total of 62 interviews and discussions were conducted, ie, expert interviews and interviews with judges and public prosecutors of both sexes at various levels: posts on entry, at first level of promotion and at different leadership levels. The inclusion of both sexes was intended to allow for comparisons between male and female career and life expectations. Further discussions on measures to promote women were conducted with judges in the function of personnel officers. Mountains of judicial documents, three files containing action plans for the promotion of women, as well as comprehensive statistical materials were scrutinised.

Before presenting key findings of this study, some basic information on Germany's judicial system is necessary for a better understanding of the context.

2. THE GERMAN JUDICIARY

2.1. Justice in Germany

Germany's judicial system, the outcome of 200 years of developments, is highly differentiated and characterised by the homogeneity of its judiciary and public prosecution service as well as a clear institutional identity. Judges in Germany are career judges and enter the judiciary at around

[1] Project team: Ulrike Schultz, Andreas Haratsch, Anja Rudek, Ilka Peppmeier and Silke Schröder.

30 years of age. As military service was only abolished quite recently, female judges tended to join the profession at a slightly younger age.

Legal education in Germany is long and tedious (Schultz, 2008). On average, young lawyers take between seven and nine years to complete their education. A minimum of four years is spent studying at university, followed by a two-year practical training organised by appeal courts. In spite of ongoing reforms of legal education, the focus of training is on skills needed for judicial office rather than practising lawyers (Schultz, 2008, 2011).[2] Each of the two parts ends with an examination set by the state justice administration. All candidates follow the same programme, irrespective of the specific legal profession they are eventually going to choose. The so-called second state examination qualifies them for judicial office as well as for an application for admission as either advocates (Anwälte), notaries (Notare) (this applies only to selected federal states), higher civil servants in local, state and federal administration or public prosecutors. Germany is the only country in the world with this model of a unitary legal profession (Einheitsjurist) (Schultz, 2005: 93–131).

Both phases of legal education have been criticised for functioning as an alienation process, an initiation ritual, comparable to rites of passage (Kvale, 1982; Rudek, 2012). They result in strong assimilation and conformity to the very traditional values and attitudes current in the legal field, which in the end builds the big homogeneous class of German jurists.

Germany has a three-tier system of courts. The first instance and the appeal courts operate under the aegis of the ministries of justice of the 16 federal states. The next higher courts are federal courts which can be appealed to on questions of law. At the top of the pyramid there is the Federal Constitutional Court (Bundesverfassungsgericht) which is the 'guardian of the constitution'. There are different jurisdictions for, on the one hand, civil and criminal matters (the so-called ordinary courts) and on the other, labour, administrative, social and tax law, these latter 'special jurisdictions' having developed in the course of the twentieth century. The first instance of the ordinary courts is split into local courts (Amtsgericht) for minor matters and regional courts (Landgericht).

Traditionally, each case was handled by three judges who were members of a 'chamber' (*Kammer)* at courts of first instance, or of a 'senate' (*Senat*) at appeal courts. This model has survived as a structural feature, although in practice, most cases are dealt with by one judge sitting alone. Exceptions are made for cases of special significance. Criminal cases are often dealt with by a bench of two judges.

Each court has a *Präsidium* consisting of the court president and a number of judges—between four and 10—elected by their colleagues. They decide annually on the composition of 'chambers' and 'senates' and on the

[2] U Schultz (2011) 'Legal Education in Germany' *RED, Revista de Educación y Derecho* 1–24, fn 4, at: revistes.ub.edu/index.php/RED.

distribution of work—a way of safeguarding the impartiality of the system and judicial independence. No cases of overt bias or bribery have been reported and disciplinary proceedings rarely lead to severe measures such as salary cuts or expulsion from office.

2.2. Women in the Judiciary: Statistical Evidence

The history of women in the judiciary is short, although in terms of the number of new appointees it has become a story of success. It was only at the beginning of the twentieth century that women were admitted as students of law at universities. The first women passed the first legal examination in 1912, accompanied by lengthy debates regarding their suitability for judicial office. They were regarded as too emotional and subjective as well as too fragile for the hard and responsible work awaiting them (Schultz, 1990: 319–59; 2003a: 271–91). In 1922, four years after the end of the First World War and the establishment of the democratic Weimar Republic, a Bill was passed granting women the right to be admitted into the 'administration of justice', ie, to the judiciary, prosecution and advocacy. However, the number of those taking advantage of this newly gained entitlement remained miniscule (Schultz, 2003a: 271–91). It was only in the 1970s that real change occurred. Since the early 1990s more women than men have studied law and already for about a decade the proportion of women taking their second state examination has been around 53 per cent.

The following table (table 1) illustrates the rapid rise of the share of women in judicial professions over the last two decades, with figures for advocates provided for comparison.

Table 1: Proportion of women in the legal professions

	Judges %	Public prosecutors %	Advocates %
1961	2.6	–	>2.0
1971	6.0	5.0	4.5
1981	13.0	11.0	8.0
1989	17.6 = 2109 of 17,627	17.6 = 661 of 3759	14.7 = 7960 of 54,108
1995	26.3	28.9	19.3
2001	27.7	30.9	25.3
2009	35.79 = 7195 of 20,101	38.71 = 1983 of 5122	31.08 = 46,736 of 150,377
2011	38.45 = 7848 of 20,411	41.03 = 2152 of 5246	32.04 = 49,872 of 155,679

Source: Official statistics, Federal Ministry of Justice, Federal Chamber of Advocates

The rise in the number of women between 1989 and 1995 was particularly striking, and then again around 2000. The slowing down in the second half of the 1990s can be attributed to an overall reduction in the number of new appointees. Developments over recent years have been breathtaking. On 1 January 2011, women's share of the number of probationary judges (ie, during their first three years in office) had risen to around 57 per cent and among public prosecutors to around 53 per cent. This has led to a corresponding rise in the number of women appointed to permanent positions. There is no significant difference between the sexes in terms of examination results, but more men than women with similar examination results apply for the more lucrative posts in the big law firms.

Among women, the judiciary is a much sought after employer, offering secure positions, high prestige, a good income, no gender-based income discrimination, social security and right to maternal and paternal leave matching that of the civil service, good chances of part-time work and a workload that is high but becomes manageable with growing routine. In addition, judges enjoy considerable workplace flexibility. In particular, sole judges at local courts (*Amtsgericht*) are only required to attend on days when they are in session—a most attractive proposition for women with children.

Figure 1 shows the distribution of judges across the various jurisdictions in Northrhine-Westfalia.

A slightly higher share of female judges in the first three jurisdictions compared with the other two can be explained by a number of factors. Social courts are the most recently created, and their expansion coincided with the steep rise in women appointees. Administrative courts have long enjoyed particularly high prestige and the reputation of selecting the best graduates. Here the higher share of women may be explained by the fact that prestige is frequently associated with masculinity, while feminisation is regarded as detrimental to status (Böge, 1994: 77ff; Schultz, 1990: 319–59; 2003a: 271–91). Financial courts are part of courts of second instance and have a different recruitment pattern.

Jurisdiction	%
Ordinary courts (civil and criminal)	76
Administrative courts	10
Social courts	6.5
Labour courts	4.5
Financial courts	3

Figure 1: Distribution of judges across jurisdictions in Northrhine-Westfalia

3. CAREERS IN THE JUDICIARY

3.1. Career Structure

Judges are appointed by the appeal courts.[3] The selection of judges and public prosecutors is based on second state examination results. On average, some 15 per cent of examination candidates achieve the results required. Today, personality factors are also tested in the recruitment procedure: professional expertise and competence, personal and social competence and leadership skills. Many are appointed directly following graduation; others start by working in industry or in the advocacy for a couple of years. There is a legal age limit for judicial appointment and in Northrhine-Westfalia this is around 35 years. Exceptions are possible but rare. After three years as probationers, judges are given permanent positions for life.

Public prosecution services as well as courts have institutional organisational structures—judges hold a status comparable to that of civil servants, although their rulings are independent in terms of their content—a feature tirelessly invoked by the judges themselves and guaranteed by the Constitution.[4] By contrast, public prosecutors work within a hierarchical system and are answerable to superiors.

Judges' careers start from judge at a court of first instance to judge at a court of appeal or presiding judge at a court of first instance (first career step) and to presiding judge at an appeal court (second career step). The latter positions are a prerequisite for a 'real' career, which leads to positions of director, president or vice-president of a court. However, as the title of 'judge' by definition presupposes active judicial functions, even those opting for a position more heavily orientated towards administrative duties are required to continue in some judicial capacity.

On their initial appointment, during the probationary period, judges are entrusted with various judicial functions at courts of first instance within their region. This is followed by an application for a permanent position. The Court President makes 'recommendations' that can also be interpreted as allocations to particular functions. Women tend to end up at local courts of first instance (*Amtsgericht*), in keeping with traditional views of women's abilities (Beck-Gernsheim, 1976) in family courts and general departments of the public prosecution service.[5]

[3] Judges at federal courts are elected.

[4] Art 97 s 1: 'Judges are independent and answerable only to the law'.

[5] Unfortunately, there is a lack of statistical data on the subject. On the gender-specific segregation in organisations, *cf* Allmendinger and Podsiadlowski (2001: 276–307).

After a minimum of five years into their permanent position[6] judges and prosecutors can be entered into the appeal court's 'list of potential candidates for promotion' (*Erprobungsliste*). For judges, a career then requires nine months' work in an appeal court 'senate' under the supervision of the presiding judge of the senate and a positive assessment on completion, for prosecutors at the appeal courts' prosecution service. This period is generally experienced as particularly stressful and nicknamed 'third state examination'.

Assessment marks play an important part in a person's career. During the probationary period, candidates are assessed after 6, 18 and 36 months, subsequently every 4 years, and on applying for career positions. Within a judge's life marks go up within a scale of 10:1 (and various sub-divisions). In order to speed up the process, a number of assessments on applications for career positions may be needed. Importantly, these marks do not reflect someone's qualities but that person's position on the promotion ladder. There is also the chance of doing a two-year stint as a candidate for promotion, especially in the Ministry of Justice.

In 2005, the Ministry of Justice issued highly detailed legal regulations on the conduct of assessment and the *Erprobung*. Although those judges responsible for personnel issues do offer information sessions, many members of the judiciary lack detailed knowledge of the process, especially as there are also unwritten rules creating differences in the way it is handled in the different court districts (that tend to have a 'culture' of their own). 'The justice system is a closely knit network', one of our female interviewees observed. For outsiders the career system is hardly transparent.[7]

R1	Basic position
R2	Presiding judge at a court of first instance
R3	Judge at an appeal court
R1–2	Director of a local court of first instance (*Amtsgericht*, ordinary jurisdiction)
R3–R5	President of a court of first instance
R5–R8	President of a court of appeal

Figure 2: Positions on the salary scale

[6] The length of the waiting period before being admitted to this procedure depends on candidates' marks leading up to it.

[7] An additional hurdle is created through the existence of a specific terminology.

3.2. The Hidden Structure

A career in the German judiciary depends on visibility and 'being asked'. Candidates apply on being encouraged because someone has been impressed with their performance and/or their personality. This may start as early as during their university studies, practical training or at interview for first appointment. To quote one person with personnel functions: 'However, being recognized and appreciated by one person isn't enough. One individual's impression needs broader support across the hierarchical spectrum'. A group of favoured candidates begins to crystallize, their chances consolidating during their time as probationers. 'Certain individuals create a buzz. That's an important criterion. A good reputation is something … that matters'. Coffee meetings in court play a considerable part in all this:

> For someone's name to crop up starts with such banalities as sitting down at 11 o'clock in the canteen. In those days there tended to be a hard core of colleagues who went to fetch a last cup of coffee from the canteen and then sat down to chat about this and that. I, too, enjoyed that … it makes such a difference. This way you get to know a lot of people. Problems, too. And if then you see that so and so gets things done, then her or his prospects start to rise.

The question is whether women stand the same chance as men of being noticed.

3.3. Women in Career Positions

At the time of this investigation, one of three presidents of ordinary courts of appeal (*Oberlandesgericht*) and two of three presidents of labour courts of appeal (*Landesarbeitsgericht*) in Northrhine-Westfalia were women. The administrative and social courts of appeal had male presidents. At first glance this might suggest that the gender distribution in leadership positions is fairly even. However, this is an optical illusion. For at the next level down there were few women, for example, only one out of 19 presidents of ordinary regional courts (*Landgericht*) was a woman.

The picture becomes even clearer from a longitudinal perspective. Between 2000 and 2010 the proportion of women in R3 and higher leadership positions had remained unchanged. Only at small (but not at larger) ordinary local courts of first instance had the share of women slightly increased. In categories R2 and R3 for the positions as presiding judges of 'chambers' or 'senates' the gender distribution was remarkably weighted in favour of men. This might be due to the fact that these posts include a leadership component and may therefore be regarded as more suited to men.

All 14 top positions (R3 and R4) in Northrhine-Westfalia's public prosecution service were held by men, while at the next level down (R2) 39 out of 208 (19 per cent) were women. (The overall proportion of women in the service is 39.9 per cent.) If one takes into account that the structure of the public prosecution service is even flatter than that for judges (only R1–R4) these figures are strikingly low.

All in all, these data show that there is no such thing as a 'trickle up effect'. Even though women only joined the professions in significant numbers in the last 25 years, simple arithmetical calculations based on the assumption of similar career progression for both sexes would suggest that the share of women in leading positions ought to have reached much higher levels than is actually the case.

4. CAREER FACTORS

With the German judicial hierarchy having a fairly flat structure, career opportunities are few and far between. Several of my interviewees reported having been warned from the start not to expect much in the way of promotion. This applies particularly to the ordinary jurisdiction because the bulk of all posts are at local courts of first instance *(Amtsgericht)* where four out of five of all female first instance judges of the ordinary courts are working. The move from there to a regional court (*Landgericht*) is rare, the two levels being separated by a kind of impermeable 'layer of clay'.

4.1. Soft Career Factors

Factors that help promotion include professional commitment beyond the call of duty, taking on special tasks (examinerships at state examinations, conducting seminars for candidates in practical training), volunteering for roles of responsibility in judicial self-government or being active in professional associations—all these difficult to fulfil for women (and men) with family duties.

One important precondition for a successful career is mobility within the court district, obviously more of a problem for women than men. Others include a stable home life and support from one's family. Many older men we spoke to still enjoyed a traditional marriage with wives wholly dedicated to home duties, thus freeing them for additional professional duties. A few women in higher positions had 'housemen', several were supported by their mothers. Some—rather more men than women—mentioned the fact that their partners had cut back on or even given up their own career ambitions.

Job satisfaction plays a significant part in career success and, as already shown in a study conducted in Germany in the early 1990s (Hassels and Hommerich, 1993) it is particularly strong among judges of both sexes. Ultimately, chance also plays its part, as conceded by the majority of interviewees at levels R2 and above, while examination results may or may not be of importance.

All this suggests the importance of availability for career success in the German judiciary, the proverbial 'being in the right place at the right time'. For top positions, certain political factors naturally also play a part.

4.2. Promotion Hurdle Number One: Administrative Experience

The first and foremost criterion for promotion in the German judicial system is administrative experience. The first opportunity for acquiring such experience occurs during one's time as probationer through periods of secondment to appeal courts. Once in a permanent position, judges can take over administrative duties at their court of first instance. A range of administrative functions are on offer, such as supervision of support staff, supervision of notaries, bailiffs and disciplinary and personnel matters.

This is an unregulated criterion giving court presidents a free hand in selecting candidates for promotion. To quote from an interview with a young female judge:

> [C]ertain people get into the administration ... That is, nobody really knows who will actually get in. Is it based purely on merit or not? ... One feels that there isn't a great deal one oneself can do, but there is someone from above making a request.

Once again, the question is whether such 'requests' relate as much to women as to men. A court president illustrated what is sometimes nicknamed 'the nose principle' by the example of career training for promising younger staff. 'Well, a kind of open circular was sent to all judges inviting applications from anyone interested'. In answer to our question of how he went about making a selection, he replied:

> Well, hmm, I actually started to wonder. Hardly anyone had put in an application to me. And on carefully listening around, someone said something that nearly knocked me over. He said, well, if it isn't the President who asks me to apply ... (laughter). In our institution people are used to being approached personally, especially if it is a matter of administrative duties.

Having only just survived the stress of law examinations, taking on such demanding duties represents yet another endurance test. Not only does it require combining normal judicial and administrative work, but it means the loss of flexitime, as administration requires constant presence at the workplace—a considerable drawback for those with family obligations. Nor does it help that there is no offer of systematic preparation for such administrative tasks. It is a matter of learning by doing and of hoping for support and guidance from colleagues, with further training only available once the task has been taken on—a case where experience has shown that women tend to be more reluctant than men to undertake such risks.

Those who take on such administrative tasks leave the familiar environment of coffee meetings with their colleagues and (albeit only temporarily) move over to join the president's circle. This may well act as a possible obstacle for developing self-confidence and a sense of belonging. Not surprisingly, judges and public prosecutors of both sexes need to ask themselves whether the move is actually worthwhile. After all, there are no financial benefits to be gained, and the option of part-time work hardly exists. Rumour has it that women in general are not interested in taking on administrative tasks. An internal survey conducted in 1999 in Northrhine-Westfalia on the professional situation of female judges and public prosecutors in their first jobs showed that around half of them expressed an interest in administrative duties, while only one out of four (ie, one-eighth of the total) had actually taken on (or been assigned to) any.

4.3. Promotion Hurdle Number Two: *Erprobung*

Most applicants for promotion are in their mid to late thirties when they face the next test, the period of probation at the appeal court (*Erprobung*). In Northrhine-Westfalia most will have to cope with a considerable commuting distance. They are expected to prove themselves through more than ordinary professional commitment—once again posing problems for those with family commitments. Also, after years of professional independence, they are working under supervision. Anecdotal evidence suggests that communication in higher court senates leaves a lot to be desired, praise is rare and regular feedback weak.

Admission to this process is based on performance *and* age. A number of younger women interviewees were critical of this approach:

> What I find really difficult in the judiciary is: there are people who kill themselves ... That may just be noted, but it is not rewarded ... I would prefer it if there were more stringent differentiations. One might say, there is someone who by seniority is younger, but (s)he has achieved this and that, copes regularly with a massive caseload, and puts a lot of effort into helping probationers. Let's simply give her/him precedence.

This trial period coincides with life's 'rush hour', an obstacle therefore for women with children. 'If you want to achieve anything here, that has to happen when you are between 30 and 40, and after that you can write off any career'. Young women also noted a paradox:

> What struck me is that many women enter the administration quite young, and then return to court service. There they get forgotten, or they become mothers.

> While with men, they are often taken into the administration at a later stage, so that in principle they can move smoothly from there into their trial period [at the appeal court]. That's quite different. They are physically present and then move on into the trial period or to the Ministry of Justice.

For over 20 years it has been possible to undergo this second probation in part-time form. But there are disadvantages: 'Well, from what I can see here, women working half-time definitely have to wait longer ... There are only two posts for part-time women'.

Our interviews showed that a not inconsiderable number of women (some men as well) decide to forego this next step. After all, job satisfaction, a prestigious position and a decent income can be had even at R1 level. Hassels and Hommerich, in their representative study of 1993, found that a third of women were aiming at a career, a third was undecided and a third wanted to forego promotion.

The question arises whether this second period of probation is an effective tool. It is meant to show whether a judge has the ability, suitability and professional performance to qualify for the first step on the career ladder. This is rather a formalistic rationale. According to our interviewees, the real aim is to perform a qualitative test of candidates' professional performance, ie, their performance as judges. Quite clearly another objective is to achieve a further homogenization of judges and to strengthen their commitment to the aims of the organisation. Younger judges in particular are critical of the additional workload connected with probation.

4.4. Promotion Criterion: Assessment

'But performance must be up to scratch', our interviewees declared unanimously. So, marks are linked to performance. But is assessment always gender neutral? According to the 2006 'Action Plans for the Promotion of Women', results for women during (initial) probation and in their first post were slightly lower than those for men. This is amazing as access to the judiciary is based on examination results, which must have been comparable for men and women. The impression is conveyed—underpinned by research on assessment of women in organisations—that the assessment of their performance as judges is affected by stereotypes and, most particularly, those of gender (Schreyögg, 1998: 1–32; Krumpholz, 2005: 23–27. See also, Höher and Höher).[8]

Assessments on application for career posts are used as a controlling mechanism in the filling of posts. A judge handling personnel issues

[8] P Höher and F Höher, *Personalprozesse—(K)Ein diskriminierungsfreier Raum?* at: www.hoeher-team.de/wp-content/uploads/2007/07/diskriminierungsfreie_diagnostik1.pdf.

commented: 'It can happen that the allocation of marks is partly used not as a function of assessing a candidate's achievement but as a tool in the distribution of posts'. That means, they are not allocated purely on the basis of individual achievement, but are geared to the requirements of a planned sequence of promotions.

Judges at the local courts of first instance (*Amtsgericht*), are assessed by the presidents of their regional court of first instance (*Landgericht*) which may be at a considerable distance from the local court.[9] The fact that the president has hardly any personal knowledge of the many judges in the district is obviously a drawback, particularly for the many female candidates at the local courts.

Although the general principle of using marks to steer the promotion process is accepted, specific assessments are often criticised, and the selection of one candidate over another formally appealed against. Here, too, it would be interesting to find out whether any gendered factors are involved, for example, if men more readily start court proceedings than women.

5. THE PROMOTION PROCESS

As described, applications for promotion are steered. One president commented: 'One doesn't normally simply apply, but does so following personal encouragement, along the lines of "Would you like to do this?"'. This also means that others may be recommended not to apply or to withdraw their applications. This process starts with the application for a first permanent post.

In the placement process a report on the candidates is produced. If two applicants have the same mark, their details in the reports are being 'squeezed' for more information, although, on the surface, the reports don't say very much. 'It is frequently much more informative to read between the lines. This is done with considerable care'. The quota regulation as per § 7 section 2 of Northrhine-Westfalia's Equality Law which is to be applied if two candidates are of equal qualification, suitability and achievement, only becomes relevant after this initial sifting process, and is therefore hardly ever used. The team only heard of one case where it had worked in favour of a female candidate. The 'squeezing' is done until differences have been discovered. Thus, the quota regulation fails to do its job as the important tool in the promotion of women for which it has been designed.

[9] With the exception of judges at the four big local courts in Northrhine Westfalia which have a court president.

A sample of 20 reports on the allocation of posts analysed by the team showed up a number of peculiarities. On average, female applicants for promotion presented better marks than their male colleagues, as they apparently refrained from applying unless their achievements were higher. Possibly, they were only 'invited' if they had these marks, or they were simply more cautious. Strikingly, women were proportionately stronger than men in terms of meeting the range of employability required for promotion. However, there were no noticeable systematic differences in assessment reports regarding the arguments for promotion for either sex.

Promotions matched the president's proposals. Interviewees repeatedly stressed this 'presidential power' resulting from the combined effect of promotion proposals, the selection for administrative duties and assessments. Regarding the filling of higher leadership posts, recent years have brought a series of appeals (mostly from men) against rejections in favour of another applicant, some of which have been widely reported in the press.

6. CAREER OBSTACLES FOR WOMEN

So what are the career obstacles for women?

6.1. Work–life Balance

Judicial work is demanding, making it difficult to achieve a reasonable work–life balance, especially in cases where there is the dual burden of work and home. An elderly female judge observed laconically that she only coped with her work by 'doing without a private life—my work is my hobby'. Another interviewee stated:

> One could have enjoyed one's children rather more. Occasionally I allowed myself the treat of ambling to the kindergarten and helping my children to make a lantern for St Martin's Day, thinking: you can't always be absent. But what I had to neglect was this unrushed pleasure of being with my young children.

6.2. Motherhood

The obstacle par excellence for a professional career is motherhood. To quote one comment, echoed again and again by younger women judges:

> I gave formal notice of my pregnancy. The reaction was, 'What a shame, so you can't make use of your administrative experience'. I responded by saying that I wouldn't quite see things in this light. Thereupon I was told, 'No, no, don't misunderstand me. I am sure it has been a very valuable experience for you'. Well, I have to confess that I had to swallow hard. And subsequently there was

> no further mention regarding any further such tasks coming my way. At some point I raised the subject saying ... that I thought even with a child a career in the judiciary should be possible. Whereupon I was told that this would, of course, be much more difficult now. For normally the next step would be to be seconded to an appeal court and there to be allocated to, for instance, the administration. But that, I was warned immediately, would not be possible with a half post and a child, the automatic assumption being that one would only return to a half post. I was never really asked whether I might have different plans ... If I had been offered something concrete—that certainly wasn't the case. If anything, it was the contrary. I rather felt that my pregnancy clinched it. That was roughly how I interpreted it.

Another female judge said:

> When I left [for maternity leave] I was told, 'Well, you just get on with having your baby' ... And then I started again, and there was really nothing to choose from. I wasn't actually told where I would end up, but simply allocated to this chamber, which saddened and annoyed me somewhat. And since then nothing further has really happened.

No doubt, the president basically meant well. But generally speaking, women with children cease to count in career terms. Such stereotypical categorisations lead to loss of potential, the phenomenon called 'leaky pipeline'.

6.3. Part-time Work

The other significant obstacle to a career is part-time work, sometimes identified with part-time commitment, more generally regarded as adding to the workload of colleagues. A male judge who had opted for part-time work for some time recollected:

> I was working part-time three days a week. A colleague said to me, 'Don't you think that I am going to deal with your files on the other two days'. I remember this as if it had happened today, it annoyed me no end, I would never have expected this.

Although part-time work has by now almost become the norm in the judiciary (a number of female interviewees called the judiciary a paradise for mothers) part-time work for women is seen as a signal that they are now going to give priority to family duties. As one interviewee stressed:

> [T]he interests of half-time women are not really taken into account [by the *Präsidium*] because no one sitting there has an interest in such matters ... On the contrary, I have heard rumours that the prevailing view is rather that these mums have to be fitted in somehow. Which makes me think it would be nice if we were seen in a different light.

Men in the judiciary who take advantage of 'months for fathers' and work part-time can have wholly different experiences. The male judge quoted above reported that:

> I was an exotic creature and ultimately benefitted from this status ... had a man's bonus. Was then allocated to a 'chamber' with three women, was pampered and spoilt, all of them thought this was cool ... Shortly afterwards, I was elected a member of the Präsidium, where I was regarded as representing part-time women. From then on, meetings were held in the morning.

Part-time work is seen as an obstacle to taking on administrative duties. Leadership tasks, where total dedication and overtime work are expected, are practically incompatible with working part-time. Job sharing happens very rarely, commented on by one woman judge as short-sighted:

> We recently held a judicial staff meeting (*Richterversammlung*)—civil law judges. And someone raised that issue saying that it was difficult. And presumably there is no desire to create half 'chambers', as this would require additional resources as well as additional organisation. Of course, I am not wholly familiar with the details, and perhaps I fail to see all that is relevant, but looking at it from the outside I do think it rather short-sighted. Once the structures have been set up, it would pay off because the number of half posts is bound to rise over the years. And surely they would fill these 'chambers'. And even if they, at some stage, decide to return full-time, they will be replaced by others. And, it's a pity because it is just these 'chambers' which we have at the moment, let me call them 'women's chambers', these halves, they work extremely well.

6.4. Discrimination

'There is no such thing as discrimination', 'discrimination is a thing of the past', 'possible as a rare exception'—these were recurring comments. Judges are objective and impartial, committed to the principle of equality. There were minor concessions:

> I do think it's sexist if people say things like 'Oh, now she, too, is broody', or 'Who, then, has to pick up the pieces at work? Obviously, that's us men again'. You can hear that sort of thing quite often, especially from younger male colleagues. And I can't help feeling that it isn't just a joke but they really think that way.

6.5. Partners' Careers

In the case of 'dual career couples' one's partner may represent an obstacle (Schmidt, 1993) especially where there are no devoted grandparents close by able and willing to look after children. Tradition has it that men's careers take precedence, although we did come across a few judges and public prosecutors who had, at least for certain periods, taken the backseat in favour of their wives.

6.6. Competition among Women

Women among themselves can place an obstacle in the way of each other's careers.

This happens, first when in certain areas they have to compete with each other, while other areas are left to men (Bischof-Köhler, 1997: 209–41). However, documentation available to us showed no clear indication of gender-specific duties (such as by legal field) within individual court instances, although we did occasionally hear some anecdotal evidence to that effect.

Secondly, some women fail to behave in a sisterly fashion if their own life plan differs from that of others. A woman in a leadership position who had internalised the traditional male model of leadership regarded quite a few of her female colleagues as unsuited for a career:

> There are simply types who may really be unsuited for leadership positions. I can think of many persons who embody what is 'typically female'—a little reserved, a little shy, and, of course, adaptable, but lacking that, let's call it, 'inner strength' needed in order to do something of that kind ... There are women like that.

Women generally hesitate in supporting other women. The older generation in particular have difficulty understanding younger ones if they choose not to follow the same hard and self-denying path as they themselves did (Schultz, 1990: 319–59; 2003a: 271–91)

6.7. Gender Stereotypes

Men and women in the judiciary are unable to free themselves from stereotypical perceptions. They themselves have them as do those they come across. This has a direct impact on the leadership structure which follows a male model. 'Leadership posts are a man's game' said one of our female interviewees. From the start, women are expected to have lower career ambitions than men, they are regarded as less suited for a career due to 'typically female qualities' and, as shown above, are impeded in their career due to the division of labour in marriage and family that is modelled on traditional gender roles.[10] They are 'the Other' who might endanger the traditional institutional image (Boigeol, 2003: 401–18).

[10] On the theory of division of labour and gender construction, *cf* Wetterer (2002) 'Gender at Work'.

6.8. Do Women Judges Judge Differently?[11]

All interviewees stressed that women in the judiciary are just as efficient as men. They laughed at the old prejudices that women are unable to judge objectively or that they are too soft. After all, on entering the profession women and men are equally qualified in terms of examination results. There was general agreement that women do not judge differently or better than their male colleagues—with a few exceptions. An elderly court president thought that, as an inveterate football fan he might, in appropriate cases, reach conclusions that were different from those of his female colleagues. One female court president thought that the presence of female judges had enlivened the judiciary; however, following up this statement by the observation that what was now needed was an increase in the appointment of efficient young men.

6.9. Inner Career Obstacles and Career Renunciation

It is true that women, on the whole, see careers differently from men. Here we observe the impact of role models and the socialisation process. Traditionally women are faced with different expectations from men. That affects the way they see themselves and restricts their scope for action. For a positive view of the world, women and girls depend much less on their careers than their male counterparts. Their social environment attributes greater significance to beauty, kindness and fulfilling their role as mothers, than to professional achievement. Expectations are created and cause women to attempt to meet them; and it is true, women do have a more clearly defined orientation towards the family. Human resources research shows that, in principle, although women's motivation to succeed in a career is just as strong as men's, they have lower perceived efficacy (Wiswede, 2007). Women's perception of self-efficacy, their trust in their own abilities, is also lower than that of men (Bandura, 1997). Besides, they are inclined to hide their light under a bushel, not wishing to appear superior to others. As one female judge observed:

> Well, that's a kind of men-women thing. I have noticed that again and again. We women have to accept that we sometimes lack self-confidence. I always find it fascinating how men can manage to look as if, through some minute idea, they had just newly invented the wheel, and how they present themselves. While women, if they have a good idea, start off by saying 'I've got an idea, but it may

[11] *Cf* Schultz (2003b: 295–321; 2005: 93–131) and my contribution to 'Do German Judges Need Gender Education?' in this volume.

not be worth a lot', or something like that. Women are, I think, made to be much more reserved and hide their achievements, thereby standing in their own way.

A female colleague commented: 'Men are better at showing that they are good at something, never mind whether that's actually true or not'. That is why women more frequently need to be encouraged. As one president stressed, 'One just needs to go up to women and say, how about it? Of course, women then need to be prepared to do it. But perhaps they need a little more wooing than men'.

7. RESULTS

This research project—located between the sociology of organisations and of professions—uses the example of the judiciary to demonstrate that organisations are gendered in the ways they are (Acker, 1991: 162–79; Wilz, 2002; 2008: 123–36) and how gender works at work (Wetterer, 2002). The report represents a complex organisational study. Opaque structures have been made transparent—which posed problems for the key players in the study. However, there was no other way in which it could have identified the factors that either advance or impede a career. Although the hidden structures are known, those who have to take the decisions did not wish to see them documented. It was therefore necessary to ask what their expectations regarding the research results had been, and whether all they wanted to achieve was to have it confirmed that women have lower career ambitions than men and that all that was required was improvements in public childcare. On the other hand, there was enthusiastic applause when the project was presented to a wider audience, including judges concerned with personnel issues, the latter expressing delight in finding that what they had always known was now at last being discussed openly.

Careers in the judiciary are a game with complex and highly differentiated rules. A career requires conforming to the system. A male judge commented: 'You think that you are independent and can structure your work accordingly, but in most things you are pretty well governed by authority, superiors, the president of the court'. In this respect judges, too, correspond to the ideal of the Prussian public servant.

A career in the German judiciary cannot be planned. The key players are the presidents assisted by judges handling personnel matters. Careers are predetermined through communication among court presidents. They are the gatekeepers and co-opt those that continue and stabilise the system. Their personnel policies are oriented on the ideal of complete availability and an unbroken career, ie, an ideal more suited to the lives of men than of women. They allocate places and career chances through the tap on the shoulder while frequently blocking, in a spirit of caring patriarchy, access to women with family duties, thereby establishing a gender hierarchy (Wetterer, 2002). Women who have children are assumed to have abandoned any career ambition.

Nevertheless, all the actors in the project—women and men alike—had a very positive attitude towards the German judicial system, combining high professional satisfaction with gratitude and loyalty. For most of the interviewees, gender was not perceived as a key criterion for a career.[12] It always appeared as an impediment in connection with family duties. Institutionally, the problem of combining family and work is rather regarded as one to be resolved by individuals. It is up to each of them to decide which way to jump—career or family. However, problems of childcare due to a lack of nursery school places are classified as concerning society at large, ie, the state or the local community and not the institution.

Gender-specific asymmetries of career structures are located below the surface[13] and are not easily identifiable. However, on closer inspection it becomes clear that the allocation of positions does not always correspond to an individual's achievement, and that it disadvantages women.

This report led to a catalogue of measures designed to modernise the system of personnel recruitment and selection, to iron out perceived deficits and to promote women's access to leadership positions.

8. REFERENCES

Acker, J (1991) 'Hierarchies, Jobs, Bodies: A Theory of Gendered Organizations' in J Lorber and SA Farrell (eds), *The Social Construction of Gender* (Newbury Park, Sage).

Allmendinger, J and Podsiadlowski, A (2001) 'Segregation in Organisationen and in Arbeitsgruppen' in B Heintz (ed), *Geschlechtersoziologie* (Opladen, Westdeutscher Verlag).

Bandura, A (1997) *Self-efficacy: The Exercise of Control* (New York, Freeman).

Beck-Gernsheim, E (1976) *Der geschlechtsspezifische Arbeitsmarkt. Zur Ideologie und Realität von Frauenberufen* (Frankfurt am Main, Aspekte Verlag).

Benschop, Y and Doorewaard, H (1998) 'Covered by Equality: The Gender Subtext of Organizations 19 *Organization Studies* 787.

Bischof-Köhler, D (1997) 'Geschlechtstypische Besonderheiten im Konkurrenzverhalten: Evolutionäre Grundlagen und entwicklungspsychologische Fakten' in R Wunderer and P Dick (eds), *Frauen im Management* (Neuwied, Luchterhand Verlag).

Böge, S (1994) 'Ungleiche Chancen, gleiches Recht zu vertreten: Zur beruflichen Situation von Frauen in der Juristenschaft' in RH Stein and A Wetterer (eds),

[12] On the gender subtext in organisations, *cf* Benschop and Doorewaard (1998: 787–805).

[13] On gender asymmetries in organisations, *cf* Kuhlmann, Kutzner, Riegraf and Wilz (2002: 221–49).

Studierende und studierte Frauen: Ein ost-westdeutscher Vergleich (Kassel, Jenior und Pressler).

Boigeol, A (2003) 'Male Strategies in the Face of the Feminisation of a Profession: The Case of the French Judiciary' in U Schultz and G Shaw (eds), *Women in the World's Legal Professions* (Oxford, Hart Publishing).

Gildemeister, R and Wetterer, A (eds) (2007) *Erosion oder Reproduktion geschlechtlicher Differenzierungen. Widersprüchliche Entwicklungen in professionalisierten Berufsfeldern und Organisationen* (Münster, Westfälisches Dampfboot).

Hartmann, A (1999) 'Integration durch Marginalisierung? Eine empirische Analyse der beruflichen Situation von Richterinnen und Staatsanwältinnen im deutsch-französischen Vergleich' (unpublished Master's thesis, Tübingen).

Hassels, A and Hommerich, C (1993) *Frauen in der Justiz* (Köln, Bundesanzeiger).

Krumpholz, D (2005) 'Wahrnehmung von Frauen bei Einstellung und Beurteilung' 5 *GiP* 23.

Kuhlmann, E, Kutzner, E, Riegraf, B and Wilz, SM (2002) 'Organisationen und Professionen als Produktionsstätten von Geschlechter(a)symmetrie' in E Schäfer, B Fritzsche and C Nagode (eds), *Geschlechterverhältnisse im sozialen Wandel* (Opladen, Leske and Budrich).

Kvale, S (1982) *Hochschulprüfung und Herrschaft. Hochschulprüfungen zwischen Ritual und Rationalisierung* (Weinheim, Beltz).

Rudek, A (2012) '*Institution und Initiation: Soziologische Schlaglichter auf die Juristische Staatsprüfung*' in T Kuhn, H Putzke and U Kramer (eds), *Fehler im Jurastudium Ausbildung und Prüfung* (Stuttgart, Boorberg).

Schmidt, M (1993) *Karrierefrauen und Partnerschaft. Sozialpsychologische Aspekte der Beziehung zwischen karriereambitionierten Frauen und ihren Lebenspartnern* (Münster, Waxmann).

Schreyögg, F (1998) 'Zum Einfluss der Geschlechtsstereotypen auf die Beurteilung der Arbeitsleistung' 1 *OSC, Organisationsberatung und Supervision* 1.

Schultz, U (1990) 'Wie männlich ist die Juristenschaft?' in U Battis and U Schultz (eds), *Frauen im Recht* (Heidelberg, CF Müller).

—— (2003a) 'The Status of Women Lawyers in Germany' in U Schultz and G Shaw (eds), *Women in the World's Legal Professions* (Oxford, Hart Publishing).

—— (2003b) 'Women Lawyers in Germany: Perception and Construction of Femininity' in *Women in the World's Legal Professions* (Oxford, Hart Publishing).

—— (ed) (2004) 'Richten Richterinnen richtiger? Zur Frage, ob Frauen die juristische Berufspraxis verändern' in *Frauenbilder. Reader für die Aktionswochen der kommunalen Gleichstellungsbeauftragten 2005* (Ministry of Health, Social Matters, Women and Family NRW, Düsseldorf).

—— (2005) 'Regulated Deregulation—The Case of the German Legal Profession' in W Felstiner, *Reorganization and Resistance: Legal Professions Confront a Changing World* (Oxford, Hart Publishing).

—— (2008) 'Legal Education in Germany—An Ever (Never?) Ending Story of Resistance to Change' in V Olgiati (ed), *Higher Legal Culture and Postgraduate Legal Education in Europe* (Naples, Edizioni Scientifiche Italiane).

—— (2012) 'Frauen in Führungspositionen der Justiz. Untersuchung von Frauenkarrieren in den Justizbehörden in Nordrhein-Westfalen' *Deutsche Richterzeitung* 9.

Schultz, U, Peppmeier, I and Rudek, A (2011) *Frauen in Führungspositionen der Justiz. Eine Untersuchung der Bedingungen von Frauenkarrieren in den Justizbehörden in Nordrhein-Westfalen.* Projektbericht (Hagen, Institut für Geschlechterforschung und Gleichstellungsrecht und –politik).

Schultz, U and Shaw, G (eds) (2003) *Women in the World's Legal Professions* (Oxford, Hart Publishing).

Wetterer, A (1993) *Professionalisierung und Geschlechterhierarchie. Vom kollektiven Frauenausschluß zur Integration mit beschränkten Möglichkeiten* (Kassel, Jenior und Pressler).

—— (2002) *Arbeitsteilung und Geschlechterkonstruktion. 'Gender at Work' in theoretischer und historischer Perspektive* (Konstanz, UVK Verlag).

Wilz, SM (2002) *Organisation und Geschlecht. Strukturelle Bindungen und kontingente Kopplungen* (Opladen, Leske and Budrich).

—— (2008) 'Die "Leistung" des Geschlechts. Zur sozialen Praxis von Geschlechterdifferenzierung und Leistungsbewertung in Organisationen' in K Dröge, K Marrs and W Menz (eds), *Wandel des Leistungsprinzips und die Entwicklung der Arbeit* (Berlin, Edition Sigma).

Wiswede, G (2007) *Einführung in die Wirtschaftspsychologie* (Stuttgart, UTB).

2.3

Women Judges and Magistrates in Kenya: Challenges, Opportunities and Contributions

WINIFRED KAMAU

Abstract

Women in Kenya are under-represented in the legal sphere, both as professionals in legal practice and in the judiciary. In particular, they have been excluded or marginalised in the higher courts and are more concentrated in the subordinate courts which have lower status and less attractive terms and conditions. There are serious structural and institutional barriers to women's selection and upward mobility in the judiciary, which need to be addressed. It is laudable that despite women being a minority in the Kenyan judiciary, they have made their mark in terms of articulation of gender issues within the judiciary, particularly through the Kenya Women Judges Association and the Jurisprudence of Equality project. The Constitution of 2010 has introduced important reforms in the structure and organisation of the judiciary, which hold out much promise for women's advancement in the judiciary and have already produced some positive results. However, there is need for more concrete policies and measures specifically targeted at ensuring gender equality and equity in the Kenyan courts.

1. INTRODUCTION

IT IS NOW broadly accepted that gender diversity in the judiciary is desirable. A rich body of scholarship has developed offering a number of rationales for diversity. These include the need for equal participation, namely that equal participation of men and women in the justice system is an inherent and essential feature of a democracy without which the judiciary cannot enjoy public confidence and legitimacy. Secondly, it has been argued that women bring to the judiciary a different perspective based on their different life experiences, attitudes and values, which add richness and texture to the judicial system. Diversity has also been advocated in order to counter-balance the traditional perception of judging as a 'masculine' enterprise (Malleson, 2003; Bratton and Spill, 2002; Feenan, 2008). This chapter examines women's participation in the Kenyan judiciary and highlights the factors accounting for women's under-representation and marginalisation in the judicial sphere, particularly at the highest levels. The chapter begins by tracing the historical roots of the problem in terms of legal and educational policies that have constituted barriers to women's access to legal education. The chapter discusses the structure and organisation of the Kenyan judiciary and looks at institutional and structural issues that pose challenges to women's recruitment and promotion into the judiciary. It takes into account current developments and promise brought about by the passing of the Constitution of 2010. Finally, the chapter highlights the contributions that women judges and magistrates have made to the administration of justice in Kenya, particularly in the area of gender equity.

2. HISTORICAL LEGAL BACKGROUND

Kenya became a British Protectorate in 1895, was declared a British colony in 1920 and continued under British colonial rule until 1963 when it gained independence. Colonial rule saw the introduction of the English legal system into the territory. The colonial government established a racially stratified legal system, one for Africans and the other for non-Africans. English style courts comprising the High Court and subordinate courts staffed by British judges and magistrates were established for the non-African population. Africans were served by 'native' courts or tribunals staffed by African traditional leaders or colonial nominees applying customary law. In addition, colonial administrators in the form of district commissioners also acted as magistrates in the African courts. It should be noted that lawyers were not allowed audience in the African court.

Legal education for non-Africans was non-existent during the colonial period as the administration adopted an overtly racist education policy which severely restricted opportunities for higher education for Africans.[1] As such there were no openings to study law in Kenya, or anywhere in Africa. The only available opportunities were in the United Kingdom and India, but the colonial government had a policy of not providing scholarships for Africans to study law. As few Africans had the private means to educate their children abroad, the legal profession was dominated by Kenyans of English and Indian descent.[2] During the colonial period, most

[1] The colonial policy was to provide only such education as to equip Africans with the skills necessary to provide a productive menial class as well as a cadre to support the administration as clerks and messengers, ie, to effect the policy of indirect rule.

[2] In 1968, of the 292 practising advocates, there were only 11 Africans compared with 224 Asians and 57 Europeans. None of these were women (Ghai and McAuslan, 1970: 403).

of the judicial officers were British, and all were men. Hence, at independence there was no professional African cadre of judicial officers who were trained lawyers. In 1967, the dual court structure was dismantled and a unified court system established.[3]

In 1961, following the recommendations of the Denning Committee on Legal Education for Africans, a law faculty was set up in Dar-es-Salaam University College, a constituent college of the University of East Africa, to provide legal training for African students from that region. In Kenya, a faculty of law was established at the University of Nairobi in 1970. This remained the only law faculty until 1994 when a second faculty was opened at Moi University.[4]

The participation of Kenyan women in the legal profession and the judiciary must be viewed against the backdrop of colonial policy concerning African education as well as prevailing attitudes towards women. While the general African population was disadvantaged in terms of legal education, the position of women was even worse. From the beginning of colonial rule, education for Africans was seen as education for men, as men were regarded as the primary source of labour. Hence, there were very few schools for girls, and the enrolment rate for girls was low and retention rates were even lower. There was sex stratification in the curriculum, with girls taking different subjects from boys.[5] The official policy was that girls should concentrate on the three B's—baby, bath and broom—to prepare them for their future roles as wives and mothers. Careers for women were therefore severely constrained and were restricted to teaching, nursing, social services and secretarial work (Ngugi, 1986).

Women's legal training was adversely affected by the general constraints in the education sector. The low enrolment and retention rates in secondary school hampered their eligibility to enter university and study law. This was more so because the entry qualifications for law faculties are among the highest. By 1980, there were only 35 women admitted to the Kenyan Bar.[6] The first woman to establish a law practice (in 1978) was Kalpana Rawal (now a judge). By the mid-1980s, the number of women admitted to study law at the university had increased significantly, though women were still in the minority.[7] This trend has continued, and in the last few years the number

[3] Vide Judicature Act (Cap 8), Magistrate's Courts Act (Cap 10).

[4] Kenya School of Law had been established in 1963 to provide legal training for non-graduates. It is now concerned with postgraduate training prior to admission to the Roll of Advocates. Several other law faculties in both public and private universities have in the 2000s been established.

[5] Girls were offered courses in domestic science, cookery and needlework, while boys were taught carpentry and metal work.

[6] Source: Law Society of Kenya.

[7] In 1986, there were 158 female law students at the University of Nairobi out of a total of 389. Source: Office of the Registrar, University of Nairobi.

of women graduating from university law schools has outstripped that of men.[8] The increase is attributable to enhanced access to secondary and tertiary education for girls, and the fact that law is an arts-based course; girls in Kenya tend to perform much better in the arts than in the sciences. In particular, the rise of parallel degree (Module II) courses at universities, where self-financing students are able to attend classes in the evenings and weekends, has contributed significantly to the opening up of access to university education. However, the population of women advocates is still quite low at 35.5 per cent.[9]

3. THE CONSTITUTION OF KENYA, 2010

Kenya acquired a new Constitution, which was promulgated on 27 August 2010 after a referendum. The Constitution of 2010 constitutes a watershed and promises a new dawn for democracy, rule of law and human rights, with positive implications for women. The new Constitution, which is the supreme law, has a number of important provisions which are of relevance to issues of gender and the judiciary.

First, the Constitution sets out national values and principles of governance, which are to form the foundation of the country as a democratic state and are to be binding on all persons, specifically state organs and state officers and public officers. These values include human dignity, equity, social justice, inclusiveness, equality, non-discrimination and protection of the marginalised, among others.[10] The Constitution also sets out values, which apply to all state organs. These values and principles include high standards of professional ethics, fair competition and merit as the basis of appointments and promotions, subject to diversity of Kenya's communities and affording of adequate and equal opportunities for appointment, training and advancement, at all levels of the public service for men and women, members of all ethnic groups and persons with disabilities.[11]

Further, the Constitution has a comprehensive Bill of Rights, which contains important equality and non-discrimination clauses. Article 27

[8] Statistics from the Kenya School of Law's postgraduate Advocates Training Programme shows a consistent upward trend in women's enrolment levels since 2008. In 2008, women made up 51.8% of the total student population; in 2011, women comprised 60.8% (512 women out of a total of 875 students). Source: Kenya School of Law, Academic Registry Office. These figures are significant as the Kenya School of Law is the only institution that provides professional legal training for law school graduates. Graduates of the school therefore go directly into the pool of qualified advocates.

[9] There are 2917 women advocates compared with 5240 men advocates registered with the Law Society of Kenya. There are 856 advocates whose gender is undeclared. Source: Law Society of Kenya, Roll Summary by Gender, at: lsk.or.ke.

[10] Art 10.

[11] Art 232.

provides for equality before the law, right to equal treatment and equal benefit of the law including the political, economic, social and cultural spheres. There is prohibition of discrimination on specified grounds, which include sex, pregnancy, marital status and dress, among others.[12] Article 27 also recognises the principle of affirmative action and obliges the state to take legislative and other measures, including affirmative action programmes and policies designed to redress any disadvantage suffered by individuals or groups because of past discrimination. Women are regarded as a disadvantaged category of people.[13]

Another important principle is the 'one-third' gender rule, whereby not more than two-thirds of members of elective or appointive bodies should be of the same gender. The state is to take legislative and other measures to implement this principle, which is intended to ensure a minimum of one-thirds representation of women in public offices.[14] The Constitution further provides that the general principles of international law and any treaty or convention ratified by Kenya shall form part of the law of Kenya.

The Constitution contains specific provisions regarding appointment of judges, including higher qualifications and more objective eligibility criteria. The principles that should guide the Judicial Service Commission in the performance of its functions are competitiveness and transparent processes of appointment of judicial officers and other staff of the judiciary as well as the promotion of gender equality. The Constitution further provides for the vetting of current judges and magistrates by a vetting board to ensure high ethical and professional standards among judicial officers.[15]

The upshot of these constitutional provisions is that the public service, including the judiciary, can no longer operate in a 'business as usual' mode, and that legislation, policies and processes must be put in place to effect and implement constitutional imperatives. This, as will be seen below, has already led to significant changes in the composition and operations of the judiciary, with important ramifications for women.

4. THE KENYAN JUDICIARY: STRUCTURE AND ORGANISATION

The current structure and organisation of the Kenyan judiciary is set out and governed by Chapter 10 of the Constitution of 2010. The constitutional provisions are supplemented by new statutes, notably the Judicial

[12] Other prohibited grounds of discrimination are: race, health status, ethnic or social origin, colour, age, disability, religion, conscience, belief, culture, language or birth.
[13] See definition of 'marginalised' group' in Art 260.
[14] Art 27(8).
[15] s 23 of Sixth Schedule.

Service Act,[16] the Vetting of Judges and Magistrates Act and the Supreme Court Act,[17] in addition to existing legislation.[18] Under the Constitution of 2010, the judiciary consists of superior courts and subordinate courts. The Chief Justice is the head of the judiciary, while the Deputy Chief Justice is the deputy head.[19]

4.1. Superior Courts

The superior courts are the Supreme Court, Court of Appeal, the High Court and special courts with the status of the High Court mandated by the Constitution to deal with employment and labour relations and environment and land matters.[20] Superior courts are courts of record and their decisions are binding in accordance with the doctrine of *stare decisis*.[21] These courts are presided over by judges who enjoy security of tenure, subject to retirement age.[22] Judges can only be removed on limited grounds through an elaborate mechanism involving a tribunal.[23] In addition to security of tenure, judges enjoy superior terms of service, including salary and leave entitlements, official vehicles, drivers, housing and security.

The superior courts are arranged hierarchically, with the Supreme Court being the highest court in the land. It should be noted that this is the first time that Kenya has had a Supreme Court. This court has exclusive original jurisdiction to hear and determine disputes relating to presidential elections, as well as appellate jurisdiction to hear appeals from the Court of Appeal and other courts. The Supreme Court consists of the Chief Justice (President of the Court), Deputy Chief Justice (Deputy President) and five other

[16] No 1 of 2011.

[17] No 2 of 2011 and No 7 of 2011 respectively.

[18] Notably the Judicature Act (Cap 8), the Magistrate's Court Act (Cap 10) and the Kadhi's Court Act (Cap 11).

[19] Art 161, Constitution.

[20] Art 162. The Industrial Court Act, No 20 of 2011 and the Environment and Land Court Act, No 19 of 2011 have been passed.

[21] This is a common law doctrine which requires that previous decisions of superior courts are binding on lower courts.

[22] The term of the Chief Justice has now been limited to a maximum of 10 years, subject to the retirement age. Judges will now retire at the age of 70 but have the option of earlier retirement on attaining the age of 65 years. Judges may now also resign from office on giving notice to the President.

[23] The grounds for removal from office of a judge include inability to perform the functions of office arising from physical or mental incapacity, breach of a judicial code of conduct (to be prescribed by Parliament), bankruptcy, incompetence or gross misconduct or misbehaviour. Such removal may be initiated only by the Judicial Service on its own motion or on the petition of any person to the Judicial Service Commission. The President may then appoint a tribunal to inquire into the matter and the Tribunal's recommendations are binding on the President, subject to a right of appeal to the Supreme Court.

judges.[24] It should be noted that the first appointee to the post of Deputy Chief Justice, Nancy Baraza, is a woman. Of the other five judges, only one is a woman. Hence out of a total of seven judges, only two are women; this falls short of the one-third gender principle.[25]

The Court of Appeal is the second highest court in Kenya. It consists of not less than 12 judges. The President of the Court of Appeal is elected by the judges in that Court from among themselves. The Court has jurisdiction to hear appeals from the High Court and any other court or tribunal prescribed by an Act of Parliament.[26] Hence the Court of Appeal has only appellate jurisdiction and cannot act as a court of first instance. It should be noted that as at the promulgation of the Constitution of 2010, there was no woman in the Court of Appeal. Since then, a number of women have been appointed to this court.[27]

The High Court is the third highest court in the land. The number of judges in this court is to be prescribed by Parliament. The Principal Judge of the High Court is to be elected by the judges of this court. The High Court has the widest jurisdiction among the superior courts. It has unlimited original jurisdiction in civil and criminal matters and any other jurisdiction, original or appellate, conferred on it by legislation.[28] In addition, the High Court has jurisdiction to determine questions of whether a right or fundamental freedom has been violated, as well as to hear matters relating to the interpretation of the Constitution. The High Court also has supervisory powers over subordinate courts, and over any person or body exercising judicial or quasi-judicial power, but not over a superior court.[29]

4.2. Subordinate Courts

The subordinate courts consist of magistrates' courts, Kadhi's courts, courts martial and other courts or local tribunals as may be established by an

[24] Art 163.

[25] See *FIDA-K & 5 Others v Attorney-General & Another* (Petititon No 102 of 2011) [2011] eKLR discussed below. Nancy Baraza resigned in October 2012 after a constitutional tribunal recommended her removal from office following an altercation with a security guard. Upon resignation, she withdrew her appeal to the Supreme Court challenging her removal: 'Nancy Baraza Resigns' *The Star* 18 October 2012.

[26] Art 164.

[27] Out of a total of 31 judges in the Court of Appeal, 9 are women.

[28] In practice, this court hears civil matters where the pecuniary values are high, and the most serious criminal matters namely murder and treason. It also has appellate jurisdiction in both civil and criminal matters, and hears appeals from the subordinate courts and administrative tribunals. In addition, it exercises admiralty jurisdiction. Specialised judicial divisions of the High Court have recently been created dealing with commercial, criminal, constitutional and family matters.

[29] Art 165.

Act of Parliament.[30] By contrast with judges, the appointment, tenure and removal of magistrates and Kadhis is not constitutionally regulated, and is left to legislation. This cadre of judicial officers is in the category of ordinary civil servants. They are appointed and removed by the Judicial Service Commission, have no security of tenure and are subject to the usual terms of service for all civil servants, including salaries (which are much lower than those of judges), leave and retirement age (recently raised from 55 to 60). They are not entitled to official vehicles, drivers or security, although resident magistrates are usually entitled to housing at the court station.

Under the Magistrates' Courts Act, the jurisdiction of magistrates is determined on a territorial and pecuniary basis. There are several levels in the magistrates' court hierarchy, with the Chief Magistrates' Court being the highest and the District Magistrates' Courts the lowest.[31] Women's representation in the magistrates' courts is much higher than in the superior courts, being currently about 41 per cent.[32] The Kadhi's courts are provided for under Article 170 of the Constitution and their jurisdiction is limited to determination of questions of Muslim law relating to personal status, marriage, divorce or inheritance in proceedings where all the parties profess the Muslim religion and submit to the jurisdiction of the Kadhi's courts.[33] They are presided over by Kadhis who must profess the Muslim religion and possess such knowledge of the Muslim law as applicable to any Muslim sects that qualifies them, in the opinion of the Judicial Service Commission, to hold a Kadhi's court. Traditionally, the Kadhi's courts have been the exclusive preserve of men.[34]

The subordinate courts' decisions do not have precedent value, and are subject to appeal in the High Court and may be reversed, varied or confirmed. The High Court has supervisory jurisdiction over these courts and may issue judicial review orders quashing their decisions, for instance on the grounds of bias or error on the face of the record. The magistrates' courts are nonetheless of immense importance as they are the first level of the judiciary available to the majority of litigants, as well as being more accessible and less costly than the higher courts.

[30] Art 169.

[31] In the order of hierarchy, the Chief Magistrates' courts are the highest, followed by the Senior Principal Magistrates' Courts, Principal Magistrates' Courts, Senior Resident Magistrates' Courts, Resident Magistrates' Courts, and the lowest being the District Magistrates' Courts.

[32] Source: National Commission on Gender and Development, 2006.

[33] Other courts currently in existence are the Children Courts set up under the Children Act, 2001 to deal with issues relating to children; anti-corruption courts have also been established under the Economic Crimes and Anti-Corruption Act, 2003.

[34] However, the new Chief Justice, Willy Mutunga, has indicated that the Judicial Service Commission will soon be recruiting women to sit in the Kadhi's courts: 'Kenya: Women Magistrates to Sit in Kadhi's Courts, says Mutunga': *Nairobi Star* (30 September 2011).

Kenyan magistrates' courts (where women are most heavily represented) handle more than 90 per cent of the country's caseload and are the first court of resort for most people coming before the courts in both civil and criminal matters. Though exercising judicial authority and being part of the judicial branch of government, they are of low status and judges at these courts are subject to much poorer terms of service than their counterparts in the higher courts. For instance, they do not enjoy the same protection of their independence as judges. Magistrates and other judicial officers, unlike judges, do not have guaranteed security of tenure. The Chief Justice has delegated powers to exercise disciplinary authority over lower judicial officers, including interdiction, suspension and reprimand. Disciplinary proceedings leading to dismissal may be carried out through a disciplinary committee or panel.

While judicial officers at all levels in Kenya experience similar constraints and challenges, such as inadequate facilities, shortage of personnel and case backlog, the position of magistrates is particularly onerous. For example, magistrates often operate in congested work stations and most of them lack basic facilities such as computers (and internet connection), library, housing and transport. While salaries and other benefits have been regularly increased for judges of the Court of Appeal and the High Court, there have been no equivalent improvements for magistrates and other judicial officers.

5. APPOINTMENT OF JUDICIAL OFFICERS

This section discusses the factors affecting the appointment of judicial officers and how they impact on women. First, it looks at the role of the Judicial Service Commission and then examines the processes for appointment of judicial officers.

5.1. The Judicial Service Commission

The Judicial Service Commission (JSC) occupies a cardinal role in the judicial appointment and promotion system. The JSC is a constitutional body vested with the function of recommending to the President persons for appointment as judges, as well as to review and make recommendations on the conditions of service of judges, judicial officers and the staff of the judiciary.[35] Hence,

[35] Art 172(1)(a) and (b). However, this does not include making recommendations on remuneration, which is done by the Salaries and Remuneration Commission under Art 230 of the Constitution.

the composition and workings of the JSC are important factors affecting women's representation and upward mobility in the judiciary.

Prior to the passing of the Constitution of 2010, the composition of the JSC was narrow and not sufficiently representative, being drawn only from appointees who were already in the service of the government.[36] At that time, the only woman representative in the JSC was Justice Joyce Aluoch. After her departure from the JSC no other female member was appointed. This lack of women's representation has meant that women have been deprived of an advocate within the JSC.

The Constitution of 2010 has introduced some significant changes in the workings of the JSC. The broad function of the JSC is now categorically stated to be to promote and facilitate the independence and accountability of the judiciary and the efficient, effective and transparent administration of justice. This is important as it serves as a guiding framework for all operations of the JSC. Other specific functions include the discipline and removal of judicial officers (other than judges) and implementation of judicial education programmes.[37] In the performance of its functions, the JSC is to be guided by certain principles, namely competitiveness and transparent processes in the appointment of judicial officers and other staff in the judiciary, and the promotion of gender equality. The Judicial Service Act of 2011 now provides an institutional framework and policy guidelines for the recruitment, promotion and deployment practices in the Judiciary. Such framework and guidelines were previously lacking.

Under the Constitution of 2010, the membership of the JSC has been broadened considerably. The JSC now consists not only of the Chief Justice (as chairperson), the Attorney-General, a nominee of the Public Service Commission and representatives from the Supreme Court, Court of Appeal and High Court, but of a magistrate, two advocates and two members of the public who are not lawyers. It is also notable that the representatives of the various courts and the advocates are not merely nominated but elected by the relevant professional associations. There is also the requirement for equal gender representation (one man and one woman each) in the elections of representatives from the High Court and magistrates' courts, the Law Society and also in the appointment of representatives from the general public.[38] In addition, representatives from the public must be approved by the National Assembly.[39] The broader representation, democratisation and gender

[36] The members of the JSC were the Chief Justice (as chairman), the Attorney-General, two judges designated by the President and the Chairman of the Public Service Commission.

[37] Art 172. These functions are further elaborated in the Judicial Service Act.

[38] Art 171.

[39] s 15, Judicial Service Act.

inclusiveness in the composition of the JSC is more likely to take into account diversity and gender equality in the appointment of judicial officers.[40]

5.2. Appointment Process of Judges and Magistrates

The President appoints the Chief Justice, Deputy Chief Justice and all other superior court judges in accordance with the recommendations of the Judicial Service Commission. In the case of the Chief Justice and the Deputy Chief Justice, the appointments are subject to the approval of the National Assembly.[41] Magistrates are appointed directly by the Judicial Service Commission.[42]

Prior to the Constitution of 2010, the criteria for appointment to the judiciary were sketchy and inadequate. They merely required that a person should either have served as judge of a court in the Commonwealth having unlimited original or appellate jurisdiction or must have been an advocate of not less than seven years' standing.[43] In that system, there were no job applications or interviews and no criteria for evaluation of qualifications. Names were simply presented by the JSC to the President with recommendation for appointment. The opaqueness and lack of specificity in the process worked to the disadvantage of women. The system encouraged patronage, nepotism and ethnic and gender bias, with women mostly excluded from the informal 'old boys' networks and clubs that play a large part in such appointments.

Similarly, the JSC's powers of appointment, discipline and removal of magistrates and other subordinate judicial officials lacked clearly defined and transparent criteria and procedures. While vacancies in magistrates' courts and minimum qualifications required by law for applicants were publicly advertised, the actual process in the selection and recruitment was not transparent. Nor were there clear criteria for the promotion and evaluation of magistrates.

The Constitution of 2010, together with the Judicial Service Act of 2011, have introduced far-reaching reforms in relation to the appointment of judicial officers. First, the Constitution has laid down more rigorous and objective criteria of eligibility for judges. The qualifications for judges are now more specific. All judges must have either a law degree from a recognised university, or be advocates of the High Court of Kenya or possess an equivalent qualification from a Commonwealth country. The experience and skills base for judges has been widened to include experience in academia,

[40] The current JSC comprises 10 members, of whom four are women.
[41] Art 166.
[42] Ibid.
[43] s 61, repealed Constitution.

the judiciary, legal practice or another relevant field, which should range from 10 to 15 years.[44] In addition to academic and professional qualifications, all judges are now for the first time required to possess a high moral standing, integrity and impartiality.[45]

The Judicial Service Act of 2011 sets out a long and elaborate procedure for the appointment of judges. The process includes public notification of vacancies, submission of applications, initial review for completeness and compliance with constitutional and statutory requirements, background reference checks, background investigation and vetting and publication of the names of applicants. There is also provision for the scheduling of interviews, criteria for evaluation of qualifications, nomination of qualified applicants and notification of nominations.

Hence, for the first time in Kenya's history, judicial appointments have been conducted using a public, competitive and transparent process. For the first time, positions for Chief Justice, Deputy Chief Justice, Chief Court Registrar, Supreme Court and High Court judges were advertised in the official Gazette and daily newspapers. Public interviews were conducted in the glare of the media with live radio and television coverage. Candidates were questioned on their academic and professional credentials, including scholarly writings and quality of judgments, moral and financial probity, contribution to legal and professional life, contribution to the community etc. Any questionable transactions or judgments were probed.[46] The names of successful candidates were then forwarded to the President to approve. The Chief Justice and Deputy Chief Justice had in addition to undergo vetting by the National Assembly. It was only after all this was done that the judges were finally sworn in.

Although this process has been criticised in some quarters as being overly intrusive and in violation of the constitutional right to dignity of the applicants, the general outcome has been a more diverse judiciary, with wide representation from academia, civil society, legal practice and the bench. The newly appointed judges seem to have more credibility in terms of integrity and professionalism. The Chief Justice and his Deputy in particular have been associated with human rights, access to justice and women's empowerment. The gender distribution of the courts is also more favourable to women, with a female Deputy Chief Justice.

However, it should be noted that the share of women in the Supreme Court, which is two out of a total of seven judges, seems to fall below

[44] Judges of the Supreme Court are required to have at least 15 years' relevant experience while judges in the Court of Appeal and High Court should have at least 10 years' relevant experience. *Cf* s 61 of the repealed Constitution.

[45] Art 166.

[46] See for instance, 'Kenya Begins Interviews for Judges', *KBC News*, 4 July 2011 (kbc.co.ke).

the one-third gender requirement for public offices. This was challenged in the case of *Federation of Women Lawyers (FIDA-Kenya) & Others v Attorney-General*.[47] The petitioners alleged that the JSC in making its recommendations to the President violated the Constitution and fundamental rights and freedoms of women in not taking into consideration the correct arithmetic/mathematics of the constitutional requirements on gender equity. As a result the recommendations fell below the constitutional mandatory minimum and maximum on gender equality. The petitioners therefore sought a declaration that the JSC's recommendation was gender insensitive, discriminatory against women, disrespectful of women and contrary to the Constitution of the Republic of Kenya and therefore null and void. They also sought an order restraining any further purported appointments of Judges of the Supreme Court pursuant to the recommendations made by the JSC. However, the High Court dismissed the petition and ruled that the JSC did not breach any constitutional provisions and acted properly and within its discretion.

While the Court's decision in this case did not favour the petitioners, the JSC seems to have subsequently become more sensitive to gender balance. For instance, in their nominations to the High Court in August 2011, there were almost an equal number of women and men (13 women and15 men), thus going even beyond the one-third gender rule. Subsequently, four other women have been appointed to the High Court. This could perhaps be attributed to the JSC's awareness of the possibility of legal challenge should they not adhere to constitutional requirements.

Another far-reaching reform introduced by the Constitution of 2010 is the vetting of judges and magistrates who were already in office before the passing of the Constitution. Under section 23 of the Sixth Schedule Parliament is required to enact legislation, within one year from promulgation of the Constitution, establishing mechanisms and procedures for vetting the suitability of all judges and magistrates already serving. This resulted in the passing of the Vetting of Judges and Magistrates Act[48] which establishes a Vetting Board with mechanisms and procedures for the vetting of judges and magistrates pursuant to the requirements of the Constitution. It lays down the criteria for vetting, which include the judicial officer's professional competence, communication skills, integrity and fairness, among others.[49] The Vetting Board has already been constituted and is made up of six Kenyans and three foreigners, of whom three are women in accordance with the one-third gender rule. The board has commenced its work and already a number of judges have been found unfit to serve in the judiciary.

[47] Petition No 102 of 2011 [2011] eKLR.
[48] No 2 of 2011.
[49] s 18.

6. WOMEN'S EXPERIENCE IN THE KENYAN JUDICIARY

6.1. Women Judges

Until 1983, when Effie Owuor was appointed to the High Court, there was no woman judge in Kenya, in the High Court or the Court of Appeal. The next woman judge, Justice Joyce Aluoch, was not appointed to the High Court until 1986. By 1993, when Justice Mary Ang'awa was appointed, there were only three women judges in Kenya.

Table 1: Some Women Pioneers in the Judiciary

Hon Lady Justice Effie Owuor (Retired) Effie Owuor has the distinction of having a series of 'firsts', being the first woman state counsel, the first woman magistrate and the very first female judge of the High Court (1982) and then of the Court of Appeal (2003). She was also an ambassador to the United Nations and chair of the Task Force on the Laws Relating to Laws affecting Women (1993) which resulted in the passing of a number of Acts of Parliament, most notably the Sexual Offences Act, 2006. She retired from the judiciary in 2008 and is currently the Chair of the Sexual Offences Task Force.
Hon Lady Justice Joyce Aluoch (Retired) Joyce Aluoch was the second woman to be appointed magistrate (1974), became a High Court judge in 1983 and a judge at the Court of Appeal in 2008. Among her outstanding achievements in the judiciary was the inauguration of the Family Division of the High Court. She is credited with simplification of litigation in family law matters, making it affordable and expeditious. She is a founder member of the Kenya Women Judges Association (KWJA) and is currently its patron. In 2003, Justice Aluoch was elected Vice-Chairperson of the UN Committee on the Rights of the Child, having previously served as the first Chairperson of the African Union Committee on the Rights of the Child (2001). She retired from the Kenyan judiciary in 2009 to take up an appointment as a judge in the International Criminal Court at the Hague.
Hon Lady Justice Mary Ang'awa Justice Ang'awa was the third woman to be appointed a magistrate (1980).[50] She considers herself a 'guinea pig' as in the following year ten more women were appointed to the bench. She became the first woman Chief Magistrate in 1990 and the third female High Court judge in 1993. She has been chair of the Kenya Women Judges Association and been at the forefront of the Association's efforts towards gender equity in the judiciary.

[50] Being a Seventh Day Adventist, Justice Ang'awa while at the Kenya School of Law (the postgraduate training institution for lawyers) refused to attend class on Saturdays. On taking the examination, she was only one of two women who passed. The Principal (Tudor Jackson) was so impressed that he insisted she had to be appointed a magistrate.

Table 2 below shows the representation of women in the judiciary as at 2006. Since 2000, the number of women judges at the High Court has increased considerably. As at 2010, there were 18 women judges, compared with 42 men judges, making up 30 per cent of the bench.[51]

Women have been noticeably absent at the Court of Appeal. Under the repealed Constitution, only two women had ever been appointed to this Court, namely Justice Effie Owuor, being the first appointee in 2003 and Justice Joyce Aluoch in 2006. After they retired they were never replaced.[52] Even during appointments to this Court in 2009 there was no woman appointee. On a positive note, after the passing of the 2010 Constitution, the JSC has recruited a total of nine women to this court. While this is encouraging, the number of women in the Court of Appeal still falls short of the one-third gender rule.[53]

The judicial appointments under the Constitution of 2010 have seen a significant rise in the number of women judges. As already mentioned, there are now two women in the Supreme Court, one of whom is the Deputy

Table 2: Proportion of Women in Judicial Service Establishments, 2006

	Men	Women	Total	% Women
Chief Justice	1	0	1	0
Judges of Appeal	14	0	14	0
High Court judges	47	12	59	20
Commissioner of Assize	2	1	3	20
Chief Magistrate	9	6	15	40
Senior principal and principal magistrates	15	11	26	42
Senior resident magistrates	63	38	101	38
Resident magistrates	83	64	146	44
District magistrates	126	92	218	42
Chief Kadhi/Kadhis	17	0	17	0
Total	376	224	600	37

Source: National Commission on Gender and Development, 2006

51 Source: Kenya Women Judges Association.

52 Justice Owuor retired from the Court of Appeal in 2006 while Justice Aluoch retired in 2009 and thereafter became a Judge of the International Criminal Court at The Hague.

53 The number of judges in the Court of Appeal is 31. However, the numbers are still fluid as some judges have been declared by the Vetting Board as unfit to serve and their appeals against removal are pending.

Chief Justice. Of the 28 High Court judges appointed in July 2011, 13 are women bringing women's representation in the High Court to 44 per cent.[54] These women judges are generally younger, and many have had careers outside the bench as practising advocates and academics. Further, while women's representation in the Supreme Court stands below one-third, it is arguably much better than in the old system where there was no woman in the highest court.

However, it has been observed that women are seemingly reluctant to apply for the higher constitutional offices and are more comfortable playing 'deputy'. For instance, when the positions for Chief Justice were advertised, only two women applied. By contrast, the position of Deputy Chief Justice (the lower post) attracted a much higher number of women applicants. During the selection of members of the Vetting Board for magistrates and judges, the relevant Act had to be amended to extend time to allow more women to apply as their numbers fell below the one-third rule. Some possible explanations are that women may feel uncomfortable with the media coverage and public scrutiny involved in the new selection process.

6.2. Women Magistrates

The entry of women into the magistracy was slow in the first decades following independence, as there was no policy of incorporating women. It was only in 1973, ten years after Kenya attained independence, that the first woman magistrate[55] was appointed. In 1974, another woman magistrate[56] was appointed, the third in 1978[57] and the fourth in 1980.[58] This slow entry is linked to the constraints facing women in legal education that have already been outlined. It may also have been due to the absence of examples of women magistrates, so that the job of a magistrate was identified with men.

After 1980 there was a significant increase in the number of women magistrates. For instance in 1981, ten more women were appointed magistrates. Today, women make up about 40 per cent of the magistracy. Thus, women's representation in the judiciary has been mostly in the lower echelons of the judiciary, ie, the magistrates' courts. Issues have arisen regarding the promotion of women magistrates, many of whom have remained in the same position despite long and capable service. Promotions seem to have

[54] Source: Judiciary website: www.judiciary.go.ke.
[55] Effie Owuor.
[56] Joyce Aluoch.
[57] Roselyne Walekhwa Nambuye.
[58] Mary Ang'awa.

been made in a haphazard manner and long-serving women magistrates have largely missed out on promotion to positions as judges. It is heartening to note that in the appointments to the High Court made in September 2011, seven women magistrates were appointed judges.

It should be noted that there are no women in the Kadhi's courts. However, the Chief Justice has indicated that the Judicial Service Commission intends to recruit women into the Kadhi's courts as part of ongoing judicial reforms. This has generated controversy as Kadhi's courts have traditionally been regarded as the domain of men.[59]

While in recent years there has been a significant increase in the number of judges, there has not been a corresponding increase in the hiring of magistrates. The Strategic Plan of the Judiciary for 2005–08 indicated that there are 245 vacant positions in the magistracy. The shortage of magistrates has led to a huge backlog of cases at magistrates' court level.[60] As part of ongoing judicial reforms, the current Chief Justice has put in place plans to hire more magistrates and positions for 160 magistrates have recently been advertised. There are also plans to recruit more Kadhis, including women. Further, the Chief Justice has also promised to look into the terms and conditions of judicial staff, particularly magistrates and administrative staff, which have hitherto been very poor. The Chief Justice has also recommended to the JSC the promotion of 278 magistrates and 12 Kadhis.[61]

Table 3: Remuneration Package for Members of the Judiciary

	Salary (Kenya Shillings)	Allowances (Kenya Shillings)
Chief Justice	531,650	452,990
Judges of Court of Appeal	214,635–277,950	287,590
High Court judges	130,314–333,320	227,290
Magistrates	18,960–84,055	
Paralegals	4425–71,365	

Source: Institute of Economic Affairs, 2006

[59] 'Kenya: Clerics Oppose CJ over Women in Kadhi's Courts', *Nairobi Star* (4 October 2011) at: www.allafrica.com.

[60] In March 2004, 32 lawyers in private practice turned down government offers of appointments as magistrates because of poor working conditions in magistrates' courts. This was followed by threats and protests by lawyers in different parts of the country against the shortage of magistrates and judicial staff. In 2005, magistrates from two areas went on strike as a protest against their low salaries and poor working conditions.

[61] 'Progress Report on the Transformation of the Judiciary: the first 120 days'. Source: www.judiciary.go.ke.

6.3. General Challenges faced by Women Judicial Officers

One of the challenges that women judicial officers have faced, particularly in the earlier years, was a lack of acceptance by members of the public.[62] This was mostly due to public perception that only men could hold positions as judicial officers. No effort was made to provide facilities for women's needs.[63] Although pay and terms of service are the same for both sexes, women judicial officers are not rewarded as well as they should be,[64] as men tend to be promoted over women, resulting in poor motivation on their part. The feeling is that there is no reward for hard work, as the pay is the same irrespective of how much time and effort is invested in the work. However, a perception among some members of the public that women magistrates are incompetent and careless is giving way to a growing recognition of their capabilities and professional dedication. For instance, a number of heads of stations in the High Court are currently women and the first Chief Registrar appointed under the Constitution of 2010 is Gladys Shollei.

Further, women also experience challenges in terms of balancing work and career,[65] compounded by the practice of frequent transfers from station to station, which forces many of them to put their children into boarding schools. There is a need to develop a transfer policy that is sensitive to the family concerns of judicial officers, particularly women.

7. CONTRIBUTIONS OF WOMEN JUDGES AND MAGISTRATES

Women judges and magistrates have made immense contributions to the administration of justice in Kenya despite the challenges they have faced. In particular, through their interpretation of the law they have promoted the advancement of gender equality in the courts and worked towards making justice more accessible to all. This has in large measure been achieved through the Kenya Women Judges Association (KWJA).

[62] For instance, a woman judge who was in her earlier career posted to be a magistrate in a rural community in the 1970s encountered initial hostility from litigants as there had never been a woman magistrate in the area. However, she was eventually able to gain their confidence once they became satisfied of her competence and fairness.

[63] For instance, there were no toilet facilities for the first woman judge. One woman magistrate had to breastfeed her baby in the car as there were no facilities in the judiciary for child care. The position has not changed to date.

[64] For instance, one woman magistrate has in the course of her career been assigned several challenging responsibilities, which she has discharged with excellence, but she has not received adequate recognition, eg, by being appointed as a judge.

[65] For instance in 2007, one woman was sworn in as a judge but subsequently declined to take up her position citing family reasons. Interestingly, she is the only person in Kenya who is a sworn judge but works as a corporate lawyer away from the courts.

7.1. The Kenya Women Judges Association

The Kenya Women Judges Association (KWJA) was formed in 1993 as an affiliate of the International Women Judges Association (IWJA).[66] Initially, Justices Effie Owuor and Joyce Aluoch were its only members, as they were the only women judges in Kenya.[67] Later, Valeria Onyango, the Deputy Chief Litigation Counsel at the Attorney-General's Chambers, was co-opted as the Founder Secretary. Gradually, membership increased as more women were appointed to the High Court, and magistrates were made full members of the association in 2005.[68] Besides women judges and magistrates, the Association's membership now includes women commissioners of assizes and women state attorneys. By 2010, the Association counted 72 full members (including all 18 women judges and 54 magistrates) and two honorary as well as a number of associate members.

Among its objectives, the KWJA seeks to urge for and encourage the appointment and recruitment of women into the judiciary, and particularly the appointment of greater numbers of women judges so that the judiciary reflects an equal role for men and women in society. Other objectives include promoting the advancement of women in general through the fair administration of justice. It also seeks to develop the rule of law and equality of all before the law, and in particular to promote and encourage gender equality in all matters relating to the administration of justice. It seeks to keep under review all aspects of discrimination on a gender basis and to work actively for the eradication of all forms of discrimination against women in the administration of judges.[69] The KWJA enjoys the support of the Chief Justice of Kenya and the Attorney General of Kenya in the running of its various programmes.

7.1.1. Establishment of the Family Division of the High Court

One of the key achievements of the KWJA was that it spearheaded the formation of the Family Division of the High Court. Following a workshop in

[66] This was after Lady Justice Joyce Aluoch had attended a meeting of 50 women jurists from every continent who attended the tenth anniversary meeting of the US National Association of Women Judges; they saw a need to act in concert to seek solutions for problems impeding equal justice for women, recognising that by speaking with a united voice they could advance gender justice for all women. The meeting eventually spurred the formation of the IWJA in 1991.

[67] The Association was registered under an exemption clause because there were only two women judges at the time. Kenyan law requires such associations to have a minimum membership of three people.

[68] The main reasons for including magistrates were to reflect international practice as well as the need for broader representation of women judicial officers. It was also felt that through a 'cross-pollination' process both women judges and magistrates would benefit from their interaction with each other. Interview with Justice Mary Ang'awa (7 August 2009).

[69] Art 2, Constitution of the Kenya Women Judges Association.

April 2000, the KWJA submitted its recommendations to the Chief Justice. He subsequently appointed an Administrative Committee chaired by Lady Justice Joyce Aluoch, and consisting of several stakeholders, to work out the modalities of forming a Family Division of the High Court. The Committee's report was accepted by the Chief Justice, and on 21 December, 2000, the Family Division of the High Court was launched.

The Family Division is a specialised division designed to hear matters relating to the family, such as divorce, probate and adoption, and is aimed at improving access to and delivery of justice in family law matters. This enables more focused judicial decision-making and provides the opportunity for judges to develop expertise in those areas of law. The Family Division has also set aside specific days of the week for specific matters, which makes the process more efficient for judges and litigants. For instance, Friday is the day set aside for adoption cases. On that day, no criminal cases are held in the High Court, creating a child-friendly environment in the court.[70]

7.1.2. *Bench-book on Family Law*

The KWJA has produced a bench-book on family law to guide judges in the Family Division of the High Court as well as other judicial officials. It contains a checklist of matters that need to be taken into account when judging different types of family cases. For instance, in adoption cases, the procedures have been streamlined in order to protect children. The Court must now liaise with the Children's Department and Immigration Department before an adopted child can be taken out of Kenya. The bench-book has proved to be very useful to judges and lawyers. However, it needs to be updated as it was prepared before the passing of the Sexual Offences Act 2006.[71]

7.1.3. *Compendium of Sexual Offences Cases*

The KWJA has compiled a Compendium of Sexual Offences Cases based on research of cases decided by the magistrates' courts. This compendium is of immense value to judicial officers as it acts as a guide on how to deal with offences under the Sexual Offences Act of 2006, as well as facilitating organised analysis of jurisprudence in this area of law.

7.1.4. *Jurisprudence of Equality Programme (JEP)*

Among the most important achievements of the KWJA is the spearheading of the Jurisprudence of Equality Programme (JEP). The JEP project was

[70] Interview with Lady Justice Mary Ang'awa (7 August 2009).
[71] No 3 of 2006.

formally begun in 1995 under the auspices of the International Women Judges Foundation.[72] The programme is designed to prepare judges and magistrates to be able to apply international, regional and national human rights norms to cases coming before them in their national and local courts, including those relating to gender based discrimination and violence. This is to sensitise judicial officials to the existence of international instruments pertaining to women, children and vulnerable persons and to enable them to implement equality principles in their decision-making.

The programme works through a task force charged with administering all operational aspects of the project. This task force is responsible for selecting a two-member team (composed of a judge and a legal academic or an NGO advocate) who go through training at a trainers workshop (3T Workshop) preparing them in turn to conduct human rights seminars in their own countries. The workshops are held twice a year, for three years.[73] At the end of each project year, the task force and the training team hold a follow-up meeting with the JEP participants in their respective countries.[74] The end result is to produce a critical mass of JEP-trained judges and magistrates—and later lawyers—who will appropriately apply human rights norms to cases before them. The KWJA has already successfully completed human rights training workshops which have had a positive impact in terms of recognition of women's rights.[75]

The JEP has now proved to be of tremendous value to those who are faced with the responsibility of making legal decisions, but are not conversant with how to apply international instruments. After attending the JEP trainings, judges, lawyers and rights advocates have come up with positive decisions that uphold human rights norms. This is significant, as Kenya, whose legal system is based on the common law had, until the Constitution of 2010, had adopted the dualist approach to international law, in which international conventions are not directly enforceable in national courts unless their provisions have been imported by legislation into domestic

[72] A pilot project was first held in Costa Rica, the Philippines and Romania. Other projects were conducted in Argentina, Brazil, Chile, Ecuador and Uruguay. In Africa, the project has been conducted in eastern and southern Africa, namely South Africa, Kenya, Tanzania, Uganda and Zimbabwe. The African Regional coordinating office is based in Uganda. (That office co-ordinates the various programmes as outlined below). The East African Judicial Training Committee consisting of Kenya, Uganda and Tanzania have also adapted this programme as part of their training curriculum.

[73] Each year, two more new trainers are selected to conduct the two workshops. They then adopt a curriculum relevant to the circumstance of their country, but as far as possible, in line with the training material.

[74] The purpose is to review the curriculum where there may be legal changes, to discuss the way in which the participants have applied the training and to elicit suggestions on ways to improve the curriculum.

[75] See: www.iawj.org/news.

law.[76] Judges who have been trained by JEP have been encouraged to have regard to international norms when deciding cases where the domestic law is uncertain or incomplete. This was done in line with the Bangalore Principles on the Domestic Application of International Human Rights Norms of 1988.[77] Principle 7 reads as follows:

> It is within the proper nature of the judicial process and well-established judicial functions for national courts to have regard to international obligations which a country undertakes, whether or not they have been incorporated into domestic law—for the purpose of removing ambiguity or uncertainty from national constitutions, legislation or common law.[78]

Kenyan courts have used this approach to hold that customary law may be excluded where it is contrary to international human rights principles. For instance, in one of the clearest and boldest articulations of gender equality, Lady Justice Wendoh in *Re Estate of Musyoka (deceased)*[79] noted that Kamba customary law, which was relied on by one of the parties, is discriminatory on the ground of sex, and contrary to section 40 of the Law of Succession Act.[80] She then proceeded to apply international and regional human rights instruments espousing principles of gender equality and non-discrimination—namely the Universal Declaration of Human Rights (UDHR), the Convention on the Elimination of All Forms of Discrimination Against Women (CEDAW), the International Covenant on Economic, Social and Cultural Rights (ICESR) and the African Charter—notwithstanding the fact that these instruments have not expressly become part of the domestic law of Kenya.

Another notable case is *Rono v Rono* (2005) where the court set the precedent of applying international human rights norms such as found in the UDHR and CEDAW in a succession case. It should be noted that although all the judges in this case were male, at least one of them, Justice Waki, had gone through the JEP training programme and was also a trainer.

[76] Examples of the dualistic approach are found in the United Kingdom, Canada and New Zealand, among others. This is in contrast with most civil law jurisdictions—such as Germany and Italy—which adopt the monist view of international law whereby international law instruments automatically become part of the domestic law.

[77] These Principles were adopted in Bangalore in 1988 by the Commonwealth Secretariat to guide judges in common law countries in the application of international human rights norms in domestic courts.

[78] However, under Principle 8, where national law is clear and inconsistent with the international obligations of the state concerned, in common law countries the national court is obliged to give effect to national law. In such cases the court should draw such inconsistency to the attention of the appropriate authorities since the supremacy of national law in no way mitigates a breach of an international legal obligation, which is undertaken by a country.

[79] In 2005.

[80] Cap 160.

Another significant decision is *JAO Homepark Caterers Ltd.*[81] where the High Court upheld the human rights of a woman who had been dismissed from her job on the grounds of being HIV positive.

The Constitution of 2010 now provides that international treaties or conventions, which Kenya has ratified, will form part of the law of Kenya.[82] Thus, the Constitution has adopted the monist approach where international instruments ratified by a country form part of the country's law without the need for domestication in the form of municipal legislation. This is a radical shift from the previous position as it means that Kenyan courts can now apply international conventions ratified by the country, such as CEDAW, without waiting for Parliament to enact domesticating legislation. The new approach has positive ramifications for the promotion of gender equality and the protection of women's rights by the courts.

8. CONCLUSION

Women in Kenya have been under-represented in the judiciary, particularly at the higher levels. A combination of structural and institutional barriers in legal education, the nature of the judicial appointment system as well as societal attitudes have worked to adversely affect the selection and upward mobility of women in the judiciary. However, despite women being a minority in the Kenyan judiciary, they have made their mark in terms of the articulation of gender issues within the judiciary, particularly through the Kenya Women Judges Association and the Jurisprudence of Equality project. The changes brought about by the Constitution of Kenya of 2010 including the current judicial reform initiatives, hold much promise for women's advancement in the judiciary and have already produced some positive results. However, there is a need for more concrete policies and measures specifically targeted at ensuring gender equality and equity in the courts. It is hoped that with the increased numbers of women judges and magistrates, there will be a critical mass that will be instrumental in consolidating the gains made and ensuring that the judiciary becomes an institution that is fair, equitable and accessible to all.

9. REFERENCES

Bratton, KA and Spill, RL (2002) 'Existing Diversity and Judicial Selection: The Role of the Appointment Method in Establishing Gender Diversity in State Supreme Courts' 83(2) *Social Science Quarterly* 504.

81 *JAO Homepark Caterers Ltd* [2004] eKLR.
82 Art 2.

Feenan, D (2008) 'Women Judges: Gendering Judging, Justifying Diversity' 35(4) *Journal of Law and Society* 490.

Ghai, YPG and McAuslan, PWB (1970) *Public Law and Political Change in Kenya* (Nairobi, Oxford University Press).

Malleson, K (2003) 'Justifying Gender Equality on the Bench: Why Difference Won't Do' 11 *Feminist Legal Studies* 1.

Ngugi, WW (1986) 'Sex Discrimination in Employment' (University of Nairobi, LLB dissertation, unpublished).

2.4

The Impact of Women on the Administration of Justice in Syria and the Judicial Selection Process

MONIQUE C CARDINAL

Abstract

Available data show that qualification standards applied to women candidates in the judicial selection process in Syria seem to be higher than those applied to men. As a result, women are among the best qualified members of the judiciary. In addition to being highly qualified, women are also known for their judicial integrity. Based on interviews conducted with 110 women judges and public prosecutors during the period 2004–08, this chapter will examine the social, economic and political conditions that enable women in Syria to be more autonomous than their male colleagues in their decision-making. Close attention will be paid to the career of the first woman appointed to the judiciary in Syria, Ghāda Murād (1975–2006), and the impact she had on the judicial appointments process as member of the High Judiciary Council.

1. INTRODUCTION

'CLEAN HANDS', *NAZĀFAT AL-YAD*. This Arabic phrase was used repeatedly by legal professionals and the public during a series of interviews to express their satisfaction with women judges and their decisions in the courts of the Syrian Arab Republic, commonly known as Syria. Put bluntly, women judges are less prone to bribery than men. On the whole, they rule according to the law and not for personal gain. There are hard facts that support this claim (to follow shortly) and allow us to conclude that women judges and public prosecutors have had a positive impact on the administration of justice in Syria. Their honesty and integrity have worked to reform the judiciary from within and to ensure that people's rights are protected by the law. Of course, the scope of this impact is limited since women make up only 14 per cent of the judiciary, in all close to 200 judges and public prosecutors.[1] Nonetheless, the contribution of women to restoring the public's trust in the judiciary has not gone unnoticed.

This chapter will first look at how the appointments process of the judiciary in Syria has the potential of ensuring that only the most qualified candidates are selected. In fact, available data show that at the different stages of the selection process, the standards of qualifications applied to women candidates seem to be higher than those applied to men. The end result is that women are, for the most part, among the best qualified members of the judiciary. Close attention will be paid to the career of Ghāda Murād (1975–2006), the first woman to be appointed to the judiciary in Syria, and the impact she had on the judicial appointments process as member of the High Judiciary Council.

In addition to being highly qualified, women are also known for their judicial integrity. This chapter will also examine the social, economic and political conditions that enable women in Syria to be more autonomous than their male colleagues in their judicial decision-making.[2] Based on interviews conducted with women judges and public prosecutors over a four-year period, it will show that women's relative social isolation, economic dependence and disempowerment as political agents paradoxically secure their independence as judicial officers.

2. METHODOLOGY

During the period 2004–08, 110 women judges and public prosecutors were interviewed at the main courthouses of Damascus and its suburbs (56), Aleppo (12), Lattakia (9), Tartus (10), Hama (4), Homs (15) and al-Suweida (4). This number represents slightly more than 50 per cent of female holders of judicial office in the major urban centres of the south, mid and north regions of Syria—women in the furthest north governorates, Deir ez-Zor, al-Raqqa, al-Hasaka and Idlib, remain to be interviewed.

The semi-structured interviews (authorised by the Ministry of Justice and the chief public attorney of each courthouse visited) contained a sequence of closed questions to obtain statistical data, which are not available in the public domain. Women were asked about their civil status, number of children, academic background, experience in advocacy (if any), age at appointment, their first office and the level and jurisdiction of court experience during their careers (Cardinal, 2008). In addition, a series of open

[1] The percentage of women members of the judiciary is based on figures of 31 December 2008 provided by the Statistics Bureau of the Ministry of Justice.

[2] This chapter owes much to Peter H Russell's theorisation of judicial independence. See Russell (2001).

questions were formulated in order to gauge the perceptions women have of their judicial functions and work environment as well as their attitudes towards these. Among a number of issues addressed, they explained why they chose to study law, if they thought women were apt to work in the criminal jurisdiction as public prosecutors, investigating judges and trial judges and whether they preferred criminal or civil law. They spoke about the impact their careers have on their family lives and were asked what impact they, as professionals, have on the administration of justice in Syria. The topic of discrimination was also raised. The interviews took place either in the judges' and public prosecutors' offices or in chambers, and sometimes in the courts. They were mostly conducted in private, but also on a number of occasions in the presence of colleagues or court staff, though rarely in the presence of lawyers and clients. They were not recorded since recording devices are not allowed on court premises and interviewees would not have felt at ease. All data are based on brief notes taken during interviews and filtered through the author's memory, interpretation and subjectivity.

3. AN APPOINTMENTS PROCESS BASED ON MERIT

As in other civil law jurisdictions, entry to the judiciary in Syria is based on competitive examinations. There are separate sets of examinations for the two court systems: the ordinary courts and the administrative courts. This chapter focuses on the appointments process of the ordinary courts since, up until today, women have not been appointed to the administrative courts in Syria.[3]

The competitive examinations for entry to the ordinary judiciary are of two types: (1) a judicial examination open to relatively young jurists—between 26 and 32 years of age in the most recent examination of 2007—who, if selected, undergo training for two years at the new Institute of Judicial Studies (IJS) in Damascus before their appointment to the lowest ranks of the judiciary as peace court judges, deputy public prosecutors or investigating judges; and (2) an examination for lawyers with either 10 or 16 years' experience who, if chosen, are appointed to the higher courts: first instance and appellate. Approximately 25 per cent of the ordinary judiciary is recruited from a pool of experienced lawyers. Every two years, members of the judiciary are promoted to a higher rank and receive a salary increase based on a fixed salary scale like other civil servants. The judiciary in Syria is a career judiciary.

[3] Fieldwork conducted in the summer of 2008 did not produce conclusive results that might explain the non-appointment of women to the administrative courts in Syria.

The competitive examination for both groups of candidates consists of two phases: written and oral. Success in the written exam allows the candidate to take the oral exam. Members of the oral exam committee sit on the High Judiciary Council. This Council supervises the recruitment, promotion and removal of all judges and public prosecutors. The highest-ranking members of the judiciary make up the Council: the President and two Vice-Presidents of the Court of Cassation, the Attorney-General of the Syrian Arab Republic and the Director of the Judicial Inspection Department. The Minister of Justice, a senior member of the judiciary, represents the executive branch of government on the Council. He is assisted by a Deputy Minister who also sits on the Council. The President of the Syrian Arab Republic officially presides over the High Judiciary Council, but delegates his power to the Minister of Justice.[4]

Like the written exam, the oral exam aims to evaluate a candidate's knowledge of the law, but it also serves the purpose of assessing his or her communication skills and professional demeanour. Of the two, the oral exam is clearly the more subjective. At the end of the training programme at the IJS, candidates undergo a last set of examinations. The lists of successful candidates at all stages of the selection process are published according to rank (Cardinal, 2008).

3.1. Higher Qualifications for Women

In 1977, women competed for the first time in the National Judicial Examination. It was the outright success of Ghāda Murād, the first woman appointed to the judiciary in 1975, which paved the way for this first generation of women judicial candidates. Of the 21 women who underwent the one-year training programme, nine were finally appointed to the judiciary in 1979, a success rate of 45 per cent. As for the men, 45 out of 163 were appointed, a success rate of only 28 per cent.[5] In 1979, 17 per cent of the appointees were women. It was said that the women candidates performed extremely well and finished in the highest ranks. Qamar Sarsar held first place and two other women, Lutfiyya 'Ubayd and Hasnā' al-Aswad, were among the top ten finalists. Given their high success rate, it is possible that the standards of qualifications applied to the women in the initial screening process were higher than those applied to the men. At the time, there was stiff opposition to women holding judicial office. The Ministry made sure

[4] Art 65 Judiciary Act (*Qānūn al-sulta al-qadā'iyya*) No 98 of 15 November 1961 (with amendments). Partial diacritics of the Arabic transliterations are provided in the chapter.

[5] *al-Mar'a al-'arabiyya* (The Arab Woman), 1978: (121) 45; *al-Jarīda al-rasmiyya l'l-jumhūriyya al-'arabiyya al-sūriyya, al-juz' al-thānī* (The Official Gazette of the Syrian Arab Republic, vol. 2) 1981: (28) 4910-12.

that the women members were highly qualified in order to protect them and the government from unwarranted criticism. Three women of the 1979 cohort still in office today—Lutfiyya 'Ubayd, Hasnā' al-Aswad and Salwā Kadīb—hold seats in the Court of Cassation.

Of the five National Judicial Examinations to follow in the 1980s and 1990s, it was only in 1993 that the percentage of women appointees equated that of 1979, with the remaining ones ranging between six and 14 per cent. It is impossible to comment on the selection process of these competitions for lack of data. However, the availability of more recent data enables a closer scrutiny of the selection process set up in 2002 with the founding of the IJS.

Judicial trainees that complete the two-year training programme at the IJS have a success rate of almost 100 per cent, with the exception of the odd drop-out. This could imply that the screening process of applicants and the written and oral entry examinations are extremely strict. When compared with past cohorts, the first four cohorts of the IJS recruited during the period of 2002–2005 are significantly different with regard to women candidates. Their percentage is relatively high, averaging 34 per cent. Equally surprising is the fifth and most recent cohort of 2007 with its rock bottom percentage of women candidates: 12 per cent (figure 1).[6] How does one explain this roller-coaster ride in the recruitment of women at the IJS? And what effect has it had on the qualification standards applied to women?

The government of Syria recommended in its Ninth Five-Year Plan for national development (2001–05) that the participation of women in the executive, judicial and legislative branches of government and other

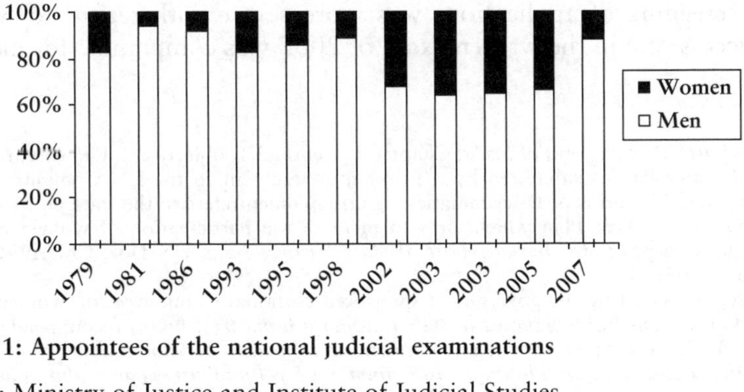

Figure 1: Appointees of the national judicial examinations

Source: Ministry of Justice and Institute of Judicial Studies

[6] A special thank you to Paul Dussault, Webmaster of the Faculté de théologie et de sciences religieuses of Université Laval, for help on past and present figures and graphs.

decision-making positions be expanded.[7] It did not, however, propose the use of compulsory quotas in order to compensate for the under-representation of women in public office.[8] The increase in the recruitment of women judicial candidates during the period of 2002–05 corresponds to the state policy of promoting women's rights and participation in the decision-making process. The Tenth Five-Year Plan (2006–10) heralds the achievements of the Ninth-Year Plan, notably the 'increase in the percentage of women [sic] participation [...] in all ministries and public sector institutions'.[9] The Tenth Five-Year Plan states that its main objective is to promote women's rights and integrate gender issues and equality in the process of development (Chapter 23: 3, 8 ff). The national working plan devised by the State Planning Commission requires that ministries 'integrate gender issues' in their agendas (Chapter 23: 14). Strategy 1 of the plan refers to the 'special efforts [required] to increase women [sic] participation in administrative, economic and political sectors at the central national level and at the level of governorates and municipalities' (Chapter 23: 15). Although there is no explicit reference to enhancing the participation of women in the judicial branch of government, the Tenth Five-Year Plan consistently refers to the need for increasing the number of women in decision-making positions and of promoting 'a culture of gender equality', the expression used in the English version of the plan.

The 12 per cent of women recruited as judicial trainees in 2007 falls short of the state's gender equality policy. It is true that the percentage of women applicants in 2007 was low, 27 per cent,[10] in comparison with the average percentage for the period of 2002–05: 39 per cent. For lack of information, it is impossible to determine if fewer women applied in 2007 or if the initial screening of applications was more severe with regard to women. The success rate in the written exam of 2007 was comparable for men and

[7] *al-Khutta al-khamsiyya al-tāsi'a*, Chapter 3, section 3.1, objective 2. Likewise, the initial report of States Parties submitted by the Syrian government to the UN Committee on the Elimination of All Forms of Discrimination against Women refers to the state policy outlined in the Ninth Five-Year Plan which aims to increase the participation of women in public decision-making positions. *Initial report of State Parties*, *Syria*, UN Doc. CEDAW/C/SYR/1 29 August 2005: 41.

[8] A report issued by the government-sponsored National Committee for Women Affairs After Pekin (*al-Lajna al-wataniyya li-shu'ūn al-mar'a li-mā ba'd bikīn*) recommended that a quota of 30 % be adopted for the appointment of women to decision-making positions. See *al-Istrātījiyya al-wataniyya li'l-mar'a hattā 'āmm 2005 fī'l-jumhūriyya al-'arabiyya al-sūriyya* (National Strategy for Women Until 2005 in the Syrian Arab Republic) section 5, objective 2. (The document can be accessed online at the following address: www.awfonline.net/arabwomanforum/page/sr/2004/es.htm). This recommendation of the committee is also mentioned in the *Initial report of State Parties*, *Syria*, UN Doc. CEDAW/C/SYR/1 29 August 2005: 41.

[9] *al-Khutta al-khamsiyya al-'āshira*, Chapter 23, section 23.1.4: 7. This quotation is taken from the English version of the Tenth Five-Year Plan.

[10] Decree No 534L of 27 March 2007/8 *Rabī' al-awwal* 1428 H (H stands for the *Hijrī* dates of the Muslim calendar.)

women: 63 per cent of the men passed the exam in comparison with 58 per cent of the women.[11] As for the oral exam, it was difficult for all candidates since their number, 850, had to be reduced to about one hundred because of the limited capacity of the IJS to train large numbers. The success rate of women in the oral exam was significantly low in comparison to their past performances and to men as shown in figure 2. However, their low success rate in the 2007 oral exam does not mean that the quality of the women candidates was poor. On the contrary; out of the 109 candidates selected, 13 were women, four of whom ranked in the top ten with one of them, Nisrīn Āghā, occupying first place. Women obtained a very high rank in the final results due to the rigorous evaluation process applied to them: 11 out of the 13 recruits were ranked in the top 50 per cent of all candidates.[12] It is a change in the recruiting practices of the High Judiciary Council, and not a change in state policy concerning gender equality in all professions and employment, which explains the much lower percentage of women candidates of the 2007 cohort of the IJS.

The deliberations of the High Judiciary Council during the selection process are confidential and it is, therefore, impossible to comment on the Council's policy regarding women candidates. However, a change observable to all occurred within the membership of the High Judiciary Council, which may explain the decrease in the recruitment of women judicial candidates in 2007. In August 2006, Ghāda Murād, the Attorney-General of Syria, retired. Thus, the High Judiciary Council lost its first and only woman member. As member of the Council, Ghāda Murād participated in the selection process of the first four cohorts of the IJS for the period of 2002–05. Although Ghāda Murād, like the other members, only had one

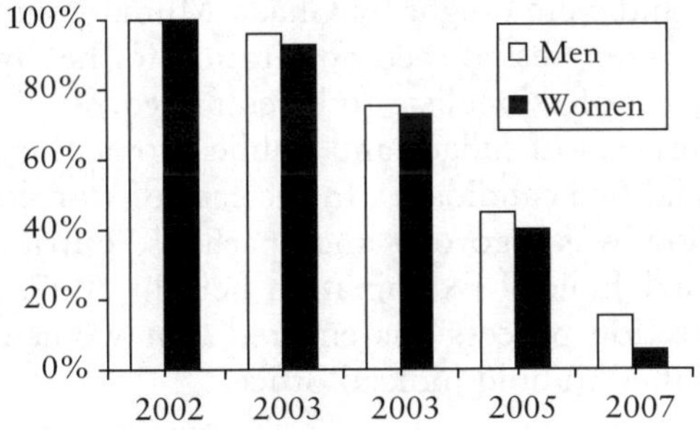

Figure 2: Success rates in the oral exam of the IJS

Source: Ministry of Justice and Institute of Judicial Studies

[11] Decree No 794L of 29 April 2007/12 *Rabī' al-thānī* 1428 H.
[12] Decree No 3864L of 11 December 2007/1 *Dhū al-Hijja* 1428 H.

vote in the selection process, her presence on the Council coincided with an increase in the number of women judicial candidates. Other researchers have observed that a woman's presence on a panel of judges or on a selection committee can change the outcome of the decision-making process (Songer and Crews-Meyer, 2000). As one researcher concluded, 'the incorporation of difference on the bench subtly changes and, ultimately, improves the judicial product' (Rackley, 2008: 49).[13] The same can be said about the judicial selection process in Syria. A different type of member on the High Judiciary Council produced a different type of result in the judicial selection process. It can be assumed that during the 2002–05 period a more equitable evaluation process was applied in comparison to the discriminatory selection process of 2007, which transpired in the very low success rate of the women judicial candidates in the entry oral examination. Biased evaluation of candidates in the oral examination phase of the judicial selection process has been observed in other jurisdictions (Boigeol, 1993: 497–98). The more equitable selection process implemented during Ghāda Murād's mandate as member of the High Judiciary Council resulted in improving 'the judicial product' since qualified candidates were not rejected to the advantage of lesser qualified candidates simply because of their gender.

In an interview,[14] Nā'il Mahfūz, President of the Court of Cassation and thereby member of the High Judiciary Council, described Ghāda Murād as 'the independent voice' of the Council, who unrelentingly defended her point of view, often one voice against six, and who sometimes succeeded in convincing her colleagues. Given the reputation of Ghāda Murād, it is not surprising that during her mandate on the Council, any form of discrimination against women candidates during the selection process was reduced to a minimum. Many young women judges and public prosecutors who trained at the IJS and were taught by Ghāda Murād—she gave the sessions on law of evidence—expressed their admiration for her and considered her a model of judicial professionalism to be emulated.

The selection process of judges and public prosecutors in Syria aims to recruit the best qualified candidates. In the case of women, it was observed that the evaluation was rigorous and, perhaps, outright discriminatory in the last National Judicial Examination held in 2007. Nonetheless, this very rigorous selection process has ensured that women members of the judiciary are qualified to hold judicial office.

[13] Here Rackley is quoting the words of Baroness Brenda Hale, the only woman law lord in the United Kingdom.

[14] Ghāda Murād was interviewed by Rawān al-Dāmin on 7 December 2007 for the series 'Women Pioneers' (*al-Rā'idāt*) produced by al-Jazīra television network based in Qatar. The transcript of the interview can be accessed online at the following address: http://www.aljazeera.net/programs/pages/dac02e8a-d486-46b0-aace-13ed8ca81e36. The author is extremely grateful to Paul Dussault for having located the interview on Youtube.

In addition to competence, integrity is a quality demanded of all judicial officers. What makes it possible for women to maintain 'an independent voice' in decision-making and be less exposed to outside influences and direct offers of bribery? The second part of the chapter will explain why women, in addition to being competent, are also known for their judicial integrity. It will also describe the measures adopted by the government and the Ministry of Justice to fight corruption in the judicial ranks and the active role women have played in securing a more independent and accountable judiciary.

4. THE SYRIAN GOVERNMENT'S FIGHT AGAINST JUDICIAL CORRUPTION

On 5 October 2005, the dismissal of 81 judges and public prosecutors throughout Syria made the front pages of the three major daily newspapers of Damascus, *al-Ba'th*, *Tishrīn* and *al-Thawra*. The respective articles stated that during the parliamentary session held in the capital,[15] members of the People's Assembly (Syria's Parliament) gave their full support to the removal of 81 judges and public prosecutors on grounds of corruption, as ordered by the Legislative Decree No 95 of 3 October 2005, signed by the President, Bashar al-Asad. In a speech pronounced before Members of Parliament, the Minister of Justice, Muhammad al-Ghafarī, described the dismissal as a step in the right direction towards judicial reform and the best way to win back the public's confidence in the judiciary.

In the weeks to follow, a number of articles appeared in the three dailies,[16] written by journalists, lawyers and members of the public, again expressing their support for the removal. Many commented that this action of judicial reform was perhaps too modest, since those removed only constituted a small percentage of the judicial corps,[17] implying that even more judges and public prosecutors should have been brought to justice for their misconduct.[18] Some people called for a general purging of the ranks of other civil servants or professionals, notably general managers of public enterprises, government inspectors, police and lawyers, well-known to be corrupt. Lawyers were especially targeted, labelled the instigators

[15] 4 October was a gruelling day for Parliament. Forty-three legislative decrees were reviewed, all in the record time of three hours: *al-Thawra* (5 October 2005) 15.

[16] Approximately 40 articles on judicial reform were published in the three dailies during October 2005.

[17] About seven per cent of the total number of judges and public prosecutors were removed according to figures provided by *Tishrīn*. The total number of judges and public prosecutors in Syria in October 2005 was 1085 (12 October 2005) 14; or 1110 (29 October 2005) 7.

[18] *al-Ba'th* (9 October 2005) 5.

of corruption (*mafātīh al-fasād*) because they attempt to bribe underpaid judges to make decisions in favour of their clients.[19]

In October 2005, the aim of the government was not only to punish the misconduct of judges and public prosecutors, but to improve the livelihood of those members of the judiciary who are honest and hard-working. Legislative Decree No 93, issued the same date as No 95, stated that judges and public prosecutors, state attorneys and judges of the Council of State (judges of the administrative courts) were to receive a 25 per cent increase in their salaries. In addition, a fee paid for every case filed at court, in the form of a stamp (*al-lazīqa al-qaḍā'iyya*), was doubled (100 Syrian pounds; two US dollars) as stipulated by Legislative Decree No 94 of 3 October 2005. This fee is used to supplement the salaries of judges and public prosecutors and is equally shared by all members of the judiciary on a monthly basis. The amount per person varies from 16,000 to 20,000 Syrian pounds (Ministry of Justice, 20 July 2006). The doubling of the fee greatly improved the incomes of judges and public prosecutors, but, as some complained, at the expense of the common citizen and not the state. It was understood that better-paid judges and public prosecutors would be less prone to bribery. Housing with preferential mortgage rates was also to be made more readily available and transportation from home to work was promised for all (some members of the judiciary already benefit from this privilege).[20]

The reaction of the dailies' readership to the increase in income was mixed. Some felt that the income of the judges and public prosecutors was now astronomically high given the living standards of Syria, and that other public sector employees, especially teachers, also deserved an increase in their salaries. Others described the poor working conditions of judges and public prosecutors: the dirt and dust of courtrooms, the shabby furnishings, the lack of air-conditioning, etc. They thought the increase was well deserved and that more should be done to improve the justice system.

The names of the 81 judges and public prosecutors to be dismissed were not published in the newspapers, and it was only in the confines of the courthouses throughout Syria that names were circulating. Would the debate have been different if the public had known that out of the 81 judges and public prosecutors removed, only two had been women (Ministry of Justice, 21 December 2005)? It is common knowledge in the courthouses that women judges and public prosecutors, in general, are more honest than their male counterparts and, as a result, the public has more confidence

[19] *Tishrīn* (12 October 2005) 14.

[20] One last decree, No 92, issued also on 3 October 2005, aimed at improving the financial situation of judges. Allowances for out-of-court inspections were increased: *Tishrīn* (8 October 2005) 5.

when served by a woman.[21] In October 2005, women made up 12 per cent of the judiciary, but only accounted for 2.5 per cent of those judges and public prosecutors removed from office. Fieldwork conducted at the Damascus courthouse in December 2004 and December 2005 shows that the percentage of women judges and public prosecutors increased at the courthouse, from 38 per cent in 2004 to 47 per cent in 2005. After the 'judicial cleansing' of October 2005, there was a slight shortage of personnel at the Damascus courthouse. The number of public prosecutors was reduced to half in order to appoint judges to the vacated courts, and the number of women was at an all time high at the end of October: 70 out of 134 (52 per cent).[22]

These hard facts show that women members of the judiciary are, on the whole, less corrupt. If this truth were better publicised then, perhaps, the more conservative factions of Syrian society would be less opposed to women holding judicial office. Since this truth is known to the Ministry of Justice, it remains puzzling that fewer women were recruited in the 2007 cohort of the IJS. Of course, nothing guarantees that women who are now members of the judiciary or members to be, will continue to conduct themselves in an ethical way.[23] Nonetheless, the figures are there to vouch for their integrity, and an increase of the women membership of the judiciary could be a more gradual way to reform the judiciary from within instead of the sudden removal of dishonest judges and public prosecutors from above.

5. JUDICIAL AUTONOMY OF JUDGES AND PUBLIC PROSECUTORS

A judiciary that is independent from other branches of government on an institutional level is not necessarily independent on the individual level. Members of the judicial corps can be exposed to outside influences in addition to pressures within the judicial hierarchy in the everyday workings of the court and in their decision-making. To evaluate the degree of autonomy of the judicial corps, many factors are to be taken into consideration. In the Syrian context, the institutional structures of the judiciary, the connections or

[21] An opinion expressed by lawyers, court clerks and women judges and public prosecutors. Interviews: 15 June 2004; 20 June 2004; 21 June 2004; 23 June 2004; 28 June 2004; 29 June 2004; 1 July 2004; 8 November 2004; 22 November 2004; 27 June 2006; 29 June 2006; 23 July 2006; 5 June 2007; 6 June 2007; 18 July 2007; 26 May 2008; 27 May 2008; 28 May 2008; 29 May 2008; 27 July 2008; 28 July 2008; 29 July 2008; 29 July 2008; 30 July 2008; 21 December 2008.

[22] Decree No 2979/L of 26 October 2005.

[23] A few interviewees said that women at the courthouse (judges, prosecutors, lawyers and court staff) are not entirely immune to bribery. In their opinion, not gender but one's education and good upbringing is the best deterrent against corruption. Interviews: 21 June 2004; 17 May 2007; 28 July 2008.

lack thereof between the judiciary and outside authorities and the personal integrity of its members, particularly female, will be described with the intention of answering the initial question of this chapter: why are women judges and prosecutors more independent decision-makers than their male counterparts?

5.1. Institutional Structures

The Constitution of 1973 guarantees the independence of the judiciary from other branches of government (Articles 131 and 133, section 1).[24] However, on 3 October 2005, this independence was momentarily infringed upon when for the next 24 hours, as stipulated by Legislative Decree No 95, the Council of Ministers had the full power to remove those judges and public prosecutors it thought unfit for office. According to the 1961 Judiciary Act (with amendments), it is the High Judiciary Council that imposes disciplinary sanctions for any misconduct on the part of judges and public prosecutors (Articles 107 and 109). The range of sanctions includes: (1) a warning; (2) a salary reduction; (3) a delay in promotion; and (4) dismissal for the most serious offences (Article 105). The decisions of the High Judiciary Council are based on reports prepared by the Judicial Inspection Department of the Ministry of Justice. This department is responsible for investigating complaints made against judges and public prosecutors. In addition, it routinely evaluates the performance, productivity and efficiency of all members of the judiciary. A positive report issued by the department results in promotion; a negative report can result in a sanction if so decided by the High Judiciary Council (Article 15, section 10). The administrative body of the Judicial Inspection Department is composed of a president and six members, all high-ranking members of the judiciary (Article 11, section 2). To assist in the routine evaluation process, senior members of the judiciary are mandated by the department to review the work of lower-ranking members. (In 1999, of the 86 judges and public prosecutors chosen to conduct the evaluations, six were women—seven per cent.)[25] Thus, senior

[24] In an interview granted to the Syrian magazine, *Syria Today* (no 51, July 2009: 40), Ghāda Murād commented that in order to better guarantee the independence of the judicial branch of government, the Minister of Justice, as member of the executive, should not be at the head of the High Judiciary Council, because certain members of the Council who disagree with him fear the possibility of a removal if they express their opinions. She suggested that Art 65 of the 1961 Judiciary Act be amended in order for the President of the Court of Cassation, the highest-ranking member of the judiciary, to act as the head of the Council and deputy to the Syrian President.

[25] Decree No 1168 of 16 June 1999. *The Official Gazette of the Syrian Arab Republic*, vol 2, 1999(42) 4468. The women delegated are among the most high-ranking members of the judiciary: Ghāda Murād, at the time, was the Attorney-General of Syria; Salwā Kadīb, the only woman to have been appointed the President of an Assize Court and President of one

members of the judiciary exert their influence and control over all members of the judicial corps and staff, holding them accountable for their conduct. After a two-year probationary period, all recently appointed judges and public prosecutors secure tenure (Article 74).[26] In the case of a removal, the High Judiciary Council must justify its decision and the person to be removed has the right to appeal the decision (Article 110). However, this is not what happened on 3 October 2005, when the judges and public prosecutors were removed on grounds of corruption by the executive branch of government and the normal channels of appeal were suspended, making the decision irrevocable. As expressed by the public debate in the press, both the government and the people felt that corrupt judges and public prosecutors were to be held accountable for their misconduct and that their dismissal was to be swift and definite.[27] A temporary violation of judicial independence was tolerated in the name of judicial reform and accountability. Nonetheless, the dismissal of judges and public prosecutors in October 2005 was an extraordinary measure on the part of the government, for statutory legislation requires that judges and public prosecutors in Syria benefit from security of tenure, 'the sine qua non of judicial independence' (Russell, 2001: 14).

5.2. Personal Connections and Powerful People

The 1961 Judiciary Act (with amendments) stipulates that a member of the judiciary should not express any political opinions or engage in political activity (Article 81). In an interview granted to the al-Jazīra television network after her retirement from the judiciary,[28] Ghāda Murād expressed her opinion about the appropriate conduct that a judge or public prosecutor should adopt with regard to politics. She first mentioned the Judiciary Act that prohibits a judge or a public prosecutor from adhering to a political party or association, this in order to maintain the neutrality (*ḥiyād*) of the judiciary. Ghāda Murād explained that even though she personally agreed with the ideology of the ruling Ba'th Socialist Party in Syria and was

of the criminal divisions at the Court of Cassation; Āmina al-Shammāt who was the presiding judge of the commercial court of first instance at the Damascus courthouse, a court some consider the most important at the courthouse; Halīma Haydar, one of the two judges of the Indictment Division, at the Damascus courthouse, that decides if a case is brought before the Assize Court; Shukrān Kallās, President of one of the civil appeal courts at the Damascus courthouse and substitute judge at the Court of Cassation; and Amīra Ahmadū, a judge on a civil appeal court in Idlib before her retirement in 2004.

[26] Art 93 mentions a three-year period.

[27] Except for judge Nizām Dahdal, who expressed his reservations about the Council of Minister's role in the dismissal in an interview granted to *al-Thawra* (7 October 2005) 4.

[28] See above (n 14) for complete reference.

approached on a number of occasions to become a party member, she never did because of her judicial functions. She hypothesised that if a judge were a member of the Ba'th Party and one of the two parties to appear in court were also a Ba'thist, the judge might feel ill at ease while adjudicating. She added, however, that it was tolerated that members of the judiciary belong to the ruling party. For example, one of the women recruited in the first National Judicial Examination open to them in 1977 was, at the time, an executive member of the Women's General Union.[29] (All executive members of the Union are members of the ruling Ba'th Party.)[30] During interviews conducted at the Damascus courthouse in 2004, a court clerk mentioned that the presiding judge was absent because she was attending a party meeting.[31] In many public services and buildings in Syria it is not uncommon for the ruling Ba'th Party to have a recruiting office. This is the case at the Damascus courthouse where party meetings are periodically held in a large conference room. Some people at the courthouse even claim that being a party member provides more opportunities for career advancement. However, it is clear that one can pursue a successful career in the judiciary without being a party member, as in the case of Ghāda Murād.

During the television interview, Ghāda Murād also spoke about the problems sometimes encountered when a judge or public prosecutor presides over a case in which one of the parties belongs to the class of 'important' people and officials (*nās muhimīn*; *mas'ūlīn kibār*). She spoke about two incidents while in office. In the first instance, she was the presiding judge of an appellate court which did not rule in favour of some important people. As a form of reprisal, she was transferred to the public prosecutor's office. This relocation had no effect on her remuneration since salaries are determined by one's rank and seniority, and not by the functions performed.

At the time of the second incident, she was the chief public attorney (*al-muhāmī al-'āmm al-awwal*) at the Damascus courthouse—the first woman in the Arab world to hold such a position—when a complaint was lodged against the son of the 'second or third' most important political figure in Syria. The accused had bought an apartment on the top floor of a building and had wrongfully taken possession of the roof, which was shared property, in order to build on it. He blocked the access to the roof and, after an investigation was conducted, the illegal construction was dismantled on the order of the chief public attorney. Ghāda Murād was immediately contacted by the powerful father who invited her to come and

[29] *al-Mar'a al-'arabiyya* (The Arab Woman), 1978: (121) 48. This periodical is the official organ of the Women's General Union of Syria.

[30] For more information on the Women's General Union of Syria, see author's PhD dissertation, 'La publicistique pour les femmes au Moyen-Orient (1980–1995)' (Université de Paris VIII, 1999) 232–337.

[31] Interview, 25 October 2004.

have a cup of coffee or tea and talk things over. She apologised saying that she was busy. Later on, the same case was assigned to the appellate court where she held office. The court finally ruled that the wall blocking the entrance to the roof was to be destroyed in order to allow all apartment owners to have access to it. The day the decision was read in court, the lawyer and son of the important politician could not believe they had lost the case. Shortly after, the Minister of Justice sent a note thanking Ghāda Murād for the decision.

As these two incidents show, sometimes a judge is reprimanded for a decision she takes and at other times she is thanked. It really depends on who is in power and the connections they have. Of course, the presiding judge must possess a certain amount of courage to make decisions that are not necessarily in favour of powerful people. Ghāda Murād was praised for her courage and integrity by her mentor, Abū al-Khayr 'Ābdīn, former president of a civil appellate court at the Damascus courthouse. However, as mentioned by Ghāda Murād, some judges and public prosecutors are basically dishonest and will ask officials to cover up for them. In return, the officials will ask for favours and, little by little, the judge will moderate his decisions. This she regards as a direct violation of the oath that members of the judiciary pronounce when they take office: 'I swear by God to judge among people fairly and to respect the law' (Article 77 of the 1961 Judiciary Act).

5.3. Personal Integrity: Sense of Duty, Reputation and Financial Security

In the interviews conducted with women judges and public prosecutors in the courthouses of Syria, it transpired that they had a high sense of moral and religious duty. Many of them expressed the idea embedded in religious education (Christian and Muslim) and the Islamic legal tradition that a judge, as every other believer, is responsible before God for the decisions he or she makes. A prophetic tradition cited in the classical treatises of Islamic law on judgeship, and mentioned by some judges and public prosecutors, states that for every three judges in office, two are destined for Hell and one for Paradise.[32] The judge who makes a decision without knowledge of the law or the judge who has the knowledge but deliberately decides against the law is destined for Hell. It is only the judge who has knowledge and respects the law who is destined for Paradise. This is the ideal of judicial conduct upheld in the Islamic legal tradition, and many women judges

[32] The tradition is found in the collections of *Abū Dā'ūd* (no 3573); *al-Tirmidhī* (no 1322); and *Ibn Māja* (no 2315).

expressed their desire to be that judge who respects the law. Some judges and public prosecutors, both women and men, also referred to the letter that 'Umar ibn al-Khattāb (d. 644), second caliph of the nascent Islamic empire, addressed to Abū Mūsā al-Ash'arī, a judge he appointed to Kufa (Iraq). The letter embodies the credo of judicial conduct and procedure of the Islamic legal tradition. Even today, at the IJS, this letter is taught and analysed in the course on judicial ethics. A judicial ethics inspired by the religious and legal tradition of Islam is still very much part of the judicial culture of Syria even if civil law (of French origin) has basically become the law of the nation. In his letter, which adorned the offices of some judges and public prosecutors (5 June 2007; 27 July 2008), 'Umar reminds judges that all persons are equal before the law and that the judge who respects the law will be rewarded in the Hereafter:

> Consider all the people equal before you in your court and in your attention, so that the noble will not expect you to be partial and the humble will not despair of justice from you. [...] For establishing justice in the courts of justice, God will grant you a rich reward and give you a good reputation (Rosenthal, 1958: 453–54).

The women judges and public prosecutors interviewed said they worked hard to maintain the high moral values associated with their office. Since the idea of women holding judicial office is still not entirely accepted in Syria, women members of the judiciary feel the obligation to do their best to remain above reproach and live up to the standards of competence and integrity expected of all members of the judiciary. Women judges and public prosecutors are, therefore, very concerned about their reputations as professionals; they are equally concerned about their reputations as women. If a woman judge or public prosecutor were to accept a bribe, it is assumed by many that she is morally corrupt (*faltāneh* in Syrian dialect) and would be willing to accept money for another type of service, perhaps of a sexual nature (28 June 2004; 8 November 2004; 26 June 2006; 28 July 2008). Her reputation as a respectable woman would be ruined let alone her reputation as a judge. In fact, a woman's personal integrity is indistinguishable from her judicial integrity. Women in all social contexts in Syria do their utmost to preserve their reputations as upright and morally honest persons in order to maintain the respect of others as observed by the author on many occasions.

With regard to social mores, though women and men do mix in the workplace, their relation is not one of proximity in Syria. If it is tolerated that women associate with men at work for professional reasons, socialising inside or outside the workplace is unacceptable (21 June 2004; 29 June 2006; 23 July 2006; 28 July 2008). In most courthouses, there is a cafe for lawyers and court staff. Women lawyers are circumspect about sharing a table with male colleagues and tend to mix solely with other women. Many of them do not even go to the cafe, a place identified as the realm of men. As for the women judges and public prosecutors, they often get together in each other's chambers over coffee or tea as noticed by the author. For the most part, after a long day at the courthouse, women go home. Of the women and judges interviewed, 74 per cent are married or divorced and almost all of them have children and, therefore, must attend to family responsibilities. A woman's narrow circle of acquaintances, namely of family and close friends, often unrelated to the work environment, has a direct bearing on her capacity to remain autonomous in her judicial functions. Most women do not belong to the informal networks of lawyers, judges and government officials that exist inside and outside of the courthouses (29 June 2004; 26 June 2006; 29 June 2006). As one woman judge mentioned, women do not transform their homes into a judge's chambers or a closed courtroom (28 May 2008). It is true that some women are the wives, daughters and sisters of influential men and may benefit from these connections. However, they are rarely implicated directly in networks of influence and, therefore, are less exposed to the pressures and demands which could have an impact on their decision-making. Rather than viewed as a handicap, a woman's relative social seclusion is an asset to her career as a judge and public prosecutor. It ensures that she decides cases as independently as possible.

Some women judges and public prosecutors explained that the willingness to accept a bribe is linked more to one's economic responsibilities, which are greater for men than women, rather than generated by a strong sense of greed. Nonetheless, they did not regard this as an excuse for the violation of one's duties and the law (17 June 2004; 28 June 2004; 26 June 2006). Generally speaking, women are not responsible for their own livelihoods. If they live with their parents, their father is economically responsible for them; if they are married and live with their spouse, it is their spouse's duty to support them (Article 154 of the [Muslim] Personal Status Law No 59 of 1953). Married women can participate in paying household expenses, but their salaries are considered a second income. Some single women contribute to the upkeep of their ageing parents, especially their widowed mothers; however, again, it is considered the duty of their brother(s) to provide for ageing parents. Women's economic independence from men is neither a social reality nor considered a goal in itself. In 2003, women constituted only 12.4 per cent of the work force (non-agricultural) in Syria (Courbage, 2007: 204)[33] and most of the women judges and public prosecutors interviewed said they embarked on a judicial career not out of economic need or

[33] The Tenth Five-Year Plan states that the participation of women in the labour force decreased from 19.8% to 16.3% (in the Arabic version the percentage is 17.3) during the period 2002–04. It is not specified whether these percentages include women who work in agriculture. See Arabic version: 847; English version : chapter 23.2.1: 5.

the desire to be economically independent, but out of a desire for personal achievement or because they wanted to defend people's rights and fight against social injustices. In fact, the women judges and public prosecutors of today constitute, on a wider scale, the first generation of career women, since 89 per cent of their mothers are homemakers (Cardinal, 2008: 129). Perhaps with time, economic considerations will become the major factor which determines if women pursue a career. Until then, women judges and public prosecutors remain the most independent members of the judiciary in Syria because they have fewer economic responsibilities and are excluded from social networks of power and influence.

6. CONCLUSION

Ghāda Murād was the first woman in Syria to be appointed to the judiciary in 1975. She was the first woman in the Arab world to act as a chief public attorney as well as the first woman Attorney-General. As Attorney-General of Syria and member of the High Judiciary Council, Ghāda Murād is the only woman to have played an active role in the recruitment and selection process of the judiciary. During her mandate, the percentage of women candidates admitted to the judiciary increased significantly, only to drop after her retirement in 2006. Her presence on the Council made a difference. The judicial selection and appointments process was implemented with greater equity and equal opportunities were provided for the best candidates, both women and men. As a result, the overall quality and professionalism of the judicial corps improved. Ghāda Murād also made a difference in the everyday workings of the courts. She ruled according to the law, disregarding the political connections and social status of the parties appearing in court. It is regrettable that only four months after Ghāda Murād retired at 65, a law was passed which prolonged the term of judicial office to 70 years of age (Law No 64 of 27 December 2006). If her term had lasted for an additional five years, the judiciary and the public could have continued to benefit from her integrity, professionalism and independent voice. Most probably, a greater number of women judicial candidates would have been selected for the 2007 cohort of the IJS. Since her retirement in August 2006, Ghāda Murād has gone back to her first career and practises law in Damascus.

The majority of women judges and public prosecutors have followed in the footsteps of this woman pioneer in their commitment to the law and equal treatment of all parties. The evidence shows that women members of the judiciary are more independent and less prone to bribery and corruption than their male colleagues. Does this mean that women are innately more ethical? Though most women members of the judiciary do not disassociate their professional duties from their religious duties—they are responsible for their decisions and actions before the judicial community and society as they are before God—this chapter did not take an essentialist stance and claim that women are 'naturally' more honest. Rather, it attempted to describe the social, economic and political factors which enable women members of the judiciary in Syria to be more independent in their decision-making.

7. ACKNOWLEDGEMENTS

The Ministers of Culture and Justice of Syria are to be thanked for granting permission to conduct the research. My thanks also go to all participants, both women and men, for generously giving up their time and the Institut français du Proche-Orient (IFPO) in Damascus for its unconditional hospitality and support. The research was funded in part by a Cardinal-Maurice-Roy grant from the Université Laval, Quebec, Canada.

8. REFERENCES

Boigeol, A (1993) 'La magistrature française au féminin: entre spécificité et banalisation' 25 *Droit et Société* 489.

Cardinal, MC (2008) 'Women and the Judiciary in Syria: Appointments Process, Training and Career Paths' 15(1–2) *International Journal of the Legal Profession* 123.

Courbage, Y (2007) 'La population de la Syrie: des réticences à la transition (démographique)' in B Dupret, Z Ghazzal, Y Courbage and M al-Dbiyat (eds), *La Syrie au présent: reflets d'une société* (Arles, Actes sud).

Malleson, K (2003) 'Justifying Gender Equality on the Bench: Why Difference Won't Do' 11 *Feminist Legal Studies* 1.

Rackley, E (2008) 'What a Difference Difference Makes: Gendered Harms and Judicial Diversity' 15(1–2) *International Journal of the Legal Profession* 37.

Rosenthal, F (1958) (trans Ibn Khaldūn) *The Muqqadimah, An Introduction to History* vol 1 (London, Routledge and Kegan Paul).

Russell, PH (2001) 'Toward a General Theory of Judicial Independence' in PH Russell and DM O'Brien (eds), *Judicial Independence in the Age of Democracy: Critical Perspectives from Around the World* (Charlottesville, University Press of Virginia).

Songer, DR and Crews-Meyer KA (2000) 'Does Judge Gender Matter? Decision Making in State Supreme Courts?' 81 *Social Science Quarterly* 750.

2.5

Skills for Judicial Work: Comparing Women Judges and Women Magistrates

KATHY MACK AND SHARYN ROACH ANLEU

Abstract

This chapter examines judging and gender by looking in depth at women in the judiciary, particularly their experiences of and attitudes towards judging. As more women enter the legal profession and the judiciary, greater attention is being paid to the experiences of women, rather than considering only male/female comparisons.

Our comprehensive socio-legal study of the entire Australian judiciary enables a comparison of the experiences and attitudes of women at different levels of the judicial hierarchy. In particular, this chapter examines attitudes towards skills and qualities needed for everyday work, comparing the views of women who preside in the first instance trial courts with those who sit in the higher trial and appellate courts.

The findings challenge the monolithic image of the generic disembodied judge as well as the binary construction of male/female differences within the judiciary. They also problematise attempts to map judging processes and outcomes onto differences of gender or court hierarchy alone.

1. INTRODUCTION

MUCH DISCUSSION OF gender and judging is based on assumptions or expectations of differences between men and women judges (Beiner, 2005: 187; Boyd, Epstein and Martin, 2007). As more women enter senior ranks of the legal profession and the judiciary, greater attention has been paid to the multiple identities of and differences among women (Boigeol, 2003: 415; Hunter, 2005; Kenney, 2010; Martin, Reynolds and Keith, 2002: 620; Mather, 2003: 34; Menkel-Meadow,

1995: 243, 264; Rhode, 2003; Wells, 2003: 238; Gastron, 2013; Kohen, 2013; Rackley, 2013 and Bartolomei, 2013, in this volume).

This chapter investigates judging and gender by looking at women's experiences of and attitudes towards judging in light of the contexts in which they undertake their work, whether first instance trial courts or the higher courts.[1]

In 2009, women constituted about 30 per cent of the Australian judiciary.[2] This is an increase from 14 per cent in 1999 (Women Lawyers' Association of New South Wales, 1999: 17–18) and nine per cent in 1995 (Thornton, 1996: 202, fn 62). Even as the proportion of women in the judiciary becomes larger, women's exclusion and limited roles continue; women tend to be in less prestigious roles, lower ranks or specialist courts, such as family or children's courts (AIJA, 2009; Hunter, 2003: 93; Thornton 1996: 204). The location of women in the Australian judiciary is similar to women in the legal profession generally or in the judiciary in other countries (Gastron, 1991: 25–28; Schultz, 2003: xxix–xxxi).

The increasing numbers of women, especially in the lower courts, is one of the few readily apparent aspects of diversity within the Australian judiciary (see Moran and Rackley in this collection for a consideration of dimensions of diversity). There is relatively little variation in race/ethnicity, age, wealth, class, disability, sexuality, professional background or marital/parental status (Mack and Roach Anleu, 2008).[3]

[1] This research was funded initially by a University-Industry Research Collaborative Grant in 2001 with Flinders University and the Association of Australian Magistrates (AAM) as the partners and received financial support from the Australasian Institute of Judicial Administration. Until 2005, it was funded by an Australian Research Council (ARC) Linkage Project Grant (LP210306), 2002–05, with AAM and all Chief Magistrates and their courts as industry partners and with support from Flinders University as the host institution. From 2006, the research has been funded by an ARC Discovery Grant (DP0665198), 2006–08 and since 2012, by an ARCD Discovery Grant (DP1096888) 2010–2012. All phases of this research involving human subjects have been approved by the Social and Behavioural Research Ethics Committee of Flinders University.

We are grateful to Russell Brewer, Carolyn Corkindale, Elizabeth Edwards, Ruth Harris, Julie Henderson, Lilian Jacobs, Leigh Kennedy, Lisa Kennedy, Mary McKenna, Wendy Reimens, Mavis Sansom, Billy Chia-Lung Tai, Jordan Tutton, Rose Williams, Rae Wood and David Wootton for research and administrative assistance.

[2] Australasian Institute of Judicial Administration (AIJA) (2009) Gender Statistics: Judges and Magistrates, at: www.aija.org.au/index.php?option=com_content&task=view&id=32&Itemid=121.

[3] The Australian judiciary has an average age of 57 years, and two-thirds are aged between 52 and 64. They identify their ancestry as Australian and/or English or Irish and their religion as Christian, equally divided between Catholic and other Christian (usually Anglican); those who do not identify as Christian indicate no religious affiliation. Nearly all spent their childhoods in Australia and most grew up in large cities and are nearly evenly divided among those who attended state schools, Catholic and other independent private schools. Nearly all their fathers participated in full-time paid work. Half of their mothers did not participate in paid work at all, and over half identify their mother's main occupation as home duties. Most report personal incomes between \$225,000 and \$325,000 and household incomes between \$225,000

A second major difference within the Australian judiciary is court hierarchy.[4] Court hierarchy is important within the legal system; distinctions are often drawn between the magistrates who sit in the lower 'inferior' first instance courts, and judges (or justices) who sit in the higher or 'superior' courts.[5] The nature and demands of the work in Australia's first instance trial courts are unlike those of the higher courts in important ways, discussed more fully below.

and $375,000. Nearly all magistrates and judges are married or partnered, and most of their spouses are in paid work, about equally divided between full-time and part-time work. Nearly all magistrates and judges have at least one child and about half the judiciary have three or more children. All have legal qualifications and most have experienced a variety of forms of legal practice, mainly in the private sector, before entering the judiciary, on average, after 15–20 years in practice. There are some gender differences in these qualities, but a detailed consideration of all gender differences is beyond the scope of this chapter.

[4] Australia has a federal system of government. This is reflected in the court system, with national courts and a court system for each state and two territories operating separately. (Territories are regions, which have some degree of self-government but do not have the full independent legal status of states.)

Each Australian state and territory has a magistrates or local court and a Supreme Court. There is also an intermediate trial court called the District Court in New South Wales, Queensland, South Australia and Western Australia (County Court in Victoria) but not in the smallest jurisdictions (the Australian Capital Territory, the Northern Territory and Tasmania).

Magistrates courts in the Australian states and territories are first instance courts of general criminal and civil jurisdiction; trials are heard by a magistrate sitting alone. District/County Courts are primarily trial courts, hearing criminal cases with juries, and civil cases, usually without juries. Supreme Courts hear the most serious criminal cases usually with juries, larger complex civil cases usually without juries and appeals. Appeals in Supreme Courts are usually heard by a panel of three judges. Some jurisdictions also have specialist courts such as land and environment courts, industrial commissions or children's courts which may operate as separate courts or as a branch of a generalist court.

Commonwealth courts are national courts which hear cases throughout Australia and include the High Court, the Federal Court, the Family Court and the Federal Magistrates Court. The High Court of Australia is the final court of appeal from state and Commonwealth courts. The Federal Court has a specialist trial and appeal jurisdiction, primarily commercial and administrative law matters arising under particular Commonwealth legislation. The Family Court deals with issues of divorce and custody of children. The Federal Magistrates Courts hear less complex matters falling under the jurisdiction of the Family Court and the Federal Court.

There are approximately 160 judges in Commonwealth courts, 400 state and territory judges and 450 magistrates totalling over 1000 judicial officers, organised into over 25 different courts for a total population of 22,000,000. This description does not include members of the many state and federal tribunals, which resolve a range of disputes arising under specific legislation. The officials who preside in tribunals are generally not regarded as judicial officers.

[5] In this chapter, the terms 'judiciary' or 'judicial officer' refer to all members of the Australian judiciary, judges and magistrates. The terms 'magistrate' and 'judge' are used to distinguish members of the judiciary who preside in the first instance, or lower courts from those who preside in the higher courts. Unlike the lay magistrates observed by Carlen (1976) and McBarnet (1981) in their studies of English magistrates' courts, Australian magistrates are paid judicial officers, nearly always full-time, with legal qualifications and appointed until a fixed retirement age, usually 65 (Mack and Roach Anleu, 2004). This is a change from the previous practice in some Australian jurisdictions in which magistrates were part of the public service, often promoted from the ranks of the clerks of the court, and sometimes without legal qualifications. The formal statutory requirement of legal qualification and separation from the public service is fairly recent, from 1969 in Tasmania to 1991 in Queensland.

As Judith Resnik has argued, feminist theories of judging should be built on the daily experiences and practices of judges (1988: 1930). This chapter concentrates on judging and the nature of judicial work as experienced by women magistrates and women judges, and in particular on the skills and qualities used in everyday work. We ask whether gender interacts differently with the experience of judging at different levels of court.

This question is addressed by drawing on findings from two national surveys conducted in 2007, one sent to the magistrates who preside in the first instance courts, the other to the judges of the higher courts.[6] Together these surveys cover the entire Australian judiciary.

Responses to the surveys track the proportion of women in the Australian judiciary almost exactly: women make up 25 per cent of the respondents to the judges survey (n=309) and 33 per cent of the respondents to the magistrates' survey (n=242), with 29 per cent of all respondents overall indicating they are women. The percentages of women and men are based on responses to a single question in the survey which asked respondents to tick one of two choices: male or female. Three people who returned surveys did not respond to this question; one was a magistrate and two were judges.

Comparing women judges and women magistrates within the Australian judiciary requires a more complex analysis than a simple dichotomous comparison. It entails comparing male magistrates and male judges along the same dimensions resulting in the construction of four cohorts—female magistrates, female judges, male magistrates, male judges—as shown in Figure 1 below and in the format of the tables used to present the survey data in this chapter.

[6] Two separate surveys were required so that each survey could contain questions and terminology appropriate to the specific level of the judiciary and to the distinctive nature of their work, as well as questions applicable across all levels of the judiciary. The surveys were conducted as mail-back questionnaires. Participation was voluntary. Because of very strong concerns from the judiciary about confidentiality of the data, no tracking or identification was used on the surveys, so that the identity of those who returned the surveys and those who did not is unknown. All completed surveys are completely anonymous.

The National Survey of Australian Judges was sent to all 566 judges throughout Australia in March 2007. The survey was printed as a booklet with a heavy bright blue cover to distinguish it from the magistrates' surveys. Responses were received into June 2007; 309 surveys were returned, giving a national response rate of 54.5%. The judges who responded are generally representative of the judges as a whole, in terms of gender, time on the bench and level of court and appear generally representative in terms of age, though that cannot be calculated fully, as complete baseline date of birth data for all judges is not available.

The second National Survey of Australian Magistrates was sent to all 457 magistrates throughout Australia in late May 2007. The survey was printed as a booklet with a heavy bright orange cover to distinguish it from an earlier magistrates' survey in 2002 and the judges' survey. Two hundred and forty-two surveys have been returned, giving a response rate of 52.9%. The magistrates who responded are generally representative of the magistracy as a whole, in terms of gender, age and time on the bench, while there is some variation in terms of jurisdiction, with a slight overrepresentation of magistrates from New South Wales, compared with magistrates from other jurisdictions.

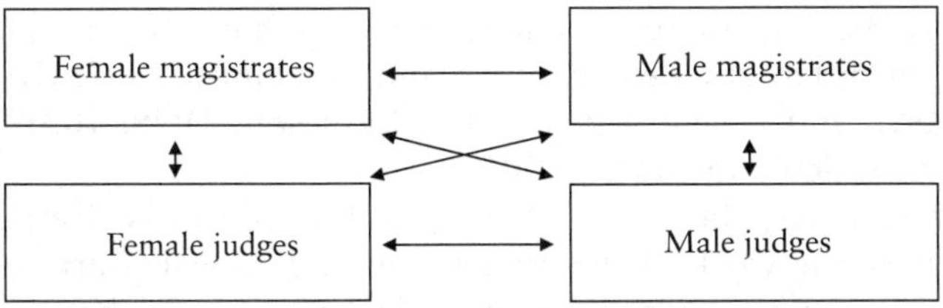

Figure 1: Four cohorts

Of course, gender and court hierarchy are not the only factors which may affect the views expressed by each cohort. For example, women are generally younger than their male colleagues and are more recently appointed to their positions in the judiciary. Male judges tend to be appointed after much longer times in practice than their female colleagues. (A detailed consideration of gender differences within the Australian judiciary is beyond the scope of this chapter. For an overview see Mack and Roach Anleu, 2010b.)

The results of these multifaceted comparisons demonstrate some complexities of gender and judging. While the dominant story is one of shared or similar attitudes on many dimensions across all four cohorts, the differences, where they exist, form varied patterns. These findings sometimes challenge and sometimes reinforce the binary construction of male/female judicial differences and the importance of court hierarchy in understanding judging. This deeper investigation of women judges' and women magistrates' experiences of the skills and qualities—which they regard as important—provides the basis for a nuanced understanding of the gendering of judging and of the performance of gender in different judicial contexts.

2. SKILLS AND QUALITIES NEEDED FOR JUDICIAL WORK

Judicial officers draw on a wide range of skills and qualities to carry out their tasks and functions. This analysis focuses on the importance to female judges and magistrates of three types of qualities: legal values, legal skills and interactive/interpersonal qualities. Each group of skills has strong potential for indicating differences along gender or court dimensions. They are also the qualities which the largest majorities of survey respondents identified as essential or very important to their everyday work.[7]

Discussions of judicial qualities tend to assume a 'generic' judge, even though judges undertake different jobs in different courts (Resnik, 1988:

[7] This analysis is based on responses to a survey question which asked respondents to indicate, from a pre-defined list of 39 skills and qualities, whether a particular skill or quality was essential, very important, important, somewhat important, or not important in the performance of daily tasks.

1909). More recently, there is some recognition that different qualities may be needed for different courts (Cowan and Hitchings, 2007; Kritzer, 2007: 334–36; Mack and Roach Anleu, 2007; Malleson, 1999: 103; Moorhead, 2007; Roach Anleu and Mack, 2005a).

In many respects, the work of magistrates' courts is distinctive when compared with the work of the higher trial and appeal courts. All trials in magistrates courts are heard without juries. Magistrates have virtually no appellate jurisdiction. They sit alone in regional and remote areas as well as in capital cities. The volume and pace of work is substantial; 90 per cent of all civil and criminal cases are initiated and finalised in the lower courts, usually within six months (Steering Committee for the Review of Government Service Provision, 2009). Those who appear in these courts are often unrepresented. The magistrates who preside must make very many judicial decisions every day, in circumstances of substantial caseload pressure; indeed, some cases can be fully resolved within minutes (Mack and Roach Anleu, 2007; Roach Anleu and Mack, 2007a).

Judicial work in this context appears to demand different qualities and skills compared with presiding at jury trials or hearing appellate cases, where presentations come primarily from legal practitioners and most interaction is with legal professionals, court staff or other judges rather than directly with parties (Roach Anleu and Mack, 2005b). Earlier Australian research suggests that interactive/interpersonal skills may be regarded as more important by magistrates than by judges (Laster and Douglas, 1995: 187–88). While magistrates may put less emphasis on conventional legal skills such as legal reasoning (ibid), legal values such as integrity or a sense of fairness might be expected to be highly valued by all judicial officers, regardless of court.

How might gender interact with these possible differences in the evaluation of skills needed for different types of courts? Will women share the views of their male colleagues at their level of court, or will women share views with each other, across court hierarchy? Some commentators on gender and judging have suggested that skills or qualities which address the role of emotions and interaction within judicial work demand capacities which are sometimes thought to be gendered (Menkel-Meadow, 1995; Neave, 1995; Resnik, 1988: 1921; Roach Anleu and Mack, 2005b). Resnik (1988) has argued that including qualities of compassion and sympathetic attention would require a shift in the conventional understanding of judging (1922–23).

More recently, considerations of women and judging have proposed conceptions of feminist adjudication which draw on feminist practical reasoning and contextualisation (in this collection see: Baines, 2013; Hunter, 2013 and Bartolomei, 2013, drawing on Katherine Bartlett, 1990). This may include elements of the ethic of care associated with Carol Gilligan's research, such as an emphasis on listening (Hunter, 2008: 13). However, feminist adjudication is not the same as an ethic of care, nor does it entirely depend on reinforcing conventional essentialist gendered stereotypes about women and emotions. Contextualisation, in this sense, is rational. It is a form of reasoning which emphasises concrete situations and contexts, though not to the exclusion of legal norms or abstractions. While empathy is important, feminist practical reasoning, as a judicial method, can also incorporate a kind of 'detached attention' (Hunter, 2008: 13). This involves a focus on the person before the court and the facts, while drawing on a wider base of legal and social knowledge as well as emotional insight (Bartolomei, 2013, in this volume). Rosemary Hunter, citing Helen O'Sullivan, describes this, in part, as a 'particularity' model of judging (2008: 12). Feminist adjudication, at any level of court, might value some legal skills such as fact finding, in order to particularise the individual or the context, or problem solving or settlement skills, as well as interpersonal qualities.

The most important finding from our research is the considerable similarity among all judicial officers, regardless of gender or court, in their relative assessment of the various qualities or skills. Nearly all respondents regard legal values as essential for their daily work, while two-thirds to three-quarters consider legal skills and interpersonal qualities as essential or very important. Many of the differences that emerge are primarily ones of intensity. In particular, women—especially women magistrates—tend to express their views of the importance of the various qualities with greater intensity, with a higher proportion rating a skill as essential, compared with responses from the other three cohorts. This pattern needs to be kept in mind when comparing views about a specific group of skills or an individual skill or quality, as indicated in the discussion below.

2.1. Legal Values

The strongest finding about the qualities and skills for everyday work is the extent to which women and men at all levels of the judiciary assess legal values as the most important type of qualities for their work. Legal values include impartiality, integrity/high ethical standards, a sense of fairness and protecting legal rights. About nine out of ten respondents in all cohorts rate two specific legal values (impartiality and integrity/high ethical standards) as essential, and around eight out of ten assess a sense of fairness as essential. The proportion in all four cohorts regarding protecting legal rights as essential varies from six out of ten to four out of ten. The only other quality to rate as high as any of the top three legal values is communication, an interactive quality discussed below.

Views about a sense of fairness and protecting legal rights show the greatest gender and hierarchical variation of the four legal values, though the differences are relatively slight.

Table 1: A sense of fairness (essential)

Female magistrates	89%	Male magistrates	76%
Female judges	84%	Male judges	76%

Three-quarters of male judges and male magistrates regard a sense of fairness as essential. A slightly greater proportion of women judges (84%) and a larger percentage of women magistrates (89%) regard this quality as essential (possibly reflecting the generally greater intensity of women's responses overall).

Protecting legal rights shows the most variation of the four values:

Table 2: Protecting legal rights (essential)

Female magistrates	63%	Male magistrates	41%
Female judges	53%	Male judges	55%

While a majority of respondents in three cohorts regard this aspect of judicial work as essential, these are notably lesser proportions than the other three legal values. This may reflect a view that the system itself protects legal rights, not the individual judicial officer. The judicial role is limited: to apply the law through a process which should result in enforcement of legal rights.

In terms of gender and court hierarchy analysis, the same proportion of female and male judges identify protecting legal rights as essential, while a larger percentage of female magistrates express this view, contrasting with a much smaller percentage of male magistrates. Theories of feminist adjudication suggest that promoting substantive equality or challenging legal doctrines that systematically disadvantage women would be an appropriate judicial role (Baines, 2009; Hunter, 2008). The strong endorsement of the importance of a sense of fairness might suggest that women share this judicial orientation slightly more than men. However, the different views about protecting legal rights indicate a less gendered view complicated by court hierarchy. The views of male magistrates, who are older and have spent a longer time as magistrates than their female colleagues, may reflect experience with limited opportunities to protect legal rights in their role. Female magistrates, who are younger and more recently appointed, may have greater expectations of the opportunities or of their own capacities to act within the judicial role. The shared views of female and male judges indicate that they agree about the potential for this in their courts or their own role, which differs slightly from the views of magistrates, whether male or female.

The two legal values that nearly all regard as essential are integrity/high ethical standards and impartiality. Integrity is an essential complement to impartiality and judicial independence (AIJA, 2007: 3–7). Judges are independent precisely on the expectation that they can and will judge impartially, without prejudgment of issues or preference for one party or class of litigants (Malleson, 1999: 73). In order for the rule of law to operate, judges must bring the highest standard of personal ethics and integrity to their everyday work.

A strikingly strong shared commitment to the legal value of impartiality appears to dominate women's and men's views about their work, whether magistrates or judges. The few who do not identify it as essential regard it as very important. This intense emphasis on impartiality among Australia's judiciary has significant implications for gender and judging. According to conventional concepts, a judge is a 'passive arbiter'. The neutral, impartial judge is disembodied, detached, unemotional and impersonal (Shaman, 1996: 610). Judicial decisions are compelled by law, fact and reason and are not the personal choice of an individual judge (Boigeol, 2003: 416; Malleson, 1999: 63; Moorhead, 2007).

The shared views about impartiality may indicate a general acceptance among women and men of the conventional understanding of neutrality as detached and objective. This may account for some of the similar views expressed by all cohorts about their work (Rackley, 2002; Roach Anleu and Mack, 2009). One advantage of this understanding of neutrality, for women and men, is to insulate the judiciary from responsibility for personal choice, internally/personally and politically/publicly. As Judge Sonia Sotomayor stated during the Senate hearings on her nomination to the US Supreme Court, 'It is not the heart that compels conclusions in cases, it is the law'.[8]

These findings suggest important reasons why women's judging may not be different from men's in many respects at any level of court. If judging has been constructed as masculine (Thornton, 1996: 201–09), and a particular understanding of impartiality underpins that construction (Naffine, 1991: 39–47), then women and men today, judges and magistrates, may be participating in an ongoing construction of judging as masculine through a shared acceptance of the belief in a fictional disembodied judicial officer (Rackley, 2002).

However, the meaning of impartiality and the generic judicial person may be different for women, or have a different value for women (Thornton, 1996: 207–08). Deference to the status quo can be a way of rebutting the presumption of incompetence faced by women judges, or indeed, any 'other'.

[8] See D Lithwick, 'What a Waste' *Slate* (2009) at: slate.com/id/2222936.

Beverly Blair Cook (1988) argued that 'regardless of other characteristics, ethnicity, class, age, family ideology, women judges are categorised first of all by their sex' (21). Claiming a disembodied professional identity may be empowering, a way of (implicitly) resisting being categorised by sex first, as a woman judge or a female magistrate. Adherence to shared norms of disembodied neutrality may be a way of resisting being gendered or raced. Sotomayor's conventional response may be the words of a wise Latina indeed, refusing to accept powerful white male attempts to reduce her to a few elements of her identity.

The claim that a male-dominated judiciary produces objective and value free rules and processes has been rejected from several perspectives: legal realism, feminism, critical legal studies, critical race theory and others (Astor, 2007: 224–25; Davies, 2008; Naffine, 1991). Thornton (2007) describes this assumed 'bifurcation between the objectivity of the judicial role and the subjective persona of the judge' as miraculous, and points out that concerns about judicial subjectivity are only raised if the judge or judicial nominee is a woman or somehow 'other' (391–92). Many possible sources of distinctively subjective judicial views—for example, a career as a prosecutor, or membership of a church—are rarely challenged in the same way as being gendered female. The inevitable deployment of male/masculine subjectivity in all the years the judiciary has been wholly male is either unnoticed or, worse, becomes the benchmark of a false impartiality.

Feminists point out that specificity of identity and voice as part of a diverse judiciary are not only consistent with ideals of legal neutrality, but positively necessary for legitimate judicial decisions (Hunter, 2008; Malleson, 2003). Rosemary Hunter (2008) argues that 'impartiality simply means a lack of partiality for one side or another; it does not have to mean indifference or disengagement' (18). Resnik (1988) and Naffine (1991: 39–47) go somewhat further and challenge the reality of a complete or pure impartiality: 'Impartiality and disengagement can never be achieved. Feminism rejects the choice between being a blank slate and imposing oneself on another, between having no interest and being corrupted by self interest' (Resnik 1988: 597). Oliver Wendell Holmes remarked long ago (1881) that 'the life of the law has not been logic; it has been experience' (1). Including the experiences and attitudes of diverse women, which will be similar to and different from men's experiences, is essential to an impartial judiciary.

2.2. Legal Skills

The elements in the survey which form this category are: legal analysis, legal knowledge, legal research, fact-finding ability, settlement skills, intellectual skills and problem-solving skills. In light of the very strong commitment to legal values, it might be expected that the judiciary would express a similarly consistent and strong allegiance to these legal skills. However, the overall emphasis on these qualities is much less than on legal values. Women magistrates express the most intense support, greater than female judges. This suggests a difference in the understanding of the nature of the work in the different courts. However, the views of female magistrates contrast very strongly with male magistrates, indicating that some male and female magistrates do not share the same view about the skills needed for their court. Female and male judges express similar views to each other, suggesting that they have a shared sense of the need for this range of skills on their court.

Table 3: Legal skills (essential)

Female magistrates	55%	Male magistrates	37%
Female judges	48%	Male judges	48%

Interestingly the views expressed by each cohort for the legal value of protecting legal rights (discussed above) are the same as for legal skills overall. While this pattern is an outlier compared with the responses for the other three legal values, it is consistent with the responses to legal skills. This suggests that the judiciary may view protecting legal rights less as a core value and more as a technical skill.

Because of the variety of skills included within this category, they need to be analysed individually, to tease out more subtle gendered or court related meanings. Some skills are more clearly specifically legal, while others reflect a wider view of what the work of a judicial officer might entail. For example, legal analysis, legal research or legal knowledge may be regarded as more technical or abstract, and possibly as more masculine (Gorman, 2005). Alternatively, they may be less important to magistrates' court work which involves more routine cases where the legal principles are well established (Laster and Douglas, 1995). Settlement and problem-solving skills may be more associated with feminist adjudication or with the more interactive work of the magistrates' courts.

Overall, judges value legal knowledge more than magistrates, and women value this skill more than men, but disaggregating the four cohorts presents a more complex picture, similar to that for legal skills overall. The same proportions of female and male judges value legal knowledge in their everyday work, suggesting that men and women in the higher courts have a shared view about this aspect of their work. However, a higher proportion of female magistrates values legal knowledge compared with male and female judges and much higher than male magistrates who have the lowest proportion regarding this skill as essential.

Table 4: Legal knowledge (essential)

Female magistrates	78%	Male magistrates	51%
Female judges	64%	Male judges	62%

The difference in views between male and female magistrates is very large and challenges any explanation of difference based primarily on the nature of magistrates court work compared with the higher courts. This is surprising as it might be expected that assessments of legal knowledge would reflect the nature of the work in each court more than any gender difference, where the higher courts may have a greater reliance on formal law, and that magistrates might value this quality less, given the different demands of their work (Mack and Roach Anleu, 2007; Roach Anleu and Mack, 2005b; Roach Anleu and Mack, 2007a).

Similarly, the shared views of female and male judges challenges an explanation for the difference between male and female magistrates on purely gender grounds. The lower proportion of male magistrates valuing legal knowledge may reflect the attitude of longer serving male magistrates for whom the job may often appear routine. Women are more recently appointed and younger as well as being outsiders as women, so they may feel that they have to prove themselves. This may be a partial explanation for why higher percentages of women magistrates (and to a lesser extent women judges) identify more skills as essential. They may be setting a standard for themselves to perform at a high level across all aspects of work, to prove they belong in the judiciary and that they were appointed on merit (Mather, 2003: 43–44; Thornton, 1996: 203). Women magistrates may be, or feel they need to be, more conscientious, taking decision-making very seriously, fully justifying decisions in law (Botelho Junqueira, 2003: 447), an experience shared with women in the legal profession generally (Easteal, 2001: 224–25).

The response pattern for legal analysis is similar to that for legal knowledge. (Table not given.) Legal research, which might be expected to be highly valued like legal knowledge and legal analysis as a specifically legal skill, or to reflect a clear difference in the nature of work of different courts is not highly valued by any cohort. (Table not given.) It was valued most highly by male judges (about one-third), with female magistrates and female judges very similar (about one-quarter) and male magistrates least.

Four legal skills diverge somewhat from the overall pattern: problem-solving skills, fact-finding skills , intellectual skills and settlement skills. These appear to be less specifically legal than other qualities in this category and they are arguably more likely to be associated with feminist adjudication.

Table 5: Problem-solving skills (essential)

Female magistrates	70%	Male magistrates	44%
Female judges	68%	Male judges	64%

The same proportions of female judges and magistrates rate problem-solving skills as essential, suggesting a possibly gendered view which transcends differences in court work. There is also a very large difference between male judges and male magistrates which might indicate a difference in the skills needed at different courts. However, similar proportions of male and female judges also regard this skill as essential, undercutting a gender explanation. There is a very large gender difference between male and female magistrates with respect to this quality. This is surprising as problem-solving skills might be expected to be especially important in the magistrates courts, with their emphasis on interaction directly with the parties, such as in small claims type cases or with many unrepresented participants.

Fact finding could be characterised as a technical legal skill, that is, part of the formal process of the court for establishing the necessary information for application of law. Alternatively it can be seen as part of contextualisation, of the particularity associated with concepts of feminist adjudication. It might be more important to magistrates than judges, as magistrates sit alone and engage directly in fact finding.

Table 6: Fact-finding skills (essential)

Female magistrates	62%	Male magistrates	54%
Female judges	51%	Male judges	54%

None of these views is clearly supported by the findings. Female magistrates have the highest proportion regarding this skill as essential, contrasting with their male colleagues, suggesting a gendered finding. However, the strongest contrast is with female judges (51%) who are essentially the same as male magistrates and male judges (54%). This response pattern is not the same as the pattern for technical legal skills such as legal knowledge, nor is it a clear gender pattern or a clear court pattern.

Intellectual skills display yet another pattern. Within each gender group, judges value intellectual skills as essential, more than magistrates, perhaps reflecting perceptions about differences in the nature and demands of their work. Within each court group, women value this quality more than men, but the gender difference between the judges is less than within the magistracy, and the court hierarchy variation among men is greater than among women.

Table 7: Intellectual skills (essential)

Female magistrates	54%	Male magistrates	36%
Female judges	68%	Male judges	57%

Intellectual skills are valued most highly by women judges—over two-thirds—followed by male judges then female magistrates, and least valued by male magistrates—just over one-third. In contrast to findings in relation to most other legal skills, female magistrates and male judges express very similar views about intellectual skills, different from their gender colleagues and their court colleagues.

Very few in any cohort regard settlement skills as a significant judicial skill. This likely reflects a view that settlement is for the parties to determine. In Australia, the judicial role is limited to case management and judges rarely have an active role in case settlement.

Overall, comparing the views of female magistrates and female judges regarding legal skills shows that higher proportions of female magistrates value legal analysis, legal knowledge and fact-finding ability, while a higher proportion of female judges value intellectual skills. The only shared views among the women are the similar proportions valuing problem-solving skills and legal research. This suggests that views about legal skills—at least those described by these categories—are not distinctly gendered.

Another important finding is the similarity between female and male judges across several skills: fact finding, problem solving, legal analysis, legal knowledge, but not legal research (where male judges value this more than any other cohort) and intellectual skills (which women judges value most). However, it is not possible to conclude from this finding that views about legal skills are largely determined by level of court, since male magistrates, as a group, value legal skills least and women magistrates value them most.

2.3. Interactive Qualities

Many interactive qualities are addressed in the surveys, including communication, courtesy, interpersonal skills, being a good listener, compassion, patience, managing the emotions of court users, sense of humour, empathy and cultural awareness. These are all qualities which may be especially important in the lower courts or part of contextualised, feminist judging and/or characteristically associated with women. Of course, these qualities are not unique to feminist adjudication, or to women. Kate Malleson (1999) identifies research which finds that the qualities judges admire in each other are 'empathy, humanity, patience, courtesy' over legal expertise (117), though professional and technical skills tend to be prioritised over humanistic skills (102).

The responses to these ten interactive/interpersonal qualities have been aggregated, to identify overall views about qualities of this type. A majority of women in the judiciary (50%) regard these qualities as essential compared with just over one-third of their male colleagues (36%). Comparing the findings by court hierarchy reveals that a slightly higher proportion of magistrates (45%) value these skills compared with judges (37%). These findings seem to confirm expectations about gender patterns as well as reflecting the need for different skills in magistrates' courts compared with other courts.

However, when the responses of the four cohorts are considered separately, a more complex picture emerges, in some respects similar to the pattern for legal skills, but also different.

Table 8: Interactive qualities (essential)

Female magistrates	57%	Male magistrates	38%
Female judges	43%	Male judges	35%

Female magistrates again appear distinctive with the highest proportion valuing these qualities compared with the other three cohorts, though as noted above this may partially reflect the generally higher proportions of this cohort regarding many skills and qualities as essential. Female judges are the next largest proportion which regards these qualities as essential. Although it is a somewhat smaller proportion compared with female magistrates, it is a slightly greater percentage than either of the male cohorts.

The differences between the women might suggest a difference in the nature of work in each level of court. However, much smaller proportions of male magistrates value these skills compared with female magistrates, only slightly less than female judges. The group with the lowest proportion regarding these qualities as essential is male judges, though there is really no difference between male judges and male magistrates.

This suggests a complex interaction of gender and court hierarchy. The distinct demands of the work of magistrates' courts, which might be expected to require greater interactive skills, appear to be reflected in the differing views of female magistrates and female judges, but are not paralleled by a similar variation between the male judges and male magistrates. Gender expectations are borne out to some extent. The percentage of women in each cohort valuing these qualities is greater than either of the male cohorts, which are nearly identical to each other. Female magistrates differ from male magistrates much more than female judges differ from male judges. This may reflect greater opportunities in magistrates' work for different ways of judging compared with judicial work in other courts (Hunter, 2004; Roach Anleu and Mack, 2005b; Roach Anleu and Mack, 2007b). Also, the strong views and larger numbers of female magistrates compared with female judges may account for the overall differences between men and women and magistrates and judges discussed above. What these numbers show is the effect, on the whole group of respondents, of the very intense views of female magistrates, who make up about one-third of the magistracy as a whole.

This data could suggest that women in the judiciary are conforming to a more gendered role. It could also be a sign of some degree of feminist adjudication approaches among the women, as their responses are more nuanced than the male responses, suggesting a greater responsiveness to the particular court context in which they undertake their everyday work. On the other hand, as suggested by Douglas and Laster (1991), it may be that the work of the lower courts is itself somewhat feminised, by demanding skills and qualities necessary for direct interaction with individuals and their emotional and personal needs.

2.4. Empathy, Communication and being a Good Listener

When each interactive skill is considered separately, in light of the 'essential' responses, it appears that women magistrates form a distinct cohort in relation to seven of the ten skills in this group: courtesy, interpersonal skills, compassion, managing emotions of court users, sense of humour, cultural awareness and empathy. Female magistrates are the largest proportion assessing each of these skills or qualities as essential compared with the other three cohorts, who have similar, lower proportions identifying these skills as essential. This pattern is demonstrated by analysing the response to the quality 'empathy'.

In the context of judging, empathy encompasses an understanding, intellectual and emotional, of the experiences and circumstances of others, whether through shared experience or conscious choice to develop the necessary attention, insight or perception (Henderson, 1987; West, 2011). Empathy is also identified in some discussions of gender and judging and is an important quality underpinning contextualisation and feminist practical reasoning (Miller and Maier, 2008; Neave, 1995; Resnik, 1988).

Table 9: Empathy (essential)

Female magistrates	41%	Male magistrates	27%
Female judges	29%	Male judges	23%

While empathy was not regarded as an especially important quality by the Australian judiciary generally, a larger proportion of women magistrates regard empathy as essential compared with the other three cohorts, who are all relatively similar to each other. The contrast is strongest between female magistrates and male judges, but the difference among male and female judges and male magistrates is slight. The contrast between female magistrates and female judges might suggest that the difference reflects the different nature of work in their courts, but there is less contrast between male magistrates and male judges than might be expected if this were the determining factor.

Communication is the interpersonal skill most highly valued by the judiciary as a whole. It is the only skill in this group identified as essential by high proportions of all categories of respondents.

Table 10: Communication (essential)

Female magistrates	91%	Male magistrates	77%
Female judges	80%	Male judges	70%

Views on communication can be divided along either gender or court lines. Women in each court value this skill more highly than their male counterparts, suggesting a gender dimension to the responses; and magistrates, whether female or male, value this skill more highly than their male judicial counterparts which may reflect differences in the nature of their everyday work. Looking at the four responses separately reveals a contrast between the proportions of female magistrates and female judges regarding communication as essential.

There is a similar difference between male judges and magistrates in the proportion regarding communication as essential, reinforcing the view that the nature of work is a factor in this difference. Very similar proportions of male magistrates and female judges identify communication as essential, while the proportions of female magistrates who regard communication as essential (91%) contrasts most strongly with male judges (71%) who value this quality less, making a gendered explanation less satisfying.

The only quality in the interaction group which appears to be equally valued by female magistrates and female judges, contrasting with their male colleagues, is being a good listener.

Table 11: Being a good listener (essential)

Female magistrates	70%	Male magistrates	57%
Female judges	68%	Male judges	47%

Nearly identical proportions of women judges and women magistrates regard this quality as essential, considerably more than males in either court. While the difference between male magistrates and male judges may reflect differences in the work of the court, these differences are not shared by the women in thinking of the work in their respective courts.

The recognition of the importance of emotional work in the courtroom, especially by female magistrates, may appear to be at odds with the traditional masculine conception of the judicial role which posits that emotions conflict with the rational nature of judicial reasoning (Roach Anleu and Mack, 2005b). Valuing interactional qualities does not necessarily require devaluing of legal skills or of legal values, as shown by the research findings.

3. CONCLUSION: SKILLS, GENDER AND COURT HIERARCHY

Women judges and magistrates may experience several possible gendered and judicial identities: assimilation to masculine judicial norms, the ideal of the disembodied neutral judicial officer who is neither male nor female, a gender-aware female judge or a feminist judge. These identities are not necessarily mutually exclusive. A woman's identity might assimilate to her male colleagues on some dimensions or in some contexts, but emphasise gendered or feminist approaches in others. As Harriet Silius (2003b) has pointed out in relation to the legal profession 'quantitative feminisation … does not equate with feminisation in the sense of demasculinastion or a change in gendered practices of legal work, culture or the profession itself' (388).

The identification of respondents as women or men for the purpose of this analysis was established by responses to a question 'Gender', asking to tick a box 'Male' or 'Female'. When responding to this question, each respondent made a choice, at some level, about gender identity. This quantitative survey research provides a basis for identifying areas where gender is experienced or performed differently among the judiciary, though it cannot fully or deeply explore the complexity of the gendered identities of each individual judicial officer. Interpreting these somewhat contradictory findings requires a pluralistic theoretical analysis, drawing on feminist, legal and sociological theory (Silius, 2003a).

Women magistrates report the greatest emphasis on interactive qualities for their everyday work, contrasting most strongly with male judges. While these differences might reflect a difference in the kind of work undertaken at the magistrates' courts, these views are not consistently shared with male magistrates, suggesting a gender difference within the lower court. Female judges value these skills less than female magistrates but slightly more than male judges, suggesting a gendered pattern within their level of court. However, the gender divergence among the judges is less than among the magistrates, perhaps suggesting that women judges are more closely assimilated to the views of male judges.

Women magistrates also report the greatest emphasis on legal skills as important to their everyday work, contrasting most sharply with male magistrates. These views may reflect a particular understanding of the distinct needs of their courts, which entail high volumes of relatively routine matters, perhaps becoming more routine the longer one sits in the court. Views of female magistrates suggest an identity distinct from male colleagues in the magistracy and from the female judges. Female judges value legal skills less intensely than female magistrates, and often the percentage of female judges regarding a legal skill as essential is the same as male judges. This further supports the view that women in the higher courts may share a judicial identity with their male colleagues regarding skills, rather than sharing a gendered identity with female magistrates.

Women magistrates' greater commitment to interactive qualities and to legal skills may reflect a complex relationship between gender and court hierarchy. Within the hierarchies of gender and court status, women magistrates are at the bottom of the ladder with male judges at the top.

A commitment to greater interactive qualities and more legal skills on the part of women magistrates may indicate an attempt to use knowledge and expertise as strategies of empowerment. This may reflect a pattern described by Elaine Botelho Junquirea (2003), who depicts women in the Brazilian judiciary attempting to be equal, to show they belong, by working harder, paying more attention to detail, giving more thorough reasons (447). As a result of this extra effort, they are different.

In spite of these differences, the research indicates elements of a shared judicial identity among all cohorts. Most important of these similarities is a nearly universal commitment to legal values and especially to the legal ideal of impartiality as essential to everyday work. Impartiality may have the same meaning for women magistrates, women judges, male magistrates and male judges—a detached, objective neutrality derived from the masculine nature of the judiciary. However, impartiality may have other meanings for women in the judiciary, as suggested by differences in views about other skills and qualities for judicial work.

Impartiality may not mean disengagement or detachment, as conventionally understood. Rather, sustaining the law's impartiality relies on some degree of personal or emotional engagement. The legal value of impartiality which is so highly valued by the judiciary often depends on the successful performance of some kinds of interaction (Mack and Roach Anleu, 2010), which is recognised by the high value put on communication as a skill, especially by women magistrates. As women judicial officers, especially magistrates, value interactive skills more, this may lead to different approaches to and performance of impartiality among women in the judiciary.

The findings from this survey provide concrete evidence for complex variations in gender ordering in different material contexts within the Australian judiciary. Analysing the views of women judges and women magistrates separately, along different dimensions or in different contexts as well as comparisons with the views of their male colleagues, provides evidence that several possible gender and judicial identities can be found among the women whose views are represented. While women and men at all levels of the court hierarchy may sometimes share in the traditional construction of judging as masculine, masculinity will not be reproduced exactly. Differences create opportunities for transformation, especially in lower courts where a higher proportion of women express distinctive attitudes and constitute a stronger gendered presence than female judges in their courts.

4. REFERENCES

Astor, H (2007) 'Mediator Neutrality: Making Sense of Theory and Practice' 16(2) *Social and Legal Studies* 221.

Australasian Institute of Judicial Administration (AIJA) (2007) *Guide to Judicial Conduct*, 2nd edn (Carlton, Australian Institute of Judicial Administration).

Baines, B (2009) 'Contextualism, Feminism, and a Canadian Woman Judge' 17(1) *Feminist Legal Studies* 27.

Bartlett, KT (1990) 'Feminist Legal Methods'103 *Harvard Law Review* 829.

Beiner, TM (2005) 'Female Judging' 36(4) *The University of Toledo Law Review* 821.

Boigeol, A (2003) 'Male Strategies in the Face of the Feminisation of a Profession: The Case of the French Judiciary' in U Schultz and G Shaw (eds), *Women in the World's Legal Professions* (Oxford, Hart Publishing).

Botelho Junqueira, E (2003) 'Women in the Judiciary: A Perspective from Brazil' in U Schultz and G Shaw (eds), *Women in the World's Legal Professions* (Oxford, Hart Publishing).

Boyd, CL, Epstein, L and Martin, AD (2007) 'Untangling the Causal Effects of Sex on Judging' 54(1) *American Journal of Political Science* 389.

Carlen, P (1976) *Magistrate' Justice* (London, Martin Robertson).

Cook, BB (1988) 'Women as Judges' in B Cook, L Goldstein, K O'Connor and S Talarico (eds), *Women in the Judicial Process* (Washington DC, American Political Science Association).

Cowan, D and Hitchings, E (2007) 'Pretty Boring Stuff: District Judges and Housing Possession Proceedings' 16(3) *Social & Legal Studies* 363.

Davies, M (2008) *Asking the Law Question*, 3rd edn (Sydney, Thomson Lawbook Co).

Douglas, RN and Laster, K (1991) 'Feminisation of the Magistrates' Courts: The Influence of Gender?' Australian Institute of Criminology Women and the Law Conference (Canberra, 24–26 September).

Easteal, PW (2001) *Less Than Equal: Women and the Australian Legal System* (Chatswood, NSW, Butterworths).

Gastron, A (1991) *Situacion Actual De La Mujer En El Poder Judicial Argentino* (Buenos Aires, 1er Premio Coca-Cola en las Artes y las Ciencias).

Gorman, EH (2005) 'Gender Stereotypes, Same Gender Preferences, and Organizational Variation in the Hiring of Women: Evidence from Law Firms' 70(4) *American Sociological Review* 702.

Henderson, LN (1987) 'Legality and Empathy' 85 *Michigan Law Review* 1574.

Holmes, M (2007) *What Is Gender? Sociological Approaches* (London, Sage Publications).

Holmes Jr, OW (1881) *The Common Law*.

Hunter, R (2003) 'Women in the Legal Profession: An Australian Profile' in U Schultz and G Shaw (eds), *Women in the World's Legal Professions* (Oxford, Hart Publishing).

—— (2004) 'Fear and Loathing in the Sunshine State' 19(44) *Australian Feminist Studies* 145.

—— (2005) 'Discrimination against Women Barristers: Evidence from a Study of Court Appearances and Briefing Practices' 12(1) *International Journal of the Legal Profession* 3.

—— (2008) 'Can Feminist Judges Make a Difference?' 15(1–2) *International Journal of the Legal Profession* 7.

Kenney, S (2010) 'Critical Perspectives on Gender and Judging' 6(3) *Politics & Gender* 433.

Kritzer, HM (2007) 'Toward a Theorization of Craft' 16 *Social & Legal Studies* 321.

Laster, K and Douglas, R (1995) 'Feminized Justice: The Impact of Women Decision Makers in the Lower Courts in Australia' 12(1) *Justice Quarterly* 177.
Mack, K and Roach Anleu, S (2004) 'Who are Magistrates Today?' 26 *Law Society Bulletin* 32.
—— (2007) 'Getting through the List: Judgecraft and Legitimacy in the Lower Courts' 16 *Social & Legal Studies* 341.
—— (2008) 'The National Survey of Australian Judges: An Overview of Findings' 18 *Journal of Judicial Administration* 5.
—— (2010a) 'Performing Impartiality: Judicial Demeanour and Legitimacy' 35(1) *Law & Social Inquiry* 137.
—— (2010b) 'Women in the Australian Judiciary' in P Easteal (ed), *Women and the Law in Australia* (Sydney, LexisNexis).
Malleson, K (1999) *The New Judiciary: The Effects of Expansion and Activism* (Aldershot, Ashgate).
—— (2003) 'Justifying Gender Equality on the Bench: Why Difference Won't Do' 11 *Feminist Legal Studies* 1.
Martin, PY, Reynolds, JR and Keith, S (2002) 'Gender Bias and Feminist Consciousness among Judges and Attorneys: A Standpoint Theory Analysis' 27(3) *Signs* 665.
Mather, L (2003) 'Gender in Context: Women in Family Law' in U Schultz and G Shaw (eds), *Women in the World's Legal Professions* (Oxford, Hart Publishing).
McBarnet, DJ (1981) 'Magistrates' Courts and the Ideology of Justice' 8(2) *British Journal of Law & Society* 181.
Menkel-Meadow, C (1995) 'Feminization of the Legal Profession: The Comparative Sociology of Women Lawyers' in R Abel and P Lewis (eds), *Lawyers in Society: An Overview* (Berkeley, University of California Press).
Miller, SL and Maier, SL (2008) 'Moving Beyond Numbers: What Female Judges Say About Different Judicial Voices' 29(4) *Journal of Women, Politics & Policy* 527.
Moorhead, R (2007) 'The Passive Arbiter: Litigants in Person and the Challenge to Neutrality' 16 (3) *Social & Legal Studies* 405.
Naffine, N (1991) *Law and the Sexes: Explorations in Feminist Jurisprudence* (Sydney, Allen & Unwin).
Neave, M (1995) 'The Gender of Judging' 2 *Psychiatry, Psychology and Law* 3.
Rackley, E (2002) 'Representations of the (Woman) Judge: Hercules, the Little Mermaid, and the Vain and Naked Emperor' 22(4) *Legal Studies* 602.
Resnik, J (1988) 'On the Bias: Feminist Reconsiderations of the Aspirations for Our Judges' 61 *Southern California Law Review* 1877.
Rhode, DL (2003) 'Gender and the Profession: An American Perspective' in U Schultz and G Shaw (eds), *Women in the World's Legal Professions* (Oxford, Hart Publishing).
Roach Anleu, S and Mack, K (2005a) 'Judicial Appointment and the Skills for Judicial Office' 15 *Journal of Judicial Administration* 37.
—— (2005b) 'Magistrates' Everyday Work and Emotional Labour' 32(4) *Journal of Law and Society* 590.
—— (2007a) 'Magistrates, Magistrates' Courts and Social Change' 29(2) *Law and Policy* 183.
—— (2007b) 'Australian Magistrates, Therapeutic Jurisprudence and Social Change' in G Reinhardt and A Cannon (eds), *Transforming Legal Processes in*

Court and Beyond: A Collection of Refereed Papers from the 3rd International Conference on Therapeutic Jurisprudence (AIJA, Melbourne).
—— (2009) 'Gender, Judging and Job Satisfaction' 17(1) *Feminist Legal Studies* 79.
—— (2010) 'The Work of the Australian Judiciary: Public and Judicial Attitudes' 20 *Journal of Judicial Administration* 3.
Schultz, U (2003) 'Introduction: Women in the World's Legal Professions: Overview and Synthesis' in U Schultz and G Shaw (eds), *Women in the World's Legal Professions* (Oxford, Hart Publishing).
Shaman, JM (1996) 'The Impartial Judge: Detachment or Passion?' 45 *Depaul Law Review* 605.
Silius, H (2003a) 'Making Sense of Gender in the Study of Legal Professions' 10(2) *International Journal of the Legal Profession* 135.
—— (2003b) 'Women Jurists in Finland at the Turn of the Century: Breakthrough or Intermezzo?' in U Schultz and G Shaw (eds), *Women in the World's Legal Professions* (Oxford, Hart Publishing).
Steering Committee for the Review of Government Service Provision (2009) *Report on Government Services: Court Administration (Chapter 7)* (Canberra, Australian Government Productivity Commission).
Thornton, M (1996) *Dissonance and Distrust: Women in the Legal Profession* (Melbourne, Oxford University Press).
—— (2007) 'Otherness on the Bench: How Merit is Gendered' 29 *Sydney Law Review* 391.
Wells, C (2003) 'The Remains of the Day: The Women Law Professors Project' in U Schultz and G Shaw (eds), *Women in the World's Legal Professions* (Oxford, Hart Publishing).
West, R (2011) 'The Anti-Empathetic Turn' Georgetown Public Law and Legal Theory Research Paper No 11-97.
Women Lawyers' Association of New South Wales (1999) *NSW Courts Gender Initiatives Review: Discussion Paper* (Sydney, Women Lawyers' Association of New South Wales).

2.6

Professional Stress, Discrimination and Coping Strategies: Similarities and Differences between Female and Male Judges in Switzerland

REVITAL LUDEWIG AND JUAN LALLAVE

Abstract

This chapter contributes towards understanding the effect of gender on judging. It examines whether the experiences of women and men judges with their profession support a gender differences or a gender similarities hypothesis. Women and men judges in Switzerland (N = 243) were asked to rank their experiences with professional difficulties, coping strategies, work–life balance, satisfaction and discrimination to determine whether there were differences or similarities due to gender. Significant differences between women and men judges' mean rankings support a gender differences hypothesis, while differences not significant support a gender similarities hypothesis. Findings upheld gender similarities for experiences with professional difficulties, the use of most of the coping strategies, most experiences with work–life balance and satisfaction. Findings upheld gender differences for some coping strategies and experiences of discrimination. Women judges reported using mediation and social support as coping strategies and experienced gender discrimination significantly more than men did. Overall, 27 per cent of findings support a gender differences hypothesis, while 73 per cent support a gender similarities hypothesis.

1. INTRODUCTION

THIS CHAPTER REPORTS on the relative psychological experiences of men and women judges with their profession in Switzerland. It involves rethinking the tension between gender differences and gender similarities. Kimball (1994) stresses the importance of both perspectives and the tension between them. Early last century when women were outsiders in most professions, Hollingworth (1918) argued for similarities and against gender differences to encourage the inclusion of women. Today, we maintain that it is reasonably clear that women and men are equally qualified to judge. Hyde (2005: 590) confronts an, 'overinflated gender differences model popular in advertising', which is saturated in public opinion, the media and many academic papers. The gender differences hypothesis holds that men and women are vastly or primarily psychologically different. Hyde finds support for a gender similarities hypothesis, which holds that while men and women may differ in some psychological variables, they are similar in most. The similarities hypothesis has not been specifically discussed in understanding judges' professional experiences.

Zuriff (2006: 641) reminds us that, 'judgments of similarity and difference are psychological, not scientific'. He stresses that one must 'determine the psychological importance of each dimension in human judgments of similarity and difference' and urges that we not dismiss 'gender differences dependent on context' and, 'consistent with social-role theory'. Davies and Shackelford (2006: 641) 'generally agree with the gender similarities hypothesis' but argue that 'gender differences may be more profound and have greater societal costs than Hyde suggested'. They recommend 'an evolutionary psychological perspective' to investigate gender differences and limit 'their associated costs'.

As clinical and forensic psychologists, we examine this controversy of general gender differences and similarities as a factor among judges' experiences. Differences in life experiences seem to support claims that women might be psychologically different from men. This may contribute to differences in their experiences of judging. In psychology, differences may lead to distancing, while similarities contribute to empathy and identification. Both of which can lead to bias as Gutheil and Datillio (2007: 34) observe 'The largest barrier to acceptance of human diversity is the deep-seated, prejudice-laden worldview of our own Ids'.

Women judges may encounter similar difficulties in their work as men judges, provided they confront similar caseloads. They both may learn and use the same coping strategies. However, as psychologists we expect that judges' psychological experiences should reflect gender differences. Women may continue to experience discrimination more often than men may observe within the profession, while increasing numbers of women judges and the profession's stance on gender neutrality may mask or silence these differences.

Women's democratic right to participate in public decision-making supports the need to increase their numbers on the bench. The presence of women judges in Switzerland is a recent development, since judges in Switzerland are politically elected and women only acquired a voice and voting rights at the federal level in 1971. While women did not have voting rights, they could not run for election as judges. However, in a short span of 39 years we note a rapid improvement.

Today, the value of gender equity is an unqualified good. In a federal census in Switzerland in 2000, women represented 30.8 per cent among judges and state attorneys, 23.2 per cent among top-level judges, 23 per cent among second and third level judges and 28 per cent among first level judges (Niquille, 2007). Most cantons began to include women as judges in 1971 and 1972 when they got voting rights at federal level—with some exceptions. In Basel, women were admitted as early as 1967 and in Appenzell as late as 1990. In 1974, Margrith Bigler-Eggenberger became the first regular federal judge (Ludewig, Weislehner and Angehrn, 2007). However while women make up over 50 per cent of all law students, they fall 20 per cent short of the 50 per cent balance for equal representation within the profession. To achieve this ideal representation of gender balance, women must want to be judges. It is therefore important to understand women's experiences as judges (Malleson, 2003).

The recent history of women's participation as judges in Switzerland may explain why there are very few studies. In this study we were interested in understanding women's psychological experiences as judges relative to that of men. Considering the recent inclusion of women, we sought information on their integration in the profession. We expected that women and men would report evidence to support a gender differences hypothesis in their psychological experiences within their role as judges. This would be an alternative to a Nil hypothesis consistent with Hyde's notion of gender similarities, consistent with Tversky (1977: 340) who observes that 'common features are weighed more heavily in judging similarities' whereas distinctive features are weighted more heavily in judging dissimilarity.

1.1. Perceptions of Emotional Experiences in Judging

This chapter focuses on women and men judges' experience with professional stress, coping strategies, work–life balance, satisfaction and discrimination, beyond the question of differences in decision-making. Judges' work is stressful. Their daily concerns involve 'workloads, sentencing, incompetent attorneys, finances and family life' (Menninger, quoted in Middleton, 1981: 1101). They confront 'cases requiring active judicial management' with 'inadequate or abusive representation' and 'vulnerable clients' (Portnoy, 2004: 131–32). Judges also worry about the consequences of their decisions, and their effective use of skills (ibid).

Although judging involves a full range of emotions, the emotions evoked by criminal and civil procedures are often negative. In criminal cases, defendants 'may be fearful or hostile, while victims are distressed or angry'. In civil cases, parties 'may feel frustrated and annoyed at having to go to court'

(Anleu and Mack, 2005: 591). Disclosures of poor financial management may prove embarrassing in cases involving debts. In domestic violence, parties may be either frightened, or openly hostile. Thus, court users experience anger, fear, uncertainty and intimidation and their emotional displays can cause judges themselves to experience—and sometimes express—strong emotions. 'Magistrates must often regulate their own emotions and those of some court users' (ibid*:* 590). Discerning how deeply judges experience their work is not a simple task and beyond the scope of this chapter.

'Order and decorum' require that judges keep a lid on feelings and 'remain objective, dispassionate, above the fray'. This adds to their burden. In response to stress, judges must 'unobtrusively and acceptably' control 'the urge to scream' (Menninger, quoted in Middleton, 1981: 1100). Judges' responsibilities make their stress worse than they might in other professions. In a study by Menninger, 50 per cent of 254 judges 'felt comfortable with how they handled stress in their lives and 11 per cent did not know how to handle that stress' (ibid). 'Judges are subject to a wide range of physical and emotional problems and stressors, but often don't get the help they need' (Zimmerman, 2006: 10). Portnoy (2004: 132) found positive correlations between internal states associated with stress and 'feelings of tension, feeling disliked by others, feeling irritable with others, not feeling appreciated, negative feelings about professional role, and difficulty in making decisions'. Menninger found 'references to internal pressures': living up to expectations, struggle for 'quality and thoroughness' and concern over the best decision. These pressures challenge judges' ability to maintain emotional balance and equilibrium because they 'can't always please everyone' but 'must also penalise or punish' (Menninger, quoted in Middleton, 1981: 1101). Negative emotions remain a source of judges' stress. Distancing and depersonalisation are often ineffective coping strategies. They can lower judges' job satisfaction and disrupt their work and family life balance. Imbalances between work and family life may cause women more stress because they experience greater responsibility for family life (Schultz and Shaw, 2008: 1; Sander and Hartmann, 2009). Most judges report that they lead happy personal lives and their most pressing task is 'to keep from being overwhelmed' in stressful circumstances.

1.2. Discrimination

Gender differences can be used to discriminate against women or to focus on 'positive human characteristics undervalued because they are symbolically associated with women' (Kimball, 1994: 389). Gender similarities can also be used to support the status quo or to 'support political and social equality for women' (ibid). Hollingworth (1918) stressed similarities' arguments towards the 'integration of women' into 'the existing social and economic system'. Kimball (1994: 388) argues that differences were 'viewed as dangerous' because in 'our hierarchical world' they were 'used to exclude women, to reinforce oppression, and to minimise the role of coercion in the subordination of women'. Differences tend to reduce 'real women and men to stereotypes'. To 'counter the preponderance of men in positions of power and prestige' similarities focus on 'intellectual skills and social competencies'. Scientific justification for political equality aims to show that gender differences do not exist or are 'too small to explain gender differences in the labour force' (ibid).

A 'sense of connectedness, concern with human relationships, and care-giving' are 'characteristics that women bring to human culture more than men' do. The political goal of differences 'is not equality, but rather a more humane world that incorporates traditional feminine values as a central human focus' (ibid: 389).

Discrimination of women in Switzerland changed with their right to vote in political elections in 1971[1] as described above. The growing presence of women judges does not automatically undo discrimination and some of the anchors persist (Ludewig and Weislehner, 2007: 69). While, 'women's presence serves as a necessary base line, some believe that the legal profession remains inhospitable to incorporating women' (Kohen, 2008: 113; see also Schultz and Shaw, 2003).

2. QUESTIONS AND METHODS

This research, conducted at the University in St Gallen, Switzerland, enquired into five factors:

1. Professional difficulties weighing heavily on judges, such as time pressure, problems with colleagues, decision-making and professional stress.[2]
2. Cognitive and behavioural coping strategies.
3. Work–life balance.
4. Pleasant experiences of satisfaction.
5. Unpleasant experiences of discrimination and perceptions of professional problems at the meta-level.

A qualitative-phase involved 31 Swiss women and men judges and 80 other members of the legal profession. A quantitative-phase employed a written questionnaire designed on the basis of an analysis of initial interviews.

[1] Of 38 Supreme Court Justices in Switzerland, 11 are women.

[2] While we briefly mentioned decision-making, it is not the primary focus of this chapter. A paper on this subject is in progress.

We enquired into gender differences and gender similarities by asking women and men judges to rank their own experiences with these factors.[3]

We tested the 'Nil hypothesis' that differences were not significant and pursued a gender differences hypothesis consistent with the common notion that women and men differ in their decisions. The sample for this questionnaire consisted of 247 professionally trained women and men from 50 Courts in German-speaking Switzerland. The analysis included 243 questionnaires because four respondents did not indicate gender. Of the replies, 28 per cent of them were from women; this percentage is well in line with the overall percentage of women judges.[4]

Using respondents' ranks, we computed the mean for each gender. Then we compared the means for women with the means for men. If we found that the means were not significantly different, we accepted the Nil in support for the gender similarities hypothesis. If we found that the means were significantly different, we rejected the Nil in support for the alternative gender differences hypothesis.

3. RESULTS

3.1. Professional Difficulties

All professions have their own particular burdens. Medical doctors feel stress dealing with death (Hohner, Grote, Hoff and Dettmer, 2003); teachers with students (Wagner, Christ and Van Dick, 2003); and judges with difficulties in legal decision-making and pressures from litigant parties. Other general stressors common to all professions include time pressures and problems with colleagues.

3.1.1. Time Pressure

Time pressure was the most frequently reported difficulty by 98.6 per cent of judges. Litigant-parties' pressure for a swift ruling, but also diligent and good judicial work takes time. Thus, judges experience conflict between quality and quantity. Working on less complicated cases may postpone work on ones that are more complex. Women and men judges ranked their experience with time pressure similarly. The mean rank for women was 3.53 and 3.6 for men. Only 1.4 per cent of all judges denied the experience of time pressure as a professional difficulty.

[3] Rankings based in a 5 point Likert scale (from 1 to 5) for most factors except 'satisfaction', based on a 10 point scale (from 1 to 10).

[4] See above p 231.

3.1.2. Problems with Colleagues

While 71 per cent of judges reported difficulties with colleagues, there were no significant gender differences among judges' rankings. The mean for women was 2.03 and 1.97 for men.

3.1.3. Decision-making

Judges engage daily in decision-making under potentially stressful conditions. In civil law, conflicts between litigant parties involve irreconcilable differences, for example, which parent receives custody of the child after a divorce. In criminal law, judges must decide between guilt and innocence. Although 98.4 per cent of judges reported difficulties in decision-making, there were no significant differences in ranking by gender. The mean for women was 2.54 and 2.56 for men. Stress from problems between litigant parties was reported by 85.7 per cent of judges; 14.3 per cent denied stress. There were no significant differences in ranking by gender; the mean for women was 2.08 and 2.05 for men.

3.1.4. Professional Stress

On leaving the office, judges do not separate easily from emotions and difficult cases and 90 per cent reported difficulties affecting their private life. They think about escalated situations, conflicting parties and legal decision-making in their free time. The mean rank for women was 2.62 and 2.47 for men. Only 10 per cent of judges denied such difficulties. Encounters with stress can lead to health impairments. While they do not occur daily, 57 per cent of women judges and 62 per cent of men judges reported difficulties sleeping due to unusual work stress such as, when dealing with custody cases involving kidnapping, highly publicised cases or strong disagreements within a five-judge panel. The mean rank for women concerning sleep disorders was 1.82 and 1.85 for men. We found no significant difference in sleep disorders due to gender independent of age.

3.1.5. Subjective Perception of Professional Problems

Judges differ in their perception that women have more difficulties in their judging role than men do. Women judges perceive they sometimes face greater difficulties than men. Men judges perceive that women seldom have greater problems than men. The mean rank for women was 2.74 and significantly higher than 2.04 for men.[5]

[5] T-Test for women having it more difficult than men: $t = 4.616$, $df = 199$, $p < .000$.

Table 1: Professional difficulties

Professional difficulties supporting a gender differences hypothesis	**Mean**	
	Women	**Men**
Do women judges generally have it more difficult than men judges do?	2.74*	2.04*
Professional difficulties supporting a gender similarities hypothesis	**Mean**	
(These differences in means are statistically not significant)	**Women**	**Men**
Time pressure	3.53	3.68
Difficulties with work colleagues	2.03	1.97
Difficulties with decision-making	2.54	2.56
Difficulties with litigant parties	2.08	2.05
Professional work stress and emotions interfere with personal life and free time	2.62	2.47
Difficulties sleeping	1.82	1.85

*Statistically significant difference $p < .000$ (Likert scale from: not at all = 1 to 5 = very much, 0 = do not know)

From seven items on professional difficulties, six items or 85 per cent conformed to the criteria for similarities and only one item, or 14 per cent, conformed to the criteria for differences. The importance of this single difference is that it represents women's self-perception and men's perception of women.

3.2. Coping Strategies

Coping strategies may facilitate reasoning, change attitudes, lower the impact of emotions and modify the influence of perceptions of stressors. These include cognitive, emotional, behavioural and tactical attempts to minimise a conflict and to reduce stress. Women and men judges, consciously or unconsciously, employ similar strategies to reduce psychological stress temporarily or permanently. We looked at four types of coping strategies (Felsten, 1998):

1. Cognitive-emotional coping strategies.
2. Emotional-avoidance coping strategies.
3. Tactical coping strategies.
4. Social support coping strategies.

3.2.1. Cognitive-emotional Coping Strategies

Cognitive-emotional coping strategies help reduce stress by restructuring the problem or by controlling emotional responses to the problem. The first facilitates reasoning by organising values in a hierarchy. The second facilitates objective detachment by distancing oneself from difficult emotions. For example, in a quarrel with a friend, one can decide that it was a small quarrel considering the value of the friendship, or that such a friendship is not important enough to ignore a principle. We expected but found no significant gender differences. Women and men use the same cognitive-emotional coping strategies to the same extent (Folkman and Lazarus, 1980).

Value-hierarchy: Constructing a value hierarchy is a cognitive strategy to cope with difficulties in decision-making by organising a set of values. For example, if a single mother with a two-year-old daughter is found guilty of a crime, in sentencing, judges must balance two values: adhering to legal penalties associated with the verdict and protecting the child's need for mother, care and education. A value-hierarchy helps determine an appropriate sentence and resolve judges' stress. In their use of a value-hierarchy, the mean for women's rank was 3.09 almost identical with 2.99 for men.

Objective distancing: This is a detachment strategy to cope with a difficult case. It facilitates concentrating on the legal criteria and goal by distancing oneself from the fate of the parties. It may simplify decision-making, but can lower justice quality by discounting emotional and perhaps more humane considerations. Women ranked using objective distancing as frequently as men did. The mean for women was 3.34 and 3.26 for men.

3.2.2. Emotional-avoidance Coping Strategies

Emotional-avoidance prevents professionally difficult and stressful situations from overwhelming judges emotionally in their personal lives. It enables disengaging from particular stressors that may persist after leaving the office. Women and men use emotional-avoidance similarly (Felsten, 1998).

Suppression: This is a cognitive strategy to dismiss thoughts associated with a negative stressor from particularly difficult cases. Men judges ranked their use of suppression slightly higher than women judges did. The mean was 2:36 for men and 2.20 for women.

Distraction: This is an action strategy, whereby persons engage in other activities in order to temporarily reduce stress. Women judges ranked their use of distraction slightly higher than men judges did. The mean was 2.83 for women and 2.70 for men. However, these differences are not statistically significant.

3.2.3. *Tactical Coping Strategies*

Tactical strategies focus on actions to facilitate resolving cases and reduce stress. In a dispute with a friend one could apologise, send flowers or talk directly to defuse the conflict. What action-strategies are available to judges in stressful situations? In a civil case, a sentence favouring either party will be stressful, if parties seem equally right. To satisfy both parties, this dilemma is better resolved by the use of court settlement (*Vergleich*) or external mediation.

Court settlement (*Vergleich*): Judges can aid parties to reach an agreement without pronouncing judgment by court settlement. Women and men judges ranked their use of court settlement similarly, consistent with a role constraint hypothesis. The mean rank for women was 3.71 and 3.75 for men.[6]

External mediation: External mediators can help resolve conflicts outside court. Using non-partisan mediators, judges can avoid the stress in sentencing, except when mediation is not successful. Use of external mediation supports a socialisation hypothesis (Ptacek, Smith and Zanas, 1992) because women and men are socialised differently, despite their similar training. Women ranked their use of this action strategy significantly higher than men judges did. The mean for women was 2.52, but only 1.88 for men.[7] This difference is statistically significant.

3.2.4. *Social Support Coping Strategies*

Social support like talking over problems with others can reduce internal stress. Research reflects gender differences in the use of social support (ibid). Therefore, we expected women to use social support more frequently than men do. We asked judges whether they used discussions of cases and/or conversations with family and friends as a means of coping with stress.

Discussions on cases: Women judges sought social support by direct discussions of cases more than men did. The mean for women was 3.94 and 3.42 for men.[8]

Conversations with family and friends: Women judges sought social support through conversations with family and friends more than men did. The mean for women was 3.54 and 2.94 for men judges.[9] These differences are statistically significant.

[6] T-Test for court settlement: $t = 2.589$, $df = 95$, $p < .003$.
[7] T-Test for external mediation: $t = 3.467$, $df = 202$, $p < .002$.
[8] T-Test for direct discussions: $t = 3.578$, $df = 203$, $p < .000$.
[9] T-Test for conversations with family and friends: $t = 3.901$, $df = 229$, $p < .000$.

Table 2: Coping strategies

Coping strategies supporting a gender differences hypothesis	**Mean**	
(These differences in means are statistically significant)	**Women**	**Men**
Women use mediation slightly more often than men do (referrals outside court)	2.52*	1.88*
Women use direct discussions for social support more than men do	3.94*	3.42*
Women use conversations with family and friends for social support more than men do	3.54*	2.94*
Coping strategies supporting a gender similarities hypothesis	**Mean**	
(These differences in means are statistically not significant)	**Women**	**Men**
Hierarchical values	3.09	2.99
Objective distancing	3.34	3.26
Men use avoidance slightly more than women do	2.20	2.36
Court settlement (*Vergleich*) ie, judge assisted agreement	3.71	3.75
Women shift to other activities slightly more than men do	2.83	2.70

*Statistically significant difference $p < .003$—(Likert scale from: not at all = 1 to 5 = very much, 0 = do not know)

Women and men judges' use of cognitive-emotional and avoidance coping strategies conforms to the criteria for a gender similarities hypothesis, while the use of tactical and social support strategies conforms to the criteria for a gender differences hypothesis. Women judges ranked their use of non-partisan mediation as social support at the action level as well as discussions on cases and conversations with family and friends higher than men did. Overall, we observed more gender similarities than differences. From eight items on coping strategies, five items or 62.5 per cent conformed to the criteria for similarities, and three items or 37.5 per cent conformed to the criteria for differences.

3.3. Work–life Balance

This study found employment rate imbalances among judges: 72 per cent of men occupied 79.3 per cent of full-time posts compared with 20.7 per cent of posts occupied by women, while 63.5 per cent of women work part-time compared with 24.3 per cent of men.

Both women and men judges struggle to maintain work–life balance. Stressful imbalances occur when professional life affects private life or private life hinders professional goals.

3.3.1. Impact of Profession on Personal Life

Women and men judges equally feel that their professional life affects their private life. The mean for women was 2.46 and 2.56 for men. This slight difference is statistically not significant.

3.3.2. Impact of Personal Life on Professional Goals

Women ranked feeling that their private life hinders their professional goals significantly higher than men did. The mean for women was 2.52 and 1.87 for men.[10]

Table 3: Work–life balance

Work–life balance	**Mean**	
	Women	**Men**
Women are more likely to feel their private lives hinder their professional goals	2.52*	1.87*
Women and men feel that their profession is at the expense of their private life	2.46	2.56

*Statistically significant difference $p < .000$—(Likert scale from: not at all = 1 to 5 = very much, 0 = do not know)

From two items on work–life balance, one item conformed to the criteria for similarities and one item to the criteria for differences. In contrast with men, women judges feel that their private life hinders their professional goals whether they have children or not and independent of the number of children.

Men judges move along career steps, while women judges progress less smoothly for the sake of their family. While both must coordinate various objectives in their lives, women may value goals in partnership, family and children more than men do. Women's conscience may limit their opportunities, when promotions conflict with their performance as good mothers:

> Women want to be perfect mothers, partners and judges. They feel more responsible in their family role to housework and private life. Their diverse goals may cause them more stress. Younger judges, regardless of gender, are more likely to feel that their private life affects their professional goals. This represents a fundamental conflict for younger women judges with smaller children who require more time and attention.[11]

[10] T-Test for effect of personal life on professional career goals: $t = 4.512$, $df = 240$, $p < .000$.

[11] ANOVA Analysis of variance for age of women and men judges: $F = 2.840$, $df = 240$, $p < .025$.

3.4. Satisfaction

Satisfaction involves conscious and unconscious expectations and actual conditions. We examined experience of satisfaction in job, family life and standard of living.

3.4.1. *Job Satisfaction*

Judging is highly valued. It combines public reputation, prestige and respect. These positive factors are available to both women and men judges. Judges enjoy greater autonomy, greater possibility for part-time work and more compatibility with family life compared with attorneys and doctors. Women and men judges ranked their satisfaction with work very high. The mean for women was 8.22 and 8.37 for men.

3.4.2. *Family Life Satisfaction*

Women and men ranked satisfaction with their family life very high. The mean for women judges was 8.39 and the mean for men was 8.32.

3.4.3. *Standard of Living*

Women and men judges are content with their standard of living. Women's mean of 8.85 is not statistically significantly different from men's mean of 8.49.[12]

While their wage scales are identical, women judges may be more satisfied with their standard of living. They have different expectations and must be more adaptable than men. Women's earnings in the judiciary are much higher than they would be in other professions. Men are accustomed to higher wages in other professions. Thus, while equally content with their standard of living, men seem less content with their incomes.

Table 4: Job satisfaction

Job satisfaction supports a gender similarities hypothesis	**Mean**	
(These differences in means are statistically not significant)	Women	Men
Very high levels of job satisfaction	8.22	8.37
Women are slightly more satisfied with their family than men	8.39	8.32
Women are slightly more satisfied with their incomes than men	8.85	8.49

(Likert scale from: not at all satisfied = 1 to 10 = very satisfied)

[12] P-value for differences in men and women's content with their standard of living: $P < .067$.

All three items on job satisfaction or 100 per cent conformed to the criteria for similarities.

3.5. Discrimination

Do women and men judges experience disadvantages within the profession due to gender discrimination or canton affiliation?

3.5.1. Canton Affiliation

There are 26 cantons in Switzerland. A small percentage of women and men judges, 7.5 per cent and six per cent respectively, reported feeling discriminated because they did not live and work in the same canton by colleagues, for example other judges, lawyers or by parties.

3.5.2. Gender

Women and men judges differ in their experiences of gender discrimination at work. Statistically significant, 52 per cent of women judges and five per cent of men judges reported experiences of gender discrimination (see figure 1 below).[13]

Table 5: Experiences of discrimination

Experiences of discrimination	%	
	Women	**Men**
Women and men experience similar discrimination due to canton affiliation.	7.5	6.0
Women experience more professional disadvantages due to gender discrimination than men do. (This difference in means is statistically significant)	52.0*	5.0*

*Statistically significant difference $p < .000$

From two items on discrimination, one conformed to the criteria for similarities due to canton affiliation, and one conformed to the criteria for differences due to gender discrimination.

[13] Mann-Whitney U-Test for differences in experiences of gender discrimination: Asymp. Sig. (2-tailed) $p > .000$.

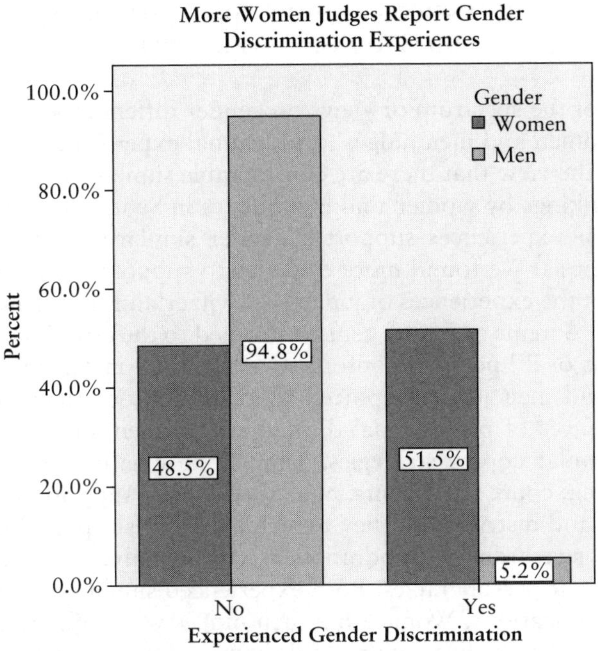

Figure 1: Experienced Gender Discrimination

Women with more than nine years of work experience reported more gender related discrimination than did women with fewer than nine years' experience. Perhaps the system has improved. Women working over 15 years were the first women judges in Switzerland and had more boundaries to overcome. They may have been exposed to discrimination more than younger women judges, who today encounter better conditions. Perhaps younger women judges may not have had time to experience discrimination and their experiences may increase in time.

However, women judges report only isolated incidents and do not want to criticise the judicial system as such. For example, one woman judge described how an expatriate male ignored her question during the court proceedings or rather only answered the male judge although she was the top judge in the case. Another woman judge reported that an older attorney did not take her seriously at the beginning, but this changed in the course of time. Women judges reported eighteen incidents of discrimination from court litigant parties, eleven incidents from attorneys, eight incidents from judges and six incidents from political parties.

4. DISCUSSION: GENDER SIMILARITIES AND DIFFERENCES HYPOTHESIS

At one end of the spectrum of views on gender differences in judging is the view that women and men judges' professional experiences are different; at the other, is the view that there are considerable similarities. Comparing the means of rankings by women and men judges in Switzerland, we examined whether their experiences support a gender similarities or gender differences hypothesis. We found more evidence to support a gender similarities hypothesis in the experiences of judges in Switzerland. From a total number of 22 items, 16 items or 73 per cent conformed to the criteria for similarities and six items or 27 per cent conformed to the criteria for differences.

Women and men judges reported more similarities than differences in their experiences of professional difficulties. Women and men judges also use many similar coping strategies. They employ value hierarchies, objective distancing, court settlements, mediation, social support and avoidance, suppression and distraction. They reported similar sleeping difficulties and professional stress due to hindrances from an inability to separate their work from their personal lives. Both experienced similar psychological and physical complications. Women and men judges were equally content with many aspects of their lives, with similarities in job satisfaction, family life satisfaction and standard of living.

Yet, we found some significant gender differences. Women judges used external mediation and social support, ie, direct discussions on cases and conversations with family and friends as coping strategies significantly more than men judges. Women judges also feel that their judging role is more difficult for them than for men. They feel that they have a harder task than men, that their personal lives interfere with their professional goals and that they experience more gender discrimination. Although these differences do not appear sufficient to support a gender differences hypothesis, they are important in an assessment of the subjective perceptions of women and men judges.

The following four considerations may help to explain why there are more gender similarities than gender differences.

First, similar professional difficulties support a role constraint hypothesis. Women and men judges have similar roles. They undergo the same legal studies and share the same socialisation. This influences their awareness, their thinking, their behaviour and their experience of stressors.

Secondly, gender does not automatically enhance a person's ability to cope with difficulties. Women appear to use some coping strategies more than men, which may be consistent with common gender differences. Social support and mediation involve seeking help to achieve greater social competence, rather than relying solely on self-confidence. Thereby they lower their own experiences of stress. This is a positive difference, which can lead to greater objectivity. It partly reflects a difference in the socialisation of women and men. Based on this social orientation we expected women would use suppression less than men would. We found this not to be the case. This may be due to the influence of men's examples as precursors on the bench. Suppression is only a short-term strategy that can be very problematic when applied consistently in coping with all circumstances because it avoids dealing with important factors.

Thirdly, work–life balance interacts with job satisfaction. Like women, men who decide to become judges tend to have a high sense of family responsibility. This does not mean that men do as much work in the home or with children as women. Although they may do more than men who choose to become company lawyers, perhaps they feel they should do even more. Thus, men judges like women experience stress when their work interferes with family life. Women, however, also feel that the stress within family life can hinder their professional goals. Thus, unlike men, women experience the challenge of a two directional stress between profession and family. They feel more obliged to cope with multiple tasks and bear the ultimate social responsibility for the family, household and child rearing or education. Therefore, they place higher demands on themselves to live up to the profession's expectation of their role and performance. This leads them to estimate their work as more stressful and more demanding than that of their male colleagues.

Fourthly, judging remains a traditionally male dominated profession. Women continue to experience gender discrimination, but may not want to alienate themselves from their male colleagues by claiming discrimination. Both men and women may tend to normalise the presence of gender discrimination. Despite the increase in numbers on the bench, women may still perceive themselves as surrogates. Men are also conscious of the controversies surrounding gender discrimination and feel that they have to treat women equally. Women may minimise the severity of their experiences and prefer not to talk about them. Men may not express or acknowledge their own feelings or tendency to discriminate and consciously control them. Both may therefore underestimate the psychological differences. Men may not want to represent views that interfere with women's potential contribution, out of collegial respect or political correctness. Women judges do not want to criticise the system and instead tend to reduce their own subjective feelings of disadvantage or discrimination to isolated single events. The younger generation of women judges who may have experienced fewer disadvantages, do not talk about their experiences or are not in touch with them. In either case, they may deny experiences of gender discrimination.

Women often attribute their successes and failures differently from men. Women attribute their success to favourable outer circumstances, to luck or to coincidence and personalise responsibility for failures (Maag, 2007).

Women may account for difficulties by their gender affiliation. Men portray the opposite pattern: they account for their success internally and attribute their failures externally; they feel they are successful because they mastered special tasks by their own skills and competence and feel that failures are due to unfavourable outer circumstances. Under the positive influence of women, men may become more socially oriented, but attribute it to their own doing. Women may feel self-conscious, underestimate their potential contribution and strongly adhere solely to an objective interpretation and application of the law. Similarities between women and men judges fit the role constraint hypothesis. Women and men judges have the same professional role with similar stressors and deal with difficulties using many of the same coping strategies. This minimises the likelihood of differences between women and men judges as they interact and mutually influence each other in their daily work.

Gender differences and similarities both have their value and the tension between them accentuates the benefits of each of them.

In the early 1900s, women were excluded from the professions because they were different. In the Western world women, as outsiders, began to stress their similarities in order to justify entering the professions. Similarities have been crucial in justifying equality and thereby increasing the number of women in the profession. In a formerly male justice system, the socialisation process of judges and judging was obviously gendered.

Today women judges have integrated well into the system. As insiders now, both genders can emphasise their differences from within the profession in order to improve the quality and values of judging. Gender differences may influence the quality of judging by including the unique contribution of women and men. Both benefit from each other's contribution whether they are different or similar. Their mutual influence in the socialisation process serves to diminish the appearance of differences and to increase the appearance of similarities in the profession. With the increase of gender diversity within the judging profession in Switzerland, we observe many similarities between men's and women's experiences. They are highly satisfied with their work, the prestige and standard of living and value many facets of the profession. Men may appear now more socially and community oriented than before, and women may seem more principled or rule oriented than formerly anticipated (Angehrn and Ludewig, 2007).

Overall, 72 per cent of the considerations in this study conformed to the criteria for similarities and 27 per cent to the criteria for differences between men and women judges' experiences with their work in Switzerland. The differences observed remain relevant and merit further consideration. The tension between similarities and differences can be compared to the tension between experiencing one's own work and perceiving the work experiences of others.

5. REFERENCES

Angehrn, E and Ludewig, R (2007) 'Erleben und verarbeiten Richterinnen Moraldilemmata anders als Richter? Literatur- und Interviewanalyse' in R Ludewig, K Weislehner and E Angehrn (eds), *Zwischen Recht und Gerechtigkeit: Richterinnen im Spiegel der Zeit* (Bern, Stämpfli).

Davies, APC and Shackelford, TK (2006) 'An Evolutionary Psychological Perspective on Gender Similarities and Differences' 61(6) *American Psychologist* 640.

Felsten, G (1998) 'Gender and Coping: Use of Distinct Strategies and Associations with Stress and Depression' 11 *Anxiety, Stress and Coping* 289.

Folkman, S and Lazarus, RS (1980) 'An Analysis of Coping in a Middle-aged Community Sample' 21 *Journal of Health and Social Behavior* 219.

Gryski, G, Main, E and Dixon, W (1986) 'Models of State High Court Decision Making in Sex Discrimination Cases' 48 *Journal of Politics* 143.

Gutheil, TG and Datillio, FM (2007) *Practical Approaches to Forensic Mental Health Testimony* (Baltimore, Lippincott Williams and Wilkins/Wolters Kluwer).

Hoff, E, Grote, S, Dettmer, S, Hohner, HU and Olos, L (2005) 'Work–Life-Balance: Berufliche und private Lebensgestaltung von Frauen und Männern in hoch qualifizierten Berufen' 49(4) *Zeitschrift für Arbeits- und Organisationspsychologie* 196.

Hohner, HU, Grote, S, Hoff, EH and Dettmer, S (2003) 'Berufsverläufe, Berufserfolg und Lebensgestaltung von Ärztinnen und Ärzten' in A Abele, EH Hoff and HU Hohner (eds), *Frauen und Männer in akademischen Professionen. Berufsverläufe und Berufserfolg* (München, Asanger).

Hollingworth, LS (1918) 'Comparison of the Sexes in Mental Traits' 15 *The Psychological Bulletin*.

Hyde, JS (2005) 'The Gender Similarities Hypothesis' 60(6) *American Psychologist* 581.

Kimball, MM (1994) 'The Worlds We Live In: Gender Similarities and Differences' 35(4) *Canadian Psychology/Psychologie canadienne* 388.

Kohen, B (2008) 'Family Law Judges in the City of Buenos Aires: A View from Within' 15(1–2) *International Journal of the Legal Profession* 111.

Ludewig, R, Weislehner, K and Angehrn, E (2007) (eds), *Zwischen Recht und Gerechtigkeit: Richterinnen im Spiegel der Zeit* (Bern, Stämpfli).

Ludewig, R and Weislehner, K (2007) 'Einstieg, Aufstieg, Entfaltung: Drei Generationen von Richterinnen in der Schweiz' in R Ludewig, K Weislehner and E Angehrn (eds), *Zwischen Recht und Gerechtigkeit: Richterinnen im Spiegel der Zeit* (Bern, Stämpfli).

Maag, R (2007) 'Haben Frauen eine andere Konfliktwahrnehmung und andere Lösungen?' in R Ludewig, K Weislehner and E Angehrn (eds), *Zwischen Recht und Gerechtigkeit: Richterinnen im Spiegel der Zeit* (Bern, Stämpfli).

Malleson, K (2003) 'Justifying Gender Equality on the Bench: Why Differences Won't Do' 11 *Feminist Legal Studies* 1.

Menninger, W (1981) in M Middleton, 'Judges Told how to Deal with Stress' 67 *American Bar Association Journal* 1100.

Niquille, M (2007) 'Richterinnen der zweiten Generation in veränderten Rahmenbedingungen?' in R Ludewig, K Weislehner and E Angehrn (eds), *Zwischen Recht und Gerechtigkeit: Richterinnen im Spiegel der Zeit* (Bern, Stämpfli).

Peresie, JL (2005) 'Female Judges Matter: Gender and Collegial Decision-making in the Federal Appellate Courts' 114(7) *Yale Law Journal* 1759.
Portnoy, SM (2004) 'The Role of Judges in Keeping Difficult Parties Contained in Court' 18(3) *American Journal of Family Law* 131.
Ptacek, JT, Smith, RE and Zanas, J (1992) 'Gender, Appraisal, and Coping: A Longitudinal Analysis' 60(4) *Journal of Personality and Social Psychology* 747.
Roach Anleu, S and Mack K (2005) 'Magistrates' Everyday Work and Emotional Labour' 32(4) *Journal of Law and Society* 590.
Sander, G and Hartmann, I (2009) 'Erhöhter Stress bei weiblichen Führungskräften' in G Frank, and WR Kromm (eds), *Leadership and Health—Weshalb die Folgen schlechter Führung kein Arzt heilen kann* (Düsseldorf, Symposion Publishing GmbH).
Schultz, U and Shaw, G (2003) (eds), *Women in the World's Legal Professions* (Oxford, Hart Publishing).
—— (2008) Editorial: 'Gender and Judging' 15 *International Journal of the Legal Profession* 1.
Sommerlad, H (2002) 'Women Solicitors in a Fractured Profession: Intersections of Gender and Professionalism in England and Wales' 9(3) *International Journal of the Legal Profession* 213.
Tversky, A (1977) 'Features of Similarity' 84(4) *Psychological Review* 327.
Wagner, U, Christ, O and Dick, RV (2003) 'Belastungen und Befindlichkeiten von Lehrerinnen und Lehrern' in A Abele, EH Hoff and HU Hohner (eds), *Frauen und Männer in akademischen Professionen. Berufsverläufe und Berufserfolg* (München, Asanger).
Zimmerman, IM (2006) 'Helping Judges in Distress' 90(1) *Judicature* 10.
Zuriff, GE (2006) 'Judgments of Similarity are Psychological: The Importance of Importance' 61(6) *American Psychologist* 641.

Part 3

Gender Perspectives in Judging

3.1

Gendered Experiences of a Judge in Germany

RUTH HERZ

WALKING UP THE wide central staircase in the hall of the palatial court building in Cologne, I felt intimidated. On my way to be sworn in as a judge I wondered whether I would ever feel at home here. Later inside a court of law, dressed in the black judge's robe with the velvet collar, I took the oath which, for decades, judges before me had recited. At that solemn moment in my life I felt I had realised my professional dream. I was now a member of the judiciary and had vowed to resolve people's conflicts fairly and objectively.

My father, a lawyer with a private practice in Düsseldorf, was especially proud of his daughter sitting on the bench. In 1933 his career was cut short when he was forced to leave Breslau (now Wroclaw) where he had been a lawyer at the Court of Appeal. By decree of the Nazi government, which had just come to power, he had like all Jewish lawyers been banned from practising his profession. The same fate had met my grandfather, as well as other family members who were also lawyers. I have often wondered how my father must have felt when he entered the court building for the last time to collect his lawyer's robe after the horrendous and violent way the Jews had been treated when—before that time—they had been an integral part of German society. In many cities across Germany they were chased out of court buildings, forced into refuse trucks and driven around the city centres ridiculed and humiliated. He never shared those feelings with us. He did tell me though that he had no wish to remain in a country where he was undesired and degraded, regardless of the fact that our family had lived in Prussia since the seventeenth century. My father left Germany for Palestine in April 1933. Becoming a judge in Germany in the mid-1970s was therefore hardly natural or unproblematic for me. I did feel, though, that by so doing I somehow restored my father's dignity.

The robe I was wearing at the swearing-in ceremony was not my own. A senior judge had lent me his robe, which was a few sizes too large and nearly reached the floor. While I struggled with the unfamiliar garment and its wide sleeves its owner remarked that I would certainly have to grow into it. It was clear to me that he meant this metaphorically. My feeling at the time was and still is, that this middle-aged and middle-class judge had not meant this as an encouragement, but that it rather reflected his scepticism as to whether a young woman, however highly qualified, would be able to adequately fulfil the task she was taking on. I had been appointed by the Minister of Justice, as is always the case in Germany, on the merit of my last exam marks. I had also by then earned a doctorate of law from the University of Cologne, which few judges had. Only later did I realise that this remark was the first piece of a puzzle that I would eventually fit together with many other pieces to form a picture of gender relations in the judiciary. In this chapter I would like to present this picture, drawn from my personal experience as a female judge in the years from 1974 to 2001.

In 1974, 90 per cent of judges in Germany were male. Since then, the proportion of female judges has gradually increased to 36 per cent. I did not see any reason why resolving conflicts between people and mending the social fabric of society should be male dominated. I wanted to take part in this enterprise. On the practical side I knew that as a judge I would be in control of my daily timetable, which is so important when juggling a profession with being a wife and a mother of two young children. My mother who had travelled alone from Tel-Aviv to Brussels to study bacteriology in the late 1920s was one of the first women to be admitted to that university. On returning she practised her profession in the state veterinary laboratory of Palestine. From her I learnt how important it was to keep a balance between professional and domestic life.

It was now up to me to reinvent the role of the traditionally male judge into one in which I could fit as a woman. Young (male) judges were advised to appear at the swearing-in ceremony wearing a black suit and white shirt. Women were expected to adapt to the male model and wear a black skirt suit with a white blouse. This was not my style. I could not bring myself to appear in such a conformist attire. After all, I had been active in the 1968 student movement fighting to modernise the state with its judiciary, which had not resisted the Nazi regime. I chose a navy coloured dress, high-heeled shoes and earrings. I am not sure what price this resistance cost me. It was my first conscious expression of femininity as a judge. I certainly did not want to appear unprofessional or unrealistic let alone unrespectable and had to negotiate my appearance, my style and my clothing as I went along.

The judiciary being a male domain, all but one of my professors and instructors during my studies as well as my practical training, was male. The only female judge I was referred to for one of the phases of my training had a reputation among the trainees as being especially harsh. In my case, this turned out to be completely untrue. But it did reflect a widespread perception of women in the judiciary which dismissed them as either exceptionally harsh or alternately as too lenient. She encouraged me in my work and trusted my judgement. She eventually became one of the few judges to whom I could later always turn for professional advice.

I quickly settled down in my chambers preparing my cases for the next day's hearings and writing my decisions. The atmosphere in court, my fellow judges, the court files and papers were, after all, familiar to me. It was now necessary to concentrate on systematically applying what I had studied at university and had learnt during my practical training. Judging is obviously not a profession governed by intuition and emotions, but one of applying the law and interpreting it with logic and knowledge. It was with dismay though, that I realised after working through the files, that what I had learnt at university was one thing and real life was another. The first case in the civil court I was assigned to was a divorce. It was not until 1977 that special family courts were installed in Germany. The middle-aged couple seeking a divorce, about 20 years my senior, were most probably nervous entering the court, but so was I. For the first time I was carrying the full weight of responsibility for the decision I would eventually have to make. I could not help wondering whether, after all, I had made the wrong professional choice. While I believed I was capable of dealing with the legal questions involved, I hoped I would also be able to solve the personal conflict of the couple. I also wondered what they thought, seeing the young female judge, lacking in life experience, about to decide on the far-reaching changes in their lives. Did I convey the necessary authority and gravitas? I was still under the influence of the reaction of a comment made by an elderly lady who had knocked on my door a couple of days earlier, taken one look at me and said: 'Excuse me Miss, I am looking for the judge as I would like a quick word before the proceedings'. Although there was a sign on the door indicating my name and my title, she obviously did not expect a young woman to be the judge but rather a middle-aged male. Looking at the couple filing for a divorce, I could not help noticing the husband's bright and airy spirit and his obviously new multicoloured tie. He claimed that his wife had led a leisurely life during their marriage, not having had to work. He did not see why, after the divorce, he should go on paying her alimony. His wife, looking tired and dejected, obviously did not consider looking after their four children and the large household a comfortable life. By now there was no way she could earn her own living. Did I colour my professional work with my gendered view seeing this woman and her future with my female eyes? Should this perspective have an impact on the judiciary as a whole?

I found myself reflecting whether university adequately equips judges for their arduous profession. Studying law at university as well the practical training at the different courts of law and lawyers' and notaries' offices, which follow academic studies in Germany, lead us to think and act in a specific, legal, way. We are trained to change life's stories into law's stories.

In the continental European legal system we are in fact trained to 'skeletonise' the 'facts' from the story of a legal case. 'Judgecraft' is thus an exercise in stripping stories of many aspects and paring them down so that they neatly fit into the judge's method of handling cases in court. I did not question this process or its effects at first, but once I was more secure in my day-to-day work at court I realised that I was sometimes hearing stories or seeing the facts differently from my male colleagues. I decided to discuss this with my few female colleagues but realised that I was having a difficult time convincing them. Law's definitions seemed to me increasingly problematic when seen from a feminine perspective. This was especially true in sexual crimes such as rape. Although this was being discussed outside the courts, predominantly by feminists, among us judges there was silence. I was disappointed when I tried to argue the case of the definition of rape in the German criminal code with a female judge. She saw nothing wrong with the definition, although it required the victim to defend herself with force against the attack by the man. Surely all women know, I argued, that using force against a man may be pointless in many instances. My interlocutor who insisted on referring to and relying on well-known decisions of the Court of Appeal was impervious to my arguments. It made me realise the extent to which male values and perceptions are unconsciously adopted by women in law. It was also a reminder of how difficult it would be to win women to a common cause in law and justice. Indeed, no active female solidarity seemed to have developed within the judiciary in Germany.

The gender issue is further complicated by the fact that judges are not only mostly male but on the whole are recruited from the same social class. Fitting in to the judiciary means acquiring the behaviour, thinking and even body language of our peers. Those who are outsiders, being female, or coming from lower echelons of society, learn to fit in. We outsiders achieve this through interaction with our peers in court, which conditions us to see the world in a specific way and to develop typical opinions, behaviour, styles and tastes as well as ways of expressing ourselves. Judges in time literally incorporate this 'habitus', as Pierre Bourdieu has called it, making it their 'second nature'. This is an explicit model of knowledge of the rules of the game and how to play it. It is therefore so important to belong and not remain an outsider.

Court rituals, its dramaturgy, language and clothing and, last but not least, the gender of the judge, rather than a charismatic personality bestow and ensure continuity of judicial gravitas. This is why the special aura often peels off as soon as the judge removes the robe and leaves the courthouse. I was intrigued by the reaction of some people at a dinner party who learned of my profession and remarked: 'You don't look like a judge! You smile, you are friendly and you are a young woman'. The image of the judge was clearly that of a middle-aged and middle-class man, the personification of authority, independence and objectivity.

Independence and objectivity are the values we judges strive for and believe we can maintain. However, a judge is not only the sum of her training and judicial habitus, but is of course a private person with her own background and history. Inevitably, the judge's personality and attitudes will surface in his or her court decisions. This is not only true for cases and issues which are the subjects of public debate. After all, judges are part of society, read newspapers, watch television and have their views. Therefore the entire societal and political climate is present in the courtroom. The notion—that judges are invariably impartial is an indispensable myth used to sustain faith in the legal system—caught up with me personally.

My own personal biography was dominated by the expulsion of my father from his legal position in the wake of the Nazi's rise to power and his enforced exile to Palestine where he could not exercise his profession. It rendered me an outsider as well as an insider, both in the judiciary as well as in society. Being the only Jewish judge in Germany, I was clearly more sensitive to the plight of the other in court. After leaving the judiciary I wrote a book about my career, my own understanding of the judge's role and my views on law and justice. In the book I revealed my thoughts and feelings while going about my profession. One of the reviews in a leading newspaper commented, 'we certainly need these judges who are genuinely committed to justice, but we don't want to know the details of their thoughts' (*Süddeutsche Zeitung*, 20 June 2007).

As a wife and mother of two young children, I wished to allot time to both sides of my life. This meant that I often went home for lunch instead of going to the court cafeteria, which did not always go down well with my male colleagues. I did not join the judiciary as a feminist looking for slights against women but I was irritated when my family name, which means 'heart' in German, seemed to be an invitation for my 'benevolent' male colleagues to refer to me as 'Herzchen', the diminutive of Herz, which is also a term of endearment. I refused to play the game and protesting that I was their equal, earned me the comments of being a 'bad sport' or lacking a sense of humour.

I felt proud and fortunate to be assigned to a civil court at the beginning of my career. This is the branch of law considered the most intellectual and I enjoyed the challenge. It would also have been beneficial for later promotion. When later I was offered the chance of promotion, I declined because I enjoyed being in the lower court where I could encounter 'real' people and deal with their conflicts rather than with their lawyers in the high court. But, alas, after two years of practice, I was transferred to the criminal youth court (*Jugendschöffengericht*). This is a criminal court dealing with young people aged between 14 and 21 charged with all offences except murder and manslaughter. Although this is considered to be a position of status and responsibility, I was not happy; I felt I had been redefined as a mother figure instead of as an intellectual judge and placed in my 'natural' habitat. This was not what I wanted in the workplace. But I had to ask myself how come I was the only female judge during most of my time at the youth court? Was it a man's job after all? I soon understood that the presence of a male judge in the juvenile court secures the continuity of the notion of the male father figure representing the state as the ultimate authority for the young, both male and female. This is precisely one of the reasons why I considered my profession to be so important for my own children, a boy and a girl. I wanted them to understand that both men and women could be models for both of them and for society. In the case of two teenage girls, first time offenders who had stolen two CDs from a music shop, I noticed that this was not the way my male colleagues thought. The prosecutor made the point that they had probably offended because they lacked paternal model and authority, as their fathers were absent from home. It did not occur to him that by so doing he was disqualifying the mothers. This seemed to me particularly ludicrous considering the trivial nature of their offences.

After my initial scepticism I grew to value and also enjoy my position in the youth court. I became interested in youth and also in the concept of a group within society defined and constructed exclusively by their age. During this phase between childhood and adulthood young people are confronted with specific problems and challenges. It is common for them to test borders and to look for adventures, especially outdoors. This is the usual definition of youth, a modern 'invention' or 'discovery' of the beginning of the last century. I learnt important lessons about the place of youth in society and also about myself. I delved into theories explaining the causes of crime and realised how society targets youth as the source of a wide array of its problems, and by so doing deflects from other causes as well as its own inability to solve them.

As a woman who had experienced that the world was a different place depending on where you came from, I was determined to listen to the stories of the people in court and not only to the legal way of thinking. The case of a 16-year-old boy, accused of stealing a tray of yoghurt pots delivered to a supermarket, is a case in point. He had been living on the street since running away from home in a small town near Cologne. His parents were present in court and agreed to take him back. The boy refused to accept the offer, which the social worker considered very generous. In fact he resembled the boy's father. Both seemed decent but narrow-minded provincial men. This type of atmosphere, the boy said in court, was exactly what he had run away from. He wanted to try and find his own way in life. I admired him for his courage and open-mindedness. I said I did not believe that anyone else in the courtroom would have been able to survive on the street on their own, for which I gained angry looks all round. I understood that none of the solutions suggested by the social worker appealed to him. I therefore suggested he find a flat for him where he could live with other youngsters under some kind of supervision.

Those early thoughts and experiments led me to ponder on the whole notion of the 'youth court' and the justification for its existence. Though often presented as a benevolent institution, it gradually became clear to me that youth courts play a more dubious societal role. Society—or more precisely the elected (overwhelmingly male) lawmakers—determines what sort of behaviour should be defined as criminal. It is hardly surprising that the majority of young criminals are to be found among young working-class males. They rarely have access to bank accounts or any other sources of monetary goods. They resort to bodily harm, robbery and breaking into cars and houses which is considered 'normal' for the '*classes dangereuses*'. Punishing young men is the way of disciplining them.

Girls are expected to behave differently and are therefore rarely targeted as criminals. The reason for this became clear to me when I was asked to deliver a series of lectures and was about to reiterate the usual definition of youth which, I realised, hardly conformed with my own. I had grown up doing exactly the same as most other girls in our culture, chatting with my girlfriends about clothes, makeup, music and boys. We, the girls, spent most of our time indoors, often called on by our mothers to help them with domestic chores or to look after younger siblings. We clearly were practising our future roles as housewives and mothers while our brothers were playing outside. The standard definition of youth was in fact confined to describing only one type of youth, male youth.

Typical offending patterns for girls are thefts of lipsticks and makeup, jeans or T-shirts and the like while strolling together with their friends through shops in the city centres. When I asked a young woman, charged with stealing a pair of jeans, why she had done this, she burst into tears. The male actors in court, her lawyer, the prosecutor as well as the social worker, were quick to reassure her that she would not be treated too harshly. They all gave me disapproving looks as I persisted in demanding a response from the girl. I explained to her that retreating into the typical female strategy of becoming weak in a male context was unwise in the long run. I wanted her to understand that she needed to act in a grown up and adequate fashion because her behaviour was only perpetuating the status quo of women in society. I was aware of this, because even I, a judge with a doctoral degree, was placed in that situation when defined as the mascot of the juvenile court judges.

I remember one case in which a 16-year-old young woman, who lived at home with her mother and her mother's new partner, had run away and was hanging out in the main railway station in Cologne. She had been caught pick-pocketing. In court she admitted being guilty of the offence. The prosecutor suggested sending the girl back home to avoid the danger of her drifting into prostitution. This, he said, is the path girls take when they are living on the street. In addition, he agreed with the social worker that community service work would get her back on the right track in life.

He 'benevolently' added that a further sanction would not be necessary. The case itself seemed simple enough, so the prosecutor and social worker in court, both male, had not thought to probe the girl further. When I questioned her about why she had run away from home in the first place—behaviour considered adventurous for boys, but unusual and even 'unnatural' for girls—she shyly revealed that her mother's partner was molesting her sexually while her mother was at work. She had not been able to tell her mother about it for fear of wrecking the relationship with the man with whom she seemed so happy. For a young girl in her situation, running away from home, far from adventurous, was a grown up and rational way of dealing with her predicament. Sending her back home would be counterproductive. What this girl needed, instead of benevolence, was a job so that she could stand on her own two feet. I sent her to the city council job training centre for professional advice instead.

Having grown into my everyday life as a judge, I was one day re-reading some of my decisions and noticed that they flowed rather well; they were lucid and logical. Where had my doubts, hesitations and uncertainties disappeared? I had ironed them out of the texts as all judges do. I also realised that we judges do not acknowledge doubts to each other, nor even to ourselves. We harbour a certain hubris, which includes a good portion of self-righteousness. I remember commenting to a colleague one day in the court cafeteria, after having tried a case of shoplifting: 'I suspect that we have all, at some point in our lives, committed a theft or some equivalent offence' whereupon he answered stiffly: 'I certainly have not'. Self-reflection poses a threat to the integrity of judicial identity.

After five years of practice in the youth court, I was asked to write a textbook on criminal youth law earmarked for university law students. I agreed on the spot because it seemed to provide me with the vehicle I was seeking for changing the way we study law. I wanted to change the way we learn about law. My experiences and reflections as a youth court judge had revealed to me again and again that, during our studies of law and our practical training, we do not learn much about reality. My book included not only a section on theories of crime, but many examples of cases from my everyday judging experience. I also started teaching a course in youth justice at the university. As part of the course I regularly took the students to observe a day in the youth court which provided them with an opportunity to perceive what their academic studies failed to convey. In one such visit we were listening to a case of three 16-year-old defendants, two boys and a girl, who were charged with breaking into a newspaper shop after hours and stealing the money—about one hundred euros—from the till, which they all admitted after hearing the letter of accusation read to them by the prosecutor. One of the boys was German and the judge asked him mainly about his school performance. He encouraged him to make better progress so that he could later aim for a good job which would allow him to become a responsible member of society; he then fined him. His best friend, born in Germany to Turkish parents who had come to Germany 30 years earlier, was dealt with more harshly. Although he had no prior record, he received a conditional prison sentence. The judge further saw fit to comment that as 'Turkish men often do not respect women' it would be right for him to have a male probation officer. Perhaps without being aware of it the judge thus perpetuated the young man's place as an outsider in society without much prospect of integration or achieving the role he attributed to the German boy. The girl, very pretty with long blond hair, was dealt with in a different way. She admitted that her poor school performance was because she was bored. The judge did not comment on this at all and decided she should only be cautioned. He thereby assigned her the role of a future housewife. The students were amazed to realise the degree to which the judge was shaped by, and was reinforcing, the societal status quo. This of course was not done consciously, nor was it part of a conspiracy, but arose simply from a lack of insight into the lives lived by people of a different class, background or sex. Would a female judge have decided in the same way? Surely her own biography would influence her decisions.

I often faced similar situations, which accentuated differences between male and female perceptions in court. One such case was an attempted robbery committed by a 17-year-old young man. He had attacked a man in order to steal his money. The male social worker harped on about the lack of a father figure in this youngster's life and was convinced that this was one of the reasons for his offending. He did not acknowledge the mother as an authority figure in the child's life. While listening to him I was watching the boy's mother who was present in court. She seemed a sensible and strong enough woman to me. I asked her about her life and she reported that the boy's father, who was an alcoholic, had been abusive to her, so she had left him when the child was very young. Her next partner had resorted to physical abuse of the child so she had left him, taking the child with her. She seemed to have made rational and right decisions; after all, rather than the men in her life being good role models for her and her child, she was taking on the responsibility of rearing the child alone.

Gradually I became aware that the existing sanctions set out in the Youth Code were not always adequate responses to the offenders and offences I encountered in court. This became especially clear to me in the case of a 15-year-old boy who had terrorised his schoolmate, forcing him to hand over his new jacket to him. The victim's mother had made her reluctant son go to the police with her and report the event. In court, both boys—the accused as well as the victim/witness—were evasive. It eventually transpired that the offender had long since returned the jacket to the owner and the boys had become friends. Obviously the custodial sentence, which the prosecutor continued to demand, following the dry letter of the law, no longer seemed appropriate. I was now set on proposing alternative sanctions.

'Alternative sanctions', as community sanctions were called in Germany, had been widely introduced in the 1980s. But community service as well as anti-aggression or outdoor motorcycling courses, did not always seem satisfactory to me. These especially did not appeal to girls. The only schemes open to girls were mother-and-child groups. Besides the fact that these schemes again simply prepare women for the traditional dependent role in society as opposed to the roles of men, it also seemed to sexualise women. My criticism was not well received by the social workers who deemed the scheme benign.

I was searching for an alternative which would have more direct implications for both parties in a conflict. During a year I had spent in the United States I had become acquainted with victim-offender mediation schemes, which were mushrooming across the country. I visited many of them, examining the way they functioned. Transferring this idea to the German legal system and culture was not an easy task. With much effort, I succeeded in securing funding and setting up such a scheme in Cologne. Invited to present the scheme before a committee at the Federal Ministry of Justice, I arrived with two male collaborators who had helped me set it up. We were very graciously received and I was treated like a lady and seated to the right of the Justice Secretary at the round table. After the preliminaries, the chairperson asked who of the gentlemen would like to present the scheme, which I had devised. I had to disappoint him by taking the floor myself. Victim-offender mediation was subsequently introduced into the German Juvenile Code as a sanction.[1]

My continued quest for alternative ways of treating offenders evoked criticism from some of my colleagues. They defined it as 'leniency', which was naturally associated with me as a female judge. Some even went further, suggesting that my approach stemmed from my late husband's strong influence over me. He was a sociology professor and this, to my fellow judges, was synonymous with political left leanings and a liberal attitude to crime and punishment. They simply could not bring themselves to credit me with my own thoughts. Female judges often have the reputation of being emotional and therefore unprofessional when deciding on punishment. It is not easy to define leniency in decision-making. Nobody had ever compared my sentences with those of other judges. In fact the only study made so far comparing decisions of male and female judges in Germany was inconclusive.[2] The act of punishing is hard to assess objectively. Is there a 'right' amount of punishment for each case? Can only male judges rightly assess it? I soon realised that labelling female judges as lenient was a way

[1] Ruth Herz was later awarded the 'Federal Cross of Merit' for her efforts.
[2] R Drewniak (1994) *Strafrichterinnen als Hoffnungsträgerinnen* (Stuttgart, Thieme).

of excluding women's values from notions of professionalism: caring is interpreted as partial and therefore unprofessional.

Before leaving the judiciary to go to Oxford to pursue further research on the nature and process of judging, I was given a rare opportunity to leave my own stamp on the image the public has of the judiciary, airing at large the lessons I have drawn from my long-drawn personal experience as a judge, including those on gender. For four years I played the part of the judge in a daily court series on German television. *Das Jugendgericht* (The Youth Court) was a presentation of fictional cases based on genuine ones tried in juvenile courts across Germany. The Ministry of Justice—under constant pressure to ensure the transparency of the judicial process, enthusiastically embraced the idea. Allowing a judge, rather than an actor, to enact the role of a judge meant that 'justice could be watched being done'. To me it provided a unique opportunity to present to millions of viewers, on a daily basis, a female judge who was in full authority and control, and yet capable of pursuing a sensible, humane and fair youth justice in Germany.

Much has changed since I was appointed to the judiciary in Germany. The numbers of women judges has risen dramatically. Now, young female judges can watch other women in court and be reassured that they do not have to behave like men. Increasing the number of women among the judiciary is not sufficient. More needs to be done. It is astonishing, that in our time of mass participation and exposure, the judiciary rarely reflects on its role in society, on its power or political attitudes. Like most male judges, female judges also tend to accept the codes and conventions of the judicial role.

3.2

Women Judges in the Netherlands

BREGJE DIJKSTERHUIS

Abstract

This chapter addresses two central questions concerning judges and gender: what is the situation of women judges in the Netherlands, and do women judge differently from men? The discussion of the first question starts with a statistical profile of the distribution of women throughout various levels of the internal hierarchy of the current Dutch judiciary. Although vertical segregation continues to persist, the share of women in the Dutch judiciary has increased to such an extent that today parity of numbers has been achieved. This so-called feminisation of the judiciary has led to a debate inside and outside the judiciary that will be analysed in this chapter.

Furthermore, this chapter contributes to the debate on possible gender-based differences in judges' decision-making processes based on original data obtained during my six years of PhD studies. I was granted access to the normally closed two-yearly meetings of the Dutch Judicial Alimony Commission, where 24 member judges of all district courts and middle level courts discuss maintenance issues and develop guidelines to apply in the judicial decision-making process. By observing the discussions I gained an understanding of how both male and female judges determine their position in the political and gender-sensitive field of maintenance.

1. INTRODUCTION[1]

IN THE DUTCH civil law system, there are 19 districts courts. Each district court is made up of a maximum of five sectors, which always include administrative law, civil law (including family law) and criminal law. Appeals against judgments of district court judges in civil and criminal law cases can be brought at the competent middle level courts, five in total. Appeals against administrative law judgments go to one of the competent specialised administrative law tribunals. Appeals in civil, criminal and tax

[1] My thanks for comment go to Jonathan Soeharno and for editing advice to Sarah Brants and Marjolijn Dijksterhuis.

law cases are lodged at the Supreme Court of the Netherlands.[2] Simpler cases are dealt with by single judges and more complex cases by three-judge sections.

I will first give an overview of the distribution of women within and across the various branches of the Dutch legal profession. Next, I analyse the debate in the media on the quantitative feminisation of the judiciary. The third section discusses to what extent female judges affect the content and outcome of judicial work (Schultz, 2003b: 313–14). I focus on divorce law, more specifically maintenance law.[3]

2. FEMALE PARTICIPATION IN THE DUTCH LEGAL PROFESSION

2.1. The Distribution of Women in the Judiciary

In the 1910s and 1920s demand for the appointment of female judges in the Netherlands had risen. The public prosecutor of the Supreme Court at the time wrote in a letter to the Dutch Parliament that although there were no formal obstacles, there were other objections: women would be more emotional than male judges and influenced by their feelings. Moreover, they were 'not normal during their menstrual period, which would make them unsuitable as a judge'.[4]

It was not until 1947 when the Netherlands had to deal with a serious shortage of judges that the first female judge was appointed, but only after the Minister of Justice had given his consent (Sloot, 1980: 1186; de Groot-van Leeuwen, 2009: 25). In 1991, De Groot concluded—on the basis of her empirical research on the Dutch judiciary—that many more women had finished their education to become judges but they hardly ever occupied top positions. She argued that this was not only due to the fact that they were female, but rather that many women limited their career possibilities by opting for part-time work (1991: 148). She also showed that in the 1980s and 1990s the participation of women in the Dutch judiciary increased steadily. In 1985, 16 per cent of the judges were women, and by 1995 the share of female judges had risen to 34 per cent (De Groot, 2003: 342). A milestone was reached in 2008 when, for the first time, female judges outnumbered male judges (1207 women compared with 1190 men). Currently, female judges are still in a majority, and this majority is growing fast with each

[2] See: <www.rechtspraak.nl/information+in+english.>

[3] This was the subject of my PhD study, which provides original data. I observed the meetings of the Judicial Alimony Commission and conducted semi-structured interviews with judges and other key persons within the group of Dutch maintenance judges (Dijksterhuis, 2008).

[4] W Sorgdrager, 'Strafklimaat harder ondanks feminisering' *Volkskrant* (5 September 2009).

age group (60–70 years: 30 per cent; 50–60 years: 45 per cent; 40–50 years: 60 per cent; up to 40 years: 76 per cent).[5]

There are two points of access to the Dutch judiciary: the first option is a six-year judicial training programme. Lawyers can apply directly after graduation from law school, but the selection is very strict. The second route is to enter the judiciary after six years of legal experience in one of the different branches of the legal profession, followed by a one-year judicial training programme also based on selection. An interesting question remains whether recruitment to the two programmes shows the same trend of feminisation, and if it is the case, whether this has led to a diversity policy to recruit more male judges. Data from previous years (2001–08) show that the proportion of women selected for the six-year judicial training programme varied between 70 per cent and 90 per cent of the total number (every year around 60) of the total. Peaks can be found around 2003 (87 per cent); 2005 (85 per cent); 2006 (89 per cent); and 2008 (85 per cent). These are future judges so one can assume that the increase of female judges will go on. Remarkably, in 2009 and 2010 the share of women dropped to 65 per cent and 62 per cent respectively.[6] An obvious explanation might be that the judiciary is aiming at recruiting more male judges, but the Coordinator Recruitment of Judges at the Council for the Judiciary rejected this claim although admitting that attention is paid to this issue of feminisation and, in the short or long term, a policy to counteract this trend will be developed. There are no data available on the distribution of women in the one-year judicial training programme; but it seems that mainly women apply. This was confirmed by the Coordinator Recruitment of Judges at a large district court who stated that currently most candidates entering the judiciary after six years of legal experience are women in their thirties and forties.

2.2. Career Opportunities

In spite of holding a majority in the Dutch judiciary, women judges are still a minority in leading positions in the judiciary. The position of judge at the Supreme Court represents the peak of a judicial career academically speaking, while that of president of the court is the highest managerial position in the judiciary.[7] In 2010, 20 per cent of the Supreme Court judges were female (total number of women: six). Equally, only a very small percentage of female judges, 12 per cent (total: three) are presidents of a district court or a middle level court. Compared with 1995, when seven per cent of

[5] Internal data of the Council for the Judiciary.
[6] All data: Council for the Judiciary.
[7] Those managers also exert a few judicial functions.

women (total: seven) occupied top positions in the judiciary, the number of female judges in these top positions has only slightly improved (De Groot, 2003: 343). The lower manager position of president of the sector is also mainly occupied by male judges, but women have their share with a reasonable 29 per cent (total: 21). Among senior court judges whose task is to improve the quality of judgments within the courts, the share is 40 per cent (total: 371).

Table 1: Distribution of women in the Dutch court hierarchy, 2010

Positions	Women total number	Women %
Supreme court judges	6	19
Special judicial colleges	65	50
Middle level judges	182	40
District court judges	989	54
Judges working part-time	**Women total number**	**Women %**
Supreme court judges	unknown	unknown
Special judicial colleges	56	47
Middle level judges	157	38
District court judges	837	51

Distribution of women in key positions (managers) in the Dutch court hierarchy, 2010

Positions	Women total number	Women %
Vice-president and President Supreme Court	0	0
President of the court	3	12
President of the sector (civil/criminal etc)	21	29
Senior court judges (district courts and middle level)	371	40
Judges working part-time	**Women total number**	**Women %**
Vice-president and President Supreme Court	0	0
President of the court	3	11
President of the sector (civil/criminal etc)	20	28
Senior court judges (district courts and middle level)	324	37

The percentage of female judges in district courts is 65 per cent (total: 989), compared with 45 per cent at the middle level courts (total: 182). Thus, male judges are still dominating the middle level courts. This is likely to change, as the number of female judges in the middle level courts has increased in the last few years. In 2008, for example, the female contribution within the district courts was 53 per cent (total: 921) compared with 38 per cent (total: 186) within the middle level courts (Raad voor de Rechtspraak, 2009). This trend of quantitative feminisation in the middle level courts will most probably go on. Compared with the situation in 1995, when female judges occupied only 23 per cent of the middle level position (total: 165), the situation of women has improved considerably.

To conclude, women are still clearly in the minority with regard to managerial positions in the judiciary as well as judges in the Supreme Court, while the situation at middle level is much more favourable—a development that is expected to continue. Overall, in all positions the share of women has increased.

2.3. The Debate in the Media on Quantitative Feminisation of the Judiciary

Feminisation of the judiciary seems to be a positive development at first sight, but has found its critics and has led to a debate within and outside the judiciary. The debate takes place in the national media, among researchers, judges and other stakeholders involved.

In 1994, judges and researchers were interviewed for the first time in one of the main Dutch national newspapers *De Volkskrant* on the subject of feminisation of the judiciary.[8] Male judge Bert van Delden, at that time president of the district court Den Haag and later the first president of the Council for the Judiciary, argued that women did not sentence differently from men, even in sexual offences. But his female colleague, senior judge J van den Steenhoven-Drion, expressed a different opinion:

> In the sixties, rapists were let off with a suspended prison sentence. I blamed the male administration of justice. This supposedly mild sentencing practice changed when women got their share in the judiciary, although changing views in society and rejuvenation of the judiciary are also important factors.[9]

Van den Steenhoven-Drion was appointed as one of the first Dutch female judges in 1975. She had applied for the position because it permitted her

[8] G van der Wal, 'Mevrouw de rechter' *Volkskrant* (2 April 1994); 'Vrouwen te soft om rechter te zijn' *Telegraaf* (1 September 2009).

[9] Ibid.

to work part-time. Her appointment, she suggests, was due to a general shortage of judges. In the *Volkskrant* of 1994 Van den Steenhoven-Drion explains that most letters are still addressed to 'Sir ', and she adds: 'Power is associated with men'. Leny de Groot-van Leeuwen, professor of sociology of law, argues in the same article: 'I am deeply convinced that it is not a single characteristic that determines the judicial culture or judicial judgments. People's acts are determined by many factors'.[10]

In spring 2009, the discussion on the feminisation of the judiciary in the media continued. The immediate cause was the annual report of the Council for the Judiciary, which stressed that since 2008 women in the judiciary outnumbered men (Council for the Judiciary, 2009). In the national newspaper *Parool*, attorneys and legal scientists were interviewed on the matter.[11] Male criminal attorney, Theo Hiddema, stated that female judges deliver judgments of the same quality as men do and added: 'The difference is that women are a bit more precise and stick to the files more than men do. Women work consistently, item by item, towards a verdict'. Interestingly enough, he indicates that women also work more efficiently: 'When a female judge is judging, you are sure to be home early, because the potatoes are waiting' (ibid). A rather left-handed form of praise. Although Hiddema himself did not consider the feminisation of the judiciary a problem, he claimed that some of his clients, especially the more 'macho' immigrant clients, found it hard to accept being judged by a woman. This applied particularly to sexual offences. If they were sentenced by an all-female three-judge bench, they considered that to be the reason for their conviction. According to Theo de Roos (male professor of criminal law) feminisation has changed the judicial culture: 'Twenty or thirty years ago, the atmosphere in the judiciary with all those men in ivory towers was more stiff and formal than it is today. Women have contributed a great deal to this process' (ibid). Marijke Malsch (female researcher and deputy judge) from the Dutch Institute for the Study of Crime and Law Enforcement finds these sentiments understandable, regardless of whether they are just or unjust. She warns of the consequences of a continuation of the fast increase of the proportion of female judges:

> It should not matter whether the judge is male or female, but in reality it does. People should recognize themselves in judges. Courts should consider this. It is questionable whether three female judges should be appointed in a sexual offence with a male suspect.[12]

[10] Ibid.
[11] J Salden, 'De rechter is steeds vaker een mevrouw' *Parool* (22 May 2009).
[12] Ibid.

In June 2008, the local television programme *rtvnoord* broadcast a case where gender ('being a woman judge') played a role in judging and even led to an official challenge of the capability of the judges. The attorney of a suspect of a sexual offence in Groningen raised objections because the public prosecutor, the judge and the clerk of the court were female. His argument was that these women would not be able to judge his client impartially. The court rejected this argument because the Constitution does not allow for discrimination.

In September 2009, Joost Eerdmans, a male former member of the House of Commons, continued the discussion on feminisation in the media, in articles on 'women are too soft to be judges' and 'Eerdmans starts a civil initiative against injustice on the part of women judges'. According to him, criminal courts paid too little attention to victims, for which he blamed female judges. Women judges' personalities, so he argued, caused them to be more lenient towards criminals and to value social rehabilitation higher than reprisal. Their female qualities were empathy, mercifulness, indulgence, tolerance, the taking of balanced decisions and searching for win/win solutions.[13] To solve these 'problems' in criminal law, Eerdmans established the 'Civilian Committee against Injustice'. In *Pauw and Witteman*, the national television current affairs programme, the famous Dutch male criminal lawyer, Gerard Spong, debated with Eerdmans on this issue. Spong argued that Dutch sentences were more severe than those in surrounding countries, thereby demonstrating that Dutch judges were not soft.

Winnie Sorgdrager, the first female chief public prosecutor at any court (in 1994) and the first female Minister of Justice (from 1994 to 1998) contributed to the discussion in the national newspaper *Volkskrant*.[14] Sorgdrager argued that Eerdman's assumption was incorrect. Since the 1980s, punishments issued by judges had become increasingly severe. At the same time, the number of female judges had increased. According to her, sentences had been independent of the gender of the judge. However, Sorgdrager did think that suspects seemed to prefer a three-judge mixed-gender bench to an all-female one. Other voices joined in the debate: I pleaded in the national newspaper *NRC* for more judges, either men or women, with female qualities, such as empathy.[15] In the current affairs TV-programme *Buitenhof* on 4 April 2010, Professor of Medical Didactics, Gerda Croiset, gave a critical view on the feminisation of social professions such as medicine, the judiciary and education.

In the media discussion on the feminisation of the judiciary, three dominant strands can be identified. Each strand is part of, or is linked to,

[13] J Eerdmans, 'Eerdmans begint burgercomité tegen onrecht' *Volkskrant* (31 August 2009); Vrouw minder geschikt als strafrechter' *Volkskrant* (5 September 2009).

[14] Sorgdrager, above (n 4).

[15] B Dijksterhuis, 'Stel juist meer feminiene rechters aan' *NRC* (11 September 2009).

broader discussions in society. The first that can be identified is 'gender perspective in judging'. This debate concerns the question whether typical female qualities can affect legal work. The perception of femininity with regard to judges plays a role in this debate. The view of Eerdmans is similar to that of the public prosecutor of the Supreme Court, expressed in 1921, that typical female qualities do affect judgments and that women's sentences were softer than those of their male colleagues.[16] Van Delden, De Groot-Van Leeuwen and Hiddema held against Eerdmans and expressed the dominant view in the discussion that women do not sentence differently from men. Remarkably, this debate on gender perspectives in judging focuses completely on criminal law and fits into a broader debate on the frequently heard call of society for more severe punishments. Another aspect—the impact of women judges' working style and culture on the judiciary—is also repeatedly mentioned, especially by male contributors to the discussion.

The second strand of the debate concerns the perceived relation between the gender of judges and the legitimacy of judgments. The central question in this debate is whether clients or suspects accept judgments when judge(s), public prosecutor, and/or the clerk of the court are female and, whether or not the judiciary should show diversity and mirror the gender composition of society. The majority of researchers and judges share the opinion that although it should not matter by whom you are judged, in practice it does. It is considered to be better for the image of the judiciary and the legitimacy of judgments that three-judge benches consist of female and male judges or, in case of a single-judge section, at least one of the professional actors, either the judge, the public prosecutor or the clerk of the court should be a man. This is especially true with regard to sexual offences. Also ordinary citizens perceive gender to be of influence on the judicial process and question the legitimacy of judgments, thereby supporting Hiddenma's and Sorgdrager's observations. The fact that in 2008 the sex of a judge led to a request to challenge the judge's authority is a striking signal of the reality of this perception. Hiddema has, as described, also raised the issue of ethnicity in this context, especially concerning immigrants from 'macho cultures' and calls for further socio-legal research.[17] This debate fits into a broader discussion on the question whether judges are or should be mirroring the population in terms of gender, race, political views etc. Within the Dutch judiciary, the political discussion currently focuses especially on the distribution of different ethnicities within and across the judiciary (Raad voor de Rechtspraak, 2007).

[16] Sorgdrager, above (n 4).

[17] In cooperation with students, I am conducting fieldwork that should give an answer to the question whether suspected persons, especially immigrants, find it hard to accept if they are judged by women only.

The third strand of the debate concerns 'feminisation of the judiciary as a trend', the question whether feminisation of the judiciary is a social problem including the danger of discrimination against the female part of the judiciary. There is the danger that media attention might have the effect of a self-fulfilling prophecy, with the public and also suspects ending up believing in the problematic nature of a feminised judiciary—the so-called spiral of amplification (Brants and Brants, 1991).

2.4. Diversity Policy in Favour of Male Judges?

A committee established by the Council for the Judiciary in 2007 to make recommendations for the improvement of the six-year judicial training programme concluded: 'The composition of the judiciary should be better connected with society: The judiciary should ensure a balanced composition of men and women, autochthonous people and immigrants'. In his preface, the chairman of the committee and president of one of the district courts phrased it as follows:

> We would want the candidates for the six-year judicial training programme to represent society. This is a utopian dream as the population at law faculties is totally out of balance in terms of the proportion of men and women. There are fewer men available and competition among legal professions is strong (Werkgroep Verbetermogelijkheden Werving Raio's, 2007).

The Council for the Judiciary's reflections on a special policy to recruit more men raises the question to what extent it is legally possible in the Netherlands to pursue a diversity policy or even an affirmative action policy. Recently, the Dutch Equal Treatment Commission made an important decision in the field of medicine. Professor of Medical Didactics, Gerda Croiset, set the stage for this judgment with her remark that when a male and a female student are equally suitable, the man should be recruited for the medical college.[18] The Dutch Equal Treatment Commission passed a judgment on 23 October 2007:

> According to section 141 paragraph 4 of the Treaty establishing the European Community affirmative action policy it is possible to prevent or compensate for disadvantages regarding sex. The Dutch government did not apply this exception of the anti-discrimination principle symmetrically. According to Dutch legislation, affirmative action policy is only permitted with regard to women. The reason is that the legislation is only meant to remove invisible barriers. Affirmative action policy is a temporary measure that ends when a certain number is reached (Judgment 2007-185).

[18] 'Meer vrouwen, minder aanzien' *Trouw* (6 November 2007).

According to the Dutch Equal Treatment Commission, there are no invisible barriers for men. The decreasing share of men is due to a lack of interest and not discrimination. In that case an affirmative action policy meets legal barriers.

3. GENDERED JUDGING

3.1. A Successful Methodological Approach

> In the Judicial Alimony Commission there were four archetypes of judges: First, the male judges who were female friendly. Secondly, there were the tough male judges who thought that women should earn their own living. They considered all expenses of the men who were obliged to pay maintenance as relevant, with the result that hardly anything was left for maintenance payments. Those male judges were the minority. Third, there were the female judges who fought for the interests of women. The fourth type were the women judges who said: come on and work. In the Judicial Alimony Commission we told each other maliciously that it was clear which judge had to pay maintenance himself. Some men even left the family law court when they had to pay maintenance themselves.
>
> Interview with a middle level judge, former member of the Judicial Alimony Commission (Dijksterhuis, 2008: 79).

The question remains whether women judges' decision-making differs from that of men. More specifically, in how far 'typical female' qualities, such as intuitiveness, empathy, emotionality, sensitivity, context-relatedness, being cooperative, being non-authoritarian and less set on competition can affect judicial work (Schultz, 2003b: 313–14). These qualities are related to the identity of the judge. According to Schultz, there are complex patterns of identity such as the cool and tough female lawyer and the motherly woman judge concerned with individuals' welfare (Schultz 2003a: viii). To what extent do Dutch female judges provide 'women's other voice', which Gilligan highlighted, in the field of alimony? To what extent are fundamental changes being brought about by the growing numbers of female judges in family law in the Netherlands? I have dealt with this question in divorce law, and more specifically maintenance (Dijksterhuis, 2008). This area deals with the redistribution of both ex-partners' incomes after the divorce. Those receiving alimony are mostly women and children, while those who pay alimony are usually men. In other words, this area of law is very suitable for research on the influence of gender on judicial decision-making. In maintenance cases in Poland and Brazil, female judges have been observed to be more inclined than male judges to be harsh on housewives, as presumably they apply their own personal standards as professional women (Schultz and Shaw, 2003: 1v; Fuszara, 2003: 376–77; Botelho Junqueira, 2003: 445–49). German divorce proceedings give similar impressions. The explanation according to Schultz is that professional women feel less sympathetic towards women who expect someone else to make a living for them (Schultz, 2003b: 315). Overall, international socio-legal fieldwork indicates that gender-specific features can be shown to exist in terms of judges' behaviours and working styles, but in most countries there is not sufficient hard evidence to prove that they affect the actual outcome of particular cases (Schultz and Shaw, 2003: 1vi; Schultz 2003b: 315)

My PhD study contributes to the methodological discussion with examples taken from maintenance law. Schultz emphasises the difficulties of researching gendered judging. Perceptions and constructions are basically individual and difficult to measure (Schultz, 2003b: 316). This methodological problem can be partly solved when judges are forced to express their opinions. I used an effective method to learn more about gendered judging. Over a period of six years, I had access to the closed meetings of the Dutch Judicial Alimony Commission, 'Werkgroep Alimentatienormen'. Twice a year, 24 member judges, women and men, of the 19 district courts and the five middle level courts, discussed maintenance issues and developed guidelines to apply in the judicial decision-making process. At the meetings in 2002 and 2003, women and men were equally represented. In 2004, 2005, 2006 and 2007, women in the Judicial Alimony Commission (total: 24) outnumbered men, varying from 54 to 63 per cent. The opinion of judges sitting in chambers was thus transferred to a broader national level. By observing the discussions I gained an understanding of how judges determined their position in the field of maintenance cases, in which gender-issues play an important role.

I will give a short overview of this typical phenomenon of national judicial cooperation in the field of maintenance law. In the past, Dutch family law judges were bound by only two criteria when determining maintenance. These legal criteria were the 'capacity' of the party obliged to make maintenance payments, and the 'neediness' of the party with the right to receive maintenance. Therefore, legislation gave the judge great discretionary freedom and little to go on. As a result, the amounts of alimony awarded by judges varied enormously. The judiciary felt obliged to solve this problem, and in 1975 the Commission was formed. Its 'alimony guidelines' gave judges something to hold on to when calculating the amount of alimony. The aim of these guidelines was to limit the role of discretion (which in some cases was mere 'guesswork') thus increasing the uniformity of judicial decisions. These guidelines are still in force today and a permanent Commission is charged with updating and revising them. It is important to stress that the alimony guidelines are used in all courts, even though formally they have no binding effect on the judges as they are not considered to be law based on Article 79 of the Dutch Judiciary Act. As such, the Supreme Court cannot test a ruling of a lower court against them.

In my research, I explored the history, evolution and actual practices of this Judicial Alimony Commission over a period of 32 years (1975–2007) (Dijksterhuis, 2008). Through the detailed presentation of complex cases, I investigated and analysed the dilemmas that judges face when producing such guidelines (Dijksterhuis, 2008: 223–24). In my fieldwork, I used a multiple method research approach. First, I attended and observed nine Judicial Alimony Commission meetings, where member judges discussed and evaluated existing guidelines and other related issues. Secondly, I conducted 54 semi-structured interviews with family law judges and other actors involved. Thirdly, I conducted a thorough analysis of all relevant historical documents concerning the Judicial Alimony Commission, such as meeting reports since 1975.

My study focused on the way in which national judicial cooperation works. Here I took a closer look at the influence gender might have on the decision-making process in the Judicial Alimony Commission. The Judicial Alimony Commission has developed more than a hundred potential criteria for the legal criterion 'capacity' of the party obliged to make maintenance payments, and the 'need' of the one who had the right to receive maintenance. Questions that were discussed in the Judicial Alimony Commission were: What part of the income should the man give to his ex-partner and children? To what extent should the alimony award be reduced when a man who is obliged to make maintenance payments finds a new partner? Should a man pay maintenance when he is seriously in debt? These issues contain a very strong gender aspect.

3.2. Gendered Judging in the Field of Alimony: The Results

A female middle level judge and member of the Judicial Alimony Commission in the 1990s expressed her ideas on female judges in one of my interviews as follows:

> We tried for years to appoint female judges as chairmen in the Judicial Alimony Commission and did so with success. We thought it was prudent. The ones who determine the law are men. For example, the length of alimony is restricted by the legislator. Most of the few women in Parliament are emancipated women, who consider it ridiculous that women receive alimony for 20 years. Female member judges of the Judicial Alimony Commission were of course emancipated women too. But we also saw daily in the courtroom the disasters happening to women.

Thus, in her view female judges were more suitable in looking after the interests of women who had the right to receive alimony.

It is indeed true that so far all chairmen of the Judicial Alimony Commission have been women, except for the current one. But a substantial proportion of female members in the Commission did actually not support alimony guidelines that were favourable to women and children; rather the reverse was true. The Commission used a technical and pragmatic approach on political issues with regard to maintenance and rationally calculated the level of alimony, using guidelines that judges found easy to apply (Dijksterhuis, 2008: 207–08). A male Supreme Court Judge and former member of the Commission put it as follows:

> The task of the judges in the Judicial Alimony Commission is to distribute the income fairly between men on the one hand and women and children on the other. This should be done in a very pragmatic way. The current Commission chairman claimed: I cannot judge which alimony system is the more just. All I can consider is which system is easier for a judge to apply.

Interestingly, on different occasions the Commission discussed the question whether the system should be altered so as to benefit women and children. I moreover observed that in meetings judges hardly ever expressed their personal views on the different aspects of maintenance. In interviews the middle level court judge and chairman in the 1990s indicated that her personal opinion about women receiving maintenance differed from her professional opinion:

> I am a working woman, I am financially independent. Actually in my opinion other women should do the same. But at the same time, many women of my age do not do that. In that case men have to pay the full price in accordance with the alimony guidelines. I do not ask: why were you not working? Such views are personal and are not relevant in my work as a judge. And moreover: I do not even think that when I see such a woman in front of me. Though I do think: if you had worked, you would not be in such trouble. And she added: People can act as if they are neutral, although they have their personal opinions. That is the reason why I am a big supporter of three-judge benches and of a Judicial Alimony Commission that filters out the personal aspect from judicial decisions.

The Commission's current chairman emphasised that his personal opinion often differed from his professional one in that it favoured men, but that he kept the two separate on principle. Only one female district court judge explicitly expressed her personal opinion as a point of professional reference:

> There was always a never-ending discussion about the question if the child's need should be related not only to the income of the man but also to that of the woman if she starts working some time after the divorce. In the district court we decided that that should be the case. I totally agreed with that decision. That also had to do with my personal situation. I started working when I was older. It would be strange if only the income of my husband were relevant.

An exception to the general abstinence regarding the voicing of personal views occurred when judges discussed the problem of high childcare costs, partly based on their own experiences. But in most cases they took their experiences in the courtroom as their tacit point of reference to determine their position on alimony guidelines.

The result of the pragmatic approach was that judges did not sufficiently take into account any longer-term political consequences of their guidelines. For a long time, the Judicial Alimony Commission failed to notice that the system favoured the (mostly male) partner who is obliged to make maintenance payments, and disadvantaged the (female) partner and children who receive maintenance payments. Although this could be considered as a political choice, hardly any political discussion had taken place in the Judicial Alimony Commission, with the result that gradually the system developed in a way that was basically against the interests of women and children.

One explanation might be that the Commission's female members, that is over half of the total, simply did not stand up for women and children. Although in their daily work they experienced that the guidelines resulted in poor alimony payments, they did not raise the issue for discussion. This was the view of attorney Van Oldenborgh who was directly involved in the development of the judicial alimony guidelines:

> The major objection against the Judicial Alimony Commission is that a discussion about the philosophy behind the system never took place. It was as if those judges all felt very sorry for those poor guys that had to pay such tremendous maintenance. In my opinion, the Judicial Alimony Commission was too 'men-friendly'.

There were also other reasons to explain the Commission's disregard for the recipients of maintenance payments (mostly women). One practical argument which judges mentioned was that in the majority of cases, alimony did not make a big difference for the women and children: regardless of any alimony payments they would still depend on the National Assistance Act, due to their low income. In other words, the judges focused on the interests of ex-partners and their children instead of on those of the taxpayer in general. A female district court judge and member of the Commission in the 1980s confirmed this in interview:

> Many judges in the Judicial Alimony Commission were of the opinion that the men had to pay less alimony when a woman depended on the National Assistance Act. In that situation the men often also had a low income. We thought that the public could bear that.

Most judges also found it undesirable if the alimony payments were such a big part of the men's income that they lost the motivation to work or that they became unable to pay their debts.

In 1996, a male district judge and at the time Commission secretary pleaded for a drastic reform of the alimony guidelines, as they were unjust to women and children. He wrote an article in *The Dutch Lawyer's Journal* (Ten Hoeve, 1996) but tried unsuccessfully to persuade his fellow judges in the Commission. His explanation:

> What happens at the moment is that the most powerful in the divorce procedure, namely the ones that have to pay alimony, are spared. That is a safe choice for the judges because it prevents many conflicts. The powerful group with the money offers greater resistance. Those men hire more expensive attorneys than their wives can afford. Most people in the Judicial Alimony Commission identify with the winners: the ones that earn the money and are obliged to pay alimony.

From 2002 onwards, a male middle level court judge and former member of the Commission published several articles in different Dutch legal journals also arguing for a reform in favour of women and children (Van Teeffelen, 2002). Although his proposal was briefly discussed by the Commission, he hardly received a response. Apart from these spontaneous calls for an evaluation of the current guidelines, three judges (two female, one male) seized the opportunity of new legislative proposals to call for a reform. In fact, the legislator had criticised the unjustness of the alimony guidelines and requested that chairmen should take action. Remarkably, only the male chairman and district court judge succeeded in 2007 in convincing the majority of the Judicial Alimony Commission to agree with the proposed reform. At long last, the maintenance payment guidelines were adjusted in favour of women and children.

Overall, this debate about maintenance payments shows that it is too simple to categorise judges as female or male-friendly according to their sex. Rather, as in Poland, Brazil and Germany, Dutch female family judges do not provide women's 'other voice'; they neither judge women's claims more harshly, nor do they offer special support for them. The few calls to change the alimony guidelines in favour of women and children came mostly from male judges. Over the years, the Alimony Guidelines had developed in a way favourable to men. But it was not the gender and values of the judges, but their technical professional perspective that appears to have been the most influential factor. In interviews, the Commission's influential chairpersons made sharp distinctions between their personal and their professional opinion. The same applied to judges' pronouncements at Commission meetings where they hardly ever expressed their values and their professional attitude always seemed to be decisive.

To conclude: although the quantitative feminisation of the Dutch judiciary has been looked at with fear by the media, this trend did not lead to a qualitative feminisation. Until now even in the 'gendered' family law a unique female sound in the Dutch Judiciary has not been found.

4. REFERENCES

Boigeol, A (2003) 'Male Strategies in the Face of the Feminisation of a Profession: The Case of the French Judiciary' in U Schultz and G Shaw (eds), *Women in the World's Legal Professions* (Oxford, Hart Publishing).

Botelho Junqueira, E (2003) 'Women in the Judiciary: A Perspective from Brazil' in U Schultz and G Shaw (eds), *Women in the World's Legal Professions* (Oxford, Hart Publishing).

Brants, C and Brants, K (1991) *De sociale constructie van fraude* (Arnhem, Gouda Quint).

De Groot-van Leeuwen, L (1991) *De rechterlijke macht in Nederland: samenstelling en opvattingen van de zittende en staande magistratuur* (Arnhem, Gouda Quint).

—— (2003) 'Women in the Dutch Legal Profession (1950–2000)' in U Schultz and G Shaw (eds), *Women in the World's Legal Professions* (Oxford, Hart Publishing).

—— (2009) 'Vrouwen in de rechterlijke macht. Van eigen hoekje naar de top' in M De Boer and W Marjan (eds), *Vrouw & recht. De beweging, de mensen, de issues.* ijers (Amsterdam, AUP).

De Groot-van Leeuwen, L, van Rossum, SU and Schuyt, KJM (1996) 'De aanloop tot de rechterlijke macht; verslag van een enquete onder raio's' 5a *Trema* 107.

Dijksterhuis, B (2008) *Rechters normeren de alimentatiehoogte. Een empirisch onderzoek naar rechterlijke samenwerking in de Werkgroep Alimentatienormen (1975–2007)* (Leiden, Leiden University Press).

Fuszara, M (2003) 'Women Lawyers in Poland under the Impact of Post-1989 Transformation' in U Schultz and G Shaw (eds), *Women in the World's Legal Professions* (Oxford, Hart Publishing).

Gilligan, C (1981) *In a Different Voice: Women's Conception of the Self and Morality* 47 *Harvard Educational Review* 481.

—— (1982) *In a Different Voice: Psychological Theory and Women's Development* (Cambridge, Harvard University Press).

Malsch, Marijke (1989) *Lawyers' Predictions of Judicial Decisions: A Study on Calibration of Experts* (Leiden, Leiden University Press).

Raad voor de Rechtspraak (2007) *Hoofdlijnen personeelsbeleid Rechtspraak* (2008–11).

—— (2009) *Jaarverslag 2008* (Den Haag).

Schultz, U (2003a) 'Introduction' in U Schultz and G Shaw) (eds), *Women in the World's Legal Professions* (Oxford, Hart Publishing).

—— (2003b) 'Women Lawyers in Germany—Perception and Construction of Femininity' in U Schultz and G Shaw (eds), *Women in the World's Legal Professions* (Oxford, Hart Publishing).

Schultz, U and Shaw, G (2003) (eds), *Women in the World's Legal Professions* (Oxford, Hart Publishing).

Sloot, BP (1980) 'Officiële uitsluiting van vrouwen in juridische beroepen' 45/46 *NJB* 1186.

—— (2004) 'Moeten rechters lijken op de Nederlandse bevolking? Over de wenselijkheid van descriptieve representatie door de rechterlijke macht' 2 *Trema* 49.

Sullerot, E (1968) *Histoire et sociologie du travail féminin* (Paris, Gonthier).

Ten Hoeve, P (1996), 'Trematologie, een beetje een zwartboek eigenlijk.' *NJB* 793.

Van Teeffelen, P (2002) 'Zijn we met de Tremanormen op de goede weg?' *FJR* 130.

Werkgroep Verbetermogelijkheden Werving Raio's (2007) *Eindrapport* (Den Haag).

3.3

Gender and Judging in Traditional and Modern Societies: A Comparison of Two Case Studies (Ivory Coast and Italy)

MARIA RITA BARTOLOMEI

Abstract

This chapter draws on two different pieces of fieldwork. On the one hand, the research relates to the specific case of the survival of traditional procedures for the resolution of conflicts in the Ivory Coast where, among the Abron ethnic group, as in the past, we can still find women judges with their own courts of justice. On the other hand, I give the results of research based on periods of participant observation at law courts in the Marche region of Italy and on 80 in-depth interviews with both female and male judges and lawyers.

Through my work I will try to discuss how, according to Hanne Petersen's theory of so-called 'home knitted law', with female judges we can easily find intuitive-unofficial legal practices, where values like bargaining, sympathy, sharing and solidarity are more and more widespread.

Special attention is devoted to 'horizontal segregation', that is to say, to gender specialisation either in family, juvenile or immigration law and consequently exclusion from important financial and political disputes and questions. Finally, the work aims to show how through women's access to judging, considerable changes take place both in scholarship and jurisprudence. To sum up, we could say that gendered legal expertise greatly contributes to developing new jurisdictional patterns and models.

1. INTRODUCTION

LEGAL AND JUDICIAL systems are historically male institutions, but in recent decades we have witnessed cultural, social and demographic changes which have led to an increasing number of women entering the legal professions, and an increase in the proportion of women in the judiciary has created diversity on the bench. According to Baroness Hale,[1] 'a more diverse judiciary incorporating a variety of perspectives will make a difference to the decision made' (Hale, 2001). Thus, after more than 30 years of feminist legal theory and jurisprudence, socio-legal scholars and researchers continue to debate the impact of women's presence on the administration of justice. Central to this debate are the questions whether women judges add a 'different voice' (Gilligan, 1982) and whether gender affects legal outcome (Coontz, 2000).

We have a large amount of literature on the subject today. Scholars either highlight how the assumption that women would make a difference simply by being on the bench is a questionable one (Hunter, 2008), or conclude that there is no evidence of clear-cut gender-based differences (Kohen, 2008). Starting with the work of pioneering scholars like Beverly Blair Cook, Sue Davis, Elaine Martin (Kenney, 2008: 87), the theoretical problems involved in this area have been acknowledged by feminist legal theory, and as a consequence the anti-essentialist critique is beginning to be taken seriously (Kohen, 2008: 112). Other contributions reject the 'different voice' as a simplistic and dangerous myth, even though admitting that diversity on the bench facilitates the understanding of the problems facing people (Rackley, 2008). Women, for example, seem to be more likely to rule in favour of gays and lesbians on their due process and equal protection claims (Smith, 2005). Others speak about an 'attitudinal model' (Beiner, 1999) or about women judges' advocacy of human rights and minority groups' claims and needs (Elias, 2006).[2]

At the same time, some scholars stress that the massive entry of women into the legal profession stems less from women's increasing gender awareness and empowerment than from structural contingencies; that is to say, from demographic, social and economic changes transforming the productive labour system and the family's organisation (Olgiati, 2006).

Without claiming definitively to settle all debates on the subject, this chapter is a contribution, from an anthropological perspective, to a better understanding of the multiple ways in which gender and law can interact (Frazier and Hunt, 1998). Focusing on the well-known controversial question, 'Will women judges really make a difference?',[3] the chapter summarises the main findings of two different experiences gathered in the field. The first case study relates to the survival of traditional procedures for the resolution of conflicts among the *Abron* ethnic group in the Ivory Coast. Special attention is devoted to the ability of the traditional female 'judges' in 'asking the women question' (Bartlett, 1990: 837) and in fighting for a

[1] The first and only female law lord in the UK.
[2] Dame Sian Elias is Chief Justice of New Zealand.
[3] A famous speech by Justice Bertha Wilson, the first woman judge of the Supreme Court of Canada (Wilson, 1990).

wider social justice through the innovative (re-)interpretation of traditional values, attitudes and patterns of behaviour.

The second study is an attempt to depict the situation of women judges in the Marche region of Italy. Here, by presenting individual experiences and different viewpoints, I will try and discuss how women judges understand their profession and its requirements, their representation of the ideal judge, their motivation to become a judge, the way they experience the power they wield, and different opinions on whether women judges decide cases differently to their male counterparts (Kohen, 2008: 120).

Drawing on the current literature on the topic and using qualitative methods, the research adopts a comparative perspective with the aim of identifying gender differences and similarities in values and attitudes. Specifically, to analyse the contributions that women judges bring, or might bring, to the judiciary, I rely on Hanne Petersen's theory about the so-called 'home knitted law' (1996).[4] When we have female judges, in fact, we can easily find intuitive/unofficial legal practices, where values like bargaining, sympathy, sharing and solidarity are more widespread. In line with many other works on the subject, my research aims to show that, while litigant characteristics do not affect judicial decisions, the gender of the judge sometimes does (Coontz, 2000: 59).

2. WOMEN JUDGES AMONG THE ABRON ETHNIC GROUP

In this section I propose drawing on fieldwork on the specific case of the survival of traditional procedures for the resolution of conflicts among the *Abron* ethnic group.[5] The *Chefferie Royale Abron* is a combined political and judicial institution present in the geographical and cultural area corresponding to the north eastern territory of the present day state of the Ivory Coast.[6] It is interesting not only because of its past characteristics, but because of the role it continues to play in the present day. The Constitution of the Ivory Coast makes no explicit provision for political and judicial institutions other than those of the state. In spite of that, the *Abron*

[4] 'The term "home knitted law"... expresses the contextual and gendered version of the most general and gender neutral term "informal law"' (Petersen, 1996: 16).

[5] This study is based on participant observation and ethnographic interviews: chiefs (25), male elders (50), female elders (20), government officials (10), the Queen Mother and lay people (60). Here I will report data collected during the anthropological fieldworks carried out during May–June 1995 and March–April 1997, but previous information and experiences are used as well. For further information, see Bartolomei (2001).

[6] The Ivory Coast is a country in western sub-Saharan Africa which overlooks the Guinean gulf. It has an area of 322,462 sq km and the population is 18 million: Muslim (55%), Christian (35%) and Animist (10%). The official language is French. It was a French colony until it became independent in 1960: www.state.gov/r/pa/ei/bgn/2846.htm; www.tlfq.ulaval.ca/axl/afrique/cotiv.htm.

institution of sacred kingship and a matrilineal kinship system persists and the administration of justice by the traditional King, Queen Mother and both male and female chiefs continues to be widespread.[7]

Even though in the *Abron* kingdom of *Gyaman* military and political power has always been exercised by men, we cannot neglect the symbolic as well as the real importance of women in social, political and judicial life. We can infer the significance attached to the feminine role either from many customary practices—the transmission of status and goods still occurs, for example, according to the system of matrilineal filiation; or from the fact that we can still find lineages' and/or villages' female chiefs and 'judges'; or, mostly, from the position assigned to the Queen Mother in keeping the balance and symmetry of the *Abron* institutional system.[8] Her major competence and powers are linked to the administration of justice. The Queen Mother, in fact, has the right to interfere in the dispensation of justice by the King and his royal council, even asking for mercy or a reduction of sentence. Furthermore, she chairs her own judicial council, which has exclusive jurisdiction in the resolution of conflicts that arise among women. She continues largely to retain her traditional monopoly in the settlement of disputes in both divorce matters and quarrels between women and foreign men. In the exercise of this role the Queen Mother avails herself of the services of the council of 'women elders' which assists and advises her mostly whenever she has to deliver a final decision on sentences of lower rank female chiefs which are appealed against.

Here I propose to examine some aspects of the dispensation of justice by the *Abron* Queen and other women 'judges' that appear of particular interest.[9] The first aspect concerns the absolutely 'informal' character of the decisions reached by women, in both a substantive and procedural sense:

> One element of differentiation from modern law is in fact the 'substantial' character of the rationality to which the role of the chief and his council conforms. Decisions, once reached, do not aim to achieve the higher degree of formal juridical correctness, but are each adapted to circumstances according to the principles of ethical equity in a substantial sense or on the basis of more practical and utilitarian needs (Bartolomei, 2000: 308).

[7] The data collected in the field show that, from an anthropological point of view, the traditional *Abron* judicial process seems to be definable, even at the present time, as an institution in the true sense of the term (Bartolomei, 2001).

[8] The Queen Mother is the symbol of femininity and the fertility upholder; she represents and acts for all the kingdom's women, defending their claims and rights at any social level. She is in charge of any ritual dances and ceremonies and manages women's public works. She runs one or more villages and co-chairs the royal council with the King, controlling and balancing his power and elders' influence as well. Her favourable opinion in the designation of a new king is a conditio *sine qua non*. See Bartolomei (2001: 151ff).

[9] I would like to make it clear that I have not been to the Ivory Coast since 1997 and I am not sure whether the situation has changed in the meantime.

In this regard, data collected in the field show that, in reaching their decision—women more than men—make a synthesis between experience and decision-making in such a way as to find the best solution for all parties. They offer situational, need-based, ad hoc settlements, which consider the specific social context: persons, means, interests and values involved. The 'informal' character of women's judgments can be inferred also from the absence of severe, ritually necessary procedural rules. Furthermore, recourse is never had to supernatural trials, such as oaths, ordeals and divinations (often present, by contrast, in male dispensation of justice).

Another aspect to point out is something we can label the 'communal' character of the judgement given by the female 'judge'. In fact, women's decisions—especially final decisions—can be regarded as taken by the whole community of participants: the trial is always open to the public and all participants are allowed to speak, thus contributing to a common norm-generating process. In contrast in the male system of administration of justice, the greater the severity of the procedures and the more important the ritual, the higher judges rise in the hierarchical scale. Often cases are heard behind 'closed doors' and each proceeding has its own specially qualified ranks assigned to speak.

Furthermore, the 'home knitted law' phenomenon can be qualified in the *Abron* society. The normative framework—the sum of normative myth, precept and precedent—to which *Abron* chiefs refer is clearly differentiated from the ideal type of 'rational codified law'. It is characterised instead, by reference to the 'law of the ancestors', sacred, orally transmitted and immutable in substance. At the same time the institutions of neither Islamic nor state law can be disregarded. In dispensing justice, women seem to be able to reinterpret this complex normative framework in original ways and adapt it to new external cultural dictates 'through complementing rationality and emotionality' (Petersen, 1996: 164). In contrast to their male colleagues, they completely put aside typical *Abron* martial values, sometimes also overlooking ancestral mysteries and esoteric knowledge condensed in proverbs. The evidence suggests, indeed, that they draw especially on traditional principles of bargaining, co-operation and solidarity. That means that they do not seek to achieve the complete elimination of difference and inequality—an extremely hard task for a hierarchical society—but try to manage them by creating mutual social obligations and reciprocal duties. Giving judgment in a kidnapping case, for example, the Queen decided that the child obviously had to be returned to his own mother, but at the same time she condemned the kidnapper (a poor infertile woman) to go to the family's house twice a week to help the mother in caring for the child and to stay with him(!). 'Settlement is always preferable to adjudication' the Queen reporting this case said to me.

The characteristics of the procedure by which justice is dispensed by women, in fact, appear more comprehensible if they are incorporated in an organisational framework where traditional forms of cooperation, interdependence and mutual assistance exist both within the production unit represented by the extended family, and between the various units of production in the same village.

Whereas male chiefs manage instability, uncertainty and insecurity stemming from increasing social change, female emancipation, modernisation of law, westernisation of culture, etc, through the introduction of new criteria of selection and decision-making, women draw from the well of traditional wisdom practising a great deal of openness and flexibility. Let me give an illuminating example:

> A constantly recurring problem in this area at the present time is that of the juridical identification of the criteria for the allocation of resources, especially those of land tenure ... [As I said before,] the *Abron* rules of succession provide for the transmission of status and goods according to the system of matrilineal filiation and in conformity with the norms that govern common property. These norms conflict with the principles of state law ... [that recognise only] individual ownership and a patrilineal system of property transmission ... The traditional [male] chief and his council have ... succeeded in establishing an effective rapport between these two types of jurisdiction ... [introducing] the distinction between properties inherited through family ties and property acquired during a person's life. The former ... are transmitted according to the rules of lineage; the latter, by contrast ... are transmitted according to the provisions of state law' (Bartolomei, 2000: 306–09).

In this manner, the traditional judicial process succeeded in preserving some of its distinctive traditional features, while at the same time showing a marked capacity for adaptation and innovation. However, this effective, interesting and clever solution inevitably brought about a loss of women's (matrilineal system) social power. In response, when settling divorce cases, the Queen and other powerful women have introduced and started to follow the (revolutionary) rule of practising a kind of 'informal' legal framework—to condemn the husband to transfer to his wife one or more shareholdings in the farmers' cooperatives or to buy her a stall in the local market. In this way they seek greater economic empowerment and independence of women.

To sum up, my findings clearly show that, through the traditional judicial process, the Queen Mother and the other women chiefs at lower level continue to spell out the law and to control and guide the behaviour of the community under their rule. Their role has undoubted juridical significance, and decision-making mechanisms are juridical insofar as they refer to normative tradition and myths. Furthermore, 'they are guided by certain conceptions and expectations about what is a right or a wrong way to act and behave' (Petersen, 1996: 33). To manage the needs of social change in everyday life, *Abron* women creatively reinterpret and adapt traditional wise practices and the key values of solidarity, cooperation, interdependency, reciprocity, sharing and sympathy. In so doing, they often develop new judicial practices and norms which constitute subversive counter-forces to modernity and modern legal thinking about rationality, certainty and predictability.

Nevertheless, to use a terminology more familiar to a Western reader, it may be said that we see a clear 'horizontal discrimination' in the *Abron* system of justice: women continue to be prevented from decision-making in policy matters, disputes with big coffee and cocoa traders, lese-majesty or witchcraft crimes, to name but a few.

3. WOMEN JUDGES IN THE MARCHE REGION OF ITALY

This research is part of a wider project begun in January 2008 and still in progress. The project aims to acquire a better understanding of the contributions which women jurists (lawyers, judges and notaries) interacting with, and practising in law firms, courts and other legal fields, are currently making to the changes and transformations of legal culture. Here I will report only some provisional findings concerning exclusively women judges in the Marche region of Italy.[10]

The study is based on participant observation at ten law courts[11] and in-depth interviews[12] conducted with female judges (40)[13] and lawyers (20),[14] as well as with male judges (10)[15] and lawyers (10).[16] For a better understanding of the findings to date I have summarised the data collected from interviewing women judges into three main topics: (1) the balance between family and work; (2) the perception of one's own role and relationships with male colleagues; and (3) the possible contributions to legal culture.

[10] The first woman member of the judiciary was appointed in Italy only in 1965. The selection process is founded on competitive examinations (the candidate must have a degree in law) and formal qualification. Given the lack of disciplinary measures and sanctions the career paths are automatic. Leading positions, instead, are elective ones. The civil law judicial system of Italy is divided into two court structures: ordinary courts and administrative courts. This study focuses on ordinary courts exclusively.

[11] I spent about two weeks in each court, observing the daily routines and interviewing people.

[12] The female and male judges' statements quoted in this section are not supported by reference to interviewees' initials as the judges agreed to grant interviews provided they could retain their anonymity.

[13] Five honorary judges; eight judges of the peace; fifteen stipendiary judges; eight investigating judges; four judges of the court of appeal, no public prosecutor because there are so few in the Marche region.

[14] They have been selected from four legal associations corresponding to the courts of Ancona (3), Ascoli Piceno (8), Fermo (5) and Macerata (4).

[15] Five gowned judges and five judges of the court of appeal.

[16] They have been selected from three legal associations corresponding to the courts of Ancona (3), Ascoli Piceno (5) and Macerata (2).

As far as other groups of interviewees (female lawyers, male judges and lawyers) are concerned, here I will give only a glimpse of their most interesting opinions on the subject.

3.1. Women Judges' Views

The sample of women judges comes from a wide variety of social backgrounds, with differing family situations and working conditions, so it is not possible to draw a uniform social profile for them.

Findings on the first topic suggest that, in the struggle to balance work and family, career and private aspirations, all women judges complain about the lack of family-friendly policies in the legal profession, institutional impediments, prejudices, a 'glass ceiling', unsuitable court schedules and so on. In any case, however, they prefer the judiciary to other legal professions because it seems easier to combine with motherhood and child care (Schultz and Shaw, 2003: 271, 281).

Women tend to experience their family and work obligations as an integrated part of their everyday life, so they often refer to chronic 'conflicts concerning competing demands for time, care and efficiency in both workplace and family' (Justice of the Peace, 30 January 2009). Sometimes, for example, the complexity and delicacy of issues dealt with in court require that case files be taken home. But simultaneously, the obligation to care for children and grown-ups, young and old, healthy and sick always falls on women.

According to interviewees, having a house to run and a family to care for is the main reason why women judges generally give up the idea of making a career. Promotion, in fact, generally means moving home to another part of the country. While formally promotion is based on length of service, in practice salary increases do not necessarily correspond to a real change in the roles that women actually fulfil.

There is another interesting finding that I would like to highlight. In the workplace generally we witness more solidarity, mutual assistance, reciprocity and cooperation among female judges and lower court personnel, who are predominantly women, than among female judges themselves. In many courts we can find patterns of collaborative behaviours among women as well as gendered practices, which could be assimilated to either Petersen's notion of 'norm of consideration'[17] or to her concept of 'home knitted law' (1996).

[17] It 'implies an informal actual obligation to consider needs and work obligations outside paid work' (time demands, needs for care, etc) in the organisation of paid work itself. The concrete realisation of this informal norm is 'contextual or situationally conditioned'. It can be viewed as 'a *feminine* contribution to law—as a norm which is produced or generated *by* women and in practice also mainly *for* women—as well as for their families' (Petersen, 1996: 46, 47, 49).

Relating to my second topic—the perception of one's own role and relationships with male colleagues—I want to stress first that more and more women in the Marche region choose the judiciary in preference to another legal profession, as it offers job security, a regular work schedule, automatic career prospects and maternity leave. Moreover, judges enjoy prestige and authority in society. Nevertheless, my interviewees also mentioned ethical and moral reasons for their choice of career, such as, for example, achieving empowerment of women and children, guaranteeing social justice, reducing the complexity of social life, fulfilling the common good, etc.[18] Most of them shared an image of the ideal judge as a person who investigates how people are treated and is concerned about their legal rights being infringed. They experienced the power they wielded as a strong responsibility and were clear that they were trying to do their very best as judges. They considered their work as a public service and aimed at maintaining the highest standards in terms of honesty, impartiality, fairness, empathy, directness, sensitivity to the context of cases, as well as knowledge of the law.

In general, women judges consider themselves more patient and sympathetic than their male colleagues and more willing to find the best solution for everybody. They take the view that their office requires great courage because of the responsibility involved in the effects of their decisions on the lives of others.

Even if young women judges have recently outnumbered men in the judiciary, there are still many exclusively male-dominated fields,[19] and challenges from their male colleagues are allowed to continue:

> In order to overcome male hegemony and to reach higher positions we have to study and work twice as hard as our male colleagues. The most difficult thing is to reduce male prejudices about our lack of legal knowledge, trustworthiness and professionalism (Appeal Judge, 23 January 2009).

As far as their relationships with male colleagues are concerned, many interviewees agreed with the following two statements:

> When you are in a joint session trying to convince male colleagues of the rightness of your opinions, reliance on either your beauty and sex appeal or on aggressiveness will not get you anywhere. In the former case they generally don't take you seriously, regarding you as an object, just a sexual object without brains, thought or will. In the

[18] In this sense see also Schultz and Shaw (2003) xxxix, quoting D Rhode and L de Groot.

[19] Despite the amendment of art 51 of the Italian Constitution and the constitutionalisation of the principle of 'equal opportunities', women judges are concentrated in the lower ranks of the judiciary (Justice of the Peace and honorary judges). There is also a lack of women in director (5%) and semi-director positions (7%). In the National Anti-Mafia Management (Direzione Nazionale Antimafia) there is no woman. Only 6% of judges in the Court of Cassation and only 1% of chief judges are women: G Casella, 'Donne in magistratura' *Diritto and Diritti* (2003): www.diritto.it/osservatori/giustizia_costituzione/ver_giustizia/mag_soc18.html.

latter, they react by becoming more narrow-minded, obstinate and aggressive in turn. The only way to bring them round is to demonstrate high standards of legal knowledge and expertise and above all to use your powers of persuasion and take into account all psychological aspects of the case' (Appeal Judge, 23 January 2009).

Often male colleagues are arrogant and accuse us of not taking sufficient account of leading cases (precedents) while presumptuously engaging in 'creative jurisprudence' (Stipendiary Judge, 18 November 2008).

Female judges themselves believe that their male colleagues tend inevitably to criticise and ostracise them. Reasons given are first, that female judges can claim daily and hourly maternity leave; secondly, that they are willing to go beyond economic issues and delve deeply into relational, emotional and psychological aspects of cases; and finally, for what male judges label 'feminine soft jurisprudence' (ie, a way of deciding cases that sometimes moves away from strictly classical legal reasoning and instead introduces extralegal concepts and principles).

This issue brings us close to our third topic for discussion, the impact of women judges on current legal culture. In my interviews, women judges initially tended to deny any difference or capacity that could be derived from gender. But this initial denial was frequently reversed later on closer reflection. Along with Kohen, I think that 'this first denial could be explained as a strategy on the part of women judges to ... avoid discrimination by asserting that they do not make any difference in adjudication and that women can administer justice as well as men' (2008: 116).

During my research, I rarely met a woman judge in disagreement with the idea that 'in any trial case multiple points of view must be articulated, recognised and considered seriously. Personally I try always to see the matter from an alternative perspective' (Stipendiary Judge, 18 November 2008). Although generally they do not represent themselves as feminist and reject the label of 'feminist judge', most of them stated the importance of 'asking the woman question' (Bartlett, 1990: 837) and of behaving in a way (contextualisation, particularity model, detached attention) that Hunter regards as typically feminist (2008: 11–13). In the words of a GIP (Investigating Judge, 20 February 2009):

I think that the experience of being female is a crucial element of being more willing and able to hear and understand the stories of women litigants and of listening carefully and respectfully about their lives. Our own experience enables us to respond sympathetically and to succeed in putting gendered experiences into legal discourse.

Interviewing women judges, I clearly perceived a strong willingness—indeed a determination on their part—to focus on the concrete situation of participants in the proceedings, to reason from the broader social context on which the legal rules in question operate and to produce a decision that is individualised rather than abstract. Taking everything into consideration, they try to approach legal issues in a way that is not strictly formalistic and goes straight to the point. They do not worry about diverging from precedent and current jurisprudence. Furthermore, they do not indulge in juridical technicalities and tend to avoid adjourning a case only for procedural or technical reasons. In my experience of courts, women judges rarely decide that a case cannot proceed.

Interviewees told me that they generally study every file with great care and try to widen their knowledge by reading and integrating material from different sources, both legal and extralegal. 'Judging is an intellectual challenge that requires lifelong learning, updating and practice' (Stipendiary Judge, 12 May 2009). Anyway, they all share the opinion that 'differences with male colleagues are to be found more in the process than the outcome of the judgment' (Appeal Judge, 12 June 2008). Thus, women's different approaches to legal reasoning are often grounded in 'informal' procedures and extralegal knowledge, principles and values. Various judges in the sample referred to their willingness to explain their own reasoning in detail to parties, and their tendency to write decisions significantly longer than those of their male colleagues.

3.2. Female Lawyers' Views

In considering women's impact on the judiciary, female lawyers agreed that the gender of a judge sometimes can make a difference to the outcome of a case. According to them, even if it is impossible to tell whether another judge deciding the same case would reach the same decision, women judges tend to show a repetitive normative pattern of behaviour, especially in family law, juvenile or immigration hearings, where they reveal a great ability to establish good relationships and to be empathetic, while also paying attention to relevant details.

All the female lawyers in the sample think that, despite stereotyped images, women are truly more able to understand relationships based on emotion and affection. Furthermore, they tend to be more inclined and ready to listen to, and keep the attention of those who are outsiders to the system of male privilege. 'In contrast to commonly shared prejudices, female judges don't always automatically settle in favour of women. In divorce cases without minors, for example, women judges tend not to order the husband to provide alimony for his wife' (CP, 11 May 2009).[20] In this regard a certain

[20] This opinion was shared by more than 10 female lawyers interviewed. On pro-wife decisions in divorce cases see, eg, Martin and Pyle (2000: 1231).

'local legal culture' has developed among some female judges from Fermo and Ascoli Piceno law courts. 'This is maybe because being female judges and working women, they don't concede the admissibility of the role of a "kept woman" and try to foster the economic independence and empowerment of women in general' (PP, 15 March 2008).[21]

In contrast, where there are minors to safeguard, they tend to be extremely severe in the penalties imposed on the husband. Women lawyers affirm that female and male judges often bring different interpretations to the same situation:

> Women generally approach cases of sexual abuse, sexual harassment, rape or domestic violence in a less legalistic way than their male colleagues, showing a somewhat empathetic attitude towards the victim as well as a deeper interest in the people involved and a greater attention to all the distinctive elements which contribute to making the single situation a specific and unique one (TM, 21 February 2009).

Along with scholars who point out that generally women are more likely than men to view certain behaviours as sexual harassment (Frazier and Hunt, 1998: 4, 10; Rotundo et al, 2001) the interviewees remarked that 'women and men judges often have differing perceptions of what constitutes sexual harassment or sexual abuse' (MR, 19 September 2008).

From the interviews with female lawyers there clearly emerge views on distinct gender differences in the way women judges approach decision-making. Female lawyers see their judicial colleagues as intent on achieving a better understanding of the whole situation, in a complete and non-schematic way. 'Women judges generally act in consideration of the concrete and specific context in a way that is flexible and balanced' (AV, 20 September 2008). And: 'Male judges generally look at and consider only the "fact", while women instead try to understand and explain the meaning attached to it' (BBC, 25 October 2008).

Women judges are also said to consider the hearing context as a whole, possibly because they are 'better at examining a witness and checking his/her trustworthiness' (BBC, 25 October 2008). Often they tend to be quicker and more resolute in decision-making than their male colleagues. 'Usually in deciding a case they avoid procedural exceptions and delays. Furthermore, they do not refer strictly to either general rules or precedents or current jurisprudence' (BB, 23 October 2008). Nevertheless, interviewees think that because women judges are more 'visible' and 'exposed' than their male colleagues, they are particularly aware of the great responsibility of their office.

[21] Schultz and Shaw (2003: lv) report a quite similar phenomenon speaking about Poland and Brazil.

Women lawyers believe that sometimes there are conflicting relationships between male and female judges. Some of them explained this situation as follows: 'A woman judge is authoritative ipso facto: her unquestionable high status and the power connected with the office of judge are constantly questioning men's virility and their traditional hegemonic position' (RA, 27 February 2009). Another added: 'It is perhaps also for this reason [women's empowerment] that almost all male judges seem to be suffering from a psychologically troubled and narcissistic behaviour' (AMV, 28 February 2009).

3.3. Male Judges' Views

Male judges agree in affirming that the judiciary is effectively experiencing the feminisation of its ranks and women today are more career-minded than in the past. For some of them, women's integration into the judiciary can have a positive impact, influencing how they (men) perceive cases involving women's issues and thus promoting gender fairness in the substantive law. 'The presence of women judges can make a difference in a male judge's sensitivity to the existence and consequences of discrimination: gender-based, race-based, status-based, etc' (Appeal Judge, 13 May 2009).

For others, women are still not ready to hold office. 'They often still find it difficult to reconcile their personal experiences and feelings with a theoretical tradition of impartiality (between litigants as well as between arguments), objectivity, rationality, legality and detachment' (13 May 2009), an elderly stipendiary judge said. Male judges present themselves as constantly expanding and updating their jurisprudential resources, while women are represented as having excessive reliance on 'psy'-disciplines and on non-legal issues and problems.

As newcomers to the profession, sometimes female judges are charged by male colleagues with being too self-opinionated, quite superficial (in their rapid decision-making) and uncertain (in their resorting to so much extra-legal expertise, reports, evidence, examinations and testimonies).

Many male judges reported that gender can sometimes impact on the process of cases although it generally has little or no effect on the outcome of most cases:

> Obviously different judges with different backgrounds and experiences can interpret the same factual matters differently. Judges, in fact, operate from their own perspective, but judicial decisions must be legally motivated and each of us has to take responsibility for his/her own decisions in presenting (legally acceptable) alternative reasoning in the case at hand (Stipendiary Judge, 6 February 2009).

> Since the principle of equal treatment is central to our concept of justice, knowing whether women judges decide a case differently to men has profound implications for equal treatment under the law. Thus we have to hope and work to avoid it (Appeal Judge, 10 February 2009).

Women are often criticised by male colleagues for taking too much leave of absence and too many sick days, as well as for sometimes using their office in the courtroom as a place to care for their children or give them somewhere to wait while they are in court.

Speaking about horizontal segregation most interviewees think that

> women themselves prefer either family law or the juvenile or immigration sector of the legal system because of their greater sensitivity for desire to help others and because they feel more suited to matters which are less difficult and complicated from the legal point of view and nearer their everyday experience and practice (Stipendiary Judge, 6 February 2009).

'Women develop both the preference and the capacities that make them more suitable to deal with family matters' (Employment Judge, 21 May 2008).

Most of the sample believe that the absence of women from senior courts and appointments is not due to clear and deliberate exclusion and discrimination from male colleagues, but 'a lack of interest on the part of women and their unwillingness to go after leading positions and mostly on their lack of availability given the need to accept moving home and longer working hours' (Appeal Judge, 6 June 2008). Only a few admit that the whole organisation of the justice system is patriarchal and women still have to fight to achieve real dignity, respect and equality.

3.4. Male Lawyers' Views

Most male lawyers interviewed agree that female judges sitting on the bench sometimes are really different from their male counterparts. 'Occasionally female judges effectively favour female lawyers' (PB, 18 September 2008). 'It depends not so much on feminine solidarity and complicity but is especially because they [women lawyers] are strong civil and human rights defenders' (JB, 18 September 2008). 'Sometimes male and female judges approach legal issues differently: whereas men aim to reach formal juridical perfection, women seek a concrete solution able to definitively settle the conflict' (SA, 23 September 2008).

Male lawyers state that women judges tend to be quicker than their male colleagues in deciding cases even though they generally allow more evidence to be called. 'To show they are equal to a situation they like working across disciplinary boundaries' (LS, 14 February 2009). 'Whereas male judges' qualifications and training are strictly juridical (doctrine and jurisprudence), women tend to improve their extra-legal knowledge' (RD, 14 February 2009).

But, according to male judges, male lawyers do not interpret these patterns of behaviour as always having solely positive outcomes. They link both of them to a sort of feminine 'juridical insecurity' which sometimes produces dysfunctional and perverted effects on single cases and also on the legal system as a whole.

From the interviews with male lawyers emerges the belief that 'women judges are usually less predictable than men judges mostly because of their tendency to moodiness and fickleness as well as of their propensity to decide each case differently to any other' (SG, 24 October 2008). They stress that whereas lawyers always have to act carefully and responsibly given that they personally answer for wrong behaviour either to clients, judges or colleagues, the judiciary enjoys a lot of discretion and freedom from criticism (*insindacabilità*). In fact, except for rare cases of serious crime or damage, they see judges as answerable to no one and only extremely rarely subjected to disciplinary measures or sanctions.

Lawyers believe that this kind of 'immunity', along with job security, certainty over income, sick days, maternity leave and the power and prestige related to the office, explains women's preference for the judiciary over a career with a law firm. Besides, in the collective mind of the legal profession, judges are considered to be of higher social status than lawyers, especially within provincial or small town courts.

Various lawyers in the sample declared that women judges generally tended to be less strict about rules and timetabling, and more conciliatory towards lawyers' claims and needs than their male colleagues. Interviewees by and large stressed that when a female judge is sitting, the chances of friction and disputes during the process are extremely rare. Male lawyers generally behave in a more conciliatory fashion, avoiding aggressiveness, conflict and opposition, persuaded that 'although sometimes they adopt a "woman's viewpoint" in the context of women's issues, generally women judges try to maintain neutrality and fairness, while eliminating sources of conflict between parties' (FG, 16 May 2009).

3.5. Overview

The civil law's nostrum that the judge must be neutral and apply the law strictly in line with judicial objectivity and laid down rules means that discussing influences of gender on judging can be unacceptable (Schultz and Shaw, 2008: 3). Nevertheless, recently socio-legal scholars have seen the issue of 'gender and judging' as one of considerable and lasting interest (Schultz and Shaw, 2008: 1). This rapid glimpse at a few provisional findings appears to confirm some interesting trends.

First to emerge is the importance which women judges assign to contextualisation, that is to say the tendency to consider the specific situation of the parties and to understand the broader social context, the so-called 'social framework evidence' (Hunter, 2008: 12). This means that they try to concentrate on the reality of people's lives rather than on narrow doctrinal issues. In both traditional and modern societies, women seem to prefer 'individualised decision-making', ie, what O'Sullivan (2007)[22] refers to as a 'particularity model' of judging.

In Italy, women lawyers stress women judges' ability is to think relationally, and with attention, compassion and concern (classical elements of the well known 'ethics of care': Gilligan, 1982) while adopting what literature on the topic labels as 'practical reasoning' (Bartlett, 1990: 849–50; Hunter, 2008: 12). In fact, currently, when the national and international legal landscapes appear totally confused and a spatial, temporal and conceptual relativity seems to scramble all the usual reference points (Delmas-Marty, 2002) the force of reasoning could be the key criterion for passing fair, effective and suitable sentences.

Speaking about gender relations it seems to me very important to specify that I often witnessed a mismatch between what women judges said and what they effectively do. In fact, observing gender interaction in law courts I noticed that—contrary to their statements—women judges often show and use their sex appeal, feminine charm and fascination to capture male attention, agreement and consensus of opinion. For example, during my periods of participant observation I noticed that some of them often dress in a scanty way, with short skirts and plunging necklines.

Male judges very much sustained the traditional stereotype. They stressed especially women's propensity to look at family problems in their full complexity with a greater sensitivity for the context, thus explaining and justifying the high number of women in family law, as compared with other sections of the judiciary (*cf* Mossman's (2009) reference to 'pink files' and 'blue files'). In fact, women are frequently in charge of areas related to the roles they have traditionally performed within the family.

Despite the large increase in Italy in the number of women receiving legal education and their advance in the judiciary, female judges are still located at the bottom of the judicial pyramid. Their domestic responsibilities affect their career choice and chances of advancement, and they still suffer the persisting phenomena of horizontal and vertical segregation (according to Schultz and Shaw (2003: xlvii, li, 281–82) this phenomenon is quite common in other European and non-European countries).

As we have seen, although women judges are the stronger supporters of women's rights claims, the areas where women judges differ from men are not always around women's issues. Besides, not all women have the capacity or the willingness to represent women's perspectives and experiences. As feminist standpoint theory has taught us, gender consciousness is acquired; it is not an automatic component of biological identity (Kenney, 2008: 103–04). It is important to stress also that women are sometimes more

[22] Quoted by Hunter (2008: 12).

transformed by institutions than they are capable of transforming them (*cf* Schultz and Shaw, 2003: lii–liv).

Admittedly, my research lacks control of individual characteristics other than gender. This might attract the criticism that what I consider as gendered differences might be rooted in other sources and therefore present a somewhat partial view of the situation. Nevertheless, the data collected suggest that all interviewed persons from the different categories seemed likely to agree that in some areas women judges do behave differently from men. Although in both Italy and the Ivory Coast, interviewees in principle seemed likely to agree with the statement that 'a wise old man and a wise old woman reach the same conclusion',[23] most of them afterwards, in answering my questions and thinking over the subject, changed their minds.

The evidence, however, suggests that gender does not operate in a self-evident fashion. In accordance with feminist legal theorists, in fact, we do not have to see sex in an essentialist way and assume gender differences. I therefore tried to investigate when gender can be seen empirically to produce attitudinal differences (Kenney, 2008: 95). Given that gender is a social process and therefore does not work in a fixed, predictable, static way, it is clear we cannot predict from the judge's gender how (s)he will decide.

4. CONCLUDING REMARKS

To sum up, three key hypotheses have emerged so far about the impact that gender has, or could have, on the judiciary.

First, the most significant contribution that women currently seem to be making to the judiciary (especially the family law judiciary) is the introduction of an interdisciplinary approach to the resolution of trial cases. Avoiding the rigid application of universal rules and narrow doctrinal issues, but taking into account the particular circumstances of the case in point and integrating material from different sources both legal and extralegal, female judges are promoting fairness, equality and substantive justice.

Secondly, women appear to be more inclined to stress the effect that non-legal factors can have on judicial decisions. Practising and disseminating values like bargaining, sympathy, sharing, immediacy and solidarity, women judges contribute to challenging the dominant understanding of what the law is or is considered to be (especially as far as Western law is concerned). In fact, if the relationship between modern law and rationality has often been discussed, the role of emotions in law and societal orders has rarely been addressed. It seems crucial that future research and practice should pay more heed to the relation between norms and feelings. As the actions and decisions of individual women will be guided by

[23] Quoting Minnesota Supreme Court Justice M Jeanne Coyne (Martin, 1993: 126).

emotions linked to values, they will inevitably contribute to the ways norms and behaviour develop (Petersen, 1996: 15).

Finally, there is another important issue I would like to point out. It was almost taken for granted—and hardly questioned by any of the interviewees in the Marche region—that women judges may effectively influence their male colleagues, either directly or indirectly, and yet in an absolutely unpredictable way. In bringing an important diversity of approaches to the decision-making process, and offering a different explanation of why a given result should be reached, women foster a shift in the male judges' attitudes, thinking and behaviour. More specifically, we witness in women a greater sensitivity to, and advocacy of, human rights and the claims and needs of minority groups. In offering a contribution of this kind, they may open up the space for novel ways of conceptualising difference and otherness and promoting substantive equality.

Despite differences and peculiarities in both the above-mentioned case studies, we can identify women's strategies for articulating an alternative vision of the real, for redrawing the boundary between the legal and the social, and for challenging how we think about the law itself, either modern or traditional. They occupy their role as judge in a constructive way to imagine and build a more complete vision of the law and its impact on people's everyday practices and experiences.

5. REFERENCES

Arden, M (2008) Address to the Association of Women Barristers' Annual General Meeting (3 June).

Bartlett, K (1990) 'Jurisprudence and Gender' 55 *University of Chicago Law Review* 1.

Bartolomei, MR (2000) 'The Traditional Judicial Process among the Abron as an Instrument for the Legal Control of Social Change' in A Febbrajo, D Nelken and V Olgiati (eds), *Social Processes and Patterns of Legal Control: European Yearbook of Sociology of Law* (Milan, Giuffrè).

—— (2001) Giustizia tradizionale e mutamento sociale (Milano, Giuffrè).

Beiner, TM (1999) 'What will Diversity on the Bench mean for Justice?' 6(1) *Michigan Journal of Gender and Law* 113.

Belleau, M-C and Johnson, R (2008) 'Judging Gender: Difference and Dissent at the Supreme Court of Canada' 15(1–2) *International Journal of the Legal Profession* 57.

Coontz, P (2000) 'Gender and Judicial Decisions: Do Female Judges Decide Cases Differently than Male Judges?' 18(4) *Gender Issues* 59.

Davis, S (1992–93) 'Do Women Judges Speak "In a Different Voice?": Carol Gilligan, Feminist Legal Theory and the Ninth Circuit' 8 *Wisconsin Women's Law Journal* 143.

Delmas-Marty, M (2002) *Towards a Truly Common Law* (Cambridge, Cambridge University Press).

Elias, S (2006) 'Changing our World' International Association of Women Judges' Conference (Sydney, 4 May).

Frazier, PA and Hunt, JS (1998) 'Research on Gender and the Law: Where are we Going, Where have we Been?' 22(1) *Law and Human Behavior* 1.

Gilligan, C (1982) *In A Different Voice: Psychological Theory and Women's Development* (Cambridge, Harvard University Press).

Graycar, R (2008) 'Gender, Race, Bias and Perspective: Or, How Otherness Colours your Judgment' 15(1–2) *International Journal of the Legal Profession* 73.

Gutek, B and O'Connor, M (1995) 'The Empirical Basis for the Reasonable Woman Standard' 51 *Journal of Social Issues* 151.

Hale, B (2001) 'Equality and the Judiciary: Why Should We Want More Women Judges?' *Public Law* 489.

Hunter, R (2008) 'Can Feminist Judges Make a Difference?' 15(1–2) *International Journal of the Legal Profession* 7.

Kenney, SJ (2008) 'Thinking about Gender and Judging' 15(1–2) *International Journal of the Legal Profession* 87.

Kohen, B (2008) 'Family Law Judges in the City of Buenos Aires: A View from Within' 15(1–2) *International Journal of the Legal Profession* 111.

L'Heureux-Dubé, C (1997a) 'Making a Difference: The Pursuit of a Compassionate Justice' 14 *Canadian Journal of Family Law* 103.

Martin, E (1993) 'The Representative Role of Women Judges' 77(3) *Judicature* 166.

Martin, E and Pyle, B (2000) 'Gender, Rise and Partisanship on the Michigan Supreme Court' 63 *Albany Law Review* 1205.

Martin, PY, Reynolds, JR and Keith, S (2002) 'Gender Bias and Feminist Consciousness among Judges and Attorneys: A Standpoint Theory Analysis' 27(3) *Signs* 665.

Mossman, MJ (2009) 'Bertha Wilson: "Silences" in a Woman's Life Story' in K Brooks (ed), *Justice Bertha Wilson: One Woman's Difference* (Vancouver-Toronto, UBC Press).

Noddings, N (1984) *Caring. A Feminine Approach to Ethics and Moral Education* (Berkley, University of California Press).

Olgiati, V (2006) 'Donne & lavoro. L'inclusione della differenza di genere nelle attività economiche e professionali' 3 *I Quaderni dell'Istituto di Sociologia* (Università di Urbino).

Palmer, B (2001) 'Women in the American Judiciary: Their Influence and Impact' 23(3) *Women and Politics* 89.

Peresie JL (2005) 'Female Judges Matter: Gender and Collegial Decisionmaking in the Federal Appellate Court' 114 (7) *Yale Law Journal* 1759.

Petersen, H (1996) *Home Knitted Law. Norms and Values in Gendered Rule-Making* (Aldershot, Dartmouth).

Rackley, E (2008) 'What a Difference Difference Makes: Gendered Harms and Judicial Diversity' 15(1–2) *International Journal of the Legal Profession* 37.

Rotundo, M, Sackett, PR and Nguyen, Dung-Henh (2001) 'A Meta-Analytic Review of Gender Differences in Perceptions of Sexual Harassment' 86(5) *Journal of Applied Psychology* 914.

Schultz, U and Shaw, G (2003) (eds), *Women in the World's Legal Professions* (Oxford, Hart Publishing).

—— (2008) 'Editorial' *International Journal of the Legal Profession*, Special Issue on Gender and Judging 1, 5.

Smith, FO (2005) 'Gendered Justice: Do Male and Female Justice Rule Differently on Questions of Gay Rights?' 57 *Stanford Law Review*2087.

Wilson, B (1990) 'Will Women Judges Really Make a Difference?' 28 *Osgoode Hall Law Journal* 507.

3.4

Gender Arguments and Gender Perspective in Legal Judgments in Argentina[1]

ANDREA L GASTRON, M ANGELA AMANTE
AND RUBÉN RODRÍGUEZ

Abstract

Based on a sample of 105 judicial judgments (including an in-depth analysis of a case of abortion on request) we try to answer the question to what extent the Argentine judges use gender arguments in their judgments, and what this tells us about their gender perspective.

We conclude that the presence of gender arguments, as well as of a gender perspective, is still rare in Argentine legal judgments: a gender perspective is far from being consolidated as an ideology operating in Argentine courts. Instead, whenever it arises, it merely reflects the opinion of individual members, rather than the opinion of the judicial organisation, which, in general, shows little or no sign of a gender-sensitive approach.

1. INTRODUCTION

> Impartiality and equidistance are not intended to eliminate all moral judgment (...), but to take distance at the moment of judgment, assuring that the judge shall not favor any of the parties whatsoever, to the detriment of the other party (Kohen, 2005: 336)

THIS IS BEATRIZ Kohen's conclusion to a highly illustrative report about the different theoretical approaches that usually justify the necessity for a greater female presence in the judiciary. We are using

[1] This research is part of the project 'Paradigms and Paradogms of Law: A Gender Point of View about Justice in Argentina' *Universidad de Ciencias Empresariales y Sociales* (University of Business and Social Sciences) BA, 2006–10. Research Team: Andrea L Gastron (director), M Angela Amante (assistant) and Rubén Rodríguez (statistical advisor).

it as a basis for our research into the extent to which men and women judges from our country use gender arguments in their judgments, and whether we can infer a gender perspective from them. This follows on from our recent descriptive type analysis of cross-gender preferences between judges and parties, based on a non-representative sample of legal judgments in Argentina (Gastron, Amante and Rodríguez, 2009).

The question posed is not value-neutral, since it is associated with the view that more women should hold offices in the judiciary and its power structure, and is part of a context of greater, though not yet consolidated visibility of women in general in decision-making positions. In 2007, for the first time in our history a woman,[2] a lawyer, was elected by popular vote as President of the Argentine nation.[3]

The debate about why it is desirable that more women administer justice is not new in gender studies: it was born in the 1980s, when the presence of women in judicial positions—although more widespread than before—was rather a recent phenomenon in the Anglo-Saxon world (Kohen, 2008: 29 et seq). Nevertheless, we are still far from finding a unanimous answer.

In fact, two very clear lines of argument have emerged (Kohen, 2005: 331): on the one hand, the democratic legitimacy argument, that stresses the legitimacy of the democratic system and the idea of representativity which, of course, includes other disadvantaged groups (ethnic, political, religious, etc); and on the other, the argument of gender differences, much more controversial, which assumes that women would make a specific contribution to the forensic world.

On considering several reasonable criticisms against the latter line of argument, we have ruled out the search for specific contributions of female judges from our work. This is not due to the lack of them: paradoxically, as Gargarella states, it is expected that certain *personal attributes*, such as gender, ideology, social status, religion or place of birth, have an influence on the interpretation of constitutional and legal rules, and, therefore, democratic system legitimacy presupposes the presence of male, female, conservative and progressive, Christian, Jewish and Muslim, 'Porteños'[4] and provincial judges, etc (2006: 125).

[2] She is Cristina Fernández de Kirchner. In 1975, the Vice-President of Argentina, María Estela Martínez, had taken over the office of President on the death of her husband, President Juan D Perón. Her removal from office was due to the coup d'état in 1976. Eva Perón, Perón's second wife, never held a formal political position and served as First Lady of Argentina.

[3] In both cases, they were wives to recent presidents of Argentina. A study of the Argentine legislative has shown that, together with traditional mechanisms of access to the parliamentary bench (most parliamentarians of both sexes hold a university degree, especially in law), women frequently still rely on social connections: out of 16 national women senators in 2002, at least eight admitted to having a close family bond with provincial party leaders (Gastron, 2002: 7).

[4] People from the City of Buenos Aires.

The problem is that we are still uncertain as to the extent to which such contributions are due to an alleged 'female specificity'.

In fact, many empirical findings deny the existence of significant differences in styles and work results of women and men judges (Schultz and Shaw, 2003: liv; Aliotta, 1995: 235; McGlynn, 1998: 184; Malleson, 2007: 40). Therefore, we have focused on trying to ascertain to what extent gender arguments and a gender perspective occur in judicial judgments in Argentina, except as the occasional reflection of personal views of individual magistrates.

The analysis unit of our research is the judicial judgment. The judgment is the highest and probably the most visible point of the entire judicial process. For this reason, its deep study becomes highly revealing regarding continuing social and gender differences in the access to Justice in Argentina.

However, judicial judgments are just one link in the long chain of social and gender inequalities in this context, as illustrated by the case of economically disadvantaged women.

A recent research carried out in the Argentine capital Buenos Aires shows that half of the low-resource women are unaware of the existence of free legal assistance services. About 12 per cent of these women acknowledge that they have heard about them, although they do not know precisely what they are. Only about 30 per cent of the women surveyed can mention an institution that provides free legal services in the city.

These results are not surprising if we take into account that in the three major cities of our country nearly 60 per cent of the women are not aware of the existence of a law against domestic violence, and fewer than three out of ten can mention some aspect of this law (Birgin and Gherardi, 2008: 94 et seq).

The situation is not very different in the rest of the Latin-American countries: women are more exposed than men to suffer injustice, discrimination and even bodily harm either within their family, or in their work, being themselves the main users of the legal system (Undurraga, 2005: 1).

To the difficulties described to access the legal system, we must add the existence of deep-rooted legal traditions with little gender sensitivity and, in general, poor sensitivity to the claims of the less protected sectors of society. This situation does not originate so much from the particular characteristics of certain magistrates, but from the *institutional mechanisms* of the judicial power, such as the ample margins of manoeuvre enjoyed by judges, the citizens' lack of opportunities for making judges accountable and the tendency of justices to decide in a consistently non-impartial way (Gargarella, 2006: 109).

These are precisely some of the institutional mechanisms we will deal with below.

2. RESEARCH DESIGN AND METHODOLOGY

In the Argentine legal system judges provide written records of their decisions. The judgment contains the beliefs, values and attitudes of the judge in a single judge court or of the judges in a collegiate court. The judgment also provides gender perspectives in its discursive chain.

In order to discover to what extent Argentine judges use gender arguments in their judgments, and whether they convey a gender perspective, we carried out a thorough analysis of judicial cases based on precedent judgments. The collection of judgments was made in Buenos Aires between September 2006 and April 2007. We conducted this research through one of the most popular electronic databases among legal operators in Argentina, Lexisnexis which contains more than 46,000 legal judgments from the whole country, both at federal and provincial (ordinary) levels.

The first selection round filtered a total of 2196 judgments, added to other relevant judgments that had an impact on academic and professional or communication media. The non-probabilistic, descriptive and reasoned sample obtained, finally included a total of 105 judgments.

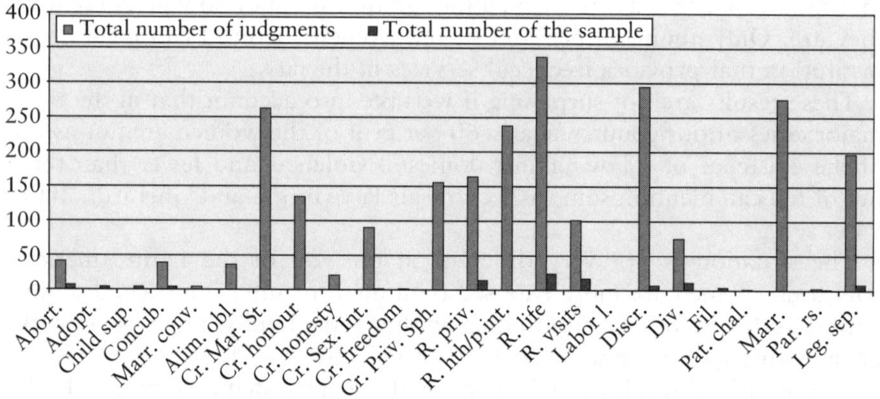

Figure 1: Pre-selection and final selection of judgments according to subject matter

The selection criteria of our units of analysis are the following:

1. We only considered judicial cases where gender issues are as a rule necessarily discussed, such as abortion, adoption, child support, concubinage, marriage conventions, alimony obligations, crimes against marital status, crimes against honour, crimes against honesty, crimes against sexual integrity, crimes against freedom, crimes against private sphere, right to privacy, right to health and personal integrity, right to life, right to

visits, labour law, discrimination, divorce, filiation, paternity challenge, marriage, parental rights and legal separation.[5]

2. The search covered the period between 2003 and 2007; most cases were concentrated between 2005 and 2006. Because of the importance of the subject three judgments from between 2001 and 2002 have been added. Nevertheless, time has not been included as an analysis variable.
3. The research included a great variety of legal fields and jurisdictions such as civil, civil and commercial, criminal and correctional, criminal cassation, family, labour, contentious administrative, social security, minority correctional, preliminary proceedings and misdemeanour, etc. However, although jurisdiction has often been a factor in the identification of cases, it has not been an analysis variable, since most of the cases selected belonged to the civil jurisdiction (family).
4. We have considered cases of single-judge courts (first instance judges), as well as of collegiate courts (chambers of appeal, higher provincial or national courts).[6] The number of judges has not been considered as an analysis variable, but most of the cases came from collegiate courts.
5. Jurisdictional scope: judgments come from federal and ordinary/provincial courts from all over the country, under the three judicial instances (first instance courts, chambers of appeal or second instance courts, and higher courts, either at provincial and national level—Supreme Court of Justice).

Taking into account these criteria, figure 2 (below) groups together the selected legal judgments. The following data have been included: verifying number (if applicable), intervening court, date of judgment, cover-sheet of the case, gender arguments and gender perspective likely to be identified by the court.

The research team was composed of three members, each of whom applied their own methods to the same textual data, thereby allowing for subsequent comparisons. The next stage planned in our research will focus on double triangulation of qualitative and quantitative methods (Cea D'Ancona, 1998: 48–50).

[5] Due to methodological requirements of a previous research stage where we discovered to what extent judges favour or not the parties of their same gender, those cases had a dichotomous outcome, where 'winner-take-all' rules apply.

[6] The number of intervening judges generally indicates judicial hierarchy: the greater the number of judges, the higher the hierarchy. Thus, first instance courts are under the charge of only one judge; Chambers of Appeal, in higher density geographical areas, are distributed in courts composed of three members each; the National Supreme Court of Justice (today it is composed of seven members due to the resignation of two of them) and the higher provincial courts are collegiate. There are certain exceptions: in the Province of Buenos Aires, family courts are collegiate, although they are first instance courts.

3. CASE STUDY

We considered one particular case that had broad media impact. The mother of a 19-year-old mentally disabled girl, who had been raped[7] by a close relative (her uncle) and become pregnant, had put in a request for authorisation to have an abortion.[8] The request was made, as often happens, after hospital authorities had refused to perform the abortion.

The technique used for the judgments analysis was based not so much on the collection of key words, but on more complete semantic units, like phrases or paragraphs,[9] which were framed taking into account the characteristics connected with the abortion problem that absolutely permeates the gender thematic in our culture.

Under Argentine law, abortion is a criminal act (sections 85–88, Criminal Code) punishable by imprisonment ranging from between one and four years for the woman who has caused or consented that someone caused it, and also for the person who has carried it out with the consent of the woman (physicians, surgeons, midwives or chemists who performed the abortion).

Argentine law considers abortion a non-punishable crime if the pregnancy has resulted from rape or sexual abuse committed against a mentally deficient or insane woman (thus exactly reflecting the case in question) for which the consent of the legal representative is necessary (section 86, subsection 2, Criminal Code).

The criminal rule is very clear regarding the abortion grounds for non-imputability,[10] and it also considers the case of an abortion performed to avoid a risk to the life or health of the mother provided the risk cannot be avoided by other means.

But in practice, although the legal text is quite clear, physicians only perform an abortion after judicial authorisation, since they are subject to

[7] Sexual abuse is always presumed when the injured party is younger than 13 years old, or has not been able to freely consent to the act.

[8] The case under analysis was sent to the Supreme Court of the Province of Buenos Aires, the highest court of the most important provincial state of the country, both from the point of view of its area, 307,571 km^2—similar size to Italy—and its economy representing 38.5% of Argentine GDP and also the number of inhabitants (nearly 37% of the whole country's population).

[9] The paragraphs included herein are in italics. They were taken from a legal case whose data are the following: Docket data- Lexis Nexis: No 35003763. Court: Province of Buenos Aires Supreme Court. Date: 31 July 2006. Parties: R, LM Published: SJA 20/12/2006. JA 2006-IV-210. Key words: Crimes against people; Abortion; Non-punishable abortion; Rape of a mentally disabled minor; Petition for authorisation.

[10] Although legal scholars have discussed whether the word 'violación' (rape) is applied to mentally competent women, in the case studied there is no doubt of its applicability since the injured party is a mentally disabled minor.

civil and criminal liability, even when the case is one of non-imputability provided for by section 86.

This seems to be a paradoxical situation, since judges might refrain from granting an authorisation that the same rule does not require. In many cases, the judicial authorisation is bound to cause a delay beyond the time when it is advisable to perform the abortion without risk for the mother's psychophysical health. As one of the judges involved pointed out:

> And this is, exactly, one of the torts that the petitioner has insistently been arguing that she has not asked for authorization since pursuant to subsection 2, section. 86, Criminal Code there is no need for such authorization in the case of abortion. The petitioner is right. I do repeat, there is no need for request on performing a medical practice to stop gestation. There has been excessive judicial intervention. There is no gap in this rule to infer that a judge may either authorize or prohibit the behaviour described herein (R, L M, 2006; voted by Judge Genoud).[11]

This state of affairs encourages the practice of clandestine abortions, which mostly affect women from marginal social groups who cannot afford a medically sound abortion and therefore run the risk of high costs to life and health. In the words of the same judge:

> It is contradictory to argue that if the abortion had been practised it would not have been punished but, due to the unnecessary intervention of Justice, the disabled shall be prevented from such possibility.
>
> Furthermore, we can follow the guidelines of the Human Rights Committee (Argentina, 11/03/2000) article 14 that reads: 'On the issue of reproductive health rights, the Committee is concerned that the criminalization of abortion deters medical professionals from providing this procedure without judicial order, even when they are permitted to do so by law, inter alia when there are clear health risks for the mother or when pregnancy results from rape of mentally disabled women. The Committee also expresses concern over discriminatory aspects of the laws and policies in force, which result in disproportionately high numbers of illegal, unsafe abortions performed on poor and rural women' (R, LM, 2006; voted by Judge Genoud).[12]

Needless to say that the criminalisation of abortion in Argentina causes great controversies and discussions between opposing groups which are not unaware of traditional influences of the Roman Catholic Church, the official state religion. Further complications are posed by the lack of efficient

[11] Male.
[12] Male.

public policies in the promotion of responsible paternity and prevention of unintended pregnancies. To quote another member of the judicial team:

> But the real problem exposed in generalised precarious situations goes beyond the judicial resolution of cases like the one mentioned herein: it conveys a structural character.
>
> Through strident statements, the lack of institutional policies that deal with the heart of the problem of maternity and childhood overall are hardly concealed. Coordination between sanitary and educational programmes is insufficient. Promotion of responsible sexuality within the framework of each individual's self-determination can be part of any legal text (it does not seem to be very clear that the effects arising from Act Number 25673 in force have been satisfactory in this field) or the government agenda; but it is difficult to achieve if social marginality and exclusion are not reversed.
>
> In the meantime, thousands of rapes, many of them domestic rapes, and clandestine abortions, especially on minors, show how distressing is the indifference to social suffering and decay (R, LM, 2006; voted by Judge Soria).[13]

4. RESULTS OBTAINED

Our sample of 105 legal judgments was analysed in terms of content in order to establish to what extent judges use gender arguments and, possibly, adopt a gender perspective.

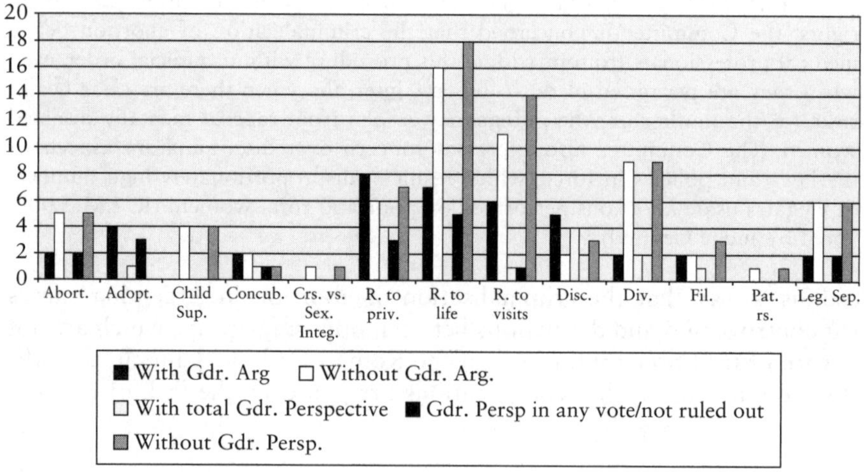

Figure 2: Gender arguments and gender perspective in the judgments analysed (in detail)

[13] Male.

Under the heading of 'gender arguments' we grouped together judges' statements about women *qua* women or about gender generally, regardless of the social roles of women and men, whether positive or negative.

Thirty-eight per cent (40 judgments) contain gender arguments. However, this number decreases abruptly when individual votes are analysed, since in the case of collegiate courts (where most of the cases studied come from) gender arguments appear isolated as argument from one judge, and not as arguments of most of the members of the collegiate court.

We paid special attention to judges' references to rules specifically related to female or gender themes, such as, for example: the Convention on the Elimination of all forms of Discrimination against Women (CEDAW),[14] the relevant parts of the Argentine Constitution and the International Covenant on Economic, Social and Cultural Rights (ie, affirmative action measures, etc), Act Number 474 of the City of Buenos Aires that has created the Plan of Real Equal Opportunities and Treatment for Women and Men, etc.

These rules are rarely expressly quoted in judgments, including those that contain gender arguments.

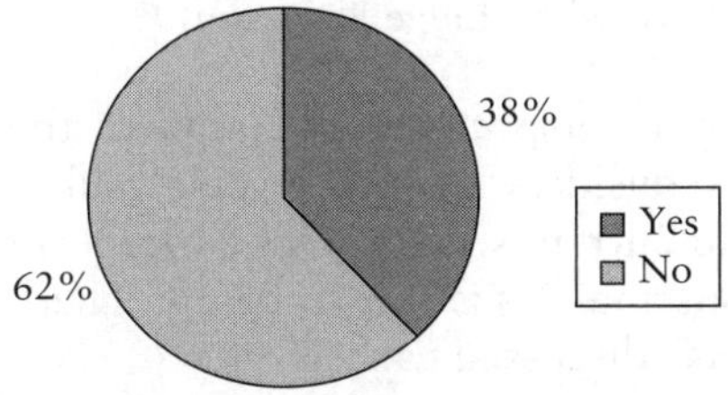

Figure 3: Number of judgments with gender arguments

Sometimes, gender arguments occur in judgments, but not to favour women's position or to take into account their social standing, but to legitimate the opposite position.

For example, in the case discussed above, judges placed greater weight on the right to life of unborn children (expressly referring to national and international rules about children's rights) than on the mother's health,

[14] In Argentina, constitutional law and international covenants have the same juridical value as national laws, being at the same level (s 31, NC); in this the Argentine system differs from countries such as Germany, Greece, France, Spain, Italy, Austria, Portugal, etc, where international covenants rank higher than domestic constitutional laws (Zuppi, 2001; García Belsunce, 2006; Badeni, 2005; Bidart Campos, 1995 etc.) On the other hand, the Argentine Constitution itself specifically lists those treaties and covenants on human rights, granting them constitutional rank. This exhaustive enumeration does include both the CEDAW and the International Covenant on Economic, Social and Cultural Rights (s 75, ss 22 NC).

without mentioning current legislation about women's rights. In the words of Judge Mahiques:

> [I]n case of an incompatibility between a mother's right to health and the right to life of the unborn child, the latter shall prevail and, to that end, she raised the argument of the unconstitutionality of any criminal rule that is invoked to justify an abortion as requested herein, where the mother's life is not in danger, because this does imply a serious violation of constitutional rights, especially the right to life.' (R, LM, 2006; voted by Judge Mahiques).[15]

Also, phrases such as 'maternal instinct', 'maternal honour', 'good housewife', 'minor's higher interest', 'natural maternal attitude', 'responsible motherhood', 'family protection', 'weak sex', etc, are frequently found in many judgments.

> The act of rape or abusive insemination is confused with maternity. While the first produces serious damages that will be reflected in the future victim's life, which are sometimes irreparable, and really damages female dignity, the latter, since it represents the transmission of life to a human being, dignifies and honors the mother (R, LM, 2006; voted by Judge Pettigiani).[16]

On the issue of 'gender perspectives', we applied the term whenever any part of a judgment considers women's social subordination within the power structure of our current society. This concept is strongly linked to the concept of gender conscious, as is shown below. There follows a paragraph extracted from the case discussed earlier:

> At the court hearing with the adolescent we also met her mother who, lucid and completely understanding the adverse situation they find themselves in, gave consent to the abortion, as required by law. Nobody knows her daughter better than she herself because they live alone together, she takes care of her, she gives her a bath, she has made sure that she attended a specialised school for people with disabilities and who now regrets that, due to this problem, her daughter is unable to attend workshops preparing young people with special needs to undergo some handicraft training. As we can see, this woman, undoubtedly, is struggling to meet the needs of the minor, within the limits of her possibilities. Needless to say this is the person best placed to say what is most beneficial for the young woman under these hard and problematic conditions (R, L M, 2006; voted by Judge Genoud).[17]

[15] Male.
[16] Male.
[17] Male.

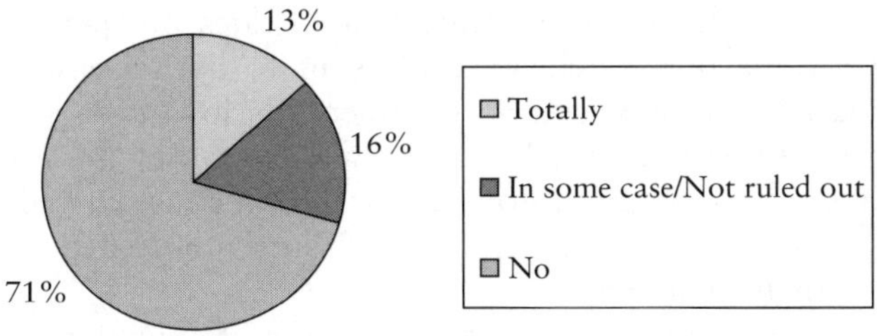

Figure 4: Number of judgments with a gender perspective

This variable is highly revealing since it clearly shows to what extent women and men judges make their gender consciousness explicit in their judgments, and it does not agree with gender argumentation.

Overall, we observed the incorporation of a gender perspective in 31 cases, but in more than half of these (17 cases) this appears in the isolated vote of one member of the collegiate court, or it is not quite clearly expressed (see figure 4).

In spite of the methodological limitations of this research (which is still at an exploratory stage) this allows us to hypothesise that a gender perspective is far from being a consolidated ideology operating in Argentine courts. Rather, whenever it arises, it just reflects the opinion of individual members. In the words of Judge Soria:

> The Argentine juridical system lacks a suitable regulation on the matter where this litis should be included. In the above-mentioned case, as soon as her mother knew of the rape, the victim could have been assisted by the Public Ministry and by practitioners. As we have seen, this did not happen due to the intervention of a District Attorney, as has been clearly pointed out by the attorney general in her report and the vote of my colleagues (R, LM, 2006; voted by Judge Soria).[18]

5. SUMMARY AND CONCLUSIONS

This chapter is the result of our attempt to establish the extent to which judges from our country use gender arguments in their judgments, and in how far current Argentine jurisprudence adopts a gender perspective in the resolution of cases.

We assume that the in-depth study of judgments containing the beliefs, values and attitudes of judges, allows us to get close to the problem of social and gender inequalities within the access to justice, particularly when we deal with unfair societies such as ours.

[18] Male.

Although the methodological strategy used does not permit the generalisation of results, our conclusions allow us to hypothesise that the use of gender arguments in Argentine judgments is low, even in those cases where they would be relevant. Where they appear, they are introduced by individual men or women, but do not represent a consolidated ideology in the judicial power.[19] It is striking that this is even accepted by the judges themselves in their judgments.

The presence of gender arguments, as well as of a gender perspective, is still rare in Argentine legal judgments: when a gender perspective arises, it merely reflects the opinion of individual members, rather than the opinion of the judicial organisation, which in general shows little or no sign of a gender-sensitive approach.

Consistent with our findings Gargarella (2006: 127) refers to the *institutional mechanisms* of the Argentine judicial power as the source of deep-rooted traditions that result in a consistently non-impartial way of solving the cases, showing a very poor social and gender sensitivity.

If we recognise the need to justify a greater presence of women in the judicial power, this presence does not guarantee by itself that women's interests shall be better represented.

What does matter is enlarging the number of women (and men) judges with gender consciousness: judges who, based on a greater identification with women's issues/problems, will be able, for example, to consider in their judgments the place of female subordination within the power structure of current societies, and how this place determines the life realities of women. However, what matters most is not individual but institutional awareness within the judiciary of the significance of gender so as to project to all social sectors a clearer idea of the role that men and women should perform in a fairer and more equal society.

6. REFERENCES

Aliotta, J (1995) 'Justice O'Connor and the Equal Protection Clause: A Feminine Voice?' 78 *Judicature* 232.

Badeni, G (2005) 'El caso "Simon" y la supremacía constitucional' *La Ley* 639.

Bergallo, P (2006) 'Un techo de cristal en el poder judicial? Selección de los jueces federales y nacionales en Buenos Aires' Jornada Académica: *Ved en trono a la noble igualdad*, organizada por la Asociación Civil por la Igualdad y la Justicia (ACIJ), en la Facultad de Derecho de la Universidad de Buenos Aires.

Bergoglio, MI (2006) 'Llegar a socia? La movilidad ocupacional en las grandes empresas jurídicas. Análisis de género' *VII Congreso Nacional de Sociología*

[19] Ideology is hereby defined according to Karl Mannheim, as a justification of the dominant status for the only fact of being dominant (Mannheim, 1993: 49 et seq.).

Jurídica, Facultad de Ciencias Jurídicas y Sociales de la Universidad Nacional de La Plata.

Bidart Campos (1995) *Los tratados de integración: derecho comunitario versus derecho interno: primacía o no de la constitución* (Buenos Aires, Academia Nacional de Ciencias Morales y Politicas).

Birgin, H and Gherardi, N (2008) 'Retos y oportunidades para mejorar el ejercicio de los derechos de las mujeres' in A Etchegoyen (ed), *Mujer y acceso a la justicia*, 1a ed (Buenos Aires, El Mono Armado).

Cea D'Ancona, MA (1998) *Metodología Cuantitativa. Estrategias y técnicas de investigación social* (Madrid, Editorial Síntesis).

Fucito, F (1999) *El abogado desde la perspectiva judicial*, Fundación Ciencias Jurídicas y Sociales, Colegio de Abogados de la Provincia de Buenos Aires, La Plata.

García Belsunce, HA (2006) *Los tratados internacionales de derechos humanos y la Constitución Nacional* (Buenos Aires, Academia Nacional de Ciencias Morales y Políticas).

Gargarella, R (2006) 'Protesta social y parcialidad judicial' in Birgin, H and Kohen, B, *Acceso a la justicia como garantía de igualdad. Instituciones, actores y experiencias comparadas* (Buenos Aires, Biblos).

Gastron, AL (2002) 'Vive la différence!? Mujeres y varones en el Senado de la Nación' ponencia, La Plata: *Jornada Internacional: Globalización y crisis de representación* (publicación en CD).

Gastron, AL, Amante, MA and Rodríguez, RJ (2009) 'Género y argumentos de género en el Poder Judicial: Lo que muestran las sentencias judiciales en la Argentina' XIII *Revista Científica de UCES* (con referato) (Buenos Aires, Asp).

Kohen, B (2005) 'Más mujeres en la justicia: los argumentos más frecuentes' 3(6) *Academia. Revista sobre enseñanza del Derecho de Buenos Aires* (Departamento de Publicaciones, Facultad de Derecho, Universidad de Bs As) 331.

—— (2008) *El género en la Justicia de Familia. Miradas y protagonistas* (Buenos Aires, Ad Hoc).

Malleson, K (2007) 'La justificación de la igualdad de género en la magistratura: por qué la diferencia no funciona' 8(1) *Revista Jurídica de la Universidad de Palermo* 35.

Mannheim, K (1993) *Ideología y Utopía. Introducción a la sociología del conocimiento* (México, Fondo de Cultura Económica).

McGlynn, C (1998) *The Woman Lawyer Making the Difference* (London, Butterworths).

Schultz, U and Shaw, G (2003) (eds), *Women in the World's Legal Professions* (Oxford, Hart Publishing).

Undurraga, V (2005) 'Acceso a la Justicia cuando las mujeres son víctimas de discriminación', conferencia, *Reunión de expertas y expertos: Una mirada al Acceso a la Justicia en los Países del Cono Sur*, organizada por la Comisión Interamericana de Derechos Humanos de la OEA, en el H Senado de la Nación, Buenos Aires.

Zuppi, AL (2001) *La Jurisdicción extraterritorial y la corte penal internacional: premio estimulo academia nacional de derecho y ciencias sociales de Buenos Aires* (Buenos Aires, La Ley).

3.5

Do Women on South Africa's Courts Make a Difference?

RUTH B COWAN*

Abstract

This chapter reports a study as to whether South African women judges have made a difference.

The South African context promises judicial gender diversity, but it is a promise not kept. The study takes from the cases decided by the Constitutional Court from 1994–2009 three women's rights cases to present the 'voices' of the three women serving on that court. It also considers one case unrelated to women's issues in which the three women each express a different view.

The conclusion is that women did make a difference on the women's rights cases, even when dissenting from the majority; that women would have made a greater difference if the promise of judicial diversity had been kept; and that the women also made a difference in cases that did not raise women's issues.

1. SOUTH AFRICA'S GENDER DIVERSITY PRIORITY

WOMEN'S PRESENCE ON the bench in South Africa began in 1994 with the end of apartheid. As Justice Yvonne Mokgoro observes in the documentary *Courting Justice*,[1] during the hundreds of preceding years 'I guess there was no thought that women could also serve'. More accurately, what kept women off the bench was the firmly embedded assumption that women were unsuited by nature and by divine

* Research assistance provided by Colleen Normile, student at the City University of New York School of Law.

[1] The documentary features seven South African women judges. Speaking from their courtrooms, chambers, homes and childhood communities, they convey their commitment to using their judicial authority to realise the Constitution's promises. See, for further information, *Courting Justice* (2008) at www.courtingjustice.com. The *Courting Justice* DVD can be ordered from Amazon.com.

intent to be any place but home. It was simply unquestioned that they could or should ever serve.

The post-apartheid Constitution, setting forth a human rights-based constitutional democracy, overrode this assumption by mandating the consideration of gender when making judicial appointments. Regarding the appointment of judicial officers, the Constitution orders that 'Any qualified woman or man who is a fit and proper person may be appointed as a judicial officer'.[2]

It asserts '[t]he need for the judiciary to reflect broadly the racial and gender composition of South Africa', further asserts this requires a gender-diverse judiciary; and thus orders that gender 'must be considered when judicial officers are appointed'.[3]

The appointments were to be made to what was now to be an independent judiciary. The apartheid judiciary had not been independent—its charge was to assure the validation of apartheid's legislation, executive regulations and official actions. Yet, these same apartheid courts were to be retained, as were their judges and court personnel whose record was hostile to the very human rights, which the judiciary was now charged to protect. The Constitution did create one new court, ie the Constitutional Court. The new court was charged with and limited to considering cases in which constitutional issues were raised.

Given the continued engagement of the apartheid judges—all but two of whom were white males and almost all of whom were energetic in support of apartheid's oppressive and repressive laws and brutal actions—the transformation of the judiciary in terms of race and gender was important to establishing the judiciary's very legitimacy. It was and continues to be verbally embraced as a high priority by leaders of the government and leaders of the legal profession. Central to the transformation was to be the appointment of Africans, Coloureds, Asians and women.

2. THE REALITY OF JUDICIAL GENDER DIVERSITY

The high verbal priority given to judicial gender diversity is not, however, reflected in the reality of appointments. At the end of 2008, which concluded 15 years under the constitutional mandate regarding the appointment of women, there were 197 judicial positions occupied by permanent appointees on South Africa's superior courts—ie, the Constitutional Court,

[2] The Constitution of the Republic of South Africa 1996, Act 108 of 1996, s 174(1).
[3] Ibid.

the Supreme Court of Appeal and the High Courts.[4] Women had been appointed to 34 positions—less than 18 per cent. In three courts there were no women at all. In four courts there was but one woman and in two courts there were but two women—hardly a critical mass in any of these six courts. In the courts' leadership positions of Judge President and Deputy Judge President there was but one woman. Jeanette Traverso, that one woman, serves as Deputy Judge President of the Cape Town High Court. She addresses the near male exclusivity in the documentary *Courting Justice*, declaring it a 'tragedy, especially since there is not a single black woman in a leadership position'.[5]

The most frequently expressed response to comments about this poor record is the pipeline-pool explanation. According to this account, there are so few women because the educational disruptions, school shut downs and sexism during apartheid denied women the opportunity to qualify for consideration. They are not in the pipeline; they are not in the pool from which qualified candidates can be drawn. Lending credibility to this explanation was the establishment by the Minister of Justice and Constitutional Development of a training programme for women who aspired to become judges (referred to as 'aspirant women judges'). It was presumed that the training would help qualify the aspirant women judges.

The pipeline-pool explanation, despite its popularity, is challenged if one but looks at the composition of the bench. Opening one's eyes one sees that more than twice as many black men have received judicial appointments during this same period. Blacks—a category which includes Africans, Asians and Coloureds—were at least as disadvantaged educationally during apartheid as were women. Yet 77 black men, contrasted with 34 women, had been appointed from 1994 to the end of 2008. They constituted 39 per cent of the judiciary, compared with to less than 18 per cent for women.

An explanation better grounded in reality than the pipeline-pool excuse is persistent sexism—about which the sitting women judges speak in *Courting Justice*.[6] Critics charge that the decision-making process of the Judicial Service Commission (JSC), which is established by the Constitution to manage the judicial appointments process, allows a lot of room for member biases to reign.[7] Sexist assumptions and comments are ample at JSC sessions. At the JSC's first public interviews, Kate O'Regan, Professor at the

[4] This statistic and the following figures are taken from charts provided to the author by the Judicial Service Commission. The charts list, court by court, the name of each permanently appointed judge and indicates for each their race and gender.

[5] See *Courting Justice*, above (n 2).

[6] Ibid.

[7] David Yutar, 'Judging those who would be judged' *Sunday Argus* (10 April 2005) 18.

University of Cape Town Faculty of Law, was a candidate for appointment to the new Constitutional Court. As reported in the *Sunday Times*:

> [S]he had bowled over the interrogators with her brilliance and her obvious capability. But, it seems, that was not enough. She had young children, one of the commissioners pointed out. If appointed, would she be able to make adequate arrangements for their care while she was at work.[8]

Sexist comments were made and discriminatory assumptions were clear at interviews of five women being considered for the Constitutional Court and one woman being considered for the position of Deputy Judge President. These were interviews I attended.

One candidate for the Constitutional Court, who at the time was not resident in South Africa, was asked what it would take for her to move back. Before she could respond, another JSC member answered she would need a South African boyfriend.

Anne-Marie de Vos, the only female judge serving on the Pretoria High Court, was being considered for Deputy Judge President position. The JSC, in my judgement, subjected her to harsh and hostile questioning. The subsequent *Sunday Times* report of her interview, headlined 'quips and marked prejudice show how much attitudes still need to change', concurred with my assessment.[9]

Another explanation grounded in reality and related to persistent sexism is the de facto, though unstated, requirement that candidates have served as Acting Judges. Though some Acting Judges are already judges who are temporarily 'borrowed' and reassigned from another court, most Acting Judges have not yet become judges. It is a position to which they aspire. The appointment to Act provides experience and legitimacy. The process for becoming an Acting Judge is unfriendly to women. The process is one of appointment by each court's Judge President. As of December 2008, all of the Judge Presidents were men.

3. SHOULD WOMEN MAKE A DIFFERENCE? DO WOMEN MAKE A DIFFERENCE?

In contrast to the assertions in the United States that judges function like baseball umpires, in South Africa a frequently expressed and undisputed justification for the appointment of those previously excluded by racism and sexism is precisely so that they would and should provide perspectives previously absent; that they would therefore be essential to advancing the

8 Carmel Rickard, 'Judging Women Harshly' *Sunday Times* (23 October 2005) 21.
9 Ibid.

Constitution's promises. African, Coloured, Asian and women judges were and are expected to add value—they were and are expected to make a difference in the decisions rendered; they were and are expected to make a difference in the development of the New Democracy's jurisprudence.

Frequently at screenings of *Courting Justice*, the documentary featuring seven South African women judges, the expectation surfaces. The question is asked, 'What difference have the women made?'

In fact, the women have made a difference. They have lent legitimacy to the judiciary, they have inspired other women to aim for judicial appointments, they have raised the comfort level of women appearing in court and they have—through their extrajudicial volunteer commitments—worked to increase access to justice. But, have they made a substantive difference; ie, have they affected South Africa's jurisprudence?

4. THE STUDY REPORTED HERE

It is this question, which the study reported here, embarked on answering. The study should be understood as preliminary even to the first step in what will require many more before an answer can be definitive.

The study focuses only on women Constitutional Court Justices. There were two among the first eleven Constitutional Court Justices appointed in 1994: Yvonne Mokgoro and Kate O'Regan. In 2005, a third woman, Bess Nkabinde, joined them.

Between 1994 and 2009, the Constitutional Court issued judgments in 356 cases. Trying to capture the Justices' 'voices' this study chose to scrutinise those cases in which one or more of the women 'spoke' in a majority opinion, a concurring opinion or a dissenting opinion. This resulted in scrutinising 130 cases—more than a third of the cases decided. In 59 or 16.6 per cent of the 356 cases, one of the three women Justices wrote the Court's opinion. In addition to the 59 majority opinions written by one of the women, they wrote 52 concurring opinions and 19 dissenting opinions. The concurring and dissenting opinions are both, in an important sense, dissents from the majority. Together they represent a disagreement with the Court's opinion in 20 per cent of the cases decided.

Table 1: Constitutional Court cases 1994–2009

	No of cases	% of 356
Women spoke	130	36.5
Court's opinion	59	16.6
Concurrence	52	14.6
Dissent	19	5.3
Concurrence + dissent	71	20.0

One might question whether the focus on Constitutional Court Justices, rather than on the judges serving in other courts, might impede identifying the jurisprudential impact of women because of the special characteristic of all those appointed to this Court: all of the judges had evidenced strong commitments to human rights before being considered for appointment. The record, however, parries the question. Despite their shared commitment to human rights, the justices when confronted with actual cases differ. Their opinions thus provide a rich diversity of views. Further, the development of those opinions is elaborate. Ever conscious that they are responsible for developing a new human rights jurisprudence, the justices provide a full and clear account of the reasoning underlying each decision, identifying the compelling principles and facts.

5. WHERE 'WOMEN'S ISSUES' ARE INVOLVED

Even in this strong human rights environment, the women nevertheless differed from all but one of their male colleagues when cases involved issues clearly related to women's rights or to matters of particular relevance to women's experiences.

The three 'women's rights' cases considered by the court during the period 1994–2009 make this point. The cases are: *S v Jordan and Others*;[10] *Volks NO v Robinson and Others*;[11] and *Masiya v Director of Public Prosecutions Pretoria and Another*.[12]

In *Jordan*, the issues relate to the criminalisation of prostitution and brothels; in *Robinson* the issue involves the widow's benefit entitlement for a woman, not legally married, living in a lifelong relationship and in *Masiya* the issue involves the definition of rape. In the *Jordan* and *Robinson* cases the women Justices were in dissent; in the *Masiya* case the three women were among the majority.

5.1. *S v Jordan and Others*

The law criminalising prostitution targets only the prostitutes and not their customers. The law also criminalises brothels. Considered here is just the former and only some of the arguments made.

The majority held that in targeting the prostitutes and not also their customers, the law is not discriminatory. It held that the law is gender-neutral: that

[10] *S v Jordan and Others* [2002] ZACC 22, 2002 (6) SA 642 (CC).

[11] *Volks NO v Robinson and Others* [2005] ZACC 2; 2005 (5) BCLR 446 (CC).

[12] *Masiya v Director of Public Prosecutions Pretoria and Another* [2007] ZACC 9; 2007 (5) SA 30 (CC).

customers are liable to prosecution under separate statutes; that in targeting the supplier—ie, the prostitute, the State is choosing an effective way to curb prostitution; that the law is not rendered discriminatory based on gender because prostitutes are overwhelmingly female; and that prostitutes have other economic options.

The dissent by Justices O'Regan and Albie Sachs acknowledged that prostitution has 'an impact on the quality of life' and that the legislature, therefore, can regulate prostitution 'so long as it does not limit other fundamental rights in a way that would not be justifiable in an open and democratic society'.[13] They then, point by point, develop their argument that the law is discriminatory.

They begin with a consideration of gender stereotypes:

> [T]he effect of making the prostitute the primary offender directly reinforces a pattern of sexual stereotyping which is itself in conflict with the principle of gender equality. The differential impact between prostitute and client is therefore directly linked to a pattern of gender disadvantage which our Constitution is committed to eradicating. In all these circumstances, we are satisfied that ... this is a case where an apparently neutral differentiating criterion producing a markedly differential impact on a listed ground results in indirect discrimination on that ground.[14]

> This distinction [between the prostitute and the customer] is, indeed, one which for years has been espoused both as a matter of law and social practice. The female prostitute has been the social outcast, the male patron has been accepted or ignored ... The difference in social stigma tracks a pattern of applying different standards to the sexuality of men and women.[15]

> Although the difference may on its face appear to be a difference of form, it is in our view a difference of substance, that stems from and perpetuates gender stereotypes in a manner which causes discrimination ... Such discrimination, therefore, has the potential to impair the fundamental dignity and personhood of women.[16]

> We see no reason why the supplier of sex for money should be treated as more blameworthy than the client. If anything, the fact that the male customers will generally come from a class that is more economically powerful might suggest the reverse. To suggest, as the law (and Ngcobo J) do, that women may be targeted for prosecution because they are merchants of sex and not patrons is to turn the real-life sociological situation upside-down.[17]

[13] *Jordan and Others*, above (n 11) para 56.
[14] Ibid, para 60.
[15] Ibid, para 64.
[16] Ibid, para 65.
[17] Ibid, para 68.

> Parliament may decide to render criminal sexual intercourse where a reward is paid, but their decision to make only purveyors of sexual intercourse and not purchasers primarily liable, entrenches the deep patterns of gender inequality which exist in our society and which our Constitution is committed to eradicating.[18]

> It is no answer ... to a constitutional complaint to say that the constitutional problem lies not in the law but in social values, when the law serves to foster those values. The law must be conscientiously developed to foster values consistent with our constitution.[19]

The dissent argues against the other conclusions contained in the majority opinion but the statements above are sufficient to indicate that Justice O'Regan (and Justice Sachs) offer a very different perspective; one which those committed to gender equality would undoubtedly applaud.

5.2. *Volks v Robinson*

The Court's judgment finds the law providing widow benefits 'incapable of being interpreted so as to include permanent life partners'[20] and goes on to distinguish between marriage and other cohabiting relationships. It references the argument in the dissenting opinion by Justice Sachs expressing 'concern for the plight of vulnerable women in cohabitation relationships'[21] and, while expressing 'a genuine concern for vulnerable women who ... become victims of cohabitation relationships',[22] it asserts this is 'part of a broader societal reality that must be corrected through the empowerment of women and social policies by the Legislature'.[23]

The joint dissenting opinion from Justices O'Regan and Mokgoro, instead of pointing to the differences between marriage and other cohabiting relationships, points to the commonalities:

> [N]ot every family is founded on a marriage recognized as such in law. Yet members of such families often play the same roles as in families which are founded on marriage and provide companionship, support and security to one another.[24]

18 Ibid, para 69.
19 Ibid, para 72.
20 *Volks*, above (n 12) para 45.
21 Ibid, para 64.
22 Ibid, para 66.
23 Ibid, para 68.
24 Ibid, para 106.

The dissent also points to the historical failure to recognize marriages solemnized by customary law and by the principles of Islam or Hinduism and asserts the

> constitutional prescript that families that are established outside of civilly recognized marriages should not be subjected to unfair discrimination.[25].... In our view, [the court's judgment] defeats the important constitutional purpose played by the prohibition of discrimination on the grounds of marital status.[26]

Rather than dismissing women's vulnerability, they argue its relevance. They describe the status of cohabiting women under common law showing, they assert

> that cohabiting partners are a vulnerable group, and that in the absence of any other forms of legal regulation, the fact that they are excluded from the provisions of section 2(1) [the section of the Act under consideration] can have a grave impact on the interests of cohabiting partners.[27]

Under the circumstances in the case before them, where there was a permanent life partnership in which the parties had undertaken mutual duties of support, and one in which the pattern of vulnerability and dependence had been established, where the surviving partner is in need and there has been no equitable distribution to the surviving spouse from the estate of the deceased spouse, 'exclusion from the provision of section 2(1) can have a grave impact'. Furthermore:

> It is our conclusion that, in the absence of any regulation in such circumstances, the effect of limiting the scope of section 2(1) to married spouses only will constitute unfair discrimination under section 9(3) of the Constitution.[28]

The cited section of the Constitution prohibits direct or indirect unfair discrimination based on marital status:[29]

> It is not clear why marriage only need be protected ... To the extent that the purpose of providing legal protection to a surviving spouse but not to a surviving cohabitant might be to preserve the religious attributes of marriage, this cannot be an acceptable purpose in terms of our Constitution ... While marriage plays an important role in our society, and most religions cherish it, the Constitution does not permit rights to be limited solely to advance a particular religious perspective.[30]

[25] Ibid, para 107.
[26] Ibid, para 118.
[27] Ibid, para 132.
[28] Ibid.
[29] The Constitution of the Republic of South Africa 1996, Act 108 of 1996.
[30] *Volks*, above (n 12) para 119.

5.3. *Masiya v Director of Public Prosecution Pretoria*

The facts in the case are that Masiya anally penetrated a nine-year-old girl without her consent. He could not be charged with rape because the common law definition included only non-consensual vaginal penetration. Instead he was charged with indecent assault, an offence carrying a lesser penalty. The questions before the Court were, whether to broaden the definition of rape to include anal penetration; whether the definition should be gender neutral (that is, whether it should include males as well as females); and whether these matters properly belong in the courts rather than in the legislature.

Justice Nkabinde wrote the majority opinion which Jutices Mokgoro and O'Regan also signed. She starts with an account of the changes in the understanding of laws regarding rape from its intent to protect the economic interests of the father, husband or guardian of the female; to perpetuate stereotypes, male dominance and power; and to perceive females as objects.[31]

With the advent of our constitutional dispensation based on democratic values of human dignity, equality and freedom, the social foundation of these rules has disappeared ... In South Africa now the 'focus is on the breach of a more specific right such as the right to bodily integrity' and security of the person and the right to be protected from degradation and abuse. The crime of rape should therefore be seen in that context.[32]

She sees no distinction between non-consensual vaginal and anal penetration in that both constitute

> a form of violence ... equal in intensity and impact ... The object of the criminalisation of this act is to protect the dignity, sexual autonomy and privacy of women and young girls as being generally the most vulnerable group in line with the values enshrined in the Bill of Rights—a cornerstone of our democracy.[33]

She declines to consider whether rape should be defined as gender-neutral because the facts in the *Masiya* case do not deal with this. That issue will be dealt with, she asserts, either by the legislature or by the courts 'when the circumstances make it appropriate and necessary to do so'.[34] It is inappropriate in this case for the court to rule because 'the development of common law ... is a power ... always vested in our courts ... exercised in an incremental fashion as the facts of each case require'.[35]

[31] *Masiya*, above (13) para 24.
[32] Ibid, para 25.
[33] Ibid, para 37.
[34] Ibid, para 30.
[35] Ibid.

Chief Justice Pius Langa concurs with the majority's extended definition of rape but dissents on the failure to extend the definition to include males. His reasoning is that the problem is about gender and not about males and females:[36]

> [T]he groups of men who are most often the survivors of rape, young boys, prisoners and homosexuals, are, like women, also vulnerable groups in our society. Moreover, they, and most other male victims, are raped precisely because of the gendered nature of the crime. They are dominated in the same manner and for the same reason that women are dominated; because of a need for male gender-supremacy. That they lack a vagina does not make the crime of male rape any less gender-based.[37]

He argues that both male and female victims are similarly situated and should be treated alike. In my view, to do otherwise fails to give full effect to the constitutional values of dignity, equality and freedom: dignity through recognition of a violation; equality through equal recognition of that violation; and freedom as rape negates not only dignity, but bodily autonomy. All these concerns apply equally to men and women and necessitate a definition that is gender-neutral concerning victims.[38]

He further argues that failure to extend the definition harms women:

> The unintended effect is to enforce the subordinate social position of women which informed the very patriarchy we are committed to uproot. The social reality of women cannot be ignored, but we should be wary not to worsen it.[39]

He responds to Justice Nkabinde's embrace of judicial restraint that although the particular survivor in this case was a female, the case is not about the sex of the victim but about gender and how we understand rape. Extending the definition to male survivors therefore goes no further than is absolutely necessary to cure the defect I have found in the common law. Even if this may be a slight departure from the facts of the case, it is not unusual for this Court to give orders, either when developing the common law or determining the validity of statutes that go beyond the exact facts but are necessitated by the underlying constitutional principles involved.[40]

His departure from Justices Nkabinde, Mokgoro and O'Regan might be considered by many to reflect a more inclusive feminist position. Or might it relate somehow to his gender?

[36] Ibid, para 77.
[37] Ibid, para 86.
[38] Ibid, para 80.
[39] Ibid, para 85.
[40] Ibid, para 90.

6. DID THE WOMEN MAKE A DIFFERENCE IN CASES INVOLVING WOMEN'S ISSUES?

Did the women justices make a difference in cases involving women's issues? The answer is clearly 'yes'. The Constitutional Court considered three cases of particular relevance to women—*Jordan*, *Volks* and *Masiya* previously identified. The women were vocal in 100 per cent of these.

The affirmative response applies even in *Jordan* and *Robinson* in which the women's opinions failed to persuade their colleagues. Their dissents, like dissents from judges in the courts of other countries, do matter. As so persuasively pointed out by Marie-Claire Belleau and Rebecca Johnson in their study of dissents by the Supreme Court of Canada's female and male Justices:

> While a dissent is not, strictly speaking, 'the law', the fact that the substance of the dissenting opinion is produced by a judge is a matter of some significance. This makes a dissenting opinion significantly different from other attempts to persuade or convince. A dissenter has the ability to force the majority to respond, to answer, to explain, to shift or to accommodate. The words of a dissenting opinion are a direct challenge, and the majority may feel required to enter into dialogue. And even where a majority does not respond directly, the very fact of the dissent often means that the majority reasons must be written differently than they would have been in its absence (2008: 59).

Even if dissents do not constitute 'the law', they provide an authorised judicial space for the articulation and exploration of angles of vision whose public expressions are sometimes denied, concealed or silenced (Belleau and Johnson, 2008: 68).

Citing examples, they further remind us that some dissents, 'with time, successfully bring about change in the law; courts may explicitly revisit particular problems, expressly overturning the law, and adopt what had formerly been a dissenting view', and others become the motivation and basis for legislative action (Belleau and Johnson, 2008: 59). In summary, dissents are important.

How much difference these women made in these cases cannot be quantified. Perhaps they provided a weightier dissent for the record than would have occurred had they not been there or they provided views that now are there to be adopted at a later time. In *Van der Merwe*, a case referred to below, the court's judgment cites Justice Mokgoro's dissenting reasoning from another case, as dispositive of an issue before the court.

How much difference these women made in the Masiya case, where they were in the majority and where the court's opinion was even written by one of the women justices, also cannot be quantified. Interviews with their colleagues at the time might be helpful but absent that information it is enough to point to the facts that they were there; their voices were heard; their votes counted.

7. WHEN WOMEN'S ISSUES WERE NOT BEFORE THEM

While agreeing in cases in which women's issues or concerns were raised, the women Justices disagreed when other matters came before them. This conforms to the study by Belleau and Johnson. Their study of dissent among the Supreme Court of Canada Justices also involved three women. Belleau and Johnson found when they counted the dissents for each of that court's nine justices, the three women topped the list in number of dissents (2008: 60). They cite other studies of these three women which show that they 'were as likely to disagree with their female as with their male colleagues' (2008: 62). Belleau and Johnson conclude 'One could be forgiven for ironically responding with the observation that, whether or not women judges will make a difference, it appears that they will certainly differ' (2008: 61).

The three women on the South African Constitutional Court did certainly differ. They differed regarding the outcome in five of the 130 cases examined; in another ten cases they differed on the reasoning, though agreed on the outcome.

The issues considered were wide ranging. In the five cases in which they disagreed on the outcome the issues included:

- criminal procedure;[41]
- voter registration documentation;[42]
- constitutional applicability to private arbitration;[43]
- property confiscation;[44] and
- legislative regulation of the private security industry.[45]

In the cases where they agreed on the outcome but differed on the reasoning, the issues were equally wide ranging. They covered:

- Electoral Commission decisions;[46]
- court procedures in 'vexatious' litigation;[47]

[41] *S v Manamela and Another* [2000] ZACC 5; 2000 (3) SA 1 (CC).

[42] *New National Party v Government of Republic of South Africa and Others* [1999] ZACC 5; 1999 (3) SA 191 (CC).

[43] *Lufuno Mphaphuli & Associates (Pty) Ltd v Andrews and Another* [2009] ZACC 6; 2009 (4) SA 529 (CC).

[44] *Van der Merwe and Another v Taylor NO and Others* [2007] ZACC 16; 2008 (1) SA 1 (CC).

[45] *Bertie Van Zyl (Pty) Ltd and Another v Minister for Safety and Security and Others* [2009] ZACC 11; 2010 (2) SA 181 (CC).

[46] *Premier of the Western Cape v The Electoral Commission and Another* [1999] ZACC 6; 1999 (11) BCLR 1209 (CC).

[47] *Beinash and Another v Ernst & Young and Others* [1998] ZACC 19; 1999 (2) SA 91 (CC).

- the constitutional compliance of a Regional Council's provisions;[48]
- property vesting from solvent to insolvent spouses;[49]
- advance payment requirements for water services;[50]
- review procedures for immigrants facing deportation;[51]
- self-incriminating evidence in administrative procedures;[52]
- the constitutionality of two criminal procedure provisions;[53]
- the constitutionality of presidential pardons for mothers but not fathers;[54] and
- the constitutionality of imprisoning an uncooperative witness.[55]

8. VOICES OF DISAGREEMENT

To hear the Justices' 'voices' where they disagreed, their words in *Van der Merwe and Another v Taylor and Others*[56] case are offered.

The issue in *Van der Merwe* was whether currency seizure constituted arbitrary deprivation of property. Justice Nkabinde wrote the majority opinion, Justice O'Regan wrote a concurring opinion and Justice Mokgoro dissented. As in most of the cases considered in this study, *Van der Merwe* poses a number of issues. In *Van der Merwe* one of the issues in dispute was whether the Court should consider the case at all; the other issues related to the seizure of money found in Van der Merwe's luggage when he was about to leave South Africa to join his family and friends for a vacation and his subsequent arrest. He had failed to file a declaration required when moving money out of the country and, in addition, the amount he was removing exceeded the amount permitted.

The initial question with which the Justices disagreed was whether the Court should consider the case at all. The Court did grant leave to appeal; Justice O'Regan disagreed:

> I do not conclude that the legal principle relied on by the majority is incorrect ... It relates to an important remedy of the common law, which should ordinarily

[48] *African National Congress v Minister of Local Government and Housing, Kwazulu-Natal and Others* [1998] ZACC 2; 1998 (3) SA 1 (CC).

[49] *Harksen v Lane NO and Others* [1997] ZACC 12; 1998 (1) SA 30 (CC).

[50] *Mazibuko and Others v City of Johannesburg and Others* [2009] ZACC 28; 2010 (4) SA 1 (CC).

[51] *Koyabe and Others v Minister for Home Affairs and Others* [2009] ZACC 23; 2010 (4) SA 327 (CC).

[52] *Ferreira v Levin NO and Others; Vryenhoek and Others v Powell NO and Others* [1995] ZACC 13; 1996 (1) SA 984 (CC).

[53] *S v Coetze and Others* [1997] ZACC 2; 1997 (3) SA 527 (CC).

[54] *President of the Republic of South Africa and Another v Hugo* [1997] ZACC 4; 1997 (4) SA 1 (CC).

[55] *De Lange v Smuts NO and Others* [1998] ZACC 6; 1998 (3) SA 785 (CC).

[56] *Van der Merwe*, above (n 45).

first be determined by the Supreme Court of Appeal. There are, too, other legal issues which may well be relevant ... upon which we have not had the benefit of argument.[57]

In my view, these complex and difficult legal issues upon which neither we, nor the courts below, have had the benefit of argument indicate that it is not in the interests of justice for this Court to entertain this appeal.[58]

Accordingly, I would refuse to grant leave to appeal. In summary, I would emphasize that it is undesirable for this Court to decide important and complex issues of the common law as a court of first and final instance, and especially ... where the issues have not been properly ventilated on the pleadings or in argument.[59]

This matter aside, all the Justices agreed that he owned a portion of the money, but disagreed as to whether he owned the rest. Also in dispute was whether the theory that property must be returned to the rightful owner applied in this case.

In the opinion written for the court by Justice Nkabinde and one other Justice, they held he was not the rightful owner of the disputed amount, but merely a custodian because he claimed he held the money on behalf of the family members he was attempting to join. The opinion also supported the State's justification that it needed to hold the money as evidence in the criminal case:

The applicants ... [ie Van der Merwe and another] have established ownership of [the portion of the money]. However, the applicants have not shown that they are the owners of the [total amount] and, what is more, they have not shown that the respondents are not entitled to hold the amount seized pending an order of disposal at the end of the criminal trial.[60]

Justice Mokgoro, in dissent, argued that the case should have been heard and, further, that the money should be returned to Van der Merwe. Her dissent builds on the Constitution's protection against arbitrary deprivation of property:

Once the state seizes private property as it did in this case, and the legal basis for the seizure and holding is in dispute, the question of arbitrary deprivation of property under ... the Constitution is clearly implicated, making the matter intrinsically a constitutional one.[61]

[57] Ibid, para 100.
[58] Ibid, para 102.
[59] Ibid, para 103.
[60] Ibid, para 137.
[61] Ibid, para 20.

Justice Mokgoro elaborated on the importance of checking arbitrary police action by connecting it to the injustices of the apartheid past:

> In this constitutional era, where the constitution envisages a public administration which is efficient, equitable, ethical, caring and accountable and respectful of fundamental rights, the execution of public power is subject to constitutional values. Section 195 ['Basic values and principles governing public administration'] reinforce these constitutional ideals. It contemplates a public service in the broader context of transformation as envisaged in the Constitution and aims to reverse the disregard, disdain and indignity with which the public in general had been treated by the administration in the past. Section 195 envisions that a public service reminiscent of that era has no place in our constitutional democracy. The remissness on the part of the [South African Police Service] is not conducive to the current effort of public service transformation. It must certainly be discouraged.[62]

There was another partial dissent but the dissenter does take Mokgoro's high ground.

9. WHAT CAN BE SAID?

This study—which was based on cases in which the women expressed agreement and disagreement—considered only a percentage of the total 356 cases decided by the Court. In the cases not examined there were permutations, with one or more of the women Justices joining their male colleagues in majority opinions, concurring opinions and dissents, though their views were not separately expressed.

What does the study show? It shows that each of the women Justices was a fully participating member of the Court. If there were to be another study counting each of the male Justices' records in authoring the majority, concurring and dissenting opinions, it would—based on my cursory examination—confirm this.

On women's issues, these women did, and certainly sought to make a difference. They provided perspectives and arguments that would otherwise have been weaker or absent. In the *Jordan* and *Volks* cases, in which only Justice Sachs also dissented, they strengthened the weight of the losing arguments advancing a women's rights perspective. In *Masiya*, the third case involving an issue of concern to women, where all but one of the men signed onto the majority opinion written by Justice Nkabinde, it would not be unreasonable to credit them with influencing some of their male colleagues. Here, again, interviews with the men on the bench would be informative. But absent this source of information, the way in which the

[62] Ibid, para 72.

Constitutional Court considers cases lends weight to that likelihood as at the Constitutional Court, the Justices when in conference thoroughly discuss the cases before them. Justice Mokgoro, in *Courting Justice*, identifies these discussions as critically important. The Justices also circulate opinion drafts to all their colleagues and receive strengthening comments, even from those who have expressed opposing views.

On all other matters, they did not speak with one voice. The women Justices, like their male colleagues, bring all they know and all that they have experienced to their understanding of the issues before them. Justice Mokgoro's reminder in *Van der Merwe* of the property seizure experiences during apartheid speaks loudly to this. While many within and outside South Africa without doubt see only that they are women—gender being all they see—they are women who are educated in the law, intelligent and articulate and who bring expertise in areas of law, who were engaged in the struggle for democracy and who are members of families and of communities and much more. On 'hearing their voices' one must see they are not one-dimensional, that they are not single minded and that they see through many lenses. Their fullness must surely be taken into account when considering their contributions as Jurists. The totality of their knowledge and experience—which includes but is not confined to knowledge and experience which informs them on matters of concern to women—has been and continues to be important to the development of South Africa's new jurisprudence. Surely this is significant.

10. REFERENCES

Belleau, M-C and Johnson, R (2008) 'Judging Gender: Difference and Dissent at the Supreme Court of Canada' 15(1–2) *International Journal of the Legal Profession* 57.

Courting Justice (2008) at www.courtingjustice.com.

Rickard, C, 'Judging Women Harshly' *Sunday Times* (23 October 2005) 21.

Yutar, D, 'Judging those who would be judged' *Sunday Argus* (10 April 2005) 18.

Part 4

Gendered Construction of Judges

4.1

'May it Please the Court'. Forming Sexualities as Judicial Virtues in Judicial Swearing-in Ceremonies

LESLIE J MORAN

Abstract

This chapter explores sexuality and gender of the judiciary by way of a case study of the texts of public swearing-in ceremonies of the Supreme Court of New South Wales, Australia. I first came across this data on the Court's website, where digital copies are published. Pre mid-1990 examples were found in the press files of the judiciary stored in the Court's law library. The sample used in this chapter is taken from the years 1973 to 2008. The texts have much in common. They have a common purpose and structure. They record a ceremony dedicated to 'welcoming' the newly-appointed judge that is made up of the swearing of oaths followed by a number of speeches. The speeches are a form of 'life writing': of biography and autobiography. As textual portraits of state officials their hagiographic style has the purpose of identifying and mapping the personal and professional qualities of the subject onto the newly-made judicial subject. They formulate and fashion the subject as the embodiment of judicial virtues. The objective of this chapter is through the lens of queer theory, to offer a reading of these texts exploring the formation of sexuality as judicial virtues.

1. FORMING SEXUALITIES AS JUDICIAL VIRTUES—A CASE STUDY

THIS CHAPTER EXPLORES the sexuality and gender of the judiciary by way of a case study of the texts of public swearing-in ceremonies of the Supreme Court of New South Wales, Australia. I first came across this data on the Court's website, where digital copies are published. Pre mid-1990 examples were found in the press files of the judiciary stored in the Court's law library. The sample used in this chapter is taken from the years 1973 to 2008. The texts have much in common. Each is made up of a number of speeches of key legal figures (the Attorney General (or his appointee), President of the Bar Association, President of the Law Society) with a reply by the new judge. They record ceremonial events, variously described as 'civic occasions' (Spigelman, 1998: 6), a 'ceremony of welcome' (Loxton, 1973: 5), a 'celebration' (Macken, 2008: 7) that take place in the Banco Court, the largest, most elaborately and expensively furnished court in the Supreme Court building, in Sydney. The face-to-face audience is fellow judges of the Supreme Court, judges from other courts, men and women of the legal profession and friends and family of the new judge. Technology, the printing press and now digitalisation,[1] potentially enhance the public nature of these events[2] though it remains the case that the audience is predominantly a 'legal audience' (Allsop, 2008: 11).

The texts demonstrate a remarkable consistency of general content and tone. They take the form of what might best be described as life writing (biography) that has a strong hagiographic quality. The speeches have a double function formulating and fashioning the subject not only as an exemplary individual life, but as an exemplary life that embodies the virtues of the judicial institution. As such, the speeches are a very specific form of life writing, being biographical accounts dedicated to the portrayal of state officials (Moran, 2008; 2009). The new appointee's response in the first instance is somewhat different, being a statement of thanks; but it also has strong life-writing qualities (this time autobiographical). As explained by one of the newly-appointed judges, 'Preparing [the speech] was like preparing my own eulogy' (Fullerton, 2007: 6). Like the speeches that precede it, the response has a double function as a form of textual self-fashioning that is also an institutional self-fashioning. Each swearing-in document offers a textual portrait that makes, and makes public, the values and virtues of the institution of the judge. The primary objective of this chapter is to explore how, if at all, sexuality is made in these texts and, more specifically, how the subject's sexuality is figured as an institutional ideal, as a judicial virtue, in this important public setting. In undertaking this task the analysis will also examine some aspects of the role of gender in the formation of the judicial subject as a sexual subject. One tool that has been invaluable in undertaking this project is queer theory. I begin with a few words about aspects of queer theory that helped to make sense of the gaps and silences that emerged as a recurring theme in my early research (Moran, 2006). Thereafter, I use these insights to examine and analyse the formation and operation of sexuality in the judicial institution.

A key insight from queer theory is that sexuality is a matter of 'culture' (Berlant and Warner, 1998: 548, fn 2) a 'sexual regime'. Seidman describes

[1] Post-1998 swearing-in texts are published on the website of the Court. The pre-1998 texts are in the Court's law library filed under the judge's name.

[2] Technology also transforms the interaction from face-to-face to mediated 'quasi-interactions' (Mawby, 2002: 73).

it as, 'a field of sexual meanings, discourses and practices that are interlaced with social institutions and movements' (1994: 169). As such, sexuality, Berlant and Warner explain, is always in play. It is always in public. Thus, the perceived and proposed absence of sexuality from the institution of the judiciary in general, and judicial diversity debates in particular, needs to be treated with considerable caution. More specifically, a requirement to be silent about sexuality is not the absence or disappearance of sexuality from individual and institutional relations and settings, but a key dimension of its mode of public appearance and operation.

Under the conditions of heteronormativity, silence is a device by which sexuality appears in public. More specifically it is one of the devices through which heterosexuality as the norm is reproduced in society in general and, I want to suggest, in the institution of the judiciary in particular. Sexuality in general, and gay or lesbian sexuality in particular, is not so much a troubling new addition, a threatening invasion, an inappropriate incivility or an irrelevant matter in judicial settings. It is always already a very public and relevant dimension of the institution of the judiciary.

Silence, absence and invisibility, all play a key role in the public fabrication of the heterosexual as privileged sexual subject. It is as the unmarked that heterosexuality is fashioned as the basic idiom of the personal, and the social. Heterosexuality is in some respects like the air we breathe—a diffuse all-pervasive presence (a sense of rightness) but at the same time out of mind, unnoticed, unrecognisable, often unconscious, and immanent to practice or to the institutions.

The attribution of absence to the pervasive presence of heterosexuality plays a central role in linking certain qualities and values to that subject's position. One characteristic attributed to heterosexuality as the unmarked is that of 'a state of nature'. This gives rise to a multitude of positive connotations; truth, self-denying, unaffected, unprejudiced, impersonal, and so on. Another is the link between heterosexuality and the ideal. And another is the assumption that heterosexuality is the very pinnacle of moral accomplishment. In short, the heteronormative regime produces heterosexuality as a rather paradoxical phenomenon, which is always present and generating a superabundance of meaning while at the same time being absent.

Thinking sexuality as a regime or culture, rather than an identity, requires us to recognise the diffusion of heterosexuality: it has no centre. There is no singular moment of operation or final moment of realisation. But its social, temporal and spatial diffusion potentially makes it much more difficult to recognise its forms of operation (Berlant and Warner, 1998: 556). At best, Berlant and Warner suggest, it is never more than a fragile, provisional unity. Finally, the study of heteronormative culture requires that we take seriously 'the metacultural work of the very category of heterosexuality'. As Berlant and Warner explain, this works to consolidate 'as a sexuality widely differing practices, norms and institutions' (1998: 553). In response, sensitivity is needed both to the way the purported totality of heterosexuality fashions and displays cohesion and singularity and to the way in which, at the same time, it marks and exposes its fragility. With all these thoughts in mind let me return to the data: the swearing-in texts.

The key finding arising from my analysis of the judicial swearing-in texts is that sexuality is not so much purely personal or private or extrajudicial and thereby missing from these textual renditions of the judicial institution, but an ever present and enduring feature in the texts and their depiction of the judicial institution and its office holders.

It appears perhaps most obviously in biographical and autobiographical references to the judicial subject's family. For example, at the ceremony to swear in Justice Priestley, Attorney General Landa commented, 'Perhaps the most outstanding characteristics you have exhibited are intellectual honesty and a deep and abiding devotion to your family' (Landa, 1983: 5). While there is no further information about the nature of this family, under conditions of heteronormativity current assumptions and expectations make it heterosexual by the very absence of a reference to sexuality. In an example taken from the following year, the swearing-in of Justice Ash, the heterosexual nature of the family is more explicitly stated: 'The step your Honour has taken is a major one ... for your Honour, but it is also an important one in the lives of your Honour's family—Mrs Ash especially and your four children' (Loxton, 1975: 8). The appearance of the family and family values in a hagiographic text devoted to writing the life of the subject as the embodiment of the qualities of judicial office is far from arbitrary. They are chosen to shape the subject's individual *and* official persona in the image of the virtues of the institution. Within the confines of this short chapter I offer only one analysis of this in action. In 2008 at the swearing-in of Justice Allsop as President of the Court of Appeal, the Attorney General explains: 'One central aspect of your life which has not been mentioned is your devotion to your children ... and your wife' (Hatzistergos, 2008: 5). The identification of 'devotion', as a personal virtue of the hetero-familial subject is at the same time the fashioning of that subject as the embodiment of a virtue of the judicial institution; a devotion to the law.

Another family also haunts these texts. This second family is the sum total of the social relations that make up the professional life of the subject that reaches its apotheosis in the appointment to judicial office. In some instances, the connection between the biological domestic family and the social (professional) family is literal: the two families coincide.[3] Space

[3] See Mendelsohn and Lippman (1979) and Thornton (1996) for research that takes note of the coincidence of biological domestic family and legal business organisations in Australia. See also Galanter and Roberts (2008) who explore the same issues in a UK context.

permits but one example. In the case of Justice Clarke, the President of the Law Society explained: 'Your Honour is one of a long line in the legal profession ... your grandfather was a solicitor ... subsequently a leading member of the Tasmanian Bar ... your Honour's father was called to the Bar in London' (McLachlan, 1983: 4). Again in the absence of explicit reference to the sexuality of these familial relations (both biological/domestic and professional) the assumption and expectation is that they are heterosexual. The coincidence facilitates the mapping of the virtues of the biological/domestic hetero-family directly onto the family that is the profession that generates and nurtures the embryonic judicial subject.

While the literal coincidence of the biological and professional families may be in decline, the connection between the biological and the social family thrives by way of metaphor. The biographical and autobiographical accounts are littered with references to the metaphorical familial ties that bind the individual subject to the legal professional family. One example is Justice Fullerton's reference to fellow judges as, 'my sister and brother judges' (2007: 6) Within the hagiographic context of swearing-in statements familial metaphors catalogue the brilliant history and successful nature of the incumbent's relationship with key family members: judges, barristers, solicitors, clerks. One important family moment that is cited again and again is intimacy between the new incumbent and now senior judges who occupy the role of 'mentor'. As the Attorney General explained at the swearing-in of Justice Priestley: 'It must be of singular pleasure to you, Chief Justice, that his Honour was the first person to read with you when you were in fact junior counsel ... he could not have had a better mentor' (Landa, 1983: 2). Another is participation in family gatherings: professional committees. The swearing-in speeches of Justice Ruth McColl, the second woman to be appointed to a position in the Court of Appeal, offer an extreme example of this. They record her 20-year membership of the Bar Council, during the course of which she was secretary (from 1987 to 1994), treasurer (from 1995 to 1997), vice president (1998 and 1999) and the first woman president (2000 and 2001). For 16 years she served as a member of the Ethics and Public Professional Conduct committees. From 1985 to 1997 she edited *Bar News*. This far from exhaustive list (McColl, 2003) offers some evidence of what Thornton describes as the 'feminist truism that for a woman to succeed she has to be better than her male counterparts'(1996: 402) A third type of family moment regularly cited in these texts is participation in manly sports with other legal colleagues, 'tennis' (Landa, 1983: 2) 'rugby' (North, 2000: 3) 'cricket' (Gaudron, 1983: 2; Harrison, 2004: 2) and 'golf' (Gaudron, 1983: 2; Barker, 1999a: 2).[4]

[4] This is the one family sporting event that crosses the gender divide.

The family metaphors take a slightly different turn in the following comment on the professional life of the new appointee Mr Justice Meagher, by the President of the Law Society. He declared:, 'I must express the view that you have been in love not only with the law, but also with the Bar and its traditions, its camaraderie, its pursuit of excellence and the skills of advocacy' (Thornton, 1989: 8). Here sentimental romantic characteristics commonly associated with the hetero-familial are mapped onto the professional world. Justice Simpson gives a slightly different spin (and more specifically a gendered spin) to being in love with the law and the Bar. In her reply to the welcoming speeches she explained that 'appointment to this, or any other court ... was properly seen as the last stage of a legal career—the professional equivalent of marriage' (1994: 12–13).

I want to linger a little longer over Justice Simpson's use of the metaphor of 'marriage' to consider its sexual connotations. Let me begin with a few general observations on the term 'marriage'. Judith Butler describes marriage as a relation of kinship and more particularly as a recognisable form of kinship that organises sexuality 'in the service of reproductive relations' (2002: 14). The legal status of marriage, she explains, gives this mode of sexual reproductive kinship a privileged status. Where same-sex reproductive relations are excluded from the legal definition of 'marriage' the latter is made to stand for reproductive relations as heterosexual.

Its metaphorical use to describe professional relations in this context highlights their kinship qualities. Legal professional social relations fit neatly into Butler's definition of 'kinship', which goes as follows. Kinship is

> a set of practices that institutes relationships of various kinds which negotiate reproduction of life and the demands of death ... kinship practices will be those that emerge to address fundamental forms of human dependency, which may include birth, child-rearing, relations of emotional dependency and support, generational ties ... (to name a few) (2002: 15).

Justice Simpson's use of the marriage metaphor not only highlights the way legal professional relations are understood and experienced as relations of reproductive kinship, but figures reproductive kinship in a particularly sexed and gendered context: male and female.[5] But to assume that the reproductive kinship of the legal profession is organised in this gendered way is premature. What is the sexed nature of the legal profession as

[5] The gender aspects of this metaphor are also relevant. 'Marriage' is a metaphor that describes the gendered terms under which women may access the male dominated institution of the judiciary. Also marriage not only gives access (sometimes limited) to a man and his capital (and to the world of men) but potentially results in the further confinement of women to the margins (in the domestic sphere) to do labour that is poorly valued effectively excluding women from the key male institutions.

reproductive kinship and more specifically how does it fashion the sexuality of the judiciary?

While neither branch of the legal profession (solicitors or barristers) nor the judiciary can continue to be defined by terms such as 'fraternity' or 'brotherhood', as single sex/gender—male/masculine organisations (Thornton, 1996) it has been and it still remains the case that men dominate legal professional kinship relations. Where men occupy all or the key positions, legal professional kinship reproduction is not hetero-sexed but homo (same) sex reproduction. This draws attention to another key dimension of the swearing-in texts: they represent legal professional kinship reproduction as same-sex (male-male) reproduction.

The judiciary are born to the legal professional family that is a family without women (Lipman-Blumen, 1976: 30). Men turn to men to negotiate all the key stages in the production and reproduction of legal professional life: economic, social, intellectual, emotional, physical. Men, in a variety of caring and nurturing roles (as teachers, pupil masters, heads of chambers, judicial mentors, clerks etc) play the dominant role in legal institutional reproduction (both professional and judicial). In the overwhelming majority of the speeches relating to male members of the judiciary the role of women in professional reproduction is formally abolished. When women do appear in the texts of male appointees, and they always do, their role is formally outside the professional family, confined to that other realm: domestic/biological reproduction. And when women do appear in the professional context they occupy 'reproductive' and 'domestic' roles, valued as marginal to the real business of the profession (as secretaries), performing menial tasks supporting the male legal professional/judicial office holder (Whealy, 2000: 5).

In thinking through the implications that same-sexed (male-male) reproduction raises for the sexual fashioning of the judicial subject, I want to turn to work on homosociality. Homosociality, Eve Sedgwick's explains,

> is a word occasionally used in history and the social sciences, where it describes social bonds between persons of the same sex; it is a neologism, obviously formed by analogy with 'homosexual' and just as obviously is meant to be distinguished from 'homosexual'. In fact, it is applied to such activities as 'male bonding', which may, as in our society, be characterized by intense homophobia, fear and hatred of homosexuality. To draw the 'homosocial' back into the orbit of 'desire' … is to hypothesize the potential unbrokenness of a continuum between homosocial and homosexual—a continuum whose visibility, for men in our society, is radically disrupted (1985: 1–2).

I resort to Sedgwick's 'homosocial' not to put genital homosexual relations at the root of other forms of male homosociality, but to draw attention to the significance of same-sex desire in professional reproduction and to highlight one of the effects this has on sexuality in that context; the production and reproduction of a demand for the radical dislocation of genital homosexual relations. In short, the institutionalisation of homosocial desire in professional kinship relations of reproduction works to secure the sexual culture of those same-sex professional relations as formally exclusively heterosexual. Resort to those professional kinship relations in the public formation of the subject's judicial qualities and virtues, is a means by which the sexual virtues of the judicial subject are also formed as heterosexual.

Same-sex professional reproduction is not a kinship theme unique to male judges. Female same-sex professional reproduction is a theme in speeches relating to female judges. Its importance is noted by the female judges, as well as by the other (male) speakers. But my preliminary analysis would tentatively suggest that it is wrong to merely conclude that reproductive kinship associated with female judicial appointees is a mirror image of that long associated with men.[6]

Justice Carolyn Chalmers Simpson was one of the first women appointed to the bench of the Supreme Court. The kinship theme in her speech opens with the following remark: 'I have reached the point at which thank yous are delivered to parents, spouses and children. I have none of these' (1994: 15). While not literally the case, this comment can perhaps best be understood in relation to the tragic loss of her mother when she was young and the time she spent away from the domestic world of the biological family, in school. Perhaps more significantly, it tends to emphasise the career importance of that 'other' family: the professional family. What reference does she make to that family? A distinctive aspect of her speech thanks 'those many women who have preceded me in the legal profession' (Simpson, 1994: 15) and singles out Jan Joy (her clerk in chambers) and her secretary, Julie Briese. A key difference between male judicial colleagues contemporary with Justice Simpson is not just that she mentions these women but that these women do not occupy elite roles. These are women on the margins of the legal professional world. In later examples the women cited are more likely to occupy elite positions: as judges, senior legal characters, who are mentors. For example, Justice Bell cites Justice Matthews, Justice Gaudron, Justice O'Connor, Justice Simpson, as important female figures, 'not just because they have served as role models ... but particularly for their personal qualities of unfailing warmth and support for women members of the profession'. She concludes: 'I have been a beneficiary' (Bell, 1999: 3). Another difference between male and female appointees is that while the swearing-in speeches of male judges continue to record the importance of same-sex reproduction (that persists in excluding or marginalising women) the biographical accounts of female appointees refer to both men and

[6] For commentary and insights on female same-sex reproductive legal professional kinship networks in Australia see Thornton (1996).

women. In good part men appear as key players in kinship reproduction as of necessity, they still control access and resources. But there is a need to be open to the possibility of a different reading; of a mode of hetero-social reproductive kinship. Heterosociality refers to an organisation of social relations that resists or refuses exclusively male social interactions and is made up of 'non sexual attractions held by men (or women) for members of the other sex' (Bird, 1996: 121, 127). However, there is yet scant evidence that such a transformation is operating in a legal professional context in general or a judicial context in particular.

If the analysis offered so far paints a picture of the cohesion and the singularity of the sexual virtues of the judicial subject made under the conditions of heteronormativity, then I must also add that the data offers evidence of a more diffuse and multiple heterosexuality and a heterosexuality that is more fragile. Let me begin by drawing on comments Justice Meagher made in his response to the usual laudatory biographical speeches that preceded his reply. He begins in familiar terms: 'Finally I must thank my wife and daughter'. But his comments then break with convention. He thanks them 'for performing handsomely the tasks for which they as women were designed; namely to provide me with domestic comfort; and also for their fortitude in embracing the new challenge which confronts them—to supply me with financial assistance' (Meagher, 1989: 11). How are we to make sense of this chilling celebration of the marginal, subordinate and exploited position of the female members of the judge's family? Justice Meagher offers a guide to their meaning. It comes from an observation he makes about the nature of the swearing-in speeches. The generous remarks, central to the hagiographic tone of the speeches, he explains are 'nonsense, ... [f]lattery ... heavily laced with mendacity' (1989: 9). One reading of his harsh and barbed comments about the burdens, trials and tribulations suffered by his wife and daughter is they expose the hagiographic fiction celebrating the domestic family and the role of the wife within it for what it is: a tale of gender exclusion and exploitation. The sentimental romantic family ideal is not the only experience of that institution. And this other experience offers a challenge to it as the metaphorical template for the institutional ideal of judicial office.

Another example that challenges the homogenous sentimental romantic hetero-familial ideal focuses on the impact of career on family. An example comes from the swearing-in of Justice Priestley. The Attorney General begins in the usual way making institutional virtues out of the subject's heterosexual family. As a 'family man' the man/judge is 'dedicated but truly contemporary' (Landa, 1983: 3). The tenor changes a little when he goes on to note the impact of professional life on family life, which takes the form of 'the sacrifice of time available to family and loved ones inherent in any successful and distinguished barrister's life' (1983: 3). The familial/institutional virtues of the hetero-family, as the moral apotheosis, are not so much fully realised in the institution of the judge as threatened by that self-same institution that demands long periods of absence by the father/judge from the biological family. This comment both acknowledges the failings and the fragility of the heterosexual ideal (the threat is connoted by way of the reference to the 'sacrifice of time'—the absent father) that underpin the judicial institution. But at the same time the threat is quickly glossed over and the link between the moral virtues of the heterosexual family and the judicial institution are remade by reference to the pride (the self-awareness of moral superiority) experienced by the family, which follows the elevation of the husband/father to the office of judge. As the Attorney General explains: 'I am confident that they will feel the sacrifice ... has been well rewarded by his appointment' (Landa, 1983: 3). And it is a recuperative theme that has enduring appeal. In the 2008 swearing-in of Justice Allsop the Attorney General explained, 'Your family share in the honour you receive today' (Hatzistergos, 2008: 5).

I now want to consider the texts of the ceremonies of three particular judges; Michael Kirby appointed in 1984 as President of the Court of Appeal, Virginia Bell appointed in 1999 and Justice Elizabeth Fullerton who became a judge of the Supreme Court of New South Wales in 2007. The texts relating to all three are barely distinguishable from all the other texts that make up this case study. The biographical expositions show all the signs of the hagiographic mode of representation noted above. All three are depicted as the embodiment of exemplary legal careers with abundant evidence of investments made in professional relations. Befitting the senior post being occupied by Michael Kirby the Attorney General sums up the new incumbent's glittering career with the comment that 'Few curricula have demonstrated so much *vita*' (Landa, 1984: 3) The usual hyperbolic tone shapes the depiction of their cognitive qualities. Kirby is 'one of the nation's ablest legal minds' (Landa, 1984: 1–2). Bell is 'more skilful and entertaining' than other colleagues at the Bar (Barker, 1999: 1), and Fullerton is 'pre-eminent ... in the present generation' of leading counsel (Slattery, 2007: 1). Their many cultural and emotional qualities coincide with the fundamental qualities of judicial office: erudition, independence, dedication, passion, generosity, fearlessness, to name but a few. What of references to sexuality?

Unsurprisingly references to family appear in all thee cases. One difference in the texts is that in two texts (Kirby and Bell) the domestic family is only mentioned by the judge, maybe in response to the lack of references in the biographical speeches. In all instances where the nature of that family is expanded upon it is by reference to parents, siblings, aunts, nephews. The unspoken of these figures of domestic reproductive kinship is heterosexuality.

References to the other family, the profession as family, are prominent in the biographical speeches and take a familiar form. President Kirby (as he then was) notes the coincidence of the biological and professional families:

'there is my family: a close and loving home environment, whose only error in fact was to spawn so many lawyers' (Kirby, 1984: 13). He also makes use of family as metaphor for the legal profession; his 'original home' is in 'the bosom of the law' (1984: 12). If neither 'family' nor 'home' necessarily excludes his long-time male partner Johan, the absence of a reference to him and the reference to the coincidence of biological and professional families (Kirby's brother is Justice David Kirby a judge of the Supreme Court of New South Wales since 1998) at least formally leaves the heterosexual assumption undisturbed.

There is a noticeable difference in the way reference is made to the familial role of judicial mentor between these three swearing-in texts. In the context of President Kirby, there is no explicit reference to the gender of the reproductive kinship network that he is made a part of. In the biographical and autobiographical accounts relating to the two women, the gender of the professional kinship networks is explicitly stated. If implicitly male same-sex reproductive kinship produces the male judicial subject as heterosexual, there is nothing necessarily in the explicit references to female same-sex reproductive kinship to suggest that these female judges are fashioned sexually as anything other than heterosexual.

So far the biographical and autobiographical fashioning recorded in the texts of the swearing-in ceremonies of Justices Kirby, Bell and Fullerton forms their individual and institutional persona according to the requirements of heterosexuality as a judicial virtue. Is this the end of their sexual formation in that context? The swearing-in texts of both women contain reference to other sexualities. In both instances it occurs by way of a reference to Sydney's gay and lesbian event, *Mardi Gras*. In the case of Justice Bell it is introduced by the President of the Law Society, forming a part of Justice Bell's professional pedigree, as a sign of her exceptional professional qualities. Justice Bell's first professional appointment was as a lawyer with the Redfern Legal Centre, 'a pioneer of the community legal service'. The President of the Law Society continues: 'The centre was known for taking cases that few others would. This includes the now historic civil liberties case involving those arrested at the first Gay Mardi Gras in mid-1978' (Hole, 1999: 2) In the speeches of Justice Fullerton's inauguration it is used to fashion her civic credentials and virtues. The President of the Bar Association explained that Justice Fullerton was 'a director of the Gay and Lesbian Mardi Gras Board and … chaired the Mardi Gras Festival committees' (Slattery, 2007: 4).

I finish with some examples of references that intrigue me. The first is a comment by the Attorney General made during his acclamation of Michael Kirby. It appears in a reference to Kirby's prolific writing, 'a ceaseless production of papers, articles, speeches and reviews'. Commenting on Kirby's preference for using opening quotes, the Attorney General observes: 'the author may remain hidden in the obscurities of erudition'(Landa, 1984: 5). The very public persona produced through his copious scholarship also, this comment suggests, leaves the subject surprisingly hidden from view. The second comment is by the President of the Bar Association in his speech at the ceremony for Justice Bell. He concludes that he 'would have to agree with [Justice Bell's] own assessment of [her personality], you are a very, very private extrovert' and he explains, 'being enigmatic can be an attractive quality in a judge' (Barker, 1999: 2). Last but not least, two extracts relating to Justice Fullerton. Both come from her reply. In closing she thanked her parents for their joint and different wisdom, ethics and their 'approval for the choices I have made in my life'. The second extract refers to hairstyles, and more specifically 'the mullet' haircut and a particular style of men's trousers that long-lingered in the wardrobe of barristers. She explains: 'I was totally uneducated in the codes of decorum expected of a barrister. Losing the mullet came first. Getting morning trousers to fit was next, but I am not sure that I've taken much in since then' (Fullerton, 2007: 7) How are we to make sense of these comments?

Michael Kirby 'came out' as a gay man in 1999, some 15 years after his appointment to the Supreme Court of New South Wales and some three years after leaving that Court to take up an appointment to the High Court of Australia. He announced his long-standing relationship with a man, Johan van Volten, in the pages of the Australian 1999 edition of *Who's Who*. In response to a question I put to him during the course of an interview, 'Would you agree that [1999] was the first moment in your professional life that everybody knew that you were gay?' he replied, 'Certainly not.' He explained, prior to that date:

> It was commonly known that I was homosexual because I had a partner from the 11th of Feb 1969 and lived together with him in the suburbs of Sydney. We lived quite openly. We went shopping and did other things that ordinary people did. Australia is quite a small society, 20 million people, and concentrated in a few cities, therefore I think it was generally known that I was gay. But that was not asserted. Remember, in the early days, from 1969 till 1974, homosexual acts even between consenting adults in private were still illegal ... that was a reason for a certain degree of discretion. As well as that, I'm quite a discrete sort of a person. Most people who end up on the judiciary are.[7]

Justice Virginia Bell has made no formal announcement about her sexuality, however, others have described her as 'an openly lesbian lawyer' (Marsden, 2005: 171), and the entry for her in the free encyclopaedia *Wikipedia* explains (giving newspaper reports as its sources): 'Bell lives in inner Sydney with her female partner, a barrister'.[8] In relation to Justice Elizabeth

[7] Interview with Justice Michael Kirby (22 February 2006). On file with the author.

[8] Anon (undated) 'Virginia Bell' *Wikipedia*: en.wikipedia.org/w/index.php?title=Virginia_Bell.

Fullerton, during the course of an interview I undertook with a district court judge based in Sydney, he described Justice Fullerton's speech as an overt statement of the judge's lesbianism. But can any of the above comments, in the hagiographic context of the swearing-in statements, be read as a reference to a non-heterosexual fashioning of the judicial subject?

In short the answer I offer is 'yes' and 'no'. How written texts were heard cannot be determined (in the still dominant manner of legal analysis) just by carefully reading the text (Sinfield, 1991: 48). It is of central importance to consider who hears and the framework of understanding. The immediate and wider context and the knowledge, history, experience, assumptions and expectations of the audience are also crucial to making sense of the swearing-in ceremony and the biographical and autobiographical objectives that shape the speeches. Justice Kirby, in his *Judicial Farewell*, on retiring from the High Court of Australia offers an example of this:

> On past occasions, when I have come to this point, I have referred to my debt to unnamed 'loved ones'. My fearless sisters-in-law would always dig my partner Johan van Vloten in the ribs to let him know that this was him. He was on (Kirby, 2009: 7).

Kirby's observation suggests that for some, if you were in the know, other sexualities might be not just represented but heard and appreciated even under conditions of censorship and exclusion. His earlier comment that prior to formally coming out many members of the small-knit community of Sydney barristers (and maybe lawyers more generally) knew he was gay might also suggest that the lack of reference to his partner's name in his swearing-in speech in 1984 may have been heard at least by some of the legal community, the main audience for the speeches, as a 'public' reference to his sexuality. For those 'in the know' references to Justice Kirby's tendency for enigmatic quotes, Justice Bell's ability to be a private extrovert may all be heard as references to other sexualities being made into the virtues of judicial office. If, as Kirby has suggested, the times of discretion or secrecy are over (Kirby, 2009: 7) I would suggest that this is a rather naive and too simplistic a position. For example, in presenting this chapter to the audience of scholars at the 'Gender and Judging Workshop' in Onati, my assumption that the mullet haircut was a well-known and very visible sign of lesbian sexuality fell flat.[9] Few knew what a mullet was, never

[9] Under the title *How to know if someone is a lesbian*, 'Step 3 explains, 'Mullet haircuts and hair clipped or shaved close to the head, have been traditional stereotypes for the butch lesbian. This doesn't mean that everyone with the hairstyle is gay, nor does it mean that all lesbians have that type of hairstyle. Female mulletheads wear the look as a symbol'. (eHow Relationships and Family Editor, undated): www.ehow.com/how_2106673_know-someone-lesbian.html.

mind that it was a style of hair associated with a particular sexual political significance.[10] The reference to the mullet suggests that it remains the case that a representation of gay or lesbian sexuality may be both simultaneously open and secret depending on the audience who may be occupying the same space (Sinfield, 1991: 50).

2. CONCLUSIONS

The biographical and autobiographical texts studied here provide ample evidence that sexuality is a very public dimension of the judicial body. Its public formation and display through these ceremonies and the texts that record them is the end-point of an intense process of selection and organisation that shapes sexuality in the service of fashioning the exemplary lives of those who take up judicial office. A study of these texts provides an opportunity to study these public performances through which sexuality is made a virtue of the judicial institution.

The sexual virtue of the institution of the judiciary has long been fashioned (and in many instances continues to be fashioned) as exclusively heterosexual. A perhaps more surprising finding is that central to the achievement of this sexual cultural formation is a set of social relations that I have described as same-sex professional reproduction.

If the illusion is the seamless realisation of heterosexuality as the crowning individual and institutional achievement, there is also evidence of its failure and patterns of hetero-relations that in the shadow of the assumed perfection are dysfunctional. If in the past other sexualities threatened to undermine the hagiographic project of subject/institution formation, then there may be some evidence that this is changing. The general hagiographic project is still in place: the subject must still be fashioned according to the requirements of life-writing and exemplary life and the life of a subject that embodies the elite attributes associated with the institution/office. But, change is taking place. It occurs, this research suggests, through shifts in what might be described as 'minor details' such as a reference to a haircut or involvement with an organisation. But the analysis of these texts also warns against any simplistic assumption that sexuality and sexual difference is reducible to that which is to be found in the performance as a movement from secrecy to full openness and transparency in the text of the swearing-in ceremony. The analysis offered here warns against the 'illusion of immanence'; that the totality of meaning is to be found in the image itself. While what appears in the speech or on the pages of the text is important, the meaning of the

[10] Others drew attention to the fact that in Australia—and Sydney in particular—the mullet haircut has strong social class connotations, being associated with poor working class communities in Sydney's western suburbs.

text is as much a product of the audiences and the social relations that they produce in and through the text. The life-writing of the individual subject/institution does play a key role in making and making public sexuality as a virtue of judicial office, but attempts to make and change the sexual virtues of that institution do not end with that process. They are also made in and through the social relations produced through the face-to-face interactions with the judge and the quasi-interactions with the text.

3. ACKNOWLEDGEMENTS

Special thanks to University of Sydney whose fellowship and funding assisted the early research and to Jenni Millbank and Gail Mason who played a key role in supporting this research.

4. REFERENCES

Allsop, JLB (2008) 'Swearing-in Speech of Allsop P' in *Swearing-in Ceremony of the Honourable James Leslie Bain Allsop as a Judge of the Supreme Court of New South Wales and President of the Court of Appeal of the Supreme Court of New South Wales* (Sydney, Supreme Court NSW).

Barker, I (1999a) 'Swearing in Speech, Ian Barker Esq, QC, President, New South Wales Bar Association' in *Swearing-in Ceremony of the Honourable Patricia Anne Bergin, SC as a Judge of the Supreme Court of New South Wales* (Sydney, Supreme Court NSW).

—— (1999b) 'Swearing in Speech, Ian Barker Esq, QC, President, New South Wales Bar Association' in *Swearing-in Ceremony of the Honourable Virginia Margaret Bell, SC as Judge of the Supreme Court of New South Wales* Sydney (Sydney, Supreme Court NSW).

Berlant, L and Warner, M (1998) 'Sex in Public' 24 *Critical Inquiry* 547.

Bell, V (1999) 'Swearing-in Speech, Bell J' in *Swearing-in Ceremony of the Honourable Virginia Margaret Bell, SC as Judge of the Supreme Court of New South Wales* (Sydney, Supreme Court NSW).

Bird, SR (1996) 'Welcome to the Men's Club: Homosociality and the Maintenance of Hegemonic Masculinity' 10 *Gender and Society* 120.

Butler, J (2002) 'Is Kinship always already Heterosexual?' 13 *Differences: A Journal of Feminist Cultural Studies* 14.

Fullerton, E (2007) 'Swearing-in Speech of Fullerton J' in *Swearing-in Ceremony of the Honourable Elizabeth Fullerton SC as a Judge of the Supreme Court of New South Wales* (Sydney, Supreme Court NSW).

Galanter, M and Roberts, S (2008) 'From Kinship to Magic Circle: The London Commercial Law Firm in the Twentieth Century' 15 *International Journal of the Legal Profession* 143.

Gaudron, MG (1983) 'Swearing-in Speech, Miss MG Gaudron, QC Solicitor General' in *Swearing-in Ceremony of the Honourable Matthew John Robert Clarke as a Judge of the Supreme Court of New South Wales* (Sydney, Supreme Court NSW).

Harrison, IG (2004) 'Swearing-in Speech, Mr IG Harrison SC, President, New South Wales Bar Association' in *Swearing-in Ceremony of the Honourable Richard Weeks White as a Judge of the Supreme Court of New South Wales* (Sydney, Supreme Court NSW).

Hatzistergos, J (2008) 'Swearing-in Speech, the Honourable John Hatzistergos MLC, Attorney General of New South Wales' in *Swearing-in Ceremony of the Honourable James Leslie Bain Allsop as a Judge of the Supreme Court of New South Wales and President of the Court of Appeal of the Supreme Court of New South Wales* (Sydney, Supreme Court NSW).

Hole, M (1999) 'Swearing in Speech, Ms Margaret Hole, President, Law Society of New South Wales' in *Swearing-in Ceremony of the Honourable Virginia Margaret Bell, SC as Judge of the Supreme Court of New South Wales* (Sydney, Supreme Court NSW).

Kirby, M (1984) 'Swearing-in Speech, Kirby P' in *Swearing-in Ceremony of the Honourable Michael Donald Kirby CMC as a Judge of the Supreme Court of New South Wales, a Judge of Appeal of the Court of the Supreme Court of New South Wales and President of the Court of Appeal of the Supreme Court of New South Wales* (Sydney, Supreme Court NSW).

—— (2009) *High Court of Australia Judicial Farewell The Hon Justice Michael Kirby AC CMG Justice of the High Court of Australia* (Canberra, High Court).

Landa, DP (1983) 'Swearing-in Speech, the Honourable DP Landa MLC, Attorney General' in *Swearing-in Ceremony of the Honourable Lancelot John Priestley as a Judge of the Supreme Court of New South Wales and as a Judge of Appeal of the Supreme Court of New South Wales* (Sydney, Supreme Court NSW).

—— (1984) 'Swearing-in Speech, the Honourable DP Landa, MLC Attorney General' in *Swearing-in Ceremony of the Honourable Michael Donald Kirby CMC as a Judge of the Supreme Court of New South Wales, a Judge of Appeal of the Court of the Supreme Court of New South Wales and President of the Court of Appeal of the Supreme Court of New South Wales* (Sydney, Supreme Court NSW).

Lipman-Blumen, J (1976) 'Toward a Homosocial Theory of Sex Roles: An Explanation of the Sex Segregation of Social Institutions' 1 *Signs* 15.

Loxton, AH (1975) 'Swearing-in Speech, AH Loxton, President, Law Society of New South Wales' in *Swearing-in of the Honourable William Percy Ash as a Justice of the Supreme Court of New South Wales* (Sydney, Supreme Court NSW).

Macken, H (2008) 'Swearing-in Speech, Mr H Macken, President, Law Society of New South Wales' in *Swearing-in Ceremony of the Honourable James Leslie Bain Allsop as a Judge of the Supreme Court of New South Wales and President of the Court of Appeal of the Supreme Court of New South Wales* (Sydney, Supreme Court NSW).

Marsden, J (2005) *I Am What I Am: My Life and Curious Times* (Camberwell, Victoria, Penguin).

Mawby, RC (2002) *Policing Images: Policing, Communication and Legitimacy* (Cullompton, Willan Publishing).

McColl, RS (2003) *Swearing-in Ceremony of the Honourable Ruth Stephanie McColl SC as a Judge of the Supreme Court of New South Wales and a Judge of Appeal* (Sydney, Supreme Court NSW).

McLachlan, DE (1983) 'Swearing-in Speech, DE McLachlan, President of the Law Society of New South Wales' in *Swearing-in Ceremony of the Honourable Matthew John Robert Clarke as a Judge of the Supreme Court of New South Wales* (Sydney, Supreme Court NSW).
Meagher, RP (1989) 'Swearing in Speech, Meagher JA' in *Swearing-in Ceremony of the Honourable Roderick Pitt Meagher as a Justice of the Supreme Court of New South Wales and as a Judge of Appeal* (Sydney, Supreme Court NSW).
Mendelsohn, O and Lippman, M (1979) 'The Emergence of the Corporate Law Firm in Australia' 3 *University of New South Wales Law Journal* 78.
Moran, LJ (2006) 'Judicial Diversity and the Challenge of Sexuality: Some Preliminary Findings' 28 *Sydney Law Review* 565.
—— (2008) 'Judicial Bodies as Sexual Bodies: A Tale of Two Portraits' 29 *Australian Feminist Law Journal* 91.
—— (2009) 'Judging Pictures: A Case Study of Portraits of the Chief Justices, Supreme Court of New South Wales' 5 *International Journal of Law in Context* 61.
North, JFS (2000) 'Swearing-in Speech, JFS North, President of the Law Society of New South Wales' in *Swearing-in Ceremony of the Honourable Anthony Gerard Whealy as a Judge of the Supreme Court of New South Wales* (Sydney, Supreme Court NSW).
Sedgwick, EK (1985) *Between Men: English Literature and Male Homosocial Desire* (New York, Columbia University Press).
Seidman, S (1994) 'Queer-ing Sociology, Sociologizing Queer Theory: An Introduction' 12 *Sociological Theory* 166.
Simpson, CC (1994) 'Swearing-in Speech, Simpson J' in *Swearing-in Ceremony of the Honourable Carolyn Chalmers Simpson QC as a Judge of the Supreme Court of New South Wales* (Sydney, Supreme Court NSW).
Sinfield, A (1991) 'Private Lives/Public Theatre: Noel Coward and the Politics of Homosexual Representation' 36 *Representations* 43.
Slattery, M (2007) 'Swearing-in Speech, M Slattery QC, President, New South Wales Bar Association' in *Swearing-in Ceremony of the Honourable Elizabeth Fullerton SC as a Judge of the Supreme Court of New South Wales* (Sydney, Supreme Court NSW).
Spigelman, JJ (1998) 'Swearing-in Speech' in *Swearing-in Ceremony of the Honourable JJ Spigelman QC as Chief Justice of the Supreme Court of New South Wales* (Sydney, Supreme Court NSW).
Thornton, BE (1989) 'Swearing-in Speech, BE Thornton Esq, President, the Law Society of New South Wales' in *Swearing-in Ceremony of the Honourable Roderick Pitt Meagher as a Justice of the Supreme Court of New South Wales and as a Judge of Appeal* (Sydney, Supreme Court NSW).
Thornton, M (1996) *Dissonance and Distrust: Women in the Legal Profession* (Melbourne, Oxford University Press).
Whealy, AG (2000) 'Swearing-in Speech, AG Whealy' in *Swearing-in Ceremony of the Honourable Anthony Gerard Whealy as a Judge of the Supreme Court of New South Wales* (Sydney, Supreme Court NSW).

4.2

Let History Judge? Gender, Race, Class and Performative Identity: A Study of Women Judges in England and Wales

HILARY SOMMERLAD

Abstract

The legitimacy of the judiciary requires that its claims to embody Enlightenment values of rationality and impartiality are credible. More recently, social representativeness has also become an essential quality, and macro social change has for some time, therefore, placed the judiciary under considerable pressure to become more diverse. But as one of the most powerful mechanisms for reinscribing the conventional social script, the law is also pivotal to both the construction of women as irrational, disorderly and hence inherently unsuited for judicial office (Thornton 1996) and the naturalisation of masculinised legal authority. As a result the judiciary is symbolic of hegemonic masculinity.

This chapter draws on research conducted with a small number of women judges which aimed to reflect on the antinomy between women and judicial office. The research explored how the respondents positioned themselves within the range of competing discourses which now circulate within the field, how they conceptualised the judicial role and how they established their authority and negotiated the collegiality they must enact as part of their bid for recognition. It investigated the extent to which, if at all, they met with resistance, and if they did, whether their capacity to contest their interpellation as women rather than judges was constrained by their habituation to the legal profession's hierarchy and cultural practices. The chapter draws on Bourdieusian and feminist post-structuralist theory to consider both these questions and also whether the entry of large numbers of women and the diversity discourse are capable of producing new judicial subjectivities.

1. INTRODUCTION

THE USURPATIONARY PROJECTS of women (Witz, 1992) and other 'outsider' lawyers, together with public pressure for a more representative judiciary, have for well over a decade generated calls for reform at the highest levels in the United Kingdom.[1] In 2005, this modernising project resulted in the Constitutional Reform Act (CRA) 2005 which, in accordance with the equal opportunities' 'script', established a Judicial Appointments Commission (JAC), substituting a formal application process for the practice of appointing on the basis of informal soundings. This reform, together with previous initiatives,[2] has resulted in significant diversification at the lower levels of the English and Welsh judiciary, partially vindicating the then Lord Chancellor's predictions that the establishment of the JAC would ensure that 'within five years' time ... every under-represented group (would be) applying in proportion to its presence in the pool. At every level. In our tribunals and in our courts. Progressing from post to post, according to ability. Regardless of gender, race, disability, sexual orientation, religion or age'.[3]

These claims fall squarely within the 'commonsense', liberal evolutionist narrative of social change which conceptualises history as linear progress,[4]

[1] Those who have called for reform have included past and present Lord Chiefs of Justice, eg Lord Taylor (1992: 9); however until 2005 it was assumed that the numbers of women judges in England and Wales would simply increase with time (the Scottish judiciary remains a separate institution). The constitution of an advisory panel represents the most recent reform initiative: see The Report of the Advisory Panel on Judicial Diversity 2010: www.justice.gov.uk/publications/judicial-diversity-report.htm); the Report also includes a 'timeline of judicial initiatives in England and Wales' which starts in 1988 with steps to formalise recruitment by publishing guidelines for appointments.

[2] The primary aim of both the Constitutional Reform Act (CRA) 2005 and previous initiatives has been to persuade, through, eg, publicity campaigns, a wider range of applicants to apply for judicial office. Any form of affirmative action has been consistently rejected. Although the most recent report on Judicial diversity recommends that the Judicial Appointments Committee (JAC) 'make use of the Equality Bill positive action provisions where the merits of candidates are essentially indistinguishable', the use of quotas has been rejected. (The Report of the Advisory Panel, ibid, 33).

[3] Lord Falconer (2005) 'Increasing Judicial Diversity: The Next Steps': www.dca.gov.uk/speeches/2005/lc021105.htm.

[4] The conceptual origins of this line of thought are to be found in the Enlightenment and 19th century Evolutionism, which posited the existence of social laws producing progressive social change; a core feature of the modernist narrative, it is exemplified by Macaulay's 'Whig' interpretation of British history, and Maine's thesis that law and society developed from status to contract (Maine, 1963: 118–19), and hence from pre-modern forms of social formation, characterised by relationships of authority based on ties of affinity and irrational beliefs, to rational capitalist modernity. Recent critics of this progressive meta-narrative include Butler (2008). The propagandist element of this narrative of social change led Marx to call Macaulay 'a systematic falsifier of history' (Marx, 1974: 671) and while few contemporary analysts would depict social change as such a straightforward process, this sort of rationale underpins the thinking behind the Ministry of Justice (MOJ) reforms, and is characterised

and individual actors as essentially rational, and hence autonomous and unencumbered, free to form associations with whomsoever they choose. In this narrative, it is therefore presumed that when contradictions within the social structure or institutions provoke a crisis, not only can a resolution be achieved, but it will be informed by principles of economic rationality and abstract justice.

As a master discourse, the legitimacy of which rests on claims to inherent rationality, objective impartiality and ideals of justice, the law (and therefore the judiciary) are both paradigmatic of this rationalist explanatory model and represent one of its primary vectors. This fact, together with the predication of conventional political economy on the neutrality of labour markets, entails assigning responsibility for the persistent under-representation of women and individuals from other historically excluded groups in the higher courts of England and Wales[5] onto the excluded themselves. Thus, the failure of the Ministry of Justice (MOJ) reforms to realise Falconer's claims is variously attributed to a lack of qualities on the part of women such as skill, merit and commitment, myths they hold about the judiciary[6] and choices, voluntarily entered into (Hakim, 2002).

These facile explanations for women lawyers' continuing difficulties in achieving parity of participation and recognition (Fraser, 1998; 2000) are challenged by extensive empirical evidence which indicates that the root cause of persistent labour market segregation and segmentation is the gendered nature of organisational cultures (for example, Acker, 1992; Cockburn, 1991; Kanter, 1977; Caraway, 2007; Potter and Hill, 2009). For instance Newman (1995: 11) argues that it is the more subtle practices, processes and discourses, which render an organisation intrinsically gendered and thus defeat even well-developed equal opportunity initiatives. Elite professions, in particular, remain saturated with masculinity (see, for example, Kuhlmann and Bourgeault, 2008) legitimising masculinity's status as the primary indicium of worth (Thornton, 2007).

by an optimism, derived from the Enlightenment, that crises will produce 'rectifying forces' (Shanin, 1985: 177–78).

[5] The 20% of judges who are female are largely located in the lower ranks; there is only one woman in the Supreme Court out of 12 judges; no female Heads of Division, 15 High Court judges out of a total of 107 and the most recent round of appointments actually saw a decrease in the numbers of women appointed: see www.judiciary.gov.uk/keyfacts/statistics/women.htm. Thus, as Justice Secretary, Jack Straw acknowledged in 2008, 'expectations that a new system of appointing judges would lead to a more diverse judiciary have so far not been fulfilled': news.bbc.co.uk/1/hi/uk/7399591.stm.

[6] The Report of the Advisory Panel, above (n 1); no evidence is adduced to support the claim that the factors which deter women are mythical. By contrast, Potter and Hill argue that the focus on women entrants to masculinised workplaces assumes them to be the problem, and argues that it is the barriers which they face in undertaking non-traditional jobs that need to be changed (2009).

A range of theories also enable us to critique the hegemonic, rationalist model of social change, and these point to the need to focus on context and process and the social relations which provide the basis for inequalities (Emirbayer, 1997).[7] For instance, one of Bourdieu's primary concerns has been with the durability and deep embedding of gender in socio-structural arrangements and cultural practice (1980; 2001). The relative autonomy of masculine domination despite historical transformations in patriarchy also shows us that new social forms do not supplant their predecessors; rather, different temporalities are co-enacted in social practice. Social change is thus simultaneously cumulative and contested. The resulting co-existence of the modern and the pre-modern is attributable, in large part, to the active resistance on the part of the powerful to the democratisation of institutional power. 'Modern' institutions and cultural practices are permeated by residual elements of patrimonial networks based on patron-client relations, where homosocial obligation and affinity do not merely trump merit, but are actually viewed as representing it.[8] The citation of enduring discourses which reproduce the devalued subjecthood of the 'Other', valorise the normative[9] and justify the maldistribution of resources, represents a further form of resistance.

Consequently, reform programmes cannot be read simply as forces of progress because within liberal democratic states, reform is the only legitimate response to challenge (Shanin, 1985: 53; Mattausch, 2003). While such programmes may in part be progressive, their framing by traditional discourses of, for instance, judicial professionalism, their reluctance to address systemic discrimination and, above all, their failure to recognise that social structures are based on affective (homosocial) bonds (Durkheim and Mauss, 1963: 85) make them largely ineffective while also blunting the demand for deep-seated social change. In this way it is possible to preserve and mask a transmutation of the status quo (although this may not be an entirely conscious objective).

Using these theoretical insights, this chapter draws on the data from a study of 16 women judges to contribute to our understanding of the

[7] There are several variants of this deconstructive sociology, ranging from Foucault's rejection of causal lines of enquiry for a genealogical approach, post colonial theory's insights into the resilience of the colonial project and the cultural production of knowledge by structures of dominance, the work of Critical Race theorists on the recursive resistance to, and abrogation of, modernising equality strategies at the point where these pose a realistic threat to the existing power structures (eg Bell, 2004) and feminism's refutation of the conceptualisation of patriarchy as an historically specific form that disappears with the establishment of the state (eg, Mitchell, 1971; Pateman, 1988).

[8] As Kanter has argued, the 'more closed the circle ... the greater the tendency for people to try to reproduce themselves, the more constraining becomes the emphasis on conformity' (Kanter, 1977: 68).

[9] Thus, racism and misogyny are not pre-modern relics, but continue to pervade social practices and discourse.

cultural practices and socio-structural arrangements which sustain the status quo, and the extent to and ways in which institutionalised relations of social subordination are contested. In the section below I discuss my methodology.

2. RESEARCH METHODS

The methodological assumptions underpinning the chapter are that agency is possible, but that its potential is constrained by the material properties, cultural practices and discourses which characterise social fields, so that these are unstable entities, producing a social world in constant flux. These assumptions implicate qualitative research with a purposive sample. The view that the experiences of professional women operating in a male sphere are likely to produce multiple positions (Baxter, 2002) means that, following Abbott (2001), I regard narrative as the best way of eliciting what I anticipated would be the processual, fragmented experience of women judges.[10] I therefore conducted in-depth interviews which aimed to elicit women's biographies. I asked my informants why and how they had come into the judiciary, which sites they occupied and what their future career plans were. I also asked about their initial experiences; how they 'imagined' themselves, and, relatedly, how they established their authority within both the courtroom and the informal, social spaces; whether they had encountered resistance; and whether they recognised and struggled with their complicity in the discursive mechanisms which reproduce the historicised subjectivities of, for instance, black and brown women. The transcribed interviews were authenticated by respondents and in most cases a follow-up interview clarified or expanded themes which had arisen in the first interview.

The (16) interviewees were aged between 45 and 60. Three were British south Asian (one British Indian and two British Pakistani) and one was British African. Five described their origins as lower middle or working class. They included a recorder in family law and a Crown Court judge. However, because the majority of women judges are located in the lower levels of the judiciary, the research focused on the tribunal service. The sample included regional tribunal judges, principal tribunal judges and tribunal chairs sitting in a range of tribunals including residential property, charity, asylum support, mental health and immigration. Five judges were fee paid (that is not salaried). Six had applied to become judges in the early

[10] As Abbott has argued, standard research methods assume a linear reality, composed of stable entities with changing attributes, and are therefore incapable of capturing the messy, processual nature of social life (2001).

to mid-1990s (at the time of the initial drive to get more women into the profession). Two women were barristers who had, for some time, been academics and sat as part-time judges. The others were either still practising lawyers (and therefore fee paid judges), or had come direct from private practice as solicitors (nine) or barristers, or following a career break, which could include government service.

3. MOTIVATIONS FOR, AND SITES OF, ENTRY

One would expect that since the majority of the sample were recent or current practitioners, they would—to a greater or lesser extent—display the habitus of a conventional lawyer, including a respect for the hierarchy and values of legal office. And it was striking that while both academics and a few of the other judges described themselves as feminist and also—when asked about their original motivation for becoming lawyers—concerned with social justice (and all the practitioners had done private client/legal aid work), neither feminism nor social justice were cited as motivations for becoming judges. On the other hand, the extent to which these women had assimilated and identified with professional values and status was, as one would expect, modified by a consciousness of being, to a greater or lesser extent, outsiders, and the resulting fracturing of voice pervaded their narratives. Thus, while several cited such motivations as 'being invited to apply' and 'judicial status', the most common theme was flexibility, which meant that 'judging works well with child care'. Relatedly, others emphasised 'push' factors and in particular the refusal by the solicitors' profession to accommodate children; for instance:

> I specialised in white collar fraud. I then had a baby and left because the practice didn't feel they could accommodate part time work, which they could have done—in white collar crime arrests are virtually by appointment. Their decision made me feel I didn't want to be in that kind of atmosphere—in which I'd be a second class citizen (immigration judge).

But, as in solicitors' firms, flexibility tends to be a component of low status work. The following comment by a barrister supports Thornton's description of the judicial arenas in which women are concentrated as 'in between' spaces and diasporas:

> Tribunals have always been considered to be the bottom of the pile and certainly till recently we've had a lot of women judges. The tribunal system is the bottom rung, so it's more accessible and flexible. Conversely most men wouldn't touch it ... for successful male barristers it would be beneath them (Social Entitlement Tribunal chair).

However, the data suggested that this partitioning of the outsider subject from the dominant judicial population[11] produces complex results. On the one hand, the lack of a 'proper career pathway for the lower level judiciary into higher judicial role' (Charity Tribunal chair) and the very 'limited nature of discretion in low level jurisdictions' (fee paid Asylum Support Tribunal chair) ensures that these women do not threaten the male monopoly over authoritative status. On the other hand, the very lowliness and separateness of the tribunal system made it possible for some women to create their own spheres of influence, detached from the wider judicial field and thus, as Baroness Hale has argued, to 'make a difference ... on at least two levels, style and substance' (2005: 288). Her point is illustrated by another Asylum Support Tribunal chair who said that her principal judge had produced a particular culture because 'she's a woman and black, and then also there are only 4 of us and only one of those is a man. There's no huge feeling of hierarchy'. Furthermore, the relatively fluid nature of the forms of law with which some women judges were working made it possible to disrupt/challenge existing assumptions about legal and judicial practice.[12] Thus, the same principal judge of the tribunal (who had herself cited 'an interest in human rights' as her motivation for becoming a judge) was described as giving the tribunal a 'thrust (which) has always been very human rights, long before the Human Rights Act'.[13]

The low status/high autonomy (for some women judges) dichotomy is a theme which ran through respondents' accounts. The uneven and shifting experiences it produced are reflected in (and also caused by) the intertextuality of the various competing discourses which currently pervade the judicial field: namely, those of judicial professionalism and gender difference, and—contra these—discourses of diversity and managerialism which are destabilising traditional ideas of what it is to be a judge. In the following section I consider how the resulting tensions are reflected in respondents' accounts of how they negotiated the judicial role in both the informal spaces and the courtroom.

[11] This segmentation of the judicial labour market is justified by one of the rationales proposed by the MOJ for needing to increase diversity—namely the need to ensure that in fields such as 'equal opportunities, immigration and asylum ... the choice of qualified lawyers ... includes some from backgrounds with which clients are likely to identify. In fields such as family law, a choice of lawyer that includes both women lawyers, and lawyers with personal experience of different cultural traditions, may make it easier for some clients to secure the services they need' (DCA, 2003).

[12] The debate over whether women might 'lawyer differently' is longstanding—see, essays in 1985 *Buffalo Law Review* (Marcus et al, 1985) discussing Carol Gilligan's proposition that women had a 'different voice'. For more recent contributions see, eg, Malleson (2003); Hunter (2008); Rackley (2009).

[13] A pervasive characteristic of the judgments in the feminist judgments' project is a concern for human rights (Hunter et al, 2010).

4. ROLE NEGOTIATION

Respondents demonstrated an acute awareness that their judicial status was mediated by discourses of gender and sometimes racial, sometimes class, difference—powerfully illustrated by the fear one woman expressed on becoming a judge shortly after having given birth that she would be seen as 'a mummy rather than a lawyer'. Identity dissonance was particularly problematic outside the courtroom. Thus, some women described the training sessions they had participated in when they first became judges as 'rites of passage'.[14] The following three accounts of such events illustrate the insight that power relations are inscribed 'as active ingredients on the bodies as well as the minds that perceive them' (Bourdieu, 2001: 31). There was a striking similarity in how the respondents experienced the overwhelming preponderance of men in the judicial field:

> After being appointed I went to this training course … and I remember there was this sea of grey men—pompous, loud voices etc. There were around 200 people there, probably around 20% of whom were women. I couldn't believe that it just hadn't changed at all in all those years. I just remember the place being full of middle aged rather straight looking males and so when I walked in, I thought 'oh god'. (immigration judge).

> All meetings outside my tribunal are still predominantly male—dominated by public school/Eton type blokes. I recall the first meeting I went to, having the impression of entering a sea of blokes, and thinking 'oh no'. They're all sort of standard blokes, with the blue shirt etc—very boring and unimaginative clothes (Mental Health chair).

> I remember walking into this sea of people … nearly all of whom were male and all over 50 and they all seemed big and imposing ... of course they are charm personified because you're one of the few women. Drank like fish, I remember … and all talking about their children's (private) education and whether they're going to Oxford or Cambridge' (chair Residential Property Tribunal).

These informal spaces and social occasions represent a crystallisation of social relations, processes, experiences and understandings. They are articulated moments of power, spatialised sites of social reproduction (Massey, 1994) in which male judges *perform*[15] those cultural practices which,

[14] Haas and Shaffir describe such processes as involving threats of humiliation and requiring symbolic changes, including in dress and demeanour, to affirm and sustain the neophyte's new identity which must then be legitimated by insiders (1991: 4–5).

[15] Following Judith Butler, gender is not something that subjects simply have but is also something that must be performed, so that the signs of gender are 'performative'—a term which Butler borrowed from JL Austin meaning that verbal expressions actually do what they say (Butler, 1993: 10), thereby reproducing patriarchal, classed and raced structures through repetition, or citation to use Butler's term, of the signs of gender, class and race.

through continual citation, both construct their judicial masculinity and symbolise their homosocial community, thereby simultaneously establishing and confirming their own internal hierarchies and the difference/inferiority of outsiders (Barth, 1969). It is in such spaces therefore—where they too must perform collegiality, involving the suppression of sexuality—that women feel themselves most under surveillance. Here they must deal with all the 'paraphernalia' surrounding the male judge which appears to be peripheral and private but in fact structures the public, the character of which is revealed by 'talk about whatever they do at the golf club' (chair of Residential Property Tribunal) or by questions which link the right to judicial status with paternal class: 'who was your father?' or which articulate the performative qualities which would characterise a proper judge, such as '"which club do you belong to?". I was asked this on my first day at the tribunal by the guy I was paired with. He then asked "do you do yachting?"' (Asylum Support Tribunal).

The relationship between the classed, raced and gendered nature of the field and its reproduction through homosocial practices and mortification of the newcomer (Goffman, 1961: 24)—who either does not know the rules of the game, or holds insufficient cards to play it (Bourdieu and Wacquant, 1992), or is incapable of performing it—is also evoked by a Crown Court judge's recollection of her sense of inadequacy when, as a junior barrister, she was unable to

> join in any of the informal chat ... everyone seemed to have a legal background and they'd all done lots of travelling, went skiing, played rugby, cricket and so on ... it was very 'clubby' ... it was about feeling not as knowledgeable, not as cultured. It was a class thing. At one stage I felt so bad about it I thought about reading the Encyclopaedia Britannica.

It is in the informal social spaces too that some women reported encountering displays of overt misogyny, such as 'grop(ing) women, after drinks and nibbles, deliberately and without any apparent consciousness that it's wrong' (immigration judge). And the consequently alien nature of these highly masculinised spaces meant that many women, despite recognising that 'being known' and socialising remain primary criteria for career progression, excluded themselves from them; for instance three women said that they did not attend social occasions such as the Council for Immigration Judges' annual dinners held in Vintners' Hall despite their important role in developing social networks. Another described such events as 'difficult—so upper class, so male—they are a throw back in that the roles are all for the men and any women are there as the decoration at the table' (senior immigration judge).

Other women said they also avoided the judges' dining rooms:

> [T]he library is where people meet for lunch—referred to as the mess and I used to avoid it at the beginning because it was the way it's called ... the service is around

> 60/40 men/women, and the ones who went to lunch in the mess were overwhelmingly men. The majority of them are middle aged—the way they come across it's how I imagine walking into a boys' public school—room full of quite large, loud men all talking either about their cases or something else I'm not particularly interested in (immigration judge).

Butler's argument that habitus is a 'citational chain lived and believed at the level of the body' (1997: 155) is again evoked by this last woman's further comments when she went on to describe these men's performances in the following terms: 'booming on about their cases ... I call it willy waggling—trying to outdo each other, but on a very boysy level ... It's just a very alien atmosphere full of puff and bluster'.

The same nexus of power, discourse and subjectification, which establishes who can speak, where and with what authority[16] is evoked by the following comments: 'the men convey that sense of self importance in their body language, there's no sense of awkwardness or embarrassment—they look you straight in the eye and demand attention'.

The corollary of men's supremely confident bodily hexis is women's careful schooling of their bodies, their interiorisation of the male gaze;[17] thus one respondent recounted how, before entering the judges' 'mess' for the first time she had felt that she had to

> demonstrate—subtly—my right to be there by being self assured—so, before I went in ... I checked myself in the corridor but then walked straight in—erect and smiling—scanned the room quickly to see if there was a space next to someone whose name I knew, and then went and sat down there, with assurance, and made a remark about the soup. The thing is I'm only 5' tall so I do try and make myself more imposing—raise myself to my full height—and I wore high heels (family law recorder).

The antinomy between judicial authority and female gender is also revealed in women's accounts of being mistaken for, for instance, a secretary. The observations of an Asian Asylum Support chair that this was particularly likely to happen to 'Asian, African Caribbean and African women ... we are always being taken for the administrator or interpreter—or client—you have to power dress to show your status', speaks to the tenacity of gendered and racialised professional structures and practices. Another black woman recalled her fear on her first day that she might not 'really look like a judge'.

[16] Bourdieu describes a process of price formation where the value of an utterance is determined not simply by its intrinsic properties, but by the objective positions that interlocutors occupy in the 'field of power', 'on the capacity of the various agents involved to impose the criteria of appreciation most favourable to their own products' (1991: 67)

[17] Women's denigratory self-regard is, Bourdieu argues, the result of their historicised fear of bodily ridicule, revealing the constancy of masculine domination (2001).

Her feelings of insecurity were echoed by the comments of an Asian woman judge in which she emphasises the alienating natural authority her fellow judges conveyed:

> I was definitely not part of the immigration judge clique, who always thought they were better than everyone else 'we do very important work'—very pompous, self-important. I just didn't relate to that pomposity.

As a result, many recalled feeling timid and being deferential when first appointed, and others spoke of challenges to their authority by some male representatives:

> [Y]ou do get some defendants who are racist but it's counsel who can sometimes be really bolshy, refuse to take your ruling as final ... and just generally behave in a way that challenges your authority in a way they wouldn't before a male judge. I know that because if you mention it to your male colleagues they express surprise and say things like 'no, surely not—Mr Smith is so polite' (Crown Court judge).

This woman's explanation for such behaviour illustrates the property rights male barristers feel they have in judicial positions:

> I sense they're resentful ... when I was appointed the comment 'she's black and female so she's ticked more of the Lord Chancellor's boxes' was made to a female colleague who told me of them; it put her off applying—she said she'd be so embarrassed to think these sorts of things were being said.

5. WOMEN'S JUDICIAL PERFORMATIVITIES

As this last quotation reveals, the entry of women and the discourse of diversity has, to some extent, destabilised the judicial field, creating a moment of 'crisis' for normative judicial authority and identity. The interplay of discourses (Baxter, 2002) which is a feature of this crisis is creating a space for contestation and the emergence of new judicial subjectivities, producing a diversity of performative responses.[18] This was revealed in my respondents' accounts of how they practised judging—the range of which reflected not only the variability of different judicial sites, but also the increasing ambiguities which inflect judicial practice, and women's own non-unitary and constantly shifting subjectivities (Leonard, 2003; Walkerdine, 1981). This nexus of subjectivities can, crudely, be categorised into two extremes. On the one hand there is a performance of judicial authority which is deferential to hierarchy, cites prior discursive practices

[18] For extensive discussion of the 'different' lawyering women judges and in particular Baroness Hale has engaged in, see Rackley (2008, 2009; Hunter 2008).

in which the traditional meaning of what it is to be a judge is sedimented and which, at its most extreme, may be described as a 'hyper' judicial performance. At the other end of the spectrum, women articulated a position which entailed a (generally subtle) contestation of both the conventional way of judging and also existing working practices. The accounts of several women of their own ways of judging spanned both extremes as well as positions in between.

Adherence to the orthodox judicial performance is easily explicable given the disciplinary techniques through which a lawyer is constituted (Kennedy, 1982), producing internalisation of the doxa of the field and development of its habitus—a tacit, practical understanding of and engagement with its practices, and a sense of oneself as an office holder rather than a 'woman'. Thus the comments: 'I'm first and foremost a judge/lawyer' (Charity Tribunal chair) and: 'I think there's little difference between male and female judging'.

These refrains explicitly situate their judicial performativity[19] within the discourse of (bleached out (Levinson, 1993; Wilkins, 1998)) legal professionalism, thereby asserting their judicial normativity:

> [If] there's a discretion to be exercised that hasn't been exercised fairly then I exercise it, but I always make sure that I stick to the law and to judicial principles and precedents—I'm first and foremost a lawyer. I think I'm fair but I could never make a sentimental decision which was wrong in law—but I feel I've always made the decision which is the right decision (Asylum Support Tribunal chair).

Further, although several women echoed the observation that in the courtroom women were generally 'taken seriously automatically, because you are then in role', and 'people see you as a judge, with gravitas', others appeared conscious that an explicitly orthodox performance was required in order to counter gendered presumptions of lack of authority and/or spoke of their sense of a disciplinary gaze:

> If an applicant has leave to appeal against your decision then an upper tier judge will look at it, they'll produce a judgment where they'll comment on the lower judge's decision making. There are more males in the Upper Tier—it's probably worse than the officers' mess. I know as a woman that if I'm seen to be particularly lenient it will be seen as a negative thing so I've always tried to administer the law directly, within the law (Regional Tribunal judge Social Entitlement).

[19] The nexus of structure and agency encompassed by Butler's performative theory of gender through its focus both on the performance of gender by an individual subject, and the work that cultural practices, discourses and management systems do on the subjectivities of individuals to produce that performance, is encompassed by the experiences reported by my informants.

Another thought that women were 'vulnerable to being labelled as feminist' (Mental Health chair); another said that 'women are perceived as being more likely to be lenient or emotional in their decision making—this is seen as a negative thing'. (immigration judge). The following comment makes it plain how this surveillance could distort judging practices:

> The feeling of being an outsider did extend to how I behaved as a judge at first. I felt terribly self-conscious, on guard, needing to make sure I was right and also be seen to be doing it 'properly'. So I may even have been harsher than white judges (South Asian senior immigration judge).

As a result, some women recounted giving a performance which was explicitly masculinised:

> I feel I am perceived differently—as a woman. I emphasize different parts of me ... I feel I'm acting I suppose. I do much more of 'right, I'm in charge' because I feel I have to overstate the fact ... And I don't smile so much, I'm quite formal; I suppose I'm trying to be like a male judge (white middle class Family Court recorder).

This account resonates with her following description of two women circuit judges who apparently sought to strengthen their claim to judicial authority by suppressing all vestiges of the feminine:

> They're both lovely fun people out of court but in their courts they're both 'ice queens' ... they suppress any expression of their personalities to an extent to which male judges never seem to ... I'm not sure if it's because they feel their personality is not 'judicial' enough. They rule their courts very strictly, far more strictly than the men.

For some women, however, it was their gendered experience of legal practice and their rejection of its disciplinary techniques which had provided the motivation to become judges. Presumably as a result, such women, at other times, recounted a performativity which, to varying degrees, *did* represent a different way of judging, or the production of a different voice. For instance, one woman distinguished her practices from her male counterparts: 'immigration and employment judges are pompous and arrogant—and part of that is running their tribunals far more like courts than tribunals'.

The most striking example of adopting a consciously different approach to judging was offered by the south Asian feminist judge who had been anxious about exercising discretion too often in favour of the appellant in immigration/aslyum adjudication early on in her career. She then proceeded to claim that now she only dealt 'with the facts—I don't particularly look at it from a political angle—if someone's got a case then that's the issue—whatever their background'. However, as the interview progressed she expanded, and the story she recounted sheds interesting light on the debate over judicial 'difference':

> [O]f course I'm more aware of some things than another judge would be—for instance, take the recent furore about women appearing wearing the nikab—I first dealt with this in the 1990s when I started out as an immigration adjudicator ...The presenting officer was having a fit about a client who was wearing the nikab and said to me 'you'll have to ask her to remove her veil because I can't cross examine her without seeing her eyes'. I said 'the only relevant issue is to identify whether she's the woman who she says she is'. I got her to come to me, with her passport, and to stand with her back to the others in the court room, with the woman clerk next to me, and to remove her veil. I was then able to identify her and I said: 'she is who she says she is and now you just have to deal with it'.
>
> It was a primary purpose case so she was asked 'why did you agree to marry this man when you hadn't met him', and she replied 'because I prayed and got advice from God'. To which the presenting officer replied 'oh you speak to God and he speaks back does he?' He was very sarcastic and I could see her solicitor also squirming, as if what she'd said was ridiculous. So I said 'please explain this to me'. She said 'there's this special prayer which I spoke and I then got an answer in a dream; the dream showed a large green flag; green is a good colour and so I knew God had answered me and that the marriage was ok'. And I said 'so that was an Istikhara?' which is the name of this special prayer. And her eyes lit up and she said 'yes'. The point is that it showed that she was not lying—the story and my understanding of it, my cultural awareness mean that her story was reasonable—it went to her credibility and I allowed her appeal and directed that she be given entry clearance as it was a genuine marriage.

At the end of the interview she said—'so, yes, in my court I make justice'.

By contrast, some women made it clear that when they exercised discretion this was not necessarily to the benefit of women:

> [Y]ou have to decide whether conduct is reasonable or credible and I think being female does affect how you look at people—but that may not necessarily be benign. Sometimes I sit with men—eg male doctors—and then I'm conscious of the fact that if someone is saying something which suggests they're trying to play the female card then I can be more judgemental. The jurisdiction is benefits entitlement, and cases are often to do with disability and the applicants are the bottom of the pile and there's a large part of me which says 'oh come on' (regional tribunal judge Social Entitlement).

This account of harsh scrutiny of women appellant's accounts was echoed by other women who said they were likely to interrogate testimonies of sexual abuse more closely than their male colleagues. However the subsequent comments of the woman just cited point to the identity dissonance which can fracture female judicial performativities:

> T]hen something else says 'come on you are a fortunate person—how would you cope if you were a single mother living in a tower block with no money'. I think because as a woman you have to have coped with some of that stuff—ie bringing up children, you're more conscious of those issues—because all women have to get on with things, so you may be both harder but then also more conscious of difficulties.

6. CONTESTATION, RESISTANCE AND CLOSURE

Barriers to promotion were a recurring theme for many respondents, and several cited the rigidity of structures and inflexible attitudes. This had provoked some women into contestation; for instance, one judge described how she had sought to persuade her head of chambers to consider alternative ways of working:

> [W]e had (a discussion) about the possibility of using conference calls to avoid everyone having to turn up for minor procedural matters. I was saying 'can't we do this—would save everyone's time and a lot of money—it would be a much more efficient process?' This was after a week of doing hearings miles away from home.

The head of chambers' response to her that her suggestion 'was impossible because "we don't have a room"' underlines the significance of etiquette and the material, symbolic trappings of status in the production of judicial authority and hence identity:

> I said that the whole point was that it was done over the phone, so it could be done from anywhere—eg from my office. He said 'you can't possibly make a call like that if you are not in a judicial setting'. To which I said 'so you can't be judicial if you're working from home?' and he said, 'that's right'.

This expression of tradition and ritual in structures which require a 'male' career path means—as this respondent proceeded to observe—that judging is 'much more difficult—impossible actually—if you have dependent children. I couldn't have done the job when my children were younger (they're now 16 and 18)'.

Other women also had accounts of the difficulties they had encountered in attempting to progress. The inflexibility of existing systems at the higher levels was a theme of another woman's story of the difficulties she had experienced in obtaining promotion:

> A new level of tribunal judges has been created so everyone involved in immigration, social security, mental health, charities tribunals are all now part of

> an over-arching tribunal ... The idea was that there would be opportunities for existing judges to move into another area so your experience as a judge would have meant something ie they'd take into account your general judicial skills and pay heed to your past history. In practice that hasn't happened, so, in sum, there's no proper career pathway for someone like me into a higher judicial role, and this is exacerbated partly because of my location and partly because of child care, but also because they, and the structure, are very inflexible. They could draw on this wealth of experienced women in the tribunal system and the tribunal system is really quite feminised at the lower levels in part because the working patterns are very flexible (fee paid immigration judge with AIT).

However, the discourse of female (and racial and class) difference represents a more deep-seated barrier than structural rigidities (although of course the two are inextricably entwined). Despite the indications of the emergence of new judicial subjectivities, women's claim to authentic judicial identity, whether it is one which is imitative of the current norm, or one which is different, must still be recognised as authentic. The refusal of recognition by those with discursive agency[20] is evidenced in the confinement of women to subordinate places, legitimised through the premise of a formal equality regime and the discourse of merit.[21]

Although merit is, of course, always contextual, subject to heuristic biases in favour of the familiar and the similar (Falkenberg,1991), its iconic status rests on its claimed objectivity. In practice, when applied to women, it is grounded in cultural stereotypes which are frequently tinged with misogyny. This is powerfully revealed by one woman's account of her repeated attempts to move out of the tribunal service, each of which was rebuffed with a new hurdle. She produced the letter which explained the grounds of her latest rejection, which stated that she should have acquired more sitting experience in crime, as this would have helped 'to provide stronger evidence supporting the necessary *authority* (author's emphasis) and communication skills'. However, in practice, her evidencing in her interview of her ability to convey authority was viewed as excessive as the letter went on to make plain: 'in this context, the panel felt that you could have been a little less forceful at interview, in order better to display the restrained nature expected of a judge in the Crown Court'.

The plasticity and hence opacity of such a key attribute as authority (like merit) means that its citation can, and probably will, draw on cultural stereotypes with the result that women can either be deemed to lack it or if they do display it, to be deeply transgressive (Silvester, 1996). The ontological

[20] This phrase signifies that discourse is not simply a translation of struggles and systems of domination but that for which and by which the struggle is waged (Butler, 1997).

[21] As Thornton observes, the concept of merit has only relatively recently been mobilised, in response to the disruption caused by outsiders' usurpationary struggles (2007).

impossibility of women enacting authority 'properly' (Thornton, 1996) is reflected in this woman's comments:

> I have no idea what 'a little less forceful' is supposed to mean! I want to ask them what evidence they have to suggest that I am not restrained. I told them I had to raise my voice in Court on one occasion to stop a man from physically attacking me and members of my panel and that by so doing I had stopped him in his tracks long enough for him to be removed by security. This was in response to them asking me if my authority had ever been challenged in court. Why ask the question, if you don't want to hear the answer? Would a male candidate have received the same response I wonder?

Other women considered that in practice masculinity continues to be the natural, legitimate property of the judicial field; for instance a mental health judge explained that despite the apparent modernisation of the selection process the sift is done by the head of chambers 'because they want someone who can work with him and because that's how the appointments for the higher levels of the Tribunal Service have been done for years and years. They know who they want, and they do the sift'.

The significance of social networks and cultural capital in being 'wanted' featured in other accounts of the appointment process; for instance:

> [W]hen I was (recently) appointed I had all the objective tests ... I was then asked if I was aware of what goes on in the tribunals and said yes because I'd discussed it with—and gave the name of the senior president for the whole country—and the whole tone of the interview changed—I had become one of them (Residential Property Tribunal chair).

This reference to the persistence of this shadow structure of archaic, personalist practices, was echoed by others; one said: 'the system of secret soundings ... old habits die hard and great weight is given to a raised eyebrow or a question mark on a piece of paper against a particular name', and a Mental Health chair argued that 'the more the rhetorical emphasis on diversity, the subtler it becomes. The point is, it's still going on'.[22]

7. CONCLUDING REMARKS

The discourse of diversity, together with women's active contestation of existing structures and practices and occasional engagement in new judicial performativities, appears to be challenging the homologous relationship between masculinity and legal authority, producing some destabilisation

[22] In fact, despite the duty to promote diversity (see above), the JAC is also empowered to take secret soundings.

of the judicial field. However, my data suggest that the extent to which cultural change is taking place is strictly constrained. In part this stems from the fact that women judges are already socialised into the rules of the profession; as lawyers they have achieved their subjectivity through the discourses and power structures which speak through them: 'in terms of the maleness of the culture, my time in private practice both helps me cope with it and also, to some extent, makes it less visible to me' (mental health chair).

The problem also lies in seeking to diversify the judiciary through bureaucratic initiatives premised on the formal equality regime,[23] since this assumes (to paraphrase Beverley Skeggs (1997)) that the resources for telling and displaying the self are equally available to all and, further, that these performances are read equally, objectively. Grounded in a rationalist ideology, such initiatives overlook the non-rational basis of society, the fact that social structures are based on affective bonds, with affective interactions creating classifications of behaviour which sustain these structures (Durkheim, 1963: 85): 'bonds, not essences, provide the bases of durable inequality' (C Tilly in Emirbayer, 1997). There is a corresponding failure to recognise that the judiciary fits the description of a 'categorically bounded network ... which hoards access ... and develops practices that perpetuate this restricted access' (Emirbayer, 1997: 292f). Or, as a senior immigration judge said of her reaction to the constitution of the recent advisory panel on judicial diversity: 'hollow laughter—because despite everything that is trotted out there's still a narrow conception of what a judge is—he's still a white, middle class, Oxbridge male'.

The data clearly illustrate the consequent resilience of the discourse of gender difference, of which, of course, the law is a major vector. The iterative process of producing identities can therefore be construed as a struggle centred around recognition and authorisation (Fraser, 1998) and the power to recognise and authorise remains with men. Consequently, the constraints on women's claims to judicial authority are exemplified by Fanon's observations that 'it is not I who make meaning for myself, but it is the meaning that was already there, pre-existing, waiting for me ... I came into the world with the will to find meaning but then found that I was an object. Sealed into that crushing objecthood' (1967: 134; 109). The iterative nature of this process is revealed by the fact that refusal of recognition, along with the denial of subjecthood and the projection of (negative) meaning, is one of the primary processes through which social divisions of class, gender and race are established and reproduced, simultaneously reaffirming the subjecthood and worth of the judgement maker, reinforcing his power to

[23] As Thornton has observed, letting women in legitimates this regime of formal equality (2007).

'recognise' or refuse identity claims. In this way masculine cultural hegemony is reproduced.

8. REFERENCES

Abbott, A (2001) *Time Matters: On Theory and Method* (Chicago, University of Chicago Press).

Acker, J (1992) 'Gendering Organizational Theory' in A Mills and P Tancred (eds), *Gendering Organisational Analysis* (London, Thousand Oaks).

Barth, F (ed) (1969) *Ethnic Groups and Boundaries* (Oslo, Oslo University Press).

Baxter, J (2002) 'A Juggling Act: A Feminist Post Structuralist Analysis of Girls' and Boys' talk in the Secondary Classroom' 14(1) *Gender and Education* 5.

Bell, D (2004) *Silent Covenants: Brown vs Board of Education and the Uunfulfilled Hopes for Racial Reform* (New York, Oxford University Press).

Bourdieu, P (1980) *Le Sens Pratique* (Paris, Minuit).

—— (1991) *Language and Symbolic Power* (Cambridge, Polity Press).

—— (2001) *Masculine Domination* (Cambridge, Polity Press).

Bourdieu, P and Wacquant, L (1992) *An Invitation to Reflexive Sociology* (Chicago, University of Chicago University Press).

Butler, J (1993) *Bodies that Matter: On the Discursive Limits of 'Sex'* (New York, Routledge).

—— (1997) *Excitable Speech: A Politics of the Performative* (London, Routledge).

—— (2008) 'Sexual Politics, Torture, and Secular Time' 59(1) *The British Journal of Sociology* 1.

Caraway, T (2007) Assembling Women: The *Feminisation of Global Manufacturing* (New York, Cornell University Press).

Cockburn, C (1991) I*n the Way of Women: Men's Resistance to Sex Equality in Organisations* (Basingstoke, Palgrave Macmillan).

Department of Constitutional Affairs (DCA) (2005) *Constitutional Reform: A New Way of Appointing Judges* (Department of Constitutional Affairs, London).

—— (2005) *Increasing Diversity in the Legal Profession—A Report on Government Proposals (*Department of Constitutional Affairs, London).

Durkheim, E (1912) 1995 *The Elementary Forms of Religious Life* (trans K Fields) (New York, Free Press).

Durkheim, E and Mauss, M (1903) (1963) *Primitive Classification* (trans R Needham) (London, Cohen and West).

Emirbayer, M (1997) 'Manifesto for a Relational Sociology' 103(2) *American Journal of Sociology* 281.

Falkenberg, L (1991) 'Improving the Accuracy of Stereotypes within the Workplace' 61(1) *Journal of Management* 1072.

Fanon, F (1967) *Black Skins, White Masks* (New York, Grove Press).

Fraser, N (1998) 'Heterosexism, Misrecognition, and Capitalism: A Response to Judith Butler' 228(1) *New Left Review* 140.

—— (2000) 'Rethinking Recognition' 3 *New Left Review* 1.

Goffman, E (1961) *Asylums* (New York, Doubleday).

Hakim, C (2002) 'Lifestyle Preferences as Determinants of Women's Differentiated Labor Market Careers' 29(4) *Work and Occupations* 428.

Hale, B (2005) 'Making a Difference? Why we need a More Diverse Judiciary' 56 *Northern Ireland Legal Quarterly* 281.
Hass, J and Shaffir, W (1991) *Becoming Doctors: The Adoption of a Cloak of Competence* (Greenwich, JAI Press).
Hunter, R (2008) 'Can Feminist Judges make a Difference?' 13 *International Journal of the Legal Profession* 7.
Hunter, R, McGlynn, C and Rackley E (eds) (2010) *Feminist Judgments: From Theory to Practice* (Oxford, Hart Publishing).
Kanter, RM (1977) *Men and Women of the Corporation* (New York, Basic Books).
Kennedy, D (1982) 'Training for Hierarchy' in D Kairys (ed), *The Politics of Law: A Progressive Critique* (New York, Pantheon Books).
Kuhlmann, E and Bourgeault, I (2008) 'Gender, Professions and Public Policy: New Directions' 27(1) *Equal Opportunities International* 5.
Leonard, P (2003) '"Playing' Doctors and Nurses?" Competing Discourses of Gender, Power and Identity in the British National Health Service' 51(2) *The Sociological Review* 218.
Levinson, S (1993) 'Identifying the Jewish Lawyer: Reflections on the Construction of Professional Identity' 14 *Cardozo Law Review* 1577.
Maine, HS (1963) *Ancient Law* (Gloucester, Peter Smith).
Malleson, K (2003) 'Justifying Gender Equality on the Bench: Why Difference Won't Do' 11 *Feminist Legal Studies* 1.
Marcus, I, Spiegelman, P, DuBois, E, Dunlap, M, Gilligan, C, MacKinnon, C and Menkel-Meadow, C (1985) 'Feminist Discourse, Moral Values, and the Law—A Conversation' 34 *Buffalo Law Review* 11.
Marx, K (1974) *Capital*, vol 1 (London, Lawrence & Wishart).
Massey, D (1994) *Space, Place and Gender* (Minnesota, University of Minnesota Press).
Mattausch, J (2003) 'Chance and Societal Change' 51(4) *The Sociological Review* 506.
Mitchell, J (1971) *Sexual Politics* (Garden City, Doubleday).
Newman, J (1995) 'Gender and Cultural Change' in C Itzin and J Newman (eds), *Gender, Culture and Organisational Change* (London, Routledge).
Pateman, C (1988) *The Sexual Contract* (Cambridge, Polity Press).
Potter, M and Hill, M (2009) 'Women into Non-traditional Sectors: Addressing Gender Segregation in the Northern Ireland Workplace' 61(2) *Journal of Vocational Education and Training* 133.
Rackley, E (2008) 'What a Difference Difference Makes: Gendered Harms and Judicial Diversity' 15 *International Journal of the Legal Profession* 37.
Rackley, E (2009) 'Detailing Judicial Difference' 17 *Feminist Legal Studies* 11.
Shanin, T (1985) *Russia as a Developing Society*, vol 1 (New Haven, Yale University Press).
Silvester, J (1996) 'Questioning Discrimination in the Selection Interview: A Case for More Field Research' 6(4) *Feminism & Psychology* 574.
Skeggs, B (1997) *Formations of Class and Gender* (London, Sage Publications).
Lord Taylor CJ (1992) 'The Judiciary in the Nineties' Richard Dimbleby Lecture.
Thornton, M (1996) *Dissonance and Distrust: Women in the Legal Profession* (Melbourne, Oxford University Press).

Thornton, M (2007) "Otherness' on the Bench: How Merit is Gendered' 29 *Sydney Law Review* 391.
Walkerdine, V (1981) 'Sex, Power and Pedgagy' 38 *Screen Education* 18.
Wilkins, D (1998) 'Identities and Roles: Race, Recognition, and Professional Responsibility' 57 *Maryland Law Review* 1502.
Witz, A (1992) *Professions and Patriarchy* (London, Routledge).

Part 5

Feminist Judges and Feminist Adjudication

5.1

Must Feminist Judges Self-identify as Feminists?

BEVERLEY BAINES

Abstract

Feminist legal scholars want judges to self-identify as feminist. Rosemary Hunter offers a compelling argument about the significance of self-identification as the marker of a feminist judge. However, few judges are willing to self-identify as feminists. Feminist adjudication offers an alternative theory. It serves three functions not met by feminist self-identification. First, it distinguishes the professional culture of feminist judges from that of feminist legal scholars, a distinction borne out in a study comparing the use of the 'f' word on the bench and in the academy. Second, it positions feminist judges to intervene in the contemporary feminist legal theory debate between dominance feminists who self-identify and postmodern feminists who disavow their approach. Third, it invites feminist legal scholars to recognise the power dimension inherent in their relationship with the feminist judges whom they study. I conclude it is premature for feminist legal scholars to rely only on the theory of feminist self-identification to credential feminist judges.

1. INTRODUCTION

FEMINIST LEGAL SCHOLARS want women who are judges to identify as feminists. Rosemary Hunter takes this aspiration seriously, transforming it into the normative claim that 'a feminist judge must identify her (or him) self as a feminist' (2008: 9). Clearly, women judges merit recognition as feminists when they self-identify. They seldom comply with this norm, however. Their reasons for non-compliance are often unknown. Some may be anti-feminist, although women who hold this view tend to be willing to acknowledge it.

More interestingly, they may be feminists who have good reasons for their unwillingness to self-identify. These reasons may include their legal culture (judicial rather than academic professionalism) and/or the feminist theory to which they subscribe (postmodern rather than dominance feminism). They also may involve dissatisfaction with the expectations that feminist legal scholars impose on self-identified feminist judges. Under these circumstances, might there be another way to identify feminist judges who share one or more of these reasons for not self-identifying?

In fact, there are two possibilities. Both involve analysing judicial decisions. Some analysts concentrate on whether the outcomes advance feminist objectives; some, on whether the judge's method of adjudication is consistent with feminist methodology. In this chapter I adopt the latter approach, focusing on feminist adjudication. First, I draw on Katharine T Bartlett's work (1990) in which she set out three feminist legal methods. She relied mainly on feminist scholarship and feminist lawyering to exemplify these methods. Nevertheless, I intend to argue that Bartlett's account of one method provides a good illustration of feminist adjudication.

Next, I set out the two major limitations of feminist self-identification theory. One is that it fails to provide a basis for distinguishing between the professional culture of feminist judges and that of feminist legal scholars. Yet such a distinction is a possibility and is, in fact, borne out by the results of a study comparing the use of the words 'feminist' and 'feminism'—the 'f' words—on the bench and in the academy. The other is that feminist self-identification constrains the positions that feminists can take in the debate that preoccupies contemporary feminist legal theorists. This debate, which arose late in the twentieth century, is between dominance feminists who must self-identify and postmodern feminists who tend to disavow identity politics (Munro, 2007). In contrast, I maintain these limitations are addressed by feminist adjudication theory which provides the alternatives that go unmet in feminist self-identification theory.

On the other hand, feminist adjudication has its own limitations, the most significant of which constrains '*expectations* about the judicial behaviour of feminist judges' (Hunter, 2008: 9, emphasis in original). While feminist legal scholars apply these expectations to self-identified feminist judges, they do not apply them to women judges who have not self-identified as feminist; imposing feminist expectations on the latter would be unfair.[1] However, this constraint fails the test of reciprocity. Feminist self-identification is a unilateral act which does not involve any scholarly analysis, unlike feminist adjudication which does. Therefore, only the latter facilitates reciprocity by enabling feminist judges to apply feminist expectations to the scholarly work of feminist legal scholars. Fairness is, in short, a question of perspective.

I conclude that feminist adjudication is responsive to the cultural, theoretical and political considerations that may deter feminist judges from

[1] Rosemary Hunter, comment made at the 'Gender and Judging Workshop', International Institute for the Sociology of Law, Onati, Spain (11 June 2009).

self-identifying. Feminist adjudication offers an alternative to feminist self-identification. Thus, it is premature to require feminist judges to self-identify as feminists; instead, feminist legal scholars can identify them by their feminist adjudication. Moreover, having more than one way of determining whether judges are feminist places an onus on feminist legal scholars to make their own theoretical, cultural and political perspectives transparent when they study judicial feminism.

2. FEMINIST ADJUDICATION

2.1. Three Feminist Legal Methods

It is not easy to explain what counts as feminist adjudication, mostly because feminist legal scholars tend to refer to it as if we share the same understanding of it. There is considerable descriptive work but a dearth of theorising. Six studies come to mind, starting with the earliest Canadian work by Christine Boyle (1985) and the earliest American study by Suzanna Sherry (1986). Three more American studies by Katharine T Bartlett (1990), Sharon Elizabeth Rush (1992–93) and Michael E Solimine and Susan E Wheatley (1994–95) followed. I rely on Bartlett's work because it is foundational to most of the studies that followed hers.

Bartlett's approach is subject to a caveat, however. It does not include all of the aspects of adjudication that might be attributed to feminist judging. She did not examine some of the more recent issues that other feminist legal scholars have studied, including whether women who are judges dissent more frequently than their brethren (Belleau and Johnson, 2004; Guinier, 2008; McClain, 2009) or whether having women on multi-judge benches influences women-centric decisions (Farhang and Wawro, 2002; Peresie, 2005; Stribopoulos and Yahya, 2007). Instead, Bartlett confined her research to legal reasoning processes.

All of her methods—asking the woman question, feminist practical reasoning and consciousness-raising—reflected 'the status of women as "outsiders", who need ways of challenging and undermining dominant legal conventions and of developing alternative conventions which take better account of women's experiences and needs' (Bartlett, 1990: 831). Although she did not specifically distinguish the work of judges from that of lawyers and scholars, nevertheless few of Bartlett's examples involved judges. This lacuna calls into question whether all three methods are apposite to adjudication.

In a recent study comparing one of Bartlett's methods, feminist practical reasoning, with Canadian Supreme Court Justice Bertha Wilson's use of the contextual method, I outlined the adjudicative features of this particular method (Baines: 2009). It is less clear, however, whether the other two methods transfer from the realms of practice and scholarship to adjudication. For instance, the method of asking the woman question, while compelling, is vulnerable to capture by forces indifferent or hostile to feminism. Similarly, the method of consciousness-raising has more purchase for feminist lawyers and scholars, with only foundational relevance for feminist judges. In this part, I assess the adjudicative potential of all three of Bartlett's feminist legal methods.

2.1.1. Asking the Woman Question

At first glance, the method of asking the woman question seems intuitively distinctive and conducive to adjudicative tasks. It involves 'examining how the law fails to take into account the experiences and values that seem more typical of women than of men, for whatever reason, or how existing legal standards and concepts might disadvantage women' (Bartlett, 1990: 837). As Bartlett observed: 'Women have long been asking the woman question in law' (1990: 838). However, when there were no women on the bench male judges responded that 'the omission was justified by women's different roles and characteristics' (Bartlett, 1990: 838). In other words, asking the woman question had no discernible impact on conventional legal method. In her study of two early twentieth century Canadian women's rights cases, Mary Jane Mossman (1986) foreshadowed this conclusion.

Nevertheless, contemporary feminists continue to 'ask the woman question in many areas of law' (Bartlett, 1990: 842). Bartlett explained that it 'confronts the assumption of legal neutrality' (1990: 847). Rush put it somewhat differently, explaining that feminists ask the woman question to expose the 'bias inherent in most of our rules' (1992–93: 613). By asking the woman question, a feminist judge 'rejects references to an objective truth and looks at situational truth' (Rush, 1992–93: 629). In contrast, 'the traditional judge draws on the abstract rules of law and applies them often without consideration of the entire factual context' (Rush, 1992–93: 630). Therefore, as Rush's work makes clear, context and its relationship to rules bulks large when feminist judges ask the woman question.

Bartlett also emphasised the importance of context, albeit from a different perspective, when she acknowledged that asking the woman question is a method which is vulnerable to the critique of essentialism (1990: 847). Her response to this critique was not to refuse to apply this method; rather she urged that it be 'extended beyond efforts to identify oppression based only on gender' (1990: 848). Adapting Elizabeth Spellman's approach, Bartlett concluded that fine-tuning the woman question 'to encompass the breadth and specificity of oppressions actually experienced by different women—and even some men—can only make feminism clearer and stronger' (1990: 849). In other words, the feminist judge who asks the woman question must enlarge her consciousness to take into account the perspectives of other women.

In sum, the contextualism inherent in applying the method of asking the woman question is indicative of overlaps with Bartlett's remaining two methods—feminist practical reasoning (or contextualism) and consciousness-raising. Absent feminist practical reasoning (or contextualism), a feminist judge asking the woman question might be unable to sustain the claim for inclusivity. Similarly, absent consciousness-raising a feminist judge asking the woman question might have difficulty challenging gender bias. My objective is not to dismiss or even diminish the feminist legal method of asking the woman question. Instead, I suggest its value is enhanced when used in conjunction with one or both of the other two feminist legal methods.

2.1.2. Feminist Practical Reasoning

Bartlett referred to her second method as feminist practical reasoning although I prefer the term contextualism, or the contextual method, because it is cognisable to more than feminist legal scholars. Practical reasoning is a philosophical concept that Bartlett dated back to Aristotle and then fast forwarded to Hobbes and Kant, as well as to some of the American legal realists (1990: 850–54). She characterised this malestream version as one that takes the legitimacy of community norms for granted (1990: 855), an approach that would be an anathema to a feminist judge asking the woman question. In contrast, feminists subscribe to the notion of many communities and reject privileging one or more over the others. Bartlett explained: 'Feminist practical reasoning differs from the other forms of legal reasoning, however, in the strength of its commitment to the notion that there is not one, but many overlapping communities to which one might look for "reason"' (1990: 855). Accordingly, feminist judges who would use feminist practical reasoning should 'seek to identify perspectives not represented in the dominant culture from which reason should proceed' (Bartlett, 1990: 855).

Although identifying perspectives that are not privileged might typically be perceived as proceeding from the experiential approach of consciousness-raising, neither Bartlett nor Justice Wilson took this route (Baines, 2009: 34). When I compared Justice Wilson's contextualism with Bartlett's feminist practical reasoning, I concluded that both women relied on the same approach: they distinguished their method from the abstract method (Baines, 2009: 35); they attached importance to the factual dilemmas that led to the litigation (2009: 36); and most surprisingly (as I observed) they contended that feminist practical/contextual reasoning encompassed abstract reasoning (2009: 36). As Bartlett put it: 'Contextualized reasoning is not the polar opposite of a "male" model of abstract thinking' (1990: 856). Rather, feminist practical reasoning (or contextualism) requires 'the process of abstraction, that is, the separation of the significant from the insignificant' (1990: 856).

Moreover, feminist practical reasoning (or contextualism) is a rational process. Bartlett explained: 'Feminist rationality acknowledges greater diversity in human experiences and the value of taking into account competing or inconsistent claims' (1990: 857). Striving to integrate emotive and intellectual factors, feminist rationality tries 'to open up the possibilities of new situations rather than limit them with prescribed categories of analysis' (1990: 857–58). However, this openness is threatening to traditionalists, prompting their critique that 'feminists' reason contextually in order to avoid the application of rules ... to which they substantively object' (Bartlett, 1990: 862). Far from avoiding rules, Bartlett responded, feminist practical reasoning (or contextualism) seeks to expose and open up debate concerning the political and moral considerations that underlie them. 'By forcing articulation and understanding of those considerations', she concluded, 'practical reasoning forces justification of results based on what interests are actually at stake' (1990: 863).

2.1.3. Consciousness-raising

Bartlett defined consciousness-raising as 'an interactive and collaborative process of articulating one's experiences and making meaning of them with others who articulate their experiences' (1990: 863–64). I entertain some doubts about the ability of feminist judges to use consciousness-raising as a method of adjudication.

To the extent that consciousness-raising involves collaborative articulation, it is difficult to see how it could be transformed into an adjudicative process as currently understood. However, I have no reservations about feminist judges practising it off the bench, 'not only in small personal growth groups, but also on a more public, institutional level' (Bartlett, 1990: 864). On the other hand, consciousness-raising is a knowledge-creation process. As such it could be incorporated into the format of a judicial opinion. In fact, I venture to suggest that Canadian Supreme Court Justice Claire L'Heureux-Dubé sometimes wrote opinions that could serve as the prototype for the knowledge-creation feature of consciousness-raising.[2]

Bartlett, too, may have been concerned about the potential of consciousness-raising for feminist adjudication. She reported that one feminist legal scholar, Judith Resnik, 'has argued that feminist judging will involve more collaborative decisionmaking among judges' (Bartlett, 1990: 865 citing Resnik, 1988: 1942–43). Continuing, Bartlett acknowledged that the primary significance of consciousness-raising is to provide 'a substructure

[2] Eg, *Symes v Canada* [1993] 4 SCR 695; *R v Ewanchuk* [1999] 1 SCR 330; *Trinity Western University v British Columbia College of Teachers* [2001] 1 SCR 772.

for other feminist methods—including the woman question and feminist practical reasoning—by enabling feminists to draw insights and perceptions from their own experiences and those of other women and to use these insights to challenge dominant versions of social reality' (1990: 866). Under these circumstances, feminist legal scholars should defer characterising consciousness-raising as a method of feminist adjudication while subjecting it to further study.

2.2. Feminist Adjudication

What does feminist adjudication mean? Bartlett maintained that the point 'of legal methods is to reach answers that are legally defensible or in some sense "right"' (1990: 867). The notions of right or justice or substantive equality are as contested in as they are apposite to feminism. For example, some feminists would rely on women's substantive equality to justify criminalising polygamy while others (myself included) would use women's substantive equality to challenge the use of the criminal law to prohibit polygamy (Bailey, Baines, Amani and Kaufman, 2005). Hunter put it well when she wrote: 'In some cases, what constitutes a "pro-woman" decision or a feminist outcome may be considerably less than obvious' (2008: 14). Still, as feminist legal scholars we ought not to give up on identifying feminist approaches to adjudication.

Clearly there may be more than one approach to feminist adjudication. In addition, some of these approaches might be combined. For example, we could begin with Hunter's preference for feminist adjudication that consists of 'a combination of feminist practical reasoning, the particularity model and detached attention in Weil's sense' (Hunter, 2008: 13). Or, we could pursue feminist practical reasoning (or contextualism) alone because, as I have argued elsewhere, 'the marriage of context and abstraction distinguishes feminist practical reasoning from the other two modes of feminist legal methodology that Bartlett described' (Baines, 2009: 37). In fact, it is exciting to imagine that feminist adjudication might offer more than one version of feminist contextualism!

My objective in this part is not to argue for a particular version of feminist adjudication, or that there is only one version. Rather, mine is the preliminary argument that there is content that feminist legal scholars can use to sustain a theory of feminist adjudication, whether that content arises from Bartlett's method of feminist practical reasoning (or contextualism) or some other approach. The next step is to distinguish the theory of feminist adjudication, however structured, from that of feminist self-identification. In part three, I explain how the former addresses two significant needs that otherwise go unmet by the latter.

3. THE LIMITS OF FEMINIST SELF-IDENTIFICATION

3.1. Two Limitations

If feminist self-identification and feminist adjudication are distinctive theories, each could fill gaps left by the other. In this part, I describe two functions—one cultural and the other theoretical—that feminist self-identification theory cannot meet. In contrast, the theory of feminist adjudication can fill these gaps.

First, there is some evidence that feminist judges and feminist legal scholars do not share the same legal culture, or at least do not share it in all respects. A study comparing the use of the words 'feminist' and 'feminism' on the bench and in the academy reveals distinctive professional cultures, suggesting feminist legal scholars should study feminist judges on their own terms before presuming to import others. Obviously having more than one approach to feminism—that is, feminist adjudication as well as feminist self-identification—is more conducive to accommodating the different professional cultures of feminist legal scholars and judges.

Secondly, I turn to the most significant contemporary debate in feminist legal theory. Typically feminist legal scholars portray this debate as a contest between dominance and postmodern feminism (Munro, 2007). There are almost no studies suggesting that feminist judges position themselves within this debate, yet why would they not? One barrier is that dominance feminism requires self-identification, which feminist judges seem disinclined to do. Another barrier is that feminist judges cannot enter the debate on the side of the postmodern feminists who disavow self-identification in the absence of another approach. Feminist adjudication may constitute this alternative. Thus, having more than one approach might also enrich our recognition of occasions when feminist judges rely on feminist legal theory to inform their decision-making.

3.1.1. Distinguishing Professional Cultures

In Canada, feminist legal scholars and feminist judges share the same initial process of legal education as they begin their legal careers. The normal pattern is first to complete an undergraduate university programme and then to attend a law school for three years to acquire an LLB or a JD degree. Thereafter the pattern allows for divergences with most scholars completing masters and more recently, doctoral programmes in law, whereas most judges do not feel compelled to pursue these graduate programmes. Instead, they usually enter the practice of law which they must practise for a minimum of ten years to become eligible for appointment to the bench. On the bench, judges are afforded opportunities to attend specialised judicial education programmes.

Although it may be counterintuitive, I do not intend to rely on the most flagrant distinction between judges and scholars, namely that only the former are expected to adjudicate cases. In Canada, some feminist legal scholars challenged this expectation by introducing the Women's Court of Canada. These scholars took their adjudicative role very seriously, 'offering alternative decisions on cases that were before the Supreme Court of Canada, following the same rules and law as the Court but applying different equality analyses and coming to different conclusions' (Majury, 2006: 6). At the same time, they did not abandon their scholarly role insofar as another objective was to satisfy the requirements of critical reflection, which they did by undertaking 'to demonstrate that the Supreme Court of Canada decision in each of these cases is but one of many decisions that could have been written' (Majury, 2006: 8). The first six cases that these feminist legal scholars issued under the aegis of the Women's Court of Canada are published as a special issue of the *Canadian Journal of Women and the Law* (2006).

Despite similarities in their legal training and the functional cross-over afforded by the introduction of the Women's Court of Canada, there is evidence that feminist judges and feminist legal scholars do not share the same legal culture, or at least do not share it in all respects. If their professional cultures are distinctive, it follows that feminist judges and feminist legal scholars may also choose to reveal their feminism in different ways. Thus, feminist legal scholars should study feminist judges on their own terms.

I decided to conduct a very simple study focusing on the use of feminist language by judges on the Supreme Court of Canada since 1982. More specifically, I examined the use of the words 'feminist' and 'feminism'—the 'f' words—in judicial decisions and in academic legal journals. The outcomes surprised me. Not only do the women who sit on the Supreme Court of Canada seldom if ever self-identify as feminist; in addition, they have never used the words 'feminist' and 'feminism' in their judgments. This lacuna covers a time span that is significant. Since the first woman was appointed to this Court in April 1982, seven women have sat and four currently sit on this Bench.[3] My research assistant conducted a keyword search for the stem 'femini-' in the Court's database of cases decided since 1982; it yielded no decision in which any of these women ever used 'feminist' or 'feminism'.[4]

This finding contrasts quite starkly with their colleagues in the academy. Feminist legal scholars make liberal use of these words in the articles and books that they publish. A similar keyword search of all texts/periodicals

[3] Bertha Wilson sat between 1982 and 1991; Claire L'Heureux-Dubé sat between 1987 and 2002; Beverley McLachlin appointed 1989; Louise Arbour sat between 1999 and 2004; Marie Deschamps appointed 2002; Louise Charron appointed 2004; and Rosalie Abella appointed 2004.

[4] C Ashbourne (19 May 2009) Westlaw search.

listed in the 'Index to Canadian Legal Literature' since 1982 resulted in 183 titles (never mind contents) containing the words 'feminism' or 'feminist'.[5] A search of all the books in the Queen's University law library turned up 106 titles with these words.[6] Thus, in what is central to their professional work—publication for scholars, adjudication for judges—their utilisation (or not) of the 'f' words suggests a significant cultural difference.

Yet both groups of women are part of the same legal culture. What explains the difference? The culture at the Court does not explain the difference. Male justices do not hesitate to use the words 'feminist' and 'feminism' in their opinions. Since women have sat on the Court, four men have used them.[7] One referred to The Toronto Women's Bookstore as 'feminist',[8] while in the same case another mentioned Customs confiscations of materials from 'Canadian feminist bookstores'.[9] A third wrote about 'feminist groups'[10] and about the activities of union members 'be they concerned with the environment, tax-policy, day-care or feminism'.[11] The fourth described both a specific male individual (the complainant) and a group as 'feminist'.[12] Taking into account that Supreme Court of Canada decisions are published in both official languages (English and French) but not double counting, the four male justices used the 'f' words seven times over 17 years. Almost invariably their usages were synonymous with 'women'. While the appearance of these words is by no means excessive, it suffices to exclude the suggestion of a rule whether formal or informal proscribing the words 'feminist' or 'feminism' in the judgments issued by this Court.

Just as the culture at the Court does not explain the difference, neither does the culture among the women justices at the Court. When not writing judgments they use the 'f' words in other kinds of formal written and oral communications. To illustrate Justice Bertha Wilson, the first woman appointed to this Court, used 'feminist' and 'feminism' four times in a

[5] C Ashbourne (27 May 2009) Westlaw search excluding law school course materials and workshop seminars. Most authors are Canadian feminist legal scholars; however, 14 are identifiably male, including three anti-feminist males.

[6] C Ashbourne (28 May 2009) Queen's University QCAT search excluding workshop seminars and theses. While most authors are feminist legal scholars, many are not Canadian; three sole and two joint authors are male.

[7] C Ashbourne (21 May 2009) Westlaw SCC database search of stem 'femini-'.

[8] Binnie J, *Little Sisters* [2000] §11: *Little Sisters Book & Art Emporium v Canada* 2000 SCC 69.

[9] Iacobucci J, *Little Sisters* [2000] §188: *Little Sisters Book & Art Emporium v Canada* 2000 SCC 69.

[10] La Forest J, *Lavigne* [1991] § 281: *Lavigne v OPSEU* [1991] 2 SCR 211.
The French version actually contains two references to 'groups feministes', one of which appears as 'women's groups' in the English translation.

[11] La Forest J, *Lavigne* [1991] § 283.

[12] Beetz J, *Brossard* [1989] § 129: *Brossard (Town) v Quebec* [1989] 2 SCR 279. The English version contains only one reference: 'The complainant, an avowed feminist'; the second is translated as 'The women's group'.

lecture delivered at the University of Manitoba at the end of her first year on this Bench. Justice Wilson referred to 'the feminist movement' (Wilson, 1983: 226); to 'a feminist perspective' (1983: 229); to 'feminist theology' (1983: 229 quoting Russell, 1974: 19); and to 'contemporary feminism' (1983: 233). In her famous lecture 'Will Women Judges Really Make a Difference?' delivered seven years later at York University, Justice Wilson mentioned 'feminist legal commentators' (1990: 514 quoting Schafran, 1987: 412–13); 'feminist scholars in Canada' (1990: 514); 'Canadian feminist scholarship' (1990: 515); 'feminist writers' (1990: 519); and 'Feminist Theory' (1990: 521 quoting Cain, 1988: title). Finally, *Touchstones for Change*, the report of the gender equality task force that she chaired after retiring from the Bench, included two references to 'the feminist movement' in sections attributed explicitly to Justice Wilson—in the 'Introduction from the Chair' (1993: 1) and in the concluding chapter's 'Postscript (The Chair)' (1993: 272).

More significantly, Justice Wilson also 'prepared' the sections in the report's chapter on 'The Judiciary' that refer to the judicial survey material because she 'alone had access to the confidential material' (1993: 185). She had written to 'approximately 200 women judges ... asking them whether or not they had personally experienced discrimination by male Chief Justices, Chief Judges or male colleagues' (Wilson, 1993: 192). 58 of the 132 respondents 'reported having personally experienced discrimination in one form or another while on the bench' (1993: 192). Some younger women described being 'asked if they were feminists and told that feminists were unsuited for the judicial role because of their radical and biased views' (1993: 192). The male judges claimed that feminists should be 'automatically disqualified' from hearing sexual assault cases 'because of their anti-male prejudice!' (Wilson, 1993: 192). Justice Wilson's criticism of the male judges was explicit and uncompromising: 'they were simply applying their own preconceived ideas and exhibiting a mindset which clearly was not based on rational evidence but on myths and stereotypes accepted and applied without critical or constructive thought' (1993: 192). Her trenchant words were consistent with a feminist perspective but not avowed as such, nor expressed in a judgment.

After elaborating a number of other forms of discrimination described by the women judges who had responded to the survey, Justice Wilson reported that some complained about not being assigned to sit on sexual assault cases because their male colleagues saw them as 'radical feminists' (1993: 194). Again she was critical, maintaining these men applied this label to any 'woman who believes in equality, publicly asserts that belief and attempts to achieve it' (1993: 194). Was Justice Wilson thinking of herself when she made this statement? If so, was she concerned about the label as a whole or only about the adjective 'radical'? In fact, it may have been the latter given her next sentence: 'Because the existing norm has always been and still is the norm of inequality, equality must inevitably seem radical to some in that it is a total rejection of inequality' (1993: 194). Being called a feminist did not merit comment; being 'radical' did.

Justice Wilson was not the only woman to speak and write about 'feminists' and 'feminism' in non-judgment communications. What is interesting, however, is that not all of the other six women justices have used the 'f' words in such communications. A search of the Index to Canadian Legal Literature produced more than 180 entries for all seven women justices.[13] Of these, 22 were attributed to Justice Wilson, 23 to Justice Claire L'Heureux-Dubé, 36 to Chief Justice Beverley McLachlin, 12 to Justice Louise Arbour, 2 to Justice Marie Deschamps, 3 to Justice Louise Charron and 34 to Justice Rosalie Abella. A keyword search of these works using the stem 'femini-' revealed that other than Justice Wilson, only Justices L'Heureux-Dubé, Arbour and Abella have written about 'feminists' and 'feminism'.[14] Their references deserve further study. For the purposes of this chapter, however, it is sufficient to assert that none were disrespectful or derogatory about feminists and feminism.

Although the foregoing survey is at best superficial, it suggests that feminist legal scholars should consider referring to at least four of the women who have sat on the Supreme Court of Canada—Justices Wilson, L'Heureux-Dubé, Arbour and Abella—as feminist judges. Admittedly they have not yet used the 'f' words in their judgments and most have not self-identified as feminist. However, their professional culture may enhance their credibility as justices if they do not self-identify as feminists or use the 'f' words in their judgments, just as the professional culture of feminist legal scholars dictates that our credibility (especially if we are second-wave feminists) would plummet were we not to self-identify and use the 'f' words.

While credibility may be personally fulfilling, it may also serve important institutional enhancement functions for feminists. Put differently, seeking it is not all bad. However, the lesson for feminist legal scholars is not about what matters as credibility or whether credibility matters. Rather it is about not finding feminist judges wanting simply because they do not meet the cultural criteria of feminist legal scholars. I suggest this is particularly true before we have some in-depth studies that compare our professional cultures. After all, self-identification is not the only mechanism at our disposal. As feminist legal scholars we can analyse what feminist judges write about feminism when they are not writing judgments. We can analyse their judgments to understand whether their method of adjudication is feminist. We can assess and critique the substance of their decisions. We can, in other

[13] C Ashbourne (3 June 2009) Westlaw search. Some studies were published before the judges were elevated to the Supreme Court of Canada.

[14] This search failed to find the 'Forward' in which Chief Justice Beverley McLachlin used both 'feminist' and 'feminism' to describe Justice L'Heureux-Dubé (McLachlin, 2004: 1, 3).

words, grant them a culture distinctive from ours without presuming to know which is more or less feminist.

3.1.2. Distinguishing Feminist Legal Theories

Feminist judges should not be precluded from participating in the most significant debate in contemporary feminist legal theory. Typically feminist legal scholars portray this debate as a contest between dominance and postmodern feminism (Munro, 2007). It may also resonate with the controversy between second and third-wave feminists, although feminist legal scholars are only just beginning to explore this relationship (White, 2008). For the purpose of this chapter, however, it is sufficient to focus only on the former.

Dominance theory, typified in the work of Catharine MacKinnon (1987; 1989), seeks to redress 'the systematic subordination of women at the hands of men' (Munro, 2007: 3). It is meta-theory, usually mono-causally explaining patriarchy and agendas for reform. Despite challenging law and the state, dominance theory evinces faith that these same venues provide 'productive avenues for improvement' (Munro, 2007: 4). Fundamental to this theory is a notion of rights, particularly equality rights, as empowerment. It is probably not too extreme to say that the notion of equality of power, as between the genders, is an end in itself in dominance theory.

Similarly, in feminist theory the slogan 'the personal is political' symbolises the empowerment that second wave feminists attributed to identifying as feminist.[15] This empowerment is both individually and collectively important. As such, it justifies the voluntariness that underlies feminist self-identification. When women in positions of power such as judges self-identify, however, empowerment is not the only consequence that follows. As Hunter argues, self-identification gives rise to expectations that feminist judges must meet (2008: 9)—expectations about their commitment to women, to challenging the treatment meted out to women by law and the State, to promoting women's equality rights and generally to their recognition of the need to disrupt malestream power. Thus feminist self-identification theory starts from a power deficit, empowers, recognises and evaluates power, critiques power and remedies power, all with gender relations in mind. It is, in short, consistent with dominance theory.

In contrast, feminist adjudication theory may appear as detached from issues of power, women, rights, equality—as detached as postmodern feminist theory. Postmodern theory has questioned 'how best to understand patriarchy, the utility of legal reform tactics, the legitimacy of women-centred

[15] See C Hanisch, 'The Personal is Political' (2006) at: scholar.alexanderstreet.com/pages/viewpage.action?pageId=2259.

methods, the merits of grand-theorizing and the contours of feminism's utopia' (Munro, 2007: 1). For example, feminist theorists such as Carol Smart (1989) and Martha Fineman (1990) 'have called for a de-centering of law and a rejection of legal reform strategies, which frequently involve reliance on rights' (Munro, 2007: 5). Other foundational dilemmas posed by postmodern theorists include whether we can talk at all about the predicament of women in collective terms (Munro, 2007: 7). While feminist adjudication is too underdeveloped to evince any of the sophistication of postmodern theory, nevertheless its sheer diffuseness makes it a better candidate than self-identification for alignment with postmodernism.

No explanation of the controversy between dominance and postmodern feminisms would be complete without reference to their critiques. Postmodern theory is critical of dominance theory for its monocausal theorising and for its essentialism; dominance theorists critique postmodern theorists for failing to address power relations and for radically deconstructing collective gender identity. Feminist self-identification and feminist adjudication are respectively vulnerable to the same critiques, albeit less intensively posed. In particular, feminist self-identification assumes a more conflictual position with malestream power, whereas feminist adjudication appears to be more conciliatory about the exercise of gendered power relations. However, these critiques do not obviate the importance of having more than one way to identify feminist judges. To the contrary they reinforce theoretical diversity.

Are the feminist legal scholars who self-identify as second-wave dominance feminists open to this diversity? Are they willing to accept the possibility that judges who do not self-identify as feminist may hold theoretical positions more consistent with postmodern feminism than with dominance feminism? The difficulties this possibility poses were amply illustrated by Ellen Anderson's recent biography of Justice Bertha Wilson (2001). Anderson maintained that Justice Wilson 'declines to identify herself as a feminist' (Anderson, 2001: xiv) while also referring to her as a 'postmodern judge' whose 'judgments may incorporate aspects of feminist theory' (2001: xv). Critics such as McGlynn (2003: 308) and Backhouse (2003: 187, fn 76) concluded that Anderson never intended to identify Justice Wilson as a feminist judge. However, what if Anderson's point was not about Justice Wilson's identity as a feminist, but rather about postmodernism's disaffection for identity politics? Might the theory of feminist adjudication, by whatever standard or standards it is constructed, offer a way out of this dilemma? Invoking feminist adjudication could provide feminist legal scholars with a method for identifying (or not) Justice Wilson's feminism without challenging her stance (if she held one) as a postmodern feminist who rejected identity politics.

3.2. Two Theories

Two theories may be better than one. It is early days to constrain the list of women judges who are feminist. The appointment of women to high courts is a recent phenomenon. In most countries, their numbers do not even come close to approximating their availability in the profession let alone in the population. To have more than one way of recognising whether these women are feminist does not preclude the application of both theories to individual judges for whom they are apposite (Hunter, this volume). On the other hand, when only one of these theories applies, it still may enhance our understanding of feminist judges and feminist judging. In sum, having more than one way to identify feminist judges is consistent with facilitating their diverse positionality in the professional culture that they share with feminist legal scholars as well as in the contemporary feminist legal theory debate.

4. THE LIMITS OF FEMINIST ADJUDICATION

4.1. Three Limitations

Feminist adjudication theory also has limitations. Two are shared with the theory of feminist self-identification while the third ostensibly is not. Both theories have to deal with interpreting judicial silence (about feminism) and resolving inconsistent (feminist) decision-making. The limitation that is ostensibly unique to feminist adjudication theory pertains to the feminist expectations that feminist legal scholars apply to the judicial behaviour of feminist judges. I conclude that an analysis of these three limitations tell us more about the power dimension inherent in feminist legal scholarship than it tells us about feminist adjudication or feminist self-identification.

4.1.1. Silence

Feminist adjudication theorists, like those who subscribe to feminist self-identification, must interpret judicial silence about feminism. For the former it takes the form of failing to use feminist adjudication; for the latter, failing to self-identify as feminist. If both forms of silence coalesce, rejection seems likely. Without more information, however, rejection is not synonymous with anti-feminism. Consistently with self-identification theory, the label 'anti-feminist' must have purchase; it should be reserved for those who 'specifically and emphatically insist they are not feminists, often by reference to the social construction or caricature of feminism as something negative, wrongheaded and/or dangerous' (Hunter, 2008: 9).

4.1.2. *Inconsistencies*

The issue of inconsistencies, like that of silence, troubles both theories. Unlike silence which is patently antithetical to self-identification, inconsistencies are more problematic for feminist adjudication. Theorists must decide whether they are prepared to demand that feminist judges use feminist adjudication in every case they decide, in every opinion they author. Or, are they willing to concentrate on women's cases, equality cases, Charter rights cases, family law cases, reproductive rights cases, etc. Hunter argued 'that a judge who identifies as a feminist cannot be selectively feminist' (2008: 14). Is the same true of a judge who does not self-identify as feminist but to whom we attribute feminist adjudication? If her approach is contextualism, might the context of the litigation temper reliance on feminist adjudication? What if feminist judges differ over the outcome of a case, one writing the majority opinion and the other the dissent, is one being selectively feminist?

4.1.3. *Expectations*

At the IISL Gender and Judging Workshop in June 2009 Rosemary Hunter argued that it is fair to have feminist expectations of feminist judges but it is not fair to have feminist expectations of women judges. More specifically, only self-identification gives rise to '*expectations* about the judicial behaviour of feminist judges' (2008: 9). Fairness demands that only self-identified feminist judges 'face challenges, demands and criticism from feminist commentators when they do not act as feminists, or do so insufficiently' (Hunter, 2008: 31). The implications of this distinction fall disproportionately on the shoulders of feminist adjudication theorists, however. If it is unfair to impose feminist expectations on women judges whose feminist credentials derive solely from scholarly identification of their feminist adjudication, their theory is emptied of all but symbolic meaning. Feminist adjudication can be used to label women judges as feminists but nothing follows.

Still, imposing feminist expectations may not be an unmitigated good. In fact, it creates a hierarchical relationship between feminist legal scholars and the self-identified feminist judges whom they study. Hunter recognises the harshness of this hierarchy. She invites feminist legal scholars to be 'more considered and respectful', more into 'encouragement and support' and more cognisant of 'obligations of *mutual* support' (2008: 31). Whatever the potential for reining in scholars, however, they cannot deny that the power to comply or not lies with them and not with the feminist judges who self-identify as feminist.

A similar hierarchy would undoubtedly arise if feminist adjudication theorists were entitled to apply feminist expectations to the feminist judges whom they study. However, this relationship is different in one significant respect. These expectations arise only after feminist legal scholars analyse the adjudication and identify it as feminist. Unlike self-identification which provides feminist legal scholars with a risk-averse free-ride, identifying adjudication as feminist puts scholarly bodies on the line. They may misidentify adjudication as feminist, or fail to credit it when it is feminist. Either way, their credibility will suffer. They will not have met the reasonable expectations of scholarly behaviour of feminist legal scholars. In other words, feminist legal scholars who use feminist adjudication to identify feminist judges submit to a more egalitarian experience. They must, in short, share some of their power with the feminist judges whom they study.

4.2. Power

The interpretation of silence, the resolution of inconsistencies, and the application of expectations highlight the power dynamic that is inherent in the relationship between feminist legal scholars and feminist judges. Moreover, these limitations constitute powerful analytic tools in the hands of feminist legal scholars. The concept of power deserves further study in this context, with both parties acknowledging their ownership of it and the ensuing vulnerabilities.

5. CONCLUSIONS

What are the goals of feminist legal scholars who study feminist judges? Can they justify requiring women judges to self-identify as feminist? Self-identification is unquestionably a fundamental tenet of the feminist movement. Hunter is not wrong to invoke it. Early feminists took the absence of women, the disappearance of women, even the silence of women and empowered them to challenge these patriarchal conditions by self-identifying as feminists. However, in the context of feminist legal scholars and women judges it is more difficult to see a parallel. The former already construe the latter as powerful simply because they are women in power. Among feminists, therefore, the context determines who benefits from self-identification. In the relationship between feminist legal scholars and feminist judges, if the former require the latter to identify as feminists, it is the feminist legal scholars who are empowered.

Do feminist legal scholars aspire to be critics of feminists judges? On the one hand, the culture of legal scholarship demands critique, the more so because feminist judges are in positions of power. On the other, feminist legal scholars also have power, both intellectual and political/activist. Who within the feminist community is tasked with critiquing scholarly exercises of power? Generally, these critics are other feminist scholars and activists, but not judges. It is not the primary (or even secondary) professional task of feminist judges to critique feminist legal scholars. There is no reciprocity.

I conclude that it is premature to require self-identification. Feminist legal scholars need time to explore alternatives such as feminist adjudication, as well as to assess the assumptions that attach to the vast majority of judges who do not self-identify as feminist. Some of these judges are anti-feminist; others are women 'judges who refuse to declare a position or remain equivocal, but whose judgments and actions evince feminist sympathies' (Hunter, 2008: 9). Although Hunter is willing to describe the latter 'as exemplars of "feminist judging"' (2008: 9), she would exclude them 'from the category of "feminist judge"' (2008: 9). However, her approach would have excluded Justice L'Heureux-Dubé for the better part of her career on the Bench. Although many feminist legal scholars revered her feminism throughout her career, Justice L'Heureux-Dubé refused to self-identify as feminist until the *Ewanchuk* controversy erupted; even then she preferred to self-identify as an 'outsider' (L'Heureux-Dubé, 2001: 24–27). I for one would not be happy qualifying Justice L'Heureux-Dubé's pre-self-identification status as 'feminist sympathiser', not least because I reserve that term for men.

My preference is to open feminism to feminist judges and feminist judging (and feminist sympathisers) whenever possible. If this means feminist legal scholars will differ over who and what counts, these are the controversies that we should entertain in considered and respectful ways, that is, without harming the justices whose bodies we put on the line. In Canada, for example, fans of Justice Wilson and Justice L'Heureux-Dubé have sparred for years over their respective feminisms. The arguments are not always of the highest calibre, but they do promote conceptualisation of feminist judges and feminist judging, not to mention highlighting the power of feminist legal scholars.

The downside of openness is the same as the downside of pursuing feminist adjudication theory. It is that feminist legal scholars appear to be without criteria to recognise feminist judges and/or feminist adjudication, or they may attribute feminism to a judge who is not feminist. Either way, they are the ones to get it wrong; they have not met the expectations of scholarly behaviour of feminist legal scholars. In sum, when feminist legal scholars use feminist adjudication they are forced to share their power with the feminist judges whom they identify.

6. REFERENCES

Anderson, E (2001) *Judging Bertha Wilson: Law as Large as Life* (Toronto, University of Toronto Press).

Backhouse, C (2003) 'The Chilly Climate for Women Judges: Reflections on the Backlash from the Ewanchuk Case' 15 *Canadian Journal of Women and the Law* 167.

Bailey, M and Baines, B and Amani, B and Kaufman, A (2005) 'Expanding Recognition of Foreign Polygamous Marriages: Policy Implications for Canada' in *Polygamy in Canada: Legal and Social Implications for Women and Children: A Collection of Policy Research Reports* (Status of Women Canada).
Baines, B (2009) 'Contextualism, Feminism, and a Canadian Woman Judge' 17(1) *Feminist Legal Studies* 27.
Bartlett, KT (1990) 'Feminist Legal Methods' 103 *Harvard Law Review* 829.
Belleau, M and Johnson, R (2004) 'Judicial Dissent: Early Reflections on Emotion, Reason and Passion in Law' in M Belleau and F Lacasse (eds), *Claire L'Heureux-Dubé at the Supreme Court of Canada, 1987–2002* (Montreal, Wilson & Lafleur Ltée).
Boyle, C (1985) 'Sexual Assault and the Feminist Judge' 1 *Canadian Journal of Women and the Law* 93.
Cain, P (1988) 'Good and Bad Bias: A Comment on Feminist Theory and Judging' 61 *Southern California Law Review* 1945.
Farhang, S and Wawro, G (2002) 'The Influence of Women and Racial Minorities under Panel Decision-Making on the US Court of Appeals' 20(2) *The Journal of Law, Economics, & Organization* 299.
Fineman, M (1990) 'Challenging Law, Establishing Differences: The Future of Feminist Legal Scholarship' 42 *Florida Law Review* 25.
Guinier, L (2008) 'The Supreme Court, 2007 Term – Forward: Demosprudence Through Dissent' 122 *Harvard Law Review* 4.
Hunter, R (2008) 'Can Feminist Judges make a Difference?' 15(1–2) *International Journal of the Legal Profession* 7.
L'Heureux-Dubé, C (2001) 'Outsiders on the Bench: The Continuing Struggle for Equality' 16 *Wisconsin Women's Law Journal* 15.
MacKinnon, C (1987) *Feminism Unmodified: Discourses on Life and Law* (Cambridge, Harvard University Press).
—— (1989) *Toward a Feminist Theory of the State* (Cambridge, Harvard University Press).
Majury, D (2006) 'Introducing the Women's Court of Canada' 18 *Canadian Journal of Women and the Law* 1.
McClain, L (2009) 'Supreme Court Justices, Empathy, and Social Change: A Comment on Lani Guinier's *Demosprudence through Dissent*' 89 *Boston University Law Review* 589.
McGlynn, C (2003) 'Book Review: Ellen Anderson, Judging Bertha Wilson – Law as Large as Life' 11 *Feminist Legal Studies* 307.
McLachlin, B (2004) 'Forward' in E Sheehy (ed), *Adding Feminism to Law: The Contributions of Justice Claire L'Heureux-Dubé* (Toronto, Irwin Law).
Mossman, MJ (1986) 'Feminism and Legal Method: The Difference it Makes' 3 *Australian Journal of Law and Society* 30.
Munro, VE (2007) *Law and Politics at the Perimeter: Re-evaluating Key Debates in Feminist Theory* (Oxford, Hart Publishing).
Peresie, JL (2005) 'Female Judges Matter: Gender and Collegial Decisionmaking in the Federal Appellate Courts' 114 *Yale Law Journal* 1759.
Resnik, J (1988) 'On the Bias: Feminist Reconsiderations of the Aspirations for Our Judges' 61 *Southern California Law Review* 1877.

Rush, SE (1992–93) 'Feminist Judging: An Introductory Essay' 2 *Southern California Review of Law and Women's Studies* 609.
Russell, LM (1974) *Human Liberation in a Feminist Perspective: A Theology* (Philadelphia, Westminster Press).
Schafran, LH (1987) 'The Success of the American Program' in S Martin and K Mahoney (eds), *Equality and Judicial Neutrality* (Toronto, Carswell).
Sherry, S (1986) 'Civic Virtue and the Feminine Voice in Constitutional Adjudication' 72 *Virginia Law Review* 543.
Smart, C (1989) *Feminism and the Power of Law* (London, Routledge).
Solimine, ME and Wheatley, SE (1994–95) 'Rethinking Feminist Judging' 70 *Indiana Law Journal* 891.
Stribopoulos, J and Yahya, MA (2007) 'Does a Judge's Party of Appointment or Gender Matter to Case Outcomes?: An Empirical Study of the Court of Appeal for Ontario' 45 *Osgoode Hall Law Journal* 315.
White, BA (2008) 'Traversing 2nd and 3rd Waves: Feminist Legal Theory Moving Forward' 39 *University of Baltimore Law Forum* i.
Wilson, B (1983) 'Law in Society: The Principle of Sexual Equality' 13 *Manitoba Law Journal* 221.
—— (1990) 'Will Women Judges Really Make a Difference?' 28 *Osgoode Hall Law Journal* 507.
—— (1993) 'Introduction from the Chair', 'The Judiciary', and 'Postscript (The Chair)' in *Touchstones for Change: Equality, Diversity and Accountability* (Ottawa, The Canadian Bar Association).
Women's Court of Canada (2006) 'Rewriting Equality' *Canadian Journal of Women and the Law* Special Issue 18(1).

5.2

Justice Marcia Neave: Case Study of a Feminist Judge

ROSEMARY HUNTER

Abstract

This chapter seeks to determine whether my previous account of feminist judging (Hunter, 2008) is borne out in the judgments of a newly-appointed feminist judge, Justice Marcia Neave of the Court of Appeal in Victoria, Australia. I analyse Justice Neave's decisions during her first three years on the bench, both quantitatively (in terms of the number and types of cases she dealt with, with whom she sat on the three-member court and what role she played in each decision), and qualitatively in terms of her reasons for decision, and how these differed, if at all, from those of her judicial colleagues. The analysis reveals that there is relatively little scope for feminist judging in the cases dealt with by the Court of Appeal, and where there is such scope, Justice Neave rarely arrived at a different result from her colleagues. In a number of cases, however, she took an identifiably feminist approach in her reasons for decision, in a way that was not reflected in the decisions of either her male or female colleagues.

1. INTRODUCTION

MARCIA NEAVE AO has had a distinguished academic career as (among other things) dean of law at the University of Adelaide (only the third woman to be appointed to a chair in law in Australia), a professor at Monash and the Australian National Universities, co-author of the first Australian casebook on property law, President of the Commonwealth Administrative Review Council and Chair of the Victorian Law Reform Commission. She also has well-established feminist credentials, ranging from heading the Victorian government's inquiry into prostitution in 1984–85, which resulted in the legalisation of prostitution in Victoria, to numerous academic articles and the support and mentoring of younger women lawyers and academics. In 1999 she was made an Officer of the Order of Australia 'For service to the law, particularly in relation to law reform in the area of social justice as it relates to issues affecting women, and to legal education' (Australian Government, 1999). On 22 February 2006 she was appointed to the Victorian Court of Appeal.

This chapter explores Justice Neave's judgments during her first three years on the Court of Appeal, in light of my previous theoretical work on feminist judgments. I was interested to find out what scope there is for feminist judgments on the Court of Appeal, to what extent and in what ways (if any) Justice Neave's judgments can be identified as feminist and in what ways (if any) her judgments differ from those of other male and female judges on the court who do not identify as feminists.

2. PREDICTIONS

The then Victorian Attorney-General, Rob Hulls, was active in appointing women to the Victorian courts at all levels. His appointments since coming to office in 1999 resulted in a significant increase in the number of women judges on the County Court (intermediate trial court: now 26 women out of 68) and the Supreme Court (now 11 women out of 43), including the appointment of the first woman Chief Justice, Marilyn Warren, in 2003. The Supreme Court comprises the Trial Division and the Court of Appeal, and Justice Neave was only the second woman to be appointed to the Court of Appeal, following a legislative amendment which broadened the eligibility criteria for judges of the Supreme Court.[1] Previously, candidates were required to have at least eight years' admission to practice in the Supreme Court, which resulted in the appointment almost exclusively of senior barristers, whereas Justice Neave's background was in academia and law reform. Her appointment was greeted warmly by many in the legal profession, with the *Victorian Bar News*, for example, referring to her 'almost unique capacity to master, quickly and confidently, very different areas of legal specialty', 'communication skills of the highest order', 'open-mindedness', 'thoughtfully founded and highly developed ethical sense' and her 'willingness and capacity to approach new problems with intellectual rigour, a commitment to arriving at conclusions based on the interrogation of evidence, self-awareness and independence of mind'. 'We all have biases', this article commented, 'But it is her Honour's ability to see and acknowledge her own, as a precondition to engaging in informed and impartial decision-making, that marks her out'.[2] This emphasis on Neave's open-mindedness, impartiality, evidence-based decision-making and ability to transcend her biases perhaps

[1] Constitution Act 1975 (Vic), s 75B, as amended by the Constitution (Supreme Court) Act 2003 (Vic), s 3. The first woman appointed to the Court of Appeal was Justice Susan Kenny in 1997, but her tenure on the Court was brief, and she left in 1998 to join the Federal Court bench.

[2] See: www.vicbar.com.au/webdata/VicBarNewsFiles/Welcomes.pdf: 14.

protests too much. Reading between the lines, is the article suggesting that although she is a feminist, that will not unduly intrude on her decisions? Others were less delicate. Amid several anonymous mutterings, *Herald-Sun* journalist Andrew Bolt directly claimed that she was unqualified for the role due to her lack of legal practice experience and her history of law reform activism, feminism and support for 'leftist' causes.[3]

In assessing Justice Neave's judicial record over the first three years of her appointment, my concern has been to investigate neither her judicial merit, nor her impartiality. Rather, I have been interested to see the extent (if any) to which her judicial practice conforms to previous accounts of feminist judging. In my 2008 article, 'Can *Feminist* Judges Make a Difference?' (Hunter, 2008), I drew on a range of secondary literature and existing judgments to produce a list of characteristics that feminist judgments might (and I argued ought to) display. These included:

— 'asking the woman question': noticing the gender implications of apparently neutral rules and practices (as well as their implications for other traditionally excluded groups);
— 'including women', both in terms of writing women's experiences into legal discourse (as individual litigants and collectively, drawing on relevant research evidence) and in the construction of legal rules;
— challenging gender bias;
— contextualisation and particularity: reasoning from context and the reality of women's lived experience; making individualised rather than categorical or abstract decisions; paying particular and careful attention to the individuals before the court; and not judging women for making different choices from those the judge herself would have made;
— seeking to remedy injustices and to improve the conditions of women's lives;
— promoting substantive equality;
— being open about and accountable for inevitably difficult choices that must be made between competing interests; and
— drawing on feminist legal scholarship to inform decisions.

Notably, this list largely concerns procedures for feminist judging rather than the kinds of outcomes that might be expected. Consequently, the presence or otherwise of these characteristics can only be determined by qualitative means—that is, it is necessary to read and analyse judgments rather than simply counting votes.

[3] A Bolt, 'Law wears a dress' *Herald-Sun* (1 March 2006); A Bolt, 'Judicial puppeteer' *Herald-Sun* (14 June 2006).

I also argued that feminist judges ought to be feminist at all times, not just intermittently, given the availability of a feminist legal analysis of just about every conceivable area of law. Even if a judge is compelled to arrive at a less than ideal outcome given the constraints of legislation and/or precedents, she can still use feminist reasoning in her opinion. A further hypothesis arising at least implicitly from my argument was that feminist judges are likely to judge differently from women judges who do not identify as feminists.

In my article I also considered at some length who might count as a feminist judge. The reason for asking this question is important to the answer. If one's aim is purely descriptive, then it is only necessary to line up any judge's actual practice with the list of characteristics of feminist judgments. Applying those criteria, it is clear that some male judges and many women judges would count as feminist. On the other hand, if one is making a normative argument, that is, contending that feminist judges *ought to* act in a particular way then, in my view, it is also necessary for the judge to actually identify as a feminist. In other words, it is only reasonable to *expect* feminist judging of someone who holds herself out as a feminist, and it is not reasonable to impose such expectations on someone who does not do so.[4] In this case, Marcia Neave clearly does identify as a feminist. Has she made the kind of difference, then, that I suggested feminist judges can and should make?

3. METHOD

The Austlii database[5] provides online access to all Victorian Court of Appeal decisions, and I focused on those delivered between 22 February 2006 (the date of Justice Neave's appointment) and 21 February 2009. The Court of Appeal sits almost always in three-judge panels, but very occasionally a case will be decided by two or five judges. I identified all of the decisions during the three-year period in which Justice Neave participated, and entered them into a database, recording the other judges on the panel, the general and specific issues involved in the case, Justice Neave's role in the decision and whether the case raised any feminist or gender issues. I took as expansive a view as possible of what might constitute a feminist or gender issue, including 'asking the woman question' (might the legal rules in question have particular gender implications?); whether the case involved a woman protagonist (as one of the parties, or as a victim in criminal cases); whether it raised any issues of equality or discrimination; and whether there were any issues of stereotypical femininity *or* masculinity involved. I automatically included all cases involving sexual offences against either adults or children.

[4] Beverley Baines puts forward a different view in her chapter in this collection.
[5] See www.austlii.edu.au.

I then read all the cases classified as involving feminist/gender issues, and made notes on all of the written reasons for judgment, whether given by Justice Neave or one of her colleagues. This material was then analysed for particular patterns, conformity with the characteristics of feminist judging outlined above and differences and similarities between the decisions of Justice Neave and those of other judges.

4. STATISTICAL FINDINGS

Statistical analysis provides an overview of and an insight into the nature of Justice Neave's judicial activity during her first three years on the bench. How many and what types of cases did she deal with? With whom did she sit and what role did she play in these cases? The findings in relation to these questions provide a framework for the qualitative analysis of judgments.

Justice Neave delivered a total of 204 judgments in her first three years on the Victorian Court of Appeal. For half of this time she was the only woman on the Court, until the appointment of Justice Julie Dodds-Streeton in August 2007. Women judges from the Supreme Court did occasionally sit on the Court of Appeal, in particular Chief Justice Warren, and Justices Betty King and Elizabeth Curtain. However, Justice Neave sat with another woman in only 35 of her 204 cases (17 per cent). The men judges with whom Justice Neave most frequently sat included Justices Frank Vincent (60 cases), Chris Maxwell (the President of the Court of Appeal: 55 cases), Geoffrey Nettle (39 cases), David Ashley (34 cases), Peter Buchanan (32 cases) and Robert Redlich (31 cases). Given that she was at the beginning of her judicial career, she acted as the presiding (most senior) judge in only 21 cases (10 per cent).

Around 60 per cent of the work of the Court of Appeal consists of criminal appeals and 40 per cent civil appeals.[6] Justice Neave's workload was similar to that of the Court in general, involving 64 per cent criminal cases and 36 per cent civil cases. Within the group of criminal cases, sentencing appeals predominated (60 per cent) over appeals against conviction (34 per cent).[7]

[6] Supreme Court of Victoria, *2006–2007 Annual Report* (Melbourne, Supreme Court of Victoria, 2007), available at: www.supremecourt.vic.gov.au.

[7] In common law systems, where a defendant has been found guilty of a criminal offence, the trial judge will proceed to impose a sentence, which involves an exercise of discretion constrained by sentencing principles and guidelines. The defendant may appeal against his or her conviction, or may appeal solely against the sentence determined by the judge: this often occurs in situations where the defendant has pleaded guilty, but believes they have received an excessively harsh penalty. In addition, it is possible (in limited circumstances) for the prosecution to appeal what they believe to be an unduly lenient sentence.

Each bench of the Court hears between three and five cases per week, and the presiding judge allocates one member of the panel to write the leading judgment in each case. This is usually done in order of seniority, unless one of the judges has a particular interest or expertise in the subject matter of the case. Broadly consistent with this allocation method, Justice Neave wrote the leading judgment in 28 per cent of the cases on which she sat.

One striking feature of the Court's judgments is that it is a very agreeable court. Most often, the other two judges simply agree with the leading judgment. They might sometimes write a relatively short concurring judgment if they disagree with or wish to supplement the leading judgment on a particular point, but it is rare to have two or three lengthy judgments giving different reasons for the same result, or dissenting from the result. This helps to explain the following statistics on the types of judgments given by Justice Neave.

It can be seen that unlike Canadian feminist judge, Justice Claire L'Heureux-Dubé, who was a noted dissenter (L'Heureux-Dubé, 2000; Belleau and Johnson, 2008), Justice Neave agreed with her (mostly male) colleagues 97 per cent of the time. This could be interpreted in a number of ways: that she did not act as a feminist; that she did act as a feminist and persuaded her colleagues to her point of view; that her colleagues were also (descriptively) feminists; or that feminism did not come into it. In fact, the latter seems to have been true in the majority of cases.

The Victorian Court of Appeal hears appeals from courts and tribunals lower in the Victorian State hierarchy, primarily from the County Court and the Trial Division of the Supreme Court. These are courts of general jurisdiction, encompassing both common law and State statute law. They do not, however, deal with family law, which in Australia is a specialist federal jurisdiction. The State does not have a constitutional Bill of Rights and its Charter of Human Rights and Responsibilities Act 2006 is justiciable only in very limited circumstances. State anti-discrimination legislation does cover issues such as sex and pregnancy discrimination and sexual harassment, but it emphasises alternative dispute resolution, and the few

Type of judgment	%
Leading judgment	28
Agreement with leading judgment	36
Joint judgment	17
Concurring judgment	8
Agreement with brief concurrence	7
Dissent	3 (7 cases)

Figure 1: Types of Judgments of Justice Neave

cases adjudicated by the Victorian Civil and Administrative Tribunal are very rarely appealed. Thus, the Court of Appeal almost never hears cases in several of the areas of law that typically raise issues of gender equality.

As a result, even on my very expansive definition of 'feminist/gender issues', only 32 per cent of Justice Neave's cases (66 cases) involved such an issue. I could not find any kind of gender angle in fully two-thirds of her cases. So much for my argument that a feminist judge should be a feminist at all times! It is true that feminist legal scholars have developed feminist analyses of contract law, property law, company law, natural resources law, competition law, insurance law and so forth, but that does not mean there is scope for the application of those analyses in any given contracts, property or other commercial case. Rather, a substantial amount of the Court's civil work appears to involve narrow issues of statutory or contractual interpretation, to which a gender-sensitive approach has no relevance. Not surprisingly then, criminal cases were overrepresented among those involving a 'feminist/gender issue'. They constituted 86 per cent of such cases, while only 14 per cent were civil matters. Within the criminal group, 51.5 per cent were sentencing appeals and 45.5 per cent were appeals against conviction.

Justice Neave gave the leading judgment in 36 per cent of the 'feminist/gender issue' cases in which she was involved. This was higher than her overall percentage of leading judgments, indicating either that she chose (or was given) the leading judgment in some of these cases due to her particular interest or expertise, or that she found feminist/gender issues in cases in which she was assigned to give the leading judgment, when other judges might not have done so. She was also twice as likely as average to write a concurring judgment in cases involving a feminist/gender issue (15 per cent versus eight per cent)—often, as illustrated below, to express a particular feminist perspective. On the other hand, in 27 per cent of the feminist/gender issue cases, she merely agreed with the leading judgment. Her dissent rate on such cases was 4.5 per cent—marginally above her average dissent rate, but nowhere near a statistically significant difference.

5. DECISIONS

5.1. Inclusivity: Creating New Legal Knowledge

In her 1995 chapter on 'The Gender of Judgments', Reg Graycar questioned the sources of judges' knowledge of the world, and suggested that such knowledge was (masculine) gendered. A feminist judge, therefore, might be in a position to correct this imbalance. And indeed, the most common and obvious way in which Justice Neave 'made a difference' in cases concerning feminist/gender issues was in making generalised statements which brought previously excluded social experiences into legal discourse, and in some instances challenged gender bias, to expand and transform law's 'common knowledge' of the world. This occurred particularly in cases concerning sexual offences and domestic violence. Apart from one other case in which Chief Justice Warren made a comment about the harm caused by sexual offences,[8] none of the other judges—male or female—made any such statements in this group of cases.

In *R v RTM*,[9] for example, Justice Neave noted in her leading judgment that: 'research reveals that some of the matters described ... are common aspects of sexual assaults against children', including delayed reporting and not disclosing all details or incidents initially, especially when the perpetrator is a family member. She observed that while each case must be decided on its own facts, 'it is equally important that myths about the "typical behaviour" of people who complain of sexual assault do not provide the basis for drawing unjustified factual inferences'.[10] Notably, another member of the Court in this case specifically dissented from these statements on the basis that counsel's submissions on those points had been peripheral to the issues on appeal and the research Justice Neave referred to was not before the court. Thus, 'As neither the applicant nor the Crown had any opportunity to comment or make submissions on it I say nothing about that research or the conclusions to which Her Honour referred'.[11]

This case marks an interesting point in Justice Neave's transition from academic to judge. As an academic, it was natural for her to refer to research evidence. But having been challenged on this approach from a judicial perspective, she subsequently avoided references to research evidence and simply made general observations, as authoritative statements of judicial knowledge. For example:

> It is common for child victims of sexual offences to have difficulty in telling others about the offences which have been committed against them. Often offenders tell victims to keep the offence a secret.[12]

> Victims of incest and other forms of intra-familial sexual abuse take years to recover from its psychological effects and sometimes never do.[13]

> People who have an intellectual disability, or an acquired brain injury, are vulnerable to sexual exploitation, because they usually have to depend on others to help them with ordinary daily activities.[14]

[8] *R v Cardamone* [2007] VSCA 77 (3 May 2007) [46].
[9] *R v RTM* [2006] VSCA 170 (28 August 2006).
[10] Ibid, [35]–[36].
[11] Ibid, [39].
[12] *R v Kovac* [2006] VSCA 229 (30 October 2006) [28].
[13] *R v DD* [2008] VSCA 15 (18 February 2008) [15].
[14] *DPP v Barnes* [2007] VSCA 51 (29 March 2007) [23].

In *R v Hester*,[15] the defendant had seriously assaulted his girlfriend on two occasions when he was drunk. The victim had submitted a victim impact statement claiming that she was partly to blame for the second incident by provoking him, and that she and the defendant had resolved their problems and wanted to continue their relationship. The defendant pleaded guilty, but appealed against the sentence imposed on the ground that the sentencing judge had failed to give due weight to the victim impact statement. Chernov JA, who wrote the leading judgment, referred to authorities which suggested that forgiveness by the victim or a supportive victim impact statement may indicate that the consequences of the offence on the victim had not been long-term or debilitating and, particularly where the offence occurs in a domestic situation, the attitude of the victim may be relevant to the question of rehabilitation.[16] He ultimately concluded, however, that the sentence imposed was not excessive. Neave JA, while agreeing with the result, added a comment on the victim impact statement from a different perspective. She noted that it was a common pattern for perpetrators of domestic violence to express penitence and persuade their victims to reconcile, that many victims were assaulted on several occasions before summoning the courage to leave an abusive relationship and that they often required considerable support to do so. She urged that sentencing judges faced with a victim impact statement from a victim of domestic violence should give these matters considerable weight, and should treat evidence of forgiveness by a domestic violence victim 'with extreme caution'.[17]

In *R v Khem*,[18] Justice Neave disagreed more explicitly with one of her colleagues over the issue of unprotected sex. The defendant had pleaded guilty to attempted sexual penetration of a child under 16. His attempt at penile penetration had been interrupted when he was discovered in the victim's bed by her brother. He appealed against the sentence imposed on a number of grounds, including the argument that the sentencing judge (a woman) had erred by holding that his failure to use a condom was a significant aggravating factor. He contended that this could not have been a significant factor given the lack of actual penetration. The leading judgment was written by Pagone AJA, who considered that attempting penetration without a condom indicated a high degree of moral culpability and recklessness on the defendant's part. Ashley JA, dissenting, would have allowed the appeal on this ground. In his view, it was doubtful whether it was legitimate to take into account the risk of a sexually transmissible disease if the defendant did not believe himself to have one, but even so, the lack of a condom and the defendant's moral culpability as a result could only have been a minor aggravating factor given

[15] *R v Hester* [2007] VSCA 298 (29 November 2007).
[16] Ibid, [9].
[17] Ibid, [27].
[18] *R v Khem* [2008] VSCA 136 (17 August 2008).

the lack of actual penetration. In her opinion, Neave JA agreed with Pagone AJA and strongly rejected Ashley JA's reasoning:

> If necessary, I would be prepared to take judicial notice of the fact that there is a risk that a number of sexually transmissible diseases, including genital herpes and genital warts, can be transmitted by genital contact falling short of penile penetration. There has been extensive community education on this issue.[19]

In any event, she continued, the sentencing judge was entitled to give weight to the fact that the defendant

> carelessly took the risk that intercourse, if completed, would expose the victim, a 14 year old girl, to the risk of pregnancy or infection. The fact that he did not have intercourse with the victim, either because he was unable to do so or because he was interrupted, does not alter his moral culpability for his irresponsible act of attempting to penetrate the victim without using a condom.[20]

5.2. Contextualisation

In other cases, Justice Neave contextualised the issues in a way that her judicial colleagues did not, both in terms of explaining the policy context for the legislation in question and paying attention to the particular circumstances of the individual parties. For example, in a stalking case, one basis for the defendant's appeal was the argument that the mental element required for the offence should be subjective, so he should only have been convicted if it was shown that he intended to cause harm to the complainant or make her apprehensive or fearful. Neave JA rejected this contention, holding that the legislation clearly required an objective intention, that is, what a person in the defendant's circumstances ought to have understood about the likely effect of his behaviour on the complainant. She added:

> The policy rationale for this provision is clear. It may be that many stalkers falsely believe that they have a relationship with the person they pursue, even though they may have never met or spoken to the victim. A provision which required proof of a subjective intention to cause harm to the victim would not apply to an alleged stalker who obsessively pursued the victim on the basis of a false belief that these attentions were welcome.[21]

In *R v RGG*,[22] the defendant, who was aged in his sixties, had sexually abused two teenage sisters, one over a considerable period of time. All three

[19] Ibid, [19].
[20] Ibid, [20].
[21] *R v Hoang* [2007] VSCA 117 (7 June 2007) [104].
[22] *R v RGG* [2008] VSCA 94 (6 June 2008).

judges agreed that the sentence imposed was manifestly excessive, but only Neave JA paid particular attention to the experience of the victims, noting that one of the girls suffered from epilepsy, and that the offending against her had continued for four years, with serious emotional and psychological consequences.[23] Although she also paid attention to the mitigating factors in the defendant's favour, this telling of the victims' story helped to counter the way in which Ashley JA and Lasry AJA in their judgments tended to minimise the offences.

In *R v Abela*,[24] the defendant had been convicted of the rape of his de facto partner. This followed an incident in which the victim had found the defendant in a bedroom lying on top of her 12-year-old daughter, and the daughter subsequently told her that the defendant had raped her. The victim was afraid of the defendant and did not directly accuse him, but that night refused to sleep with him. The next day, he insisted on having sex with her, and although she did everything to avoid it and said 'no' several times, she did not physically resist because of her fear of him. One of the defendant's grounds for appeal against his conviction was that the trial judge should not have admitted the evidence of his sexual assault on the victim's daughter because its prejudicial effect outweighed its probative value. In her leading judgment, however, Neave JA held that this evidence had a very high probative value, noting that 'it is difficult to envisage an event which is likely to have a greater effect on the complainant's willingness to participate in sexual activity with the applicant'.[25] Since there was no other, less prejudicial way of placing the act of sexual intercourse with the victim in its proper context, the judge had not been in error in admitting this evidence. In his concurring judgment, Nettle JA observed that he would have been inclined to hold that the trial judge should have excluded the evidence of the defendant's sexual assault on his stepdaughter, but on reflection, he was persuaded by Neave JA's reasoning that the evidence had such a high degree of cogency and probative force as to exceed its prejudicial effect.

5.3. No or Non-generalisable Difference

In the majority of the cases involving feminist/gender issues, however, Neave JA did not particularly stand out. In 17 cases, she simply agreed with the leading judgment delivered by one of her colleagues, joining in both the result and the reasoning offered in that judgment. In a further 16 cases, she either made her decision, joined in a joint judgment or delivered a concurring judgment on purely technical legal grounds. This may, at least

[23] Ibid, [12].
[24] *R v Abela* [2007] VSCA 22 (28 February 2007).
[25] Ibid, [75].

in part, have been in the interests of managing her workload. With almost 70 cases decided each year (well in excess of one per week, in addition to hearings), it may not have been possible to write a feminist concurrence in every case, but rather to select the cases which seemed to require specific feminist input. In addition, the task of writing a leading or joint judgment involves providing reasons that are likely to command the assent of the other members of the court, which may operate as a restraint, particularly if any gender issues in the case are relatively marginal.

In some of her leading judgments Justice Neave stressed the seriousness of the offences involved (such as domestic homicide, attempted murder, rape and child sexual abuse) and considered that the defendant deserved severe condemnation and a heavy sentence as a result, but other judges (particularly Justices Vincent and Kellam) did the same in some cases. By contrast, in other cases, despite stressing the seriousness of the offences, Justice Neave was nonetheless also sensitive to mitigating factors and ultimately sympathetic to the defendant in the sentencing process, along with other members of the court.

Greater sympathy for the defendant than her colleagues also accounted for two of Justice Neave's dissenting judgments. In *R v Toms*,[26] the defendant had introduced his much younger girlfriend to intravenous drug use, which ultimately led to her death from an overdose while he stood by and failed to seek help. His appeal against sentence was upheld due to an error by the sentencing judge, however Buchanan and Vincent JJA agreed in re-imposing the same sentence, while Neave JA would have given greater weight to mitigating factors, particularly the defendant's genuine remorse and the fact that he had sought treatment for his drug use, and would consequently have imposed a lower sentence. In *DPP v Derbey*,[27] the defendant had spent an evening drinking with his girlfriend, but she left the pub without him, and when he later could not find her he reacted angrily, went to her home and set it on fire, completely destroying the unit. The DPP appealed against the lenient sentence imposed on the defendant (a 12-month intensive correction order) and Vincent JA and Kellam AJA upheld the appeal and imposed a new sentence of two years' imprisonment. Both strongly condemned the defendant's behaviour. According to Kellam AJA:

> Regrettably, it is far from uncommon that one party in a domestic, or other relationship, as here, takes out their anger, resentment and frustration upon the other party by destruction of property. Those who do so, particularly by fire, should be under no illusion other than that they will face salutary punishment.[28]

[26] *R v Toms* [2006] VSCA 101 (5 May 2006).
[27] *DPP v Derbey* [2007] VSCA 92 (14 Mary 2007).
[28] Ibid, [46].

And Vincent JA:

> The employment of violence, almost invariably by disappointed males, whether directed against the person or property of a former or desired partner to express anger or as a form of retribution in consequence of a relationship failure or perceived rejection simply cannot be tolerated.[29]

Despite the domestic violence context, Neave JA would have dismissed the appeal, on the basis that the trial judge had not erred in concluding that, since the defendant was a youthful first offender, was remorseful and had made an early confession, his overall rehabilitation—and hence the protection of the community—would be best served by an intensive correction order. It could be said that Justice Neave's sentencing decisions were indeed individualised rather than abstract or categorical, and that she did pay particular and careful attention to the person before the court. However, this made it difficult to discern any particular pattern as to the cases in which she was inclined to be severe or merciful towards the defendant.

5.4. Classic Feminist Issues

Only three of the cases heard by Justice Neave in her three years on the Court were centrally concerned with oft-rehearsed issues in feminist legal theory. The two criminal cases are discussed here and the third—a civil case—is considered at greater length in the following section. In *R v Goodall*,[30] Justice Neave challenged gender bias and drew on feminist legal scholarship in a concurring judgment on the issue of whether a juror's particular experience gave rise to a reasonable apprehension of bias. The defendant had been tried for child sexual offences. During the prosecutor's closing address, a jury member became emotionally distressed, the jury was sent out and the juror disclosed that he had been a victim of childhood sexual abuse, but said he now felt able to continue. The trial judge discharged the individual juror but proceeded with the remaining 11 jurors, who convicted the defendant. The defendant appealed, arguing that the trial judge ought to have discharged the whole jury, on the basis that the discharged juror was not impartial and may have tainted the rest of the jury. Redlich JA dismissed this argument, noting that juries are routinely invited to assess the evidence in a case in light of their own experience, and that the jury system is premised on the notion that a juror's life experiences or their use of them in evaluating the evidence does not give rise to a reasonable

[29] Ibid, [2].
[30] *R v Goodall* [2007] VSCA 63 (13 April 2007).

apprehension of bias. Neave JA agreed, but added some more specific remarks of her own:

> I do not accept the submission that a person who has had a particular life experience cannot serve on a jury in a trial which concerns matters to which that experience is relevant. In this case the argument, put simply, amounts to the generalisation that victims of sexual assault are incapable of bringing an objective mind to the issues to be resolved in the trial of an accused for sexual offences, while other members of the jury who have not had such an experience are capable of doing so. It should not be assumed that a person who has been sexually assaulted is more likely to be prejudiced against the accused than other jurors.
>
> It is to be expected that juries will, at times, include persons who have been victims of crimes ... As Professor Martha Minow points out in an excellent article on bias and impartiality, the purpose of selecting juries from a cross-section of the community is intended to ensure they bring a variety of perspectives and experiences to the task of fact-finding.[31]

And she went on to quote from Minow's article (1992: 1217). The defendant sought to appeal further to the High Court, but special leave was refused.

R v RW[32] was the one case in which Justice Neave clearly felt compelled to arrive at a result with which she disagreed. In my 2008 article, I observed that lower and intermediate level judges may in some cases be compelled to reach a non-feminist conclusion by clear legislation or precedents, but I argued that in such cases, it is open to the feminist judge in her opinion to express her concerns about the law to which she must nevertheless adhere. This is what Justice Neave did in this case. The defendant was convicted in two separate trials of indecent assaults against two girls aged 11–14, and the rape of one of them. The offences had occurred 25–30 years previously. One of the defendant's grounds for appeal was that in both trials the judge had failed to give the jury an adequate 'Longman warning'. In *Longman v R*,[33] the High Court held that a judge must warn the jury of the dangers of convicting on the uncorroborated evidence of the complainant in a case of rape or sexual assault if the circumstances of the case (such as delay in reporting, the nature of the allegations, the age of the complainant) require it, thereby effectively reversing the effect of statutory amendments which had abolished the old requirement for a corroboration warning in sexual offence cases. In *Crampton v R*[34] the High Court added that where there has been a lengthy delay in the complaint, the warning must be given in clear

[31] Ibid, [3]–[4].
[32] *R v RW* [2008] VSCA 79 (16 May 2008).
[33] *Longman v R* (1989) 168 CLR 79.
[34] *Crampton v R* (2000) 206 CLR 161.

and unmistakable terms, since the jury may not fully appreciate the effects of delay on the memory of the complainant and of other witnesses, and may also not fully appreciate the forensic disadvantage faced by the accused in defending himself against the allegations due to the passage of time since the alleged offences (see also *Doggett v R*).[35] Justice Neave concluded, with regret, that the trial judge's Longman warnings were inadequate, noting previous Court of Appeal decisions in which more extensive directions than the ones given in these cases had been found to be inadequate:

> If I were not constrained by authority I would have been inclined to consider that her Honour adequately warned the jury of the forensic difficulties faced by the accused [by reason of delay] ... However, having regard to the High Court and Court of Appeal decisions to which I have referred, I consider that I am obliged to hold that her Honour did not give the jury sufficiently clear warning of the forensic difficulties faced by the accused in the circumstances of the case.
>
> Although I consider that the application for leave to appeal must be granted and the appeal allowed I note that there has been considerable criticism of the way in which the requirement to give a *Longman* warning has been interpreted and applied.[36]

She also noted that: 'Since the accused was presented for these offences Victorian law on Longman warnings has been substantially modified by amendments to the Crimes Act 1958'[37]—presumably implying that the unjust result in the present case should not be repeated in future.

6. *GILLER v PROCOPETS*

Giller v Procopets[38] was Justice Neave's most significant feminist judgment in her first three years on the Court of Appeal, involving just about all the techniques of feminist judging identified in my theoretical article. The case was quite complex, arising out of a failed de facto relationship in which the couple had cohabited for three years and had twin sons (Ms Giller also had a daughter from her previous marriage). After separation, the couple continued to see each other for a further three and a half years before the relationship completely broke down. Ms Giller was claiming an interest in the property owned by Mr Procopets under Victoria's de facto property regime (Property Law Act 1958 (Vic), Part IX), damages for serious assaults to which Mr Procopets had subjected her during the course of the relationship, and damages for emotional distress caused when, in an effort to

[35] See also *Doggett v R* (2001) 208 CLR 343.
[36] *R v RW* [2008] VSCA 79 (16 May 2008) [55]–[56]).
[37] Ibid, [58].
[38] *Giller v Procopets* [2008] VSCA 236 (10 December 2008).

embarrass and humiliate her near the end of the relationship, Mr Procopets had shown a video of the two of them having sex to some of her friends and relatives. The trial judge made serious adverse findings about the credibility of both parties and dismissed most of Ms Giller's claims, other than the award of $5000 for five assaults that he found to have occurred. She appealed to the Court of Appeal which, by majority, upheld all of her claims and substantially increased the damages awarded for the assaults. Justice Neave wrote the leading judgment, Maxwell P concurred, and Ashley JA dissented.

In relation to the property claim, Neave JA found that the trial judge had interpreted the scope of the legislation in an unduly restrictive manner, and that Ms Giller's relevant contributions to the welfare of the family were not confined to the period of cohabitation. She was also concerned to ensure that Ms Giller's contributions—as homemaker and as primary and later sole carer of the couple's children—were not undervalued in comparison with Mr Procopets' financial contributions. In this respect, she considered that the trial judge had tended to minimise Ms Giller's contributions while overestimating those of Mr Procopets, and she set about correcting this bias and describing Ms Giller's contributions differently by reference to the concrete reality of women's lives. For example, the trial judge's

> conclusion that Ms Giller's contributions [during the period of cohabitation] 'did not exceed the cost of her keep and that of her daughter' tended to equate her position with that of a domestic servant rather than that of a domestic partner. Characterising her contributions in that way had the effect of 'devaluing those contributions which are not readily capable of evaluation in monetary terms'.[39]

And in relation to the period after the couple had separated:

> Between 1993 and 1996 the children were quite young and must have required considerable care. The fact that Ms Giller 'maintained her own household and independence' does not detract from the value of her contributions in caring for the twins, for whom she took primary responsibility, though she received some assistance from Mr Procopets. During this period, Ms Giller undertook the double load of caring for the children and earning an income. Mr Procopets assisted her by picking up and collecting the children on some days of the week, but these contributions to the welfare of the children were no more than incidental. On no view could they be regarded as equivalent to the responsibility borne by Ms Giller. She was, for practical purposes, a sole parent, shopping, cooking and caring for twins aged between 3 and 6 years old.[40]

[39] Ibid, [354] quoting Brereton J, *Kardos v Sarbutt* (2006) 34 Fam LR 550, 561.
[40] Ibid, [337].

In addition, Neave JA accepted, contrary to the trial judge's conclusion, that Ms Giller's contributions had been rendered more arduous by the domestic violence to which Mr Procopets had subjected her. In doing so, she drew on the work of feminist legal scholars who argued in the mid-1990s that violence should be taken into account in family law property cases.[41] She said that she regarded it as 'self-evident' that the violence and threats to kill found by the trial judge would have made it significantly more difficult for Ms Giller to act as a homemaker and parent:

> Plainly, the effects of domestic violence are not limited to physical injury. The assaults on Ms Giller made her fearful, apprehensive that she would be assaulted again, and anxious to avoid provoking Mr Procopets.[42]

In conclusion, she awarded Ms Giller a lump sum of $45,000 by way of adjustment of property interests between her and Mr Procopets.

Ms Giller's claim in relation to the sex video involved technical legal issues concerning the availability of damages for breach of confidence, on which Neave JA found in Ms Giller's favour, contra the trial judge. The judge had also considered that the injury suffered by Ms Giller in this incident had been fairly minor, and did not merit an award of aggravated damages. Again, Neave JA rejected the trial judge's minimisation and told the story differently:

> It may be accepted that Ms Giller is a person of some resilience. This does not, in my view, preclude the making of a compensatory award which includes an element for aggravation. The fact that Ms Giller's friends and family knew that she had had a sexual relationship with Mr Procopets was, in my view, irrelevant to an assessment of the impact on her of knowing that others had seen her actually engaging in sexual activity ... The showing of the video was inevitably humiliating and distressing. Mr Procopets well knew from his telephone conversations with Ms Giller that she was disturbed and upset by his threats. That, evidently, was his purpose. He is fortunate that she appears not to have suffered any lasting injury.[43]

She awarded Ms Giller $40,000 damages for breach of confidence, including $10,000 aggravated damages.

In relation to Ms Giller's third claim, Neave JA looked at each assault found to have occurred by the trial judge, and once more retold the story in a manner that stressed the seriousness of the assaults and their effects, and counteracted the trial judge's minimisation. Thus, for example, where the trial judge focused only on the physical injury resulting from one assault

[41] Ibid, [293], citing Behrens (1993, 1995); Australian Law Reform Commission (1994); Wiegers (1994).
[42] Ibid, [299].
[43] Ibid, [441].

(bruising and discomfort for about a week), Neave JA also stressed the pain, shock, emotional upset and fear experienced by Ms Giller.[44] Where the trial judge had considered that Ms Giller's complaints about the effects of the assaults were exaggerated, and found that Ms Giller was 'a determined woman who is not over sensitive', Neave JA noted that:

> Ms Giller's determination and her failure to be cowed by Mr Procopets' assaults is not inconsistent with her fearing him and suffering mental distress as a result of the violence she suffered. It cannot be doubted that the victim of such an assault would have feared for her own safety. Nor are the mental distress and fear caused by such an assault diminished by the fact that she did not seek medical treatment.[45]

Neave JA not only increased the damages awarded for each assault, but awarded exemplary damages, and strongly condemned Mr Procopets' violent behaviour in a manner reminiscent of sentencing remarks. This resulted in a total award of $50,000.

By contrast, Ashley JA characterised Mr Procopets' assaults on Ms Giller as 'relatively isolated incidents'[46] which did not justify a conclusion in relation to Ms Giller's property claim that her contributions to the welfare of the family had been rendered more arduous. He also criticised Justice Neave's accounts of the assaults as going beyond the evidence that the trial judge had been prepared to accept, and introducing inferences and assumptions about their effects on Ms Giller that had not been put in evidence.[47] Neither could he take as seriously as Neave JA the threats to kill Ms Giller that Mr Procopets had made during one of the assaults:

> I should think that it was no more than a wild threat made in the course of an altercation between two excitable people. There is no difficulty in concluding that both of them were excitable and given to a variety of anti-social behaviours which many in the community would find unacceptable.[48]

In addition, he inferred from the fact that Ms Giller had resumed a sexual relationship with Mr Procopets soon after obtaining an intervention order against him that she could not have been in fear of him,[49] although clearly, quite the opposite inference could be drawn on this point.

But if Justice Neave failed to persuade Ashley JA about the seriousness of the violence, Maxwell P did agree with her fully on these aspects. Indeed he would have gone further in relation to Ms Giller's claim concerning the sex

[44] Ibid, [484].
[45] Ibid, [486].
[46] Ibid, [79].
[47] Ibid, [190]–[92].
[48] Ibid, [193].
[49] Ibid, [195].

video, and would have recognised a separate basis for the award of damages in the tort of intentional infliction of emotional distress, previously unrecognised in Australian law. In her reasons for not agreeing with him on this point, Neave JA noted that such a tort could potentially apply to a very broad range of situations, including harassment on the basis of race, sex or sexuality, 'bullying, practical jokes, unkindness in family and social relationships and the insensitive management of medical patients, employees, and consumers'.[50] Yet compensation or other remedies for much of this behaviour was already available under other common law claims, or under domestic violence, anti-stalking or anti-discrimination legislation or statutory complaints schemes. Thus, she was hesitant to create a new cause of action in the context of an individual case. In this respect, she demonstrated a feminist openness and accountability in making difficult choices between competing interests, considering carefully the possible implications of the development of a new legal claim, rather than simply retreating behind conventional arguments about the lack of precedent or the appropriate roles of courts and the legislature.

7. CONCLUSIONS

The quantitative analysis of Justice Neave's judgments suggests a disappointingly narrow scope for the application of any theory of feminist judging to the Victorian Court of Appeal. But where this scope existed, the qualitative analysis demonstrates above all the importance of feminist reasoning in writing judgments. Justice Neave was far more likely than not to reach the same result in a case as her brother (and occasionally sister) judges, but significantly often, her reasons for arriving at that result were different from those of both her male and female colleagues. This was not usually due to a different legal analysis, but rather, in the application of the law to the facts, she told the story differently or expanded the law's stock of common knowledge in a way that wrote the realities of women's lives into the legal text. What, of course, must remain unknown from a reading of published judgments, is how often Justice Neave persuaded the other members of the bench to arrive at a result which she advocated but which they would not have reached without her presence on the bench. Such an outcome was momentarily visible in the *Abela* case, but generally remains invisible.[51] Thus, while we cannot tell the extent to which this feminist judge made a difference to the outcomes of cases, and we can observe that she did not often change existing legal rules, she clearly did make a difference in cases

[50] Ibid, [474].
[51] For an analysis of the effect of women judges on the decisions of federal appellate panels in the US, see Peresie (2005).

involving feminist/gender issues by means of her reasons for judgment. In the major case of *Giller v Procopets*, she almost certainly did all three.

8. REFERENCES

Australian Government (1999) Special Notices Gazette S214: Queen's Birthday 1999 (7 June).

Australian Law Reform Commission (1994) *Report No 69, Part I – Equality Before the Law: Justice for Women* (Sydney, Australian Law Reform Commission).

Behrens, J (1993) 'Domestic Violence and Property Adjustment: A Critique of No-Fault Discourse' 7 *Australian Journal of Family Law* 9.

—— (1995) 'Violence in the Home and Family Law: An Update' 9 *Australian Journal of Family Law* 70.

Belleau, M-C and Johnson, R (2008) 'Judging Gender: Difference and Dissent at the Supreme Court of Canada' 15(1–2) *International Journal of the Legal Profession* 57.

Graycar, R (1995) 'The Gender of Judgments: An Introduction' in M Thornton (ed), *Public and Private: Feminist Legal Debates* (Melbourne, Oxford University Press).

Hunter, R (2008) 'Can *Feminist* Judges Make a Difference?' 15(1–2) *International Journal of the Legal Profession* 7.

L'Heureux-Dubé, C (2000) 'The Dissenting Opinion: Voice of the Future?' 38 *Osgoode Hall Law Journal* 495.

Minow, M (1992) 'Stripped Down Like a Runner or Enriched by Experience' 33 *William and Mary Law Review* 1201.

Peresie, JL (2005) 'Female Judges Matter: Gender and Collegial Decisionmaking in the Federal Appellate Courts' 114 *Yale Law Journal* 1759.

Wiegers, W (1994) 'Compensation for Wife Abuse: Empowering Victims?' 28 *University of British Columbia Law Review* 247.

5.3

What's in a Label?[1] *Argentine Judges' Reluctance to Call Themselves Feminists*

BEATRIZ KOHEN

Abstract

Inspired by Rosemary Hunter's proposal, this chapter attempts to flesh out the concept of a feminist judge in the context of a group of highly-placed Argentine judges. Faced with their refusal to identify with the feminist label, I was obliged to find a common denominator for their orientation; it was their admitted tendency to work from a gender perspective, commitment to equality between the sexes and empathy with feminist goals and methods. In a second step, I attempted to understand their reluctance to identify with the feminist label, their strong prejudice with respect to feminism and feminists. The answer was a reluctance to be associated with a stigmatised label, fear to be identified with the most extreme forms of feminism, a misunderstanding of feminism and its tenets, and fear that the public might see them as partial. This calls for an intense and persevering dialogue between feminists and judges empathising with feminist goals.

1. INTRODUCTION

THE SIGNIFICANT INCREASE in the number of women entering the judiciary that has occurred across jurisdictions over the last 30 years has awakened an interest in the study of women's impact on the administration of justice and has triggered research projects on the difference women might be making to the judiciary. Inspired by Gilligan's (1982) theory of the 'different voice', these studies have searched for that voice in judicial decisions, as well as in judicial dissent, attitudes, process and courtroom behaviour (Beiner, 2005; Feenan, 2009; Kohen, 2004, 2008a, 2008b; Kenney, 2008; Malleson, 2003; Menkel Meadow, 2009).

[1] I am paraphrasing Janice McCabe (2005).

Although such studies have considerably enhanced our knowledge on gender and judging, research findings have been inconclusive. While some studies have shown certain differences in certain areas of the law, others have not. Furthermore, various authors have warned against the essentialist risk involved in taking gender differences in judging for granted. Accordingly, a substantial shift was made in terms of the questions asked.

Thus, Schultz (2003) advises considering other variables besides gender and to relate research to specific contexts; Malleson (2003) recommends avoiding justifying women's presence on the bench on grounds of the difference they might make, in case this cannot be verified; and Kenney (2008) invites us to think of gender differences in judging in ways that are theoretically sophisticated, empirically true and do not lead to women's disadvantage.

Along similar lines, in order to escape from essentialism and other disadvantages, Hunter (2008) suggests we should move the focus of our attention from 'women judges' to 'feminist judges'. That is to say, instead of speculating about the contribution women judges might make to the judiciary, we should enquire into the impact of the presence of 'feminist judges'. She invites us to reflect on who would qualify as a 'feminist judge' and what we could expect from her or him.

Although I was uncertain about the extent to which Hunter's scheme would apply to the Argentine context, with a civil law system and a strong cultural tradition of 'machismo',[2] the idea of testing this suggestion (as someone who is at the same time a researcher working on gender and judging and a member of the feminist movement) appealed to me. This is more so since, as happened in the US and Canada earlier, in the last few years a small number of organisations working on gender justice have come forward in Argentina that maintain that the increase in the number of women entering the judiciary constitutes an opportunity to advance the process of incorporation of a gender perspective among members of the judiciary, both as a means to attain a more egalitarian judicial system in terms of women's place within its hierarchy and to attain judicial services better prepared to respond to the needs and demands of women litigants. Thus, they advocate the promotion of strategic alliances between feminist organisations working on gender justice and women in high positions within the judiciary. They believe that such an association may accelerate a process through which increased awareness among women about discrimination affecting their own position within the judiciary might lead to recognition of how women's social subordination shapes their access to justice and their experience as

[2] 'Machismo' usually translated as male chauvinism stands for the ideology sustaining male domination and women's subordination.

litigants. They are hopeful that such increased awareness might lead to changes in women judges' professional outlook and activities.[3]

In North America, in particular, these ideas have inspired interesting experiences and projects.[4] In Argentina, in the 1990s, AMJA (the Argentine Association of Women Judges), with the support of Inter American Development Bank, had organised workshops intending to introduce a gender perspective and foster the use of the international conventions. However, this initiative remained embryonic and its impact was not properly assessed. It is only in the last couple of years that local women's organisations have started to consider the strategies mentioned above.

Finally, what also encouraged me to pursue this study was the public discussion in 2007 in connection with the so called 'Tejerina' case about what can be expected from a 'feminist'. A girl, Tejerina, had in 2003 hidden her pregnancy[5] and subsequently stabbed her newborn baby to death, claiming that she saw the face of her rapist in the baby's face. Women's groups have extensively and persistently campaigned during the years while the file was decided and then appealed through courts, from local to national level all the way up to the Supreme Court of the Nation. The local Supreme Court charged Tejerina with aggravated murder and gave her a sentence of 14 years in prison—a charge that can lead to a sentence of 25 years in prison. Her lawyer, having had an appeal to the Highest Criminal Court rejected, decided for an Extraordinary Appeal (Remedy of Complaint) before the National Supreme Court. Feminist groups had hoped that, given its composition, with two women within its ranks and one of them having

[3] See, for instance, Abrahamson (1998) and Wald (2005). Both authors argue that women judges' experience of discrimination enables them to identify with the position of other victims of discrimination and this might influence their judging.

[4] I am referring, for instance, to the National Judicial Education Program, involving both research on gender bias in the courts and training for judges and other legal operators aimed at mitigating gender bias and promoting equality among women and men within the judiciary. These 'task forces' have been working for 20 years and have now covered most US states. Also, with the aim of sensitising the judiciary around legal issues that most affect women's relationship with the law, the associations of women judges all over the world have organised conferences and seminars on the subject. I am also referring to initiatives that aim to rewrite judgments from a feminist standpoint, such as the Women's Court in Canada and in the UK. The latter is being undertaken by Hunter, McGlynn and Rackley, feminist legal scholars from the universities of Kent and Durham. Most recently, Women's Link Worldwide, an international NGO has implemented a Gender Justice Observatory as a means of uncovering progressive and discriminatory court decisions, as part of this initiative; they invite citizens to nominate the best and worst judgments involving gender justice.

[5] Abortion is legally available in Argentina only when a seriously mentally handicapped mother has been raped (Art 86 Argentine Criminal Code) and even in those circumstances the practice of an abortion is contested because Catholic doctors from public hospitals often voice conscientious objections. This impossibility to resort to termination makes Tejerina's case more dramatic and represents the reality of thousands of girls who become pregnant after being raped. It is important to note that the de-penalisation of abortion is one of the most important pending legal issues for Argentine feminism.

publicly declared her feminism, the National Supreme Court would finally modify the charges and order Tejerina's release from prison. However, the National Supreme Court returned the file to the local Supreme Court and upheld the sentence. This led to great turmoil and much media discussion among women's groups.

2. THE STUDY

This chapter conveys the results of part of a larger ongoing research project aiming to explore the relationship between judges—mostly, but not exclusively women—and feminism, particularly what in the judges' opinion can be expected from a feminist judge.

In this exploratory examination I planned to interview a small sample of high ranking male and female judges who I expected to be sympathetic to the feminist cause. Following Hunter's suggestion[6] in her 2008 article 'Can Feminist Judges make a Difference?', I wanted to invite them to reflect on two issues: (1) what makes a judge a feminist?; and (2) what impact may such a feminist approach have on the judicial process and decision?

However, this posed an initial problem. As I had learned from personal experience, my 2002 previous research with family judges (Kohen, 2004 and 2008a and 2008b) and pilot interviews performed a few weeks before starting this study, Argentine judges—as much as Argentine women in general[7]—are very reluctant to label themselves as feminists. Even when they believe in much of what feminism stands for—human dignity for all, repairing social injustices, offering equal opportunities and respect for women and even if their judicial activity exhibits allegiance to feminist values—they often prefer not to call themselves feminists. Such a tendency was later confirmed in the course of the research, as only one of the judges interviewed—a justice from the National Supreme Court—declared her feminism.

While many of the judges approached were quite ready to give me an interview, once I voiced that it had to do with feminist judges, they emphatically stated that they were not feminists. Agreeing with McGlynn (2003)

[6] The questions posed by Hunter are: who is a feminist judge? Is it necessary for a feminist judge to be a woman? Is it necessary for a feminist judge to identify as a feminist? Considering central elements of the judicial role such as independence, impartiality, decision-making according to law, is feminist judging permissible? When applied to the legal problems affecting women the most, she asks what would be the consequences of feminist judging, in terms of process; in terms of the writing of judgments and its foundations; in terms of the effect a feminist judge may produce in her colleagues in the same court; in terms of feminist judges' participation in extrajudicial and community organisations.

[7] The 2006 ELA survey on women in the largest Argentine cities shows that only a very small percentage (3%) of Argentine women participates in the feminist movement.

that the controversy around whether one is a feminist or calls oneself a feminist can distract us from more important issues, I decided to prioritise the possibility to proceed with the research with this group of judges, regardless of whether they were ready to call themselves feminists. Nevertheless, all of them seemed comfortable with defining themselves as 'working from a gender perspective, with a commitment to advance women's rights and equality between men and women'. Thus, with the exception of the self-declared feminist, I found I had to rephrase my first question avoiding the use of the expression 'feminist judge'. Rather, I used the above minimalist operational definition, while in order to make sure that their understanding was in consonance with my own I, at some point, asked each interviewee what (s)he meant by a gender perspective. Then, I asked the judges, whether a judge with that orientation should be a woman, if she or he should declare his or her orientation and what were the consequences of such an orientation on their judicial and extrajudicial activities. Did they identify with feminism? And why, in their opinion, was there such resistance among Argentine judges to identify with feminism? Whenever it seemed relevant in the context of the conversation, I also asked them about their relationship with the feminist movement.

On the recommendation of the only self declared feminist, a justice from the National Supreme Court, I approached two women justices from two provincial Supreme Courts, a male judge from a Second Instance Criminal Federal Tribunal, a woman from a second instance Civil Commercial Federal Court, a woman from a Second Instance Civil National Court and a female judge from a Second Instance Criminal Court from the city of Buenos Aires. The interviews, which lasted between forty minutes and an hour, were mostly conducted at the judges' chambers.

3. THE CONSEQUENCES OF WORKING WITH A GENDER PERSPECTIVE AND A COMMITMENT TO EQUALITY BETWEEN MEN AND WOMEN

All the judges interviewed described themselves as working from a gender perspective and with a commitment to equality between men and women. They considered this particularly important in the field of law, where rules and practices though appearing as gender neutral, frequently respond to the male bias of the law. They mentioned as desirable an empathetic attitude towards the persons involved in legal conflicts and vigilance with respect to how the specificities of women's gender lives impinge on their relationship with the law, without substituting the andro-centric bias by a feminist bias.

Most judges in the sample stated that the gender perspective had been useful and beneficial in several respects. It had changed their attitude, had made them more sensitive to gender issues, more attuned with the particularities of each case and more aware of certain details that previously could have been omitted or passed inadvertently. This deployment of an empathetic contextual attitude towards litigants of both sexes reminds us of the 'women's voice' and the 'ethic of care' identified by Gilligan (1982) and Menkel Meadow (1989, 1997).

All the judges interviewed spoke of the crucial impact of the incorporation of the gender perspective, not only in their decisions and the writing of judgments, but in various other dimensions of their work, especially in those areas of the law, such as 'family law' and 'juvenile law', where women appear more often as litigants. They mentioned how they introduced changes in the way they approach women involved in legal conflicts, taking into account and making room for their special needs derived from the specificities of their gendered lives. Among the different examples they pointed to 'introducing changes in terms of procedure to take testimony from women and children victims of abuse in order to avoid their re-victimization by the system' or, 'an awareness about the right hours for requiring the presence of a battered wife to give testimony, thus intending to prevent conflicts with the perpetrator that might result in additional harm'. One of the judges also spoke of the need to pay attention 'to the centrality of the mother role in the family, particularly in cases referring to youth, like for instance, drug cases'. However, in their view this impacted not only on their attitudes towards litigants, but on the way they organised work in the court, from how they arrange the space, to how they plan the timetable since, as one of them said, 'most court employees are young women with family responsibilities'.

3.1. Does a Judge with that Orientation need to be a Woman?

The following testimony represents the general opinion of the judges interviewed on the issue:

> I would not deny that the experience of growing up female may foster greater sensitiveness to women's issues, however it does not necessarily work that way. For instance, while I believe that it may be easier for a woman to understand what a woman litigant giving testimony is going through, I think that being a woman is no guarantee for the embrace of the gender perspective. Proof of this is the large number of women in the judiciary that are not in the least interested in gender issues.

In fact, on the same lines, the male judge argued that:

> Although for men, the incorporation of a gender perspective may be more surprising, I know men colleagues with a strong commitment to equality and knowledge

> of human rights, who, probably, without mentioning the fact that they work from a gender perspective, write decisions that show a clear understanding of how gender works to produce social inequality and thus, have the capacity to disrupt the monolithic patriarchal legal discourse.

In addition, he also offered examples of judgments produced by men with those characteristics. Similarly, one of the women judges interviewed explained that, in her view applying the gender perspective had little to do with the sex of the judge, but to 'work with a gender perspective is rather to know what it is about and apply it adequately to concrete cases'. Moreover, she made a point of distinguishing between 'understanding and expressing the gender perspective'. Pointing to the difficulties women might have in voicing such an allegiance she argued that 'women's long-established subjection acts as an obstacle deterring women's expression of the gender perspective, even for those who have incorporated it into their professional activities'.

3.2. The Public Declaration of the Judges' Sympathies with Feminist Goals

When asked whether judges working with a gender perspective and a commitment to women's rights should make public this allegiance, most of the judges stated that although strictly speaking they had no obligation to do so, it would be desirable that they did. Moreover, the judges emphasised that, given the high authority and prestige of their offices, they were in a privileged and legitimated position in terms of influencing their colleagues.

Likewise, the judge from the National Supreme Court who, as a result of having declared her feminism had to face a great public controversy that, at a certain point, even endangered her nomination, said that it was important that

> [a] person occupying such a high-ranking office should declare his/her sympathy with feminism because, as a consequence of the power judges wield, they are 'role models', in a position to educate and encourage others and thus contribute to promote public debate around the issue and legitimate feminist discourse.

Along the same lines, a woman judge from the High Civil and Commercial Federal Court vigorously articulated that

> [a] judge is not only selected and nominated on the basis of competence, his/her philosophical beliefs are very important too, and thus, it is a duty for the judge to be honest about them and make them clear through his/her public declarations and activities, judgments, academic writings and teaching activity.

Moreover, she recommends judges working with a gender perspective and a commitment to equality between the sexes

> to pay significant attention to the section of the foundations of the judgment, where judges explain the reasons for their decisions, to take some extra time to spell out the gender analysis underlying their decisions … Although I understand that this could result in considerably overburdening women who are the main supporters of the gender perspective, I am persuaded that it is a good way to disseminate gender theory and its legal implications among colleagues and lawyers, so relevant at this early stage, and to promote the incorporation of gender analysis into the legal debate ... the possibility to introduce a discourse, still considered as alternative to a prestigious post, should help to legitimate it, and hence, it should not be disregarded ... I have been militant in that respect, so much so that, when a gender sensitive case reaches my court, my male colleagues invite me to be the first to produce an opinion and, in general, they follow my decision.

The last statement of the testimony of this woman judge points to the significance of disseminating the gender perspective among both men and women, so that women judges do not become stereotyped as the specialists in 'women's cases', as seems to be the case in the previous testimony and, at the same time, women's cases acquire relevance for both men and women judges.

The male judge in my sample maintained that '[t]he dissemination of stories, narratives showing the advantageous effects of working with a special sensitivity to women's issues and a will to redress injustices suffered by women litigants is more effective than a discursive declaration'.

By contrast, a judge from the Supreme Court of one of the provinces expressed some hesitation. Her opinion was that 'this type of declaration could confuse litigants, who might as a consequence become increasingly unsure of the judge's impartiality'. While her comment reveals a particular engagement with ordinary people involved in legal conflicts, it also shows that, as a judge, she feels threatened by the potential suspicion of partiality on the part of the public.

Indeed, a number of judges expressed the view that the existence of the Argentine Association of Women Judges was instrumental in this respect, since it allowed for collective declarations that individual judges could not make without being accused of judicial activism. I will come back to this point in the next section.

4. UNDERSTANDING THE JUDGES' REFUSAL TO IDENTIFY WITH THE FEMINIST LABEL

4.1. The Difficult Position for Women in Argentina

In this section I attempt to identify certain factors that may help us understand the judges' rejection of the feminist label. One such factor is the fragmentation of the local feminist movement. A recent anthropological study on Argentine feminism depicted it as both a complex and a much divided movement. The author suggests that in our country 'there are as many "feminisms" as feminists', emphasising the lack of a consensus about what being a feminist means (Masson, 2007). In her research, Masson discovered a great multiplicity of categories within feminism standing in opposition to each other in a relationship marked by conflict and mutual accusations. Accordingly, she enumerates 'pure feminists'; 'academic feminists'; 'political feminists'; 'independent feminists'; 'institutional feminists'; 'lesbian feminists' and so on.[8]

Moreover, she discovered various subjective identity dimensions often interrelated: one is internal—feeling as a feminist; another requires exteriorisation—calling oneself a feminist; a third requires external recognition—being considered a feminist by others. According to the author, different combinations of these dimensions can give shape to four possible standings regarding one's feminism: first, a woman can be considered by others as a feminist without accepting her feminism; in the second case, the opposite may occur; the woman can call herself a feminist while the others do not recognise her as such; the third combination refers to those cases where the woman may consider herself a feminist but does not declare it publicly as a means to avoid inconveniencies; the fourth position refers to the perfect combination where the woman declares her feminism and is considered by others as a feminist.

However, if the characteristics of the women's movement might explain the judges' reluctance to identify with feminism, one could identify in the Argentine reality a set of concurrent events suggesting that a different attitude re self-identification with feminism might have been expected from local judges.

In spite of the movement's fragmentation, the political-juridical structure has been a key domain for feminist activism. In particular in the years that followed the restoration of democracy in Argentina, feminists were instrumental in promoting a comprehensive legislative reform aiming to put women on equal terms with men, in tune with the global human rights agenda, fundamentally within the family and the political domains and in the area of sexual and reproductive rights (Kohen, 2009). Additionally, in 2003 and 2004, on the occasion of the process of selection and nomination of magistrates for the Supreme Court of the Nation, women's organisations actively campaigned in favour of women candidates.

A second relevant feature is the persistence of women's under-representation in the judiciary. Actually, in spite of the large increase in the numbers of

[8] In addition to the need to identify through opposition and separation, competition for funding contributes to the movement's fragmentation and weakness.

women that have entered the law in Argentina, inequalities between men and women persist. Even though many women have excelled in their academic and legal careers, women's participation in the judiciary is characterised by a vertical and a horizontal segregation. As statistics show, women's participation in the legal realm has made huge progress: 61 per cent of all law students at the University of Buenos Aires—the largest in the country, totalling a number of 27,000 students—are women; likewise, they now constitute half the lawyers registered in the Lawyer's Association; and, since 2004, there have been two women at the Supreme Court of the Nation and there are some women in the supreme courts of the provinces and in the higher courts of second instance. However, women only constitute around 30 per cent of the judiciary and are concentrated in the lower courts and in the branches with less prestige, such as the family and labour courts, while the proportion of women in the more prestigious courts such as the federal courts is quite low.

Finally, as all of the female judges interviewed were affiliated to the Argentine Association of Women Judges founded in 1999, a member of the International Association of Women Judges, which without having an explicit feminist standing has a clear pro woman orientation, their reluctance to identify with feminism seems quite odd and difficult to elucidate.

4.2. The General Reluctance to Self-identify as Feminist

This phenomenon is neither local nor new. The incongruity between people's beliefs about gender and their self-identification as feminists has been studied predominantly in more developed nations such as the United States where feminism has been more prominent. Authors such as Faludi (1991) and McCabe (2005) have argued that reluctance to identify as feminists stems in part from the anti-feminist backlash, in part from the image of feminists as radicals and militants, and in part, ironically, from the fact that some younger women are quite successful in their lives and hence feminism is not that relevant to them.

Scholars such as Botelho Junqueira (2003) and Thornton (1997) have observed similar tendencies with respect to women in the legal professions in Brazil and Australia, respectively. Botelho Junqueira tells of a judge who expressed horror at feminist language, while Thornton, using Cockburn's expression, referred to this phenomenon as the 'sustained anathematizing of feminism'. Clare McGlynn (2003) starts her review of Bertha Wilson's biography stating that: 'A remarkable and regrettable phenomenon of feminism is that, in spite of its undoubted role in improving women's lives, it is a label rejected by many'. And Hunter (2008) claims that 'Some women judges specifically and emphatically insist that they are not feminists, often by reference to the social construction or caricature of feminism as something negative, wrongheaded and/or dangerous'.

4.3. The Attitudes of the Judges Interviewed

Most of the judges interviewed expressed that, in spite of the fact that they worked with a gender perspective and had, as already stated, a strong commitment to further women's rights and the advancement of women's status within society, they would feel uncomfortable identifying with such a stigmatised label. The main reasons adduced by the judges were related to the pejorative images circulating around feminism, mostly related to the most extreme versions where feminists are often caricaturised as men-hating, bra-burning types. They also referred to what they thought an illegitimate feminist expectation that the judges should always favour women litigants, irrespective of whether they were right or wrong.

Irrespective of whether such views are correct or incorrect, they were shared by the judges interviewed, presenting the feminist movement with an important challenge. Hence, in their approach to judges and women judges' associations, feminist organisations working on gender justice should seek to untangle this linguistic conundrum by fostering discussion with women judges around feminism and its tenets.

In other parts of the world—mainly societies within the common law Anglo-Saxon world—prominent women judges have openly admitted their feminism and incorporated the principles of legal feminism into their work. Anne Boigeol (2008), having made very interesting suggestions regarding both the uneven progress of women within the judiciary and the asymmetrical development of theorisation about women judges across jurisdictions with common law and civil law legal system, has looked for possible alternative explanations to account for those differences. Among those, are the different conceptions of a judge within each system, the diverse development of feminist theory—particularly feminist legal theory—and the significance ascribed to gender in legal education in the Latin and Anglo-Saxon world.

The only self-proclaimed feminist in the sample affirmed that, personally, she had never had difficulties in openly declaring her feminism. She had first publicly done so on the occasion of her nomination as a candidate to the Supreme Court of the Nation, a pronouncement that brought a lot of turmoil among conservative groups (Kohen and Ruiz Núñez, 2009).

The only male judge said that, strictly speaking, he would not mind being called a feminist, as long as he did not have to agree with some extreme positions he did not share. The woman judge from the Civil Second Instance Commercial Federal Court referred to the multiplicity of feminist positions as an obstacle for her identifying as a feminist. She said that she would not like to be associated with a feminist position that did not account for difference. A very prestigious woman judge from the Supreme Court of one of the provinces, who saw feminist analysis as an instrument to redress inequalities through equity, indicated that only in those precise cases she would not mind being called a feminist.

Thus, in this sample, I could identify three positions concerning calling oneself a feminist: one judge who assertively declared her feminism; three judges who said that with certain specified restrictions they would not mind being addressed as feminists; two of them specifically referred to the need to know which feminism one would be referring to, while the third argued that she would only deploy a feminist analysis once she had perceived inequalities. Finally, the three remaining judges strongly expressed that they did not identify with feminism and would not like to be called feminists. One among those said that feminism had been historically superseded, that gender was as important as other categories such as race, ethnicity or sexual orientation. The second judge strongly rejected not only feminism but also any discussion about it, while the third declared that her refusal was 'linguistic', due to the fact that, in her mind, 'the word feminism has come to mean the contrary of 'machismo',[9] a means to substitute one form of oppression by another'. Along similar lines, as I mentioned before, many among the judges interviewed referred to what they thought as an illegitimate feminist expectation that the judges should always give reason to women litigants, irrespective of whether they were right or wrong, and strongly stated that this would mean a breach of the judges' commitment to impartiality. She added that, in her experience

> when a woman finds herself before a woman judge, she anticipates a certain complicity from the part of the magistrate, while men litigants expect exactly the opposite.... Thus, the judges attempt to avoid being identified with a position provoking inequality, on top of being impartial, judges are always concerned to appear impartial.

Not only must judges be impartial, they must also appear as such! As Pompeia,[10] Julius Caesar's wife, the judges must be above suspicion of partiality. I would think that, as a consequence of the fact that women have entered the judiciary relatively recently, they feel insecure and vulnerable to

[9] See above (n 2).

[10] 'Caesar's wife must be above suspicion, those in public life should not put themselves in the position of having their behaviour questioned'" Recorded from the late eighteenth century, the saying alludes to a story in Plutarch's *Caesar* about Caesar divorcing his wife Pompeia after the scandal surrounding the affair in which Clodius, who was in love with Pompeia, smuggled himself into the house in which the women of Caesar's household were celebrating the festival of the Bona Dea (the Good Goddess). Caesar refused to bring charges against Clodius, but divorced Pompeia; when questioned, he replied 'I thought my wife ought not even to be under suspicion'.

suspicions of partiality; this adds to their tendency to feel threatened if they identify with feminism.[11]

The judges' perceived urge to safeguard their reputation of impartiality points to a contradiction in their discourse: while, in agreement with feminist theories on judgment (Cain, 1988; Resnik, 1988) all the judges interviewed declared that impartiality was not at stake when the judges incorporated the gender outlook into their work, since it did not mean to incline the balance in favour of women systematically, but to redress existing inequalities. Even though most of them saw the need to educate men and women judges on gender issues and disseminate the gender perspective according to the mandate of the international conventions[12] ratified by the Argentine State, they felt uneasy about acknowledging their feminism and consequently articulated a concern with the public perception of their impartiality. This attitude suggests that the gender perspective has not yet been sufficiently incorporated by the judges and points to the requirement of additional training on gender for the judiciary and to the need for further theoretical discussion between feminists and judges concerning the feminist challenges to the traditional model of the role of the judge so as to become acquainted with the 'tugs, the pulls and the burdens of judging' (Resznick, 1988). This debate may contribute to strengthen women judges' professional identities as they consider their loyalties towards the law and towards their gender, and how these loyalties may compete with each other (Hale, 2001).

Paradoxically, the only judge in the sample who openly affirmed her feminism was also the one who complained of the pressures and criticism she received from feminist groups after the National Supreme Court decision in 'Tejerina'. This event suggests, on the one hand, that feminism does not exclude impartiality and on the other, that there is something in the judge's perception that might substantiate a certain caution regarding feminists. Implied in 'Tejerina' was the issue of abortion, one of the main concerns of Argentine feminists and the main obsessions of the Roman Catholic Church. As the magistrate in question had declared her allegiance to feminism and her position in favour of the de-penalisation of abortion,

[11] This is not surprising since opinion polls show that Argentines in general do not trust the judicial system. According to the reports, confidence in the judicial system has been declining since the country returned to democracy, ranging from 30% at its highest down to 18%. TNS- Gallup Argentina (2006) In Información y Justicia II: Datos sobre la Justicia argentina, Buenos Aires (Fundación Konrad Adenauer); FORES (Foro de Estudios sobre la Administración de Justicia) and Fundación Libertad (2005–06) 'Indice de Confianza en la Justicia' www.foresjusticia.org.ar.

[12] International Human Rights Conventions such as the CEDAW (Convention against all types of Discrimination against Women) and the American Convention of Belém do Pará on Violence against Women have become positive law through their incorporation to Argentine law with constitutional rank (art 75 of the Constitutional Reform in 1994).

they anticipated a different decision; instead, she judged independently according to what she thought was fair.

5. SUMMARY

This chapter originally attempted to flesh out the concept of a feminist judge in the context of a group of highly placed Argentine judges. As I found myself before a group of judges quite reluctant to identify with the feminist label, I decided to pursue the research using an alternative that allowed me to proceed and, at the same time, made the judges interviewed feel more comfortable. I thus changed the expression 'feminist judge' for a judge 'working from a gender perspective and sympathy towards the ideal of gender equality'. As I found the judges' reluctance puzzling in the context of the Argentine judiciary, I decided to make it the focus of this chapter.

I first analysed the meanings the judges accorded to the phrase mentioned above. Although the majority of the judges was not ready to call themselves feminists, their conceptions showed a clear identification with feminist goals and methodologies. As such, I feel reassured about having initiated an enquiry centred in this 'proxy' for a 'feminist judge'.

In general, the judges interviewed envisage this approach as an extremely useful critical theoretical tool that makes it possible for the judge to understand, and attempt to redress gender inequality as it appears when women are involved in legal conflicts. Even if they saw this approach as a paradigm that allows them to visualise how the law has excluded women's perspectives, they were against substituting the 'andro-centric' point of view for the women's point of view and rather thought that its incorporation was meant to complete the picture.

As I looked for possible explanations of the judges' resistance to being associated with the feminist label, in spite of their adherence to feminist goals and methods, I noticed that this aversion ran along the great dislike of feminism prevailing within Argentine society. This is strongly due to the traditional culture of machismo and to the divisions and antagonisms within the Argentine women's movement, despite the very important achievements of Argentine feminists in the area of legislative reform improving women's lives, the successful campaign for the nomination of women to the Supreme Court of the Nation and regardless of women's under-representation within the judiciary and that all the judges in my sample were members of the Argentine Association of Women Judges. I also mentioned their refusal to be associated with a stigmatised label; an apprehension to be identified with the most extreme forms of feminism; and a misunderstanding of feminism and its tenets and a fear that the public might take them as partial because of their adherence to feminism.

I came to the conclusion that this points to a strong need to promote a more intense and sustained dialogue between feminists and judges sympathetic towards feminist goals and to insist on the training of judges on gender issues. Those findings increased my awareness of the need for further research and made me more appreciative of the work of organisations working on gender justice and associations of women judges embarked in this endeavour. They certainly have a great potential to demystify feminism, generate a virtuous circle contributing to bridge the gap between judges, feminist legal scholars and feminist activists and thus promote equality before the law for men and women.

6. REFERENCES

Abrahamson, S (1988) 'On the Bias: Feminist Reconsiderations of the Aspirations of our Judges' 61 *Southern California Law Review* 1928.

—— (1998) 'Do Women Judges Really Make a Difference? The American experience' in S Shetreet (ed), *Women in Law* (London, Kluwer).

Baines, B (2009) 'Contextualism, Feminism, and a Canadian Woman Judge' 17(1) *Feminist Legal Studies* 27.

Beiner, TM (2005) 'Female Judging' 36(4) *The University of Toledo Law Review* 821.

Boigeol, A (2008) 'Gender and Judging in Common Law and Civil Law Countries' draft presentation (Montreal, LSA Conference).

Botelho Junqueira, E (2003) 'Women in the Judiciary: A Perspective from Brazil' in U Schultz and G Shaw (eds), *Women in the World's Legal Professions* (Oxford, The Oñati International Institute for the Sociology of Law, Hart Publishing).

Cain, P (1988) 'Good and Bad Bias: A Comment on Feminist Theory and Judging' 61 *Southern California Law Review* 1945.

ELA (Equipo Latinoamericano de Justicia y Género) (2007) *Como nos vemos las mujeres: Actitudesy percepciones de las mujeres sobre distintos aspectos de sus condiciones de vida*, Buenos Aires.

Faludi, S (1991) *Backlash. The Undeclared War Against Women* (US, Vintage).

Feenan, D (2009) 'Women and Judging' 17 *Feminist Legal Studies* 1.

Gilligan, C (1982) *In a Different Voice: Psychological Theory and Women's Development* (Cambridge, Harvard University Press).

Hale, B (2001) 'Equality and the Judiciary: Why Should We Want More Women Judges?' *Public Law* 4 (Ad HOC/UBA, Buenos Aires).

Hunter, R (2008) 'Can Feminist Judges make a Difference?' 15(1–2) *International Journal of the Legal Profession* (Ad HOC/UBA, Buenos Aires).

Karst, K (1988) 'Judging and Belonging' 61 *Southern California Law Review* 1966.

Kenney, SJ (2008) 'Thinking about Gender and Judging' 15(1–2) *International Journal of the legal Profession* 87.

Kohen, B (2004) 'Gender Differences in the Family Courts: A View from Within' (Unpublished thesis, University of Durham Library).

—— (2008a) *El género en la Justicia de Familia. Miradas y Protagonistas*

—— (2008b) 'Family Judges in the City of Buenos Aires: A View from Within 15(1–2) *International Journal of the Legal Profession* 111.

—— (2009) 'The Effectiveness of Legal Strategies in Argentina' in J Jaquette, *Feminist Agendas and Democracy in Latin America* (Durham, NC, Duke University Press).

Kohen, B and Ruiz Núñez, H (2009)'Las dos primeras mujeres en la Corte Suprema Argentina: el proceso de su nombramiento en la prensa' in M Rodríguez and R Asencio et al, *Una agenda para la equidad de género en el sistema de justicia* (CIEPP- Editorial del Puerto).

L'Heureux-Dubé, C (2001) 'Outsiders on the Bench: The Continuing Struggle for Equality' 16(1) *Wiscosin Women's Law Journal* 28.

MacMillan, L (1991) in B Wilson, 'Will Women Judges Really make a Difference?' (1990) 28 *Osgoode Hall Law Journal* 507 and in A Harvison Young (1997) 'Feminism Pluralism and Administrative Law' in M Taggart, *The Province of Administrative Law* (Oxford, Hart Publishing).

Malleson, K (2003) 'Justifying Gender Equality on the Bench: Why Difference won't Do' 11 *Feminist Legal Studies* 1.

Masson, L (2007) *Feministas en todas partes. Una etnografía de espacios y narrativas feministas en la Argentina* (Prometeo libros, Buenos Aires).

McCabe, J (2005) 'What's in a Label? The Relationship between Feminist Self-Identification and 'Feminist' Attitudes among US Women and Men' 19(4) *Gender & Society* 480.

McGlynn, C (2003) 'Book Review Ellen Anderson, Judging Bertha Wilson—Law as Large as Life' (Toronto, University of Toronto Press); (2001) 11 *Feminist Legal Studies* 307.

Menkel-Meadow, C (1989) 'Feminisation of the Legal Profession, the Comparative Sociology of Women Lawyers' in R Abel and P Lewis, *Lawyers in Society, Comparative Theories* (Berkeley, University of California Press).

—— (1997) 'Portia in a Different Voice: Speculations on a Woman's Lawyering Process' in H Barnett (ed), *Sourcebook on Feminist Jurisprudence* (London, Cavendish Publishing Limited).

—— (2009) 'Asylum in a Different Voice? Judging Immigration Claims and Gender' paper presented at LSA conference (Denver, May 2009).

Resnik, J (1988) 'On the Bias: Feminist Reconsiderations of the Aspirations of our Judges' 61 *Southern California Law Review* 1877.

Schultz, U (2003) 'Introduction' in Women in the World's Legal Professions: Overview and Synthesis' in U Schultz G and Shaw (eds), *Women in the World's Legal Professions* (Oxford, Hart Publishing).

Thornton, M (1996) *Dissonance and Distrust: Women in the Legal Profession* (Melbourne, Oxford University Press).

Wald, P (2005) 'Six Not-So-Easy Pieces: One Woman Judge's Journey to the Bench and Beyond' 36 The *University of Toledo Law Review* 979.

5.4

A Feminist Adjudication Process: Is There Such a Thing?

REG GRAYCAR

Abstract

This chapter brings together two separate but related areas of my research: first, my work on gender and judging (or adjudication) and secondly, work I have done with Jane Wangmann (Graycar and Wangmann, 2007) on legal responses to systemic injuries or historical harms. One of the focuses of our research on historical harms was an agreement made in the mid 1990s between a group of women survivors of childhood abuse and the government of Ontario (the 'Grandview Agreement') that established what has often been described as a 'feminist' process for addressing the injuries that these women sustained. This chapter interrogates the suggestion that creative redress packages could enhance gender equality. Specifically, I ask whether a model such as that which the Grandview Agreement put in place can appropriately bear the ascription of a 'feminist' adjudication process. More broadly, the chapter considers whether there is such a thing as a 'feminist' adjudication process. The chapter asks the following questions:

— *Has the feminist inquiry—often presented as 'will women judges/decision-makers make a difference'—been misplaced? Are we failing to ask whether adding women, or more specifically feminists, or indeed, any jurisprudential outsiders to the existing legal structures can itself bring about any effective change?*
— *Should we instead focus on whether there is space for feminist insights to be introduced into the legal decision-making process, and if there is, at what stage? Can feminist insights assist in designing adjudication processes, rather than being introduced only at the decision-making stage?*
— *What, if anything, distinguishes a 'feminist' process from a 'good' process?*

1. INTRODUCTION

THIS CHAPTER BRINGS together two separate, but related areas of my research: first, my work on gender and judging (or adjudication)—the key focus of this collection (Graycar, 1995; 1998; 2004; 2008) while the second relates to a recent research project that considered legal responses to systemic injuries or historical harms (see Graycar and Wangmann, 2007). In the course of the latter work, Jane Wangmann and I undertook a case study on the 'Grandview Agreement'. This was a Canadian redress package designed to respond to the harms perpetrated on the women and girls who had been held in the Grandview Training School for Girls in the middle of the twentieth century. The Agreement[1] was made between the provincial government of Ontario (Canada) and the Grandview Survivors' Support Group in 1994 (see also Vella, 1995; Leach, 1997). It gave rise to a process widely seen as one that developed, and put in place, an *alternative* and, it has been suggested, 'feminist' process for addressing complex harms of this kind. The Agreement has been described as

> the most advanced attempt to involve survivors in identifying their own needs and in directing their end of the negotiations. It is respectful, attempts to address the individual and collective needs of survivors, and aspires to make the world a better place for survivors to live (IHRD, 1988: [6.3].)

It has been suggested that a crucial element of the perceived success of the Grandview Agreement was the adjudication process itself, described in more detail below. Since the Grandview Agreement was concluded and the adjudication process undertaken in the early to mid-1990s, there has been a burgeoning (and long overdue) international literature on reparations (see, for example, Ferstman et al, 2009; Pete et al, 2007; De Greiff, 2006) and most recently, on gender and reparations (see, for example, Rubio-Marin, 2006; Rubio-Marin, 2009). But—with perhaps one exception—the Women's International War Crimes Tribunal (WIWCT, discussed below) which is arguably quite distinguishable, there has not been another process that has so emphatically been described as one that is (or perhaps looks) 'feminist' (though see the discussion by Chinkin, 2006: 212–13). The purpose of this chapter is to interrogate the suggestion that creative redress packages that claim to move beyond the common law's emphasis on matters such as burden of proof, causation, validation and witness credibility, and instead focus on healing and reparation, could enhance gender equality. Specifically, this chapter asks whether a model such as that which the Grandview Agreement put in place, can appropriately bear the ascription of a 'feminist' adjudication process. More broadly, the chapter considers whether there is such a thing as a 'feminist' adjudication process: or is the juxtaposition of 'feminist' and 'adjudication' an oxymoron?

[1] A copy of the Agreement is on file with the author.

This chapter will address the following issues (though not necessarily in this order):

— Has the feminist inquiry—often presented as 'will women judges/ decision-makers make a difference'—been misplaced? Are we simply counting the number of female participants and failing to ask whether adding women, or more specifically feminists, or indeed, in a broader context, any jurisprudential outsiders (*cf* Thornton, 1996: 268–69) to the existing legal structures can itself bring about any effective change?
— Should we instead focus on whether there is space for feminist insights to be introduced into the legal decision-making process, and if there is, at what stage? Can feminist insights assist in designing adjudication processes, rather than being introduced only at the decision-making stage? If it is possible to incorporate feminist insights at the design stage then can we perhaps put in place a more appropriate and perhaps 'feminist' method of responding to that harm?[2] If not, are we left with coming into the process after the framework has been set, without reference to the types of harm with which we might be concerned? (*cf* Sheehy, 1991).
— One of the key features of the Grandview redress scheme was the design of the adjudication process (indeed, of the whole package) by the women themselves. Does this tell us that the starting point of any consideration of feminist adjudication may well be prior to adjudication itself?
— What if anything distinguishes a 'feminist' process from a 'good' process? Are there particularly 'feminist' ways of hearing evidence, of evaluating it and responding to it?

In the first part of this chapter, I will identify and describe some of the (now well established) problems of existing (particularly common law) systems of responding to a variety of harms. While these are general problems, particularly for the most disadvantaged of potential litigants, they have particular resonance in the context of group harms, rather than individual ones, and perhaps even more resonance in the context of gendered groups harms. Leaving aside any gender context, the very nature of group harms itself poses a fundamental challenge to the one-on-one paradigm of accidental encounters between strangers for which the tort system seems best suited and indeed, for which it was designed. While not all of the group harms to which I refer are gendered harms, many of them have some or all of the characteristics of gendered harms. So what are gendered harms?

2 As, eg, through the use of concepts such as 'gendered harms': discussed further below: see Graycar and Morgan (1990, 2002: part 4); Howe (1987 and 1994: 171–77).

2. GENDERED HARMS

As Jenny Morgan and I described them in our book, *The Hidden Gender of Law*, gendered harms are the kinds of harms or injuries that happen to women because they are women (see Graycar and Morgan, 1990; 2002: part 4; and see also Conaghan, 1996, 1998; Bottomley, 1996). We suggested there that there is a spectrum or range of harms that happen to women along a continuum: at one end are those harms that are individually invasive of individual women (such as individual sexual assault,[3] or medical injuries to women's bodies) while at the other end are those that happen to all women, for example public displays of misogynist advertising or pornography.

Of course, many gendered harms occur to women because of the operation of a range of intersecting forms of disadvantage (*cf* Crenshaw, 1989; Duclos, 1993). This was graphically described by Chinkin, writing about the 'comfort women' who were the subject of the WIWCT hearings:

> The comfort women had been subjected to sexual slavery because they were women, because of their race, because of their status as colonized or defeated peoples, and in many instances because they were poor: all factors that militated against their receiving justice (2006: 205).

Returning to redress schemes, many, though not all, respond to harms that have a gendered dimension. These include:

- — forced eugenic sterilisation (occasionally, though much more rarely, performed on young men/boys);
- — taking of indigenous children from their families, often accompanied by sexual abuse; and
- — broader forms of institutional abuses, often for gendered reasons such as 'being in moral danger' (for example, Grandview).

Not only are these kinds of harm perpetrated on people who are generally disadvantaged, but the fact that they happen to people as members of those groups itself served to distinguish them from the types of injuries for which the tort system was developed, namely, accidental injuries arising from a sometimes random encounter between two individuals, such as road accidents, industrial injuries or medical malpractice.

Attempts to seek remedies for these types of harms—in particular tort remedies which have traditionally been seen as the appropriate remedy for personal injury or harm—regularly confront a number of barriers which

[3] And here I am also distinguishing between a group version of sexual assault such as rape in war; and the harms that happened via sexual slavery to, for example, the women in respect of whom the WIWCT hearing, discussed below, was held.

help to demonstrate how difficult it is to achieve redress for gendered harms through the tort system. Some of these barriers are outlined below. (For a general discussion, see Conaghan and Mansell (1998) especially chapter 7.)

2.1. Limitation of Actions Rules

These are the time limits within which a legal claim must be commenced (Mathews, 2003; Graycar and Morgan, 1995).[4] The traditional rationale for the existence of such rules was explained by Justice McHugh in the High Court of Australia as follows:

> The enactment of time limitations has been driven by a perception that '[w]here there is delay the whole quality of justice deteriorates' … The effect of delay on the quality of justice is no doubt one of the most important influences motivating a legislature to enact limitation periods. But it is not the only one. Courts and commentators have perceived four broad rationales. First, as time goes by, relevant evidence is likely to be lost. Second, it is oppressive, even 'cruel', to a defendant to allow an action to be brought long after the circumstances which gave rise to it have passed. Third, people should be able to arrange their affairs and utilise their resources on the basis that claims can no longer be made against them. Insurers, public institutions and businesses, particularly limited liability companies, have a significant interest in knowing that they have no liabilities beyond a definite period …
>
> The final rationale for limitation periods is that the public interest requires that disputes be settled as quickly as possible.[5]

In recognition of these difficulties, some jurisdictions have either abolished these time limits for certain kinds of harm, such as childhood sexual abuse, or have extended them or waived them via some kind of moratorium for a defined period.[6]

2.2. Evidentiary Issues

Related to the concern about limitation periods (and one of the matters specifically identified by Justice McHugh) is the problem of evidence. If the

[4] See: *A v Hoare* [2008] 1 AC 844, [2008] UKHL 6 (HL); *Stingel v Clark* (2006) 226 CLR 442 (High Court of Australia). For more detailed accounts of the barriers posed by limitation periods for survivors of childhood sexual abuse, see Graycar and Wangmann (2007: fn 90).

[5] *Brisbane South Regional Health Authority v Taylor* 186 CLR 541; [1996] HCA 25 (High Court of Australia) 551–52 (McHugh J); citations omitted.

[6] For references to some North American jurisdictions that have removed or amended limitation periods in child sexual assault cases, see Graycar and Wangmann (2007: fn 90).

harm in relation to which recourse is being sought happened many years ago, how reliable and/or even available is evidence that would support any claim?[7] And even if, prima facie, some evidence is available, there are also closely related forensic issues about how trials proceed, and in particular what happens to women who have experienced sexual violence in the context of litigation.[8]

2.3. Problems in Attributing Responsibility

Another constraint that has played a key role in limiting any possible redress via the tort system are the rules about the allocation of blame as between individuals and the organisations that either employ them or for whom they carry out work as contractors. Specifically, this refers to legal rules about vicarious liability that have generated considerable litigation in the context of cases particularly involving sexual abuse of children in a number of different jurisdictions (see Luntz et al, 2008, 17.3.18–17.3.11; discussing cases decided on this issue by the House of Lords, the Supreme Court of Canada and the High Court of Australia; see also Wangmann, 2004).

2.4. Jurisdictional Issues

Sometimes it may be difficult to identify the appropriate forum in which to seek a remedy, or the plaintiff or organisation might be in a jurisdiction that limits or excludes tort claims altogether (for example, New Zealand).[9]

Irrespective of any of these identified constraints, or the heavy financial cost that might accompany seeking legal remedies (especially with limits on the availability of legal aid, at least in Australia, outside the criminal law, some of which are themselves gendered: see Mossman, 1993; Graycar and Morgan, 1995), there may well be other distinct disadvantages for the victims/survivors in having to relive some of the traumatic experiences of their past in an adversary context. This is not to suggest that there may

[7] For a clear illustration of some of these difficulties, see the *Cubillo* cases: *Cubillo v Commonwealth* (1999) 89 FCR 528, [1999] FCA 518; *Cubillo v Commonwealth (No 2)* (2000) 103 FCR 1, [2000] FCA 1084; *Cubillo v Commonwealth of Australia* (2001) 112 FCR 455, [2001] FCA 1213.

[8] For a discussion about women's credibility in law, particularly in terms of sexual assault criminal trials, see Mack (1993); Hunter (1996).

[9] New Zealand established a 'no fault' personal injury compensation scheme on 1 April 1974, administered by the Accident Compensation Commission. For the current legislative scheme, see the Injury, Prevention, Rehabilitation, and Compensation Act 2001. For some discussions of the scheme see Todd (2000 and 2002). The ACC website provides a history and chronology of the amendments to the scheme at: www.acc.co.nz/about-acc/overview-of-acc/introduction-to-acc/ABA00004.

not in some cases be some benefits in doing so, as researchers in the field of therapeutic jurisprudence have suggested, but there is a need for caution about exposing persons, whose traumatic experiences have made them vulnerable, to further trauma (see, for example, Feldthusen, Hankivsky and Greaves, 2000; Feldthusen, 1993. See generally, Graycar and Wangmann, 2007, references cited at fn 29 *et seq*).

I mentioned above that the tort system was ill-suited to dealing with group harms because of the assumptions that underlie it, particularly the idea that the harms with which it is concerned flow from a random encounter between two strangers. So, for example, an ongoing pattern of domestic violence or sexual assault, or indeed any type of (ongoing) harm between people in an ongoing relationship, has difficulty fitting into this one-off event paradigm, and this may be even more striking when the victim/survivor is a child (see Conaghan, 1998). Of course, not all types of harm fall at one end or the other of this individual to group continuum. Some types of harm or injury are both individual and group harms: for example, there may be a clearly identifiable group that was harmed in a particular manner or place, where the rationale of the harm was their membership of a particular disadvantaged group, while at the same time some individual group members may have incurred distinct harms as individuals. The Canadian Indian Residential Schools Settlement is a good illustration of this, where those who can show they were taken to the schools are eligible for what is known as a 'common experience payment', while those who can demonstrate some specific kind of injury that occurred to them as an individual may receive compensation for that as well.[10] This is another indication that we need to think not only about a continuum of forms of harm, but about a continuum of forms of response, rather than trying to fit things into a system such as the tort system which did not contemplate these kinds of harms when designed.

3. SYSTEMIC INJURIES AND FEMINIST ADJUDICATION: SOME BACKGROUND CONCERNS FROM FEMINIST LEGAL THEORY

Before engaging directly with the question of whether the Grandview adjudication process was a 'feminist process', it is important to reflect, if only briefly, on some of what we have learned from the past quarter century of feminist legal scholarship in order to contextualise such an evaluation. While it is not possible in this chapter to do justice to that work,[11] I am nonetheless indebted to Margaret Davies whose recent article, 'Feminism and the Flat

[10] To view the Residential Schools Settlement, see: www.residentialschoolsettlement.ca/settlement.html.

[11] For an overview of some of that work, at least up to 2002, see Graycar and Morgan (2002).

Law Theory' (Davies, 2008) has very much informed this discussion about the connections between the two different strands of my work that this chapter is attempting to bring together.

In her discussion, Davies examines two modalities of law: the vertical and the horizontal. For her, vertical law is hierarchical and seen as 'emanating from a single authoritative centre and among other things, it sets boundaries, such as the limits determining some arguments or reasons as "legal" while others are "non-legal"' (2008: 283). By contrast, flat or horizontal law 'replaces the values of superiority and certainty with the values of contiguity and contingency ... and replaces the limited spaces of law-state unity with the more expansive, illimitable and multi-dimensional (or stratified) spaces of intersubjective actions' (2008: 287). Davies' purpose in the article is to ask how 'flat' or horizontal law might be useful for feminist legal theory and practice.[12] In particular, she considers ways in which horizontal or flat approaches to law might transgress vertically determined perimeters of the nation state and its legal system.

To place these issues in context, Davies (2008: 284) summarises some of the difficulties that feminists have identified with vertical law. These include:

— the detachment of positive law from everyday realities;
— its wilful blindness to gender as meaningful social difference; and
— the construction of legal subjects as idealised white, masculine, heterosexual, masculine types.

Davies reminds us that much feminist work in law has historically focused on exclusion. While the current situation with respect to vertical law is that exclusion on the basis of gender is no longer necessarily explicit (by contrast, say, with laws that denied married women legal status: see Graycar and Morgan, 2002: 91–96), nonetheless gendered exclusions are still alive and well. Perhaps more insidiously than those that were clearly stated, such as Blackstone's notorious 'husband and wife are one, and the husband is that one' (Blackstone, 1765: 432), contemporary forms of exclusion occur via

> gendered values read into [law's] so called 'neutral' doctrines, the selectivity of legal doctrine in addressing harm, the normalising effects of law on socio-political movements, the silencing and stereotyping of certain voices and narratives in court-based dialogue, the gendered nature of legal culture, and so forth (Davies, 2008: 284).

Or, to quote an old book, it is the 'hidden gender of law' (Graycar and Morgan, 1990) that plays such a significant role in maintaining gender hierarchy (and see also MacKinnon, 1987: chapter 3).

[12] The reference to 'practice' is significant, and not often encountered in much of the scholarship about feminist legal theory: Davies' work is a rare exception. See also Davies (2003).

Davies (2008: 284) notes that it is easy to see why engagement with positive, ie, top-down or vertical law has been regarded, while essential, as only a partial solution by feminists and critical legal scholars. And I would suggest that this applies equally, or perhaps even more forcefully, to projects concerned with addressing gender inequality that seek to respond to that inequality by having more women included among the decision-makers. As I have argued over many years, having more women in legal decision-making roles is absolutely essential, but it is nonetheless only a partial solution (Graycar, 1995: 266–67 and 268–69; Graycar, 1998: 9–10). As Davies (2008: 284) reminds us: 'the remedy for exclusion is not simply formal inclusion, and ... disempowerment cannot be addressed only by a conferral of rights'.

Significantly, Davies concludes this part of her article as follows:

> Whether or not the officials who populate law's hierarchy are demographically diverse is not the issue; the issue is rather the monopoly held by this hierarchy on constructions of legal truth. That is not to deny the evident and positive impact which feminism has had upon the content and culture of law (2008: 285).

While I am unequivocally in favour of the idea that there should be more women judges and, more broadly, a much more diverse judiciary, at the risk of being somewhat heretical, I would suggest that if we do not interrogate and clarify the reasons for pursuing this project, we may be in danger of simply 'adding women and stirring'. That is, the call for increased participation by women and increasing diversity in judicial decision-making must be seen as an essential, but nonetheless only a small part of a much bigger strategy, rather than as an end in itself.

Before concluding with some thoughts about the possible rationales for seeking greater diversity in the judiciary, I will turn to the Grandview Agreement and adjudication process, and briefly look at another possibly 'horizontal' intervention in law: the Women's International War Crimes Tribunal (WIWCT).

4. THE 'GRANDVIEW AGREEMENT'

The Grandview Training School for Girls was a residential institution that operated from 1933 to 1976. Girls were sent there for reasons that were largely related to gendered and racialised notions of delinquency and deviance—often because of precocious displays of sexuality, but just as likely because they were abused and/or had no-one to look after them properly (see Sangster, 2001: 148). On average, there was an annual population of 120 Aboriginal and non-Aboriginal girls who resided there for periods ranging from a few months to several years. There was a clear racialised element to the abuse experienced by the Aboriginal girls, and there were also reports of anti-lesbianism and anti-Semitism. Girls who were at Grandview experienced a range of harms from psychological to physical and sexual abuse. Perhaps the most egregious was the use of a secure facility for placing the girls in solitary confinement (Churchill House, though better known as the 'screaming house': see Graycar and Wangmann, 2007: 9).

Stories about the abuse experienced by many of the girls at the school first emerged in the 1990s. A psychologist who was treating two women recognised the similarity in their stories and—with their permission—arranged for them to meet. These women went public with their stories, and shortly thereafter the Grandview Survivors Support Group (GSSG) was formed. There was a lengthy police investigation and while charges were eventually laid against a small number of people, there were only two convictions. This is not surprising, given the difficulties of engaging with the criminal law, where the burden of proof requires that charges be proved 'beyond reasonable doubt'. There is a certain irony in the fact that the very harms that flow from institutionalisation of this nature, such as life experiences that are coloured by mental illness, criminal activity, substance abuse etc, are the very things that significantly impair women's capacity to be accepted as credible witnesses. In other words, the nature of the harm is itself a barrier to any legal remedy, not only, but perhaps most dramatically, via the criminal justice system.

The GSSG eventually grew to over 200 women. The group hired a lawyer, and with the assistance of that lawyer commenced negotiations with the Ontario Government toward establishing some kind of redress mechanism. During the lengthy negotiation period (10 months) as a sign of its good faith the Ontario Government set in place a dedicated telephone line for advice, information, support and counselling, and also funded the support group. Eventually, an agreement establishing a redress mechanism was formally approved by the government in June 1994 after being voted on and accepted by the members of the GSSG.

The preamble to the Agreement stated:

> This Agreement is based on ... a recognition that society has a direct responsibility to provide the support necessary to facilitate the healing process of survivors of sexual and institutionalized abuse, particularly when such abuse arises in the context of an institution housing children. It also recognizes the current individual-based solutions offered by the civil justice system are inadequate responses to institutionalized and sexual abuse. These problems are prevalent enough in our society so as to warrant a social based response which seeks, ultimately, to facilitate the healing of survivors (Grandview Agreement, overview).

The two key elements of the Grandview Agreement that are relevant for the purposes of this discussion are the fact that the Agreement was negotiated by the women themselves; and, arising from that, the nature of the adjudication process.

4.1. The Benefits

The Agreement put in place a range of benefits. First, there were group benefits, available to all women who had attended Grandview, irrespective of whether they had suffered any specific particularised physical or sexual abuse. In other words, the payment was simply for the harm of having been there. The group benefits included the provision of a crisis telephone line and payment for the removal of tattoos which the women saw as an ongoing reminder of their time in the institution. As one of the adjudicators[13] remarked:

> [Y]ou can see this was an Agreement negotiated by the women when you see that [*the removal of tattoos*] ... you just know that mattered to them. I would never have thought of it (interviewee 3 in Graycar and Wangmann, 2007: 14).

Significant among the group benefits was an apology that was eventually provided by the government in Parliament.

Next, there were general benefits which, while not specifically directed at Grandview survivors, were aimed at assisting survivors of sexual assault and institutional abuse more broadly. These included proposed changes to the statute of limitations for certain sexual offences and related tort actions; research initiatives (including funding for an evaluation of the Agreement and the adjudication process) and a proposal for a healing centre.

Finally, there was a range of individual financial benefits available to those women whose claims about physical or sexual abuse were validated via the adjudication process. Those women received amounts ranging from $3000 up to $60,000, based on a matrix that considered the type of harm and its impact. Moreover, once a claim had been validated, services such as financial counselling and therapy and assistance for vocational training were also available, as was an individual apology.

4.2. The Adjudication Process

A central aspect of the Grandview process—and one that was emphatically designed by the women survivors themselves—was the adjudication process. There were six adjudicators appointed, all of whom were women. Five were white and one was Aboriginal. All had a background in work on violence against women, most had previous experience in adjudication processes, five were law professors and one was a practising lawyer. The adjudicators described their collective expertise as being in 'human rights, feminist legal

[13] For the purposes of the case study that Jane Wangmann and I undertook into Grandview Agreement, interviews were conducted with five of the six adjudicators and the lawyers for the GSSG and the Ontario Government, and each interview is numbered: see Graycar and Wangmann (2007).

theory, tort law, criminal law, family law, constitutional law, property law, access to justice, health law, Aboriginal legal rights, minority language rights and adjudication in administrative tribunals' (*Report of the Grandview Adjudicators*, 1998: 5). Specifically, the adjudicators brought to the hearing and decision-writing process knowledge about the gendered harms that are directed at women and children, knowledge about the prevalence of violence against women, and an understanding of the ways in which experiences of violence or abuse may impact on women, including affecting their ability to recount what they have experienced. As experienced lawyers, they also brought to this process knowledge of the ways in which women and children's claims about violence have historically been dealt with within the legal system. The adjudicators saw the process as having 'multiple goals':

> First, it was a forum for the review and assessment of evidence relating to 'validation' and the assessment of quantum of damages. To this extent, the hearings did not differ from other, more traditional legal proceedings where judges review exhibits, listen to evidence, and make findings of fact based on legal standards and principles, including the onus of proof. Second, the Grandview hearings were intended to offer the applicants an opportunity to describe their experiences in their own words to someone with authority. The goal of adjudication pursuant to the Agreement was to empower the survivors of institutional abuse to define the wrong that was done to them, to explain the repercussions on their lives, to demand accountability and the restitution of their dignity, and to claim official recognition of injustice. The Grandview adjudication process was designed to accomplish all these goals (*Report of the Grandview Adjudicators*, 1998: 10).

Of the six adjudicators, four commenced in 1995 and the two others at a later time. Those four were provided with training by a feminist therapist who also had Grandview survivors as her clients, aimed at assisting them in dealing with people with multiple personalities and in learning 'ways to be more respectful as an adjudicator in responding to testimony', as well as more practical issues like what to wear to make claimants feel more comfortable (see Graycar and Wangmann, 2007: 25 and see generally des Rosiers, Feldthusen and Hankivsky, 1998; Feldthusen, Hankivsy and Greaves, 2000). One of the survivors said:

> I have nothing but the highest praise for every single person I came into contact with. They never once said to me 'I understand what you went through'. They were never disrespectful. That touched my life (Feldthusen, Hankivksy and Greaves, 2000: 88).

4.3. The Hearings

The claims were determined by way of an oral hearing and the nature of the hearings and their structure was determined by the adjudicators. The only guidance provided by the Agreement was that the model for the adjudication is the 'administrative law system' and that it was expected that each hearing would take around half a day to conduct. The four original adjudicators formulated the process, including the way that decisions would be written. The hearings were designed to be 'informal and non-confrontational'. Once appointed, the Aboriginal adjudicator also incorporated measures that made the hearings more accessible to Aboriginal survivors. While she noted that the Agreement had not been explicitly designed to take account of the needs and cultural requirements of Aboriginal claimants, it was 'most receptive to Aboriginal women, perhaps because of its underlying principles of healing and flexibility' (*Aboriginal Adjudicator's Report on the Process of the Grandview Agreement*, 1998: 1).

The hearings were held around Canada in many different venues. Generally, they would be held in an office setting, but some took place in the homes of applicants and in some cases, in prisons. The adjudicators stressed the importance of the physical layout of the hearing rooms. Efforts were made to ensure that the setting was non-hierarchical and there was a clear concern not to cause the participant stress, trauma and feelings of re-victimisation.

All the hearings were private and confidential (ie, closed to the public) though the women were free to bring someone with them as a support person (for example, their counsellor, family members or friends). While legal representation was permissible, few women chose to be represented. No transcript was made (though the adjudicators took notes that were eventually destroyed). The adjudicators emphasised that this privacy was essential to many claimants' willingness to participate in the process—given the need to reveal harms of a sexual nature, and the fact that they may not have revealed to anyone their background of institutionalisation:

> Some of [the applicants] would have chosen to forgo any compensation for the abuses they experienced if it had meant that they had to appear in a public forum to give their evidence (*Report of the Grandview Adjudicators*, 1998: 8).

The adjudicators asked each of the applicants to 'promise' to tell the truth (instead of 'swearing on the bible' or 'solemnly declaring') as follows: 'Do you promise to tell the truth, the whole truth and nothing but the truth to the best of your ability to recollect it?' (*Report of the Grandview Adjudicators*, 1998: 11).

As one of the adjudicators put it:

> The wording of the oath was intended to reassure an Applicant that the purpose of the hearing was to speak only about what she remembered and to identify memory gaps where they existed; and that it was anticipated that there might be problems recalling the full details of abusive events (*Report of the Grandview Adjudicators*, 1998: 11).

Aboriginal claimants could 'pledge their truth telling with an eagle feather, a traditional way of giving such an undertaking' (*Report of the Grandview Adjudicators*, 1998: 11).

Applicants were then invited to tell their story in a manner that suited them. This might involve the woman recounting her experiences in a narrative format, or it could involve a series of questions and answers:

> Care was taken ... not to interrupt the Applicant in the flow of her narrative, and to wait for an appropriate point to intervene with queries. The intent was to allow the Applicant a broad scope to define the way in which she could give her evidence about the Grandview experiences (*Report of the Grandview Adjudicators*, 1998: 12).

In their final report, the adjudicators reflected on this process:

> [It] ... seemed to enable Applicants to give difficult evidence. In the absence of constant interruptions and questioning by adversarial lawyers, some Applicants were less likely to become confused or defensive. As a result, Applicants were able to speak in detail about complex and emotionally-charged events. Applicants appeared to be comfortable explaining when their recollection of events was clear, when it was confused or foggy, or when they could not remember what happened. Indeed, it was striking how many times Applicants acknowledged a lack of clear recollection of some events while recalling others, knowing that their veracity would reduce the level of compensation to be received. Many Applicants took great pains to explain that they did not experience certain forms of abuse, or to describe and to distinguish clearly that part of their experience that was positive from that part which was abusive (*Report of the Grandview Adjudicators*, 1998: 12–13).

Survivors indicated in the evaluation of the Grandview Agreement that the hearing process was the most positive feature of the Agreement, albeit it was still traumatic:

> The most positive thing about [the hearings] was the opportunity they offered, in a relatively safe context, for women to tell their stories and have their experiences acknowledged. The most difficult thing was the 'horror of remembering' and describing their lives at Grandview (Leach, 1997: 31).

As the practical centrepiece of the Agreement, it is significant that the hearing process was assessed so very positively by victims/survivors (see also Feldthusen, Hankivsky and Greaves, 2000. For example, women commented:

> We were allowed to speak freely about what happened. We were able to express our feelings totally without being looked down upon.

> I was simply glad to have it over. I felt most satisfied with myself being able to tell what happened.
>
> She was strong, yet caring—non judgmental.
>
> I finally felt that I had been acknowledged; I was not bad. There had been something very wrong—this was finally confirmed (Leach, 1997: 31).

This is not to suggest that there were no criticisms: a small number of survivors raised concerns about the hearing process. For example, some were concerned about confidentiality and anonymity, and in particular were worried about the notes that were being taken by adjudicators during the hearing and what would happen to those notes afterwards. Others found the hearing room small, cold and clinical (Leach, 1997: 32).

The Agreement provided that the adjudicator will 'assess the claim on the basis of a finding of credibility of the applicant' (Grandview Agreement, cl 4.2.3). In considering their decisions, the adjudicators relied on the written application of the applicant and any supporting documentation (for example, therapist/counselling reports, medical records), the oral testimony of the applicant and other witnesses such as the woman's therapist, the Crown Ward file and any material supplied by the investigators.[14] The adjudicators recognised that while

> the Grandview file provided some helpful information, ... they represented only a partial view, and perhaps a deliberately distorted description of the Applicant's stay at Grandview, recorded from the perspective of the institution (*Report of the Grandview Adjudicators*, 1998: 13).

In the end it was the oral testimony that was the prime focus of the validation process. Like other legal processes, this involved assessing the woman's credibility. In their report on the Grandview hearing process, the adjudicators made a number of comments about the assumptions that often lay behind assessments of credibility in traditional legal processes and the way in which it was decided to approach 'credibility' under the Agreement. For example, the adjudicators noted that demeanour—commonly relied on to assess credibility—has a complex relationship to truth-telling: 'Demeanour may vary depending upon a witness's race, gender, cultural background,

[14] Every claim made under the Grandview Agreement was 'investigated' by a small team from the Criminal Injuries Compensation Board (CICB). While this was referred to as an 'investigation', it was 'largely conducted on the face of documentary evidence and generally involved comparing the woman's application with the Crown Ward files, any statements to the police and other documentary evidence that might be available': Graycar and Wangmann (2007: 16–17).

class, personality and emotional or psychological state and these variations may have no bearing on the witnesses' truth telling' (*Report of the Grandview Adjudicators*, 1998: 14). The adjudicators were aware that for many survivors, the process of having to recount these, frequently explicit, events was embarrassing and traumatic and that this may have a negative impact on the ability to convey the full story in a 'convincing' manner. For example, women would often 'speak in a halting manner and avoid eye contact' (*Report of the Grandview Adjudicators*, 1998: 14). The adjudicators were also cognisant of the ways in which survivors of institutional abuse might present as poor witnesses due to their experiences and the long-term consequences of those experiences. Factors such as a criminal background, drug and alcohol dependency, inability to recall events with accuracy, are frequently used to discredit plaintiffs in tort (and criminal) cases. As one of the interviewees graphically put it:

> [T]he primary barrier ... [faced by] women who have lived lives of abuse is the disintegrated nature of the lives they lived ... antithetical to what's required [by] the litigation process (interviewee 4 in Graycar and Wangmann, 2007: 27).

This difficulty was further captured by one of the adjudicators when asked whether she thought that the Grandview survivors would have been successful in a civil trial:

> I think they would have been victims on the altar of the justice system in Canada. They would have been re-victimised all over again, they would have been ridiculed, their dirty laundry would have been held up to the light and with no understanding of why. I think probably, there were some people who could have done it but they were very minimal, there were very few (interviewee 7 in Graycar and Wangmann, 2007: 33–34; see also *Report of the Grandview Adjudicators*, 1998: 22).

5. THE WOMEN'S INTERNATIONAL WAR CRIMES TRIBUNAL (WIWCT)

The second example I wish to raise is one that was also considered by Margaret Davies in her 2008 paper referred to earlier in this chapter. Davies uses as an illustration of a 'horizontal process' the Women's International War Crimes Tribunal (WIWCT) which has also been described as a civil society, rather than state based response (see Dolgopol, 2006). There are aspects of that process that, in addition to being 'alternative' are also arguably 'feminist' in nature and for that reason warrant consideration alongside the Grandview Agreement.

The WIWCT was convened in 2000 as a 'peoples' court' or 'peoples' tribunal' to hear a case against Japan and some individuals in relation to the sex slavery perpetrated during the Second World War on what have come to be known as 'comfort women' (see Dolgopol, 2003, 2006;[15] Chinkin, 2001, 2006; *WIWCT Judgment*, December 2001).[16] Chinkin explains that while the concept of peoples' tribunals is well established as a 'civil society' response to a range of international harms to which states have not responded effectively (Chinkin, 2006: 211–12), given the gendered nature of the harms that were perpetrated against the women, there was a need for a response that was able to take effective account of gendered experiences. This role has been taken in some contexts by 'Women's Courts', which have been described as a 'place where women can tell their stories in a safe place' (Chinkin, 2006: 212, referring to a description of the World Court of Women held in Cape Town in 2001).

Chinkin explains that after the failure of the original war crimes bodies that were established immediately after the Second World War to engage at all with the harms perpetrated against the women, the failure of the Japanese government to acknowledge responsibility for those harms and, more recently, the failure of some attempts at litigation by women who had been 'comfort women':

> The idea developed of combining the different approaches to transitional justice that were being pursued by states and international organisations with the models of civil society—peoples' tribunals, the Courts of Women, forms of truth commissions—into a Women's International War Crimes Tribunal to provide some form of justice where none had been available (2006: 213).

The Tribunal was constituted by Gabrielle McDonald, former President of the International Criminal Tribunal for the Former Yugoslavia (ICTY) (US); Carmen Argibay, President of the International Women's Association of Judges (Argentina); Christine Chinkin, Professor of International Law (United Kingdom); and Willy Mutunga, President of the Commission on Human Rights (Kenya). It sat for five days, including a day to deliver a preliminary judgment.[17] A key concern was the issue of evidence: clearly, as with the Grandview scheme, or indeed any form of response to historical harms, the injuries that had been perpetrated had occurred many years before and for that reason, there were serious limitations on the evidence that could be adduced. It was also suggested that records had been deliberately destroyed (Chinkin, 2006: 214).

[15] Note that Dolgopol discusses the terminology of 'comfort women' and explains why she continues to use it, notwithstanding hesitation about the term: see Dolgopol (2003: 242, fn 1).

[16] WIWCT: *The Prosecutors and People of the Asia Pacific Region v Hirohito Emperor Showa, et al and the Government of Japan*, full judgment delivered 4 December 2001: www1.jca.apc.org/vaww-net-japan/english/womenstribunal2000/Judgement.pdf.

[17] See WIWCT 2000 (preliminary judgment) WIWCT: *The Prosecutors and People of the Asia Pacific Region v Hirohito Emperor Showa, et al and the Government of Japan*, oral judgment delivered 2000: www1.jca.apc.org/vaww-net-japan/english/womenstribunal2000/oraljudgement.pdf; WIWCT 2001 (final judgment), above (n 16).

Some of the 75 survivors who attended the trial gave evidence orally; others made statements through videos or by affidavit. There was also documentary and expert evidence presented, and amicus curiae briefs outlining the legal steps that had previously been taken (unsuccessfully) (Chinkin, 2001: 337). The Tribunal decided that the evidence proved that 'Emperor Hirohito and other named defendants were guilty of rape and sexual slavery as a crime against humanity and that the government of Japan incurred responsibility under international law for its establishment and maintenance of the comfort system'.[18]

In her review of the process, Chinkin, one of the judges, observed that legal responses to atrocities such as the wartime 'comfort system' had given rise to 'innovative international and national proceedings' over recent years, including war crimes tribunals and models for truth and reconciliation:

> While a peoples' tribunal admittedly cannot provide the due process guarantees of a state-administered national or international court of law, this limitation should not lessen its usefulness. There is no more reason to question the veracity of evidence given under oath to global society than to question that given before a formal court of law ... Where previously there was only silence and evasion, such a forum constitutes a form of public acknowledgment to the survivors that serious crimes were committed against them. Such acknowledgment has been recognized as essential to redressing feelings of shame and guilt and providing healing and closure. A peoples' tribunal can thus combine in a single process elements of both war crimes trials and truth commissions. The diversity and complexity of the situations where atrocities are committed means no single definitive response can be fashioned. Instead processes must be devised that are feasible and conducive to the achievement of justice in each particular situation (Chinkin, 2001: 339).

Chinkin takes up this theme—of the importance of the design of the particular scheme—in her further reflections on the process. She attributes the ability of the organisers to design the tribunal to give effect to the dual objectives of assigning individual criminal culpability and state responsibility for wrongful acts under international law and the duty to accord reparation, to the 'freedom from the constraints of state mechanisms for international adjudication' (2001: 340). She also emphasises the centrality of its having been a '*women's* tribunal' (the emphasis is in the original), and more particularly the fact that it was established by grass roots activists, and notes that this itself is distinctive as previous peoples' tribunals did not always provide for the inclusion of women's voices.

[18] E/CN.4/Sub.2/2002/NGO/27, 2002: 2. This is from the written statement submitted to the Economic and Social Council Commission on Human Rights by Asia-Japan Women's Resources Centre, a non-governmental organisation in special consultative status on 4 August 2002, at: www.unhchr.ch/Huridocda/Huridoca.nsf/(Symbol)/E.CN.4.Sub.2.2002.NGO.27.En?Opendocument.

Yet at the end of the day, however powerful this was as a process, and however symbolically important, the WIWCT judgment could not be enforced: it was unable to order any reparation; it was unable to force the Japanese government to apologise; and it was unable to punish any perpetrator or to compensate any victim.

In her consideration of the process, Davies (2008: 297) pointed out:

> The tribunal redefined justice in relation to civil society rather than only in relation to government (Dolgopol, 2006; Chinkin, 2001) and although its findings could not be binding in any official legal sense, it nonetheless provided a space for the foregrounding of some extreme harms otherwise unacknowledged by law.

She went on to consider some of the advantages and disadvantages of a process such as this. First, and perhaps centrally, nothing decided by the WIWCT could be legally binding; it could not deliver any reparations; and the 'quality of its findings was largely moral' (2008: 297). Nonetheless, she suggests that 'such an activist intervention in the formal law' is an 'attempt to relocate and redefine it beyond the state and the government, and beyond the spaces and institutions formally constituted by vertical law' (2008: 297). And while lawyers were important to the process (as were the judges who all had considerable gravitas given their respective positions etc), the trial could simply not have occurred were it not for the work done by the victim/survivors; by non-governmental organisations (NGOs) and by the grassroots activists. These were some of the factors that, for Davies, rendered it 'horizontal'.

5.1. 'Not a Mock Trial but a Real Trial without Legal Force'

Davies immediately anticipates the criticism that this is not a horizontalised manifestation of law, but a 'non-legal repetition of law' and suggests that this depends on one's view of formal law. She notes that the WICWT pointed out that the peoples' tribunal 'was not a mock trial, but a real trial without legal force'.[19] Davies suggests that the

> tribunal participates in a broader feminist project to re-imagine law as … pushing the conventional boundaries of law, its methodological innovation was to 'combine traditional women's organising methodologies; networking, consciousness-raising, alliance-building with procedural initiatives that have established legitimacy among states and within civil society' (2008: 298).[20]

[19] WIWCT judgment, 2001, above (n 16) para 70.
[20] See also ibid, para 72.

> Thus the tribunal provides a forum for gender-based critique *and reconstruction* of the legal processes of the state. In this sense the tribunal envisions a future participatory law, at the same time as it tries to reconstruct an appropriate legally defined version of the past (2008: 298).

6. SOME CONCLUDING REFLECTIONS

In this chapter, I have examined aspects of two different processes, both of which we might call alternative, and both of which might appeal to our sense of the importance of approaching legal processes with a gendered sensibility. The first arose from an agreement made within (indeed, with) the formal legal system—after all, the agreement was with a Canadian provincial government—but which established a dispute resolution process that was informal and external to the court process (the Grandview Agreement). The second, which more closely resembled a formal trial, was conducted outside the purview of a formal justice process. Instead, it was in effect, a process designed and conducted by civil society, and while it had enormous symbolic importance, it had no actual legal traction (the WIWCT). These two examples both reflect considerable input of feminist ideas or principles. But what can we learn from them, or indeed perhaps more appropriately, what can we learn from their obvious limits?

The first, Grandview, has never been reproduced in Canada or elsewhere and the Grandview Agreement has been accorded scant, if any, attention as a model for later redress mechanisms. That may be for a number of reasons, not least perhaps because of concerns expressed by some about the forensic process.[21]

The second example, while in some ways perhaps even more powerful because of its public standing and public hearings, was quite simply extra-legal, that is, it took place entirely outside the (vertical) state institutional legal system. This is not to deny its extraordinary power and symbolic importance.

However, both processes shared one essential characteristic, and that is that they were designed specifically from the point of view of responding to a particular kind of (gendered) harm. Neither of them appears to have considered it sufficient to hope that some pre-existing legal process, one that was designed without any consideration of responding to gendered harms, would have been of value. Nor does it seem to have been contemplated that such an existing system would respond more effectively if only it had on it (more) women decision-makers.

[21] Some of these concerns, including those that led to an inquiry in Nova Scotia (the Kaufmann) inquiry, are discussed (and critiqued) in Graycar and Wangmann (2007: 31–35).

What this seems to suggest, at least tentatively, is that having women decision—makers is only a part of a bigger process that requires us to redesign the forms of adjudication in order to make them more responsive to women and to gendered harms in particular. Adding women adjudicators—indeed, adding any outsider decision- makers to adjudicative bodies is essential, if only from the most basic democratic point of view—we are entitled to participate in processes that are properly reflective of the society within which they function. But essential as that is, until we more radically transform the way we respond legally to gendered harms, we make only tiny (though necessary) inroads.

While I would never oppose any measure to bring about a more diverse judiciary, it is worth remembering that this is something that, while necessary, is not sufficient. We will not have feminist judges (*cf* Hunter, 2008) or feminist adjudication until we have the opportunity to redesign the forums in which we want those people to participate as well.

7. REFERENCES

Aboriginal Adjudicator's Report on the Process of the Grandview Agreement (24 March 1998) (copy on file with the author).

Blackstone, W (1765) 1 *Blackstone's Commentaries* (Oxford, Clarendon).

Bottomley, A (1996) *Feminist Perspectives on the Foundational Subjects of Law* (UK, Routledge Cavendish).

Chinkin C, (2001) 'Women's International Tribunal on Japanese Military Sexual Slavery' 95 *American Journal of International Law* 335.

—— (2006) 'Peoples' Tribunals Legitimate or Rough Justice?' 24 *Windsor Year Book of Access to Justice* 201.

Conaghan, J (1996) 'Gendered Harms and the Law of Tort: Remedying (Sexual Harassment)' 16 *Oxford Journal of Legal Studies* 407.

—— (1998) 'Tort Litigation in the Context of Intra-familial Abuse' 61 *Modern Law Review* 132.

—— (2002) 'Law, Harm and Redress: A Feminist Perspective' 22 *Legal Studies* 319.

Conaghan, J and Mansell, W (1998) *The Wrongs of Tort: Law and Social Theory* (London, Pluto Press).

Crenshaw, K (1989) 'Demarginalizing the Intersection of Race and Sex: A Black Feminist Critique of Antidiscrimination Doctrine, Feminist Theory and Antiracist Politics' *University of Chicago Legal Forum* 139.

Davies, M (2003) 'Legal Theory and Law Reform: Some Mainstream and Critical Approaches' 28 *Alternative Law Journal* 168.

—— (2008) 'Feminism and the Flat Law Theory' 16 *Feminist Legal Studies* 281.

De Greiff, P (ed) (2006) *The Handbook of Reparations* (New York, Oxford University Press).

De Rosiers, N, Feldthusen, B and Hankivsky, O (1998) 'Legal Compensation for Sexual Violence: Therapeutic Consequences and Consequences for the Judicial System' 4 *Psychology, Public Policy and Law* 433.

Dolgopol, U (2003) 'The Judgment of the Tokyo Women's Tribunal' 28 *Alternative Law Journal* 242.

—— (2006) 'Redressing Partial Justice—A Possible Role for Civil Society' in U Dolgopol and J Gardam, *The Challenge of Conflict: International Law Responds* (The Netherlands, Martinus Nijhoff Publishers).

Duclos, N (1993) 'Disappearing Women: Racial Minority Women in Human Rights Cases' 6 *Canadian Journal of Women and Law* 25.

Feldthusen, B (1993) 'The Civil Action for Sexual Battery: Therapeutic Jurisprudence' 25 *Ottawa Law Review* 203.

—— (2007) 'Civil Liability for Sexual Assault in Aboriginal Residential Schools: The Baker Did It' 22 *Canadian Journal of Law and Society* 61.

Feldthusen, B, Hankivsky, O and Greaves, L (2000) 'Therapeutic Consequences for Civil Actions for Damages and Compensation Claims by Victims of Sexual Abuse' 12 *Canadian Journal of Women and the Law* 66.

Ferstman, C, Goetz, M and Stephens, A (eds) (2009) *Reparations for Victims of Genocide, War Crimes and Crimes Against Humanity: Systems in Place and Systems in the Making* (Leiden, Martinus Nijhoff Publishers).

Freeman, M (2006) *Truth Commissions and Procedural Fairness* (New York, Cambridge University Press).

Graycar, R (1995) 'The Gender of Judgments: An Introduction' in M Thornton (ed), *Public and Private: Feminist Legal Debates* (Melbourne, Oxford University Press).

—— (1998) 'The Gender of Judgments: Some Reflections on "Bias"' 32 *University of British Columbia Law Review* 1.

—— (2004) 'Claire L'Heureux-Dubé: Some Reflections from Down Under' in E Sheehy (ed), *Adding Feminism to Law: The Contribution of Justice Claire L'Heureux-Dubé* (Toronto, Irwin Law).

—— (2008) 'Gender, Race, Bias and Perspective: Or, How Otherness Colours your Judgment' 15 (1–2) *International Journal of the Legal Profession* 73.

Graycar, R and Morgan, J (1990) *The Hidden Gender of Law* (Sydney, The Federation Press).

—— (1995) 'Disabling Citizenship: Civil Death for Women in the 1990s?' 17 *Adelaide Law Review* 49.

—— (2002) *The Hidden Gender of Law*, 2nd edn (Sydney, The Federation Press).

Graycar, R and Wangmann, J (2007) 'Redress Packages for Institutional Child Abuse: Exploring the Grandview Agreement as a Case Study in "Alternative" Dispute Resolution' *Legal Studies Research Paper No 07/50* (Sydney, Sydney University Law School).

Howe, A (1987) '"Social Injury Revisited": Towards a Feminist Theory of Social Justice' 15 *International Journal of the Sociology of Law* 423.

—— (1994) *Punish and Critique: Towards a Feminist Analysis of Penalty* (London, Routledge).

Hunter, R (1996) 'Gender in Evidence: Masculine Norms v Feminist Reforms' 19 *Harvard Women's Law Journal* 127.

—— (2008) 'Can *Feminist* Judges Make a Difference?' 15(1–2) *International Journal of the Legal Profession* 7.

Institute for Human Resources Development (IHRD) (1988) 'Review of the Needs of Victims of Institutional Abuse', paper prepared for the LCC (copy on file with the author).

Leach & Associates (1997) *Evaluation of the Grandview Agreement Process: Final Report* (copy on file with the author).

Luntz, H, Hambly, D, Burns, K, Dietrich, J and Foster, N (2008) *Torts: Cases and Commentary*, 6th edn (Chatswood, LexisNexis Butterworths).

Mack, K (1993) 'Continuing Barriers to Women's Credibility: A Feminist Perspective on the Proof Process' 4 *Criminal Law Forum* 327.

MacKinnon, C (1987) *Feminism Unmodified: Discourses on Life and Law* (Cambridge, Harvard University Press).

Mathews, B (2003) 'Limitation Periods and Child Sexual Abuse Cases: Law, Psychology, Time and Justice' 11 *Torts Law Journal* 119.

Mossman, MJ (1993) 'Gender Equality and Legal Aid Services: A Research Agenda for Institutional Change' 15 *Sydney Law Review* 30.

Pete, S and Du Plessis, M (eds) (2007) *Repairing The Past? International Perspectives on Reparations for Gross Human Rights Abuses* (Antwerp, Intersentia).

Report of the Grandview Adjudicators (13 May 1998) (copy on file with author).

Rubio-Marín, R (ed) (2006) *What Happened to the Women? Gender and Reparations for Human Rights Violations* (New York, Social Science Research Council).

—— (2009) *The Gender of Reparations: Unsettling Sexual Hierarchies while Redressing Human Rights Violations* (New York, Cambridge University Press).

Sangster, J (2001) *Regulating Girls and Women: Sexuality, Family and the Law in Ontario, 1920–1960* (Canada, Oxford University Press).

Sheehy, E (1991) 'Feminist Argumentation before the Supreme Court of Canada in *R v Seaboyer; R v Gayme*: The Sound of One Hand Clapping' 18 *Melbourne University Law Review* 450.

Thornton, M (1996) *Dissonance and Distrust: Women in the Legal Profession* (Melbourne, Oxford University Press).

Todd, S (2000) 'Privatization of Accident Compensation: Policy and Politics in New Zealand' 39 *Washburn Law Journal* 404.

—— (2002) 'Negligence Liability for Personal Injury: A Perspective from New Zealand' 25 *University of New South Wales Law Journal* 895.

Vella, S (1995) 'The Healing Package Negotiated by the Grandview Survivors' Support Group: An Example of Alternative Dispute Resolution and Societal Accountability in Action' in Canadian Institute, *Civil Liability for Sexual Assault in an Institutional Setting* (copy on file with the author).

Wangmann, J (2004) 'Liability for Institutional Child Sexual Assault: Where does Lepore Leave Australia?' 28 *Melbourne University Law Review*169.

Part 6

Quotas and Diversity

6.1

Which Judicial Selection Systems Generate the Most Women Judges? Lessons from the United States

SALLY J KENNEY

Abstract

Do certain judicial selection systems produce a more diverse and representative judiciary than others? Studies of electoral systems show that when voters elect more than one person at a time or rank their preferences rather than vote only for one person, voters are more likely to elect women and minority men to office. Some claim so-called merit judicial selection systems are superior because they bypass voters who discriminate and constrain appointers, thereby eliminating politics and bias from the selection process. Social science research, however, shows that merit systems are not better than elective systems in producing a diverse and representative bench. The evidence shows few systemic effects. The systems with the highest numbers of women judges are civil law systems that recruit judges to the career civil service by examination. The common law jurisdictions that enjoy the greatest increases in the numbers of women judges serving have made the gender diversity of the bench a clear priority and set goals, rid the system of indirectly discriminatory standards, trained selectors about the dangers of implicit bias and actively recruited women. Alternatively, a particular governor, president or prime minister with the power to appoint judges has made a diverse and representative judiciary a priority and chosen women and minority men accordingly. Even the best systems have substantial room to improve. After examining the many explanations for women's under-representation, I review the evidence on systemic effects in the American states. I then look at three jurisdictions that have made impressive progress in increasing the number of women judges serving—Ontario, Scotland and South Africa—to discover the ingredients of their successes.

1. INTRODUCTION[1]

Scholars have offered many explanations for why so few women serve as judges. Jurisdictions, states and countries vary enormously in the percentages of women serving. Carefully analysing variation among American states and between the United States and other countries provides a laboratory for determining which of the many variables explain differences. Two of the most popular explanations—size of the qualified pool and method of selection—do not explain the variation. After briefly reviewing the many explanations, this chapter argues that the evidence shows that adopting a so-called merit selection system does not in and of itself produce a more gender diverse judiciary.

2. WHY SO FEW? EXPLANATIONS

Twenty-six per cent of state court judges in the United States are women.[2] Yet states vary enormously in the number of women serving between Vermont (which ranks first with 41 per cent) and South Dakota and Idaho (tied for last with 13 per cent).[3] Perhaps even more puzzling than this variation is its erratic nature over time (Bonneau 2001). Examining the social scientific evidence does more than offer a comprehensive literature review. Looking back can show how a popular idea—that merit selection systems were better for women—came to be conventional wisdom and how difficult such ideas are to dislodge. Moreover, such a review shows how easily ephemeral gender effects—effects at one point in time, when women judges were few, or at one geographic location—are generalised when the cumulative weight of evidence shows the opposite. Lastly, a comprehensive review of the literature refutes scholars who say that studies fall on both sides so we cannot discern which position the evidence best supports.

The first political scientist who sought to explain why so few women served as judges, Beverly Blair Cook, tried to explain the large variation in number of women trial court judges in the 58 largest US cities (1980: 42). Legal academic Karen Tokarz, too, wondered about the large variation, from Alaska where then 21.9 per cent of its judges were women to 1.3 per cent in Tennessee (1986: 915), but she asked particularly why Missouri lagged behind. Alaska is now a laggard, not a leader, ranked thirty-eighth with 18 per cent, but the state variation is as puzzling as ever. Despite

[1] Thanks to Malia Reddick and Mark Hurwitz for their helpful comments, and to Lura Barber and Rebecca Moskow for research assistance.

[2] See www.nawj.org/us_state_court_statistics_2009.asp.

[3] Ibid.

the fact that states' rankings move around wildly, scholars asked whether culture could be an explanation for state variation. Political scientists have long debated whether differences in political culture—the values and norms about how to conduct politics—could explain differences between nations. Daniel Elazar posited that states, like nations, had distinctive political cultures that he grouped into three large categories: moralist, traditionalist, and individualist (1972). Cook asked whether Elazar's categories could explain differences among states in the number of women judges serving. She found that moralist states (states that run clean governments and believe in a collective good, such as the upper New England states, the upper Midwest and several states in the West) had significantly higher percentages of women on appellate courts, but she found Elazar's typology could not explain variation among states in the number of women general jurisdiction trial judges (1980: 53) nor could it explain variations among the cities of those states.

Cook tried to refine Elazar's model by considering whether states had distinctive gender political cultures. She added two additional variables: the number of women participating in political party conventions and a feminist public policy variable. The women's political participation measure explained some of the variation, while the policy measure explained little. Cook found a significant but weak relationship between the population of a state's answer to the Gallup Poll question of whether you would vote for a woman for president (1978: 98) and the number of women judges. After Cook, other scholars found region not to explain variation (Alozie, 1990, 1996; Hurwitz and Lanier, 2003, 2008). Bratton and Spill's study of state courts of last resort showed that relatively liberal states were particularly likely to have gender diverse courts (2002: 515), but Williams found liberal states to have more women judges only on their trial not their appellate courts (2007: 1198) and Bratton and Spill's study of federal trial courts showed that ideology had little predictive effect (2005: 130). In short, political scientists found political culture to offer little explanatory power.

If culture could not explain differences in the number of women judges serving, perhaps more simple demographic variables could? Cook observed (what legislative scholars have more recently discovered) that women were more likely to represent suburban and urban than rural constituencies (1984b: 203). Cook also found that the higher women's incomes and the lower the birth rates in a state the greater the number of women judges (1978: 98). Carbon et al also found, as early as 1980, that women were much more likely to serve in large metropolitan areas than rural districts (1982: 298).

The third explanation is the size of the qualified labour pool. Many have justified women's absence from high judicial office because it is only relatively recently that women entered legal education in large and now equal if not greater numbers than men. Apologists reassured advocates that women would 'trickle up' to higher judicial office as cohorts with equal numbers of women accrued seniority. Cook conducted the first pool analysis, asking how many women judges we should have expected to see serving on the bench given the pool of 'eligibles' assuming no discrimination, a question familiar to equal employment opportunity analysts. Cook found little change between 1920 and 1970 (1978: 90). In 1977, Cook used the number of women law graduates and the number serving in the state attorney-general's office to predict 81 per cent of the variation in the number of women serving on state courts (1978). By 1984, the evidence had changed, and Cook rejected the 'trickle up' hypothesis (1984a: 574–75). Cook found a disparity of 50 per cent between the numbers of women judges we might expect based on the number of women lawyers. If women were 10 per cent of the lawyers in a state, about five per cent of judges would be women (1984b: 199). Cook concluded that 'time is not the only barrier' (1984a: 606); rather, gatekeepers kept women out. Other scholars drew the same conclusion (Alozie, 1996; Martin and Pyle, 2002; Hurwitz and Lanier, 2003; Bratton and Spill, 2005). Moreover, the huge variation among states in how long it took after the admission of women to the state Bar for a state to appoint its first woman to the state Supreme Court (Cook, 1984a: 598), as well as the large differences between states as to when they named their first woman Supreme Court justice, suggested that something other than simply the number of women lawyers was at work. Minority men could increase their likelihood of selection by increasing their numbers, but women could not (Hurwitz and Lanier, 2003: 346). Williams seemed to be alone in her finding that the number of women lawyers did help to predict the number of women on state trial and appellate courts, although it could not explain women's under-representation (2007). She did, however, find that the number of women trial judges did not help predict the number of women appellate judges (2007: 1200). Reddick, Caufield and Nelson's study of a sample of trial judges and all state appellate judges established that the number of women attorneys in a state had no predictive power for the number of women Supreme Court judges but it was significantly and positively related to women appellate judges and trial court judges (2009: 14). Bratton and Spill found that women could not ensure a diverse highest appellate court by increasing women's presence on lower courts (2002: 514). To conclude, we cannot explain women's under-representation on courts by the absence of women in the qualified labour pool.

Fourthly, size matters. Cook showed that women were more likely to serve on larger rather than smaller courts (1980: 54); also that a superior court had to have at least 25, a municipal court five judges before selectors chose a woman (1984a: 581; 1987: 153). Her finding was consistent with what scholars of legislative elections know: when voters or other selectors choose more than one at a time and have many places to fill, they are more likely to present a balanced slate, while choosing one at a time for a small number of slots yields more homogeneity and representation from the dominant group. Size of court may partly explain the few women in rural courts, which are smaller. Other scholars confirmed Cook's finding (Alozie, 1996; Bratton and Spill, 2002, 2005; Hurwitz and Lanier, 2003; Williams, 2007, 2008b). President Clinton appointed a higher percentage of women to the larger courts than the smaller courts (Bratton and Spill, 2001: 261). If Clinton's principal goal was to diversify the courts, he would have appointed women to the smaller rather than the larger courts.

A fifth explanation I call breaking the mould. Cook found in 1978 that as a solitary token woman moved up the hierarchy, she would not necessarily be replaced by another woman (1978). Recent examples of both Justice Sandra Day O'Connor and Chief Judge Judith Kaye of New York,[4] who were replaced by men, suggest no fixed women's seats exist. Bratton and Spill's research showed that President Clinton was likely to replace African-American judges with other African Americans, but he only replaced one of the five women who left the bench with another woman (2001: 258). Gould and Merola found that judges who were 'first' (minority or woman) to hold a seat felt less confident about winning (2009: 31). The evidence also undermines the argument that the number of women in the pool drives the number of women serving, if the ceiling consists of merely one woman no matter the size of the pool. Bratton and Spill found it was more likely that a governor would choose a woman for the state Supreme Court if the court had no women members (2002). Their research suggests that selectors wanted at least token representation, and the credit and attention for appointing a first. But their research bodes ill for women's prospect of increasing their representation on courts if selectors are less likely to pick women for positions if a woman already sits on that court, ie, if the ceiling for women is one position.

The sixth explanation is that women lack the elite credentials selectors deem necessary. Women are herded into the lower status corners of the legal and judicial professions and then judged lacking in the prestigious credentials selectors value. The American Bar Association's Committee on the Judiciary, for example, valued large firm experience yet, famously, when Sandra Day O'Connor sought employment with her third place ranking from Stanford Law School in 1952, firms openly said they would not hire women. Cook documented women's exclusion from high prestige courts

[4] Judge Judith Kaye was the Chief Judge of the State of New York and the first woman to hold that position. When she retired in 2008, the nominating commission sent the governor a list of three men's names. The governor chose one from the list, as state law required.

and the efforts of judges to shunt women into special jurisdictional courts (1978). From Northern Ireland[5] to Argentina (Kohen, 2008) women are pressed into family law (with the exception of Islamic family law courts such as in Syria which bar women from service (Cardinal, 2008)) then told that family law is not a prestigious enough area of specialisation for a judge, as was said of Lady Brenda Hale (Kenney, 2004a).

A seventh explanation, rarely discussed in the literature, is homophobia (Kenney, 2010). One reason it took until 1981 to see a woman on the US Supreme Court is that the candidate who had the best chance of the job was a lesbian. Florence Allen was the first woman on the Ohio Supreme Court, the first woman on any federal appeals court (Sixth Circuit), the only woman on a federal appeals court for 32 years and the first woman any president seriously considered for the US Supreme Court (Cook, 1981). Over the course of Allen's career, elites turned against unmarried women partnered with other women (Faderman, 2000; Organ, 1998: 228, 242). In 1982, Cook compared Florence Allen's 12 unsuccessful attempts to reach the Supreme Court to the process that yielded the first woman Supreme Court justice, Sandra Day O'Connor. Cook set their credentials against other Supreme Court justices and found elite education, politically active and connected families and comfort if not affluence in both Allen and O'Connor's backgrounds, as in nearly all of the justices. Noting that only eight of 101 male justices were unmarried, Cook contrasted Allen's unmarried status (without remarking on her two lengthy partnerships with women) with O'Connor's marriage, three children and break from work when her children were small, making her life experiences closer to the experience of most American women (1982: 318) than Allen's and therefore more acceptable to her appointing authorities.

Eighth, gatekeepers discriminate against women. Vital gatekeepers, such as the law professors who suggest law clerks to Supreme Court justices, do not recommend women in proportion to their increasing numbers, closing off this important pathway (Cook, 1984a: 589). Another important gatekeeper has been the American Bar Association's Standing Committee on the Judiciary that evaluates nominees (Cook, 1982, 1988).[6] The ABA's standards have placed a premium on large firm and trial court practice, required many years of practice, and disqualified older candidates. It has rated women as unqualified, delayed women's nominations, or vetoed them

[5] D Feenan (2005) 'Applications by Women for Silk and Judicial Office in Northern Ireland' A Report Commissioned by the Commissioner for Judicial Appointments for Northern Ireland: cjani.courtsni.gov.uk/CJANIResearchReport.pdf (27 February 2008).

[6] See also S Ness, 'Sexist Selection Process Keeps Qualified Women off the Bench' *Washington Post* (26 March 1978). President Bush suspended the practice of referring names to the ABA prior to nominating a candidate in 2001, but President Obama has restored its role.

altogether. Nominating commissions, for the federal appeals courts or state courts, also serve as gatekeepers. In 1981, Dunn found that nominating commissions in merit selection jurisdictions consisted predominantly of white men (see also Henschen, Moog and Davis, 1990). Cook argued as early as 1984 that the more women on the nominating commissions, the more women on the lists (1984b: 209). Gatekeepers frequently impose different standards on men and women candidates, although what those standards are varies. Githens documented how a state nominating commission regarded women as 'uppity' and 'undesirably ambitious' in seeking judgeships, while simultaneously regarding men as lacking in ambition in seeking those same positions—any self-respecting man surely would seek more lucrative employment in a large firm (1995).

Ninth, selectors use 'neutral' criteria other than gender that fewer women than men can comply with, what in employment discrimination we call disparate impact, or indirect discrimination. Martin (1982) demonstrated how the ABA's criteria had a disparate impact on women by validating men's career patterns and by valuing large firm experience—difficult if not impossible for women to acquire because large firms refused to hire women attorneys (Slotnick, 1983a and 1983b). The ABA tended to favour older, well-to-do, business-oriented corporate attorneys. Martin's first study (1982) analysed the background of President Carter's appointees. In an interesting parallel with England, where the Lord Chancellor appointed senior judges after canvassing the higher judiciary in 'secret soundings' (Kenney, 2004b), Martin explored the disparate impact of using the criterion of being well known to senior judges for judicial appointments. Her survey found that 43 per cent of the women felt that they would not have been considered under the previous system rather than under merit selection because they lacked the political influence and credentials (Martin, 1982: 308). Like Carter's, Clinton's women appointees were more likely than men to have judicial experience and less likely to come from private firms. More women, however, now have experience as prosecutors, particularly in the US Attorney's offices, a traditional pipeline to the bench (Slotnick 1984). Presidents seem to hold women to a higher standard of experience either as a judge or a prosecutor than men.

The tenth barrier is that selectors are not likely to appoint women unless women demand it (Clark, 2004). Cook (1982) found Allen's chances for a US Supreme Court appointment were best when a network of women social reformers had the ear of first lady Eleanor Roosevelt. Despite an early 1938 Gallup poll that 41 per cent of Americans favoured a woman on the US Supreme Court, Presidents Roosevelt and Truman felt little real pressure to appoint one. President Truman at least canvassed the sitting justices who did not like the idea, fearing a woman in their midst would crimp their informal style of discussion with shoes off and collars undone.[7] Cook plotted modern women's groups' first involvement in the process in recommending three women candidates for the Arthur Goldberg vacancy (1982: 324). The National Women's Political Caucus and National Organization for Women spearheaded a process in 1977 that facilitated President Carter's breakthrough success in increasing the number of women federal judges (Clark, 2002; Goldman, 1997; Kenney, 2013). The National Association of Women Judges, formed in 1979, achieved its goal of securing the appointment of a woman to the US Supreme Court (Cook, 1988).

Eleventh, a gender gap may exist in political ambition for judicial office as it does for legislative office. Lawless and Fox (2005) documented that well-qualified women were less likely than their male counterparts to say they had considered running for office or been asked to do so. In 1983, Cook reported higher levels of ambition for judicial office among younger cohorts of women, although much of that ambition was focused on state courts. Women may have wisely ascertained that applying for judgeships in the past (or running for judicial office) was pointless despite their ambitions. Williams found 68 per cent of the women attorneys surveyed believed women faced barriers to becoming a judge (2008a: 75). Williams's survey of women lawyers in Texas did not show a large gender gap in political ambition for state judicial office in a state with partisan election (2008a). Jensen and Martinek's 2006 survey of trial court judges in New York State found women to be more ambitious than men (Jensen and Martinek, 2009). Encouraging women to run for judicial office has more effect on women than men and conversely, a perception that women face barriers to judicial office may depress women's political ambition.

Lastly, electoral politics and public opinion determine whether presidents or governors will choose women judges. Cook analysed poll data to show that Nixon's consideration of Judge Mildred Lillie for the US Supreme Court was not ahead of its time (Cook, 1982: 324–25; Dean, 2001).[8] Carter appointed more women than all previous presidents combined (Martin, 1987, 2004).[9] Reagan responded to the emerging gender gap among voters by promising to appoint a woman to the US Supreme Court, which deflected attention from the fact that he appointed only half as many women as Carter had. The first President Bush's record of appointing

[7] Chief Justice Rehnquist, Sandra Day O'Connor's law school classmate, apparently advised President Ford to exercise extreme caution in considering a woman while screening candidates to replace Justice Douglas because 'There aren't any women in sight with impressive qualifications for the job' (Cook, 1978: 71, citing Dacey). Justices Marshall and Brennan, however, reportedly welcomed the appointment of a woman, 'the sooner the better' (Cook, 1978: 71, citing Williams).

[8] SJ Kenney (2009) 'Nixon Gaffe Sparks Era of Judicial Advance' *Women's eNews*, 4 May www.womensenews.org.

[9] See also Kenney, ibid.

women improved on Reagan's and even Carter's, and he appointed half the women in the year he ran unsuccessfully for re-election (Martin, 2004: 117). Clinton appointed the largest number of women and the largest percentage of women to the bench of any president (Martin, 2004: 117). The second President Bush's numbers receded to 22 per cent from Clinton's high mark of 28 per cent (Diascro and Solberg, 2009: 290).

3. DOES METHOD OF SELECTION EXPLAIN THE VARIATION?

If practitioners were most fond of the supposedly insufficient numbers of women in the qualified labour pool as an explanation for women's absence from the bench, the explanation that most intrigued political scientists (and proponents of merit selection) was the method of selection. In 1977, only nine women served on state courts of last resort and 21 on intermediate appellate courts, and Flango and Ducat (1979: 30) found the evidence on whether one system produced more women inconclusive as the women were divided between systems. As early as 1979 analysts proclaimed the appointive methods of selection to grant women and minority men greater access than elective measures (Warden, Schlesinger and Kearney, 1979). Henry et al (1985) restated that claim for the Fund for Modern Courts. Philip Dubois (1983) found women fared as well under elections as under appointment in California from 1959 to 1977. In 1980, Susan Carbon et al surveyed women state court judges, about 25 per cent of whom had reached their post through nominating commissions and another 23 per cent had been appointed by the governor (1982). Judges tended to declare whichever system produced them to be their preferred system, the same as Gould and Merola found in their interviews with state judges of colour (2009: 18). By 1988, Cook had concluded that no one judicial selection system produced more women; instead, what mattered was a commitment on the part of gatekeepers to considering women, jettisoning discriminatory criteria and prioritising a commitment to equal justice under law.

Tokarz's analysis of all states showed that a slightly higher percentage of women, between 9.3 per cent and 9.5 per cent, had achieved state judicial office through an appointive process than by elections, which ran between six per cent and 6.7 per cent. Although dated, her study of Missouri (1986) merits closer consideration for several reasons. First, Missouri was the birthplace of the Missouri Plan for merit selection in 1940. Secondly, by choosing its appellate judges and trial judges for the two large urban counties by merit selection while also keeping elections for trial judges in so-called outstate Missouri, Missouri provided a way to test for systemic effects holding political culture relatively constant. Thirdly, Tokarz's findings contradicted conventional theories of the time. Women should have done better under a merit system, in urban rather than rural areas, and on larger rather than smaller courts. Tokarz's findings that women were more likely to serve as judges in outstate Missouri under an elective system than in the two cities under merit selection was damning to the argument that women did better under merit systems. Voters received outstate women judges well and generally gave them a higher percentage of 'yes' votes than their male counterparts. Fourthly, Tokarz, in over 30 in-depth interviews with judges, showed how the selection system shut out women: no women served as governors, appellate judges, or attorney (rather than lay) members of the nominating commission. Fifthly, she proved Missouri to be a laggard, as the selection rate of 3.5 per cent of women was far below the 9.2 per cent of lawyers over 30 in the state who were women as well as contrary to a growing tendency to appoint younger judges, and Governor Ashcroft had appointed no women at all but 19 men (1986: 942). Sixthly, Tokarz identified ways to improve Missouri's poor performance (1986: 918).[10]

Tokarz's findings demolished several core arguments in support of merit selection by demonstrating that politics pervaded the selection of judges under the Missouri Plan and the partisan election plan it replaced. The Plan simply rebalanced the political interests of the Bar, the bench, the governor, political parties and the voters (1986: 946). She concluded that merit systems were insufficient to guarantee women's full representation, if not indeed an impediment, and that 'without leadership, commitment, and vigilance by elected officials, the legal community, and the public, even a nonpartisan, merit plan inhibits access to women to the bench' (1986: 907). Missouri's Women's Bar Associations reorganised in the mid-1970s to contest the lawyer seats and to press the case for the appointment of women (Tokarz, 1986: 939). A Missouri Bar Committee undertook an intensive study of the plan and specifically criticised the small number of women selected. Shortly thereafter, Governor Ashcroft appointed the first woman, Ann Covington, to the Missouri Supreme Court in 1987. Tokarz offered a prescient warning that women, having assumed they were unlikely to be chosen, would rarely apply for judgeships, creating a self-fulfilling prophesy (1986: 949).

Subsequent analyses confirmed Tokarz's finding of no systemic effect. Alozie found a weak relationship between selection method and higher

[10] It took twice as long as the 50-year average for other states (Cook, 1984a: 598), 110 years, from the time Missouri admitted women to the Bar until a woman lawyer held a full-time position in a Missouri trial court of general jurisdiction (Tokarz, 1986: 928). Maine was the longest at 111 years. The percentage of women judges in Missouri, 5.3%, was below the national average of 7.2–7.3% and ranked Missouri 33rd out of 50 states (Tokarz, 1986: 926). In 1985, 18 of the 342 state court judges in Missouri were women (5.3%) and Missouri was one of 14 states that had never had a woman judge at the appellate level (Tokarz, 1986: 923). Only 3.5% of Missouri's merit-selected judges were women, compared with a national average of 9.5%.

numbers of women judges in his study of state judges in the 1980s, but declared judicial selection methods 'not to be the major agents some analysts think they are' (1990: 318); instead, '[j]udicial selection methods alone do not explain differential representation of women, blacks, and Hispanics on state judiciaries' (1990: 321). His study of state courts of last resort in 1993 showed 'no disparities on the effects of formal selection systems' (1996: 123). Brown's 1998 study of New York City judges from 1992 to 1997 established that elective systems produced more women jurists than appointive systems. Esterling and Andersen (1999) investigated nine state merit selection systems and found that nominating commissions selected women and minority men for judicial vacancies proportionate to their representation in the pool, but that governors did not select them. One of their most intriguing findings was that racially diverse commissions attracted greater numbers of minority applicants, but that gender diverse commissions did not. Martin and Pyle (2002) examined the background of 325 state Supreme Court justices. While they agreed that no one method of selection favoured women or minority men, they did note that African-American judges serving in systems of partisan or nonpartisan election tended to first obtain their seats by being appointed as an interim. With six African-American women justices, it was hard to generalise, but governors might have been diversifying the bench through the use of interim appointments. States with nonpartisan elections had courts with a higher percentage of women, but nearly half of those women first came to the bench through interim appointments (Martin and Pyle, 2002: 50).

Hurwitz and Lanier (2001) studied the composition of state Supreme Courts and intermediate appellate courts in 1985 and 1999 and found that women were more likely to achieve a position in the most prestigious state courts than the less prestigious ones, contrary to the idea that the higher the prestige, the lower the likelihood of women serving. They found no influence of judicial selection system. They also recommend that scholars disaggregate the data. The percentage of African-American judges serving was going down, while the percentage of women was going up. Lumping together 'women and minority men' obscures the results (2001: 92).

Holmes and Emrey found no support for the claim that women reached their judgeships through interim appointments rather than election in elective systems between 1964 and 2004 (2006: 7). The first woman on a state Supreme Court, however, was more likely to have obtained her seat by gubernatorial appointment (2006: 13) than by election (2006: 5). Democratic governors were slightly more likely to have diversified an all-male court by making an interim appointment (2006: 11).

Recent studies on gender and judicial elections continue to show contradictory results (Reid, 2004; Williams, 2007). Reid (2004) examined women's electoral performance in races for North Carolina District Court between

1994 and 1998. Women raised more money for their races than men, but 'men received significantly more electoral bang for their campaign buck than women' (2004: 834). Women running for open seats spent much more than men to do less well. Lucas examined partisan and nonpartisan state Supreme Court elections between 1990 and 2006 and found that women won more often than men in both partisan and nonpartisan elections (neither system, however, favoured women) and Republican women won most of all (84 per cent of Republican women won compared with 60 per cent of Republican men) (2007: 15).

Williams (2007) examined women serving on state trial courts, intermediate appellate courts, and courts of last resort in 2003. She found that nonpartisan elections increased women's representation on trial courts, while merit selection decreased women's representation on appellate courts (2007: 1200), a difference she could not explain. Nor could she explain why her model showed a selection system effect when so many others had not.[11] Williams rightly urged scholars to model appellate and trial courts separately so that trial court numbers do not swamp the results. Yet Williams's model is limited by being a snapshot of only one year and its results are less reliable because she classified each state by how a majority of its judges were selected rather than coding each individual judge's route to the bench. Grouping all appellate courts together may have also distorted the findings as intermediate appellate courts tend to have more members than courts of last resort and we know size of court affects the number of women serving.

Reddick, Caufield and Nelson's study (2009) carefully classifies each state according to how each judge was selected rather than by the state's formal system. Minnesota, for example, has nonpartisan elections, but most judges resign before the end of their terms, the governor appoints a replacement and that person runs uncontested in the election as an incumbent. Of Minnesota's Supreme Court justices, then, 92 per cent were initially chosen by the governor rather than elected. They included all appellate judges and a sample of trial judges. Their study did not find that the judicial selection system significantly altered the likelihood that the judge was a woman.[12] Preliminary findings from Kenney and Windett's study of state Supreme Court justices suggest that states with non partisan elections and appointments, either gubernatorial or legislative, have an expected value of female judges close to 0.25 percentage points higher in all three decades compared to states with partisan elections and merit selection processes (2012).

[11] Williams (2008b) also argued that OECD countries where a president appoints judges saw the largest numbers of women serving.

[12] Gould and Merola's 2009 study reached the same conclusions for minority judges (2009: 9).

4. WHAT DOES INCREASE THE NUMBER OF WOMEN?

One hope was that women stood a higher chance of obtaining new seats as courts grew in size. In the United States, the expansion of the federal judiciary during the Carter Administration facilitated the appointment of women. A similar expansion in the judiciary of the United Kingdom, however, witnessed no parallel growth. Bratton and Spill noted that although new seats are sometimes associated with increased diversity, they found no statistically significant relationship (2005: 128).

Individual idiosyncratic differences may explain why a US state suddenly moves up or down in the rankings. Governors such as Jerry Brown in California (Cook, 1984b: 208) or Rudy Perpich in Minnesota (Kenney 2009) catapult their states forward. The rates of presidential appointments have varied from Reagan's low of seven per cent to Clinton's nearly 30 per cent.[13] The Fund for Modern Courts found women to have fared better through elections than through appointments in a five-year period in New York City (55 per cent versus 50 per cent), but 70 per cent of Mayor Dinkins's appointments were women versus 44 per cent for Mayor Giuliani (Brown, 1998). Differences between presidents, governors or mayors swamp any possible systemic variation in the United States. Torres-Spelliscy, Chase and Greenman's study (2008) of 10 state nominating commissions in the US for the Brennan Center found that some nominating commissioners saw themselves as headhunters who made it their task to recruit a diverse candidate pool and some saw themselves as background checkers who passively waited for candidates to apply. The report recommended encouraging commissioners to actively recruit diverse candidates, train commissioners on implicit bias, appoint a diversity compliance officer or ombudsperson and make diversity of commissioners and judges an explicit statutory goal.[14]

Canada has served as a beacon of relative success; at the federal level, the proportion of federally appointed women judges grew from just over three per cent in 1980 to 26 per cent by June 2003. For provincially appointed judges, the province of Ontario led the way. The opportunity arose from growing concern that political patronage rather than merit was driving judicial appointments (Ziegel, 1987) but the goal of increasing the representativeness of the judiciary became firmly attached to judicial selection reform efforts. In 1988, an Ontario pilot project to choose provincial judges by a judicial appointments advisory committee (JAAC) began its work

[13] President Obama has been nominating women at 46.3%, 31/67, including two women to the US Supreme Court. 'A Snapshot of Women in the Judiciary as Three Women Poised to Sit on the Supreme Court of the United States' Alliance for Justice at: www.afj.org.

[14] US federal courts have declared two American states' statutory requirement of race quotas, however, to be unconstitutional: *Mallory v Harkness*, 895 F Supp 1556 (1995) and *Back v Carter*, 933 F Supp 738 (ND Ind 1996).

under the chairmanship of political scientist Peter H Russell[15] and became institutionalised in legislation in 1995. Ontario's JAAC was the only one in Canada to be made up of a majority of lay members. The criterion for appointment stated, 'The Judiciary of the Ontario Court of Justice should be reasonably representative of the population it serves' (JAAC, 2006: 10) and the amended statute required 'gender balance' (JAAC, 2006: 21, quoting subsection 43(3)). The JAAC took a proactive approach. It placed advertisements and actively encouraged under-represented groups to apply and contacted groups who represented those persons. The chair, Peter Russell, wrote to every woman lawyer with 10 years or more of experience urging her to apply. Russell recalls a flood of 50 applicants for the first five openings. Several women the committee interviewed said until they received the letter they never thought it possible for them to be a judge because they had no political connections.[16] The JAAC decided against using quotas, but it did interview a wider pool of candidates. Chief Justice Beverley McLachlin of the Supreme Court of Canada, speaking generally of judicial appointments, reported 'we only started to make progress when we started to re-think the definition of merit' (quoted in Mackay, 2005: 33) considering women who started later or interrupted their careers and who may not have had as much trial experience, but who had served as general counsel or on tribunals. Out of the first 75 appointments to the Ontario provincial court made on the basis of the JAAC process, 37 were women and 38 men. When the Committee began its work, only 10 (four per cent) of the provincially appointed judges were women (Russell, 1990: 10). Ontario created 35 new provincial judgeships in 1991.

In Scotland and South Africa, feminist hopes have not been realised. Scotland preceded England in creating a Judicial Appointments Board in 2002 and expressly repudiated the process of 'secret soundings', the vetting of judges by informally canvassing senior judges. The proportion of women in the judiciary increased from one to four of 32 judges (12 per cent), 12 to 23 out of 136 Sheriffs (17 per cent) and 10 of 58 part-time Sheriffs (17 per cent). The proportion of women applicants rose from 11 per cent to between 20–25 per cent (Mackay, 2005: 3). Mackay faulted the Scottish Executive's dual remit for charging the board with making appointments on merit irrespective of the candidates' social characteristics and background as well as recruiting a judiciary which is as representative as possible of the communities it serves, while receiving no training on recruitment and implicit bias, nor any opportunity for strategic planning about how to meet diversity goals. Without any explicit attention, and with the crush of work, Mackay feared further progress would be unlikely.

[15] See www.ontariocourts.on.ca/jaac/en/index.htm.

[16] Personal correspondence (6 July 2009). See also Omatsu (1997).

Commission member and legal academic, Alan Paterson, agreed that the Commission had not tackled the tough diversity issues as had Ontario (2006: 31).

The 1996 South African Constitution set an explicit goal to have a diverse and representative bench as did the statute creating the judicial nominating commission. Two of the 11 initial justices of the Constitutional Court were women. Progress has slowed to 'woeful' (Cowan, 2006). In 2004, only 13.3 per cent of the judges in the superior courts were women (Cowan, 2006: 303). An explicit goal may be necessary, but the South African case shows that it is not sufficient. The male-dominated Judicial Appointments Commission put forward the names of men who have anti-feminist views on sentencing in rape, customary law and polygamy, as well as asked women interviewees sexist and homophobic questions (Andrews, 2006). The Minister of Justice hosted a conference in 2006 to consider the poor performance in appointing women judges.

5. CONCLUSIONS

Apologists for women's low representation in the judiciary argue the qualified labour pool simply contains too few women. In time, women will enjoy representation proportional to their numbers. The evidence shows otherwise. A considerable lag exists and, in the case of women in the US federal judiciary, women lost ground during the Bush Administration as the gap between women's representation in the legal profession and their numbers in the judiciary grew even larger. Women will not inevitably nor steadily increase their representation in the judiciary without a concerted and intentional effort. If social science has discredited the 'trickle up' hypothesis, by now another misconception should also be put to rest. Contrary to political scientists' finding that some electoral systems facilitate a higher representation of women legislators, the evidence suggests that no one method of judicial selection promotes a fully gender representative bench. It clearly helps to eliminate requirements that indirectly discriminate against women, such as being politically well-connected, being known to senior judges, being young or having served as a partner in a large firm. If nominating commissions choose judges, it helps to have women attorney members, to encourage commissioners to actively recruit rather than to merely vet, to train about implicit bias and to make diversity an explicit goal and a benchmark for which commissioners are held accountable. The evidence from Ontario shows that a gender representative bench is achievable. The evidence from South Africa and Scotland is sobering. Gains can easily be reversed. Women's groups need to continue to demand progress. A representative judiciary will not come about of its own accord.

6. REFERENCES

Alozie, NO (1990) 'Distribution of Women and Minority Judges: The Effects of Judicial Selection Methods' 71(2) *Social Science Quarterly* 315.

—— (1996) 'Selection Methods and the Recruitment of Women to State Courts of Last Resort' 77(1) *Social Science Quarterly* 110.

Andrews, PE (2006) 'The South African Judicial Appointments Process' 44(3) *Osgoode Hall Law Journal* 565.

Bonneau, C (2001) 'The Composition of State Supreme Courts 2000' 85(1) *Judicature* 26.

Bratton, KA and Spill, RL (2001) 'Clinton and the Diversification of the Federal Judiciary' 84(5) *Judicature* 256.

—— (2002) 'Existing Diversity and Judicial Selection: The Role of the Appointment Method in Establishing Gender Diversity in State Supreme Courts' 83(2) *Social Science Quarterly* 504.

—— (2005) 'Diversifying the Federal Bench: Presidential Patterns' 26(2) *Justice System Journal* 119.

Brown, G (1998) *Characteristics of Elected Versus Merit-Selected New York City Judges 1992–97* (New York, Fund for Modern Courts).

Carbon, S, Houlden, P and Berkson, L (1982) 'Women on the State Bench: Their Characteristics and Attitudes about Judicial Selection' 65(6) *Judicature* 294.

Cardinal, MC (2008) 'Women and the Judiciary in Syria: Appointments Process, Training and Career Paths' 15(1–2) *International Journal of the Legal Profession* 123.

Clark, ML (2002) 'Changing the Face of the Law: How Women's Advocacy Groups Put Women on the Federal Judicial Appointments Agenda' 14(2) *Yale Journal of Law and Feminism* 243.

—— (2004) 'One Man's Token Is Another Woman's Breakthrough? The Appointment of the First Women Federal Judges' 49(3) *Villanova Law Review* 487.

Cook, BB (1978) 'Women Judges: The End of Tokenism' in W Hepperle and L Crites (eds), *Women in the Courts* (Williamsburg, National Center for State Courts).

—— (1980) 'Political Culture and Selection of Women Judges in Trial Courts' in D Stewart (ed), *Women in Local Politics* (Metuchen, NJ, Scarecrow Press).

—— (1981) 'The First Woman Candidate for the Supreme Court – Florence Allen' in *Supreme Court Historical Society Yearbook* (Washington DC, Supreme Court Historical Society).

—— (1982) 'Women as Supreme Court Candidates: From Florence Allen to Sandra O'Connor' 65(6) *Judicature* 314.

—— (1983) 'The Path to the Bench: Ambitions and Attitudes of Women in the Law' *Trial* 49.

—— (1984a) 'Women Judges: A Preface to Their History' 14(3) *Golden Gate University Law Review* 573.

—— (1984b) 'Women on the State Bench: Correlates of Access' in J Flammang (ed), *Political Women: Current Roles in State and Local Government* (Beverly Hills, Sage).

—— (1987) 'Women Judges in the Opportunity Structure' in L Crites and W Hepperle (eds), *Women, The Courts, and Equality* (Newbury Park, CA, Sage).

—— (1988) 'Women as Judges' in B Cook, L Goldstein, K O'Connor and S Talarico (eds), *Women in the Judicial Process* (Washington DC, American Political Science Association).

Cowan, RB (2006) 'Women's Representation on the Courts in the Republic of South Africa' 6(2) *University of Maryland Law Journal of Race, Religion, Gender and Class* 291.

Dean, JW (2001) *The Rehnquist Choice: The Untold Story of the Nixon Appointment that Redefined the Supreme Court* (New York, Free Press).

Diascro, JS and Solberg, RS (2009) 'George W Bush's Legacy on the Federal Bench: Policy in the Face of Diversity' 92(6) *Judicature* 289.

Dubois, P (1983) 'The Influence of Selection System and Region on the Characteristics of a Trial Court Bench: The Case of California' 8(1) *Justice System Journal* 59.

Dunn, PW (1981) 'Judicial Election and the Missouri Plan' in S Ulmer (ed), *Courts, Law, and Judicial Processes* (New York, Free Press).

Elazar, D (1972) *American Federalism: A View from the States* (New York, Thomas Y Crowell).

Esterling, KM and Andersen, SS (1999) 'Diversity and the Judicial Merit Selection Process: A Statistical Report' in *Research on Judicial Selection* (Chicago, American Judicature Society).

Faderman, L (2000) *To Believe in Women: What Lesbians Have Done for America – A History* (Boston, Mariner).

Flango, VE and Ducat, CR (1979) 'What Difference Does Method of Judicial Selection Make?' 5(1) *Justice System Journal* 25.

Githens, M (1995) 'Getting Appointed to the State Court: The Gender Dimension' 15(4) *Women & Politics* 1.

Goldman, S (1997) *Picking Federal Judges: Lower Court Selection from Roosevelt through Reagan* (New Haven, CT, Yale University Press).

Gould, J and Merola, L (2009) 'Improving Diversity on the State Courts: A Report from the Bench' (Washington DC, Lawyers' Committee for Civil Rights Under Law).

Henry, ML, Koslow, E, Soffer, J and Furey, J (1985) *The Success of Women and Minorities in Achieving Judicial Office: The Selection Process* (New York, Fund for Modern Courts).

Henschen, BM, Moog, R and Davis, S (1990) 'Judicial Nominating Commissioners: A National Profile' 73(6) *Judicature* 328.

Holmes, LM and Emrey, JA (2006) 'Court Diversification: Staffing the State Courts of Last Resort through Interim Appointments' 27(1) *Justice System Journal* 1.

Hurwitz, MS and Lanier, DN (2001) 'Women and Minorities on State and Federal Appellate Benches, 1985 and 1999' 85(2) *Judicature* 84.

—— (2003) 'Explaining Judicial Diversity: The Differential Ability of Women and Minorities to Attain Seats on State Supreme and Appellate Courts' 3(4) *State Politics and Policy Quarterly* 329.

—— (2008) 'Diversity in State and Federal Appellate Courts: Change and Continuity Across 20 Years' 29(1) *Justice System Journal* 47.

Jensen, JM and Martinek, WL (2009) 'The Effects of Race and Gender on the Judicial Ambitions of State Trial Court Judges' 62(2) *Political Research Quarterly* 379.

Judicial Appointments Advisory Committee (JAAC) (2006) *Annual Report* (Toronto, Judicial Appointments Advisory Committee).

Kenney, SJ (2004a) 'Britain Appoints First Woman Law Lord' 87(4) *Judicature* 189.

—— (2004b) 'Equal Employment Opportunity and Representation: Extending the Frame to Courts' 11(1) *Social Politics* 86.

—— (2009) 'Women Judges in Minnesota' 32(1) *With Equal Right: The Official Journal of Minnesota Women Lawyers* 4.

—— (2010) '"It Would Be Stupendous for Us Girls": Campaigning for Women Judges Without Waving' in J Castledine and K Laughlin (eds), *Breaking the Waves: Women, Their Organizations, and Feminism, 1945 to 1985* (New York, Routledge).

—— (2013) *Gender and Justice: Why Women in the Judiciary* Really *Matter* (New York, Routledge Press).

Kenney, SJ and Windett, J (2012) 'Diffusion of Innovation or State Political Culture? Explaining the First Women State Supreme Court Justices' paper presented at the Law and Society Association Annual Conference (Honolulu, Hawaii).

Kohen, B (2008) 'Family Law Judges in the City of Buenos Aires: A View from Within' 15(1–2) *International Journal of the Legal Profession* 111.

Lawless, JL and Fox, R (2005) *It Takes a Candidate: Why Women Don't Run for Office* (Cambridge, Cambridge University Press).

Lucas, J (2007) 'Is Justice Blind? Gender and Voting in Judicial Elections' paper presented at Midwest Political Science Association Annual Meeting (Chicago, Illinois).

Mackay, F (2005) 'Gender and Diversity Review: Critical Reflections on Judicial Appointments in Scotland' prepared for the Judicial Appointments Board for Scotland and Scottish Executive Justice Department.

Martin, E (1982) 'Women on the Federal Bench: A Comparative Profile' 65(6) *Judicature* 306.

—— (1987) 'Gender and Judicial Selection: A Comparison of the Reagan and Carter Administrations' 71(3) *Judicature* 136.

—— (2004) 'Gender and Presidential Judicial Selection' 26(3–4) *Women & Politics* 109.

Martin, E and Pyle, B (2002) 'Gender and Racial Diversification of State Supreme Courts' 24(2) *Women & Politics* 35.

Omatsu, M (1997) 'The Fiction of Judicial Impartiality' 9(1) *Canadian Journal of Women and the Law* 1.

Organ, JE (1998) 'Sexuality as a Category of Historical Analysis: A Study of Judge Florence E Allen, 1884–1966' PhD Dissertation, Department of History (Case Western Reserve University, Cleveland, OH).

Paterson, A (2006) 'The Scottish Judicial Appointments Board: New Wine in Old Bottles?' in K Malleson and PH Russell (eds), *Appointing Judges in an Age of Judicial Power: Critical Perspectives from Around the World* (Toronto, University of Toronto Press).

Reddick, M, Caufield, RP and Nelson, MJ (2009) 'Explaining Diversity on State Courts' paper presented at the Midwest Political Science Association Annual Meeting (Chicago, Illinois).

Reid, T (2004) 'The Competitiveness of Female Candidates in Judicial Elections: An Analysis of the North Carolina Trial Court Races' 67(3) *Albany Law Review* 829.

Russell, PH (1990) *Interim Report – Judicial Appointments Advisory Committee* (Toronto, Judicial Appointments Advisory Committee).

Slotnick, E (1983a) 'The ABA Standing Committee on Federal Judiciary: A Contemporary Assessment – Part 1' 66(7) *Judicature* 349.

—— (1983b) 'The ABA Standing Committee on Federal Judiciary: A Contemporary Assessment – Part 2' 66(8) *Judicature* 385.

—— (1984) 'The Paths to the Federal Bench: Gender, Race and Judicial Recruitment Variation' 67(8) *Judicature* 371.

Tokarz, K (1986) 'Women Judges and Merit Selection under the Missouri Plan' 64(3) *Washington University Law Quarterly* 903.

Torres-Spelliscy, C, Chase, M and Greenman, E (2008) *Improving Judicial Diversity* (New York, Brennan Center for Justice).

Warden, R, Schlesinger, T and Kearney, J (1979) *Women, Blacks and Merit Selection of Judges* (Chicago, Committee on Courts and Justice).

Williams, M (2007) 'Women's Representation on State Trial and Appellate Courts' 88(5) *Social Science Quarterly* 1192.

—— (2008a) 'Ambition, Gender, and the Judiciary' 61(1) *Political Research Quarterly* 68.

—— (2008b) 'Women's Representation on High Courts in Advanced Industrialized Countries' 4(3) *Politics & Gender* 451.

Ziegel, J (1987) 'Federal Judicial Appointments in Canada: The Time Is Ripe for Change' 37(1) *University of Toronto Law Journal* 1.

6.2

Gender Quotas for the Judiciary in England and Wales

KATE MALLESON

Abstract

Despite over two decades of official activity, very slow progress has been made in achieving gender balance in the judiciary in England and Wales. Women have not 'trickled up' into the judiciary as many anticipated they would. As a result, it has become increasingly possible to revisit some of the more fundamental tenets which have underpinned the approach to the problem to date. In particular, there is a greater willingness to question the inflexible commitment to the principle of equal treatment as the foundation for all judicial diversity policies and the rejection of any role for quotas. Against this background, this chapter asks whether the time has come to introduce gender quotas in the judiciary in England and Wales. It argues that, in contrast to most other diversity policies, quotas have a proven track record in bringing about a significant change in the gender balance of powerful institutions.

1. INTRODUCTION

THE LACK OF gender balance in the judiciary in England and Wales has attracted growing political attention over the last 20 years. There is now a clear consensus, both on and off the bench, that 'a diverse judiciary is an indispensable requirement of any democracy' (Hale, 2006: 2). As a result, a range of policies has been developed to reform the judicial appointments process and encourage a wider range of applicants for judicial office; the most recent and radical being the creation of a new Judicial Appointments Commission which started work in 2006.[1]

[1] For a full overview of the reforms to the judicial appointments process in England and Wales see Maute (2007). The current Ministry of Justice statement on increasing diversity in the judiciary sets out its goals as follows: 'In partnership with the Judicial Appointments Commission and judiciary, our aim is to increase public confidence in the justice system through

Yet despite two decades of official activity, the pace of change has been far slower than anticipated by many in the judiciary, the government and the legal profession and there remains little prospect of any significant shift in the composition of the bench in the near future. There is still only one woman in the Supreme Court, four women (out of 38) in the Court of Appeal and 16 women (out of 108) in the High Court. The figures are slightly higher for the lower courts, but are still very far from parity at any level of court.[2] The official approach to the problem has been dominated by a belief that it will resolve itself naturally and inevitably with the need for only modest intervention. However, as the intransigence of the problem has become clearer it has become increasingly possible to challenge the orthodoxies which inform the debate and to revisit some of the more fundamental tenets which have underpinned the approach to the problem to date. In particular, there is a greater willingness to question the inflexible commitment to the principle of equal treatment as the foundation for all judicial diversity policies and the rejection of any role for quotas. Against this background, this chapter asks whether the time has come to introduce gender quotas in the judiciary in England and Wales. It argues that, in contrast to most other diversity policies, quotas have a proven track record in bringing about a significant change in the gender balance of powerful institutions.

The focus of enquiry is on the particular legal, historical and political context of judicial appointments in England and Wales, but the arguments explored have wider implications both geographically and institutionally. The ongoing lack of diversity in the judiciary is a problem which is currently being addressed, with more or less success, across many different jurisdictions around the world.[3] Quotas have been adopted in other areas of public life, particularly in relation to elections to legislatures and are starting to be used in some courts, particularly in the newer international courts. The relevance of quotas as a tool for promoting gender balance in the judiciary therefore has implications beyond the judiciary in England and Wales.

a judiciary which better reflects and has a greater understanding of the society it serves', at: www.justice.gov.uk/whatwedo/judicialdiversity.htm. The most recent developments in the judicial appointments process in relation to diversity are set out in the Judicial Appointments Commission Annual Report 2010–11.

[2] Statistics as at April 2011. Annual Statistics for the Judiciary of England and Wales 2011, at: www.judiciary.gov.uk/publications-and-reports/statistics/judges/gender-statistics.

[3] In relation to the issue of gender diversity among judges in a range of jurisdictions, see special issue *Women of the Courts Symposium* (2005) 36(4) *University of Toledo Law Review*; (2008) 15(1–2) *International Journal of the Legal Profession* special issue on Gender and Judges; and (2009) 17(1) *Feminist Legal Studies* special issue on Women and Judging.

2. DIVERSITY POLICIES IN THE JUDICIAL APPOINTMENTS PROCESS IN ENGLAND AND WALES

Concerns about the low numbers of women appointed to the judiciary have generally been addressed by the argument that women would naturally 'trickle-up' from the legal profession to the bench leading to significant change in the composition of the judiciary within a relatively short period of time (Hale, 2006: 2; House of Commons Constitutional Affairs Committee 2003–04: paras 137–43). By the turn of the millennium it had become clear, however, that predictions of relatively fast and extensive change were wide of the mark as the numbers of women lawyers appointed to the judiciary remained stubbornly low.[4] The reasons behind this failure are complex and multiple. A wide range of factors have been identified as contributing to the lack of progress, some located in the judicial appointments process, some in the working practices and culture of the legal profession and the judiciary and others in wider societal arrangements. While a number of these are particular to the judiciary many are common to other institutions of power (Walby, 1997; Payne and Abbott, 1990; Crompton and Sanderson, 1990). The continued dominance of white men in public appointments across the board has been well documented (Childs, Lovenduski and Campbell, 2005; The Hansard Society, 2005).

Increasingly, academic and policy work on diversity has concluded that despite concerted official efforts to develop and implement a range of policies to increase the diversity of decision-making bodies, 30 years of equal opportunity policies have not produced the results which policymakers had hoped for (Squires, 2007: 2; Burrows, and Robison, 2006: 39; Equality and Human Rights Commission, 2008).[5]

Yet, despite the growing awareness of the entrenched problem of the lack of diversity in the judiciary, the dominant view in the debate in England and Wales has been that policies based on positive action are a potential threat to selection on merit. Official support for positive action has been limited to a number of modest initiatives designed to widen the recruitment pool. These include 'road shows' by the Judicial Appointments Commission directed at women and black and minority ethnic lawyers and judicial job shadowing targeted at those who are not from traditional recruitment groups or career paths).[6]

The first evidence of the emergence of a wider debate about the need for more positive action to address the lack of diversity in the judiciary arose

[4] For a full review of the changing approach to the problem of gender diversity in the judiciary in England and Wales see Kenney (2008) and Malleson (2009).

[5] See also, Fawcett Society, at: www.fawcettsociety.org.uk.

[6] Judicial Appointments Commission Annual Report (2007–08) *Selecting on Merit and Encouraging Diversity* 3, at: jac.judiciary.gov.uk/about-jac/1376.htm.

during the passage of the Constitutional Reform Bill in 2004. Critics of the current system argued that the new judicial appointments commission should be placed under a statutory duty to promote diversity. Exactly what form this duty should take was the subject of considerable disagreement. Ultimately section 64 of the Constitutional Reform Act 2005 held that 'The Commission, in performing its functions under this Part, must have regard to the need to encourage diversity in the range of persons available for selection for appointments'.

The provision was a disappointment for those who had sought a stronger statement of the Commission's role in promoting diversity. The duty relates only to applications and not to the appointments themselves and is limited to the 'encouragement' of diversity. It is also specifically subject to an overriding duty in section 63 to select on merit alone.

Within two years of the Commission starting work in 2006, concern about the continuing lack of progress on diversity led to further debate about the need for more positive action. A government consultation paper which preceded the Constitutional Renewal Bill in 2008 proposed for the first time that the executive should be given the power to set diversity targets. The Commission objected to these proposals on the grounds that they undermined its independence. This argument was accepted by the government and the proposals were dropped. However, the fact that the idea of targets was raised at all is in itself indicative of the changing boundaries of the debate.

2.1. The Use of Quotas in England and Wales

While diversity targets are widely used in public life and are generally considered relatively uncontroversial, quotas have traditionally been regarded as the rubicon of positive action. There is still considerable official resistance to the use of any form of quota, most particularly in relation to the judiciary. In 2005 Lord Falconer, the former Lord Chancellor, stated definitively that 'we won't have quotas'.[7] Yet this opposition is coming under pressure. The quotas Rubicon has already been crossed in two important areas of public life in the UK more widely. The first is the use of time-limited gender quotas in national elections to the Westminster Parliament and the devolved legislatures of Scotland and Wales.[8] The second exception to the general exclusion of quotas in the legal system in the UK is the '50:50'

[7] 'Increasing Judicial Diversity: The Next Steps', speech at the Institute of Mechanical Engineers (2 November 2005) 6.

[8] The UK is now one of a growing number of countries which have allowed quotas to be used to increase the political representation of women. See the Global Database of Quotas for Women, at: www.quotaproject.org/aboutQuotas.cfm.

quota policy introduced in the Northern Ireland police service which was designed to promote equal representation in police appointments between the Catholic and Protestant communities. This use of quotas was partly justified on the basis of the very particular need for equality in the region in the light of the long and bitter history of conflict. It was also justified because of the very particular nature of police powers since the exercise of such explicit and visible control over one section of the community by representatives of another is extremely politically sensitive (McHarg and Nicolson, 2006: 7).

In both the cases above, it is widely accepted that the use of quotas played a significant part in bringing about further and faster change than would have happened without them. The use of gender quotas in legislatures both in the UK and elsewhere is now widely regarded as being the most effective means of increasing the representation of women in public life (Squires, 2007: 25). A report by the Hansard Society on 'Women at the Top' concluded in 2005 that all women shortlists were the 'quickest and most effective means of delivering equal representation' noting that:

> After four decades where women's representation averaged around three to four per cent, in the space of three elections, a step-change at nearer 20 per cent seems to have been established ... they may not be 'fair', they may grate against liberal principles, they may, as critics claim, cast aspersions on the merit of the women elected, but one thing cannot be denied, measures that guarantee women's election work, and work quickly (The Hansard Society, 2005: 7, 96).

As the Hansard report illustrated, one of the strongest arguments in favour of quotas is that they are effective in the short term. Until recently, however, significant legal barriers have inhibited their use in England and Wales.

3. THE LEGAL FRAMEWORK GOVERNING THE USE OF QUOTAS IN ENGLAND AND WALES

The legal framework, both domestic and EU, governing equality and diversity policies in England and Wales has traditionally been based on an equal treatment model within which quotas have been generally viewed as anomalous (Barmes, 2010). The difficulties raised by moving to the use of policies based on positive action within this framework have been well documented (McHarg and Nicolson, 2006). The law has generally lagged behind the changing political agenda with examples of equality developments in the workplace moving ahead of, or being stymied by, the law. It is only very recently that the legal framework has gradually shifted to allow first for exceptions to the equal treatment principle and then for the use of more wholesale policies designed to address the ongoing under-representation of women in public and professional life.

An important shift in the domestic legal landscape was the imposition of legal duties on certain public bodies to promote equality and diversity. In relation to the judiciary, the Judicial Appointments Commission has, since 2007, become subject to the general duty to promote equality in relation to gender and disability (though not yet to the race equality duty). Most recently, the Equality Act 2010, for the first time, allows employers to apply preferential decision-making designed to promote equality when choosing between equally qualified candidates provided that they do not have a general policy of appointing the under-represented candidate in every case (Barmes, 2010: 13–15). However, despite this gradual trend towards relaxing the equal treatment principle in a way which opens legal space for positive action, particular problems remain in relation to the use of quotas. The first attempts by the Labour Party to introduce gender quotas in the selection of election candidates were blocked in the courts and required legislation to allow them to be used in the 1997 election.[9]

At the EU level, a similar pattern can be seen of successful legal challenges to positive action followed by changes to the content and interpretation of the law to allow for their use (McHarg and Nicolson, 2006; Barmes, 2010). Although the legislation introducing quotas in the Northern Ireland police force withstood a challenge in the domestic courts as being in breach of the European Convention on Human Rights (ECHR) and European law, it was passed only with a specific exception from the relevant EU legislation.[10] However, more recent European Court of Justice (ECJ) cases on the use of quotas in the ECJ suggest that the requirement that such measures be 'proportionate and justifiable' is being applied in such a way as to allow for their use, provided the quota systems are framed so as to allow for exceptions if their application would lead to the appointment of under-qualified candidates or undue hardship or injustice to those candidates passed over (Burrows and Robison, 2006: 33).

Relatively few cases specifically concerning the use of gender quotas in the judicial appointments process have reached the European courts. However, in 2007, the European Court of Human Rights (ECtHR) considered their use in the nomination lists for appointments to that Court and held that they were not, in principle, objectionable. The case was brought by Malta which sought an advisory opinion challenging the decision of the Parliamentary Assembly rejecting a list of three male candidates which it had submitted. The Assembly had held that Malta's list was in breach of its rule requiring that at least one woman should be included

[9] The Sex Discrimination (Election Candidates) Act 2002.

[10] *In the Matter of an Application by Mark Parsons for Judicial Review* [2002] NIQB 46. See McHarg and Nicolson (2006: 7).

in the nominations from each state.[11] The Court held that the provision was lawful but that the requirement for a mixed list could not override the general judicial qualifications requirements so that a state would not be in breach if it put forward an all-male list where it was not possible to identify a well-qualified female candidate:

> [A]lthough the aim of ensuring a certain mix in the composition of the lists of candidates is legitimate and generally accepted, it may not be pursued without provision being made for some exceptions designed to enable each Contracting Party to choose national candidates who satisfy all the requirements of Article 21.

Although of course distinct from the ECJ legal framework, this ECtHR decision indicates that, if introduced in the UK, gender quotas for judicial appointments might not fall foul of the provisions of the Convention provided they were not rigidly drawn.

A similar decision was reached in a 2004 judgment of the UN Human Rights Committee which considered a complaint regarding a gender quota introduced for the Belgian High Council of Justice.[12] Although not directly analogous—in that the High Council is not a judicial body but an advisory body involved in judicial appointments—many of the issues raised in the case were pertinent to the arguments regarding quotas in the judiciary. The complainant claimed that the provision was discriminatory and could lead to the appointment of less qualified women over more qualified men. This argument was rejected by the Committee on the following grounds:

> Given the responsibilities of the judiciary, the promotion of an awareness of gender relevant issues relating to the application of law could well be understood as requiring that perspective to be included in a body involved in judicial appointments. Accordingly, the Committee cannot conclude that the requirement is not objective and reasonably justifiable.[13]

The key common feature of these and other cases at UK, EU and international level which deal with quotas in the judiciary and other areas of public life, is that to be lawful they must be not be rigidly formulated in a way which might result in disproportionate hardship to rejected well-qualified male candidates or the appointment of less well-qualified female candidates. The requirement that such provisions are justified is increasingly likely to be satisfied where it can be shown that other policies have been tried and failed and that there is evidence that quotas, in contrast, are effective. It will also

[11] The rule states that at least one member of the under-represented sex should be included in the nomination list where the court is made up of less than 40% of one sex.

[12] *Guido Jacobs v Belgium* (Com No 943/2000) (17 August 2004). The provisions which required that in selecting the members no fewer than four should be men and four women.

[13] Para 9.4.

be important to show that the need for gender balance is a pressing one for the legitimacy and public confidence in the institution in question.

These arguments are now increasingly easy to make in relation to the judiciary where the failure of a range of measures to bring about significant changes has given rise to widespread concern about the impact on the legitimacy of the bench. Nevertheless, judicial decisions about what constitutes proportionate and justified action are highly contextualised. Legal challenges to quotas will still be likely to succeed where the political culture is hostile to their use. The key to removing the legal barriers to the use of quotas therefore lies in the formulation of persuasive intellectual arguments which can counter the official resistance to quotas shown by government, the judiciary and the legal profession.

4. QUOTAS AND MERIT: RETHINKING THE RANKING MODEL OF MERIT SELECTION IN THE JUDICIARY

Arguments against quotas are based primarily on principles of equity and merit. The former concerns the potential unfairness to well-qualified candidates from outside the quota group who are not selected when a quota system is applied. Although such fairness arguments are still voiced in both legal and political discourse, they have become far less forceful in light of the ongoing failure to achieve a gender balance across so many areas of public and professional life. One effect of the growing importance of the notion of proportionality is that the potential unfairness suffered by an unsuccessful male candidate is more likely to be outweighed by the collective and ongoing unfairness being suffered by women candidates and the damage, in turn, suffered by the judiciary in terms of loss of legitimacy and public confidence. Provided the individual unfairness is not disproportionate or unjustified, it is now less often accepted as a blanket reason to reject the use of quotas.

As equity arguments have receded, merit-based objections have become the focus for resistance to the use of quotas. Fears that measures to increase diversity in the judiciary would undermine the merit principle were the driving force behind the formulation of section 63 of the Constitutional Reform Act 2005 which states that selection must be 'solely on merit'. There is no elaboration in the Act on what this provision means, but from the debates during the passage of the Bill it would seem that the insertion of an overriding merit provision was intended to ensure that the duty placed on the Commission in section 64 to encourage diversity could never be relied on to justify the appointment of a less qualified over a more qualified candidate. Given the mantra-like status which selection on merit has acquired in the debate on judicial selection and diversity (as in so many other areas of public life), establishing a case for quotas is dependent on demonstrating that they can be integrated into a merit-based system. The first step in making this case requires engagement with what is meant by merit selection in the judiciary.

The argument that quotas may undermine the merit principle depends significantly on whether a ranking (maximalist) model or a threshold (minimalist) model of merit system is adopted. The former requires that all candidates are ranked and the best are appointed. Thus, if 100 candidates apply for 10 judicial posts a ranking-based merit system would list the candidates in order of merit from 1 to 100 and the first 10 would be selected. The alternative to this model is a threshold-based merit system which applies a predetermined quality level which all candidates must meet in order to be appointed. Once this threshold has been reached, diversity factors can be taken into account in selecting between well-qualified candidates.

By their nature, quota systems are difficult to reconcile with a ranking merit system because it is not necessarily possible to predict what proportion of the top candidates will be in the quota group. Thus, in the example above, the introduction of a quota might lead to the appointment of women who rank outside the top 10 best candidates. The women appointed would be qualified but not necessarily the most qualified. The implicit assumption in relation to the judicial appointments process in England and Wales, as in many other appointments processes, is that a ranking merit system is and should be applied. There are, however, good grounds for challenging this belief. This is because such a system requires that the qualities which make up the components of merit and the factors used by candidates to evidence those qualities, can be quantified and objectively compared so that the candidates can be ranked in order of merit. An obvious example of a system in which a ranking model of merit is applicable is one in which a relatively technical set of skills is required and/or where selection is based primarily on examination results or some other form of formal assessment. The sort of judiciary, which fits with a ranking merit model of judicial selection, is the career judiciary common in many European civil law systems. Candidates in these jurisdictions are selected at a very early stage in their career soon after leaving university and the key evidence used to demonstrate merit is their performance in formal legal examinations and assessments. In such a system, young judges are required to undertake relatively limited and clearly defined legal tasks and are then gradually trained for further more advanced, varied or complex elements of the work as they move up the promotion path.

This model is very different from the judicial system found in many common law jurisdictions such as England and Wales where judges are recruited from legal practice 15 or 20 years into their career. In a selection process where candidates are being appointed directly from one career into relatively senior roles in another, the components of the post generally require a range of less predetermined, varied and more generalised skills.

The result is that a ranking merit system is very difficult to apply because candidates do not come with comparable and quantifiable skills, experiences and knowledge which can easily be ranked. In systems such as the judicial appointments process in England and Wales, merit is an umbrella term which covers a very wide range of different qualities. The nature of these will inevitably differ very considerably between individuals after a decade or two of legal practice and life experience. Moreover, the qualities required of a judge in a common law system encompass a far wider range of characteristics than technical legal knowledge. The Lord Chief Justice, for example, has recently talked of the need for judges to be 'wise to the ways of the world' and to have 'moral courage'. Such qualities are not easily susceptible to quantitative measurement and comparative ranking.[14]

The Judicial Appointments Commission has tried to address the problems of operating a ranking merit system in light of the very varied qualities required of judges who must be selected from a pool of candidates with potentially very diverse characteristics, knowledge, skills and experiences. It has done this by constructing six broad sets of qualities and abilities, which provide evidence of merit. These cover: intellectual capacity (for example, the ability to quickly absorb and analyse information); personal qualities (for example, integrity and independence of mind); an ability to understand and deal fairly (for example, a willingness to listen with patience and courtesy); authority and communication skills (for example, the ability to inspire respect and confidence); efficiency (for example, the ability to work at speed and under pressure). These different qualities and abilities are intended to provide a more objective basis for ranking candidates. Yet they are still essentially qualitative in nature and difficult to measure in the sort of precise comparative way which is required for a rigorous ranking merit system. Moreover, the creation of a list of qualities and abilities does not help with the problem of how these should be ranked against each other. Candidates will score more highly in some categories than others according to their different individual strengths and weaknesses. The selectors must therefore decide whether, for example, a high score in authority and communication skills and a low score in efficiency equals or betters a middle ranking score of another candidate in both these two. In addition, should some qualities and abilities be weighted more heavily than others? Do any of the qualities and abilities trump the others? Are some essential and others merely desirable? These sorts of assessments inevitably require the exercise of judgement based to some extent on different legitimate views

[14] Lord Judge, Lord Chief Justice of England and Wales (2008) *Equality in Justice Day*, Royal Courts of Justice, London (24 October 2008) 3, at: www.judiciary.gov.uk/Resources/JCO/Documents/Speeches/speech-lcj-equality-justice-day.pdf.

about the relative values of different characteristics, knowledge, skills and experiences.

Even applying advanced and sophisticated selection assessment methods, decisions as to how the different types of evidence of merit should be ranked in any particular case will always be more of an art than a science. Such decisions are less problematic where there is a clear quality and ability gap between many of the candidates. But the more highly qualified the overall pool and the more clustered the candidates, the more difficult they become. In relation to the judicial appointments process in England and Wales, this problem is acute. Judicial posts are highly coveted and oversubscribed. By definition, many of the applicants for these posts are relatively similar in terms of abilities and qualities even if their skills and experiences are different. The graph pattern of applicants for judicial office is therefore generally U-shaped. In any one cohort of applicants for a judicial post there will usually be a small number of exceptionally strong candidates whose characteristics, knowledge, skills and experiences place them above others. These will always be appointed in any merit-based system. At the other end of the spectrum there will usually be a small number of candidates who fail to meet the minimum standards for appointment and would never be appointed. The space in between these two will be occupied by a large group whose members have a generally high level of qualities and abilities which may be evidenced by a wide range of different knowledge, skills and experiences accrued over 10 to 25 years in legal practice. Deciding which of these candidates has more 'merit' than others is highly problematic.[15]

These difficulties are, moreover, compounded in relation to the judiciary in England and Wales by historical patterns of appointment decision-making which still strongly influence the judicial appointments process today. Traditionally, the components of merit in judicial selection have been very closely correlated to the power relations in the legal profession and the working arrangements which have flowed from these. Because the judiciary has historically been a highly prestigious and powerful institution, its members (particularly in the higher ranks) have been drawn almost exclusively from a narrow group of the most elite and powerful commercial barristers practising in a relatively small number of London chambers. As a result, the selection criteria that developed in order to rank candidates were closely linked to the experiences and working practices of that group. Thus, advocacy experience in the higher courts—until recently the exclusive preserve of barristers—was regarded as a prerequisite for judicial office, whereas

[15] Wilkins and Gulati have made similar points in relation to the hiring of black lawyers in US corporate law firms arguing that the majority of candidates are in the average range and that the evidence that these applicants use to demonstrate their merit will be 'noisier'—that is less reliable predictors of quality—the nearer the applicants are to the mean (Wilkins and Gulati, 1996: 520).

case management skills—as possessed by solicitors—were not. Similarly, commercial law experience has, until very recently, been consistently valued above areas such as criminal and family law. Many judges presiding over criminal trials in the past were appointed with little or no experience of the criminal courts.

Although the Judicial Appointments Commission has sought to address these biases, in practice the legal profession and the judicial recruitment pools in turn remain highly segmented and stratified. The result is that judges in England and Wales are not and have never been drawn from across the brightest and best of all areas of the legal profession.[16] Despite more recent attempts to produce a definition of merit which more closely corresponds to the competencies required of the judges, the outcome of the judicial appointments process in terms of the composition of those appointed has remained remarkably stable with the higher posts continuing to be filled by candidates from the most socially and economically powerful groups in the legal profession. It is now widely accepted that for the judicial appointments process to ensure that the very best candidates from across the legal profession are selected, the relationship between the profession and the judicial selection pools needs to change so as to include all highly able candidates. However, if this difficult task is ever achieved then, paradoxically, the problems of applying a ranking merit model will become even more acute. The consequence of opening up the recruitment pools to a wider cross section of talented lawyers would be that more well-qualified candidates with an even wider range of backgrounds and experiences will apply so making the task of comparing and ranking them even harder.

Given the inherent and intractable problems in applying a ranking merit system in the judicial appointments process in England and Wales, the only viable option is to acknowledge that the use of a threshold merit system is both inevitable and necessary. Indeed, it is arguable that this system has, in practice, been in operation both under the new judicial appointments process and the old. Such a system does not represent a downgrading of merit, but rather acknowledges that the determination of merit beyond a threshold of key measurable qualities and abilities is a contexualised and dynamic process which involves a significant qualitative and subject element. This requires judgements to be made between a large number of differently qualified candidates where the question of which one is 'best' is a highly difficult judgement call and where reasonable selectors will (and no doubt already do) disagree.

16 Some groups of lawyers, such as those in the Crown Prosecution Service, are still not fully eligible.

In a threshold merit model, once candidates have been identified as well qualified by reaching the abilities and qualities threshold, choices can be made which take account of the broader collective requirements of the judiciary including the need for greater diversity. For example, candidate A and candidate B may both be well-qualified candidates who fulfil the merit threshold. Candidate A may have a certain set of skills, experiences and characteristics while candidate B has another, neither of which is inherently superior to the other. However, if candidate A's set is more like those of many current judges while candidate B's are less common, then the value candidate B brings in added diversity in the judiciary would argue for their appointment.[17]

If these arguments in support of a threshold merit model are accepted, then the merit-based objections to the application of a quota system fall away provided it is possible to show that the quotas do not undermine the threshold test. This requires a more detailed consideration of the nature of different quota models.

5. DIFFERENT QUOTA MODELS

Having established that quotas can, in principle, be both lawful and compatible with a threshold merit selection process, the next step is to articulate how they can be 'proportionate and justifiable' as well as effective. Contrary to the widespread view that quotas are relatively blunt instruments, there are, in fact, many different models of quotas which can be adapted and refined to meet the particular needs of different selection processes. In Germany, for example, at least four different gender quota systems have been developed in the field of employment, ranging from the very flexible and discretionary to the more strict and formal. The most widespread use of gender quotas globally has been in elections to the legislature and here too a wide range of different models has been developed.[18]

Quotas can be applied at the application stage of a selection process, the appointment stage or both. A key variable in the various models is the level at which the quota is set. There is no requirement that quotas be set at 50 per cent. Austria has, for example, set a gender quota for the selection of High Court judges at 30 per cent.[19] This flexibility might be

[17] The argument that the judicial appointments process must by necessity apply a threshold merit test so that diversity considerations are fully compatible with a merit-based system is not unique to England and Wales but has been made by Kenney in her work on gender mainstreaming in the European Court of Justice (Kenney, 2002: 267).

[18] See Global Database of Quotas for Women, at: www.quotaproject.org/aboutQuotas.cfm.

[19] UN Committee on Elimination of Discrimination against Women, Report of Meetings, 2007, available at www.un.org/womenwatch/daw/cedaw/committee.htm.

particularly valuable for the judiciary in England and Wales where it might be appropriate to set different quota levels for different ranks which have different recruitment pools. Determining the optimum quota level for any particular post requires an assessment to be conducted before the selection process of the likely ratio of women candidates in the pool who will meet the threshold to the quota. It does not matter (for merit purposes) whether there are as many equally well-qualified women as men in the pool. For example, if 10 judges are to be appointed from a candidate pool which includes four women and 12 men who meet the threshold, imposing a minimum gender quota of 40 per cent would mean that all the well-qualified women and only half the well-qualified men would be appointed. This outcome might raise objections in terms of fairness for the individual well-qualified men passed over, but it would satisfy the requirements of merit-based selection. The two relevant variables are therefore the quota level and the number of women in the pool who meet the merit threshold—the former being dependent on the latter. This means that the quota level must be raised or lowered according to a prior assessment of the relative size of the pool of women who will pass the threshold merit test. A cautious approach would set the quota level low so reducing any danger that an insufficient number of women would meet the threshold. But such an approach would also reduce the impact of the quota and might only lead to a small improvement in gender balance.

Setting a low quota threshold is not, however, the only way to respond to the potential problem of insufficient numbers of women meeting the quota threshold. Alternatively, the quota system can allow for the quota to be disregarded where, in any particular round of appointments, there is an insufficient number of well-qualified women in the pool. In such a case, there are two options; either appointments can be made from the well-qualified male candidates, so effectively suspending the quota system for that round of appointments, or the posts can be re-advertised and a second selection round can be instituted. The latter would be the preferred option unless there was an objective ground for believing that a second round would not lead to an increase in the number of qualified women in the pool. The provision of such exception clauses in the case where there are insufficient numbers of qualified women is an important factor in ensuring that the quotas are compliant with EU law. This approach has been applied in the quota system used to select the members of the Belgian High Council of Justice discussed above.[20] The judgment of the UN Human Rights Committee on the legality of the Belgian arrangements specifically

[20] The Belgian system required that in selecting the members no fewer than four should be men and four women.

referred to the possibility of a second selection round in assessing the possible outcomes of the quota system:

> [E]ither the female applicants were better qualified than the male, in which case they could justifiably be appointed; or the female and male applicants were equally well qualified, in which case the priority given to women would not be discriminatory in view of the aims of the law on the promotion of equality between men and women, as yet still lacking; or the female candidates were less well qualified than the male, in which case the Senate would be obliged to issue a second call for candidates in order to reconcile the two aims of the law.[21]

A second key variable in the different quota models is the timescale for their operation. Many quotas are time-limited, an example being the UK legislation, passed in 2002, allowing women-only shortlists for candidates to the Westminster elections which included a 'sunset clause' by which the provisions would expire—unless renewed—in 2015. The Equality Act 2010 includes a provision to extend this to 2030.[22] Likewise, a comparative example is found in Austria where temporary provisions for gender quotas for judges expired in 2010. The use of such time-limited systems can be an effective way of demonstrating that quota provisions are proportionate, in that they are designed to be used only as long as the disadvantages faced by potential women candidates are present.

An alternative approach to creating a flexible timescale for quotas is to link quota levels and timeframe so as to create a system in which quotas are initially set at a lower level but increase over time as the candidate pool widens. Such a system would fall into the category of 'result' or 'outcome' quotas which seek to develop the quota system in a way which is responsive to the changing context in which they operate. In some parts of Germany, for example, quota systems are used for public posts which require employers to draft six-year equality plans. These plans must set goals and timetables to achieve a gender balance in the composition of different ranks. The use of stepped-up gender quotas over set periods of time is also a feature of the Austrian judiciary gender quota provisions. These require that where the number of women employed in an organisational unit within the judiciary is below 40 per cent, binding requirements for quotas are introduced for periods of two years. These are set in such a way that the quotas are raised, step by step, up to 40 per cent (Parliamentary Assembly of the Council of Europe Committee on Equal Opportunities for Women and Men, 2009).

Another approach is for enabling legislation to allow for (or require) quotas to be used where the overall gender balance of the institution falls

[21] Para 9.5.

[22] This extension was justified on the grounds that, despite the improvements in gender balance brought about by the Act, women still only constituted one in five MPs.

below a certain ratio. This would allow quotas to be introduced or dropped in the light of the changing composition of an institution. An example of such an approach in relation to judicial selection is found in the appointments process to the European Court of Human Rights. Under gender provisions passed by the Parliamentary Assembly, the shortlists of three candidates put forward by Member States must include a member of the under-represented sex, where under-representation is defined as less than 40 per cent of the membership of the Court. Provided the proportion of members of each sex falls within a 40:60 ratio, the shortlist gender requirements do not apply. Women currently make up 33 per cent of the ECtHR, so that it is quite possible that the provisions may be dropped in the near future if women continue to be appointed in significant numbers. Similarly, if they fall back below 40 per cent, the provisions would apply again.

The use of a ratio such as the 40:60 rule also ensures that a genuine gender balance is maintained. At first glance the suggestion that there should be no less than 40 per cent no more than 60 per cent of either sex, as opposed to a simple statement that gender quotas for women will apply when women make up less than 40 per cent, might seem formalistic or contrived in the context of the judiciary in England and Wales where men have always significantly outnumbered women. However, it is important to recognise that this might not always be the case and that the development of a judiciary which is dominated by women is as undesirable as one dominated by men. A review of composition of judiciaries in other jurisdictions, most particularly in other European jurisdictions, reveals that the problem of disproportionate numbers of women is a real one. In France, for example, women make up approximately 70 per cent of the judiciary. Nor is this problem wholly restricted to civil law systems; Israel has similar, and increasing, proportions of women in the judiciary.

Such reverse gender imbalance is objectionable on the same principled grounds of equity and legitimacy which apply to the under-representation of women. But it also raises another concern which is specific to the issue of so-called 'feminisation' in the judiciary. The evidence suggests a strong inverse correlation between female presence and the status of an institution. Where women are present in large numbers, the status of the institution generally declines. It is notable that women tend to outnumber men in judiciaries which are low status and poorly paid such as in eastern and central Europe. Moreover, even in these states in which the judiciary is a high status occupation, women almost never outnumber men in the higher status, upper ranks. This clustering of women in lower paid, lower status professions and the lower ranks of higher status professions is not unique to the judiciary. The medical profession in the UK has been experiencing significant feminisation in its lower ranks as more young women have entered the profession, leading to a public expression of fears in 2004 by the (female) President of the Royal College of Physicians that the changing demography would lead to a devaluing of the medical profession (McGeoch, 2005).

To date, the only ranks in the judiciary in England and Wales where women outnumber men are the unpaid and relatively low status lay magistracy. Given that women now outnumber men among newly qualified lawyers, it is quite likely that among the lower ranks of the professional judiciary women will, in time, come to outnumber men with negative implications for the women who work at these ranks and the status of the judiciary as a whole. Unless and until the presence of a majority of women in a professional or public institution is not correlated to the loss of status and power of that institution, the need to maintain at least 40 per cent of men in all judicial ranks is, in itself, a justification for the 40:60 rule.

6. CONCLUSION

Quotas have traditionally been regarded as a relatively crude instrument for promoting equality overlaid on developed and complex selection processes in a way which distorts outcomes and undermines merit. Their use in the UK has been restricted to the electoral system and the very unusual context of policing in Northern Ireland. To date, the judiciary has generally been seen as particularly unsuitable for such measures. However, the very marked failure of alternative approach to gender (and other) equality measures to produce the expected 'trickle up' into the higher ranks of the judiciary has opened space for this traditional opposition to be challenged, while the legal framework, in turn, is becoming more receptive to their use.

The case against quotas rests largely on the misconception that the judicial appointments process is and can be a ranking merit system. In reality, such a model is not applicable given the particular nature of the judiciary and the candidate pools from which it is selected. Marginal decisions will always need to be made between well-qualified candidates drawn from an increasingly diverse recruitment pool. Such decisions must inevitably prioritise different qualities which cannot be numerically quantified one against the other. In the past, the characteristics which were prioritised often led to self-replication at best and discrimination at worst. By contrast, a selection system which has an open commitment to the values of equality and diversity can quite legitimately apply quotas within a threshold merit system. This ensures that only well-qualified candidates are selected while allowing space for the promotion of gender balance in the judiciary.

The devil lies in the detail when constructing an effective and merit-based quota system and a debate is now needed about the strengths and weaknesses of different models in the field of judicial selection. The overriding principles of proportionality and justifiability are key guides in this work given their increasing importance in the emerging domestic and legal framework.

Developing a proportionate and justifiable quota model requires the creation of a flexible and responsive system which is tailor-made to suit the context and particular needs of the judiciary today. There is scope for the use of different ratios such as 40:60 or 30:70 and the imposition of time frames which allow for the review and adjustment of the quota level up or down at regular intervals. Creating a system that is a good fit in the particular context of the judiciary will ensure that the quota system is compliant with domestic and EU law and will also help to persuade opponents that its use does not conflict with merit selection.

In time, it may also be possible to do more than simply defend gender quotas against the charge of undermining merit and instead to demonstrate that quotas can play a positive role in promoting merit. To date we have very limited empirical evidence, either from the UK or elsewhere, on the longer term or more indirect impact of gender quotas. One possibility is that they might 'ratchet up' the political discourse and policymaking so that some of the underlying factors reinforcing the 'glass ceiling' are more vigorously addressed. In relation to their use in the judiciary, the Equality Committee of the Council of Europe has, for example, suggested that the use of gender-balance quotas in the judiciary in Austria appears to have had a positive impact on the makeup of the Constitutional Court (to which the quota regulation does not apply) by creating an environment in which it is expected that more women are appointed to the highest judicial office. However, until systematic comparative research is conducted on this question, we can only speculate as to the indirect impact of their use. An optimistic hypothesis would be that the use of quotas creates a dynamic virtuous circle in which setting down predetermined benchmarks feeds back into the application process and the legal profession encouraging all those involved in the process of judicial selection to be more proactive in finding ways to draw well-qualified women from outside the traditional judicial career routes into the recruitment pool. If this were to happen, quotas might come to be seen not just as a necessary evil but as a way of actively expanding the pool of well-qualified candidates for judicial office and so driving up the quality of the judiciary.

7. REFERENCES

Barmes, L (2010) 'Navigating Multi-Layered Uncertainty: EU, Member State and Organizational Perspectives on Positive Action' in G Healy, G Kirton and M Noon (eds), *Equality, Inequalities and Diversity—From Global to Local* (Basingstoke, Palgrave Macmillan).

Burrows, N and Robison, M (2006) 'Positive Action for Women in Employment: Time to Align with Europe?' 33(1) *Journal of Law and Society* 24.

Childs, S, Lovenduski, J and Campbell, R (2005) *Women at the Top 2005: Changing Numbers, Changing Politics?* (London, The Hansard Society).

Crompton, R and Sanderson, K (1990) *Gendered Jobs and Social Change* (London, Routledge Press).
Equality and Human Rights Commission (2008) *Sex and Power* (EHRC, London).
Hale, B (2006) *The Appointment and Removal of Judges: Independence and Diversity* International Association of Women Judges 8th Biennial Conference (Sydney, Australia).
The Hansard Society (2005) *Women at the Top 2005: Changing Numbers, Changing Politics?* (London, The Hansard Society).
House of Commons Constitutional Affairs Committee (2003–04) *Judicial Appointments and a Supreme Court (Court of Final Appeal)* First Report of Session 2003–04, vol I HC 48-1 select committee report.
Kenney, S (2002) 'Breaking the Silence: Gender Mainstreaming and the Composition of the European Court of Justice' 10(3–4) *Feminist Legal Studies* 257.
—— (2008) 'Gender on the Agenda: How the Paucity of Women became an Issue' 70(3) *Journal of Politics* 717.
McGeoch, G (2005) 'Women Doctors and the Decline of Medical Professionalism' 57(1) *Oxford Medical School Gazette* 1.
McHarg, A and Nicolson, D (2006) 'Justifying Affirmative Action: Perceptions and Reality' 33(1) *Journal of Law and Society* 1.
Malleson, K (2009) 'Diversity in the Judiciary: The Case for Positive Action' 36(3) *Journal of Law and Society* 376.
Maute, JL (2007) 'English Reforms to Judicial Selection: Comparative Lessons for American States?' 34 *Fordham Urban Law Journal* 387.
Parliamentary Assembly of the Council of Europe Committee on Equal Opportunities for Women and Men (2009) *Nomination of Candidates and Election of Judges to the European Court of Human Rights* Doc 11798 (26 January).
Payne, G and Abbott, P (1990) *The Social Mobility of Women: Beyond Male Mobility Models* (London, Routledge Press).
Squires, J (2007) *The New Politics of Gender Equality* (Basingstoke, Palgrave Macmillan).
Walby, S (1997*) Gender Transformations* (London, Routledge Press).
Wilkins, DB and Gulati, GM (1996) *Why Are There So Few Black Lawyers in Corporate Law Firms—An Institutional Analysis* 84 California Law Review 493.

6.3

Rethinking Judicial Diversity

ERIKA RACKLEY*

Abstract

Despite significant political commitment to ensuring a judiciary that better reflects the society it serves, judicial diversity in the UK remains some way off. Taking the UK Government's definition of diversity as its starting point, this chapter argues for a rethinking of what we mean by, and understand as, 'diversity' in the context of the judiciary. To this end, it outlines two distinct, yet related, concepts typically understood as 'diversity'—inclusive diversity and transformative diversity—which work together to ensure a more varied bench. While inclusive diversity has the more familiar aim—to increase the number of those from under-represented groups on the bench—it is argued that progress toward this will be a harder and slower journey (as we are seeing) without the acceptance of transformative diversity, that is a concept of diversity that allows for differences in understandings of the judge and judging.

1. INTRODUCTION

JUDICIAL DIVERSITY—OR more specifically the lack thereof—is, in the words of Mrs Justice Dobbs, 'a hot topic … getting warmer by the day' (Dobbs, 2007). In the UK, successive Lord Chancellors have acknowledged, and sought in various ways to redress, the judiciary's (and the legal professions' more generally) apparent predilection toward white, privately schooled, Oxbridge-educated men (Irvine, 1998; Falconer, 2005; Straw, 2008). It has been the topic of numerous extrajudicial lectures and speeches by senior judges, as well as various reports, conferences and seminars.[1] And yet, despite considerable political and judicial recognition of the importance of and commitment to ensuring a judiciary that better reflects and, as such, is

* This chapter forms part of a larger project 'From Difference to Diversity: An Imaginative Critique of the Judicial Appointments Process in England and Wales' funded by an Arts and Humanities Research Council (AHRC) Research Leave award (AH/G002975/1).

[1] See Rackley (2013: ch 3 and references therein).

better able to recognise and respond to the needs and experiences of its diverse users, the reality of a diverse judiciary in the UK remains some way off.[2]

While justifications for a more diverse judiciary—broadly encompassing arguments grounded in equal opportunities, democratic legitimacy and the potential benefits of including different judicial perspectives—abound (Hale, 2001), explanations for the slow progress typically focus on the appointments process and one of two arguments: the lack of diversity in the pool from which the Judicial Appointments Commission (JAC)[3] must 'fish'—either because women and other under-represented groups are not putting themselves forward or because of the general lack of diversity in the legal profession from which the pool is drawn (Prashar, 2007: [48])—and the restricting effects of the 'false dichotomy' between judicial diversity and appointment on merit (Monaghan, 2008: 6). The first, despite problematic associations with debunked trickle-up arguments, is relatively straightforward. The JAC can only appoint to the judiciary those who are not only eligible but also, crucially, willing to apply for the job. It is therefore important to make sure that judicial entry requirements are not unduly prohibitive, to encourage highly qualified candidates to apply and to take an interest in the reasons why they might not.

The second argument is more complicated. Here the point is not whether there exists *in reality* an inevitable or essential tension between merit and diversity (JAC, 2009). It is, of course, *possible* to appoint on the basis of both: to seek 'diversity in the field [and] merit in the selection' (Prashar, 2007: [65]). And certainly in a similar vein arguments that an individual's 'merit' can be understood, and assessed, with at least one eye on what they may—or may not—contribute to the diversity of the whole are not to be downplayed (Malleson, 2003, 2006). Rather the point is this. Prioritising

[2] Of the senior judiciary in the UK (that is, members of the Supreme Court, Court of Appeal and High Court) 13.3% are women, just five out of 165 judges identify as having a Black and Minority Ethnic background (BME) and just one practiced as a solicitor before joining the Bench. Women and BME groups fair better in the lower echelons of the judiciary: for example, 28.4% of magistrates are women and around 5% of Recorders are from a BME group (Judiciary of England and Wales 'Diversity Statistics', April 2012, available at: www.judiciary.gov.uk/publications-and-reports/statistics/diversity-stats-and-gen-overview [accessed 19 December 2012]). There are no official figures available in relation to other indicators of diversity although it is, of course, possible to glean this information from other sources. Thus, we know, for example, that there are two openly gay men in the senior judiciary: R Verkaik, 'Gay judge shatters "pink glass ceiling"' *Independent* (20 September 2008) and that three-quarters of the senior judiciary (in 2005) went to fee-paying schools and 81% went to either Oxford or Cambridge Universities (Sutton Trust Briefing Note, 2005).

[3] The JAC was established in 2006 as part of the Labour Government's programme of constitutional reform, replacing a system of so-called 'secret soundings' and appointment by the Lord Chancellor. It is an independent commission, which selects candidates for judicial office primarily, but not exclusively, in England and Wales. See further, JAC website: www.judicialappointments.gov.uk/index.htm and article by its chairman [sic], Baroness Prashar (Prashar, 2010).

merit as the *sole* criterion for judicial appointment effects the *appearance* of opposition between merit and diversity which—though we might dismiss it as 'false'—has a significant impact on understandings of the judge, judging and the judiciary. Put simply, even if we recognise that the dichotomy isn't real—that the focus on merit (and the specific attention paid to its relationship with diversity) is, if you like, a knee-jerk reaction that arises as Baroness Hale has wryly noted 'whenever there is talk of changing or expanding the pool from which the judiciary are appointed' (Hale, 2003)—what we fail to recognise is that, like the image of the judge who inhabits our imagination, its status as fiction does not prevent it from having operative effects (Rackley, 2002). Questions such as how to define and measure merit, its compatibility or otherwise with diversity, the appropriateness of the JAC's ongoing strategy to 'select on merit and encourage diversity' and so on haunt diversity debates, with the result that merit—in whatever guise suits—becomes the favoured explanation for the slow progress to date *and* the solution to ensure future improvements in the quest for judicial diversity. For better or worse merit has, it seems, assumed the position of chief fall guy and great white hope. But what about the other half of the merit/diversity dichotomy? What of diversity?

That the judiciary—particularly in its upper echelons—should be more diverse has in recent years become a truth almost universally acknowledged. Judicial diversity—whatever that might entail—is increasingly seen as an almost unqualified good. And, by corollary, any impediments to it (such as unreconstructed definitions of merit, opaque appointments processes, small pools and so on) are—all things being equal—'a bad thing'. Clearly, if we're going to start making such bold claims—diversity good, uniformity bad—we need to be sure of our ground. And yet, while arguments expounding the benefits and necessity of judicial diversity flourish, discussion as to what 'diversity' means in this context—for example, what form a more diverse judiciary might take or, crucially, the impact it might have on understandings of the judge and judging—have to a large extent been silent. There is a sense that as with obscenity we, like Justice Potter Stewart, will 'know it when we see it'.[4] Frankly, in either circumstance, this is not good enough.

Taking the UK Government's definition of diversity as its starting point, this chapter seeks to unpack what we mean by, and examines the potential effects of realising, a more diverse judiciary. To this end, it outlines two distinct, yet related, concepts typically understood as 'diversity': inclusive diversity and transformative diversity. The former focuses on inclusion—letting people in—so that a previously homogenous institution or group is populated by an assortment of individuals with varied backgrounds, perspectives and experiences. So understood, diversity is a formal concept, concentrating largely

[4] *Jacobellis v Ohio*, 378 US 184, 197 (1964).

on procedural matters such as the appointments process and is grounded in arguments for equality of opportunity. Transformative diversity, in contrast, calls for a more radical approach. It, as the name suggests, is about change—about letting go; diversity is achieved through the transformation of the status quo (Cooper, 2004). It is, in essence, an argument for diversity *in* judging. It seeks the creation of conditions in which substantive (as opposed to merely formal) diversity can thrive—that is an environment that allows for difference in the style and substance of judging. This may be considered valuable in and of itself, in that the incorporation of different perspectives on the bench will lead to better justice (see, for example, Hunter, 2010; Etherton, 2009; Hale, 2008) or valuable simply because without it those who do not match the current judicial norm will either be dissuaded from joining in or will face greater difficulties and opposition if they do. Either way, it is argued, both conceptions of diversity—inclusive and transformative—work together to ensure a more varied bench. While inclusive diversity has the more familiar aim of simply increasing the number of women and those with black, Asian and minority ethnic (BAME) backgrounds (as well as other non-traditional groups) on the bench, it will be argued that short of simply parachuting them in, for example through the introduction of quotas or similar (Malleson, 2009),[5] progress toward this will be a harder and slower journey (as we are seeing) without the acceptance of transformative diversity. It will be more difficult for the non-traditional judge to gain acceptance on, if not admission to, the bench *and* they are less likely to wish to join in the first place given the prevailing (albeit fictional) images of the judge, which transformative diversity seeks to break down. Until this happens, however many fishing trips the JAC embarks on, judicial diversity, however so conceived, will remain (at least for the foreseeable future) the one that got away.

2. A WORKING DEFINITION OF DIVERSITY

'Diversity', suggest Ben-Galim, Cambell and Lewis, 'has a number of dimensions that leave the meaning of the word somewhat ambiguous' (2007: 29). Certainly, as will be seen, the concept of diversity can have a number of different meanings for different people according to the circumstance or situation at hand (Rush, 1990: 2). Nonetheless, it is important, if we are to speak meaningfully about diversity, to attempt to define what we mean when we say that our judiciary is or is not diverse, however fluid and multifaceted that definition may turn out to be. To ask, for example: which identity characteristics are relevant to diversity? Is the inclusion of some features of identity more strategically important than others? And,

[5] See also contributions to this volume by Kate Malleson and Ben Sloot.

crucially, to pose the obvious, yet typically unspoken, question: when we say we want our judges to be more diverse, diverse from what or, more accurately, whom exactly?

Diversity is often used as a synonym for variety, divergence and miscellany and in contrast to uniformity, sameness, monotony. At an individual level, it celebrates and respects the plurality of perspectives and the 'multiple forms of difference'—most obviously sex or race, but also sexual orientation, social background, political viewpoints and so on—experienced by an individual (Ben-Galim, Cambell and Lewis, 2007: 19). Its reluctance to focus on any particular character trait allows 'for a heterogeneous understanding of identity and the components that compromise it' (ibid: 22), which in turn provides an opportunity to recognise and explore the fluidity, intersection and divergence of identity characteristics (Weeks, 1993: 202). At the macro or group level, again, heterogeneity not homogeneity is crucial. Here diversity, rather than being intrinsic to the individual is, like difference, the 'product of comparison' (Minow, 1989: 3). There is no such thing as a 'diverse individual' understood in isolation from others. Thus, the diversity credentials of particular institutions are established through a comparative assessment of whether its members are sufficiently different from, or relevantly distinct from, each other.

Any number of identity characteristics may be important here, depending on the goal to be achieved. Thus, while what Rush terms 'facial diversity' concentrates largely on appearances—most obviously by ensuring a balance between the sexes and those with different racial backgrounds—'hardship diversity' focuses more broadly on ensuring the inclusion of experiences or attributes which deviate from those displayed or experienced by the group 'norm', for example, disability, age, sexual orientation, socio-economic and professional background and so on. Finally 'ideological diversity' seeks to involve those with different viewpoints, such as differences in perspective and approach which stem from political, religious or cultural affiliations (1990: 2–4). Alternatively, identity characteristics might be grouped under the categories 'visible' and 'invisible' (Moran, 2006). Here the label applies directly to the characteristics themselves as opposed to the goals the inclusion of those characteristics seeks to achieve. So, when looking at the makeup of a particular group, factors such as sex, race, physical disability, age are typically, but not always, 'visible', in contrast to the 'invisibility' (either by necessity or design) of other identity characteristics, for example, professional or socio-economic background, religious belief, mental disability, sexual orientation, membership of a political organisation and ethnicity.

Of course, the diversity categories adopted here are neither exclusive nor exhaustive; rather they are fluid, indicative and imprecise. Overlap and movement between the categories is inevitable and welcome, as are efforts to highlight characteristics necessarily excluded by the process of categorisation. In the meantime, my purpose is to provide a common—though basic—framework from which to navigate around the various attributes of diversity; to put together a somewhat crude photofit of diversity and the various guises it might adopt.[6]

Unsurprisingly given its stated aim to 'bring about a more diverse judiciary with increased understanding of the communities it serves, in order to ensure a judiciary of the highest quality which contributes to increased public confidence in the justice system' (JAC, 2006: [4]), the working definition of diversity adopted by the Department of Constitutional Affairs (DCA, now the Ministry of Justice) in their 'Increasing Judicial Diversity' consultation paper allows for the possibility of catching all potentially relevant identity characteristics within its net. Diversity is explicitly defined in the glossary as '[t]he presence among a group of individuals of a wide variety of backgrounds, cultures, opinions, styles, perspectives, values and beliefs' (DCA, 2004: 57). Accordingly, a diverse judiciary is one in which there is a mixed—albeit strategic—collection of individuals on the bench with an array of different personal circumstances and experiences, each with their own style, values, beliefs and so on. This typically translates into calls for a judiciary which, in apparent contrast and response to the profile of our current senior judges, welcomes the presence of more women, more people from BAME groups, more solicitors, more homosexuals, more state-educated, red-brick university graduates and fewer white, male, straight, barristers from Oxbridge. At its most straightforward: a diverse judiciary is an *inclusive* judiciary.

3. INCLUSIVE DIVERSITY

Diversity is not then—as the Equality Act 2006 would have it—simply the recognition of 'the fact that individuals are different' (section 8(2)). The DCA's concept of diversity adopted by the Ministry of Justice and the JAC requires more. At its heart lies the necessity of inclusion. Without inclusion, there is no diversity. Diversity requires the *presence* of difference within a group. It is about the process of *including* difference, of letting people in (Cooper, 2004: 35).

[6] A note of caution: the uncritical adoption of the language of 'diversity' risks not only conflating the many and varied reasons for under-representation of various groups in any given institution (Arden, 2008), but also constraining the identification and exploration of potential avenues for progress in relation to specific groups. That is, though there may well be some correlation across and between such groups, we should not assume that the specific difficulties faced by women, for example, are necessarily the same as those faced by members of BAME groups, let alone BAME women. Nor should we allow a focus on 'diversity' to silence debates about the representation, and discrimination, of *all* women, by far the largest under-represented group, in the judiciary (see further: the Equal Justices Initiative: www.law.qmul.ac.uk/eji/index.html).

Predictably then, the JAC has focused on ensuring equality at the point of entry, primarily through the creation and operation of a judicial selection process that is fair, open and effective. Gone are the days of taps on the shoulder, of secret soundings and an appointment process run on intuition and gossip. In their place are job advertisements, application forms, qualifying tests, selection days and so on (Prashar, 2010). This change has not happened quietly or, indeed, overnight. Far from jumping speedily on the diversity bandwagon, the JAC spent two long years considering the qualities it would be looking for in members of our judiciary, making sure these, like the selection procedures it has put in place, are 'equality-proofed', whatever that might mean (JAC, 2008: 12). Moreover, in the tradition of Lord Irvine who spent much of his time as Lord Chancellor attempting to 'break down the culture of not applying because "they'd never have the likes of me"' by haranguing lawyers from under-represented groups with the call: 'don't be shy; apply' (Irvine, 2007) the JAC regularly goes 'on tour' dropping in at conferences and meetings to spread the word that judicial change is not only afoot, it has come. And, once this message is heard, individuals from under-represented groups will start applying—judicial diversity, we are told, will follow.

Inclusive diversity ensues when procedures are fair and transparent, when equality is formal and when open, yet targeted, invitations are issued. It is about letting the previously excluded—whether formally or informally—know that they are now welcome to join in (as long, of course, as their curriculum vitae is sufficiently meritorious). Unlike the more contentious 'group-focused' affirmative action programmes, in the 'politically palatable' language of diversity the individual bears the weight of diversity objectives (Ben-Galim, Cambell and Lewis, 2007: 22). Diversity initiatives are grounded in individualistic arguments, usually in relation to equality of opportunities and experience (although these typically feed into institutional goals such as, in the context of the judiciary, democratic legitimacy and increased public confidence). And yet while the 'encouragement' of diversity is a key motivation and targeted outcome for the JAC (section 64(1) Constitutional Reform Act 2005 (CRA)), crucially it forms no part in the appointments process itself, which remains wedded to the concept of merit (section 63(2) CRA). The dichotomy between merit and diversity may be false, but the hierarchy is real. Matters of diversity are excluded from the selection process and criteria. The priorities of inclusion, it seems, only go so far. Judicial appointments continue to be made 'strictly on merit, regardless of age, disability, gender, ethnicity, marital status, political affiliation, religion or belief, sexual orientation, gender identity or other irrelevant factor' (Falconer, 2005).

We may also note here that, although the definition of diversity allows for the inclusion of a wide spectrum of identity characteristics within its remit, in the context of the judiciary (as well as other government departments) 'diversity' tends to be equated with sex, race and, to a lesser extent, disability.[7] The 'Diversity Statistics', collated and published online by the Directorate of Judicial Offices of England and Wales, focus exclusively on the sex and ethnicity of the judiciary with the result that the visibility or otherwise of members of these groups within the judicial hierarchy has become the key indicator or measure of success.[8] This practical narrowing of the focus of diversity to the inclusion of the visible identity characteristics of sex and race has a number of consequences. On the one hand, it focuses our attention and provides a relatively solid place from which to start thinking about diversity. Moreover, given the position of women and members of BMAE groups in the legal professions and/or society, their inclusion may bring with it greater educational, professional and socio-economic diversity. Similarly, casting the net too wide, it is suggested, may prove strategically disadvantageous. Any number of identity characteristics may be caught within it, some of which may bear little or no relevance, and may actually prove a distraction or impediment, to diversity aims in this context (Dobbs, 2007). Put bluntly, unless we are willing to say and, crucially, act as though *all* identity characteristic are *equally* important—that it is, for example, *as* important to ensure a reflective combination of individuals from a variety of political persuasions or geographical locations within the judiciary as it is that we achieve equal numbers of men and women—a hierarchy topped by sex and race is (at least at the outset) not only useful, but essential.[9]

On the other hand, a practical focus on sex and race must not blind us to the presence of other significant identity characteristics. It is important to note, with Mrs Justice Dobbs, that while our judiciary is clearly 'not very diverse in the traditional and visible sense, it is comprised of individuals who bring their different life experiences to the job' (2007). And so, although it is tempting to suggest that, at present, these life experiences are likely to be somewhat similar—that the potential for diversity of thought and experience embedded in similitude is likely to be restricted—we must not fall into the trap of presenting our current 'judges as an amorphous

[7] Although *cf* the Advisory Panel on Judicial Diversity Report which in its definition of diversity suggests the Panel 'considered all aspects of diversity, but have focused particularly on gender, ethnic origin, disability, sexual orientation, geographical location, socio-economic background, and the implications of being a solicitor rather than a barrister' (2010: [17]).

[8] Since this chapter was submitted, the Judicial Office has begun publishing data relating to the professional background of judges. The JAC has monitored the sexual orientation and (religious) beliefs of candidates (where given) alongside sex, ethnicity, professional background and disability of applicants since 2011. However, the Judicial Office has not yet followed suit.

[9] There is one caveat to this: By convention two members of the House of Lords (now the Supreme Court) are from Scotland and one from Northern Ireland. This is noted (although not explicitly restated) in s 27(8) CRA, which ensures the continuation of a collective 'knowledge of, and experience in, the law of each part of the United Kingdom'. However, this is better understood as matter of competence and political representation rather than one of jurisdictional diversity.

body, unable as individuals to think outside some kind of "establishment box"' (Dobbs, 2007). Despite their obvious and avowedly problematic similarities, we do our current judges—and us—a disservice to deny them their difference to each other. Not least because it falsely implies and reinforces the view that the white, male judicial norm entails a uniformity, and neutrality, of perspective and approach distinct from the troubling 'bias' and 'prejudices' of sex and race (Minow, 1992). Further, while it might make strategic sense to concentrate on the more visible indicators of diversity—at least to begin with—this strategy is not unproblematic. As Moran has argued in the context of discussions about sexual orientation and the judiciary, so long as quantitative data is used for evidencing lack of diversity, the absence of such data in relation to certain characteristics can be, and is, given as a reason for not recognising, and in turn addressing the want of such identity characteristics on the bench (2006: 566). There are, of course, many reasons—why someone might want to keep certain identity characteristics hidden, such as a wish to maintain one's privacy or fears of continuing discrimination as well as practical difficulties concerning the collection of such data. Nonetheless, the dangers of effectively reducing diversity to a two-horse race remain real.

And yet, despite all its good intentions, inclusion as a strategy for diversity is falling somewhat short of the mark, whichever identity characteristic we might focus on. Seven years since the establishment of the JAC, although figures are up, we are yet to see, as Lord Falconer intended, members of under-represented groups consistently applying (let alone being appointed) in proportion to their presence in the pool, especially in the upper echelons of the judiciary (Falconer, 2005). In particular, the strategy of diversity through inclusion has had little or no effect on those who are unaware of the possibility of judicial appointment, typically senior women solicitors. This claim is underlined by relevant statistics. Just one in five solicitors who responded to the JAC's 'Barriers to Application for Judicial Appointment' research expected to apply for judicial office, with only six per cent suggesting that it was 'very likely' in comparison to almost half of barristers surveyed, 22 per cent of whom thought it was 'very likely' that they would apply (JAC, 2009: 12–24).

More worryingly, evidence suggests that increasingly for both the traditionally under and over-represented groups, appointment to the judiciary is not a particularly attractive proposition. Research for the Judicial Executive Board found that many highly qualified candidates with good diversity credentials simply don't want to be included; they have no intention of joining the judicial ranks, however often they are asked:

> I have no interest in full-time appointment. It is the conditions of service. Five-fold reduction in income. Less control over professional life and I would feel

> bound to go on Circuit ... I have young children and I am not willing to do that. I'm married and I like to have dinner with my husband and friends rather than talking to a load of High Court judges. And also the social milieu ... The idea of spending the next 15 years of my life being a High Court judge doing rubbish work is frankly too depressing to contemplate (female silk in Genn, 2008: 21).

The JAC research similarly found that the most common reason given by respondents for not applying for judicial appointments was that they were happy in their current job (51 per cent) (although a comparable number of respondents had not applied because they did not think they would be appointed (JAC, 2009: 20)).

Of course, it may well be that responsibility for introducing any changes in response to these and other issues falls outside the diversity remit of the JAC, although it clearly has a stake in any changes that may be made. The JAC can do little, if anything, to respond directly to the comparative inadequacy of judicial pay or to demographic changes (such as an increase in second-families and responsibility for elderly parents) which, for many, make the practicalities of judicial appointment a less attractive and indeed less financially viable option (Genn, 2008: 27). It may also take a reasonable amount of solace from the fact that, while they might not enjoy the process, the changes to the judicial appointment system introduced by the JAC would not dissuade the 'vast majority' of those inclined towards judicial office from applying (ibid: 24–26). And, as Lord Judge notes, the work of the judge does not have a universal appeal: 'not everyone wishes to assume the heavy burdens of responsibility which are concomitant of judicial office' (Judge, 2008a: 3). After all, as one of Genn's interviewees remarks:

> It's a very jolly life not being a judge. Getting loads of money, making jokes and doing interesting work. You do really unusual, fascinating things working with people you like. There's lots of flexibility, long holidays, no bureaucracy. Why would you stop? (female silk in Genn, 2008: 16)

The JAC does, however, have a responsibility to provide information about the judicial appointments process and to ensure that antipathy toward and rejection of the judicial role is not grounded, as Lord Judge fears it may, in 'misapprehensions about life as a High Court judge, which may once have been but are no longer true' (Judge, 2008a: 4). Put another way, the JAC needs to ensure that its diversity strategy addresses the myths of judicial office, as well as the realities.[10] Simply opening the door to under-represented groups may not be enough.

[10] As noted by the Advisory Panel on Judicial Diversity (2010: recommendations 49 and 50).

4. TRANSFORMATIVE DIVERSITY

There is a second concept of diversity. Transformative diversity effects substantive change. It recognises that inclusion alone is not enough. As the story of the woman judge tells us, introducing diversity is a risky process (Rackley, 2007). Diversity in judging acts as a direct challenge to the 'the myth that, merely by putting on a black robe and taking the oath of office as a judge, a man ceases to be human and strips himself of all predilections, becomes a passionless thinking machine'.[11] Of course, we recognise that the image of the passionless judge is not real; that the myth is not true (however much we might want it to be). However, his status as fiction does not prevent him from having operative effects (Rackley, 2002: 618). Not least because the myth does not (typically) extend to the judge who is female, black, gay and so on. The outsider judge faces a stark choice: keep her head down and speak as a judge, unencumbered and unbracketed, or risk hostility and censure by allowing her experiences to (or, at least, to be seen to) inform their judgment as a *woman* (or some other prefix) judge (Berns and Baron, 1994: 127).

Of course, this is not to deny that there are exceptions—men and women from under-represented groups who buck the trend and who (eventually) emerge intact and unscathed. My point here is this. In the context of efforts to secure a more diverse judiciary, the pull of the image of the disinterested judge informs and shapes (positive and negative) perceptions and expectations of the judiciary as a whole (see, for example, Moorhead, Sefton and Scanlan, 2008; Gervais, 2008) including its attractiveness to those looking to join. Whatever the reality—which we are told is one of 'warm collegiate support' (Judge, 2008: 3)—in contrast to the interaction and excitement of life in practice, life on the bench is seen as 'more remote and solitary, and less collegiate' (Genn, 2008: 21). And the image of the isolated, personality-less judge and current JAC initiatives do little to counteract this.

Tried against the standard of transformative diversity, the strategies of inclusive diversity—its attitude of 'Let *us* give *them* a chance'—are found wanting (Thomas, 1990: 114). At its most straightforward, transformative diversity requires that we change (or at least acknowledge the reality and effects of) the way we think about the judge and judging. That we tackle head-on, rather than blithely dismiss, the dangerous myths that accompany traditional understandings of the judge in order to, in Human-Resources-diversity-speak, 'create an environment where everyone will do their best work' (Thomas, 1990: 114). It requires us to recognise that judges are constituted, and their judgment informed, by their individual backgrounds and perspectives. Transformative diversity takes seriously the reality that 'every

[11] Jerome Frank J in *In re J P Linahan Inc* 138 F2d 650, 652–53 (fn omitted).

decision maker who walks into a courtroom ... is armed not only with the relevant legal texts, but with a set of ... experiences that are thoroughly embedded'.[12] It embraces an understanding of the judge and judging in which these experiences and perspectives are utilised rather than denied. In other words, where an individual's diversity credentials are not (explicitly or otherwise) limited to their mere presence on the bench, but rather extend to the effect the inclusion of their perspectives and experiences might have on their (and others') judgement. Simply put, while inclusive diversity is concerned simply with bringing a wider variety of backgrounds or attributes to the bench, transformative diversity seeks to ensure that these diverse characteristics and experiences are actually tapped into, that they lead to diversity *in* judging, making 'it more likely that the decision, and the reasoning which underpins it, will reflect the evolving values and institutions of the community, and that relevant arguments are not overlooked or brushed aside, and that insupportable preconceptions are challenged' (Etherton, 2009: [70]).

If this is hard to swallow, then we must work harder to 'explode the myth of the disinterested, disengaged, and distant judge' (Hale, 2008: 320), to recognise *and embrace* the reality that who the judge is, their background and experiences, impacts on and informs their decision-making (see further Hunter, 2010). In failing to harness the potential of *transformative* diversity, the JAC and Ministry of Justice initiatives have yet to confront fully instinctive, yet limiting, images of the judge which operate to prevent members of currently under-represented groups both from *becoming* judges and from allowing them to make a difference *as* judges. Thus, while it may well be 'perfectly obvious' to Lord Judge (and others) 'that background, ethnicity, religion, sexuality and gender are utterly irrelevant to the *ability* of an individual to be a good judge' (Judge, 2008b, my emphasis), what is often missed in the rush to inclusion and the suggestion which typically accompanies it—that these factors are therefore 'utterly irrelevant to the selection and appointment of the judge' (Judge, 2008b)—is the extent to which these factors are utterly *essential* to the act of judgment, in that, as integral, constitutive aspects of the individual, they cannot be divorced from the process of judging. And moreover, in his haste to dismiss the idea that certain identity characteristics are *barriers* to appointment, Lord Judge risks reinforcing the myth whereby such factors are, at best, irrelevant to and, at worst, a distraction from the process of judging.

Transformative diversity necessitates institutional change rather than simply 'changing the faces of people performing old roles': 'It invites exposure of taken-for-granted practices and rituals, incentives and habits,

[12] Arden LJ in *Denton v London Borough of Southwark* [2007] EWCA Civ 623 [21] quoting Canadian Supreme Court Justice, Rosalie Abella.

relationships, and unspoken cultural norms that may contribute to the difficulties in hiring and promoting women and people of colour' (Guinier and Minow, 2007: 277, 273). It matters then that those purporting to promote judicial diversity continue to say that a judge's sex, age, race, class, educational background and so on *do not* matter, when they do. It matters because it is disingenuous to encourage currently under-represented groups to apply *on the basis that they are members of these groups* and then to deny the relevance of those very characteristics *both* when selecting judicial candidates *and* later when they come to judge. It matters because Lord Judge in telling delegates at the Minority Lawyers' Conference under the guise of 'encouraging diversity' that '[i]n the end *your* gender, the colour of *your* skin, *your* religious belief, *your* social origins, are all utterly irrelevant because it is the individual who is the judge' (Judge, 2009), casts himself (and others like him)—and the judge—as *without* gender, *without* colour, *without* religious belief, *without* social origin. It matters that *certain* potential judicial candidates (like merit, 'diversity' typically only arises when talking to (or about) groups currently under-represented in the judiciary—women lawyers, minority lawyers and so on) are being told that their gender, ethnicity, religious beliefs and so on are extraneous to the act of judging, that they must leave them at the door on the way into the judiciary.

It matters because who the judge is matters (Berns, 1999). It matters not only for reason of inclusion—equality of opportunity—and group survival (arguments relating to democratic legitimacy and the like) but also for the difference diversity might make, 'the kind of story ultimately told, and for the way that story reaches the law and the law reaches that story' (Berns, 1999: 8). And, once the reality that *all* judges bring their own world view to bear on their decision-making is acknowledged, it follows that it is crucial (in absence of very good reasons to the contrary) to ensure the inclusion of a range of differing perspectives and experiences on the bench.[13] To welcome, for example, that the perspectives and experiences of women judges *as women* so that they are 'just as much part of the background and experience which shapes the law as the experience of leading men's lives has been for centuries' (Hale, 2003).

This is not to suggest that there is an essential 'women's' world view, but rather to recognise that the experience of being a woman does offer something distinct from that of being a man, as do the experiences of those—male or female—from a BAME background and so on (Arden, 2008). It

[13] Clearly, not all viewpoints are of equal value. And there is a difficult question as to which we would want to include. However, on any view the inclusion of the viewpoints/experiences of sex along with race, sexual orientation, professional and educational background should be represented.

is to recognise that judicial knowledge and, in turn, judgment is informed by their 'embodied context' (Gatens, 1996) and, from there, to acknowledge that a more diverse bench might generally be expected to empathise and respond better to the diverse array of perspectives and experiences of those who come before them. United States Supreme Court Justice Sonia Sotomayor, in her discussion of the influence of her Latina identity on her judicial role, put it thus:

> Justice O'Connor has often been cited as saying that a wise old man and a wise old woman will reach the same conclusion when deciding cases ... I am ... not sure that I agree with the statement ... I would hope that a wise Latina woman with the richness of her experiences would more often than not reach a better conclusion than a white male who hasn't lived that life (2002: 92).

Her point is clear. A more diverse judiciary leads to *better* judging. Baroness Hale puts is more bluntly: 'a more diverse judiciary is a *better* judiciary' (2008: 330).

The point then is not how we might attempt to excavate partiality from judgment, but rather to consider the consequences for understandings of the judge and judging of recognising it as an essential part of judgment. In other words rethinking diversity requires us to rethink how we want our judge to judge and

> challenge[s] the notion that the only person who can be taken seriously as a neutral and fair-minded person is the judicial equivalent of a tall man in a suit ... and establish[es] the claims of people who are recognisably women, and of people of colour and people with disabilities ... as serious and responsible (Hale 2005: 288).

So viewed, arguments that the judge who openly acknowledges the role their gender, ethnicity, class and so on play in judgment—the woman or Latina judge—is in some way acting or judging inappropriately fall away. Instead, to the extent to which claims that such judges subvert traditional understandings of disinterested, dispassionate and detached judging, they are to be accepted *and embraced*. The perceived bias of the woman judge is recognised—and, crucially welcomed—for what (more often than not) it is: good judgment (Cain, 1988).

5. FROM INCLUSIVE TO TRANSFORMATIVE DIVERSITY AND BACK AGAIN

There are good reasons for adopting the second, broader notion of diversity, for seeing diversity as bringing gains beyond increased representation of currently under-represented groups. However, even if our concern was only to see a judiciary more reflective of the society it serves, transformative diversity must still play a crucial role. Diversity *in* judging is not only an important end in itself; it is also a vital means to the end of inclusive diversity, that is, a diverse judiciary.

We have already seen that simply opening the doors of the judiciary to traditionally under-represented groups has not led to them flooding in. Although generally men and women give similar reasons for *not* becoming a judge (Genn, 2008: 16–21), there is an additional sense among women practitioners—at least until a sufficient number of women are appointed to the High Court bench—that the environment of the senior judiciary is likely to be 'hostile', rather than 'supportive' towards women and members of other under-represented groups (Genn, 2008: 22). As Genn notes:

> For some female barristers, the Bench is merely seen as an extension of a male-dominated and conservative Bar, with the same culture of male self-confidence and intellectual posturing but with no respite ... female solicitors who had reached partnership in Magic Circle firms ... were reluctant to begin again ... in a world that they perceived to be even more antediluvian than city commercial practice (2008: 23).

At one level, it is all a bit catch-22. The main occupiers of the High Court bench, like those above it, are men. And, obviously, if women are deterred from applying simply *for this reason* it is, as Lord Judge notes, likely to remain so for some time yet (Judge, 2008a: 4). So viewed, responsibility for change lies exclusively with women (and others who think similarly) rather than the judiciary (and the legal profession more generally). They need to get over it, move on and join in; the possibility of diversity is in their hands. After all, it might be suggested why would the judiciary be hostile (even if it once was) towards those whose participation they are actively encouraging?

Of course it is not as straightforward as women wishing to eschew the (exclusive) company of men. (Although, crucially, the absence of a 'posse' (Guinier and Minow, 2007: 273) of women role models to provide support and encouragement does little to subvert this and may in fact work to reinforce potential women candidates' sense of unease.) Rather, it is a wish to avoid the trappings of a judicial culture that is not only male dominated, but a milieu informed, shaped and sustained by masculinity (Thornton, 1996). Related to this is the fact that prevailing images of the disinterested judge which, combined with perceptions of a hostile culture, mean that the sorts of people we want to see joining the judiciary are not seen, and do not see themselves, as fitting in.

Again this view is borne out by relevant statistics. Women are slightly more likely than men to view judicial office as 'not for people like me' (38 per cent compared with 30 per cent) as are solicitors compared with barristers (35 per cent and 21 per cent respectively), although this latter point may reflect, at least in part, the fact that only 45 per cent of solicitors expect that their firms would be supportive of their application for judicial office in comparison to the support expected by 80 per cent of barristers from their chambers (JAC, 2009: 31–35). Moreover, evidence suggests that residual *perceptions* of the 'old-boys' network' remain. Women and BAME respondents are more likely than white males to rate 'being known by senior judiciary', 'having the right educational background' and 'being in the right social networks' as positively influencing appointments (JAC, 2009: 71).

The concern of women practitioners about 'working in an old-fashioned, fustian atmosphere with old-fashioned, fustian colleagues' may well be 'outdated' (Judge, 2008a: 3–4)—a myth even. However, as Lord Judge acknowledged on another occasion, '[t]he trouble with myths is if people believe them, they tend to allow themselves to be influenced by them' (2008b). In fact, the trouble with this particular myth is that while aspects of the story may no longer be true—it may well be that life on circuit is no longer marked by outdated social practices and that High Court judges are a spritely bunch of warm, independently-minded individuals—other parts of the story (particular in relation to hostility toward the woman judge) remain much the same (Rackley, 2007).

Thus, it is vital that the JAC responds to this and other 'myths'. It is clear that the effects of the myth of the disinterested judge as well as perceptions of life on the bench (both in terms of judicial practice and culture) play a significant role in deterring well-qualified candidates from applying. It is not enough then to attempt to bat them away as 'misapprehensions', to suggest that those who believe them are misguided or uninformed, or as having 'not caught up with the reality' however tempting this may be (Judge, 2008a: 3–4). Rather, they need to recognise these apparent myths for what they are: barriers to diversity.

My point is not (simply) that women (and members of other under-represented groups) do not fit the physical image of the judge; rather it is that this physical image is mirrored by, and supports, the view that good judges possess a closed set of characteristics resulting in turn in an apparently uniform and neutral approach to judging. This in turn informs views from those not fitting this mould of the judiciary as a fusty and lonely place to be. It is this traditional view of the judge, and how *he* judges, which women and other currently under-represented groups are seen to threaten and which underlies accusations of radicalism and/or bias, as well as making being a judge an unattractive proposition to these groups. Transformative diversity is important here because it challenges this image of uniformity. In other words, the point of transformative diversity is to say there is no single approach to judging. Instead, diversity among members of the judiciary should be reflected in how individuals do the job of judging, in the perspectives and experiences they draw on to judge. In embracing the idea of diversity in judicial approach, transformative diversity ensures that women and other under-represented groups are no longer seen as dangerous outsiders as there is no longer a uniform image for them to fall outside of and to threaten. Thus, transformative diversity, in removing this barrier and creating in its place conditions in which difference can thrive, leads to an increase in inclusive diversity, as judicial office and the judiciary itself—no longer accompanied by the threat of marginalisation and open hostility—becomes a more attractive proposition to members of traditionally under-represented groups.

6. CONCLUSION

My purpose here has been to broaden understandings of diversity and to suggest that we take seriously and give closer consideration to where calls for a more diverse judiciary might take us and the effect the collective life experiences and perspectives of a diverse judiciary might have on judgment. Both transformative and inclusive diversity seek to disrupt the status quo, but in different ways. While inclusive diversity seeks to ensure the presence of diversity on the bench and the inclusion of outsiders within the traditional fold, transformative diversity looks to see what effect they might have when they get there. Transformative diversity seeks diversity in, and of, judging.

In fact, on both views diversity requires transformation. And this, in turn, requires the JAC and others seeking to ensure a more diversity judiciary to take diversity seriously. It requires them to think as deeply not only about *how* we might get a more diverse judiciary and *why* we want one, but also about what it *really* means to say that a judiciary is or is not diverse. It requires them to look beyond the selection and appointments process and consider the reality and myths of being a judge in order to see what light it might throw on why certain groups aren't applying. To, if you like, switch their attention from the effectiveness of their hooks and bait and to ask why they decided to go fishing in the first place. Then, perhaps, the JAC may have more success next time they go fishing for diversity.

7. REFERENCES

Advisory Panel on Judicial Diversity (2010) *The Report of the Advisory Panel on Judicial Diversity 2010* (Ministry of Justice, London).

Arden, Lady Justice (2008) 'Address to the Association of Women Barristers' Annual General Meeting' (London).

Ben-Galim, D, Cambell, M and Lewis, J (2007) 'Equality and Diversity: A New Approach to Gender Equality Policy in the UK' 3 *International Journal of Law in Context* 19.

Berns, S (1999) *To Speak as a Judge—Difference, Voice and Power* (Dartmouth, Ashgate).
Berns, S and Baron, P (1994) 'Bloody Bones: A Legal Ghost Story and Entertainment in Two Voices—To Speak as a Judge' 2 *Australian Feminist Law Journal* 125.
Cain, P (1988) 'Good and Bad Bias: A Comment on Feminist Theory and Judging' 61 *Southern California Law Review* 1945.
Cooper, D (2004) *Challenging Diversity: Rethinking Equality and the Value of Difference* (Cambridge, Cambridge University Press).
Department for Constitutional Affairs (2004) 'Increasing Diversity in the Judiciary' (DCA Consultation Paper, CP 25/04).
Dobbs, Mrs Justice (2007) 'Diversity in the Judiciary—Lecture' Queen Mary, University of London (17 October).
Etherton, Lord Justice (2009) 'Liberty, the Archetype and Diversity: A Philosophy of Judging' [2010] *Public Law* 727.
Falconer, Lord (2005) 'Increasing Judicial Diversity: The Next Steps' lecture at Commission for Judicial Appointments (Millbank Tower, London, 2 November).
Gatens, M (1996) *Imaginary Bodies—Ethics, Power and Coporeality* (London, Routledge).
Genn, H (2008) Report to the Judicial Executive Board, *The Attractiveness of Senior Appointment to Highly Qualified Practitioners* (Directorate of Judicial Offices for England and Wales, London).
Guinier, L and Minow, M (2007) 'Preface to Responses: Dynamism not Diversity' 30 *Harvard Journal of Women and Law* 269.
Hale, B (2001) 'Equality in the Judiciary: Why Should We Want More Judges?' *Public Law* 489.
—— (2003) 'Equality in the Judiciary: A Tale of Two Continents' 10th Pilgrim Fathers Lecture.
—— (2005) 'Making a Difference?: Why We Need a More Diverse Judiciary' 56 *Northern Ireland Legal Quarterly* 281.
—— (2008) 'A Minority Opinion?' 154 *Proceedings of the British Academy* 319.
Hunter, R (2010) 'An Account of Feminist Judging' in R Hunter, C McGlynn and E Rackley *Feminist Judgments: From Theory to Practice* (Oxford, Hart Publishing).
Irvine, Lord (1997) Speech to the Minority Lawyers' Conference (London, 29 November).
—— (1998) 'Speech to the Association of Women Barristers' (The Barbican, London, 11 February).
Judicial Appointments Commission (JAC) (2006) *Judicial Diversity Strategy*.
—— (2008) Annual Report 2007–2008: *Selecting on Merit and Encouraging Diversity*.
—— (2009) 'Barriers to Application for Judicial Appointment Research' (Judicial Appointments Commission, London).
Judge, Lord (2008a) 'Foreword' to H Genn, Report to the Judicial Executive Board, *The Attractiveness of Senior Appointment to Highly Qualified Practitioners* (Directorate of Judicial Offices for England and Wales, London).
—— (2008b) 'Equality in Justice Day' Royal Courts of Justice (London, 24 October).

—— (2009) 'Encouraging Diversity in the Judiciary' Minority Lawyers' Conference (London, 28 April).
Kenney, SJ (2008) 'Thinking about Gender and Judging' 15(1–2) *International Journal of the Legal Profession* 87.
Gervais, M (2008) The Drivers of Black and Asian People's Perceptions of Racial *Dscrimination by Public Services: A Qualitative Study* (Communities and Local Government, London).
Malleson, K. (2003) 'Justifying Gender Equality on the Bench: Why Difference Won't Do' 11 *Feminist Legal Studies* 1.
—— (2006) 'Rethinking the Merit Principle in Judicial Selection' 33(1) *Journal of Law and Society* 126.
—— (2009) 'Diversity in the Judiciary: The Case for Positive Action' 36(3) *Journal of Law and Society* 376.
Minow, M (1989) 'All the Difference: Three Lessons in Equality, Neutrality and Tolerance' 39 *De Paul Law Review* 1.
—— (1992) 'Stripped Down Like a Runner or Enriched by Experience: Bias and Impartiality of Judges and Jurors' 33 *William and Mary Law Review* 1201.
Monaghan, K (2008) 'Diversity in the Judiciary: Where we are and why it Matters' 180 *Equal Opportunities Review* 5.
Moorhead, R, Sefton, M and Scanlan, L (2008) *Just Satisfaction? What Drives Public and Participant Satisfaction with Courts and Tribunals* (Ministry of Justice, London).
Moran, LJ (2006) 'Judicial Diversity and the Challenge of Sexuality: Some Preliminary Findings' 28 *Sydney Law Review* 565.
Prashar, Baroness (2010) 'Judicial Appointments: A Work in Progress' *Law Society Gazette*, (18 February).
—— (2007) 'Judicial Appointments: a New System for a New Century' Centre for Crime and Justice Studies, King's College London (March).
Rackley, E (2002) 'Representation of the (Woman) Judge: Hercules, the Little Mermaid, and the Vain and Naked Emperor' 22(4) *Legal Studies* 602.
—— (2007) 'Judicial Diversity, the Woman Judge and Fairy Tale Endings' 27 *Legal Studies* 74.
—— (2013) *Women, Judging and the Judiciary: From Difference to Diversity* (London, Routledge Cavendish).
Rush, S (1990) 'Understanding Diversity' 42 *Florida Law Review* 1.
Sotomayor, S (2002) 'A Latina Judge's Voice' 13 *Berkeley La Raza Law Journal* 87.
Straw, J (2008) 'Launch of Law Society "Markets, Justice and Legal Ethics" Campaign', London (6 March).
Sutton Trust Briefing Note (2005) 'The Educational Backgrounds of the UK's Top Solicitors, Barristers and Judges'.
Thomas, R (1990) 'From Affirmative Action to Affirming Diversity' March–April *Harvard Business Review* 107.
Thornton, M (1996) *Dissonance and Distrust: Women in the Legal Profession* (Melbourne, Oxford University Press).
Weeks, J (1993) 'Rediscovering Values' in J Squires (ed), *Principled Positions: Postmodernism and the Rediscovery of Value* (London, Lawrence & Wishart).

Part 7

Gender and Judicial Education

7.1

Gender and Judicial Education in India

ANN STEWART

Abstract

The chapter reflects with the benefit of hindsight and new research material on an innovative gender and law education project in India, which took place between 1996 and 2002. It locates the project and subsequent developments in India within two linked but differing debates: the first involves the wider development discourse relating to the contribution of judicial reform to the pursuit of social justice and equality; and the second relates to feminist discussions on the contribution of women within the judiciary to meeting these objectives. The present research results from, but is not part of, the original project. The chapter argues nevertheless that this informal longitudinal study can contribute to debates over the effectiveness of gender training for judicial officers and the position of women within the judiciary of developing states, where they face enormous challenges in the pursuit of social justice and equality.

1. INTRODUCTION

THE CHAPTER REFLECTS with the benefit of hindsight and new research material on an innovative gender and law education project in India which took place between 1996 and 2002 and which had as its central focus 43 high ranking but 'subordinate' (trial) judges: 31 men and 12 women. It locates the project and subsequent developments in India within two linked but differing debates: the first involves the wider development discourse relating to the contribution of judicial reform to the pursuit of social justice and equality; and the second relates to feminist discussions on the contribution of women within the judiciary to meeting these objectives. While the former tends to focus on institutional development, the latter tends to assess the role of agency albeit within particular institutional settings.

In 2010, the author (the UK director of the original project) undertook in-depth interviews with members of the original group of judges to seek their reflections, after the passage of time, on the training and their assessment of the longer term impact, if any, of the project. These interviews are set within an assessment of the career trajectories of the male and female members of the group and the institutional framework in which they now work. They are senior members of the judiciary, many sitting in their respective High Courts (the final appellate body in each state).

The research therefore results from, but is not part of, the original project which was evaluated on completion and formally passed into history. The chapter argues, nevertheless, that this informal longitudinal study can contribute to debates over the effectiveness of gender training for judicial officers and the position of women within the judiciary of developing states, where they face enormous challenges in the pursuit of social justice and equality.

2. THE ORIGINAL GENDER AND LAW EDUCATION PROJECT

The Supreme Court in *Judges Association v Union of India* (1991) Suppl 11 SCR 230 issued a direction to set up an all India institute for the training of higher officers of the judiciary, including district judges, and a state level institute for training the 'subordinate' judiciary within each state or union territory. The institutional development of this decision took time. Although nominally in existence in the Supreme Court, the National Judicial Academy (NJA) appointed its first director and moved to its palatial new facilities in Bhopal in 2002. Its inauguration coincided with the completion of the project. Very few High Courts had operational training academies in the 1990s. More have since been established so that now training facilities exist, to differing degrees, in most.

In August 1995, the Department of Women and Child Development of the Government of India convened a seminar to discuss whether the legal system dealt fairly with women. The chief guest was the Chief Justice of India. The seminar was also attended by very senior stakeholders in all aspects of the legal system, including several legally focused women's organisations. The Indo-British Gender and Law Education for the Judiciary project was one product of this seminar.[1] It aimed to facilitate discussion of gender issues through the use of national and international research and experience; to develop suitable training materials which would be used initially to train a core of key judicial staff and be modified thereafter for incorporation into the common curriculum for judicial officers being developed by the NJA; to develop training skills of key judicial staff to facilitate

[1] Professor Menon of the National Law School of India, and subsequently first Director of the NJA, and the author attended the meeting. They produced the programme to meet the identified issues.

the institutionalisation within the judicial system; and to encourage the development of organisational change.

The project was funded through the UK's Department for International Development in conjunction with the Indian government. It therefore was a development project, involving collaboration between the NJA (which in effect was the Chief Justice of India and the Registrar General), Warwick Law School and the British Council which acted as management agents. This high level support ensured collaboration throughout the judicial system.

2.1. The Institutional Context

Below the all India Supreme Court (with an establishment of 31 judges) there are 21 High Courts (18 in 1995) with an establishment of 886 judges; and 16,721 judicial officers in subordinate courts. However in July 2009, the Supreme Court had a deficit of seven; the High Courts of 234 and the subordinate judiciary of 2998. India has approximately 10.5 judges per million people (compared with the UK which has 50 and Australia 46). The judiciary handles 'over 45 million cases a year on average, disposing of some 18 million cases a year' (Gopal 2009: 70).

The target group was not High Court judges but the most senior ranks of the subordinate judiciary, the district and sessions judges, who undertake both criminal and civil matters and can also be posted to a range of administrative postings, such as within High Court registries or to government service as law secretaries or, in large states, to the legal services commission. In the states with formal judicial training arrangements, they can be also posted to direct these activities. Judges change posts every three years. Although the Union is responsible for the overall administration of justice, each state through its High Court is responsible financially and administratively for its subordinate judiciary. There are therefore some institutional variations.[2] However, generally there are a number of judicial grades—the most senior of which is principle judge—who has responsibility for a whole district. Then there are a number of district and sessions judges presiding over courts dealing with serious criminal and substantial civil matters in the districts of each state. Below these there are civil judges and magistrates sitting in separate courts. India has a mixed entry process for judicial service: a route whereby judicial officers start as magistrates and civil judges and work their way up through service; and direct entry from the Bar which is possible at defined stages. Eligible practising lawyers can be appointed to

[2] These matters are covered by Arts 124 and 217 of the Indian Constitution. See also the First National Judicial Pay Commission (the Shetty Commission) report 1999, at: delhijudiciary.blogspot.com/2006/02/shetty-commission-recommendations.html

higher judicial service as district judges or directly to the High Court. There are quotas for recruitment from the different streams. Opportunities for elevation to the High Court for the career judiciary (which includes those recruited directly as district judges) are limited because there is a quota (usually 25 per cent) and an effective cut off age of around 58 because the retirement age for High Court judges is 62 (65 for the Supreme Court; 60 for subordinate judiciary). Seniority (with merit) is generally the basis for promotion for the career judiciary although there is now a merit only fast track route. Further elevation to the Supreme Court is therefore rare although significantly the Chief Justice at the time of initiation of the project came from the career judiciary.

The NJA invited all High Courts to select participants. All agreed and generally sent officers drawn from the most senior ranks. The academic project director, although not directly involved in selection, was keen to encourage the High Courts to consider the gender composition of the group, while stressing the need to identify those with an interest in both gender and training issues if at all possible. Twelve participants were women (28 per cent), an over-representation of women at this level. See, as an example, the position in Kerala, a small southern state renowned for its progressive social policies and very high literacy levels (table 1 below). In the Muslim majority north western state of Jammu and Kashmir there are at present 12 women judges (eight per cent) out of approximately 150 in post in the subordinate courts (where there is a sanctioned strength of 225 judges).

Table 1: Gender composition judicial officers, Kerala 2010

	Gender composition judicial officers, Kerala 2010			
	Munsif/magistrate	**Sub-judge**	**District judge**	**High Court**
Male	155 (74.1%)	60 (84.5%)	124 (87.9%)	27 (93.1%)
Female	54 (25.9%)	11 (15.5%)	17 (12%)	2 (6.9%)
Total	209 (100%)	71 (100%)	141 (100%)	29 (100%)

2.2. Project Design

Although set within prevailing development policy paradigms, the project's design was innovative in a number of ways.

Involving members of the subordinate career judiciary to develop the curriculum and skills which would be used across states was very unusual in the traditional judicial hierarchy. The career judiciary, despite being viewed as the essential backbone of the system, is also regarded as of uneven or inferior quality by the majority of High Court judges who are drawn from the ranks of the Bar. Thus, the project enjoyed the support of the Supreme Court, in particular the Chief Justice of India, but involved a group which did not necessarily command respect within High Courts.

As Oxner argues, it is important to appreciate the difficult position of all judges in developing countries, but in particular the position of the subordinate court judge. The subordinate court has the greatest public contact, and so the opinion held of it 'colours the reputation of all courts' (2001: 291). Yet in many countries such judges are poorly paid and made vulnerable by lack of the visible signs of professional status, such as housing and private transport:

> In some jurisdictions their decision making is interfered with by some of their many superiors. They often must watch the people who come before them wait in dirty and rundown court houses, without information services, unable to provide even copies of documents, and they know that the poor record keeping and lack of case flow management are invitations for corruption for which they will be criticized (2001: 292).

They are exhausted by the expectation that they can solve issues 'that are social and economic and usually beyond their state's capacity to fund' (Oxner, 2001: 293).

While the senior subordinate judiciary in India is well protected by a strong culture of independence and professional standing—including the provision of cars and housing—their salaries have been very low and they generally work in the type of under-resourced conditions Oxner describes.[3] In 2009, there were an estimated 30 million matters pending nationally. The Allahabad High Court (Uttar Pradesh, India's most populous state of 192 million people) estimates that there are 850,000 cases pending with criminal appeals outstanding from 1982. There are therefore extreme pressures to dispose of cases. Historically, judicial officers have had few if any in-service professional development programmes to build competency and confidence and little or no contact with judges from other states, let alone internationally, through which to share common problems. This project offered undreamed of opportunities to such judges, including not only access to out of state residential training and highest level professional interactions, but a substantial period of overseas training and professional interaction; opportunities not provided institutionally to High Court judges.[4]

[3] The Supreme Court has recognised these problems with pay which has led to the establishment of two National Pay Commissions (Shetty reported 1999 and Padmanabhan reported 2009) both of which have recommended significant increases in salaries which have been implemented in general.

[4] Of the 43 participants, only two had travelled abroad before, in both cases through family rather than professional connections. Some had travelled little within India.

Judiciaries feel strongly that judge-led training is necessary to protect their independence from outside interference and sectional interests (Malleson, 1997). It has generally been 'top down', particularly in cultures which accord high and automatic respect for teachers, with learning imparted by senior members of the community. The emphasis is on learning rules and procedures. Yet training to produce reform involves changing the behaviour of a community which is traditionally conservative and strongly resistant to change. Further, such change is not easy because it is often perceived to be contrary to personal and vested interests. Many resist and soon revert to their former patterns of behaviour (Oxner, 2001: 273). This was the first project on gender—a culturally contentious issue in India—with a considerable amount of 'outside' involvement not only from non-judges but from non-Indians.[5] There was no predetermined gender curriculum to be imparted. The programme was designed in consultation with, but not by, the Indian judiciary, primarily to tackle attitudinal and behavioural change and was to be delivered in a highly participatory manner, relying on the judges themselves to appreciate and then develop a participatory curriculum which they could in turn learn to deliver in a participatory manner. The emphasis was on the process of judging, not on influencing individual judgments (Malleson 1999: 172). The outputs (curriculum and training skills) were non-hierarchical, yet judge-led, although much of the specific programme was facilitated by 'non-judge' resources, such as experienced gender trainers, women's organisations and other professionals associated with the administration of justice.

The project, again unusually, involved both intense and sustained levels of activity and participation. It built up over the initial four years and involved some participants in activities for a further two years. Thus, for some this amounted to six years of association with the project. Each participant's key involvement took place over a whole year and involved three elements: a three-day briefing held in India; a six-week intensive programme in the UK; and a five-day follow up seminar in India. The Indian briefing was addressed by Supreme and High Court judges to cement the legitimacy for this unusual project. For many participants, this was their first professional activity outside their own state. After the first year, the briefing provided an opportunity for the participants in the previous year to interact with the next group. This interaction built confidence in the programme and the accumulation of collective knowledge, providing increasing depth to the programme.

[5] At about the same time, Sakshi, a Delhi based women's organisation, with support from the Canadian International Development Agency, initiated an Asia Pacific Advisory Forum on Judicial Education on Equality which undertook gender training.

The intensive study programme conducted at Warwick Law School in the UK involved a number of elements designed to develop different skills, including awareness of gender issues. The participants analysed international and comparative material to identify catalysts for change and considered both the likely timescales and complexity involved in implementation. The educational challenges involved in training judges are substantial, (Stewart, 2001) but this programme had to go the further step of enabling participants to gain sufficient pedagogical skills to impart participatory training.[6] Initially, many of the participants resisted: they openly doubted whether they were learning anything worthwhile. However, eventually, methods based on self-learning proved very successful for the majority—a significant number of participants became very enthusiastic supporters of these methods over the years of the project and subsequently. Each participant developed a training session with materials which could be adopted institutionally by the NJA and by state level training bodies, but also by the judges themselves for their own training activities. Each session was evaluated by the group, the trainers and in most years by a representative of the NJA (including two Chief Justices of India who came specifically to participate in these sessions). Each participant also undertook a week-long placement with an organisation or court of their choice. These placements proved very successful. Gaining first-hand experience of another system of justice stimulated considerable insight into their own, provoking thought about what exactly they were trying to achieve and how they were doing it. We regarded this as an important—but often misunderstood—aspect of internationally-based training.

Each judge prepared a 'plan of action' which involved a realistic assessment of what they might do to put their training into practice. A follow-up seminar in India was held to assess the progress of all participants matched against this plan, and which also enabled the judges to share with each other and with the NJA representatives the extent to which they were able to implement their training once they had returned to their hugely burdensome judicial postings.

Most of the participants were involved in a final stage involving collective implementation via regional 'pilot' one-day seminars attended by between 35 and 50 fellow district and sessions judges from local and neighbouring states, at which they tested their materials and training capabilities. At the end of the four years, the British Council obtained funding from the UK British Foreign and Commonwealth Office to conduct 'roll out' seminars across India. Over the course of the next two years, 3000 judges attended

[6] See A Stewart, 'Judicial Attitudes to Gender Justice in India: The Contribution of Judicial Training' (2001) *Law, Social Justice and Global Development*, at: elj.warwick.ac.uk/global/issue/2001-1/stewart.html.

three-day workshops conducted by the most capable trainer judges using the collective materials.

2.3. Evaluation

Few gender training projects have this level of financial support, investment over time and backing from senior judiciary for the acquisition of new pedagogical skills in subordinates. However, it embodied many of the limitations associated with judicial reform projects undertaken in a development context. This issue will be explored further below; however, two points can be made here.

First, the project formulation did not involve much formal consideration of the relationship between objectives and evaluation. The act of faith was that the activities described above would equip this group to contribute to the development of gender justice within the judiciary in India—that there would be positive outcomes as well as outputs. Nonetheless, the evaluation which took place at the end of the four-year project was thorough by prevailing standards.[7]

Had the training started to tackle the initial general cause of anxiety: the lack of gender justice in the courtroom? Evaluation took place at the end of the four-year project. The last batch of participants had been back in their posts for roughly six months, while the first batch had been working for over three years post-training. In theory, 43 judges were in possession of basic training skills, in practice a majority, but not all could be used as a judicial training resource throughout India. Over 20 participants had taken part as trainer/facilitators at regional seminars and had received formal assessments from participants: all were considered more than adequate, and many assessed as good or excellent. Three volumes of training materials had been tested at the initial regional seminars and judged to be useful or very useful by the overwhelming majority of participants (some 250 judges). The institutional response (activities undertaken with a gender focus; use of materials and participants in such activities) within the 18 High Courts was documented and a rough and ready rating for each state was produced. The project received considerable praise from a range of women's organisations, individual lawyers working with women in the courts and some High Court judges.

As is now recognised, measuring the immediate learning achieved in a training programme is relatively simple, but capturing attitudinal and

[7] It roughly followed the Kirkpatrick four-levels approach: reaction of participants to the training; learning (increase in knowledge and capability); behaviour (extent of improvement and implementation); and results (effects on the environment resulting from participant performance) (Kirkpatrick, 1976, 1994). See Holton (1996) for a critique.

behavioural change is much more difficult (Oxner, 2001: 282). The programme relied on detailed qualitative material (self-reflection, sample judgments, examples of individually instigated training activities, meetings held and talks given, reported changes in practice) provided by the participants themselves. Whereas the responses to wider impact questions were triangulated through other means, the behavioural change responses were not. However, within these obvious limitations, the evaluation provided very positive results. The project's 'client-centred' method—which emphasised self-direction and agency to implement training in practical ways in whatever their day-to day-court work involved—was successful. Participants identified the need to take a more proactive role in proceedings to ensure fairness between the parties, rather than simply responding to material presented by the lawyers. They were more aware of the impact of the use of discretion, in particular that it could be used to ensure such fairness wherever appropriate. On this key aspect of attitudinal change, the participants' own evaluations provided strong evidence of success. They could identify inequalities faced by women which they now recognised they had before ignored as 'mere routine behaviour'. This new understanding translated into actions, such as a fresh approach to the appreciation of evidence. They took care to avoid stereotyping.

Secondly, the project was in many ways incomplete. Despite crucial judicial support, the programme was conducted at a time when there was still only a rudimentary institutional framework for implementation at individual High Court level and no such framework at national level. A bid was prepared for the further 'implementation' phase to institutionalise this investment in human capital within the newly functional NJA and the developing state judicial training academies and to support the group itself. Based on the highly positive way in which the project had been received by all stakeholders, such further funding was expected. However, as with the fate of so many such development projects, the UK funder's priorities changed and the funding did not materialise. The absence of a project-specific collaborative institutional phase, given the structural resistance of High Courts to training for themselves and their suspicions of the subordinate judiciary, shifted the focus from institutional development to individual agency.

However, how exactly was this group of judges to continue to fulfil the expectations generated by the substantial investment in them as individuals, as 'representatives' of their High Courts and as catalysts for change? They were subordinate career stream judicial officers who returned to existing posts to work under immense pressure due to huge numbers of pending cases. Responsibility for any continuing 'success' seemed to rest heavily with this tiny group. What level of individual agency could be expected of them in the particular institutional contexts of their respective states? Did the gender of the judges make a difference to agency? Would the effects of the training 'wear off' over time, given dominant societal norms relating to gender relations and institutional pressures, or have there been changes within Indian society and within the judicial sector more specifically which provide reinforcement? Is Oxner correct in arguing that the 'behavioural change which is the basis for sustainable judicial reform is likely, however, 'to take one or two decades to have an impact' and a 'project is not unsuccessful if the seeds for change have been planted and nurtured?' (Oxner, 2001: 282).

3. LOCATING THE PROGRAMME

3.1. The 'Development' Framework: Judicial Reform Projects

There has been 'rule of law revival' within international development assistance in recent years, resulting in a huge growth in legal and judicial reform programmes:

> These reforms are widely seen as being foundational to all governance and economic development strategies because they consolidate state capacity to provide public order, safety and security; build the legal framework to secure the investment environment; strengthen judicial independence and the rule of law; and promote human rights, access to justice and (it is hoped) alleviates poverty (Armytage, 2006).

Partly because the primary focus has been on post-conflict, transitional and 'failing' states, the emphasis has shifted from project-based interventions, such as the one under discussion here, to large-scale sectoral programmes, funded through general financial support to governments wherever appropriate, aimed at comprehensive reforms of legal and judicial systems. Judicial reform has become big business, involving billions of dollars, large numbers of donors in hundreds of programmes (Trubek, 2006; APJRF, 2009: 5). Programme specifications usually require gender issues to be integrated across the sector, albeit delivered through specific projects.

Yet confidence in the efficacy of these programmes is not strong, partly because there are few reliable and universally recognised indicators of whether they work, and because such indicators as there are tend to suggest that substantive improvements in justice are very elusive (see contributions to APJRF, 2009; Armytage, 2006). Those working in the field are increasingly recognising the need to invest resources in developing methodologies which will facilitate 'evidence based' policy development and performance monitoring, and refining their approaches in the light of what has not worked.

There is a rich seam of critical analyses, from a range of perspectives, regarding this global development approach to justice (Carothers, 1998,

2006; Faundez, Footer and Norton, 2000). Some reflect on the fate of earlier modernist law and development movements (Trubek and Galanter, 1974; Trubek 2006). Others—often those with interests in gender justice—point to the continuing concentration on legal centralism and formal legal institutions, even though some account is now taken of post-colonial pluralism (Gopal, 1996; Tamanaha, 1995; Rittich, 2004–05; Stewart, 2002). The ideological assumptions which underpin this form of globalisation are criticised for undermining alternative forms of popular or local justice (Santos and Rodríguez-Garavito, 2005; An' Naim, 1999; Golub, 2003) or as forms of Western imperialism (Carothers, 2006). The more recent incorporation of compliance with human rights and liberal democracy can also be seen as a new form of imperialism (Rajagopal, 2007–08: Merry, 2006), although Sen's work on development as freedom (1999) and justice (2009) would seek to rehabilitate aspects of development discourse by focusing on 'unfreedoms', such as poverty, absence of economic opportunities and neglect of public facilities and the role of the State to enable individual capabilities (see also Nussbaum's (2000) gender-focused contribution to these developments). 'Access to justice' and 'justice for the poor approaches', dubbed the Third Moment, which seek to combine Sen's freedom approach with more pluralistic, less top-down institution centric approaches, are emerging (Kennedy, 2006; Trubek and Santos, 2006; APJRF, 2009).

3.2. Judicial Reform in India

While India may be emerging as a world power, with one of the fastest growing major economies, over 25 per cent of its population lives below the poverty line, giving rise to an understandable interest in issues of distribution and justice. The NJA has recently developed a vision for judicial reform under its present director. Gopal (2009) argues that India has developed a strong postcolonial legal and judicial system which is renowned for its capacity to innovate. It has the capacity to develop the internally devised and administered conceptual 'tools' with which to tackle the many challenges it faces. '[J]ustice should be defined as a standard of human conduct which includes, at the core, the following five norms: freedom; equality; dignity; equity; and fairness' (Gopal 2009: 46).

The normative content of 'just conduct' is defined in India by the Constitution, reinforced by those provided in international treaties and generally accepted principles of international law (Gopal, 2009: 56). 'The core role of courts should be to promote the general acceptance of the norms/standards of human conduct that comprise justice and to operationalize and apply such standards or norms to specific situations' (2009: 61). Such an approach enhances public confidence in the judiciary and strengthens support for judicial independence. Gopal argues therefore that gender justice is realised when 'women actually experience human conduct towards them that conforms to standards of equality prescribed by law', not merely 'when a court renders a decision upholding equality for women' (2009: 46–47). Thus, judges are expected to exercise—within what is presumed to be a supportive institutional context—a proactive role in which they set aside any 'non-conforming' social values they may hold and judge through the application of these just conduct values.

The development collaboration paradigm used for the original project is clearly no longer acceptable in contemporary Indian circumstances, although there are similarities in aims. As the present author wrote at the time of the original evaluation:

> One objective is to provide an atmosphere and environment within the court that is as conducive as possible to obtaining substantive rather than formal justice. Substantive justice involves a consideration of the context of the case and an emphasis on achieving a just outcome. The Indian constitution ensures that all citizens are equal before the law—formal equality. However social and economic forces make citizens unequal in practice. Thus while men and women are legally equal in court if seen as abstract legal persons, as social beings they are unequal. To achieve substantive justice these historical differences which are structural to any society and often discriminatory must be a matter of consideration for the judges (Stewart, 2000).

The NJA does not conduct gender-specific training and therefore has not made use of the materials from the project or the skills of the subordinate judicial officers. It does provide ad hoc sessions with specific gender content and has occasionally invited individual participants who have been elevated to the High Court to contribute to sessions not necessarily relating to gender issues. Each state judicial academy has its own programme for training for entry level officers and in some states some continuing education sessions. Interaction between the NJA and these state bodies is increasing and the latter are encouraged to reflect the wider NJA vision. However, the content of the training depends to a large extent on the directors, usually a posted district judge, and the High Court judges who constitute the oversight committee.[8] Specific gender training is not undertaken for entry level training within state academies, although individual sessions can be included and significant issues such as implementation of the new domestic violence legislation may be covered.

India has probably the most robust legal and judicial system within the Asia Pacific region, and the state—and the senior judiciary in particular—is

[8] The (seconded) director of the Delhi Judicial Academy is an academic who specialises in gender and law issues. The High Court judge responsible for the Institute is very supportive. There is therefore considerable gender content in the training modules.

attempting to tackle the manifest problems that it faces in securing justice for the majority of its people.[9] Some of these have been described earlier, but the lack of investment in legal education and in the legal and judicial system has undermined capacity. Despite its considerable legitimacy, the judiciary is under attack for its lack of accountability in relation to appointments to High and Supreme Courts and transfers within High Courts. These decisions are made by a collegium of senior judges, with a very limited role since 1993 for the executive.[10] There is no transparency to the process. A number of recent decisions have been challenged publicly. While the absence of any women on the Supreme Court is raised, the main concern relates to allegations of favouritism, undue influence and corruption. There are growing demands for a transparent appointments process with a greater role for Parliament and/or the executive reflecting international debates over accountability of, and diversity within, the judiciary (Malleson and Russell, 2006; Verma, 2010).[11]

3.3. Women in the Judiciary

The project was not concerned directly with the position of women in the judiciary or in increasing the numbers of women in post. However, the desire for a reasonable number of women participants raises the wider issue of justification: would gender equality within the judiciary be an 'unqualified good'? (Malleson, 2003: 1). Is it because more women on the bench improves the quality of justice by bringing 'something different to the adjudication process', or because their 'absence undermines the democratic legitimacy' of 'public decision making institutions'? (Malleson, 2003: 1–2). Varying opinions on these matters reflect different schools of thought within feminism and beyond (see Wilson, 1990; Schultz and Shaw, 2003; Malleson, 2003; Feenan, 2008; and contributors to (2008) 15(1) *International Journal of the Legal Profession*). The presence of a minimum of two women in each group had a very positive impact on the conduct of the programme, although it is important to note also the influence of intersectional identities (religion; caste; class) (Grabham, Cooper, Krishnadas and Herman, 2008).

[9] The Home Ministry in October 2009 provided states with an additional 130 billion rupees to improve courts, appoint judicial officers and set up judicial academies.

[10] See the three 'judges' cases in the Supreme Court: *K Veeraswami* case 1991 (3) SCC 655; *Supreme Court Advocates on Record Association v Union of India* 1993 4 SCC 441; *Opinion of Supreme Court Presidential Reference* (Sp Ref no 1 1998) 1998 7 SCC 739. See also recommendations in the 214th Law Commission Report 2008.

[11] The Supreme Court has also called for the introduction of an All India Judicial Service (on similar lines to the Indian Administrative Service) to improve and standardise the quality of the subordinate judicial service. However, this move is resisted by many of the High Courts and is presently shelved.

On the whole they recognised the issues more swiftly than their male colleagues and were happier with the adoption of new methods of thinking and behaving. 'They were willing to share their experiences. As others have found, male judges hearing for the first time the difficulties that their female colleagues have experienced in their professional lives were amazed and then concerned' (Stewart, 2000).

Of the 12 women, ten were highly motivated and demonstrated considerable agency. They formed the bulk of the most enthusiastic trainers during the project implementation stage, although a smaller number of the male judges showed equal commitment and sensitivity in the delivery of this participative gender training. However, many of the responses could be due to their 'other' status as women holding senior positions. These ten seemed to act as 'outsiders': having attained their position by breaking into a new group, they are less worried about conformism once they have arrived, although all were very aware of the dominant hierarchical ethos in which they worked (Allen and Wall, 1987; Martin, 1990).

3.4. Where are they Now?

Of the 43 judges, six (50 per cent) out of the original 12 women are or have been High Court judges (one has retired but went on to serve as the first female judicial chair of the All India Appellate Electricity Tribunal). Two hold high rankings and are potential candidates for Chief Justice of a High Court or possibly appointment to the Supreme Court (given the absence of any woman). Of the 31 men, 19 (65 per cent) are or have been High Court judges (two occupy post-retirement positions on specialist appellate tribunals), four hold high rankings and are potential candidates for Chief Justice of a High Court and possibly the Supreme Court. Of the remainder, most are serving principal or district judges; some hold specific postings such as registrars to the High Court, directors of training or within specialist courts. The number of High Court judges among the group marks them out currently as an exceptional group in at least two ways. As the table below (table 2) indicates, there are only 43 (seven per cent) women High Court judges.[12] The women from the project represent 12 per cent of the current total. However, given that it is difficult for members of the career judiciary to gain promotion to the High Court due to the 25 per cent quota, this group of career judicial officers has been very successful, particularly as

[12] This information was obtained through the official websites of the High Courts in July 2010. A table produced in answer to part (a) of Lok Sabha Unstarred Question No 2400 for answer on 03.12.2009 produced a total of 51 women. The discrepancy can probably be explained by the relatively rapid turnover of judges due to a retirement age of 62.

Table 2: Women in superior courts

		Total	Women
Supreme Court		33	0
High Court			
1	Allahabad	77	1
2	Andhra Pradesh	33	2
3	Bombay	60	7
4	Calcutta	38	1
5	Chhattisgarh	11	0
6	Delhi	41	8
7	Gauhati	21	1
8	Gujarat	24	2
9	Himachal Pradesh	11	0
10	Jammu and Kashmir	9	0
11	Jharkhand	11	1
12	Karnataka	36	2
13	Kerala	29	2
14	Madhya Pradesh	35	3
15	Madras	52	5
16	Orissa	16	1
17	Patna	29	3
18	Punjab and Haryana	47	3
19	Rajasthan	23	1
20	Sikkim	2	0
Total		605	43 (7%)

it includes a number who began their careers as magistrate/munsifs rather than joining the service as higher judicial officers.

Were they exceptional when they were selected by the High Courts for the project? Interviews conducted in 2010 with 27 of the original batch, which asked them to reflect on why they were chosen, indicate that they could identify such factors.[13] For instance, one was the first woman advocate in her state; the first to be appointed to be district judge and currently

[13] There were 27 interviews with judges from 11 states spread throughout India: nine women and 18 men. Of the women, six were or had been High Court judges; of the men, 14 were or had been High Court judges.

the first principle judge. Two men from different states were the first local judicial officers to be appointed to their respective High Courts. Others identified their excellent performance reviews generally, or more specifically the successful conduct of high profile cases where they had demonstrated their judicial skills and sensitivity towards women.

Did the training contribute to subsequent career development? All the participants now in the High Court feature the training prominently on their public web based profiles. It clearly represents an important facet of their careers. The interviews with participants reinforce this very clearly. All the respondents pointed to the significant and lasting impact that the project has had on them. This was not confined to their understanding of gender issues, but was generalised into a confidence to pursue their judicial responsibilities proactively—to make what they perceived to be unpopular judgments or to instigate administrative changes—the boldness sought by the 'commissioning' Chief Justice and underpinning the NJA vision.

It may be possible to speculate that the training enhanced their agency which contributed positively to their careers. However, the institutional framework and culture of the judiciary remains deeply hierarchical, highly conservative and rigid in its practices. Probity and conformity are core values. Progression is through seniority, with merit playing a subsidiary role for this group. Very significantly, every interviewee denied that involvement with the project had affected their careers. Thus, they sought and considered that it was appropriate that they had received no professional gain from the training.

3.5. Individual Agency and Institutional Development

Is it possible to make any assessment of whether the project made a difference? If so, to whom, in what ways and for how long? Not many gender-based training projects involving the judiciary are so intensive; involve so much international collaboration; enable participants to sustain some form of involvement over four to six years; or involve the particular emphasis on attitudinal and behavioural change. However, the project was not granted the crucial institutional development phase. All activities formally associated with the project ceased in 2002. Although a high profile 'home grown' reformatory institutional framework has emerged within the NJA in the last few years, there is now little institutional memory of this earlier initiative, despite two of the male participants serving as registrars general (administrative posts) in the early years of its development.

Thus, the burden of any subsequent implementation has fallen heavily on the participants and initiatives within individual High Courts. Informal contact between a number of the participants—mainly but not exclusively with the women and the author—has continued, which provided information of activities over the years. The recent interviews provide more detail. It seems that investment in these judges has been recognised institutionally within State High Courts, although the extent of the activity which flows from recognition varies considerably across the states. Much has depended on the support of individuals within a High Court, particularly the Chief Justice. Some, particularly in the immediate post-project period and those elevated to the High Court, have been called on to undertake ad hoc activities associated with gender justice and/or training within their states. One male participant on return was appointed as director of his state judicial training academy. One female participant has recently been appointed as the director of a high profile judicial training academy. High Court judges, including sometimes the Chief Justices, are still aware of their colleagues' involvement, and within a particular state know which district and session judges took part.

A number of the participants at the end of the project exercised a high level of continuing commitment to implementing the wider project objectives. For instance, three women participants from one state took it on themselves to organise (with the permission of their High Court and in the state judicial academy) gender training sessions for every subordinate judge in this very large state. This was undertaken in their very limited 'spare' time. A male judge in another state undertook a similar exercise with all court and legal services personnel in his district. There are many more individual examples of activities initiated by the participants within their particular institutional contexts and undertaken with limited but sufficient institutional support.

All judges face high levels of pending cases with the major imperative being to get through as many cases as quickly as possible. All the interviewees stress these workloads and the performance indicators that they must meet in relation to them. Some suggest therefore that they have had little opportunity to do much in relation to implementing the wider project objectives; others that they can do so despite this load. Thus, much has depended on the individual's level of agency within an institutional context which has not necessarily facilitated the use of their acquired knowledge and skills.

In relation to judging, a number of the female participants have shared key judgments at High Court and district level with the author which they consider to be innovative in pursuit of gender justice. The interviews attest to the continuing recognition of gender awareness within the participants' judging more generally. In particular, they reveal similar innovative judgments by male participants. Nonetheless, when discussing matters of violence against women, particularly in the context of new provisions relating to domestic violence (which only come before these judges on appeal), most reflect prevailing attitudes: that maintenance of the family takes priority unless the violence is extreme; that the laws can be abused by women (and their families). The female interviewees tended to have far more nuanced understandings of what constituted abuse of the law, and some were willing to place women's interests before those of the family, while recognising the very limited practical alternatives available to women.

4. CONCLUSIONS

The project has had a long-term effect on the individual participants. It has changed attitudes and encouraged behaviour change. Its innovative nature has proved to be a success. The project stimulated considerable long-term commitment and agency—boldness—within a cadre of judges not structurally associated with these characteristics, although the career trajectories of the group mark them out as exceptional. They may have been selected because they were exceptional but investment in them probably contributed to their subsequent development. As a tiny group they have produced outcomes way beyond what might be expected of them. The factors which have impacted on their progression and their agency in implementing the project objectives have become clearer with the passage of time. The support of their High Courts has been crucial in the facilitation of wider objectives. In general the women evidenced far more sustained commitment to the wider objectives, although there seems to be less differentiation within their individual judging. This, however, is a subject for further analysis.

The lack of a project institutional phase greatly affected the desired wider outcomes, particularly because of the structural location of this group. As career judicial officers they required a positive creative institutional framework within individual High Courts which was willing to recognise the contribution that these 'subordinate' judges could make and to capitalise on their agency. The present focus on and approach to judicial reform within India may be producing such a framework, although there are huge challenges ahead.

The project's location within a development framework ensured less than optimal outcomes, due to changes in international funding priorities and a lack of local institutional embodiment. While it reflects therefore the wider critiques of such judicial reform projects, it does provide valuable insights into the role of judicial education on gender and its impact over time. However, whether located within a development framework or part of an indigenous process, there is still need for more evidence on the contribution such activities can make to 'justice outcomes'.

Charting the longer-term impact of such training is important. The subsequent research sheds light on the difference that women make to such programmes and the importance of ensuring that women are properly represented within the judiciary. While it is clear that gender is not the only factor influencing agency, here it remains a crucial one.

5. REFERENCES

Allen, D and Wall, D (1987) 'The Behavior of Women State Supreme Court Justices: Are They Tokens or Outsiders?' 12(2) *The Justice System Journal* 232.

An' Naim, A (ed) (1999) *Universal Rights, Local Remedies: Implementing Human Rights in the Legal Systems of Africa* (London, Interights).

APJRF (Asia Pacific Judicial Reform Forum) (2009) *Searching for Success in Judicial Reform* (New Delhi, Oxford University Press).

Armytage, L (2006) 'Monitoring Performance of Legal and Judicial Reform in International Development Assistance—Early Lessons from Port Moresby and Phnom Penh' (International Bar Association, Chicago Showcase Governance and Social Development Resource Centre).

Carothers, T (1998) 'The Rule of Law Revival' *Foreign Affairs* 95.

—— (2006) *Promoting the Rule of Law Abroad: In Search of Knowledge* (Washington DC, Carnegie).

Faundez, J, Footer, M and Norton, J (eds) (2000) *Governance, Development and Globalization* (London, Blackstone Press).

Feenan, D (2008) 'Women Judges: Gendering Judging, Justifying Diversity' 35(4) *Journal of Law and Society* 490.

Golub, S (2003) *Beyond Rule of Law Orthodoxy: The Legal Empowerment Alternative* (Washington DC, Carnegie Endowment).

Gopal, M (1996) 'Law and Development: Toward a Pluralist Vision' *90 American Society of International Law Proceedings* 231.

—— (2009) 'Development and Implementation of Reform Initiatives to Ensure Effective Judiciaries' in *Searching for Success in Judicial Reform* (New Delhi, Oxford University Press).

Grabham E, Cooper, D, Krishnadas, J and Herman, D (2008) *Intersectionality and Beyond: Law, Power and the Politics of Location* (London, Routledge-Cavendish).

Holton, EF (1996) 'The Flawed Four-level Evaluation Model' 7(1) *Human Resource Development Quarterly* 5.

Kennedy, D (2006) 'The Rule of Law, Political Choices, and Development Common Sense' in D Trubek and A Santos (eds), *The New Law and Economic Development: A Critical Appraisal* (Cambridge, Cambridge University Press).

Kirkpatrick, DL (1976) 'Evaluation of Training' in RL Craig (ed), *Training and Evaluation Handbook* (New York, McGraw Hill).

—— (1994) *Evaluating Training Programs: The Four Levels* (San Francisco, Berrett-Kochler).

Malleson, K (1997) 'Judicial Training and Performance Appraisal: The Problem of Judicial Independence' 60(5) *Modern Law Review* 655.

—— (1999) *The New Judiciary: The Effects of Expansion and Activism* (Aldershot, Ashgate).

—— (2003) 'Justifying Gender Equality on the Bench: Why Difference Won't Do' 11 *Feminist Legal Studies* 1.

Malleson, K and Russell, PH (eds) (2006) *Appointing Judges in an Age of Judicial Power: Critical Perspectives from around the World* (Toronto, University of Toronto Press).

Martin, E (1990) 'Men and Women on the Bench: vive la difference?' 73(4) *Judicature* 204.

Merry, SE (2006) *Human Rights and Gender Violence: Translating International Law into Local Justice* (Chicago, University of Chicago Press).
Nussbaum, M (2000) *Women and Human Development: The Capabilities Approach* (Cambridge, Cambridge University Press).
Oxner, S (2001) 'The Many Facets of Training' in RV van Puymbroeck (ed), *Comprehensive Legal and Judicial Development: Towards a Just and Equitable Society in the 21st Century* (Washington DC, World Bank).
Rajagopal, B (2007–08) 'Invoking the Rule of Law in Post Conflict Rebuilding: A Critical Examination' 49 *William and Mary Law Review* 1347.
Rittich, K (2004–05) 'The Future of Law and Development: Second Generation Reforms and the Incorporation of the Social' 26 *Michigan Journal of International Law* 199.
Santos, B De Sousa and Rodríguez-Garavito, CA (2005) *Law and Globalisation from Below: Towards a Cosmopolitan Legality* (Cambridge, Cambridge University Press).
Sen, A (1999) *Development as Freedom* (New York, Random House).
—— (2009) *The Idea of Justice* (London, Penguin Books).
Schultz, U and Shaw, G (eds) (2003) *Women in the World's Legal Professions* (Oxford, Hart Publishing).
Stewart, A (2000) 'Implementing Gender Justice through the Judiciary: A Case Study of Judicial Training in India' in J Faundez, M Footer and J Norton (eds), *Governance, Development and Globalization* (London, Blackstone Press).
—— (2002) 'Juridifying Gender Justice: From Global Rights to Local Justice' in J Hatchard and A Perry-Kessaris (eds), *Law and Development: Facing Complexity in the 21st Century* (London, Cavendish).
Tamanaha, B (1995) 'The Lessons of Law and Development Studies' 89 *American Journal of International Law* 470.
Trubek, D (2006) 'The Rule of Law in Development Assistance' in D Trubek and A Santos (eds), *The New Law and Economic Development: A Critical Appraisal* (Cambridge, Cambridge University Press).
Trubek, D and Galanter, M (1994) 'Scholars in Self Estrangement: Some Reflections on the Crisis in Law and Development Studies in the United States' *Wisconsin Law Review* 1062.
Trubek, D and Santos, A (2006) *The New Law and Economic Development: A Critical Appraisal* (Cambridge, Cambridge University Press).
Verma, JS (2010) 'Judicial Independence: Is it Threatened?' First S Govind Swaminadhan Memorial Lecture at the Madras High Court Bar in Chennai (29 January 2010).
Wilson, B (1990) 'Will Women Judges Really Make a Difference?' 28 *Osgoode Hall Law Journal* 507.

7.2

Gender and Judicial Education in Japan

KAYO MINAMINO

Abstract

After briefly describing the purpose and the background of the research project, this chapter examines the gender bias in employment discrimination litigations in Japan to demonstrate how gender bias is systematically reproduced in this context in judicial decisions. First, the working conditions of judges themselves are totally based on the 'male breadwinner model', a feature that is widely accepted and shared with the private sector. Secondly, gender bias is reproduced by the bureaucratic regulation governing judicial work. In the case scrutinised here the bias arose from the informal and closed nature of the judicial conference (the norm in Japan) whose topic, attendees and conclusion were determined beforehand by the General Secretariat of the Supreme Court. In conclusion, this chapter argues that authoritarian control should be replaced with open, voluntary, social context oriented education programmes emphasising the accountability of the judiciary.

1. INTRODUCTION: JAPAN'S RANKING IN INTERNATIONAL GENDER INDICES

THIS IS AN interim report of a three-year research project on 'International Comparative Research on the Process of Development, Implementation and Institutionalization of Gender Curricula in Continuing Legal Education (CLE)'.[1] The research focuses on the gender programmes of CLE systems in 10 countries (Korea, the Philippines, Cambodia, Germany, France, Finland, Australia, Canada, the United States and Japan).

After briefly describing the purpose and the background of this research project, this chapter will examine the gender bias in employment discrimination litigation in Japan to demonstrate why it is necessary to draw comparisons with these countries that have different legal traditions and

[1] Grants-in-Aid for Scientific Research Basic Research B, Assignment No 19330027, 2007–09.

find themselves at different stages of development in terms of gender awareness.[2]

1.1. Why is CLE a Subject for International Comparison in Japan?

There are two main reasons from the Japanese point of view. First, there is a concern about Japan's legal structure/system, although Japan may be thought of as an economically advanced country. As table 1 (below) shows, the gender-related indices locate Japan in an extremely unbalanced position compared with its economy. One of the main reasons for this situation is the delayed improvement of the legal status of women. This is caused, or seems to be caused at least partly, by the lack of sensibility in the judiciary to gender issues as a matter of social justice. The aim is to find out why the Japanese judiciary lags behind global standards in this respect, in spite of the fact that Japan has always been eager to learn from foreign law.

Table 1: Countries ranked by international gender related indices based on UNDP report 2008 World Economic Forum Gender Gap Index 2008)

GDI	GEM	GGI
Australia 3	Finland 3	Finland 2
Canada 4*	Australia 8	Philippines 6
Japan 8*	Germany 9	Germany 11
France 10	Canada 10	France 15
Finland 11*	United States 15	Australia 21
United States 12*	France 18	United States 27
Germany 22	Philippines 45	Canada 31
Korea 26	Japan 54	Cambodia 94
Philippines 90	Korea 64	Japan 98
Cambodia 131	Cambodia 83	Korea 108

Key:
GDI: economically advanced countries get higher ranks (highly ranked by HDI)
GEM: Korea and Japan drop in rank compared to GDI
GGI: Korea and Japan drop in rank, and Cambodia is raised by 4 points
UNDP = United Nations Development Programme; GDI = Gender-Related Development Index, comp;[3] GEM = Gender Empowerment Measure, comp;[4] GGI = Gender Gap Index of the World Economic Forum, comp[5]
*These countries are yet to be researched (as at December 2009)

[2] As to the research in Cambodia and the Philippines, see the chapters by Keiko Sawa and Atsuko Miwa respectively.
[3] See: hdr.undp.org/en/media/HDR_2009_EN_Table_J.pdf.
[4] See: hdr.undp.org/en/media/HDR_20072008_GEM.pdf.
[5] See: www.weforum.org/en/initiatives/gcp/Gender%20Gap/index.htm.

Starting some 1500 years ago, Japan has repeatedly adopted/amended/applied foreign laws, first ancient Chinese statutes, then over the last 150 years laws from European countries as well as the United States. In other words, the Japanese law of today is largely the product of repeated additions to the existing body, most recently based on the constitutions, the judicial systems and the systems of private and criminal law of France, Germany and the United States. The laws and legal systems of France and Germany, and also England/the United States have been major subjects of research and legal education, and studies abroad have been part of the training of Japanese judges though the number of the judges who are given the opportunity is limited.[6]

By contrast, comparative research regarding the systems of Asian and other developing countries has been neglected. This is why we have taken for our comparative study a number of civil law and common law countries, but also some Asian countries, taking gender indices into account. As a result, the ten countries shown in table 1 were selected.

1.2. Limited Accessibility to Information on Judicial Education

Secondly, information related to judicial education in Japan is extremely limited, although the Bar Association's publications give the general information of CLE for lawyers, and the Prosecutors Office's periodical 'Training' (reports by the Research and Training Institute of the Ministry of Justice) does the same for prosecutors.

In the hearing of the Japanese government's reports for CEDAW (UN Convention on the Elimination of all forms of Discrimination against Women) in 2003,[7] the UN Committee asked a question regarding 'the implementation of education for judges especially focusing on indirect discrimination'. The government representative, Mariko Bandou, answered that there is (only) a one-hour lecture about 'women's rights' of as yet unclarified content in the fifth-year of training for judges. The exchange revealed that the individual educational contents had not been disclosed and also that it became reasonably questionable as to whether the judiciary

[6] As of 2002, 26 assistant judges (ie, judges in the first 10 years of their career) are sent abroad as part of their training (eight for one year to the judiciary in the US, the UK, Germany and France; 11 for one-year studies at a university or law school in the US, the UK and Canada; seven for two years of research at a university or law school in the USA and the UK). Overall, there were 3049 judges in 2002: www.kantei.go.jp/jp/singi/sihou/kentoukai/seido/dai17/17siryou-sai2.pdf.

[7] Countries that have ratified or acceded to the Convention are legally bound to put its provisions into practice. They are committed to submitting national reports, at least every four years, on measures they have taken to comply with their treaty obligations: www.un.org/womenwatch/daw/cedaw/reports.htm.

was even trying to comply with the international human rights monitoring body's recommendation.

Hence, this research aims at accumulating basic material for the implementation of a gender responsive legal system in Japan through international research, taking into consideration systems, methods and contents. This is of particular importance for the coming reform of legal education in Japan (although the timing for it is still unknown).

Law schools for legal professional education in Japan started in 2004 and only a few of them offer gender-related courses.[8] There is no gender-related education for legal professionals who are already in practice, not even for judicial officers who are most important for the implementation of gender-related laws. After passing the Bar examination, trainees mainly practise drafting (letters of complaints, bills and judgment documents) in the 15-month practical training set by the Judicial Training and Research Institute which is affiliated with the Supreme Court.[9] In Japan, judicial education does exist, but its practice is not known the the public because the training schedule, trainer, materials and the issues and topics addressed are not disclosed to the public. In Japan, judicial education is a closed system and in the few cases where external instructors are hired, their names are likely to be disclosed, but information about the contents is rarely accessible.

2. GENDER BIAS IN THE JUDICIARY HOLDING BACK WOMEN'S EMPOWERMENT

2.1. Employment Discrimination Lawsuits in Japan

The issue of gender bias among judges has been raised again and again by NGOs, lawyers and scholars concerned with the human rights situation in Japan. Gender bias was drawn into question in recent employment discrimination lawsuits, which were part of activities of citizens groups (NGOs) for women's rights. When a particular presiding judge had been elected for a series of trials, these citizens' groups filed a motion to refuse the judge and at the same time ran a campaign for institutionalisation of corrective education against judicial gender bias observed in judgments. They invited

[8] The 74 law schools were established in 2004 (72) and 2005 (2) as a part of judicial reform. This was meant to introduce an American model of legal professional education, substituting the traditional faculty of law for a general legal education and several years of individual efforts to pass the Bar examination: www.kantei.go.jp/jp/singi/sihou/kentoukai/seido/dai17/17siryou-sai2.pdf.

[9] The trainees have to pass the final examination in the Institute before they are licensed to practise. Those hoping to be appointed as judges normally have to pass in the top 10% of this 'second Bar examination'.

the director of the National Judicial Education Programme (NJEP) from the United States and held a symposium on the subject. In addition, they submitted an alternative report when the Japanese government's report was discussed by the CEDAW Commission in 2003 and united with other NGOs for information activities (Japan NGO network for CEDAW, JNNC, 2003: 42–46).

Judges were recognised as individuals who needed to be educated about gender. This was far from the traditional self-identification of the Japanese judiciary according to which judges' primary collective mission is to secure integrity, unity in conclusions and legal stability (Foote, 2006: 174–88, 206–09).[10] This understanding of the principle of independence of the judiciary has been repeatedly criticised. It has been argued that it costs individual judges their independence and civil liberty. For example, a court president 'interfered' with a trial by sending a letter to instruct the judge on the content of the judgment; the judge who disclosed the letter was degraded/ill-treated. Judges who were members of certain organisations which were considered to be 'political' (or politically progressive) were asked to withdraw from the organisations and, if they failed to do so, were refused reappointment. Some argued that this proves that judges are controlled by the courts (Kisa et al, 2009: 151–227) However, since data of personnel evaluation and education are not disclosed by courts, objective examination of these arguments has so far been difficult.

The gender bias in the judiciary can be exemplified by employment discrimination lawsuits, so-called, 'Sumitomo Lawsuits', since 1995[11] (Mitsuko Miyachi, 2001: 28–29). To put it briefly, the courts saw working women not as individuals, but as belonging to 'women' collectively and their working contract and conditions as a result of voluntary self-selection. This needs to be seen in the context of the 'women's return to household' policy introduced after the war to bring unemployed men back into paid employment and as part of companies' employment strategy which, though profitable for the short term, was gender-biased and problematic in the long term.

[10] The Supreme Court itself defines as the characteristic of the Japanese judiciary the unified system and homogeneous judicial service in other words, unity in the conclusions. 'Judicial System in the 21st Century: A Report to Judicial Reform Council' Supreme Court (2001): www.courts.go.jp/about/kaikaku/sihou-21.html.

[11] In the trials it was disputed if there was an employment discrimination against women based on gender. The defendants were Sumitomo Electric Co, Ltd, Sumitomo Chemical Co, Ltd, Sumitomo Metal Industries, Ltd, and the general manager of the Osaka Women's and Young Workers' Problems Council of Ministry of Labour. The judgment of the first trial determined that the discrimination in salary/promotion based on the employment classification was not a violation of public order and good morals according to the working trend at the time of the plaintiffs' employment (in the 1960s).

The judgment of the district court of Osaka on 31 July 2000 in the *Sumitomo Electric* case was referred to as a clear example of this issue. Even though the court found the disputed treatment of the plaintiffs to be unconstitutional—against the equity (equality under the law) clause, it argued:

> In the period between 1965 and 1974, Japanese society still had a strong consciousness of separate roles of men and women in the family context. Men were supposed to be economic providers, while their wives were supposed to stay at home and devote themselves to caring for their children. Although women were employed to work for companies, they tended to set a limit of working until marriage or childbirth and quit after a short time of employment. Many companies in Japan took this into consideration and, in return, gave men opportunities to improve their capacity and enhance their productivity through internal training based on the premise of long-term employment until their retirement. Since it was likely that women would retire after a short time, companies did not want to spend money on their training but often hired them only for routine, supplemental and simple labour. There were other reasons, such as legal constraints against women working late at night and the possibility of maternity leave ...
>
> During this period it was held that the defendant company had no choice but to manage personnel in the most effective way based on the premise of the prevailing social consciousness and women's then usual period of employment. Therefore, the company was not found to have violated public order and good morals when they allocated only routine and supplemental labours to women high-school graduates.[12]

2.2. NGO's Action to Protest against the Gender-biased Decision

When it became clear that the same judge would preside over the whole series of the Sumitomo cases, the plaintiffs in the *Sumitomo Metal* case filed a motion to recuse the judge. However, on 18 May 2001 the district court of Osaka did not find 'conditions hindering a fair trial'.

After this judgment, the Working Women's Network WWN held conferences in Osaka and Fukuoka in June 2001, inviting as speaker the director of the NJEP in the United States, Lynn Hecht Schafran. She explained that the goal of the NJEP is 'to provide facts and new sensibilities which assist judges in administering justice with greater fidelity to their own ideas on how to deliver objective/fair/just trials' (Schafran 2001: 26) This education programme is to assist judges as individuals.

Moreover, an article published in the *Yomiuri Shimbun*, the Japanese newspaper with the highest circulation, on 10 August 2001 made public

[12] Osaka District Court Judgment 2000/7/31, case no Heisei 7(wa) 8009; Hanarei Taimuzu no 1080, 126; Roudouhannrei no 792, 48.

a disclosure request by a lawyer against the Supreme Court. It had used the following conclusion of the Conference of Judges (27 October 1998) published in *Administration, Labour, and Intellectual Properties Related Incident Times* (Gyosei, Rodo, Chitekizaisanken Kankei Jiken Jiho): 'Wage differences are acceptable if labourers are engaged in the same work under different employment conditions (which means this circumstance is not a violation of public order and good morals)'. This suggests that in the lost trial the Court simply followed this conference's conclusion, holding that: 'There is unconstitutional gender discrimination, but it is not a violation of public order in terms of the Civil Code'.

These circumstances have been reported by NGOs. In its consideration of reports submitted by Japan, the UN Committee on Economic, Social and Cultural Rights (CESCR) in its session on 13 August 2001 expressed concern about the actual indirect discrimination by companies in respect of the principle of equal wages for equal work (paragraph 17 of the concluding observations). In paragraph 35, the UN CESCR stated: 'The Committee also recommends that the State party improve teaching and training programmes on human rights for judges, prosecutors and lawyers in order to enhance knowledge, awareness and application of the Covenant'.[13]

2.3. Settlement following CEDAW Concluding Observations 2003

In 2003, when the Sumitomo cases were appealed, Japanese NGOs joined forces in submitting an alternative report to the one expected from the Japanese government for the CEDAW and held a lunchtime briefing for the committee members.[14] In their concluding comments the Committee report, at paragraph 358, stated that:

> The Committee recommends that a definition of discrimination against women, encompassing both direct and indirect discrimination in line with Article 1 of the Convention, be included in domestic legislation. It also recommends campaigns to raise awareness about the Convention, in particular the meaning and scope of

[13] In its concluding comments on the fourth periodic report by the Japanese government in November 1998, the Council of the International Covenant on Civil and Political Rights (ICCPR) made the following recommendation (para 32): 'The Committee is concerned that there is no provision for the training of judges, prosecutors and administrative officers in human rights under the Covenant. The Committee strongly recommends that such training be made available. Judicial colloquiums and seminars should be held to familiarize judges with the provisions of the Covenant. The Committee's [general comments] and the [Views] expressed by the Committee on communications under the Optional Protocol should be supplied to the judges': (www.unhchr.ch/tbs/doc.nsf/MasterFrameView/5a2baa28d433b6ea8025 66d40041ebbe?Opendocument).

[14] See also WWN (2004) 1–65.

indirect discrimination, aimed, inter alia, at parliamentarians, the judiciary and the legal profession in general.[15]

In paragraphs 369 and 370, the Committee also recommended amending the existing gender discrimination in wages and promotion due to the difference in employment classification, and to reform the government guidelines to the Equal Employment Opportunity Law which is the main cause of the discrimination.[16]

As a result, in December 2003, the appeal in the *Sumitomo Electric* case in the series of Sumitomo related lawsuits was 'settled in favour of the plaintiffs' (WWN, 2004: 91–92). The government admitted liability and the plaintiff's promotion and compensation were awarded. The court settlement referred to efforts of the international community, the Japanese Constitution and accomplishments through the women's movement, and also mentioned the doctrine of indirect discrimination. The presiding judge of this settlement (Judge Toshio Igaki of the Osaka High Court) attracted much public applause not merely in this case, but in other civil actions. Lawsuits against Sumitomo Chemical, Sumitomo Metal Industries and Sumitomo Life Insurance (the so-called 'trials for discrimination against moms') also followed the precedential settlement in favour of the plaintiffs.

3. JAPAN'S JUDICIAL EDUCATION AND GENDER ISSUES

As described above, the Japanese government has been recommended by each monitoring body to provide the judiciary with educational training regarding international human rights law. However, it is obvious that the Japanese government has not yet complied with the recommendation, since the Committee of the International Covenant on Civil and Political Rights in 2008 in its concluding observation on Japan repeated the same recommendation (Asia-Pacific Human Rights Review, 2009: 122).

3.1. One-hour Lecture on Women's Human Rights

It is clear that a one-hour lecture on women's rights for judges in the fifth year of further training after their appointment is insufficient to remove

[15] CEDAW concluding comments on Japan (2003): www.un.org/womenwatch/daw/cedaw/cdrom_cedaw/EN/files/cedaw25years/content/english/CONCLUDING_COMMENTS_ENGLISH/Japan/Japan%20-%20CO-5.pdf.

[16] The 'settlement in favour of the plaintiffs' in the lawsuits against Sumitomo Electric reflected these recommendations. Also, the Ministry of Health, Labour and Welfare amended the Equal Employment Opportunity Law additionally prohibiting indirect discrimination. However, this failed to eliminate the guideline of employment management classification, which is still used as 'justification' for the discriminatory management practices against women.

any gender bias. What, then, is precisely the content of further training for judges?

The report submitted by the General Secretariat of the Supreme Court to the Judicial Reform Council in 2001 states that for both assistant judges and judges, 'On the Job Training' (OJT) represents a main educational and training role, as well as an additional occasion for continuing legal education, but does not specify its content. The website of the Supreme Court explains that their training involves over 1000 people every year. They see continuing legal education as 'a support for self-improvement of judges' and a supplemental measure to OJT.[17]

It seems that judges are forced to apply superhuman efforts in terms of their self-improvement to allow them to understand diversified and complicated social and legal situations, and obtain the social-scientific knowledge, which is one of the most important tools for fact finding and decision-making. In fact, at the Legal Training and Research Institute, in the course of training, several trainees are reported to have lost their lives each year, and although in these cases the cause of death has not been disclosed by the Institute, some of their colleagues suspect it is from overworking; so-called 'karoshi' (Japan Young Lawyers' Association, 1997).[18] Taking into consideration the deficits in judges' training, the current mismatch between the number of judges and the number of lawsuits only seems to leave two alternatives: judges either work themselves to death or they process lawsuits as routine.

3.2. Administration of Justice and Bureaucratic Judiciary

What apart from systematic training could influence the decisions of judges? Important occasions in this context are the 'Conference of Judges' and the 'Gathering of Judges' organised by the General Secretariat of the Supreme Court. These were referred to in newspaper articles about the Sumitomo related lawsuits but are not organised as formal education. Koichi Yaguchi, former Chief Justice of the Supreme Court, mentioned that 'these are precious opportunities in which judges exchange information and opinions' (Foote, 2006: 281–84). However, these 'opportunities' seem so far to have been used to produce certain integrated results in specific types of cases (Foote, 2006: 174–88, 206–09). This approach is extremely efficient in terms of human/time resources of judges in Japan, since it enables judges to quickly make 'fair' decisions and consequently increase predictability,

[17] Summary of continuing education and training system for the judges as of 2001, a report submitted by the Supreme Court to Judicial Reform Council: www.courts.go.jp/saikousai/about/iinkai/asu-kondan/asu-siryo3/pdf/siryo4.pdf.

[18] Japan Young Lawyers Association, 'Research on overworking and other problems in the Judicial Training and Research Institute': www.2s.biglobe.ne.jp/~jinkenha/kenshuu.html.

presumably leading to a reduction in the number of lawsuits. However, it can be questioned if these places for 'opinion exchange' allow judges to express their opinions freely and to refine their legal interpretation. In the Japanese system, judges are reappointed every ten years, which means that the life tenure of judges is not secured. Therefore, the possibility of dismissal by rejection of reappointment in the judicial bureaucracy could make the General Secretariat's opinions in the conference hard to resist, as personnel management is controlled by the General Secretariat of the Supreme Court. Moreover, the proceedings of the conference are not disclosed unless a disclosure request is approved. As stated, in the first trial judgment in a Sumitomo lawsuit the district court of Osaka gave the following reasoning: 'This is unconstitutional discrimination but not a violation of public order and good morals'. This statement could have been intended to conform to the conclusion of the General Secretariat presented in the Conference of Judges which also read 'not a violation of public order and good morals'. We could also infer that the judge of the first trial chose this evidently inconsistent reasoning to resist the 'integrated' behaviour in judgments influenced by the Conference, giving a cause of appeal to the plaintiffs.

3.3. Gendered Working Conditions of Judges

A look at recent legal history is revealing regarding the issue of judicial independence. In the 1960s, judgments to protect working women's rights established a legal doctrine in which the clause of equity (equality under the law) in Article 14 of the Constitution could be applied to private human relationships through section 90 of the Civil Code (public order and good morals). In recent years, however, the doctrine of public order and good morals was used to reject working women's rights. The 'liberal' judgments in the 1960s were made by the judges who were employed before the war and protected by life tenure. The new judicial reappointment system which was introduced after the war enabled the Supreme Court to control judges' decisions.

There is another way of looking at the issue. In the 1960s, direct discrimination and formal equality were easily identifiable for judges, while recent legal theory of indirect discrimination and substantive equality seems hardly persuasive to those whose frame of reference is shaped by traditional social norms. Another argument is delivered by Foote (2006: 239–48). He concludes that employment conditions for Japanese judges conform to those of employees in major Japanese companies.[19] In other words, even

[19] Big Japanese companies traditionally hold the discretion over employment practices. Employment, reassignment and promotion are within the employers' discretion, but dismissals are rather restricted. In the courts, the employment practices seem much the same; the General Secretariat of the Supreme Court holds the discretion over appointment, reappointment, promotion and transference, but dismissals are rare.

judges are not free from their individual experiences in everyday life. They, too, operate according to the principle that requires men to be breadwinners. Therefore, judicial education is needed to show them that current social norms are full of gender bias and stereotyping, including their own.

4. CONCLUSION: JUDICIAL INDEPENDENCE FROM A GENDER PERSPECTIVE

'Traditional' approaches to maintain the independence of courts—such as their integrity, unity of their judgments and their closed nature—contradict the necessity of information disclosure and transparency required to secure accountability and public trust and support. The public no longer accepts as the basis of the judicial system a political philosophy which can be summarised in the following sentence: 'Do not let the public be informed but let them rely on the government'.

There are a number of reasons for the current situation of self-isolated judicial independence in Japan.

First, the analysis of conditions in a number of other countries (table 1 above) has shown that judicial education in these civil and common law countries is similar in terms of openness, transparency and accessibility. Following interviews with judges, prosecutors and education directors, it would appear to Japanese researchers that the transparency in the standards and process of evaluation and promotion of judges appears especially high. In addition, life tenure of judges in civil law countries makes for secure working conditions; in other words, independence, protection of human rights, development of professional skills and working conditions of judges complement each other. In view of the fact that judges are not even free from being influenced by personal, subjective experiences, it is uncertain whether Japanese working women can hope for a better future when their last resort is to the courts where judges themselves suffer from the strict workplace norm of the male breadwinner model with extraordinarily heavy caseloads on the very small judiciary, resulting in working conditions that are inflexible and unwelcome to familial responsibilities. In the face of these labour practices, it cannot be wholly surprising that gender bias in the judiciary still persists 30 years after Japan ratified CEDAW.

There is, furthermore, a possible structural reason for the gender bias that is pervasive in the judiciary. It is conceivable that judges are overconforming to the perceived will of the Secretariat or the Supreme Court given the insecurity of their tenure, the bureaucratic personnel management and the closed or unspecified nature of the evaluation. The current interpretation of Article 80 of the Constitution, which articulates in its English draft that 'All such judges shall hold office for a term of 10 years with the privilege of reappointment' may be questioned as reading the term 'privilege' too restrictedly. It also should be noted that the Japanese judiciary is very deferential to the political and administrative branches, self-restraint being a vital ingredient of constitutional judgments in 'highly political' and controversial cases. The judiciary also seems to show deference to the administrative branch in the interpretation of the equal employment opportunity legislation, upholding the Ministry of Labour's guideline, which makes the legislation's equal treatment requirement almost meaningless.[20]

The third and undeniably very important reason for the persisting gender bias in the judiciary is the lack of sufficient and regular opportunities for gender-related training for the judiciary. It has been recommended that Japan should introduce such training by every human rights treaty monitoring body, over and over again, each time the government's reports undergo review. So far, the situation still leaves a great deal to be desired. This research is meant as a starting point for urgently needed further comparative research relating to other countries that import foreign laws.

5. REFERENCES

* Japanese titles are translated for the purpose of this publication only.

Asia-Pacific Human Rights Information Center (2009) 'Materials: Human Rights Committee Concluding observations summary'.

Foote, D (2006), 'Systemic Factors, Political Situations and Judicial Ethics'; 'Creation of Judicial Norms and Policy Making in Japan'; 'Reflections on Policy Making by the Judiciary' in *Judiciary and Society: Common Sense about Judiciary in Japan* (Tokyo, NTT Shuppan).*

Kisa, S and Miyazawa, S (2009) 'Working Conditions and Control of the Judges' in Kisa, S, Miyazawa, S, Satou, T, Kawashima, S, Mizutani, N and Ageishi, K *Japanese Judicial System* (Nihon Hyoronsha).*

Miyachi, M (2001) 'Gender Bias in Employment Discrimination Cases in Japan' in *Toward Elimination of Gender Bias in the Courts* (Working Women's Network and Working Women's Voice).*

Schafran, LH (2001) 'Promoting Gender Fairness in the Courts through Judicial Education' in *Toward Elimination of Gender Bias in the Courts* (Working Women's Network and Working Women's Voice).

[20] This is why the Sumitomo plaintiffs lost their first trials. The courts upheld the guideline in conforming to the conclusions in the conference, ie, that it is not unlawful to treat women differently even though the work is the same but only the job classification is different. That is precisely what the Ministry of Labour articulated in its guideline of equal employment opportunity law of 1992.

Tanaka, K (2003) 'Collaboration of Japanese NGO's for CEDAW 2002', Japan NGO Network for CEDAW, JNNC *CEDAW and NGO: Networking for Action for the Review of the Government's Report* (Akashi Shoten).*
Working Women's Network (WWN) (2004) 'Statement on the Court Directed Settlement in Sumitomo Electric Lawsuit' *CEDAW and Sumitomo Employment Discrimination* Cases.*

7.3

Engendering the Judiciary—Lessons from the Philippines

ATSUKO MIWA

Abstract

In the Philippines, efforts to make the judiciary gender responsive have seen considerable progress since the 1990s but finally gained a strong momentum after the turn of the century when the Chief Justice Hiralio G Davide spearheaded various important initiatives in order for the judiciary to deliver gender-fair justice. The creation of the Committee on Gender Responsiveness in the Judiciary chaired by two Associate Justices was the highlight of his actions and a comprehensive policy to mainstream gender in the judiciary was formulated. As the most prioritised initiative, gender training for lawyers and judges has been conducted by the Philippine Judicial Academy of the Supreme Court as well as through Mandatory Continuing Legal Education (MCLE), though it is still elective. Gender bias and stereotypes are deeply embedded in one's unconscious and therefore take a long time to eliminate. Gender training is an important tool for change, but for maximum impact to be brought about it needs to be combined with other strategic initiatives, such as the Gender Justice Award. However slow the change might be, committed leadership and well-designed and strategised programmes on the ground are critical.

1. INTRODUCTION

THIS CHAPTER TRACES efforts and initiatives to make the Philippine judiciary gender sensitive and responsive.[1] The Philippines is a country located in the eastern part of the Asian continent. It ranks forty-fifth in the Gender Empowerment Measure (GEM) of the

[1] The research is part of a comparative study on 'the Role and Impact of Continuing Legal Education toward a Gender Sensitive Judiciary'. I conducted field research in the Philippines in January 2009 and interviewed staff of the Supreme Court of the Philippines as well as those who were instrumental in promoting a gender-responsive judiciary, including staff of the Ateneo Human Rights Center, the University of the Philippines, the National Commission on the Role of Filipino Women and several NGOs.

Human Development Report 2007–08 of the United Nations Development Programme (UNDP),[2] which rates women's presence in major decision-making arenas, including seats in national parliaments and equal shares in earned income. In terms of various initiatives towards women's empowerment and, more importantly, substantive progress achieved so far, it is one of the most progressive countries in Asia.

In the Philippines, as in many other countries, efforts to achieve women's empowerment and gender equality became a solid and collective movement in the 1970s. The National Commission on the Role of Filipino Women (NCRFW), the National Gender Equality Machinery of the Philippines, was created in 1975 under the Office of the President to spearhead the government's efforts toward women's advancement.[3] The NCRFW played a key role in formulating gender policies of the Philippine government, namely the Philippine Development Plan for Women 1989–1992 (PDPW) and the Perspective Plan for Gender-Responsive Development 1995–2025 (PPGD). Since the time span of the PPGD is rather long, the Framework Plan for Women (FPW) has been formulated to serve as a guiding framework of gender policies under the Medium-Term Philippine Development Plan 2004–2010 (MT-PDP).

Three major areas of interventions identified in the FPW are: (1) women's economic development; (2) women's human rights; and (3) gender-responsive governance (Southeast Asia Women's Watch, 2008: 111–33). A mechanism is also instituted to secure financial resources in order to facilitate implementation of the gender policies through Gender Budgeting. Since 1995, according to the General Appropriations Act all departments including their attached agencies, offices, bureaus and government owned and controlled corporations shall formulate a Gender and Development (GAD) Plan in accordance with the PPGD, and the cost of implementation of the GAD Plan shall be at least five per cent of the agency's total annual budget appropriations. They are required to submit annual reports to Congress, the Department of Budget and Management and the NCRFW.[4]

2. EARLY EFFORTS TOWARDS A GENDER-RESPONSIVE PHILIPPINE JUDICIARY

The judiciary in the Philippines has been under the influence of the judicial systems of Spain and the United States due to its history of colonisation by both

[2] See: hdrstats.undp.org/en/indicators/279.html. Norway ranks at the top, followed by Sweden and Finland. Japan ranks 54th, although it ranks eighth in the Human Development Index.

[3] It was reorganised with expanded mission and mandate in 2009 and renamed the Philippine Commission on Women.

[4] General Appropriations Act 1995 (Republic Act No 7845) and General Appropriations Act 2000 (Republic Act No 8760).

countries. The Philippine judiciary consists of four levels: (1) Metropolitan Trial Courts, Municipal Trial Courts in cities, Municipal Trial Courts, Municipal Circuit Trial Courts and Shari'a Circuit Courts; (2) Regional Trial Courts and Shari'a District Courts; (3) the Court of Appeals; and (4) the Supreme Court. Shari'a Courts apply the Muslim Code on Personal Laws to deal with family disputes and contractual conflicts within the Muslim population in southern states such as Mindanao.[5] The Supreme Court is composed of a Chief Justice and 14 Associate Justices. The members of the Supreme Court and judges of the lower courts shall be appointed by the President from a list of at least three nominees prepared by the Judicial and Bar Council that is created under the supervision of the Supreme Court.[6] All in all there are 2287 judicial positions in all these courts throughout the country (UNIFEM, 2009: 19). There is no jury system in the Philippines.

Initiatives towards a gender-sensitive judiciary did not proceed with the equivalent amount of enthusiasm compared with other government agencies such as those in charge of employment or social welfare. As is noted candidly by Justice Austria-Martinez, 'gender was never seen as a significant factor affecting the function of the judiciary'.[7] In 1975, there was a study on discrimination in the Philippine legislation initiated by Irene R Cortes who served at the CEDAW (Convention on the Elimination of All Forms of Discrimination Against Women) Committee as a member from 1982 to 1986, and was later appointed Associate Justice of the Supreme Court of the Philippines. The study analysed laws from three perspectives, namely language, implementation and impact on differential treatment between women and men. Myrna Feliciano of the University of the Philippines Law School recalls this study as the beginning of interventions towards a gender sensitive judiciary. They had, however, to wait some time before such initiatives resulted in gender-responsive legislation.

Even though the coherent efforts towards a gender-responsive judiciary finally gained momentum only after the turn of the century, the 1990s saw substantial progress in terms of legislation, which addresses gender specific issues and concerns. Such legislation includes the Anti-Sexual Harassment Act 1995 (Republic Act No 7877), the Anti-Rape Law 1997 (Republic Act No 8353) and the Rape Victims' Assistance and Protection Act 1998 (Republic Act No 8505). Prior to this legislation, the Women in

[5] See: sc.judiciary.gov.ph/PhilJud.swf.

[6] The Judicial and Bar Council is composed of the Chief Justice as ex officio chairperson, the Secretary of Justice, a representative of Congress, a representative of the Integrated Bar of the Philippines, a professor of law, a retired member of the Supreme Court and a representative of the private sector (1987 Constitution of the Republic of the Philippines, Art 8, s 8). The Integrated Bar of the Philippines is the official national organisation of lawyers.

[7] See: apjr.judiciary.gov.ph/news_2007/archive_featurearticle002.html.

Development and Nation Building Act 1992 (Republic Act No 7192) was also promulgated, which mandates all government departments and agencies to review and revise all regulations and procedures to remove gender bias and to ensure that women benefit equally from and participate directly in development programmes and projects. (Guanzon et al, 2006a: 57) Though the term 'mainstreaming' was not yet used, this law was a manifestation of the government's intention to mainstream gender in its policies, which was one of the earliest legislative initiatives of this kind in Asia.

3. PROGRAMME OF ACTION TO MAINSTREAM GENDER IN THE JUDICIARY AND COMMITTEE ON GENDER RESPONSIVENESS IN THE JUDICIARY (CGRJ)

The enactment of the above-mentioned legislation did indeed represent progress, but 'gender bias continues to affect the government's delivery of basic services and gender inequality persists in employment and income rates, decision-making and leadership, as well as in quality health and medical care'[8] and 'a very serious gap in efforts of the government to promote the welfare and status of Filipino women and children, particularly those who belong to the poorest of the poor, is in the eradication of gender bias in the court system'.[9] Based on this understanding, a study was conducted jointly by the Law Centre and the Centre for Women's Studies of the University of the Philippines and was compiled in a book, in 2002, entitled *Gender Sensitivity in the Court System*. In the foreword to this book, Hirario G Davide, Chief Justice of the Supreme Court of the Philippines, gave his strong support to the study. He wrote:

> For the Judiciary, the study can be a painful look in the mirror, but it is nonetheless necessary. Here we have a tool which can guide the Supreme Court in fashioning more effective means of eliminating gender bias in the courts. The ultimate objective is a Judiciary that delivers fair justice and which is perceived to be able to do so.[10]

The findings and recommendations of the study contributed to the formulation of the Programme of Action to Mainstream Gender in the Judiciary, which was approved by the Supreme Court in 2003.[11] The programme constitutes a part of the comprehensive reform package of the Philippine

[8] Carolyn Sobritchea, quoted in Feliciano et al (2002: 4).
[9] Ibid.
[10] Ibid, viii.
[11] Supreme Court Administrative Circular No 22-2003, 27 March 2003.

judiciary, which was spearheaded by Chief Justice Davide and promulgated in the Action Program for Judicial Reform (APJR).[12]

Specific actions of the Programme of Action to Mainstream Gender in the Judiciary are:

— the formation of a Committee on Gender Responsiveness in the Judiciary (CGRJ);
— a Gender and Development orientation for the members of the CGRJ;
— a gender assessment workshop of the Action Program for Judicial Reform (APJR);
— a Gender and Development Plan formulation workshop; and
— the formulation of a comprehensive Gender and Development Plan for the judiciary by the CGRJ (Guanzon et al, 2006a: 57).

It has to be noted that the Programme of Action to Mainstream Gender in the Judiciary was instituted through the strong commitment of Chief Justice Davide but was, at the same time, a measure to comply with the already enacted General Appropriations Act mentioned earlier. The Supreme Court had not achieved the required allocation of five per cent of the annual budget to gender programmes by that time, which indicated its inability and inertia to substantively implement gender responsive initiatives.

The most important initiative under the Programme of Action to Mainstream Gender in the Judiciary was the establishment of the CGRJ, which is attended by the heads of all departments of the Supreme Court. The CGRJ consists of nine members and is co-chaired by two Associate Justices, which demonstrates a firm institutional support to the Committee from the Supreme Court.

The main tasks of the CGRJ were the formulation of a comprehensive Gender and Development Plan and a review of the gender responsiveness of the APJR, the programme for judicial reform of the Philippines. In formulating the Gender and Development Plan, several workshops were held so that major issues and concerns became clear. This process itself served as an assessment of progress and challenges in terms of gender responsiveness in the judiciary. For example, among the six components of the APJR, only the component of 'Access to Justice by the Poor' explicitly mentioned gender equality (Guanzon et al, 2006a: 60).[13] It was in a way itself a sort of training, and also an opportunity to acknowledge progress achieved.

[12] The APJR has been implemented by six components, namely Judicial Systems and Procedures, Institutional Development Reforms, Human Resource Development, Reform Support Systems, Institutional Integrity Development and Access to Justice by the Poor: apjr.judiciary.gov.ph/apjr_about.html.

[13] The other components are: judicial systems and procedures, institutional development reforms, human resource development, the reform support systems and institutional integrity development.

Table 1: Justices in Judiciary as of 31 December 2004

Court	Male	%	Female	%	Total
Supreme Court	10	66.7	5	33.3	15
Court of Appeals	49	72.1	19	27.9	68
Court of Tax Appeals	4	66.7	2	33.3	6
Regional Trial Court					
National Capital region	110	58.8	77	41.2	187
1st–12th regions	473	80.6	114	19.4	587
Metropolitan Trial Court	34	47.9	37	52.1	71
Municipal Trial Court in cities	110	73.3	40	26.7	150
Municipal Trial Court	155	68.9	70	31.1	225
Municipal Circuit Trial Court	163	72.1	63	27.9	226
Total	1119	72.2	430	27.8	1549

Source: Supreme Court Statistical Reports Division 2005 (quoted in Guanzon et al, 2006a: 62)

Table 1 illustrates the female ratio among justices in the Philippine judiciary. At the end of 2004, women comprised 27.8 per cent of all judges.

In one of the workshops conducted by the CGRJ for formulation of the Gender and Development Plan, the 'inclusion of gender courses and integration of gender sensitivity into non-gender related courses in the Mandatory Continuing Legal Education (MCLE)' was identified to be included in the plan, together with the 'development of gender sensitive court rules and policies' and a 'fast track of the implementation of gender-responsive court rules and policies' (Guanzon et al, 2006a: 61).

Out of these workshops, the 'Strategic Gender and Development Mainstreaming Plan for the Philippine Judicial System' was formulated and finally adopted in December 2003. Its vision was stated as follows: 'A judicial system that is sensitive and responsive to gender equality and empowerment in all its policies, programs, and activities, thereby providing effective, efficient, and accessible justice to all' (Guanzon et al, 2006a: 62). Following this, core strategies were put in place to achieve the vision, and for each core strategy a sub-committee was established. The core strategies were identified as follows:

- To transform the paradigm and enhance the commitment of the judicial system to gender equality through training and capability-building.
- To review or conduct a gender audit of policies, programmes and practices to make these more gender-responsive.

— To establish a gender-responsive database on the judicial system.
— To promote the use of gender-fair language, core gender messages and rituals for higher gender awareness.
— To enhance partnership and networking with other gender and development advocates.
— To organise regular family courts throughout the country.
— To create a Committee on Decorum and Investigation (CODI) in each court station and train CODI members (Guanzon et al, 2006a: 63).

As such, gender training is listed as the first strategy in the Strategic Gender and Development Mainstreaming Plan for the Philippine Judicial System. It has been, at the same time, identified in publications on gender sensitivity in the judiciary as the first priority to make the judiciary gender sensitive.[14] It is in line with this recognition that several initiatives on gender training have been undertaken so far.

4. GENDER TRAINING FOR THE JUDICIARY

There are principally two courses at the moment which offer gender training to members of the judiciary: (1) gender curricula of Mandatory Continuing Legal Education (MCLE); and (2) training on Gender Sensitivity and CEDAW conducted by the Philippine Judicial Academy (PHILJA) of the Supreme Court.

4.1. Gender Curricula of Mandatory Continuing Legal Education (MCLE)

Mandatory Continuing Legal Education (MCLE) is a recurrent training course that was promulgated by Bar Matter No 850 in 2000 and was started in 2001. MCLE is managed by the Supreme Court through the Philippine Judicial Academy (PHILJA). PHILJA, established by the Supreme Court in 1996, is a 'training school for justices, judges, court personnel, lawyers and aspirants to judicial posts'.[15]

The purpose of MCLE is to ensure that throughout their careers, lawyers keep abreast with law and jurisprudence, maintain the ethics of the profession and enhance the standards of the practice of law.[16] Every three years, all lawyers are required to complete at least 36 hours of continuing legal

[14] Those include Feliciano et al (2005: 164) and Guanzon et al (2006b: 70).
[15] See: philja.judiciary.gov.ph/about_us_academy.htm.
[16] Rule 1, Bar Matter No 850—Supreme Court of the Philippines.

education activities approved by the MCLE Committee constituted by the Supreme Court.[17] The curriculum of the course requires the following:[18]

— at least six hours shall be devoted to legal ethics;
— at least four hours shall be devoted to trial and pre-trial skills;
— at least five hours shall be devoted to alternative dispute resolution;
— at least nine hours shall be devoted to updates on substantive and procedural laws and jurisprudence;
— at least four hours shall be devoted to legal writing and oral advocacy;
— at least two hours shall be devoted to international law and international conventions; and
— the remaining six hours shall be devoted to such subjects as may be prescribed by the MCLE Committee.

Though optional, gender is included as a subject prescribed by the MCLE Committee and three units (equivalent to three hours) are credited. MCLE courses are conducted by law schools and private institutions authorised by the Board of MCLE[19] and each institution is required to submit a curriculum to get approved as a provider of MCLE.

4.2. 'Seminar-Workshop on CEDAW, Gender Sensitivity and the Courts' conducted by the Philippine Judicial Academy (PHILJA) of the Supreme Court

Training on Gender Sensitivity and CEDAW has been conducted by the PHILJA of the Supreme Court in collaboration with the Ateneo Human Rights Center (AHRC) of Ateneo de Manila University. It started as part of a project funded by the United Nations Development Fund for Women (UNIFEM) and the Canadian International Cooperation Agency (CIDA). Between October 2006 and January 2009, 15 courses were conducted at the Supreme Court attended by a total of 525 participants.[20]

As training was being developed, there was a discussion whether gender-related issues should be integrated into regular training sessions or be conducted as a stand-alone module (UNIFEM, 2009: 24). PHILJA already

[17] Rule 2, Bar Matter No 850—Supreme Court of the Philippines.

[18] Ibid.

[19] The Board of MCLE consists of representatives from the Supreme Court, PHILJA, the University of the Philippines Law School Law School Association and the Integrated Bar of the Philippines.

[20] Seminar Workshops on CEDAW and Gender Sensitivity, handout from Arianne Olegario-Galope, the Supreme Court of the Philippines (5 January 2009).

ran many training courses, and the staff of AHRC who were in charge of designing the Training on Gender Sensitivity and CEDAW was not confident that stand-alone training on gender would attract participants. Purificacion V Quisumbing, chairperson of the Commission on the Human Rights of the Philippines and also of the Sub-Committee on Training and Capacity Building of the CGRJ, played a central role in the decision to hold it as a separate course (UNIFEM, 2009: 24). It was proposed and approved as a stand-alone module by the CGRJ and PHILJA.

'The Seminar-Workshop on CEDAW, Gender Sensitivity and the Courts' is comprised of four major units, namely: (1) gender sensitivity training; (2) gender-fair languages; (3) CEDAW and the courts; and (4) case studies which are offered as a two-day course in workshop style led by (normally) five resource persons and five facilitators and attended by approximately 45 participants. Compiling the methodology, resources and handouts, a manual entitled the 'Training Manual on Gender Sensitivity and CEDAW' was published in 2007.

Of those interviewed, the role of NGOs and leadership at the top, were identified as factors which led to the implementation of these two gender training courses. In the Philippines, NGOs and Civil Society Organisations (CSOs) have been playing an important role in society since the time of the oppressive government of the 1970s. They were among the main actors, together with the Catholic Church, in opposing human rights violations under martial law and in throwing out the Marcos regime in 1986. Because of their significant contribution to restoring justice and realising human rights, they became acknowledged as partners of the judicial branch. After the re-establishment of democracy in the country through the so-called 'People Power Revolution', the focus of the NGOs and CSOs that worked for the restoration of justice has been widened to include issues and concerns of former marginalised social questions such as gender. The role of leadership, through Chief Justice Hilario G Davide, was also quite instrumental in formulating the CGRJ and subsequently introducing training on gender sensitivity.

Delivery of the courses needs to take into account several practical issues especially in relation to the characteristics of the target group. Since the judiciary is one of the most respected professions in the country, they have a tendency not to welcome speakers from non-judicial backgrounds. In order to overcome this problem, course organisers try to invite prestigious speakers from the judiciary to encourage participants to achieve a positive attitude toward the course. Context-based and experience-oriented structures and contents are needed so that the messages are articulately and persuasively delivered to the audience. Learning through dialogue and discussion that focuses on specific cases has proved effective. For example, participants are exposed to the court hearing of an incest case, with questions like 'What did you wear? A pair of pyjamas or a night gown?'. Dealing with such practical cases makes it easier for participants to understand gender bias in the judicial system. Documentation of the training, 'Going CEDAW in the Philippines' states:

> The AHRC professors agreed that their strategy in making the seminar-workshop very interactive and including 'very personal issues' such as relationships among husband and wife, father and daughter, and employee–employer resulted in lively and fun sessions (UNIFEM, 2009: 34).

Even then, participants sometimes express resistance and/or opposition towards messages from the training. Those interviewed commented that it is important not to condemn their conventional attitudes and biases and that the workshop style—which encourages reflective learning deliberately avoiding judgmental evaluations—had proved effective.

With regard to substantive results and the impact of the gender training, systematic evaluation has not yet been conducted; this is on the agenda for the future. Those interviewed commented that the impact of the gender training will show in court decisions and sentences which reflect gender-sensitivity and in responsiveness in the behaviour towards handling cases, for example, in how enquiries and investigations are conducted, including the use of gender-fair language.

Though slow and as yet without systematic evaluation, progress has already been recognised. For example, Carolyn Sobritchea of the University of the Philippines mentioned that in cases of rape, domestic violence and child abuse, the jurisdiction has become faster and the process is more gender-conscious than before. Confidentiality of information in cases of sexual violence started to be taken into account and names of victims are no longer mentioned in court decisions. Guidelines of the CGRJ reflect gender responsiveness, and laws on domestic violence and anti-trafficking have been passed. Through these efforts, decisions have increasingly shown improvement in gender consciousness.

5. GENDER JUSTICE AWARD

Building on the above-mentioned progress and to further strengthen the efforts towards a gender-sensitive judiciary, a 'Gender Justice Award' was introduced in 2004.

Organised by the Center for Women's Studies at the University of the Philippines with the collaboration of the National Commission on the Role of Filipino Women (NCRFW), the National Gender Equality Machinery of the Philippines and the United Nations Development Fund for Women (UNIFEM), the Gender Justice Award is a strategic initiative to promote gender-fair justice systems through praising judges who have written gender-responsive decisions in cases of violence against women. According to Myrna Feliciano of the University of the Philippines, this award itself is a clear reflection of positive results from various efforts towards a gender-sensitive judiciary. The award has also been recognised as an incentive to promote affirmative action in cases of gender-based inequality (Guanzon et al, 2006b: 6). The specific objectives of the award are identified as follows:

— to help raise the quality of court decisions on Violence Against Women;
— to inform the judges of the state obligations under the CEDAW;
— to inspire trial judges to be gender sensitive in the way they conduct hearings and make decisions on Violence Against Women cases; and
— to raise the level of expectation of the public for a gender-fair justice system (Guanzon, nd: 2).

The organisers wrote to a total of 1562 judges[21] to request nominations of possible awardees. The letters were also sent to public officials as well as to NGOs and parish priests throughout the country and 56 nominations were submitted. According to the qualification criteria set by the organisers, nominees should be judges who are either incumbent or retired judges of trial courts, including Shari'a courts; those who have not rendered a decision that clearly violated the rights of women; and those do not have either a pending or a prior conviction in an administrative case involving violence against women, such as sexual harassment (Guanzon et al, 2006b: 7).

A review team—which was composed of lawyers and the board of judges—led the process. The criteria for the selection of awardees are that:

— their decisions show gender sensitivity and a keen understanding of VAW;
— they address the issue of discrimination against women; and
— they have not shown insensitivity to women litigants in the conduct of trials in any of the cases heard in their court (Guanzon et al, 2006b: 6).

Out of the 56 nominees, the review team selected 20 finalists, eight women and 12 men. The board of judges then chose nine awardees, two women and seven men. The most outstanding award was given to Judge Ma Nimfa Penaco-Sitaca of the Regional Trial Court (Family Court) of Oroquieta City Branch 13. Other awardees included a judge who rendered the first sentence

[21] Myrna Feliciano, 'Crafting Advocacy for Gender-related Issues', lecture for the MCLE Programme, New Jersey, October 2008 (unpublished) 70.

for a marital rape under Republic Act No 8353 (Anti-Rape Law 1997); a prominent businessman; and a judge of a Shari'a Court who protected the rights of Muslim women and children (Guanzon et al, 2006b: 9).

This was an initiative that strongly promoted awareness of gender-based violence and the role of the judiciary for its redress. It is remarkable that the Supreme Court joined and firmly supported this initiative through the commitment of Chief Justice Hilario G Davide.

6. CONCLUSION: FURTHER CHALLENGES

The creation of the Committee on Gender Responsiveness in the Judiciary (CGRJ) chaired by two Associate Justices clearly indicates a commitment toward a gender-fair justice in the Philippines. There are training courses on gender for lawyers, judges and court staff. The establishment of the CGRJ and the introduction of gender training are mainly the result of a commitment on the part of the top management, and in the case of the Philippines, of Chief Justice Hilario G Davide, as was repeatedly pointed out by the people interviewed. However, gender classes of Mandatory Continuing Legal Education (MCLE) are elective and their influence is not yet very obvious. Moreover, it is still too early to state that training on gender sensitivity conducted by the Philippine Judicial Academy (PHILJA) of the Supreme Court has become institutionalised.

To achieve the goal of making the judiciary more gender sensitive and responsive, it is important to facilitate a change of attitudes and behaviours in handling cases, such as in the language used and investigations and outcomes of court decisions. Interviewees regarded training as the single most important initiative for this change to take place. In the case of the judiciary, the mode of delivery of training should be carefully and strategically designed.

To improve gender training, it is important to conduct and then act on a systematic evaluation. Evaluation indicators should focus on court decisions, enquiries, language and processes (for example, the protection of confidentiality and privacy).

What then would be the best strategy? Gender bias and stereotypes are strongly associated with the culture of specific times and places, and are deeply embedded in one's unconscious and therefore take a long time to eliminate. Gender training is an important tool for change, but for maximum impact, it needs to be combined with other strategic initiatives, such as the Gender Justice Award. What is then crucial for such measures to be successfully implemented is a genuine commitment on the part of the leadership. The process of change might be slow, as judiciaries are notoriously authoritarian, but it can be achieved if committed leadership and well-designed and strategised programmes are put in place.

7. REFERENCES

Feliciano, M et al (2002) *Gender Sensitivity in the Court System* (Manila, UP Center for Women's Studies).

—— (2005) *Gender Sensitivity in the Family Courts* (Manila, UP Center for Women's Studies).

Guanzon, R (nd) 'The Gender Justice Awards: An Advocacy Strategy for Judicial Reform' (unpublished).

Guanzon, R et al (2006a) *The Davide Court: Its Contributions to Gender and Women's Rights* (Manila, UP Center for Women's Studies).

—— (2006b) *Engendering the Philippine Judiciary* (Manila, UP Center for Women's Studies).

Southeast Asia Women's Watch (SEAWWatch) (2008) *Sex Segregated Data and Gender Indicators: Making the MDGs Work for Asian Women* (Manila, Miriam College-Women and Gender Institute).

UNIFEM (2009) *Going CEDAW in the Philippines* (Bangkok, UNIFEM East and Southeast Asia Regional Office).

7.4

Gender Training for the Judiciary in Cambodia

KEIKO SAWA

Abstract

This chapter outlines gender training for the legal profession in Cambodia. Since the 1990s, new legal and judicial systems have been introduced in Cambodia, with training being assisted by Japan and some other countries. Consideration is given to gender education in the government-provided judicial school and the school for lawyers, and training for judges and prosecutors regarding the anti-domestic violence law, including problems arising in the context of the global trend of exporting judicial training systems from one country to another. A number of gender and judging issues in Cambodia are also briefly discussed.

1. INTRODUCTION

1.1. The Aim of the Collaborative Research

WHILE JAPANESE COURTS are generally believed to enjoy a considerable degree of credibility, they remain unable to render appropriate judicial judgments in newly emerging legal issues associated with gender. The purpose of Minamino's collaborative research was to conduct a comparative examination of how gender issues are addressed in continuing legal education so as to propose a framework for improving the current situation (see Minamino and Miwa in this volume). The questions are: how can an open response to gender and related law become possible in the education and training of the legal profession, especially for judges? If it is not possible, why? And what is significance this? By taking gender as its subject matter—a type of knowledge still prone to be marginalised—the study attempts to understand the legal profession and, ultimately, the role of justice.

This chapter looks at Cambodia, where the fundamental introduction of a new legal and judicial system has been carried out rapidly since the 1990s after its people and society were utterly destroyed by a series of civil wars. One of the countries which offers assistance is Japan. In the following sections, after sketching the reasons why Cambodia was chosen as a subject we describe and assess gender education in Japan's training for the Cambodian judiciary and the government-provided training for judges and prosecutors in the anti-domestic violence law; a brief description of gender and judging issues in Cambodia then follows.[1]

1.2. Why Cambodia?

In our comparative study of some ten countries, the Philippines, South Korea and Cambodia have been chosen as subject countries as recipients of foreign law in Asia and because of their gender index status.

As has been discussed in Minamino's contribution to this volume, Japan—as many other Asian countries—should also be regarded as a recipient of foreign law rather than a conventional civil law or common law country. Cambodia, a French colony for nearly one hundred years, has been categorised as a civil law country. After going through a number of administration and regime changes, including the Pol Pot era, the country currently finds itself with what is called a 'patchwork of laws'. For instance, it has recently received aid and support from Japan in civil law areas and from France in criminal law areas, while adopting common law in the economic sphere. It can thus be seen as a recipient, or 'transplantee', of laws from multiple countries, and this on a regular basis. Both its legal profession system and legal professional training system have only just taken off, with assistance from donor countries in the area of legal system development.

As Cambodian society is traditionally strongly influenced by Theravada Buddhism, its people believe that it is the outcome of virtuous acts accumulated in one's previous life that determines one's character and social standing. This makes social inequalities the norm. In a society where it is considered a virtue for a woman to support her husband patiently and obediently in accordance with a strict 'code of conduct', women are oppressed by the traditional gender-based division of roles as well as male-centred social practices. Given that the gap between rich and poor is expected to widen even further, establishing a fair and stable judicial system, which arguably serves as the foundation of a country's growth, is regarded as a big challenge.

Interestingly, the Philippines—a country with a very different history but also in receipt of foreign aid—presents a very different picture regarding gender-related matters. (See Miwa in this volume and also Minamino's table 1).

[1] This chapter also forms part of the report developed out of interviews conducted in Cambodia in 2008, which itself is part of the international comparison presented in Minamino's chapter in this volume.

Table 1: Extracts from Minamino's Table 1

	GDI 2007	GEM	GGI
Japan	8	54	98
Philippines	90	45	6
Cambodia	131	83	94

GDI = Gender-Related Development Index[2]
GEM = Gender Empowerment Measure[3]
GGI = Gender Gap Index of the World Economic Forum[4]

In GDI, the Philippines ranked 90th, 45th in GEM and sixth in GGI. In the meantime, Cambodia, which is also currently receiving aid from Japan, is ranked 131st in GDI (Japan is ranked eighth) and 83rd in GEM (Japan is ranked 54th), while it outranks Japan in GGI, albeit by a slight margin: Japan is ranked 98th and Cambodia 94th. As far as GGI showings alone are concerned, Japan is part of a low-ranking group consisting of Cambodia, Japan and Korea (ranked 108th). While it may naturally be too extreme to draw a comparison by referring solely to GGI, which attracts a fair deal of criticism, the foremost reason why Cambodia has been chosen as a study subject is the possibility that there may be something in the area of gender, which might possibly help to understand Japan's gender situation.

The second reason for choosing Cambodia is its 'visibility' in the context of international trends. Just as is the case with the legal profession training system in Japan, CLE (Continuing Legal Education) actually lies in the global regime trend and thus has the potential of changing constantly. By contrast with Japan, in Cambodia the transplantation of law and social systems as a whole is the product of the direct influence of its aid sources, including a large number of international organisations, countries, NGOs and other donors. It was expected that international impact that is hard to discern in Japan where social and economic systems, including the judicial system, have a certain degree of robustness, could be seen in a more direct way in Cambodia.

[2] See: hdr.undp.org/en/media/HDR_2009_EN_Table_J.pdf. The components of GDI are: life expectancy at birth (years) 2007; adult literacy rate (% aged 15 and above) 1999–2007; combined gross enrolment ratio in education (%) 2007; estimated earned income (PPP US$) 2007.

[3] See: hdr.undp.org/en/media/HDR_20072008_GEM.pdf. The components are: seats in Parliament held by women; female legislators, senior officials and managers; female professional and technical workers; ratio of estimated female to male earned income.

[4] See: www.weforum.org/en/initiatives/gcp/Gender%20Gap/index.htm. The sub-indexes are: economic participation and opportunity; educational attainment; health and survival sub-index; political empowerment.

In Cambodia, one can see the actual process of how the law, judicial system and legal training system (including gender-related measures) are being transplanted from other countries. It is interesting to note in this context that Japan which is a donor country is rapidly falling in the area of gender as many aid recipients are improving on their gender indicators.

The interviews in Cambodia were conducted by Minamino and me in August 2008, and mostly set up by the Japan International Cooperation Agency (JICA). They involved the Ministry of Justice, the Ministry of Women's Affairs, the Royal School for Judges and Prosecutors, the Centre for Lawyer Training and Professional Improvement of the Kingdom of Cambodia, the Cambodian National Council of Women, Deutsche Gesellschaft für Technische Zusammenarbeit (GTZ, which changed its name into GIZ in 2011), the United Nations Development Fund for Women (UNIFEM) and some NGOs. We are most grateful to all actors for their invaluable assistance.

2. GENDER TRAINING IN CAMBODIA

2.1. Japan's Support for Lawmaking in Cambodia

From 1863, the year Cambodia became a French territory, during its colonial days, throughout its independence from 1953 and up until 1975, the country remained under the strong influence of France in terms of its legal system. However, in the years of the Pol Pot regime between 1975 and 1979, Cambodia's legal system was totally destroyed and people in the legal profession were massacred. In the years which followed, socialist policies were adopted. In 1989, the Constitution was amended and the country began to shift towards the market economy system. In 1993, a Constituent Assembly election was held under the supervision of the United Nations Transitional Authority in Cambodia (UNTAC). Following the subsequent enactment of the Constitution of the Kingdom of Cambodia, work has rapidly been under way to develop the country's political, economic, legal and social systems.

Since the 1990s, various international organisations—with the World Bank being a prominent example—and many countries, have given Cambodia sizeable financial assistance as well as physical and technical support under the banner of good governance promotion, one form of which is legislative support. As lawmaking was also an international aid conditionality, laws were developed in and after 1994 in the areas of investment, lawyers, tax, land and commerce, with support from those organisations and national governments (United States, Canada, Australia, Germany, France, Finland, Denmark, etc). Other laws that concern the field of action of international organisations, including UNICEF, have also been developed, such as the international adoption law, juvenile law and law against human trafficking and sexual exploitation.

Japan, somewhat belatedly, joined in this 'war of legal assistance' (Matsuo, 2009: 39) that had begun in 1990s, and its support activities got into full swing during and after 1999.

This endeavour in legislative assistance was backed by a high degree of expectation and attention in Japan, a country with no experience in legislative transplantation, save for that imposed on the colonies of Imperial Japan, and historically a receiver of law from China, Germany, France and the United States. While Japan is currently giving legislative assistance to Vietnam, Cambodia, Laos, Uzbekistan and China, its support for Cambodia stands out in that it is not confined only to 'lawmaking assistance' but also involves 'judicial system assistance' and support for 'legal profession training', which represent a framework for ensuring smooth law enforcement in real settings. The donor organisation is the Japan International Cooperation Agency (JICA).

First, JICA launched a legal system assistance project for the four-year period from 1999 to 2003, in which the Ministry of Justice of the Kingdom of Cambodia took the counterpart role. The project achieved the drafting of a civil code and civil procedure code and the subsequent submission of both Bills to the Justice Minister in March 2003. In its Phase 2 that began in April 2004, the project dealt with various coordination works and procedures needed in stages following the Bill drafting. The civil procedure code was promulgated and enacted in July 2006 and came into force in 2007. The civil code also became law in December 2007. Phase 2 ended in 2008, and the project is now in its Phase 3 and is scheduled to extend over another four years.

2.2. Overview of Judicial Education Support

The Cambodian Ministry of Justice had previously commissioned the Bar Association of the Kingdom of Cambodia (BAKC) to train the legal profession, but it resolved to educate judges and prosecutors under its own system and founded the Royal School for Judges and Prosecutors (RSJP) in 2002. When the RSJP was founded, the number of judges and prosecutors in Cambodia totalled a little short of 200. These were people with no judicial education who used to be school teachers, etc, but nevertheless had been appointed as judges or prosecutors after being trained briefly by the government, given that virtually everyone in the legal profession had once been eliminated by the Pol Pot regime. Therefore, there was a strong need not only for initial, but for continuing education. Following a structural reform, the RSJP is now run by the Royal Academy for the Judicial Profession (RAJP).

Assistance in criminal code and criminal procedure code education was to be given by France, while Japan was to provide support in civil law areas. Japan's assistance in judicial education began in November 2005 as Phase 1 of the civil law education improvement project; Phase 2 started in 2008 and is to continue until 2012. To serve as specialists on a short or long-term basis, there are always several JICA members, as well as Japanese judges, prosecutors, etc, sent from Japan who work as staff responsible for aid in developing and administering curricula and training instructors on site.

Although Japan and France both work in the same school, they operate totally independently of each other. Other aid donors have also proposed giving special seminars: for example, a land law seminar by the Asian Development Bank and a juvenile law seminar by UNICEF. In the present state, the whole school operation is virtually dependent on donor assistance in every aspect, including curriculum administration and facilities.

In order to be admitted to the RSJP, one has to pass a screening test that consists of written and oral exams. The main exam prerequisites are either both a university law degree and a maximum age of 30, or a graduate school diploma and maximum age of 35. Education stretches over a two-year period. Approximately 60 graduate each year. As the school had its first graduates in 2005, the number of graduates outnumbered all others in the whole body of judges and prosecutors nationwide by 2009. Of the 55 first graduates, six were women. As legal education in universities lacks professional expertise, everything has to be taught from scratch and, therefore, the school's policy is to give a basic legal training only.

The RSJP's continuing education for judges and prosecutors is compulsory, but the school relies on donors to actually offer it. It is given in Phnom Penh and an allowance is paid. Participants receive a certificate, but it carries no real life significance and therefore has no effect on seniority or promotion. In 2007, the course was held for one week with five sessions given per day. Civil law is taught on four days (of which JICA is responsible for a half-day and Cambodia for three and a half days) and the anti-domestic violence law is taught on one day (with Germany serving as the donor). As of August 2008 when we carried out interviews, however, the programme has remained postponed due to the failure to get instructors. Continuing education in criminal law areas is given by France. The Ministry of Justice also independently offers seminars in new legislation.

As for lawyer education, following the establishment of the lawyers act in 1995, lawyer training was once the mandate of the Bar Association of the Kingdom of Cambodia (BAKC) with support from the United States. However, it was discontinued and the Centre for Lawyer Training and Professional Improvement of the Kingdom of Cambodia (LTC) took over in 2002. Admission is determined through screening on an examination basis among applicants with a bachelor of law qualification, and the school runs on a two-year curriculum that includes a one-year internship period in a law firm. As of 2002, the registered lawyer body consisted of approximately 250, approximately 180 of whom were in actual practice. Up until 2007, 50 people graduated every year but the figure dropped to around 35 in 2008.

BAKC has been receiving assistance from the Japan Federation of Bar Associations (JFBA) since 2001. The need for continuing education for lawyers has also been raised as an issue and is on JFBA's project list, but by 2008 no training had been offered. Training is scheduled to be offered in the future, but in civil law areas only.

Both the RSJP and LTC are faced with many issues, such as study material shortages and the lack of personnel responsible for curriculum administration, but the most serious issue is the lack of instructors. For instance, the RSJP does not have even a single full-time instructor. Its current instructors are those who were involved in legislative work and their posts at RSJP are, though important, not their sole position. If Japanese staff directly served as instructors, JICA would have to continue sending instructors. For that reason, the Japanese staff try to limit their actual teaching as much as possible to the training of instructors. While top students have been chosen among the small number of RSJP graduates to be trained as instructors, they all hold another position, making it difficult for the school to secure instructors. Furthermore, it has been pointed out that the societal norm in Cambodia of bowing to seniority makes it difficult for young people to teach those older than they are, even when they do have the knowledge.

2.3. Gender Training for the Judiciary in RSJP and LTC

Although the school curricula of the RSJP do not offer any overarching lectures on gender issues, they do include a lecture on the law on the prevention of domestic violence against women, which was promulgated and enacted in October 2005. As the law came to be established with strong backing from Germany, a German aid agency called Deutsche Gesellschaft für Technische Zusammenarbeit (GTZ) became a donor and is currently in charge. The first graduates had 26 hours of study in 2005; there was no course in 2006 due to the lack of a donor; there was one in 2007; and, as it stands now in 2008, a request for a course has been forwarded to GTZ.

The JFBA established a gender section in its aid project from September 2002 to August 2005, in which BAKC was the counterpart. In May 2005, lawyers from Japan gave a two-day gender seminar to an audience of 152 people consisting of lawyers, graduates and students. In addition to lecturing on gender, they explained sexual harassment and domestic violence cases by showing legal consultation role-plays. They also distributed educational leaflets on gender written in Khmer. Unfortunately, though, it appears that this is not reflected in the current lawyer training exercise: only two or three of the eight students that we interviewed said that they had heard of the word 'gender'.

2.4. Training for Practising Judges and Prosecutors by the Ministry of Women's Affairs

The anti-domestic violence law was passed in 2005 with strong support from GTZ. According to the interviews at the Ministry of Women's Affairs (MWA), it cooperated with the Ministry of Justice and the donors in drafting the Bill and in its enforcement. The MWA also offers anti-domestic violence law training for practising judges and prosecutors, which is a form of continuing education for the judiciary.

Cambodia ratified the International Convention on the Elimination of All Forms of Discrimination against Women (CEDAW) in 1992, enacted the Constitution containing a gender equality clause in 1993, founded the Women's Ministry in 1996 and established the Cambodian National Council for Women, a national agency serving women, in 2000. In 2003, it also submitted first, second and third session reports to CEDAW. Since 1999, the MWA has adopted gender mainstreaming measures as its policy, by which it aims to incorporate a gender perspective in all intra-government policies and development plans and projects.

Multiple countries and agencies, for example, those from Japan and Germany, offer assistance in this regard in various forms. In a GTZ project launched in 2000 that was designed for the MWA to improve its ability to monitor the gender mainstreaming measures, GTZ is working with MWA officials, with those who apply the law such as judges and others in the legal profession and police authorities, and with NGOs, to make it clear that violence against women is not purely a domestic matter but a crime. GTZ has developed a manual in English for trainers engaged in such awareness-raising activities, which appeared to us to be very specific and easy to use (Coren, Maridet, Rasmei and Schmutzler, 2005).

In the meantime, the MWA, with cooperation from GTZ, USAID (United States Agency for International Development), the Canadian International Development Agency, UNIFEM and others, conducted a detailed survey and published a report in 2005 on violence against women in Cambodia. (Ministry of Women's Affairs, 2005). With support from GTZ and CMI (Centre of International Migration and Development), it also published a guide—numbering over 300 pages—on the anti-domestic violence law (Ministry of Women's Affairs, 2007).

According to the interviews, the MWA gives training on domestic violence law to practising judges and prosecutors, to lawyers and members of the police force and in universities. It has sent ten lecturers to the police because the police particularly need training. Post-training results gained by monitoring the courts reveal that the level of understanding is highest among practising judges, followed by lawyers and then prosecutors. Prosecutors, although required to hear relevant cases even in civil courts, often failed to come to hear any domestic violence cases; accordingly, training for prosecutors is currently being stepped up. However, it is likely that, in actual training, the manual developed by GTZ will be used, and the role taken up by GTZ personnel is considerable.

3. THE SIGNIFICANCE AND RANGE OF GENDER TRAINING IN CAMBODIA

3.1. Issues in Gender Training for the Judiciary

Both training practices are wholly dependent on donors. At the RSJP in particular, in the face of serious personnel shortages, the JICA staff stressed the difficulty of developing personnel, ie, main staff members and teachers responsible for curricula development and teaching.

Dependence on donors in training is accompanied by conflict between donors in terms of teaching contents. At the RSJP, each donor proposes a seminar in the area of law that concerns them. However, the JICA staff responsible for aid in curriculum development complained that they could not accept every proposal because a considerable amount of time would have to be spent by the professor specialising in basic civil law which had been newly enacted.

In the meantime, general dependence on donors has another more positive outcome: a certain level of quality has been secured in support activities associated with gender. This can be seen, for example, from, the high quality of GTZ's training manual. All donor representatives were in agreement regarding the need to raise competence on the Cambodian side.

3.2. Gender Training for the Judiciary in the Cambodian Context

A study on the significance and range of gender training for the judiciary in a number of countries has shown up a variety of issues. For example: in Australia, diminution of gender courses in CLE accompanied by focusing on CLE; in Japan, internal control of courts as an objective of continuing education; and in France, ways of introducing gender considerations into legal ones. Whether a common law country or a civil law country, most of the subject countries of our research were undergoing their own judicial reforms, during the period of which the phrase 'increasing the citizen's trust in the judiciary' was frequently repeated. According to Minamino, this discourse often

> appears itself as one so useful for the judiciary to minimize the intervention of the administrative or political branch into it and to enhance its independence. As a mean to gain trust, the fulfilment of CLE for the judiciary is proposed from within the judiciary itself, CLE being incorporated into the reforms (2010: 7).

Under this circumstance and for this purpose, the study materials of CLE must include, for example, courses that aim in helping to increase judges' ability to understand 'social contexts', one of which is 'the variety of society', and sometimes courses that help to cultivate the humanity of judges. In contrast to this overall picture in other countries, we see a context totally different in Cambodia.

First, in Cambodia, CLE for the judiciary is in much more real and urgent need because new laws are being enacted one after another including basic laws. Moreover, some practising judges lack basic judicial training. The need for CLE is enormous, but this chapter has shown the difficulties involved in providing practising judges with additional training.

Secondly, judicial independence being weak in Cambodia and interventions of the administrative and/or the political branch in the judiciary being the norm, the need for an enhancement of the independence of the judiciary in general and of individual judges goes without saying. Whether it concerns Japan or any other international agency or national government, current support for Cambodia is given on the premise of establishing good governance and the 'rule of law'. It is of course true that the concept itself is not easily defined. Also, in the international aid context, it is often associated with the World Bank's use of the rule of law for promoting the common law system and institutionalising American ways of rule of law at the expense of a country's internal situation and of co-ordination with other laws imported especially from civil law countries.[5] Nevertheless, there remains the core meaning that it is the law and not individuals' discretion that should determine the way a country is ruled, and the rule of law in this sense is strongly needed.

Thirdly, as for citizen's trust, some literature shows that in present-day Cambodia people have little trust in the judicial system and therefore sometimes seek to resolve a problem out of court. Stories of corruption among civil servants, the police, teachers and even judges, abound. A corrupt judge would act as a middleman himself and end a dispute out of court for a small sum of money. An attempt was made to fight such corruption by raising judges' salaries, which were said to be 40 dollars a month,

[5] As for the World Bank Model, see Upham (2006).

but there seems to have been no tangible effect. Moreover, under certain circumstances, availability of lawyers or recourse to law might be present unevenly, potentially creating even further inequality in terms of access to law. In fact, a survey conducted by the JFBA in 2002 found that 90 per cent of the Cambodian people do not have sufficient financial means to hire a lawyer (Japan Federation of Bar Associations, 2002)

Considering the fact that judicial education is offered amid the risk of a diminished judicial system, any discussion about such education in Cambodia, unlike other countries surveyed, requires a constant reminder of the issue of the 'rule of law' and 'access to law'. These are ultimately issues that can be addressed successfully not by any donor, but only by a concerted effort on the part of the recipient country. A big challenge is to steadily strengthen civil society, while maintaining a clear idea of where the limits lie at a given time.[6]

Given this situation in Cambodia, the significance and range of training for the judiciary can not easily be exaggerated. Yet, as violence—including not only domestic violence but also rape and human trafficking—is rampant especially against women and that there are many people whose human rights could be given minimal protection only by the existence of gender law, it goes without saying that a need to give real teeth to such laws as the domestic violence law and the law prohibiting human trafficking is urgent, as is a need for CLE on these laws.

3.3. The Acceptance of Gender Law in Cambodia

Another important point in considering the significance and range of gender training in Cambodia is to understand the acceptance of gender law in Cambodia. Generally speaking, laws of donor countries that comply with international standards on gender have been introduced to Cambodia. However, the specific contents of the civil code, anti-domestic violence law, etc, still need to be examined.

A number of theoretical issues are likely to emerge with the progress of gender law transplantation.[7]

First, modern law itself can work to further the structure of sexual discrimination. Sometimes this takes the form of exclusion or discrimination historically embedded in liberal modern law concepts of human rights and citizenry or the idea of family. At other times, it lurks behind the neutrality of law, as when it is imbedded in the very classification of law, such as

[6] There are donor countries that target their aid specifically at stronger rule of law and civil society development and, for that purpose, mainly give aid to NGOs.

[7] As for the issues of gender studies in Japan from the point of view of Asia, they have been summarised by Kamio (2006).

classification of public law and private law. Transplanting Japanese law or Western law can mean increasing the possibility of transplanting such a structure of sexual discrimination as well.

Secondly, there is a problem of possibly transplanting an outdated system, a problem that is particularly acute with regard to Japan.

Thirdly, there is a risk of creating a legal patchwork, Cambodia being an obvious case in point. This is a result of conflict among donors and is sometimes unavoidable in aid settings. However, since internationally shared norms are dominant in the gender field, the problem of donor friction at the legal level in this context seems less likely.

The fourth issue is that gender-related laws will, unlike economic laws, entail considerable changes in traditional power structures, especially those close to home and in societies where the power and the positions of women are traditionally limited. It is worth remembering that gender law at the international level and gender law that, for example, Japan is in the process of accepting now, both contain ideas and propensities that are strongly Western in character.

The fifth issue is whether the gender law to be transplanted fits actual circumstances in Cambodia. This can of course be said about transplantation of laws overall.

Finally, as explained above, there are many people in Cambodia whose human rights could be given minimal protection only by the existence of gender law. The international community must address this in a concerted fashion, and the most effective form of support in that context should quickly be sought by way of international cooperation. Movements towards such actions do in fact appear to exist.

In introducing such gender-promoting law, one must reflect on the need to form a gender-conscious self that can at times withstand a clash with local traditional culture in order to secure its effectiveness in a substantive sense. In order for someone to feel victimised in the gender context, the awareness of realising that what has been done is victimisation (rather than some inevitable consequence due to one's gender) must be introduced, which is a point before the claiming stage; it is hence necessary to have a perspective before steps can be taken to institutionalise such an awareness. More specifically, this involves forming a sense of rights entitlement and claiming rights from a micro and local level upwards, starting from recognising rights of individuals, then claiming rights in daily life in relation to families and relatives and claiming rights in more formalised settings of a community or local politics, as well as any human rights protection claim system that enables the above (*cf* Merry, 2006; chapter six).

According to fieldwork conducted in India, women who live in a conventional, traditional culture become more confident as a result of repeated experience of success in claiming their rights (Hashimoto and Miwa, 2007).

This has been taken on board by the GTZ gender training manual as well as by some Japanese NGOs working in rural parts of Cambodia.

4. CONCLUSION

Gender training for the judiciary reaches a point at which the role of a judicial system and the acceptance of gender concepts converge. In the case of Cambodia, in contrast to other countries surveyed, the judicial system itself is still in its early formation stages, and as evident in rampant cases of corruption stemming from the country's historical development, social customs and traditions have retained an overwhelming influence on the administration of justice. Yet, according to informants such as JICA, GTZ and UNIFEM, various laws on gender that follow international standards seem to have been infused, on the whole, into Cambodia in their original form. For how long such developments will endure, whether they will be internalised by society, what roles civil law and other newly-enacted laws will play in them, are questions that remain to be answered.

As the assistance for legal system and legal profession training has been taking up a significant place in the aid setting since the 1990s under the banner of the rule of law, CLE (Continuing Legal Education), which is rapidly gaining weight most notably in common law countries, can be expected to develop into an international movement. In fact, in common law countries there are experts and consultants specialising in the area of legal professional training in developing countries. We should begin to appreciate the legal assistance of Japan in a picture of this worldwide trend of assistance because experts from these countries begin to exchange their expertise with a view to giving better training in assistance, which may produce a sort of world standard. However, in these newly-institutionalised systems of CLE, the theme of 'gender' is likely to have already been partly absorbed under the general heading of 'social contexts', as has already happened in some countries researched in our comparative study.

Cambodia is, today, faced with a strong need to create a fair legal and political system and, at the same time, to strengthen its civil society. The way ahead is, however, long and arduous. Gender training for the judiciary is just one thing among others which will help in this process.

5. REFERENCES

Aikyo, M (ed) (2009) *The Handbook of Asian Legal Systems* (The University of Nagoya Press).

Coren, M, Maridet, M, Rasmei, R and Schmutzler, C (2005) *Domestic Violence, A Training Manual to Raise Awareness* (Phnom Penn, GTZ).

Hashimoto, H and Miwa, A (2007) 'The Development of a Rights-based Approach and Empowerment of Women in Asia', *Kitakyushu Forum on Asian Women.*
Minamino, K (2010) 'Role of Judiciary and the Significance of Continuing Legal Education in Judicial System in Gender and Legal System': Report on International Comparative Research on the Process of Developing, Performing, Systematizing Continuing Legal Education Programmes Concerning Gender Issues.
Issues of Legal Assistance (2010) 82(1) *Horitsu- Jiho.*
Japan Federation of Bar Associations (2002) report 'For the Continuing Development of Legal Aid in the Kingdom of Cambodia' 5 *ICD News* 31.
—— (2006) *Final Report on Bar Association of the Kingdom of Cambodia Judiciary Aid Project.*
Kamio, M (2006) 'Gender Studies and Asia' in Yasuda N and Kochu N, (eds) *New Frontier of Asian Law Study* (Tokyo, Seibundoh Publishing).
Matsuo, H (2009) *Good Governance and the Rule of Law: A Challenge of Law and Development* (Nippon-hyoron-sya).
Merry, SE (2006) *Human Rights and Gender Violence: Translating International Law into Local Justice* (Chicago, University of Chicago Press).
Ministry of Women's Affairs (2005) *Violence Against Women: A Baseline Survey* (Cambodia, Ministry of Women's Affairs).
—— (2007) *Explanatory Notes on the Law on the Prevention of Domestic Violence and the Protection of the Victims* (Cambodia, Ministry of Women's Affairs).
Sakano, I (2005) 'Current Situation and Problems Regarding the "Rule of Law" in Cambodia: From the Experience of Legal Technical Assistance' *Asia-Pacific Human Rights Review.*
Upham, F (2006) 'Mythmaking in the Rule-of-Law Orthodoxy' in Carothers T (ed), *Promoting the Rule of Law Abroad* (Washington DC, Carnegie Endowment For International Peace).
Yasuda, N (2000) *An Introduction to Southeast-Asian Law* (Nippon-hyoron-sya).
Yotsumoto, K (2007) 'Women's Rights in Cambodia-Focusing on Domestic Violence Prevention Law' *Asian Minorities and Law II.*
Legal Assistance in Asia and the Role of Japan (2008) *Jurist* 1358.
www.jica.go.jp/project/cambodia/0701047/01/index.html

7.5

Do German Judges Need Gender Education?

ULRIKE SCHULTZ

Abstract

This chapter poses two questions: Why are gender education and training so unpopular in Germany and why is the judiciary so reluctant to tackle the issue? German society at large lacks sensitivity to gender problems and even tends to deny their existence. They hardly play more than a marginal role in university law curricula. And yet, as is shown by reference to historical as well as topical examples, gender does matter in judicial decision-making. Although judges in civil law countries have less room for discretion than their counterparts in the common law world, they nevertheless are engaged in the interpretation of legal terms and in the application of rules. Therefore, the need for gender training and education is not limited to underdeveloped and developing countries, but is of integral relevance to the teaching of law wherever it occurs.

1. INTRODUCTION

GERMANY HAS VERY comprehensive equal opportunities legislation, gender mainstreaming is a recognised and legally binding principle for the public sector, there are equal opportunities officers and women's advancement plans and gender concepts throughout public institutions. But in the judiciary there is little gender awareness and almost no gender education. Judges tend to ignore the need for any such thing.

The chapter asks why this is so and how much is actually needed. This has to be seen and evaluated in the context of the legal system in Germany. After an overview over judgments with gender bias, mainly historical ones, the effects of feminisation in the judiciary are discussed, and the changes in law, which have taken place in the past 60 years to adapt the regulations to the gender equality principle of the Constitution are summed up. I describe the way gender is dealt with in legal publications, what is offered as gender contents in legal education and what is done in terms of gender education for the judiciary. In my conclusion I provide an outline of what may be lacking.

2. THE LEGAL SYSTEM IN GERMANY

Due to the model of *Einheitsjurist*, as described in my other chapter in this book, Germany has a judge-centred legal culture. Germany is also said to have the highest ratio of judges per head of the population. In 2009—for an overall population of 82.3 million—there were 20,101 judges, 5122 prosecutors and 150,377 practising lawyers. At the beginning of the twentieth century there were as many judges as lawyers—just under 10,000—for 64 million inhabitants, still 30 years ago there were just twice as many lawyers as judges. The enormous increase in lawyers in the past 30 years has changed these proportions. Now there are almost eight times as many lawyers as judges, whereas the number of judges per head of the population has kept remarkably stable over the past 130 years (Schultz, 2005).

Germany is a civil law country. In the course of the nineteenth century with the emergence of the nation state the big codes were created: the Commercial Code, the Criminal Code and on 1 January 1900, the Civil Code. There are Codes for procedural law and finally in the 1980s and 1990s the different books of the Social Code came into existence. In all fields of law the legislator still today tries to find systematic solutions.

Young lawyers are trained in the application of statutory law. One reason why judges do not see a necessity to be trained in gender questions is that judges think of themselves as technicians of the law. Judges do not understand their role as mouthpiece or interpreter of the law as common law judges do, although the application of statutory regulations is less literal than in common law countries with their interpretation acts. Judgments are passed 'in the name of the people'. The personality of the judge is hidden behind the institution. When judgments are published in the legal journals or in case collections, they are marked as judgments of, for example, the local court of Cologne, regional court of Munich, appeal court of Hamm.[1] Even the judgments of the federal courts do not give the names of the judges. Therefore it is not apparent whether women or men have passed the judgment. The only exceptions are decisions by the Federal Constitutional Court, which interprets the Constitution. Here the two chambers sit with eight judges each, and the published reasoning is signed by the judges who may also give dissenting or concurring votes.

[1] Of course the original judgments as documents are signed by the individual judges. Germany has at all court levels a culture of detailed written judgments: this comprises the description of the facts ascertained by the judge and the reasoning. Many judgments also from lower courts are published and critically discussed in legal publications.

Of course in Germany judges have a space for discretion and interpretation, and courts are not bound by precedents. It even happens that different senates of an appeal court or of a federal court decide differently on the same question of law. A joint senate of the federal courts can be asked to create uniformity of law. If the interpretation of the Constitution is involved the cases can be referred to the Federal Constitutional Court.

The rules are applied in a process called 'subsumtion' comparing the established facts to the rule. The interpretation of the rules takes into account the motives of the lawmaker (historical interpretation) and spirit and purpose of the law (teleological interpretation). Legal terms may be 'indeterminate' and therefore open to scope for interpretation.

3. GENDER BIAS IN JUDGING

There can be no doubt that there is, in fact, gender bias in some judgments, but it is not easy to find overt gender bias. Gender stereotypes and gendered life experiences can easily have a bearing on the outcome of a case. In family law, the notion of gender roles is important, for example, to decisions on alimony and custody. In criminal law, the personality of the accused has to be evaluated in the verdict. In labour law, models of male and female competencies may define the working capacities. As will be shown—in the following salient examples—even in administrative, social and tax law gender issues can play a role.

In the 1950s the 'old men' at our highest federal court applied a backward family picture (Schultz, 2003a). One of the worst cases dealt with a widow who had allowed her daughter's fiancé to share the room with his highly pregnant wife a couple of days before the wedding and who got a verdict for serious procuration, a crime with a minimum of one year imprisonment (BGHSt 6, 46 ff). The judges argued that the moral law demands that sex is performed only in marriage as its purpose and consequence is procreation and the dignity of both the child and the two partners in marriage as well as their responsibility follow from it. In opinions for a decision on parental rights the husband was proclaimed as head of the family, which they derived from concepts of natural law, and labelled as 'a predetermined rational order of the family'. To abolish the patriarchal leadership would lead to 'matrimonial anarchy', to arbitrariness and violence (1954, BGHZ 11 (1954) appendices 66, 67). The Federal Constitutional Court overruled this kind of reasoning in a decision of 1959 stating drily that the equal rights rule in our Constitution of 1949 demands full equality of mother and father with regard to parental rights (BVerfG 10, 59 ff).

In a divorce case of 1966, the federal court judges dealt with matrimonial sex, stating, 'The wife does not fulfil her conjugal duties if she lets the cohabitation happen listlessly'. 'Matrimony demands that she grants the intercourse with connubial affection and dedication'.

Decades have passed. Society has changed and different views of gender roles and morality have developed. Judgments of the described calibre cannot be found any more. But still, today, gender issues remain on the agenda. They may change, and new ones arise, such as distributionary social justice, the mini-job as a woman's trap, new forms of domestic violence, cyber stalking and mobbing, wearing of the headscarf in public. Also, many questions of reproductive medicine have been taken to the courts. Judgments in these cases have to be read critically to establish whether the judges were gender sensitive. There are enough examples to the contrary. A current problem is whether asylum or refugee law is applicable to women threatened by female genital mutilation in their home countries (Lembke and Foljanty, 2012). German administrative courts have come to different results with different reasoning.[2]

4. DO WOMEN JUDGE BETTER OR DIFFERENTLY?

The question is whether feminisation of the judiciary has led to changes in the adjudication. Is the increase of women in the judiciary having the effect of a better quality of judgments leading to more gender equality? (Schultz, 2003a).

The first female president of the Federal Constitutional Court, Jutta Limbach, dealt with this question in a speech on the German Judges Day 1995, asking: 'Do women change the third power (ie, the judiciary)? Are we witnessing in our administration of justice the emergence of a feminine element, articulated through empathy and leniency?'

So far there exist only two (by now rather dated) comprehensive empirical studies dealing with the possible effects of the feminisation of the judiciary on the outcome of cases in German courts, both in criminal law (Schultz, 2003a).

The essence of these studies is that women judges basically do not judge differently, which means that a difference in the outcome cannot be measured. The long process of legal education makes them adapt to the norms of the profession ('formation professionelle') and fit into the system. But Oberlies (1995) in line with findings by Bogoch (2003) from Israel found that there is a slight correlation between the involvement of women public prosecutors and more lenient sentences, and between female defence

[2] See P Baum (2005) 'Weibliche Genitalbeschneidung vor Gericht. Die erste Anerkennung von FGC als Asylgrund in der Bundesrepublik Deutschland': www.gender.hu-berlin.de/forschung/publikationen/gender-bulletins/texte-28/bulletin-texte-28/?searchterm=weibliche Genitalbeschneidung.

lawyers and higher sentences for women. Watched closely this means that both have problems in achieving their professional aims. This is not a question of application of law but of good communication, mutual respect and acceptance in court proceedings. And here gender matters.

In my interviews with the judiciary in Northrhine-Westfalia in 2009 (Schultz, Peppmeier and Rudek, 2011) I asked all my 62 interview partners across all the different jurisdictions and levels of court whether they knew or had heard of any differences in judging between male and female colleagues. The only positive answer I got was by judges at the state social court (which is a court of appeal) who told me independently that their female colleagues had opposed health insurance coverage for Viagra, whereas the men in the court had voted for it. It is obvious that the judges lacked gender sensitivity. In further training sessions I had offered in the Academy for the Judiciary, judges had frequently mentioned that they had observed that in alimony matters women judges indeed tended to be stricter with female plaintiffs than their male colleagues, which is very much in line with research reported from Brazil, Poland and Israel (Schultz and Shaw, 2003). But it was difficult to get any other example.

My question 'have women changed the judiciary?' was answered by the top female judge in the country with 'yes, they have made it livelier'. Later she added:

> I also believe that the debate in chambers is livelier. I am fond of mixed teams. Each brings in different experiences and that must enhance quality. That does not mean that each woman is a good judge. We have failures here as well as with men, the mixture is what matters.

Her point was that there may be differences between men and women, but more importantly there are individual differences and that it is not necessarily the outcome that is influenced, but the atmosphere and style at court (cp also Schultz, 2003a).

5. CHANGES IN LAW

Agents of change towards a more gender equal society were therefore less judges than lawmakers. The famous clearly phrased clause in the German Constitution: 'Men and women have equal rights' (Article 3, section 2) has been the foundation for fundamental changes in the law considering gender equality between men and women. Change gained momentum in the 1970s with the second women's movement. The key issue for debate was women's right to abortion. It led to a series of decisions by the Federal Constitutional Court, and the Court had to decide on many other cases involving gender equality issues. In particular, members of the German Women Jurists' Association have launched constitutional complaints against legal regulations, which appeared to be in breach of Article 3 section 2 and Parliament was asked to adapt the law to a changed gender agenda.

To give just a few extreme examples: until the 1950s, a celibacy clause prohibited female civil servants from keeping their positions when they married. In 1957, the matrimonial property regime was changed, as until 1953 a man was normally entitled to administer his wife's assets. Until the 1960s, there were wage deduction clauses for women, as they were considered to be second earners in a family with a man as breadwinner. The first Equal Rights Act in 1958 abolished the opportunity for a man to cancel his wife's employment contract. Yet until the revision of marital law in 1977, women kept the statutory duty to give priority to their family and children. Section 1356 of the Civil Code only allowed them to work if it was compatible with family duties. The male breadwinner model has remained deeply ingrained in German society; it is the basis for the German model of family insurances and pensions and a tax scheme which gives preferential treatment to couples with a sole earner and creates a high threshold for the secondary wage earner to make work profitable.

The list of deficits was long. In 1985, I started a series of lectures at my university called '*Frauen im Recht*' which has the dual meaning of 'women in law' and 'women in the right'. Over 10 years prominent women lawyers, the few law professors with gender consciousness we had at the time, top women politicians some of them having been judges before and ministers and feminist practitioners dealt with gender questions in law. Over time we tried to chart the salient issues across all legal fields and we discovered many white spots on the map. For some subjects like pension law and tax law it was difficult to find female experts, and some discrepancies and disparities were very difficult to detect, particularly if they were a result of structures and not single sections in the law, like the consequences of the breadwinner model in law and ways to change it.

In the second half of the 1980s, institutionalisation of women politics started, which helped to promote requests for change. The first equal opportunities officers were installed, at first in big cities then, in the 1990s, it became a statutory duty for all public institutions. Federal and state equality laws have come into force, women's advancement plans have to be issued regularly, there are meanwhile numerous—although still a limited number of—experts on gender questions in law. The best allies for women were the growing number of female politicians and MPs and ministers who have often, in alliances across parliamentary parties, initiated legislation on women's issues like abortion, marital rape, protection against violence, prostitution and trafficking, recognition of child care years for the pension, paid paternity leave etc.

The development in the 1990s was breathtaking, the first decade of the new millennium showing a consolidation process under the heading of gender mainstreaming. This means that over the past 25 years there has been an intensive and vivid discussion and a flourishing legislation process which has led to an extended revision of law to adapt it to the equality rule and to close gender gaps in the law to give equal chances to men and women and to hopefully create the basis for an equal distribution of goods.

Since the 1980s, the process has been supported by the anti-discrimination legislation in the European Union and judicature of the European Court of Justice. The foundation had been laid in the EEC-Treaty in 1957 with the equal pay for equal work rule in Article 119. The next milestone was the Equal Treatment Directive in 1976, followed by the introduction and subsequent application of the principle of indirect discrimination by the European Court of Justice, crowned by the five anti-discrimination directives, which have been passed in the last 10 years. In Germany these directives were transformed into national law mainly by the general Equal Treatment Act in 2006. Consequently, there is a refined and extended legislation but—of course—this is not the end of the story. The rules have to be applied in practice on a daily basis, and a continuous process of adjusting legal regulations to the changing living conditions in society and changing notions of gender roles and gender equality is necessary. And there are some cracks in the nice picture. To cite the most salient issue—the gender pay gap in Germany in 2011 is set at 23 per cent.

In spite of these developments, the importance of gender issues has often been ignored. Only very recently has there been a rising acceptance of their significance mainly resulting from the lack of women in leading positions in German companies. This has led to an alliance of women from all parties—including the conservative Minister of Labour and Chancellor Angela Merkel—demanding quota regulations.

An important pressure group in the lawmaking process was—and is—the German Women Jurists' Association and its specialist working groups commenting on and criticising pending legislation and proposing necessary changes.

6. GENDER IN LEGAL PUBLICATIONS

Where can gender knowledge be found? Not much of the discussion on gender questions is to be found in mainstream legal publications.

The sections on gender questions in law books and leading law journals are slight, if any. It seems that the only legitimate place for them is considered to be within commentaries on constitutional law. Commentaries are a typical civil law legal tool in which each section of a code, statute, act or byelaw is explained and interpreted in detail citing the relevant judgments. In Germany, they seem to be of particular importance. Of course the commentaries also sum up relevant decisions on gender questions in civil law, criminal law, social law etc, but these are not necessarily labelled as gender questions and background information tends to be limited. The big commentaries are written by the 'legal establishment' at law faculties, mainly by older men. The bulk of work on gender questions in law has appeared in grey papers and in book series from less well-known publishers. Women lawyers with gender expertise prefer commenting on judgments and discussing legal regulations and the need for change in critical legal journals, for example, in the feminist legal journal *STREIT* (which means conflict or quarrel).

7. GENDER IN LEGAL EDUCATION

Judges will not have learnt about gender issues at university. Older women judges will remember the times when overt discrimination was practised in lecture halls and when women were ridiculed (Schultz, 1990: 319–59). This happened until the late 1990s. Gender is still not a subject in the teaching of law and law faculties are still male dominated. The first woman law professor got her chair in 1965. Of the 926 law professors in Germany there are only 127 women (data from 2008), very few of them in the top positions of the hierarchy, and not much more than a handful of them are interested and specialised in gender questions. Out of a total of 42 faculties, four are still without a female law professor. Of the 40 gender chairs, which were established in Northrhine-Westfalia in the last decades, only one was in law and—due to a disagreement in the law faculty to which it had been given—it was never filled.

A specialisation in gender is—as can be easily guessed from the above—not conducive to careers. Although the former president of the Federal Constitutional Court and former law professor Jutta Limbach identified herself as a feminist, being labelled as a feminist or using this label remains a problem; it is associated with bias and unfriendly attitudes towards men. The culture in law faculties has long been extremely paternalistic and conservative, and has only just started to open up and change.[3]

German law students are mainly taught legal doctrine with details of judicature in the core subjects—civil law, criminal law and administrative/constitutional law. Nowadays, there are very few introductory law courses, which in former times gave a systematic overview of the structure and general principles of the German legal system and which could be a place for gender questions. Courses in foundation subjects like sociology of law,

[3] Women law professors' careers and law faculty culture are the subject of our new research project JurPro. Comp: www.fernuni-hagen.de/jurpro.

philosophy of law, legal theory, legal history, law and economics, which all could explicitly include gender questions are not obligatory. Students tend to choose rather courses at an early stage of their legal education on specialist subjects like internet law, copyright law, intellectual property law, which are modern and market viable. The idea of a good general educational background, in Germany called '*Allgemeinbildung*', and a solid knowledge of social reality—which had always seemed of particular importance for law students—is getting lost. It is up to each student to learn about and deal with social policy.

Equal rights issues have to be discussed in constitutional law and in European law, but the question is how much space is given over to them. For the teaching of criminal law, sexual offences and crimes are as a rule considered of little doctrinal importance. Social law and tax law are marginal subjects in legal education. Also labour law is by and large a subject of specialisation and not part of the regular curriculum. Indeed, it is doubtful whether anti-discrimination law is ever taught in any detail. Rather, it is left to individual law tutors whether gender questions are taken into account.

My own experience reflects the general situation, characterised by considerable reluctance both among law students and university curriculum planners to engage with the subject of gender. Since 1990, I have offered lectures and seminars on women or gender and law at different universities. In law faculties I attracted only few participants, whereas my seminars were most popular among students of humanities and human resources. Law students were afraid of being stigmatised when they attended these 'sectarian' courses.

In 2006, updated in 2011, I wrote a gender curriculum for law[4] in the context of the introduction of accreditation procedures for the new Bachelor and Master's qualifications created in the course of the Bologna process in Germany.[5] I defined educational objectives and identified which issues should be taught in which subjects or fields and also proposed adding an introductory course to give students an overarching picture of the relevant questions and structures. I never got any reaction to it from law faculties.[6]

[4] *Gender Curriculum Rechtswissenschaft*: www.gender-curricula.com/gender-curricula/. An English language version can be obtained from me.

[5] The purpose of the Bologna Process is to create the European Higher Education Area by making academic degree standards and quality assurance standards more comparable and compatible throughout Europe. Law is meanwhile the only subject in Germany which is still exempt from the process. Although universities offer Bachelor and Master's qualifications in law, students still have to go the traditional route with two state examinations to be able to practise in the classical legal professions.

[6] The only positive result was that when my university asked for an accreditation of the new Master of Law, a feminist colleague in the expert group demanded the inclusion of gender issues which gave me the chance to offer a gender module in the Master's programme of my university.

In the gender studies programmes which have been established in recent years at some universities in Germany, law is almost completely left out which may be due to a lack of experts that can engage with these interdisciplinary programmes.[7]

At many universities, gender concepts or gender action plans have started to recommend the inclusion of gender aspects in research and teaching and as part of gender budgeting money is provided for this and gender prizes are awarded, but the result for law faculties is still meagre.[8]

8. GENDER TRAINING FOR THE JUDICIARY

There is no gender training for the judiciary.

Young judges have to work as judges from the first day of their appointment, thus leaving no time for any regular additional training, which might include gender issues. They only have to attend a series of accompanying introductory courses (between three and five days) on practice skills.

The range of further judicial training on offer is vast, but it comprises no element relating to gender. There is a national Academy for the Judiciary which can train around 3000 or more judges and prosecutors annually.[9] Some federal states in addition have academies of their own, or at least organise further training sessions; by far the largest of these is Northrhine-Westfalia, the biggest federal state with 18 million inhabitants and 4820 judges.[10]

There are many courses for judges in the national and state academies about practice related problems and recent legal developments. Twenty years ago so-called behaviour-oriented courses started, mainly focusing on communication and including courses on self-reflection. Attendance is voluntary. In this year's (2011) programme of the national academy I found the following subjects which have gender implications: new developments in divorce law for family lawyers (numerous courses); violence in families; how to deal with victims of sexual violence; international trafficking. The focus of these will, however, be rather on legal than on gender questions.

[7] Although there are meanwhile thousands of equal opportunities officers in Germany, there is not a regulated qualification for them. I had offered one over 6 years from 2002–08 which my university shut down as it was not in their list of priorities although I had government funding for it.

[8] In 2011 I gained a grant from our State Ministry for Research and Science for a website 'RechtundGender' presenting 20 video recorded interviews with experts on gender questions in law and providing a comprehensive overview of salient relevant issues: www.fernuni-hagen.de/rechtundgender.

[9] The programme is accessible via the internet at: www.deutsche-richterakademie.de.

[10] Its programme is also on the internet at: www.jak.nrw.de/.

The academies also offer courses in leadership for judges and prosecutors. In none of the related course descriptions of the Justice Academy NRW did I find any hint of gender questions. Although the organisers told me that gender aspects are to be included, it is not clear whether they really are and in what way. The question is also how well they are received by the participants who, in my experience, are unlikely to show much interest.

A couple of years ago a psychologist and I organised two gender training courses at the national academy which seem to have been the only ones ever offered. They were to deal with gender aspects in judicial careers, the perception and construction of gender in the practice of law and gendered professional communication but too few enrolled and the course was soon discontinued.

Whenever I am involved in further training for lawyers and judges I refer to gender questions, which is well received by some, met with disinterest by others and openly rejected by a sizeable number. In general in the established part of German society there is a kind of fatigue if the subject of women's rights or the need for women's advancement are discussed or demanded, as if this would involve giving women an unjustified advantage over men.[11]

It is interesting to note that, with the exception of lawyers, many members in the top management of the public sector, including universities, have gone through gender training during the last decade. Admittedly, these courses were, in any event, never very popular as they were associated with ideological re-education.

9. CONCLUDING OBSERVATIONS

How do judges acquire gender knowledge? Germany is a very open society in which political matters as well as equality issues are widely discussed. Each educated newspaper reader knows by and large what the issues are, but this does not necessarily create gender sensitivity or—as mentioned—it might even have the opposite effect.

In the 1970s, sociology of law dealt with the problem of preconceived opinions, and although judges are aware of it, they are not keen on the subject as it means questioning their objectivity which is the foundation for their professional work. This is why there is also a resistance to discussing

[11] Overall in Germany there is a remarkable reluctance to use the word 'gender' outside social sciences and academia although we have no other German word for it. The term 'gender mainstreaming' has been introduced officially but even educated people still do not know what it means. In the German language, we do not distinguish between sex and gender and the German translation for gender is the word for gender as well as genitals. Maybe that is another explanation why the expression is not liked.

gender questions. In the two gender training courses I offered (mentioned above) judges were asked to list gender stereotypes common in society. From their answers it was clear that each of them had their own gender notions or prejudices (Schultz, Peppmeier and Rudek, 2011).

Another question is whether this leads to biased or unjust judgments. German judges, as described, are a very homogeneous class adapted in a long and tedious process of education to the values of their Constitution.[12] The judiciary as such is conservative, although this does not necessarily apply to individuals. Labour law judges tend to be a little more on the political left than judges in other jurisdictions. Political inclinations may also play a role. Gender is just one other factor.

The extensive legislation in the legalistic German legal culture determines many questions, which may be open in other countries although, of course, enough space exists for individual interpretations and decisions do remain.

There are other mechanisms—which can also relate to gender questions—that can counterbalance individual bias, for example:

- The chamber (bench) principle, as far as it is still applied; even if a judge who belongs to a chamber sits alone in a case, he may discuss the case with others in the chamber.
- The three-tier system which gives the opportunity for appeal (2nd instance) and revision (3rd instance).
- The commenting on and discussion of judgments in legal publications and the press.
- The growing number of women who bring in life experiences which differ from those of their male colleagues.

However, there are deficits. By way of illustration, just one case from 2007: a female judge denied a premature divorce (which is possible in cases of hardship) to a woman who had suffered massive violence from her husband. Both were Muslims from Morocco married according to Muslim law. The judge held that there was no hardship because the Koran gives the husband the right to corporal punishment of his wife. There was uproar in the press, and the lawyer in the case had the judge recused.

As mentioned before, judges do not only need gender sensitivity in family law, but in labour and social law, in criminal law and also in tax and pension law, but this is often lacking. After changes in the alimony rules, judges tried to resist the intentions of the legislator. In custody cases the European Court of Human Rights overruled decisions of German judges. Cases of same-sex marriages were taken to the Federal Constitutional

[12] *Cf* my other contribution in this volume.

Court and recently to the European Court of Justice. In the application of anti-discrimination rules judges had heterogeneous views. This clearly shows that gender is a subject which has to be addressed. Furthermore, gender knowledge is not only important for unbiased decision making but, as stated, for a good atmosphere and behaviour at court and the respect owed towards women.

Gender questions should be integrated into whatever is taught—where it is necessary—and should not be artificially highlighted as specific courses relating to gender alone are inclined to cause aversion. The problem is that there is still no tradition of how to achieve this and too much reluctance on the part of the legal 'establishment' to consult experts in the field.

Judges overall could do with more social scientific knowledge. Astonishingly—and this is my experience from the many courses I have given—they distrust social scientists, always questioning the reliability and validity of relevant research, but they are very open to any findings from psychology. Perhaps it is a matter of who can define social reality—both sociologists and lawyers obviously compete as to who is entitled to define it.

All in all, I see still more deficits in initial legal education than in further training. What has not been sown in the early years may not ripen later. We have to go on making public where gender problems in law exist and what should be learnt and done about it. Slowly gender knowledge will diffuse into the classical canon of teaching, but we should try to speed up the process.

10. REFERENCES

Bogoch, B (2003) 'Lawyers in the Courtroom: Gender, Trials and Professional Performance in Israel' in U Schultz and G Shaw (eds), *Women in the World's Legal Professions* (Oxford, Hart Publishing).

Lembke, U and Foljanty, L (2012) 'Migration, Flucht und Geschlecht' in L Foljanty and U Lembke (eds), *Feministische Rechtswissenschaft*, 2nd edn (Baden-Baden, Nomos).

Oberlies, D (1995) *Tötungsdelikte zwischen Männern und Frauen* (Pfaffenweiler, Zen-taurus).

Schultz, U (1990) 'Wie männlich ist die Juristenschaft' in U Battis and U Schultz (eds), *Frauen im Recht* (Heidelberg, CF Müller).

—— (2003a) 'Women Lawyers in Germany: Perception and Construction of Femininity' in U Schultz and G Shaw (eds), *Women in the World's Legal Professions* (Oxford, Hart Publishing).

—— (2003b) 'Geschlechterleitbilder der älteren Herren des Bundesgerichtshofs' in MGFFS NRW (ed), *Handbuch 'Frauen und Recht'*.

—— (2005) 'Regulated Deregulation—The Case of the German Legal Profession' in W Felstiner, *Reorganization and Resistance: Legal Professions Confront a Changing World* (Oxford, Hart Publishing).

—— (2008) 'Legal Education in Germany—An Ever (Never?) Ending Story of Resistance to Change' in V Olgiati (ed), *Higher Legal Culture and Postgraduate Legal Education in Europe* (Naples, Edizioni Scientifiche Italiane).

—— (2012) 'Frauen in Führungspositionen der Justiz. Eine Untersuchung von Frauenkarrieren in den Justizbehörden in Nordrhein-Westfalen' *Deutsche Richterzeitung* 9.

Schultz, U, Peppmeier, I and Rudek, A (2011) *Frauen in Führungspositionen der Justiz. Eine Untersuchung der Bedingungen von Frauenkarrieren in den Justizbehörden in Nordrhein-Westfalen. Projektbericht* (Hagen, Institut für Geschlechterforschung und Gleichstellungsrecht und –politik).

Schultz, U and Shaw, G (2003) *Women in the World's Legal Professions* (Oxford, Hart Publishing).

Index